Imitation and Imagination:
THE ART OF THE THEATRE

Edited by Loren K. Ruff

Authors:

Carole P. Brandt

Susan F. Clark

Ivan E. Hess

Jackson Kesler

Loren K. Ruff

Walter R. Stump

Ronald A. Willis

Steve Woods

Hunter Textbooks Inc.

For Adam Ruff
Who finally gets his turn at bat

Cover Photo: Cybis Porcelains, Trenton, New Jersey. Court Jester, 15 1/2 inches tall. An issue of 500 sculptures, Portraits in Porcelain Collection. Copyrighted by Cybis Porcelains, Trenton, New Jersey.

Design for cover and divider pages by Deborah Dale.

 Hunter Textbooks Inc.

823 Reynolda Road
Winston-Salem, North Carolina 27104

Preface

Einstein said that "imagination is more important than knowledge." This suggests that imagination is necessary to produce knowledge. Theatre and drama have always been a source for gaining and producing knowledge. As a barometer of society, they reflect what is happening politically, socially, and economically. If you are interested in a society of any country and at any time, read the plays of that period. Better yet, try to see the plays when they are produced. Theatre and drama reflect a society and its people.

Theatre and drama serve the same master—the representation of an action. Actions concern characters and characters in action is what theatre/drama is all about: it is an art form which not only imitates the actions of life but imaginatively put those actions into a meaningful and entertaining form. That is why we call this book *Imitation and Imagination: The Art of the Theatre.*

The devil is in the details and so it was with this book: physically coordinating the work of eight writers, making sure that the integrity of their work was maintained, and insuring that the intended material was covered. This manuscript's focus was solely on western theatre and was not intended to delve into the eastern aspects of theatre; that may come later. In order that this manuscript's focus would not be construed as too heavily weighted in terms of history, a balance needed to be struck in the historical section. Thus, in the majority of instances, brevity became the byword. It is important to leave enough latitude for the teacher to examine, elaborate, and explain. Too much detail tends to defeat that purpose. This is not intended to be a theatre history book but it is intended to be current. For example, the latest discoveries about the Globe and the Rose theatres, post-structuralism, feminist theatre, new theatrical movements, and bringing the musical into the 1990s are included. The chapters on theatre history are not designed, therefore, to be inclusive but rather to convey salient material in the hopes that the teacher and the student will seek a larger picture. In addition, each chapter has a suggested reading list and study questions. A pronunciation guide is included in those chapters where it is warranted. Students as well as professionals in the field mispronounce names and items; this guide is an attempt to solve this problem. Ronald J. MacDougall, reference librarian at the University of Maine, has been an immeasurable source of help in arriving at the correct pronunciation.

This book is the outcome of years of teaching theatre and drama at numerous universities. The eight authors have given of their time, experience, and expertise in contributing to this manuscript. On the surface, this book may appear to be the work of the authors, but in reality, the finished manuscript is a contribution of many individuals. With deepest gratitude, we offer our thanks to Ernestine Godfrey and her staff, Janie Bishop and Kim McGrath, without whose insight, perception and attention to detail this book would not have seen the light of day. We owe them a great deal of gratitude for their hard work. Others who have been a factor in helping this book to its completion have been David Young, a force in the theatre community and who created the network that made this book possible, Jeanne Newlin, the Harvard Theatre Collection, R. Sylvester, Q. Quat, James Secat and Michael Bigelow Dixon at the Actors Theatre of Louisville, the University of Texas Theatre Arts Collection, El Teatro Campesino, the Omaha Magic Theatre, and last but not least, MK, who really cared about the integrity of this book.

The Authors

CAROLE P. BRANDT, Professor and Head of the Department of Theatre Arts at The Pennsylvania State University, is currently President of the Association for Theatre in Higher Education and a past national chair of the Kennedy Center American College Theatre Festival. A member of the Society of Stage Directors and Choreographers, Brandt has directed over two hundred professional and academic productions and has been honored with two Kennedy Center Medallions and the Amoco Gold Medallion of Excellence. *(Chapter 17)*

SUSAN F. CLARK, Assistant Professor of Theatre History and Criticism at Smith College, specializes in American theatre. She also serves as Executive Director for Kristin Linklater's Company of Women, Inc., a non-profit multicultural theatre company. *(Chapter 14)*

IVAN E. HESS, Chair of the Theatre Arts Department at Humboldt State University, also heads the Kennedy Center American College Theatre Festival in his region. He is a scenic/lighting designer for theatre and film, and his past work includes design for numerous professional productions. Hess, a graduate of Stanford University, previously taught at Tufts University and the University of London. *(Chapter 18)*

JACKSON KESLER, Professor of Theatre and Dance at Western Kentucky University, has designed costumes for more than two hundred productions, including ballet and opera. He has also directed over seventy-five productions, including outdoor drama and period dance/movement for which he is especially noted. Kesler is the author of *Theatrical Costume: A Guide to Information Sources.* *(Chapter 19)*

LOREN K. RUFF, Professor of Theatre and Dance at Western Kentucky University, has taught theatre history, acting for the camera, American and modern drama, stage management, and introductory theatre. Ruff has served as acting judge for the American Theatre Festival, written for *The Hollywood Reporter* and *Variety*, and has acted and directed professionally for stage, film and television. He is the author of numerous articles and reviews. *(Editor; Chapters 2, 3 , 4, 5, 6, 7, 11, 13. 21, 22)*

WALTER R. STUMP, Professor of Theatre at the University of Southern Maine, received his Ph.D. from Indiana University, specializing in Dramatic Literature, Criticism, and Theory. He has won the distinguished scholar award at his university twice, and a Kennedy Center Medallion for his work in educational theatre. He is a member of the College of Fellows of the New England Theatre Conference. *(Chapters 8, 9, 10, 12, 15, 16)*

RONALD A. WILLIS, Professor of Theatre and Film at the University of Kansas, directs productions and teaches introductory theatre courses, dramatic script writing, and American theatre history. *(Chapter 1)*

STEVE WOODS, Lighting Designer, U.S.A.A., teaches at Louisiana State University. His international work has taken him to London, Mexico City, Berlin and Prague. In New York, he worked with Theatre for a New Audience and the Limon Dance Company. Premiere productions include *Rachel, Tennessee Strings, Women of Troy, A Confederacy of Dunces* and *All the King's Men.* Among his regional credits are work with the Shakespeare Theatre and the Kennedy Center; television credits include PBS, ESPN, MTV, BBC, and Showtime. *(Chapter 20)*

Imitation and Imagination:
THE ART OF THE THEATRE

ॐ

Contents

PART I: FORM AND FUNCTION

PART II: HISTORICAL PERSPECTIVES

(Continued)

CONTENTS, *Continued*

PART III: CREATIVE INSIGHTS

PART IV: PRACTICAL CHOICES

Pronunciation Guide

A vocabulary at the end of several chapters provides a guide to pronouncing words and phrases which may be unfamiliar to students.

The method used in this pronunciation guide is that of the *NBC Handbook of Pronunciation* which re-spells words according to their sound. This system is somewhat easier to deal with than the diacritical marks employed by dictionaries of the international phonetic alphabet familiar to students of linguistics. In our method the words, names or phrases are broken into their various syllables with the accented syllable appearing in capital letters. No attempt is made to reproduce such foreign sounds as the French *u*. Instead, a double *o* sound is given; thus the writer Camus becomes *kah MOO:*, a pronunciation not very French sounding but one which has gained accetance in English-speaking countries.

Here are the letters used for vowel sounds. Each letter is accompanied by a familiar English word which will indicate the appropriate pronunciation.

These are the natural vowel sound that occurs in many unaccented syllables of English words. The letters used for consonant sounds should all be readily apparent with the possible exception of *zh* which is the French *j* (or sometimes *g*). This sound is heard at the end of a few English words such as garage and rouge.

Finally, we should point out that in many cases two or more pronunciations of a word may well be considered "correct." In such instances, we have tried to select the one most commonly used throughout the United States. However, when it comes to dealing with foreign words we have tended to choose a version which retains some of the flavor of the original. For example, although the Greek word *himation* will be pronounced to rhyme with *my nation,* when one anglicizes it to the extreme, the Merriam-Webster dictionaries give the pronunciation as *him-'at-e,an.* But we have chosen to used a broad *a* or *ah* in the second syllable, this being the standard sound denoted by the letter *a* in nearly all European languages.

a	cat	*igh*	fly
ah	father	*oh*	grow
ai	fair	*oy*	boy
aw	awful	*ow*	Now
ay	hate	*oo:*	food
e	jet	*oo*	good
ee	feet	*uh*	away
i	it		

Part I
FORM AND FUNCTION

CHAPTER ONE

❧

Theatre:
The Reflective Template

A theatre event is the result of the collaboration of many artists, who create the fictive world experienced by the spectator. (Production of Ibsen's *Peer Gynt* by the University Resident Theatre Company of the Pennsylvania State University, directed by Carole Brandt with associate directors Manuel Duque and Jane Ridley. Photo by William Wellman.)

Approaches to the Study of Theatre

Theatre is an amazingly diverse enterprise and studying it, while always interesting and often demanding, is similarly varied. Each investigative strategy has value; each can be useful. However, each approach emphasizes different data, promotes its own perspective, and appeals to slightly different constituencies. We'll look at four different approaches before centering attention on the one to be pursued in this chapter.

The Dramatic Literature Approach

Approaching the study of theatre by focusing on its dramatic literature is popular and potent. The playwright's words are examined, the play's characters analyzed, and its themes identified and explicated—all in order to understand something about the nature of theatre and the way it generates meaning. The written text is clearly a key embodiment of theatrical expressiveness.

The written text offers an advantage for academic study. Its words are stable and convenient. A reader can leaf back through a written text to reread something that was confusing, or skip sections that don't hold interest. In this regard, the play on the page is studied in ways unlike the play on stage. On stage, the play resolutely unfolds at enactment speed, refusing to arbitrarily pause, repeat itself, or speed up.

Still when it comes to stability of meaning, the written text fares no better than the performed play. Though written words seem constant, the meanings we attach to them are not as obliging. People's perceptions differ, especially over time. Meanings change, topical concerns change, and when it comes to theatre, preferred styles change. Just look at an old movie, one regarded as "very realistic" in its day. Note how today's audiences respond. Often what was found satisfying now seems dated and lacking in credibility. Our time-bound cultural experiences, especially our technologies, shape our acceptance of "reality" and our sense of appropriateness in art—just as they did for our forebears. Really studying a play means considering its relevant linguistic and artistic contexts, as well as our current views on the same topics. The written text gains its meaning from its relation to all those larger contexts.

Studying a play as literature tends to downplay one very important aspect of theatre. A play, typically, is written to be produced. It is, in part, a blueprint for a production to be built, much as a complex building is built, by many collaborating specialists. The collaborators search the play for clues that shape the plans and executions of their own theatrical specialities. Then together they all, the designers—scenic, costume, lighting, sound—along with actors and directors, create an alternate world. They supply audiences with stimuli that are themselves as suggestive as the words of the play. The absence of those nonverbal stimuli puts the reader of the written text in the position of either ignoring important dimensions of theatre found only in performance, or of engaging in an amazingly adept act of imagining them and estimating their impact.

The Theatre History Approach

One way to consider a play's life in performance is through theatre history. The play and its historical milieu both at the initial performance and in revivals can be examined in detail. Such study is, for many, the most satisfying way to approach theatre.

Historical knowledge of theatre provides important access to the play in its cultural contexts. We study the play's text, the production conditions that determined its performance, the society it grew out of, and the responses of observers—both contemporary and subsequent. We can even appraise the ongoing impact of an historical theatre event.

Theatre history easily goes beyond the study of particular plays. It probes the nature of the

focuses on theatre events directly experienced only by others. As with literary study, history considers theatre's quality of immediacy only at a distance and speculatively.

The Practical Production Specialties Approach

Another approach foregrounds the complex effort of producing plays. In this strategy focus is on the theatre workers. Because theatre is a collaborative art it integrates the efforts of many specialists, among them actors, directors, designers, playwrights and other interpretive practitioners.

Because it is also a profession wherein people make their livelihood, theatre also embraces the talents of managers, agents, lawyers, and business specialists. By examining what goes into creating and marketing theatre one can learn about theatre's inner workings and its place in our society.

Theatre curricula in many colleges and universities offer production and management courses. Students develop both hands-on skills and keen insights through specialized and practical training. Additionally, many further hone their skills in an active production program.

The Spectatorship Approach

But making and marketing theatre are not activities suited to everyone. Many people are drawn to theatre strictly as audience members. They want to experience theatrical performance richly, but from the safety and comfort of the auditorium seat. They derive a special pleasure from attending the theatre. They thrive on its immediacy. They also gain illuminating insights from attending, intellectually, to the way theatre reflects and shapes their lives. They want to learn about its capacity to move them and their capacities to respond. But, at the same time, they aren't content simply to read plays and they don't aspire to be theatre historians.

For these people the most satisfying approach to theatre focuses on the dynamics of theatre atten-

Scene from Shakespeare's *The Tempest*, performed at the Champlain Shakespeare Festival, directed by Judith Williams. *(Photo by Richard Currie)*

larger social and political enterprise of theatre including its function in ages other than our own. It reveals how our idea of theatre, when compared with those of different eras and societies, remains similar in some respects and differs in others. By studying theatre history, our knowledge base is expanded, and so too is our tolerance for alternative world views.

Of course, fashions in historical methodology change along with other modes of human endeavor. Consequently, historical investigation is never really finished. New historical methods generate new insights. Students who approach theatre through history always have new discoveries even though the theatre events studied seem long in the past. But historical investigation, no matter how illuminating and stimulating,

dance. Such is the strategy in this chapter. We will approach theatre by investigating the role of the spectator. The goal is to delineate the behaviors, attitudes, skills, and knowledge embraced by responsive, able, informed, and discerning audience members. Naturally, all persons interested in approaching the study of theatre, whether from a literary, historical, or practical production perspective, can profit from examining the complex nature of audience/performance interaction. They, too, are welcome, but it is the spectator's viewpoint that dictates our approach here.

At this juncture, a crucial observation is in order. Simply stated, it reads: in the hierarchy of experiences, direct and sensitive experience with theatre is more important than talking or reading about it. This chapter is geared to that end. It seeks to facilitate a rich perception of theatre performances, both those which seem already accessible and those which seem remote (and therefore likely to be more challenging). No one can anticipate the specific nature of the next performance you will attend, but this chapter's intent is to help you find a way to enter into its spirit and share its energy and perspectives. So remember, regardless of what is said here, in the final analysis, it is your full and rich perception of that next performance, plus all subsequent ones, that most matters.

Characteristics of the Spectatorship Approach

The spectator is the last link in the creative theatre process chain. What playwrights, directors, designers, actors and others set in motion assumes its rightful form only when appropriately observed by audience members. While all the others are trained in their tasks the spectator proceeds largely by hit or miss. But until the theatre event is observed by an audience member it is not a work of art; it is only an aesthetic object on the verge of becoming a work of art. Theatre exists to be witnessed by audiences; it does not reach frui-

tion until it is witnessed. The able spectator is obliged to witness it appropriately, in all its fullness, with all its implications rendered potent and lively. This leads to three focal concerns.

Focus on the Theatre Event

The knowledgeable spectator possesses an understanding of the overall theatre event, its essential traits and its potency. Because theatre events are complex and pursue various objectives simultaneously the student is often led in many directions at the same time. Data gathered from the study of dramatic literature, theatre history, and practical production assist the spectator to develop the sophisticated sensitivity that leads to a comprehensive awareness of the theatre event. But, it must be stressed, the spectator is most interested in learning how all these data and forces coexist in the complex time/space phenomenon wherein the audience member actively confronts them.

Focus on Spectator Perceptivity

Since comprehension of the live theatre event depends on the abilities of the spectator to perceive fully and then reflect meaningfully on these perceptions, one is led to consider the nature of personal and group discernment. "How do we witness things while members of an audience?" emerges as an important topic. So, too, does "How do we come to trust that what we have witnessed qualifies as an appropriate building block of knowledge?" While both of these topics could command full-time study in their own right, the thoughtful spectator is nonetheless concerned with the relevance of issues such as these to the dynamics of theatre spectatorship.

Focus on Enhancing Responsiveness to Live Theatre Events

In analyzing the interactive nature of audience involvement and artists' expressiveness the theatre spectator amasses information about both the nature of perception and the parameters of the theatre event. But such knowledge can actually inhibit immediate responsiveness to theatre events if it imposes an intellectual grid that distances an audience member, especially the beginner, from the more holistic, immediate, and intuitive—if you will—experience of theatre. The apt spectator distinguishes between the aesthetic experience *of* a theatre performance and the thinking *about* that transaction that one pursues for intellectual satisfaction and growth. Though the two are intimately linked, they are not entirely synonymous. The developing spectator strives to increase both aesthetic responsiveness and intellectual development.

Benefits Accruing from Spectatorship Study

Even this brief consideration of theatre spectatorship reveals that the traits of a good audience member closely resemble those of a liberally educated member of society. A good audience member, like a liberally educated person, is observant, open-minded, tolerant of alternate viewpoints, able to embrace new visions, and sensitive to the multitudinous influences that shape perception and thought. All these traits are activated as spectators vicariously explore challenging fictive worlds created by imaginative theatre artists. It is no wonder that theatre is regarded as the most humanizing of the arts, often a society's crowning achievement.

The Dual and Extended Nature of the Theatre Event

The live theatre event has an intriguing dual nature which interests the discerning spectator. The theatre event is always both social and aesthetic. That is, its "event-ness" assures it a place in society. Even the process of making theatre reflects in some measure the forces and crosscurrents of its society. Attending the theatre is

obviously a social act. What may be less obvious is the fact that a spectator's fundamental ability to perceive the theatre event is also influenced by society's concerns and its endorsed habits of thought.

Simultaneously, the theatre event's aesthetic nature, its "theatre-ness," dictates the expressive form and suggests the manner in which it is to be meaningfully perceived. While one might again stress a specific society's power to shape the aesthetic nature of its theatre, what are at least equally apparent are those features which transcend the boundaries of particular cultures and make of theatre a powerful and eloquent cross-cultural art form.

The theatre event's larger social dimension extends well beyond the bounds of the actual performance. All of us have some awareness and attitudes about theatre—whether accurately formed or not—that precede our actual experience with a specific performance. Those prior impressions greatly influence our perception of particular theatre events. They become part of the emotional and intellectual baggage we carry in with us. They determine the extent to which we are willing and able to open ourselves to theatrical experiences. They also determine how we feel about and value those experiences.

Theatre's aesthetic nature is similarly powerful. It influences us both as individuals and as group members, and it does so at the deepest levels of our being. It can subtly reinforce or radically reshape our fundamental sensitivities and powers of perception. Consequently, its emotional and intellectual influences persist long after the performance itself is over. It is primarily for these reasons that the theatre event, while it may initially seem to be neatly bounded by time, has powers that extend both backward and forward, influencing us before we witness an event as well as long after we have left it.

Clearly, considerations of the multiple aspects of the theatre event and the fluctuating dynamics of theatre spectatorship lead the student to attend to much more than what simply happened on stage. The dual and extended nature of theatre coupled with the perceptual habits of the spectator create a natural matrix of interconnected intellectual concerns. At the very least, the student is led to ponder issues related to society, theatre aesthetics, details of theatre practice, and personal awareness and growth. These issues, and others, inform our basic approach to learning about theatre spectatorship.

The Theatre Event's Para-aesthetic Nature

Definition of Para-aesthetic

Theatre's social nature is complex. Its most significant elements form theatre's "para-aesthetic" dimension. They qualify as para-aesthetic because they are adjuncts to theatre's aesthetic nature, influencing its impact, but without being part of the core aesthetic occurrence we call the performance. However, that does not diminish the importance of para-aesthetics. For the spectator the para-aesthetics of a theatre event are potent influences on the perception of theatre's aesthetic nature.

Para-aesthetic Matters Important to the Spectator

Prior to Performance Attendance

Some Practical Theatre Matters. A performance inevitably involves various groups of people. For example, theatre workers form a group in order to produce a show. A social dynamic among the theatre workers results. The producing group is then perceived by the public as having a certain character and perhaps even a social or artistic credo.

The producing group does not exist in a vacuum; it is part of a larger social construct and as such interacts with other agencies and groups. For example, the producing group must inform others, potential audience members (another group in the making) of the production's existence as well as each performance's location and time so they can make plans to attend. If tickets are sold, consideration must be given to pricing and to the potential audience member's capacity to buy.

Thought must be given to making them available at convenient and well-advertised locations. The advertising used to promote the production and its ticket sales, too, has a character that makes it part of the social milieu.

Of course, each theatre must meet basic safety and health regulations for both its workers and its patrons. In short, a producing theatre operates within the same guidelines that control other enterprises in an ordered society. It interacts with many social groups to inform the public, facilitate the audience's attendance and to protect its safety and comfort.

Audience Expectations. Expectations determine, to a large extent, what we are willing to see in a theatre event and, consequently, how we appraise it. Expectations are of several kinds and derive from several sources.

There are, for example, expectations that come from our assumptions about theatre itself. That is, what do we regard as the legitimate functions of theatre? How should it involve us? What shape should the theatre event have? What part should we play in the event?

There are also expectations that arise from what we may have read or heard about a particular theatre event, its creators, or its constituent elements. For example, if we read a review of a performance, the reviewer's attitudes may shape what it is we want to see in the piece. Similarly, if we have read the play being performed, or know other works by the same author, that may precondition us as to what the piece "should" be like. The same holds true regarding our foreknowledge of each of the other theatre workers bringing the performance into being. Do we expect things of a certain actor based on other roles we have seen? Do we recognize and have special feelings about the work of particular designers or directors? Is the producer associated with particular kinds of theatre that make us expect this one to fall into a consistent pattern? Do we know any of the actors personally so that we compare their characters to their real life personas?

In other words, expectations figure prominently in our response matrix. Sensitive spectators must be willing to identify their expectations and consider their aptness. Do they lead us in a fruitful direction or do they close down the ways we are able to think about the theatre work? Are there some expectations which are inappropriate or inhibiting? In what ways do the theatre artists play upon our expectations and incorporate their influence into the work itself? Are there clues placed in the work to mislead us in some fashion and for some purpose?

Knowing our tendency to let prior expectations influence our perceptions of the performance itself, theatre publicists shape our early awareness of the event through newspaper stories, posters, and ad campaigns. All are calculated to build in us that sense of anticipation the theatre management thinks will help us enter into the theatre event. Of course, sometimes their plans backfire and we are disappointed when the performance is not as daring as we were led to believe or does not seem as funny as we expected.

Naturally, the more sophisticated our understanding of theatre is, the more diversified our expectations will be. If we believe that all theatre should do is make us laugh, our response to a somber, thoughtful piece is not likely to be very rich or satisfying. If we think issues in a comedy should not be taken seriously, if we think that laughter is only for diversion, then many of the works of social satire will lose their kick for us. If we regard all anachronisms as mistakes, such as, for example, combining Elizabethan costumes and modern rifles in the same production, then a director's attempts to use that technique to link an historic play to our immediate life experiences will categorically fail—for us. If we believe that all characters are to be fully-rounded, psychologically complete mock-ups of human beings, then much fantasy and allegory will be dismissed immediately. On the other hand, if we recognize diversity in theatre and are willing to adjust our expectations to accommodate that diversity our responses are much more likely to enhance our experiences.

Nowhere does the need for sophisticated awareness of theatre make itself felt more evidently than in confronting theatre events from specialized cultures or subcultures outside our own. Their goals and expressive methods test our flexibility of thought. Especially for these events our expectations must be carefully reexamined and, if necessary, set aside so that we can see and hear with an attitude of maximum freshness and tolerance.

Immediately Prior to and During Performance

Many para-aesthetic stimuli occur at the performance site. Some, like the informative program, are under the direct control of the theatre workers, others are often less manageable.

For example, the neighborhood where the performance takes place has perceived characteristics such as accessibility, safety, convenience, and hospitality—all traits which influence the audience's willingness to attend the theatre as well as their sense of the event once they do decide to attend. But once a theatre is situated, its workers can do little beyond joining in efforts to create the kind of neighborhood ambience they regard as appropriate to their enterprise.

Of course, each audience member attends a performance along with others. That means each audience member affects and is affected by the "other's" behavior. For example, it is usually easier to laugh at a comic situation when others are laughing. On the other hand, it is harder to pay attention when others distract you. Apart from ejecting unruly patrons, however, theatres offer little direct management of spectator responsiveness.

A theatre performance is typically identified by its relationship to real world events around it, thus making theatre's social or para-aesthetic nature loom even larger. Some performances comment on or suggest intervention in political matters. Others provide audiences who seek escape from such "real world" concerns a respite, an emotional distraction or a hiding place. Either way, theatre's perceived link (or lack of it) to society's issues defines it for the spectator.

Some expectations, usually socially derived,

influence our tolerance of what we perceive in the performance. If the setting is realistic, do we expect the acting to be realistic as well? And what do we mean by "realistic"? Do we expect the story to develop a certain way because of its early features? Are all the production languages—e.g., costuming, acting, lighting—expected to employ the same "rules of the game"? If the story first seems to be asking us "Who did it?" or "Why did these incidents happen?" can we be satisfied if a clear answer is not given? Clearly, many para-aesthetic influences come from the societal web the theatre and its audiences inhabit mutually. These often seem to be marginally controllable at best.

Some stimuli come directly from theatre workers. For example, box-office personnel interact with patrons prior to the performance. Suppose they were to treat them gruffly? Their behavior could induce antagonism in the spectator that would seriously inhibit performance response. Similarly, ushers' courtesy and efficiency as well as their knowledge of the seating plan can make the spectator feel relaxed and secure—or the opposite. Often theatres feature lobby displays that focus on careers and personalities of the theatre artists whose work spectators will witness, or alternatively, on information that sharpens their anticipation of the onstage fictive world.

Auditorium conditions such as seating comfort, sightlines, heating, ventilation, lighting, and freedom from distracting outside noises, all influence a spectator's ability to make the transition to the imaginative world of the performance.

In short, the on-site theatre experience contains numerous para-aesthetic determinants, some directly under the control of theatre workers and others not. All affect every audience member's experience of the overall event. The knowledgeable spectator correctly seeks to understand this aspect of theatre's para-aesthetic nature as a way of enriching theatre awareness.

After the Performance

It might seem that once the performance is completed the spectator is immune to para-aesthetic influences. Such is not the case. A good portion of the theatre experience is memorial. The ways a spectator remembers and relives the onstage incidents have much to do with the enjoyment and impact of the event. They also condition the

The Mermaid Theatre, London

spectator for the next event. As we will also see, one reason the memorial experience is important derives from theatre's aesthetic nature. Consequently, a spectator's behavior following a performance is worth taking into account.

The Theatre Event's Aesthetic Nature

Definition of Aesthetic

Some people mistakenly maintain that the term *aesthetic* cannot be defined. Undoubtedly, what they mean is that the term can be, and has been, variously defined. Each definition reveals a great deal about the definer's assumptions. In fact, the many ways artists, philosophers, critics, and thinkers of all ages and cultures have defined "theatre's aesthetic" and the appropriate standards for judging it form the body of knowledge known as theatre theory and criticism. Unavoidably, our consideration of spectatorship and the apt ways of achieving it sets forth one such theory at an introductory level and even articulates certain critical standards. However, it is to our larger advantage to embrace a definition of aesthetic open enough to tolerate wide variations in practice.

The aesthetic nature of theatre is its artistic aspect. Just as a theatre event shares "event-ness" with all other nonartistic happenings in the world, it shares its "artistic-ness" with all other artistic undertakings. But theatre's aesthetic nature can be differentiated from those of painting, music, dance, sculpture, and other arts. We can describe the kind of illusion that is created and we can list the materials used. To the extent that we do these things, we define important traits of theatre's aesthetic nature.

But our difficulties are not over. Recall that each society has its preference for the way theatre is to be shaped. These preferences often strain at the edges of definition. When they do, arguments about whether or not a particular undertaking is "really theatre" abound. Currently, for example, many question whether "performance art" is really

one face of theatre or an entirely different art form. Uncounted opinions exist. We will here side-step such problems of finite classification and concentrate instead on the behaviors of a spectator confronting any of a wide range of events that display at least some key theatrical aspects.

Any consideration of theatre's aesthetic nature can call into question many fine points of definition. If, however, we remember that our goal is to forge an intellectual tool that will open us to possibilities rather than sharpen an ideational weapon to hold other definitions at bay, the chances are we can make ongoing minor adjustments and still keep a clear understanding of what we mean by theatre and its aesthetic nature.

Aesthetic Matters Important to the Spectator

Illusion. All theatre is, to some extent, founded on illusion. Whether it offers a close approximation of the world we already see and accept—our consensual reality—or an alien image that thrills or amazes us, it is still an illusion manufactured for our perception. Since it is a fictive world, all things are possible. Characters can fly, like Peter Pan, or grow younger as time progresses, like Merlin, or be rocks that talk, trees that dance, or personality traits that assume human form. In other words, because the fictive world is produced by imagination(s), we can find in it attributes that remind us only glancingly of what we find in our nonfictive worlds.

Temporal. All illusions in theatre's fictive world undergo change during the time of their enactment. At no instant during our perceiving it is the whole theatre event before us. Instead, it goes by us at enactment speed, always in the perpetual present. We may anticipate the next occurrence, but until it happens it is not yet part of the demonstrated fictive world. Moreover, it is only in memory that we can reconstruct all that transpired in the theatre even recently completed; at this point the theatre experience becomes memorial. Our memories come from our experiences as witnesses. They determine our understanding.

Spatial. All theatre events take place in a space that accommodates both performers and audience members. Often the space is subdivided, made separate and distinct, with each achieving a kind of sacred status. Other times it is unitary. Each configuration causes audiences and actors to act and interact differently, both physically and psychologically.

Synergistic. Theatre events are also synergistic. That is, they seem to be more than the sum of their parts. The way the constituent parts relate to each other unleashes a special energy that melds them into a comprehensive whole. It is one of theatre's paradoxes that although its bombarding stimuli are so numerous they can never be fully accounted for, their overall impression is usually unified and singular. When, as theatre people are fond of saying, the theatre event "works," a fictive world is created wherein the parts relate to each other as if by some invisible natural law.

Computer technology assists today's scenic designers to envision fictive worlds. Pictured above is Mark Reaney's computer-based design for Stephen Sondheim's and John Weidman's *Assassins* produced at the University of Kansas. *(Photo by Mark Reaney)*

Spectator's Responsiveness to the Theatre Event

One practical way to focus on issues discussed thus far is to outline a procedure to be followed by a spectator. Obviously it should encourage the theatre spectator to account for and honor those characteristics we regard as crucial and enriching. As with all process outlines, its animating spirit is more important than the particular examples listed. The examples merely suggest some concerns in considering the elusive, complex and varied nature of theatre performance.

Nonvaluative Description

The single most important undertaking for the spectator who wishes to become more openly responsive and discerning is nonvaluative description. "Nonvaluative" simply means without judgment. Some might argue the impossibility of being absolutely nonvaluative. Nonetheless, spectatorship improves whenever that condition is invoked as a behavioral and attitudinal goal. Why? Let's look briefly at the behaviors and attitudes we combat by striving for nonvaluative description.

Template Thinking

Admittedly, every spectator experiences social conditioning. The result is a series of mental templates used to evaluate experiences. A template is a commonly used device that serves as a gauge, a model, or a mold. Used by architects and designers, it speeds the drawing process. It allows them to duplicate shapes exactly. A pattern we trace around is a template. A cookie cutter is a template.

If while working in the garden we use a screening template that allows small items to pass through and larger ones to remain on top of the screen, we are able to sift through a lot of sand, at least according to size. To separate the grains by color, we need another kind of template, perhaps a spectrometer—or we can rely on our own mental image of color correctness.

We all carry templates in our heads. They are the gauges that help us replicate past experiences. With them we recognize the familiar parts of new experiences and separate them from what is out of the ordinary. The great benefit of templates is that they speed things up. We can sort things quickly and make things uniform.

The disadvantage of templates, at least simple ones, is that they don't work very well with individual uniqueness. Things that don't fit the template must be considered more slowly if sense is to be made of them. This can be frustrating if what we want is rapid and superficial replication of uniform experience; some find this reassuring. If, on the other hand, what we seek is the understanding of something for which there is no ready template, every aspect must be faced anew. There is no shortcut.

Many of the expectations we have about theatre events come from our socially determined mental templates. When plays were expected to have five acts, other patterns seemed unsatisfying to audiences. Now that the two act structure has given us a new template, five act plays seem overlong or too complicated for many audiences.

Television shows, at least in the United States, all seem to end or start on the hour or half-hour. A time template is at work that makes all shows seem largely interchangeable. Something similar operates with the length of a college class.

Many templates affect other than time expectations. All are subject to question. For example, the hero in a drama is expected to win, whether winning means defeating the villain, overcoming a major obstacle, capturing the affections of a worthy partner, or all three. Stories are expected to proceed chronologically, according to cause and effect, and come to a definite conclusion. In fact, it is a mental template that says the serious theatre event is supposed to display a story in the first place, rather than a series of incidents or impressions coordinated according to some other principle. Many theatre-like events that don't meet story expectations, such as circuses, variety entertainments, and performance art, are considered sub-literary and are often ignored by many scholars, historians, and (consequently, but lamentably) by students of theatre.

As general theatre awareness grows, two things happen to mental templates. First of all, the number of available templates increases. Instead of regarding all theatre as being the same, you can measure what you see against a variety of templates

The original Broadway production of Arthur Miller's *Death of a Salesman*, directed by Elia Kazan and designed by Jo Mielziner, opened February 10, 1949.

until the one that is appropriate is located. Appropriateness, itself, will be determined by how much insight into the event the template generates.

The second thing that happens is that templates lose their rigidity. Their increased flexibility allows and enables you to encounter more and more unique ventures with greater and greater confidence. Whether a particular production or performance fits any known template exactly will seem less important than the moment by moment experience of that event. Of course, even in this instance a template of sorts is functioning, but it is a template that measures the intensity of the interaction between the audience member and the object of attention. It is a template that is activated by levels of interest or fascination. It is a template that gives privilege to immediacy—one of theatre's most distinctive traits.

Functionally, a template's value lies in the enriched experience and the depth of understanding it promotes rather than the orderliness it engenders. The enlightened audience member is seeking heightened, memorable, and meaningful theatre experience, not well-sifted sand.

By becoming aware of your judging tendencies, you can review your functional mental templates. You can then appraise their aptness. Nonvaluative description both promotes such self-awareness and allows open access to the theatre event.

Describing the Theatre Event's Para-aesthetic Nature

Describing the theatre event's para-aesthetic elements helps the spectator become aware of the influences—positive and negative—that influence perception of theatre's aesthetic nature. A frank review of personal attitudes about the appropriate role of theatre in society is in order. Balancing those beliefs against what is known of a particular production company's production goals stimulates awareness of any personal biases that may inhibit an open response to that company's work.

Other questions to ask yourself regarding the upcoming theatre event include such things as the following: What does the publicity regarding the production lead me to expect? Do I know anything about the play, its author, the director, the designers, and the other theatre workers that influences my expectations? What about the location of the theatre, the cost of the tickets, my sense of anticipation about the celebratory (or obligatory) traits I associate with going to this event; how are they influencing me?

Once you arrive at the theatre site, consider another cluster of questions. How comfortable and secure am I made to feel in this environment? Do the front-of-house personnel (box-office and ushers) make me feel welcome? Are there any displays that clue me in to the spirit of this event? What kind of performance/viewing space is being used? What clues does it give me about the nature of the performance? Is there a program and if so does it provide me with information that helps me appreciate the performance? What is the atmosphere in the auditorium before the show? How do my fellow audience members behave and what does this do to my expectations?

Of course, during the performance the bulk of your attention will be devoted to the aesthetic nature of the event, but take time to note some of the following: How attentive or restless is the audience? Is the auditorium (seating, temperature, ventilation, etc.) comfortable enough to not distract me from the onstage events?

Following the performance, both immediately and later, reflect on your own and others' responses. Did the audience seem to have a common spirit as they left the theatre? Were there things in the performance that I find my mind continually returning to, either because I couldn't relate to them easily or because they seem to have special meaning for me?

In all these questions and others like them there is a single intention. It is to make the spectator aware of influential para-aesthetic aspects of the theatre event. There are no right or wrong answers to the questions; there is only the hope for heightened awareness, the kind that leads to increased sensitivity. Judgment is not yet called for because the many constituent elements of the theatrical event have not all been experienced and allowed to seek their own level of impact.

The Festival Theatre in Chichester, England.

London's Aldwych Theatre, home to the Royal Shakespeare Theatre.

Premature valuation has the undesirable effect of screening the spectator from aspects of the theatre event that may prove important to its overall integrity. There is a time for critical evaluation, but common sense tells us that it ought to be when all the evidence, fairly gathered and thoughtfully considered, is in mind. That cannot happen if inattention and bias so color the data gathering process that what is being judged is not a full experience of the event but only a superficial scanning based on shallow preferences and snap decisions.

Describing the Theatre Event's Aesthetic Nature

Theatre's aesthetic nature is more important than its para-aesthetic nature. It is, after all, the aesthetic nature of theatre that gives it its prime identity. Describing a theatre event's aesthetic nature nonvaluatively, even when frustrating, is always illuminating. It clarifies things about activities outside the spectator's mind and it offers clues as to what is going on inside as well. Pursued

honestly, it expands theatre awareness and the crucial ability to process new data. Although it is easy to list general categories of description, it is not easy to predict where particular descriptions will lead. Of this much, however, we can be certain. An exciting exploration of imaginative capabilities—the spectator's and the theatre artists'—lies just ahead.

The discerning spectator should offer nonvaluative descriptions that fall into three basic categories: the fictive world set forth in the performance, the theatrical means used to create that fictive world, and the mental and emotional experiences engendered by the fictive world in the spectator.

Describing the Fictive World

The fictive world description focuses on all that can be perceived by a willing spectator of performance. Two closely related attitudes conspire to make the spectator "willing." One is the renunciation of valuation during the actual witnessing of the performance, which has already been discussed, and the other is the often-quoted "willing suspension of disbelief." Together they assist the spectator to get past the skepticism and aloofness that frequently inhibit perception of imaginative works. Instead, the spectator is empowered to mentally enter the imaginative world in order to vicariously experience the life depicted there.

Remember, anything is possible in a fictive world. By staying fully attuned to what is being witnessed the spectator allows the fictive world full credence. This is "the willing suspension of disbelief" in action. It is equally important to note the way impressions of the fictive world change as time goes on. Part of the change undoubtedly comes from the spectator's increasing familiarity with the onstage world. What seemed audacious in the beginning becomes more familiar later. But the more important sense of change will come from the alterations within the fictive world. You can highlight them by asking such questions as: How do the characters develop and grow? What discoveries and decisions do they come to? What do they do as a result of these discoveries and decisions? In short, What happens?

The spectator seeking to become more sensitized to the elements of the fictive world can employ just such a series of questions—a comprehensive template of sorts—as a guide, but should do so with caution. This template, to be useful, should be a tool rather than a weapon. It should not be artificially and relentlessly imposed on fictive world data, but should lie in reserve in the spectator's awareness, with relevant parts waiting to be activated by the onstage stimuli should that prove appropriate. In other words, it is best construed as a sensitizing device for helping the spectator stay alert.

Upon reflection, we can see that most of the questions are rather commonplace. They are like those you might imagine yourself interested in were you to suddenly wake up in an unfamiliar locale.

For example, you might begin by asking: Where am I? What year is it? What season? What day? What kind of a place is this? Thus sensitized

you would naturally be alert to any data, from any source, that would provide you with even tentative answers.

So it is with the fictive world, that alternate reality where anything is possible. The place might be an amalgam of several remembered locales all rolled into one, or it might be a fantasy space quite unlike any place you had ever imagined before. Time could be equally unusual; it could be both the year 1600 and today. Time might also rush by quickly or be slowed down to a snail's pace. In other words, time and place in the fictive world— as well as the rules that seem to control them— may be at considerable variance with what you normally encounter.

Were you to see any creatures in the unfamiliar place you awakened in, you might ask: Who are these beings that inhabit this place and what are they like? What ages are they? What attitudes does each display? What motivates them?

In the fictive world, characters demand equivalent attention. But again, the characters are not limited by real life constraints, so you have to be especially open to the possibilities they present. They may be animals or even inanimate objects that perform deeds and talk, expressing thoughts, desires, and emotional needs. Most often they will be human, but their intensity will make them bigger than life. In pursuing goals, living through challenging events, contending with obstructing forces, they will display a purity and clarity that people we meet outside of the fictive world seldom manifest.

While the characters' demographic data—their gender, their nationalities, and the like—can be duly noted, the things that are undoubtedly of most interest are aspects of their inner lives. You will want to determine their motivations and the mental and emotional traits that determine what they want and why they react as they do. You will want to monitor their discoveries and decisions, and—probably most intriguing of all—what price they are willing to pay to succeed and whether or not they do. Of course, you can only fathom the inner lives of these characters by closely observing their outer traits. The way they behave (both what

The fictive world can be based on images rather than literal reality. Pictured above is Eric Bruce's setting for the University of Kansas' production of Marcus Richey's *The Story in Frank*. It creates an imagined locale in which a young man's memories infuse his parent's home. *(Photo by Earl Iverson)*

they do and how they react to what others do), what they say, the way they look and sound—all will be used by you as indexes to those fascinating inner lives you are sure exist.

The circumstances the characters find themselves in and then seek to modify through their actions create a series of unfolding incidents. The apt spectator pays attention to the dynamics of that unfolding. There is always a special importance assigned to the pattern of how things happen in a play.

But it is not always as easy to summarize what has happened in a play as some might think. A handy template to use is the "description of polar conditions." It states how things are different at the beginning from the way they are at the end. It compares the circumstances at the "poles" of the play. The same template can describe, in shorthand fashion, any polarities of change in a character, a situation, or in the fictive world as a whole. With

the analyzed polar conditions in mind, the spectator next reconstructs the steps that transpired to bring the change about. When we do this, we begin the reflective analysis of the movement—or action— captured by the theatre performance. We reconstruct in memory the moment by moment theatrical immediacy.

An apt summary of the demanding task of fully witnessing the fictive world notes that the spectator stays alert to every possible contingency and dynamic in that world and treats it as initially credible. Deferred judgment is important to a full aesthetic experience of theatre. The spectator does that best by treating all that is observable as virtual fact and then nonvaluatively describing it. Informing all that takes place in a well-crafted fictive world is a rhythm and an unfolding pattern—a rationale—that is accessible only if it is embraced willingly. The spectator's initial step in experiencing the fictive world is to become vulnerable to elements without editing them from consciousness or from their possible potential significance.

Describing the Theatrical Means

"Theatrical means" refers to all the theatre materials, equipment, and techniques used to create a fictive world. Another way to refer to them is as theatre languages. Each collaborator responsible for forming the fictive world employs a language.

For example, it is obvious that the playwright uses words to communicate through speeches spoken by the characters; that is the simplest, most conventional use of the term "language." But a brief look at the other collaborators illustrates other language vocabularies. The actor's language uses personal behavior, sound and gesture which, when added to the words supplied by the playwright, create a sense of a character carrying out a task. The costume designer uses garments which further communicate a sense of character, but also suggest a time, a place, and perhaps a set of climatic conditions (heat, cold, rain, etc.). The scenic designer arranges space and the presence or absence of objects to provide a sense of the locale and its significant features. The lighting designer uses light, its intensity, color, direction, and changeability (plus the absence of light) to augment the work of the costume and scenic designers as well as to add a strong sense of mood. The sound designer uses recorded or live sounds to also create a sense of place, time, and mood. All collaborators use different languages to do their jobs.

It immediately becomes obvious that any single impression generated in the mind of the spectator is undoubtedly the result of many collaborators working in concert. For example, a character is perceived to be of a certain age and demeanor because of the efforts of the playwright, the actor (working along with the director), the costume designer, the makeup designer, and maybe others as well. The resulting impression may be all of a piece, that is, singular and unified, but it took many theatre workers to bring it about. Such is the nature of collaboration. It gives rise to theatre's

synergy, the powerful presence the spectator perceives—in this case, a character—constructed out of many constituent parts and transcending all of them in its potency.

The sense of a fictive world's locale, season, mood, and the like are similarly created from collaborative efforts. For example, you can be led to assume it is a cold winter from the shivering behavior of the actor, the heavy fur-trimmed parka supplied by the costume designer, the frost on the window pane provided by the scenic designer, the sound designer's wind effect, and the lighting designer's choice of light devoid of any but cool blue colors. Intersecting collaborative effort makes it difficult for the spectator to isolate the theatrical means used to create a particular illusion. But the effort to do so attunes the spectator to the way theatre operates and does much to promote sensitivity to the stimuli present in the complex fictive world.

It may be fairly argued that describing the materials and techniques theatre artists use in creating a theatrical illusion is not, strictly speaking, a consideration of theatre's aesthetic nature. That is, the description of theatrical means does not address the illusion per se. However, the judicious and skillful use of theatre's means is so closely linked to the illusion created that the wise spectator thinks of them in tandem. Recognizing how theatre artists communicate is an important step toward fuller receptivity of theatre's power and meaning.

Describing Mental and Emotional Responses

Just as the spectator monitors performance stimuli to unlock the way theatre artists generate their contributions to theatre experiences, so too does the spectator monitor any mental and emotional responses to those stimuli. But a special caution is in order.

The responses referred to here are not valuative responses to the artistic work of the creators. They are responses generated by the inner workings of the fictive world. That is, it is appropriate—in this context—to say that a character is selfish, mean-spirited and you dislike her. It is inappropriate to say that the actor who played the character is disciplined, inventive and you admire her. All the responses the spectator is describing here are apropos of the fictive world, and only the fictive world. This descriptive technique is, in effect, a way of deepening the spectator's memorial experience of the immediate theatrical illusion. It gives voice to the spectator's involvement without prematurely separating from theatre's aesthetic nature by invoking distanced critical standards.

An important way the spectator promotes involvement is to bond with the fictive world. The spectator thereby derives the special kind of experiential meaning that is the hallmark of aesthetic communication. The connection with the fictive world is achieved through the twin processes of identification and empathy.

By common consent, identification is reckoned to be an important phenomenon in the theatre. Identification is thought to be the basis of audiences' empathetic responses to characters. Similarly, it is identification which allows the actors to "live the parts" that they play. In both cases, identification proceeds from an assumption that the character is to be construed as a real person.

To so construe a character is a pleasant and enabling conceit. It allows the audience members to envision the play as a fragment of reality extending out from the time and space of the performance in all directions. It thus betokens a fictive world similar to the real world in many, but not all, ways.

The actor approaches the task of playing the character by plumbing the presumed motivations for each of the character's acts. The actor often invents an extra-textual character biography to help ground that imagined being in the fictive world. The goal is to increase the character's seeming dimensionality as a living and volitional being.

But such identification, though both pleasant to audiences and useful for actors, is a kind of mental trick we willingly play on ourselves. Just as in the clear light of reality we know that the actor is not the character, so too do we know that the character is not a real person but a theatrical device designed by theatre workers such as the playwright, actor, director, and designers to represent some otherwise ineffable quality. Thus the creation of a character as a person is merely one means for eliciting a response from audience members who join in the game by embracing the same mental trick.

Actors and directors know that there is more to a character than its "real human traits." So too do audiences when they take time to reflect on the matter. Actors and directors orchestrate the character's "behavior" in such a way as to provide focus and structure to the play and its constituent scenes. It is this structuring that enables the play to climax or come to a moment of irreversibility when the end appears inevitable. In other words, the actors and director respond to a performer's abstract patterning needs in a way that transcends the illusion of the character as a person.

It is a mark of sophistication to be able to conceive, perceive, and discuss the various abstract patterns that overlay the play envisioned as a fictive world peopled by characters who possess the traits of real human beings. To do so, however, is not to lose sight of the gateway effect provided by identification with the character as a real person. In a harmonious work of theatre art the relationship among the various abstract patterns and the entry-level fictive reality is symbiotic. Each level functions gracefully in the context of all the others.

Because the fictive world of the performance is not a natural occurrence but is a constructed image, designed to be perceived, the patterns that undergird it are also of interest to the spectator because they can reveal and validate the nature of the aesthetic choices made. Perhaps the overall pattern of what transpires suggests that it is the revelation of inner, felt experience that informs the performance rather than the adherence to literal external reality. In such a circumstance the characters might fly rather than walk because flying would make their inner feelings more evident metaphorically. Or perhaps being paralyzed might represent—metaphorically—the character's feeling of psychological impotence. In both cases what is being shown the spectator is an observable behavior designed to make clear an otherwise hidden state. This kind of "stand-in representation" makes the observable behavior a metaphor for the inner state. By remaining sensitive to the pattern of informing impulses in the fictive world the spectator develops another level of informed appreciation. The aesthetic rationale that shaped the theatre event comes into focus and becomes part of the spectator's response.

Spectator's Evaluation of the Theatre Event

At some point, all spectators will feel a need to evaluate the theatrical event. It is important when developing spectatorship abilities that such evaluation not occur too soon, that it not interfere with full observation and balanced reflection. If the developing spectator can delay coming to judgment too soon, the likelihood is increased that more theatrical elements and more subtle but interesting linkages among those elements can be perceived. Such an expansion of vision empowers the spectator to see richly varied depictions of what it means to be human, each a discrete image set forth in accordance with the diverse aesthetic preferences of its creators. Since humanizing growth is one of the theatre's most precious offerings, both to an individual and to a society, it makes good sense to become increasingly adept at receiving that offering in whatever guises it assumes.

Another observation about evaluating is in order. Any summary judgment the spectator offers may seem at first glance to be directed solely toward the theatrical event. However, strictly speaking, that is never the case. Instead, any appraisal inevitably depends as well on the transaction whereby the theatrical event was perceived. In other words, the perceived "event," even the memorial one which the spectator is "judging," always owes a measure of its existence to that spectator's ability and willingness to perceive the event.

As we grow in our capabilities as spectators our sensitivities and standards change. Interestingly, we do not simply develop higher standards, although to some extent that may be true. Rather, we develop more sophisticated standards that are increasingly appropriate to the varied events we witness. This observation has particular relevance to the learning behaviors of the developing spectator. As we reflect on a particular performance in order to evaluate "it," we are presented with a rare opportunity to reflect also on the otherwise invisible standards and premises we have within us that enable us to evaluate a work in a particular fashion in the first place. As developing spectators we have a rare chance to reshape our theatre tastes by addressing them directly.

Often someone asks, "What are the standards that tell a spectator whether a performance is good or bad?" Frankly, every valuation is a partisan statement expressing a preference for a particular aesthetic vision. You recall that earlier we noted that society helps shape an individual's tastes. Factions within society do the same: teachers, established artists, exponents of avant-garde expression, moralists, political watchdogs among them. It is less important that the developing spectator embrace a specific set of standards than it is that the spectator seek to understand whatever aesthetic and social vision was operative in shaping the event.

Some of the questions you might employ as a temporary template to help keep you alert to the performance's informing vision can be listed. Did the performance create a sense of a controlled rather than an accidental fictive world? Were the several theatre languages informed by rationales that created a clear impression? Was what happened unified in some evident way? Did it have variety? Were the "rules" of the fictive world made clear by the work of the collaborating artists?

Did what I observe have any resonance in me; that is, did it stimulate me to reflect on things in any way? Did the performance make me see things freshly? Did it urge me to behave differently in regards to those things I saw? Was what I witnessed challenging to me in any way?

Naturally, you are going to "like" some performances more than others. But, frankly, "liking" (or disliking) a performance is not enough. We all tend to like what we are familiar with, those things that reinforce our beliefs and values. Theatre events that offer the chance to expand our being will almost always go beyond what we, at first, find familiar and comfortable—at least, they should. Soon we become more able to explore ideas and experiences through theatre because we know how it operates and we realize we needn't

feel personally threatened. When we do, we will grow to "like" that experience and theatre will assume new importance in our lives. For the developing spectator, it is less important that a performance be "good" according to some codified standards than that it be illuminating. Therein lies the enduring magic of theatre.

Final Observations

While this chapter introduces you to the study of theatre as an audience member, it is not a final pronouncement. Part of spectatorship's power is that it both grows and promotes growth. Exploration of theatre through spectatorship need

"The Weeping Audience," an engraving historically depicting spectator response in the eighteenth century.

never stop. As you venture further afield into performances designed for the tastes of cultures other than your own, or for action groups who hold radical views not to your liking, you will be challenged. Meeting the challenge successfully means you will continue to learn about how theatre operates and how openly you can witness it fully before evaluating it. Finally, you will find that you grow as a theatre spectator in ways that parallel and facilitate your growth as a liberally educated human being.

Selected Readings

Beckerman, Bernard. *Dynamics of Drama*. New York: Alfred A. Knopf, 1970.

Beckerman, Bernard. *Theatrical Presentation*, edited by Gloria Brim Beckerman and William Coco. New York: Routledge, 1990.

Bennett, Susan. *Theatre Audiences*. New York: Routledge, 1990.

Carlson, Marvin. *Theories of the Theatre*. Ithaca, New York: Cornell University Press, 1984.

States, Bert O. *Great Reckonings in Little Rooms*. Berkeley, CA: University of California Press, 1987.

Styan, J. L. *Drama, Stage and Audience*. New York: Cambridge University Press, 1975.

CHAPTER TWO

❧

Origins:
Theatre and Drama

Primitive mask used in the winter ceremonials by North American Indian tribes. From Ridgeway's *Dramas and Dramatic Dances of Non-European Races*, 1915.

This is a book about theatre. More precisely, it is about theatre and drama which are two closely related but separate professions. They even have their own unions. Drama (the dramatist) has the Dramatist's Guild. As a profession, the dramatist is concerned with the script—the written word. This means the writer creates characters, their thoughts, their words, their physical actions. That is what the Greek work *drama* means—activities or actions.

Theatre has a variety of unions, the oldest being the Actors Equity Association (Equity). Theatre represents a variety of activities, the actor, the physical plant, the sets, the costumes, the lights, etc.; drama is concerned only with its one union. Together theatre and drama function to create the human experience. One experiences theatre as one does life—through the senses. That is why theatre and life are so closely bound.

Theatre is not life, however. It is an imitation. But stage life has the capability of transcending into actual life, making the action on stage real and meaningful to the audience. Whereas a person's life consists of diverse action, drama consists of structured action—that is, a dramatist condenses activity into a few hours. Within those few hours, a play is presented that focuses on the significant events and ideas in the lives of certain people. The significant events and ideas do not merely entertain but also make a statement about the human condition. It may be a profound comment about man and God, or it may be a simple observation about right and wrong. The point is that the events and ideas are selected by the dramatist who entertains while making a statement about life. The noted South African dramatist, Athol Fugard, for example, stated that life was "a dance floor full of collisions," whereas Shakespeare termed it "a walking shadow."

Each generation seeks to answer the same haunting questions: Who are we? Why were we born? What is life? What is death? In exploring these questions, we are expressing our innermost thoughts—thoughts about who we are and what we are. And it is through art that we have learned to express ourselves best.

Whether music, painting, dance or theatre, these self-expressions are a record of man's search for an identity. Throughout the centuries man has posed many questions with few answers in an effort to find his identity. Each generation reads, examines, ponders, and asks, leaving the next generation no answers but only records of their search. These records tell us that people are not very different. The questions asked by the Greeks are the same questions asked by modern Americans. Perhaps it is in the asking that humanity finds its greatest solace, for in raising these questions we have created a way of expressing our thoughts. And look what these thoughts have created: music, art, literature, theatre, medicine, and other devices for the benefits of mankind. But humanity's thoughts have not always been for the good. We have created war, bombs, guns, hatred, and similar tools of destruction which have hindered progress. Whether for good or evil, thoughts are the sum and substance of being. They give rise to actions. Theatre and drama are about actions, human actions. Of all the art forms, none express the actions of people better than theatre and drama. Only in the theatre can people watch their fellow beings live as though it were happening for the first time.

Aesthetic Distance

A factor aiding dramatic appeal is a psychological state defined as aesthetic distance. This unique condition allows audiences to view events on stage with a semi-objective attitude (detachment). It is somewhat akin to tunnel vision in that audience members block out the world around them and immerse themselves into the world of the stage. Physically, they are in the audience, but mentally they have entered into the world they are viewing. Samuel Taylor Coleridge termed this phenomenon "the willing suspension of disbelief." Audiences willingly give up their world (their reality) for that on stage, television, or the film. It is a curious psychological state which allows the audience to absorb the reality of one life while being temporarily suspended in their own world. Theatre and drama involve, therefore, more than observing fundamental truths about life; they require psychological participation (see Chapter One). That is why we laugh, cry and get emotionally involved. Shakespeare recognized this when he had Hamlet stage the "mousetrap" play. From man's first use of theatre/drama (ritual and myths), psychological participation has always been a cornerstone of the theatre's appeal. Primitive man used it to sort out his universe; we do the same.

The Function of Theatre and Drama

In its ritual form, theatre imitated as well as reflected primitive society: its hopes, its fears, its institutions, indeed its way of life. Today the theatre and its drama continue to sum up society's institutions, hopes, fears, and attitudes. The theatre is the pulse of human experience; it captures the growth of men and women—their goodness as well as their evilness. It allows us, the audience, to experience what past, present and future civilizations have experienced and might experience. Theatre is much like a bridge, providing insight not only to other worlds and people, but to ourselves. It enables man, as does all art, to look into himself and say, "I Am."

Inasmuch as theatre and drama imitate life, the question arises as to why we prefer imitation to the real thing. What function does art serve? To answer this question, we must first define art. A definition is better understood after an inquiry into how the term *art* has evolved.

Antiquity considered art to be a "useful skill which is systematically applied." This was a broad definition and included areas such as war, medicine, mining and agriculture. Aristotle's treatise, *The Poetics* (c. 335-323 B.C.), was written to prove that art as a "species" was a useful skill which could be applied systematically. In other words, he wanted to prove that poetry was an art.

In the eighteenth century, art was divided into two categories. The first was fine arts, also called polite or elegant arts, which focused on the creation of art objects for beauty and pleasure. The second group was concerned with useful, practical, or industrial arts, and thus concentrated on creating useful art objects. Concomitant with this division of art was the notion that fine arts could not be taught and were products of genius. This placed the fine arts on a plane with the gods who communicated to a select group. Fine arts thus were thought to be products of inspiration (genius), whereas practical arts were considered the creation of perspiration.

The writing habits of two eighteenth century German writers, Goethe and Schiller, exemplify the differences between the useful and polite arts. Johann Wolfgang von Goethe (1749-1832) relied greatly on perspiration in his creative efforts. He wrote, rewrote, and polished. Writing was a useful skill which he applied systematically. His contemporary, Johann Christoph Friedrich von Schiller (1759-1805), on the other hand, divined his writing; that is, he relied on inspiration from the gods. To acquire this inspiration, Schiller was said to have shut himself in an airtight room; whereupon, he would sniff a box of rotten apples until he reached what is popularly referred to as a "high." Then he would write.

Despite the separation and different approaches, art can and generally does serve two masters: it is both aesthetic and functional. Thus the chief function of fine arts is not only to "seek expression through beautiful or significant modes," but also to serve as a teaching tool. It is through imitation that we learn. As fine arts, theatre and drama fulfill both functions.

Theatre's functions of teaching and pleasing (entertaining) have served society in many ways. Theatre is useful, for example, in rehabilitative therapy for the emotionally disturbed and physically handicapped. A teaching tool, theatre serves to gain and sustain the interest of students. The business world has also utilized theatre. The theatre and its drama reflect the political, social and economic attitudes of any society at any given time. Theatre audiences provide consumer information on standards and tastes, as well as political ideas and economic levels. Social sciences are also an outlet for theatre. African American and Chicano theatre, for example, dramatize problems, fears and aspirations of minorities. When you dramatize minority problems, you must take into account social sciences such as sociology, economics, politics, history, and religion. No other form of communication affords us such an opportunity to interact visually, aurally, spiritually, and mentally with our fellow beings. Theatre and drama have universal appeal. They communicate to all people, regardless of the generation, language, or society, certain fundamental truths about life.

Hamlet (1601) and *A Death of a Salesman* (1949) are two outstanding tragedies and wherever they are produced, audiences, recognizing their merits, generally attend them in greater numbers than lesser-known works. The reasons underlying the strength of these dramas can be debated, but no doubt one of their strengths is that they communicate truths of life. These are fundamental truths to which audiences of any generation can relate; these have a universal appeal.

Theatre Origins

When we discuss theatre, we are discussing the presentation of a play. Prior to theatre being formally recognized and plays being structured, theatre and drama were one in the same. The origins of drama predate written texts. The play's focus was to be seen; it was not a written script designed to be read. The performance did not make use of the spoken word. Drama was essentially a nonverbal form as was theatre. Thus, to discuss theatrical origins is to consider dramatic origins as well. In either case, both are obscure and the theories surrounding their beginnings are diverse. Inasmuch as theatre and drama were formally recognized and organized in Athens, Greece, the theo-

ries have centered on some aspect of Athenian society.

The ritual theory has been the most widely discussed theory as to the origins of theatre. This concept was developed by the Cambridge School of Anthropologists and forwarded by Sir James Frazer (1854-1941) in his twelve-volume work, *The Golden Bough* (1890-1915).

Frazer's idea was to establish a relationship between the rituals and myths of primitive man and the theatre of the Greeks. Frazer suggests that all societies go through similar patterns of development and, consequently, one need only examine present-day primitive tribes to discover evidence about the rituals used in tribes a thousand years ago. It is in the development of ritual and myths that Frazer sees the origin of theatre. According to Frazer, primitive man, in dealing with his environment, was ignorant as to natural causes and their effects and, therefore, ascribed supernatural powers to those forces in nature which he did not understand. In seeking to gain the favor of these forces of gods, he developed systematic acts which were designed to curry favor. We term these systematic acts rituals. Some members of the tribes were more adept than others in dealing with rituals and they became known as the priests or chief actors. The stories that developed around the rituals were myths. The rituals disappeared, but the myths remain. They are the subject matter for drama.

These rituals were designed basically to insure fertility; that is, an abundance of children, crops, water, and animals to hunt. Underlying the concept of fertility was a recognition of death and man's desire to offset its powers. Death thus became evil and life (fertility), good. In many tribes, these two opposing forces became the subject of a mock battle called "The Year." One member of the tribe (the reigning king) would become an actor by representing the forces of winter (death, evil, etc.), and another member of the tribe (the king-to-be) would act the role of summer (fertility, good). This enactment or dramatic ritual was staged yearly,

Dramatization of "The Year" ritual. From Ridgeway's *Dramas and Dramatic Dances of Non-European Races*, 1915.

with good always winning. Although the winter king is slain, he is resurrected and spiritually lives on in his successor.

The relationship between ritual and theatre is established through the worship of the god Dionysus, who was slain and resurrected. He was worshipped by the Greeks at festivals held throughout the year, as the god of wine, fertility, insanity, and catharsis. Inasmuch as drama originated in connections with one of these festivals (City Dionysia) held at Athens, Frazer sees the fertility rituals practiced by primitive man as having an influence on those rituals performed by the followers of Dionysus.

Contrary to Frazer's ritual theory were the anthropologists Bronislaw Malinowski, who was a functionalist and one of the founders of modern

anthroplogy, and Claude Lévi-Strauss (b.1908), the noted French structuralist. Both reject Frazer's cultural Darwinism, both recognize that societies develop along individual lines (some are static and some are dynamic), both are interested in how societies function, and both reject the single origin theory. These arguments have relevance for theatre and drama when one considers that not all societies developed theatre and drama past the ritual stage. While some societies remained static, others were dynamic in the use of theatre and drama. In these dynamic societies, the evolutionary stages of drama are unknown. A possible explanation as to the reason underlying the different stages of development in a society may be the particular methods used in a society to transmit ideas from generation to generation. Historically, anthropologists recognize that rites which evolve in the course of human civilization are not hereditarily fixed, but rather are transmitted by tradition and must be learned anew by each succeeding generation. It seems, therefore, that societies generally have a fixed culture which is passed on from one generation to be learned by the next. A factor in maintaining that fixed culture is habit. When habit becomes ingrained in a society, it becomes a custom which traditionally creates fear when broken. Consequently, it appears that the static societies relied on ritual drama as part of the customs of their society; whereas the dynamic societies broke with old customs and developed newer forms of drama in keeping with their needs and purposes.

The Egyptians and the Greeks offer a comparison of static and dynamic societies. Although the Egyptians were an extremely sophisticated society, they never developed (formalized) theatre and drama past the ritualistic stage. The Greeks were the first to recognize theatre's potential as a specialized adjunct to their culture. The theatre provided the Greeks with a media whereby they could express their thoughts about life, death, and those forces which they believe shaped their destiny. A performance thus became an expression of feelings, thoughts, and a way of life.

Origins of Drama

Similar to theatre, the origins of drama, specifically tragedy and comedy, are equally conjectural. Ancient Greeks defined tragedy to mean "goat song," perhaps implying that either a goat was sacrificed or that a goat was given as a prize for best chorus performers. Aristotle states that tragedy originated out of the mimic representations by the leaders of the dithyrambic chorus (exarchon). The dithyramb was a story about the suffering and death of Dionysus and was sung by the chorus members who sang the refrain. The dithyramb is thought to have been developed in Phrygia (near or in Northwest Turkey) and to have come to Greece with the cult of Dionysus. Arion (c. 625-585 B.C.) is credited with changing dithyrambs into literary compositions at Corinth, a major city for the Dorian Greeks. What he probably did was to create a stationary chorus and have the chorus sing a titled poem on a well-defined subject matter. As a form, the dithyramb developed fully in Athens at the festivals of Dionysus.

Javanese historical masks and puppet. From Ridgeway's *Dramas and Dramatic Dances of Non-European Races*, 1915.

The first dithyrambic contests were held at the City Dionysia about 509 B.C. Thespis is thought to have improved upon the dithyramb by adding a prologue and dialogue, thus developing the first role for an actor. This innovation was probably responsible for his winning in 534 B.C. the first contest for the best writer of tragedy.

Aristotle credits the origins of Greek comedy "out of those who led the phallic procession." Phallic refers to the penis, which was adopted by the Greeks as a symbol of fertility as part of their religious ceremony honoring the god Dionysus, god of fertility. Further, each Athenian house had a bust of the god Hermes mounted on a flat stone slab with a large erect penis projecting from its center. Also, the City Dionysia festival had a procession in which large, erect penises made of terracotta were carried while songs were sung to phal-

lus. How a sexual ritual was transformed into formal comedy is not known. Epicharmus, who lived in Sicily, is credited with making the transformation about 480 B.C. It is also asserted that another influence was the mime from which the Athenians borrowed certain elements which they combined with their phallic choruses to develop comedy. By 486 B.C. Greek comedy was given official recognition when contests for writers of comedy were instituted at the City Dionysia festival. The first winner was Chionides.

A reaction to Frazer's ritual theory was that of archaeologist and writer, William Ridgeway (1853-1926). Ridgeway developed the tomb theory, which maintains that tragedy originated in performances at the tombs of deceased heroes. Based upon the hero-cult aspect of Greek religion, Ridgeway contends that dramatic dances and hero-cult lamenta-

Turkish karagoz shadow-play puppets. From Ridgeway's *Dramas and Dramatic Dances of Non-European Races.*

tions were performed at these hero-tombs by a priest who became a medium for the hero's spirit. The priest was thus an actor playing a part. It is thought that rituals at the tombs were later absorbed by the worshippers of Dionysus who utilized similar ceremonies and concepts. Inasmuch as Aristotle contended that drama developed out of the worship of Dionysus, the rituals at the tombs, according to Ridgeway, were factors in shaping the form of drama. Aeschylus' *Persae* (472 B.C.) serves as a good example of a drama supporting Ridgeway's theory. Darius, the dead king, is to be summoned (second episode, lines 598-851) by a hymn of reverence sung by the chorus. When

Darius' ghost appears, he addresses the chorus. Of importance to our discussion are his lines: "You are keening [lamenting] as you stand near my tomb and you are summoning me in piteous manner, singing the high-noted laments that raise the spirits of the dead." These lines indicate that a funeral ritual is being performed at the tomb of Darius, and hence involves the necessary dances, incense, incantations, and digging at the ground. The ritual seems to be much the same as that performed by the dithyrambic chorus in their worship of Dionysus.

Another theory which deserves mention is Gerald Else's (b.1908) artistic theory. A classics professor and scholar, Else's theory attributes the origin of theatre solely to the Athenians' artistic ability, which he contends was the deliberate creation of Thespis and Aeschylus. Else sees no evidence to connect the worship of Dionysus with the origins of tragedy. The only relationship that exists, he contends, is that tragedy was presented at festivals honoring the god Dionysus. Furthermore, the fact that Aristotle contends that tragedy developed from the improvisation by the leaders of the dithyramb (a song or hymn in honor of the God Dionysus) does not warrant consideration. In Aristotle's era, the dithyramb's connection to Dionysus was nil and it was simply a "narrative poem on heroic subjects." Historians have sought to transfer ritual performances from other countries to Greece in an effort to account for the influence on the Greek formation of tragedy. But as Else asserts: "Athens in the sixth century B.C. is the only place in the world that has ever given birth to tragedy. We must . . . take a closer look a Athens."

William Arrowsmith's (b. 1924) judicial metaphor theory is based upon the idea that the Greek tragic theatre's ritualistic origins warrant reexamination. Arrowsmith, an author and a scholar in the field of classics, argues that the origins are to be found in "a theatre shaped more by the law-court than by the altar." He points to the dominance of trial scenes in Greek tragedy and the plays of Euripides. In Euripides' plays, suggests Arrowsmith, the absence of a single hero can be observed. Instead Euripides creates a formal clash between two central characters in the form of a debate (agon). The theatre, then, is a metaphor for the Athenian courts, which may not have been the original creative force but certainly seem to have been a vital influence in the shaping of Greek tragedy.

There are other origin theories, but the focus of this book is simply to make the reader aware of the ambiguity surrounding the origins. Although the origins are obscure, the search for the theatre's roots has provided some insightful information concerning societal development.

Theatre and Drama: Relevance

As cultural phenomena, theatre and drama form valuable assets to our society. Why should theatre and drama continue to be valued without any obvious practical purpose? A partial answer is offered by Aristotle who contended that imitation is natural and pleasurable and that man learns better from imitation. Another explanation is offered by the Swiss psychologist Carl Jung (1875-1961), who asserted that the value of theatre and drama is that they help us analyze our immediate environment. "A great work of art is like a dream," suggests Jung. That is, there is more to it than what is immediately seen. Moreover, the great work of art requires that you perceive it according to your own experiences and hence make your own value judgments (interpretations). Like Aristotle, Jung sees art as organic and related directly to man's nature.

It is not farfetched to suggest that we still retain a strong tie with primitive man and his use of ritual. A look at our religious services, political campaigns, parades, and sport events will testify to this. Our daily lives are ritualistic, as were those of primitive man. The relationship between ritual, symbol, and man is fundamental to theatre and drama. Although theatre and drama are not actual life, their ability to imitate life enables them to

penetrate into the lives of the audience. On the one hand, audience members can respond emotionally to a situation. On the other hand, they can react intellectually to a particular social, political, or economic situation. In either case, the audience identifies and empathizes with the theatrical production through the characters, the settings, or the events. If characters in a drama are viewed as symbols of a society, then theatre and drama can be thought of as being expressions of a culture—that is, the meeting place where man's experiences are enjoined to symbolic representations. The characters, the settings, and the events are simply symbols; they represent life with all its problems and unanswered questions. The symbols of a theatre are developed according to the needs and purposes of a society. The complexity of modern society requires many more symbols that were required in a primitive society. This has led to newer forms of theatrical experimentation and a return to ritualistic drama in an effort to find some basic answers to some basic questions.

Selected Readings

Campbell, Joseph. *The Masks of Gods: Primitive Mythology.* New York, 1959.

Frazer, J. G. *The Golden Bough.* 12 Vols. London, 1913-1915

Kirby, E. T. *Ur-Drama.: The Origins of Theatre.* New York, 1975.

Lévi-Strauss, Claude. *The Savage Mind.* Chicago, 1966.

Ridgeway, William. *The Drama and Dramatic. Dances of Non-European Races.* Cambridge, 1915.

Vocabulary

1. Dionysus   digh uh NIGH suhs
2. dithyramb   DI thuh ram
3. agon   AH gawn
4. Lévi-Strauss   LE vee strows
5. Carl Jung   yoong
6. Malinowski   MAL in ow ski

CHAPTER THREE

Dramatic Structure: Form and Style

Aristotle (384-322 B.C.). Born in Macedonia, he came to Athens where he studied with Plato. Considered the founder of science, his work *The Poetics* has had a significant impact on theatre and drama.

Writing a play is like making an apple pie. Not only do all the parts have to blend together, but the parts should be in proper proportion. In the case of the apple pie, if one puts in too much sugar (or for that matter, not enough sugar), the desired apple pie will be ruined. The same idea is true for a play. The dominance of any element, say for example, the setting (spectacle), over that of the other elements that go into constructing a play will have a similar effect, meaning that the play will not be constructed well. In order to understand the elements of a play and how they operate it is important to define the elements.

A key term that requires defining is the word *drama*. This term is much used and much abused. The abuse stems from not knowing its definition, especially by the television networks, talk-show hosts, newspapers, journals, and, worst of all, many self-styled drama critics. When this term is used in the media, it is usually juxtaposed to comedy. That is, the advertisement will inform the public that they will see comedy and drama on a certain night. Juxtaposing these two gives the implication that comedy is not drama and that drama is something akin to but different from comedy. The point is that comedy is drama. *Drama* is a Greek word meaning deeds or activities. When a playwright arranges these deeds or acts in a specific way with specific characters, the writer creates (forms) either a comedy, tragedy, or melodrama. Comedy, tragedy and melodrama are forms of drama. The writer has formed the deeds or activities (drama) in such a way that a comedy, tragedy, or melodrama is the result. To say, therefore, that comedy and drama are separate is misleading and false. Comedy is drama, just as tragedy and melodrama are drama. The reasoning behind the media's misuse of the word is purely economical. Remember that in this era entertainment is a product to be marketed and sold. Most of the entertainment presented, especially on television, is melodrama. To use this term would suggest villains with stovepipe hats, fair damsels in distress, and last minute rescues. Even though these and other ingredients of a melodrama are still presented to viewers, the media disguise this form by advertising it as drama in order to lead viewers to believe that they are seeing a dramatic production that is different from comedy and thus more sophisticated—a tragedy. In reality, what is being presented is melodrama. By using the term *drama* (or misusing the term), the media pander to the masses in order to sell a product (the show). Furthermore, the advertisers are suggesting that melodrama is an inferior form. In actuality, one form is not better than another. Tragedy is not superior to comedy or melodrama, and the converse is equally true. Each form's worth is determined by the individual writer and the particular work written.

Inasmuch as drama focuses on characters and their actions, drama can be said to be about what people think, say, and do. Anytime characters think, talk, or do something, they are undergoing a change. To make a change means to create a different course, position, or direction. To do this, a character must alter by force or natural means that which the character wishes to change. This means that something must be done; in other words, some sort of action must be implemented. Thus, change involves action. Drama is about change; it involves action. Action is change, change is action.

In drama as in life there are two kinds of changes (action): mental and physical. The basic difference is that life consists of a variety of changes; drama consists of structured changes. The total change or action of a play, therefore, consists of both external and internal changes that are structured by the writer. The action of a play is not the physical aspect only; characters thinking are involved in action. Aristotle defined this aspect of action as *suffering*. Today we define suffering in terms of pain or distress. This is a restricted meaning for the term. Anything that goes on inside the character is considered suffering. It can be mere awareness or more intense, such as physical pain. The best suffering is psychological, which occurs in a tragic situation but not a comic. Inasmuch as suffering is change, it is action. Suffering leads to discovery and discovery is the basis or beginning of a complication.

Plot

To say that drama consists of structuring actions (changes) is to say that drama is organized via *plot*. Anytime you undertake to structure an action you are forming plot. As a term, plot is misunderstood and thus misused, especially when referring to story. Plot and story are not the same. All stories have plots but not all plots have stories. To understand these two concepts, it is necessary to know their definition and how each functions.

Plot is the overall organization of any action, meaning that it orders the incidents in a play, arranges those incidents in a specific pattern and gives the reasons for that arrangement. A *story* is the narrative, the sequence of events. All stories have some sort of organization but not all plots use story as a means to arrange the incidents. Sometimes plots organize travelogues, ideas, or sometimes the material is ritual. Story refers to a full account of an event or events. Plot selects and arranges parts of the story for presentation on stage, television, or in a movie. There are two basic ways for plot to unify the action for presentation. One is *linear*, also known as cause-to-effect (causality). A linear plot means that the events are sequential and chronologically in order. Hence, the use of the term linear. Another way of unifying the action is via an *episodic* plot. This type of construction is non-linear and unifies the events either through an idea or characters. Examples of this type are biography, absurdist drama, ritual drama, or travelogues. Whether the plot is linear or episodic, when the play's plot is completed, it is said to have a whole or unified action. A unified action has a beginning, middle, and end. Aristotle's dictum that a play should have a beginning, middle, and end means that a play should be complete and self-contained; that is, everything you need to know about the characters, events, and the actions should be included within the play's framework.

Beginning

The beginning of a play includes not only the beginning of the story but also the beginning of the main action. When a dramatist writes a play, the author must choose which events of a story he will show the audience. He can show the entire story or he can show the middle or the end of the story. For example, in *The Three Bears,* the author could start the story as it is usually told with Goldilocks entering the three bears' house, or he could start the story with the bears coming home. If he begins the play with the three bears coming home, then all the prior information must be told to the audience. Such information is *exposition*, which could be presented through a monologue by Goldilocks or perhaps in a dialogue between the bears and Goldilocks. Exposition is additional information given throughout the play about events that have happened before the play started. This information is needed if the audience is to understand the present situation. In film the use of a "flashback" is a method to give the audience exposition. It is part of the technology of movies which the stage cannot duplicate. That place where the author chooses to start the story is known as the *point of attack*. Points of attack are either early or late. If you have an early point of attack you will have very little exposition and for a late point of attack you will have a lot of exposition. Shakespeare uses an early point of attack; he tells the story from the beginning. In contrast, Greek tragedians use a late point of attack; they begin the play by dramatizing the final events in a story and use exposition to tell the audience what events have already transpired.

In addition to including the point of attack, the beginning of a play includes the start of the main action, the *inciting incident*. The inciting incident is in actuality a complication. In a linear construction it is the most important of all the complications because all the complication in a play stems from this one. Like all complications, the inciting incident begins with a discovery made by the protagonist (the central character) that forces that character from a static situation into an active one. In other words, everything is in balance or harmony until the inciting incident occurs and, like a see-saw, this incident causes an imbalance. The inciting incident is that incident in a story that causes everything in the play to happen. It should be pointed out that inciting incidents occur only in linear plots. Non-linear (episodic) plays make use of a *focal point*. Absurdist dramas are examples of plays which do not contain inciting incidents.

An example of traditional drama using a late point of attack and an inciting incident is Euripides' *Hippolytus* (428 B.C.). The play opens with Aphrodite's prologue giving us exposition about her hatred of Hippolytus, who refuses to honor her and who favors Artemis. She further describes how Phaedra, the wife of Theseus (Hippolytus' father), fell in love with Hippolytus. Angry over Hippolytus' refusal to honor her, Aphrodite plans to punish Hippolytus as well as kill Phaedra by revealing Phaedra's love for Hippolytus. The fact that Euripides begins the play after all the events described by Aphrodite have occurred indicates that this play has a late point of attack. Had he started with the first refusal of Hippolytus to honor Aphrodite or with Phaedra's marriage, then the play would have had an early point of attack. In Scene III the Nurse reveals Phaedra's love to an unsuspecting Hippolytus—this event is the inciting incident. It causes all the subsequent action.

Middle

The action created by the inciting incident (in a linear construction) constitutes the middle of the play. To create this action involves developing a series of complications. *Complication* is a Latin term meaning to entwine and that is exactly what it does: it entwines one event with another. Further, a complication is made up of three parts: a beginning (the discovery), the middle (crisis) and the end (climax). It functions only by changing or altering the course of action and it does so when a character learns (discovers) something.

Two points need to be made about *discovery*. First, discovery is the basis or beginning of a complication and thus creates interaction. Second, as noted earlier, the first or initial discovery is

usually labeled the inciting incident and provides the reason for the play.

When a character makes a discovery, that character is forced into making a decision. Not making a decision (doing nothing) is still a decision. This decision-making process is the *crisis* or turning point in the action. Crisis comes from the Greek *krises*, meaning decision. The decision that a character makes, whether big or small, must be one that is logical, consistent, and believable with that character's behavior as well as with the play's logic (see Probability). While the audience awaits to determine what decision a character will make, tension is created. Thus crisis creates tension, and it is the climax that relieves that tension.

Let's examine how complications operates, again using *Hippolytus* as our model. Phaedra has a tremendous problem. She loves her husband's son. A question is raised. What is she doing to do? Phaedra's struggle to solve her problem has caused her unhappiness and she, therefore, decides to die. Maintaining silence about her love, she starves herself and becomes ill. Another question is raised—why is she sick? The Nurse discovers the answer, but the answer raises another question. What will the Nurse do? The Nurse reveals Phaedra's love to Hippolytus, thus answering one question but raising another. What will Hippolytus do? Raising questions and answering them constitutes the basis for a complication. Discovery precipitates the beginning of a complication—Phaedra's self-discovery of her love for Hippolytus. In seeking to solve her question, a number of alternatives are considered—to die, reveal her love, or do nothing. The consideration of the alternatives, or the middle of the complication, creates tension and conflict (crisis) which lead to the climax (high point) of the complication—her enactment of one of the alternatives. When she decides to reveal her love, Phaedra answers the initial question but in so doing raises another. Answering one question marks the end of one complication and begins another. Beginning complications lead to middle complications and, in turn, prepare or lead to the final portion of the play.

End

The end of the play includes the resolution or *denouement*. It starts with a major crisis which leads to a climax. A *climax* always follows a crisis, and is considered the high point of the play's action. Climax comes from the Greek and means ladder, staircase. That is why it is referred to as the high point of the action. Actually, climax can be thought of as the answers to the decisions that the characters make when they are in a crisis situation. In other words, the central character or characters (protagonist) is placed in a situation where the answer or solution to the play's major problem depends upon the protagonist's decision. That decision and the uncertainty as to the final outcome create the tension. The result of that decision is the climax. After the climax, all problems are resolved. Traditional linear constructed dramas are structured to have all the unanswered questions as well as the battle between the protagonist and antagonist resolved in an obligatory scene. The obligatory scene follows the crisis and serves to restore the norm in the play. The climax is in this scene. Plays by writers such as Bertolt Brecht (1898-1956) are exceptions, since they are designed to end with a question which the audience is to resolve outside the theatre.

In summary, the parts that constitute the beginning, middle, and end are parts of plot. These are devices by which plot organizes the action. They are: (1) exposition; (2) inciting point; (3) point of attack; (4) complication; (5) discovery; (6) crisis; (7) climax; (8) denouement.

Probability

Unity is a device used by the dramatist to make the play's action effective and understandable. Action in drama must not only employ unity, but that action must be probable as well. Probability means logical, believable, and consistent, that is, believability, logic, and consistency in terms of the play and not necessarily in terms of the audience. A dramatist may be inconsistent in the use of

Henry Strozier (sitting) and Ronald Frazier in a scene from the Milwaukee Repertory Theatre's 1978 production of *Namesake* by Amlin Gray. *(Photo by Mark Avery)*

characters, ideas, and action, but as long as he or she is consistently inconsistent then the play is consisent, hence, probable. Each play has its own probability, and it is the dramatist who determines it. For example, Superman, with his incredible feats of strength and his ability to fly, is believable to audiences only within a drama. Such a person does not exist nor do we as audience members believe he exists. Superman is not natural to us, but to the world created by the dramatist he is natural as well as real. Therefore, when an emergency arises and the only way it can be remedied is with Superman's help, his appearance becomes probable—that is, logical and believable. Superman serves as an example of how probability in our lives differs from that in a drama. Probability in drama should be thought of also in terms of the characters, the thoughts, the setting, the costumes, and the lights.

In creating probability, a dramatist depicts a

series of events that combine to make up one major event. If the writer has created the play correctly, each event raises a question that can be answered in a variety of ways. Eventually all answers are ruled out but one. This is the necessary (logical) answer. It is the only one left.

Looking at probability another way, it is a way of creating or dispelling dramatic illusion, that is, the impression that actual life is occurring on stage. If the probability of the play is natural to our world, if the events and characters are logical within the play's framework, then we tend to identify with those characters and events. A bond is created by way of empathy. Aristotle called this identification process likeness. It is through likeness that we mentally enter into the feeling or spirit of a person or thing. This bond allows audiences to mentally escape into another world. Then too, the probability may be unnatural and deal with elements of fantasy. Although unnatural, the fantasy and make-believe world become probable if they are logical within the play's framework. Inasmuch as each play has its own probability, dramatic illusion may also be dispelled by this device. In a Brechtian drama, for example, dramatic illusion is broken by making the probability so unnatural as to alienate us. We are prevented from escaping into another world. Probability is concerned with the believability of the world that a dramatist creates within the framework of his or her drama.

If a play is to be effective as well as understandable, it should gain and sustain audience interest. Devices such as unity and probability do much in attaining that goal. But if the dramatist hopes to strike a responsive chord with the audience, he or she must create characters, ideas, events, and an environment that the audience will find meaningful.

Character

Although character refers generally to people, that term may also refer to animals, ideas, or unseen forces in a play. Thus, when we speak of the play's action we must include the concept of character as well. For characters express the play's action and thus the action helps us know the characters and, conversely, the characters depicts the action. Action and character are closely related.

Since a plot is concerned with structuring a play's action (the physical and mental activities of the characters), it arranges characters: what they say, do, and think. In this way, characters are the material for creating plot. The way a dramatist chooses to differentiate characters is known as *characterization*. Although the following categories may be expanded, there are four basic levels of characterization: biological, social, moral, and psychological. The higher level of characterization is psychological. For it is at that level that conflict is created.

If a character is to serve adequately as an element of plot, the character must have not only varied traits but the traits must fit together. A character must first of all be good, that is, functionally good. In this sense, good means that the decisions the character makes advance the action. In a tragedy, a character must make moral decisions if that character is to be *functionally good.* This means that the character must make good decisions according to his ethical behavior which is dependent upon whether the character's behavior is that of a villain or a hero. The decisions a character makes must be *congruent.* That is, each new trait must fit with the other traits in terms of the kind of person the character is—what that character says or does and what others say about him. When traits follow this pattern, they are termed *appropriate*. In addition, a dramatist strives to create characters who have likeness or unlikeness, and the author tries to create characters who would likely appear in the situations devised. Lastly, the character's traits should be *consistent*. The character should exhibit a continuity throughout the play. Whatever happens to the character's situation, the character's traits should remain consistent to his or her nature. If the character is inconsistent by nature, then the dramatist should dramatize that character as consistently inconsistent. For a character to be acceptable, he must be characterized in terms of being good, congruent, appropriate, like or unlike, and consistent.

Thought

Characters form thoughts. What characters think or feel is based upon their thoughts, which are expressed by words and actions. Not only do characters form thoughts, but thoughts are material for character. Therefore, characters form thoughts and, conversely, thoughts are the reasons (material) for the character's actions. Thought appears in the play not only through the actions of the characters but also as the overall meaning of the play. The character's reactions, decisions, desires, emotions, attitudes, sayings, and doings all suggest relationships. These relationships help establish the play's meaning—the overall thought or argument. Plays should be considered arguments. For it is the writer's argument about which the play is organized and, therefore, it is the basis for different viewpoints—hence conflict. Thus thought is the play's significance, which in many plays is directly expressed through or by a character. If the play is organized totally upon a basic concept or thought, thought becomes the source of the play's unity. This is true of much modern drama, such as the plays of the absurdist writers or the works of Bertolt Brecht.

Diction (Words)

By shaping words into desired patterns, the dramatist creates a character's thoughts. Diction (dialogue) is how these thoughts are expressed. Diction can do much to affect a play's form. For example, Aeschylus's use of metaphor in *The Oresteia* serves to shape the play's action into a tragedy. Pace or speed help establish the play's form (tragedy, comedy, melodrama) as well the characters within that play within that form. Pace in comedy is usually more rapid than in a tragedy. In a Greek tragedy, for example, the actor must be aware of pace as he may be required to deliver a rapid-fire exchange known as stychomythia. Keep in mind, however, that speed in language must never be such that the meaning is lost or misunderstood. Clarity is thus another important aspect of diction. Diction reveals the character's mood for the moment as well as his mood in terms of the entire play. For example, an actor saying "You killed him" may deliver the line fearfully or angrily, and thus reveal the character's present state of mind. Similarly, more in-depth dialogue or soliloquies would serve to reveal the character's mental state or emotional stability. Another function or usage of diction is characterization. What sort of person is the character? What motivates him? A dramatist assigns a particular pattern (rhythm) of speech to a character. The character may use the words in a clever way or in a boring manner. The character may use slang or be extremely formal or his physical actions may contradict everything that the character says. A character's diction does much to provide clues to the character's environment, education, social position, and motives.

In drama a character's speech patterns (choice of words, pace, and phrasing) underlie that character's lifestyle as well as the style of the play. A realistically styled play seeks to create characters whose speech is that of a contemporary society. Thus, the speech is conversational and is designed to relate to the speech patterns (rhythms) of everyday life. This means that if the dramatist creates characters that are realistic, the language should be realistic as well. However, if the play's probability is such that a realistic character might speak in nonsense syllables, then the use of nonrealistic diction is acceptable and believable. Directors and actors should note a character's speech rhythms (recurring patterns), pace, and probability as the diction will provide clues not only to characterization but to the play's overall form and style.

Sound (Music)

As an element of drama, sound can also mean music. Within the sound of an actor's voice is a tonal quality which is analogous to music. In response to a door knock (which is also a use for sound effects), a character may say "Come in" angrily or fearfully. The tonal quality (music) of the words suggests a character's state of being at that particular moment. In *Cyrano de Bergerac*, Cyrano states that Roxane's name is like a bell. The actor can deliver these lines so that the musical quality of a bell is transmitted. The same concept is true also in poetry and verse dramas. Additionally, music can be used as background music or as music to forward the play's action. This is known as signature music as it identifies characters or events. For example, in the movie *Jaws*, the music announces when the shark is present, or in another situation when a character walks down a dark hall, the music lets you know if harm will befall that character. Sound as pure music, as tonal quality, as a dialogue, or as sound effects is an integral part of the play's structure.

Spectacle

Whereas plot, character, thought, and diction (when properly utilized) create structured action (drama), spectacle is the representation of that action.

In representing the dramatic action, all the aspects that help transfer the written word to the stage are brought into force. The actor uttering dialogue, the set designer, the lighting designer, the costumer, the propmistress, and the theatre itself are considered part of spectacle. Spectacle is theatre. It represents the structured human action of the drama. The object of the specialists in theatre and the specialist in drama (the playwright) is to complete a whole. For example, the set designer, the lighting designer, and the costumer will try to complement (integrate) each other rather than seek to be individually outstanding. The functions of each part of spectacle will be discussed later, but it is important to note that each aspect seeks to enjoin itself as part of the whole and never seeks to be the completed whole. Only when the actor is present is that whole completed.

A scene from *Die Fleidermaus*, directed by Walter R. Stump, set by Charles Kading, costumes by Sue Picinich.

Form

To form means to arrange, to organize action that characters perform. When a dramatist forms, he is organizing characters. He organizes the characters (usually human) in his play via the six basic elements of dramatic structure: plot, character, thought, diction, sound (music) and spectacle. The parts are arranged according to the author's purpose; specific arrangement will give a specific form such as tragedy, comedy, or a third form, the most dominant of which is melodrama. Although specific arrangement of the basic elements will create a tragedy, comedy, or melodrama, no two plays, whatever their form, are alike. Each play is unique and, although classified as a specific form, is nonetheless to be considered not in terms of the form but rather as an individual work. Many tragedies, for example, are inferior to many melodramas; conversely, a melodrama should not be judged superior to a comedy or a tragedy. Each play must be judged for its merits. Then too, some dramas defy labeling or do not fit into the traditional molds. Harold Pinter's early plays, for example, are labeled by him as comedies of menace; Ionesco's plays are called anti-plays and tragic-farces. The plays of Pinter and Ionesco do contain the six elements of drama; they have been arranged to create a seemingly different form. The difference lies in how the author perceives his world and how he chooses to dramatize that perception. Traditionally, authors have sought to place their plays in the molds of tragedy, comedy, or melodrama. Modern plays have sought to depart from that tradition as modern dramatists perceive life differently. Nevertheless, all plays display aspects of the three major forms—tragedies, comedies, or melodramas.

Tragedy

Traditionally, tragedy is concerned with a *genuinely serious action*, one of extreme importance in the lives of one or more characters. It is an action that is long-lasting and raises questions about man's existence, his moral nature, or his social and

A scene from the Moscow Art Theatre's production of Gorsky's *Lower Depths*. Pictured are Konstantin Stanislavski as Satan (hands up) and Vassili Kachalov as the Baron in a 1902 staging of the play. *Courtesy Sovfoto.*

psychological relationships. The action is therefore one that extends past the limits of the play; it is a universal action. For the action to be genuinely serious, it must involve a protagonist whom we can admire who possesses admirable traits but is not perfect. The protagonist is thus an above average person, although he is subject to error by not being perfect. The protagonist possesses traits which make him a believable character as well as one with whom the audience can identify. Aristotle termed it likeness; the character must be like us. A note needs to be said about the term protagonist. The protagonist is not necessarily the hero; it is the central character or competitor or all the characters. Thus it may be every character in the play such as Hauptmann's *The Weavers*. The key to this term is *AGON* (prot-AGON-ist) which basically means content or competition. *Pro* means *for*, and suggests primary position. Thus, the term indicates primary competition.

At this juncture it is important to point out that purists argue that a true tragedy is a thing of the past. Their disapproval with modern tragedies lies in what constitutes the protagonist. In a period of history when rank divided society, Aristotle's dictums as to what constitutes a tragedy, ergo, a tragic protagonist, were prescribed with the idea that the tragic protagonist had to have rank. Obviously, society has changed and class has replaced rank as a method of dividing society. Although tragedy's universal concerns are applicable to modern society, present day writers, theorists, and practitioners recognize that the tragic protagonist need not hold rank in order to command respect, display moral and ethical behavior, evoke tragic feelings in the audience, and above all, display nobility. As Arthur Miller has pointed out in his essay, "Tragedy and the Common Man" (1949), "the tragic right is a condition of life" and that condition exists today as it did 2000 years ago. Furthermore, that condition existed with characters of rank and exists today with the common man. Whereas kings and queens ruled society and kept the world in motion, the common man is the orb of society and it is he alone who is the focus of all modern dilemmas. In keeping with Aristotle's precept that characters must have likeness, modern writers have fashioned their plays in terms of the common man. Characters like Willie Loman (*Death of a Salesman*) spark responses in the audience and thus Willie's struggles are their struggles, making the common man worthy of being a tragic protagonist.

Unlike comedy and melodrama, tragedy is concerned with probing the nature of good and evil; that is, investigating what represents good and what represents evil. More traditional viewpoints suggest that evil is a real aspect of our world, that a universe of absolutes in terms of justice and order exists. On the other hand, contrasting ideas are that characters in a tragedy do not deal with absolutes but rather live in a universe of relatives. This suggests that life is not a choice between right and wrong but between the lesser of two rights or two evils. In either case,

tragedy is concerned with man's response to his destiny; a response that is hopefully based on freedom of choice.

Like all dramatic forms, tragedy arouses specific emotions. It is important to remember that these emotions are created in the play and the audience responds to them. Thus, audience identification with the characters and events arouses emotions. In the case of tragedy, the specific emotions are *pity, fear* and *their catharsis*. Pity and fear are rooted in two human instincts: self-concern and concern for others. We pity others but fear for ourselves. Pity is aroused when we witness someone with whom we identify encountering bad luck (*undeserved misfortune*) which is life-threatening. Why do bad things happen to good people? Were we in a similar situation we would fear for our safety. When a protagonist encounters undeserved misfortune, he struggles to overcome his fate. The struggle is complicated because the protagonist is forced into making what is termed a *moral decision*—a decision that is not really a decision because the choice is always wrong. Moral decisions are fundamental to tragedies; they make the action *genuinely serious*. Thus the decision has lasting import, and its results will continue to affect the life of the protagonist long after the play has ended. A moral decision, then, is a decision of a universal nature (life, death, and man's relationship to a god are examples). It is made by the protagonist out of ignorance and thus contributes to the protagonist's undeserved misfortune. Moral decisions are preceded by the protagonist's deliberation about the pros and cons of his choices. In spite of the deliberation, the decision will lead to the character's downfall because it is based on an error in judgment on the part of the central character. That error in judgment stems from a weakness in the character; that is, a flaw in his nature. This is known as the *tragic flaw (hamartia)*. In Shakespeare's *Othello*, Iago is able to destroy Othello by arousing Othello's jealousy. Once his jealousy is aroused, Othello is convinced emotionally (not logically) that his wife is unfaithful. He therefore kills her. Another way to look at tragic flaw is simply the character acting

The large strong chorus from the tragedy *Heracles* on opening night at the ancient theatre of Epidauraus.

on emotion rather than logic to make a decision. With the advent of Darwin, Aristotle's *hamartia* was redefined to mean *tragic fault* rather than tragic flaw. The argument is that the character is placed in these circumstances and is a victim of his environment rather than his mental processes. *Oedipus Rex* illustrates this concept. Oedipus unknowingly kills his father and marries his mother. The murder occurs when Oedipus and Laius (his father) arrive simultaneously at the three crossroads in Phocis. Each refuses to yield the right of way and Oedipus, in a fit of temper, kills Laius. If Oedipus had arrived at the crossroads five minutes sooner or later, he would *not* have encountered his father and subsequently killed him. To quote Shakespeare, "There's a destiny that shapes our ends."

When the protagonist is threatened and is defeated in his struggle, the emotions of pity and fear are aroused. Aristotle used the term "such emotions," which indicates that pity and fear include a whole range of emotions—uncertainty, suspense, foreboding, apprehension, compassion, horror, and terror. For the action to be complete in

tragedy, the emotions aroused must be reduced or removed. The concept of reducing or removing the emotions produced by a dramatic action is termed *catharsis* or *purgation*. To purge emotions created within a play, however, does not mean that the audience's emotions must be purged. Purgation is an internal principle that must occur within the structure of the play if the play's action is to be complete and satisfying. Purgation occurs in the audience only after it has occurred within the play. To purge emotions, the initial cause for arousal must be determined. In the case of a tragedy, the threat to the central character creates fear. As audience members we identify with the leading character and thus feel fear for that character's safety. When the character suffers undeserved misfortune, we feel pity for the character. If we were in a similar situation we would be afraid. In order to remove fear in a tragedy, the threat must be removed. In a tragedy this usually involves the defeat of the central character; this represents one way to remove the fear. With the defeat of the protagonist, the threat is removed. Pity, however, is not completely removed; it is changed. With the demise of the protagonist, we no longer pity but instead rationalize about the protagonist's defeat as well as his fate. Thus pity is usually changed to admiration. We admire the heroics of the chief character or are satisfied that his name and image will survive and give meaning to his death.

Comedy

Comedy requires a *deviation* or contradiction from what is normal (a normative). What is normal to you or your friends may be different, however. Norms also differ between countries, cultures, and generations. Normal is therefore relative. This is why a comedian from one country may not succeed in another. His comic references may be in terms of his own country and culture; this dictates his concept of what is normal. A joke about a president who plays the saxophone may create laughs in present-day America but such a joke may be ineffectual in another country.

In addition to deviations from social norms, the comic action produced must not render any lasting harm to those involved. Any threat of a serious nature will preempt laughter. Dramatists

Portrait of Henri Bergson, French philosopher.

as well as audiences must be objective about writing and viewing comedy. Henri Bergson, in his essay "Laughter" (1900), suggests that we cannot have sympathy with the events on stage and must, therefore, have an "anesthesia of the heart." That is, we cannot be emotionally involved or identify

Les Fourberies de Scapin (The Pranks of Scapin) by Molière. Set by Suzanne Lalique, directed by Jean Meyer. Shown below are Denis d'Ines and Georges Baconnet. *Photo by B. M. Barnand.*

with the characters or their situations as we do in tragedy. Dramatists must play down the empathetic aspect in a character in order to arouse laughter. A prime example of Bergson's concept is the comedian Vaughn Meader. During the early 1960s, Meader's imitations of President John F. Kennedy and jokes about the president and his family had earned Meader immense fame. With Kennedy's assassination, however, Vaughn Meader's career ended abruptly. The jokes were no longer funny; people were too emotionally involved. It took fifteen years for Vaughn Meader to resume his career and even then he was not the success he had been before the assassination.

As with all drama, comedy is unified through character, thought, and action. A comedy of character may have normal characters in an eccentric world, have eccentric characters in a normal world, or even create characters who contradict expectations. The latter is a device of the Irish dramatist, George Bernard Shaw (1856-1950), and a good example is his *Arms and the Man*. The opening scene is devoted to establishing a stereotyped image of a soldier in war. The image is created through a description of the exploits of Major Sergius Saranoff, who is depicted as charging into battle, being patriotic, and cruel to his enemies. This image is satirized by Captain Bluntschli, who enters backwards through the window into the bedroom of the heroine, Raina. Contrary to Sergius's image, Bluntschli is running from battle, cringes when Raina scolds him, and carries chocolate candy instead of ammunition.

Another form of comedy is that of thought, better known as satire. The use of language to deride or ridicule some abuse in society by means of irony, sarcasm, puns, or double entendre creates a deviation from the normal or literal meaning of words and their intended meaning. A third way of unifying comedy is deviating from accepted behavior—comedy of incident or farce. In such comedy the emphasis is on the character's physical actions and not the character or his thoughts. Although many plays emphasize one element, many comedies will use a combination of any two or all three.

The Comedy of Errors by William Shakespeare. Directed by Cary Libkin; scenic design by Geoff Williams; costume design by Lisa Zinni; lighting design by Charles H. Firmin; and sound design by Delbert Boarts.

Inasmuch as comedy is a deviation from the norm and reaction to that deviation is laughter, it seems then that laughter serves as a corrective force, a type of catharsis. Laughter is aroused by emphasizing abnormal characters, situations, or creating characters whose behavior can be held up for ridicule or who are placed in a ridiculous situation. Ridicule is by definition designed to arouse laughter; it is a cause to create laughter. Thus *ridicule* and *laughter* and their *catharsis* are the emotions aroused by comedy. If the abnormality aroused these emotions, then the catharsis of these emotions will restore the abnormal back to normal. Or, to look at it in another way, restoring the norm will eliminate the ridicule and the subsequent laughter. Audiences do not find the norms funny.

Unlike tragedy, the action in comedy is not of a highly serious nature. It does not focus on man's relationship to his god, morality, or life and death. The issues involved in comedy are concerned with the vices and follies of man—his mores, manners, and societal institutions. The action tends to be of a temporary nature, which means that it will be resolved before the play's end. Consequently, the action is only deemed serious, and not highly serious as it is in tragedy. Since the action is only serious, the characters make decisions which are *expedient* rather than moral. The decisions made will affect the characters only momentarily and throughout the play. At the play's end, however, the decisions will have little or no bearing upon the characters' lives. They are not catastrophic.

Melodrama

Whether in the theatre, movies, or television, much of what we see today is melodrama. Because the name *melodrama* suggests the villain in the stovepipe hat who demands the young maiden if the mortgage is not paid, it has fallen into disrepute. Inasmuch as the term melodrama has become pejorative, the term given to melodrama today is drama, but structurally it is melodrama. As discussed in the opening of this chapter, melodrama is a term that is misused.

Unlike tragedy, melodrama focuses on a *serious* (not a genuinely serious) *action*. The fact that tragedy and melodrama focus on almost similar type actions has led to these two being mistaken for each other—they are twins, but they are different! The action in melodrama is not catastrophic or long-lasting; it is only temporary. Its serious nature will no longer be serious at the end of the play; whereas in tragedy the serious nature will continue past the play's end. There are no moral decisions in melodrama, only expedient ones. The play's action is initiated by the villain who threatens or poses a threat to the hero. This threat arouses the basic emotions found in melodrama—those of fear and hate. Throughout the play, the hero or heroine is placed in situations in which escape seems impossible. Yet escape does occur.

The continual escape of the hero or heroine is termed *chance probability*, which is unlike the natural probability found in tragedy. Inasmuch as the hero displays character traits with which we can identify (in other words, he is like us), we fear for the hero's safety and hate the villain for causing trouble. The emotions aroused by melodrama are thus *fear*, *hate*, and their *catharsis*. The catharsis, or the purging of fear and hate, is affected by what is termed *the double ending*. The double ending occurs at the conclusion when the villain is punished and the hero is rewarded.

Melodrama is concerned with upholding society's moral values, and therefore evil must be punished and good rewarded. No other form of drama distinguishes more clearly between the concept of good and evil than does melodrama. In tragedy good and evil are probed, but in melodrama they are *represented* by the villain and the hero. This concept of good and evil extends to other aspects of melodrama. The use of signature music, for example, is a trademark of melodrama. It is background music which identifies whether characters are good or bad, and whether the situation a hero is about to enter will produce harm. We are all in tune to this use of music, and the moment we hear it during a production, we are able to determine if the ensuing events will be anxiety producing. This is a characteristic of melodrama—good triumphs over evil. Good winning over evil not only characterizes melodrama but underlies its purpose of teaching a moral lesson.

Style

Tragedy, comedy, and melodrama are all considered forms, whereas literary movements such as romanticism, realism, naturalism, and other "isms" are termed style. (These movements will be discussed in later chapters.)

Style may be defined as a distinctive or characteristic mode of construction or execution in any art or work. Style in theatre and drama encompasses not only literary movements but anything which in execution displays unique definable properties. This would include the style of the individual dramatist, for each writer has a particular method of writing. In theatre and drama, style affects also the theatrical production—the director, actor, costumer, lighting designer, set designer and others who make up a production. Not only is style far-ranging in theatre, it is also relative, especially in the literary movements. The styles of romanticism or realism serve as two examples.

A Midsummer Night's Dream performed at The University of Southern Maine, directed and designed by Minor Rootes. Note the shift in focus as Albert Duclos (Oberon) moves downstage. This shift is accomplished both by the head and the body. *Courtesy Don Johnson.*

What is romantic or realistic to one generation is not usually appropriate to other generations. Nineteenth century melodrama, with its stereotype villain who wore a black mustache, cloak and hat, aroused fear in the audiences of that time. Today such a figure is not real to us and we tend to be amused by his appearance. Similarly, what we consider romantic today may not be romantic in the next generation or the perception of what is real or romantic may vary with the viewer. Hence, realism and romanticism are relative.

Considering the variables in a theatrical production and the relativity of style, it is the task of the director to determine what style he or she wishes to use in staging the production. Each specialist contributes in part according to the style that the director has suggested in order that the overall production will demonstrate the characteristics of that style or styles selected. The director may suggest stylizing the production, which means deviating from what is considered realistic at the time. Stylizing (stylism) is often referred to as a style and is defined as a departure from realism. Realism, however, is a style, and departures from realism can be conceived in a number of ways. To stylize a production thus does not define precisely in what manner the production's departure from realism will be shaped. Stylizing can mean any style and to refer to it as a style is paradoxical and confusing. Stylizing in terms of expressionism or naturalism can be thought of as being more precise. Although many plays will display more than one style, most plays lend themselves to one particular style, and that style has been determined by the dramatist or director. Thus a play may have a dramatic style as well as a theatrical style. A tragedy, for example, may be written in a realistic style but the director may choose to represent the dramatic action in an expressionistic style. Form and style are thus two separate entities affecting the staging of a play.

Inasmuch as dramatic form and style vary from generation to generation, and inasmuch as dramatic form and style reflect the social, political, and economic institutions of a society, theatre and its drama must always be viewed as both reflecting and influencing a particular society's social, political and economic ideas.

Selected Readings

Heffner, Hubert C., Samuel Selden, and Houghton D. Sellman. *Modern Theatre Practice: A Handbook of Play Production.* 4th ed. New York, 1959.

Olson, Elder. *Tragedy and the Theory of Drama.* Detroit, 1961.

Smiley, Sam. *Playwriting: The Structure of Action.* Englewood Cliffs, NJ, 1971.

Teleford, Kenneth. *Aristotle's Poetics: Translation and Analysis.* Chicago, 1961.

Vocabulary

#		
1.	Castelvetro	kahs tel VE troh
2.	Eugene Ionesco	ee uh NE skoh
3.	Aphrodite	a fruh DIGH tee
4.	Theseus	THEE see uhs
5.	Bertolt Brecht	BAIR tawlt BREKT
6.	stichomythia	stik uh MITH ee uh
7.	*Oresteia*	aw RES tee uh
8.	Cyrano de Bergerac	SEE ruh noh duh BAIR zher ak
9.	catharsis	kuh THAHR sus
10.	Henri Bergson	AHN ree BAIRG suhn
11.	Denouement	DAY noo Mahn
12.	Hamartia	hah MAHR tee uh

Part II
HISTORICAL PERSPECTIVES

CHAPTER FOUR

❧

The Greek World:
From Ritual to Formalized Drama

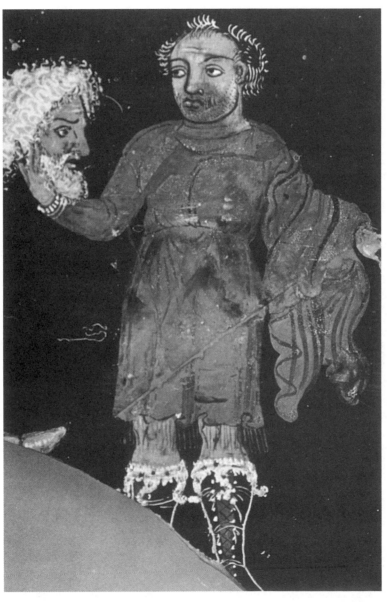

A tragic actor looking at his mask. Note the high boot (cothurnus) and long sleeves of the costume. This fragment of a vase from Tarentum dates from the fourth century B.C. *Courtesy Martin von Vagner Museum of the University of Wurzburg.*

Customarily the beginning of western theatre and drama dates with the Greeks in 534 B.C. During this time, Greece was divided into three culture centers: Ionia, Sparta, and Athens. Athens had the most influence on the theatre's development. That influence was not felt, however, until the fifth century. Before the fifth century, Ionia and Sparta dominated. Whereas Ionia developed the arts, Sparta fashioned an army. No two cultures were more diverse than these two.

Always the efficient fighting machine, Sparta ruled Greece in the fifth century. Indeed, during the seventh century Sparta identified herself with the development of art and industry. But at the end of that century plagued by population problems (8000 in 480 B. C.) Sparta chose to colonize its neighbors as a means of solving this problem. Once the lands were conquered, Sparta needed an army to maintain these colonies, which led Sparta to restructure its society in 600 B.C. to a military state, and the subsequent development of a society that took control of its citizens' lives with the specific intention of creating a war machine. Consequently, Sparta isolated itself, forbade foreign visitors, and created a regimented lifestyle for its citizens.

For males this new control meant that at age six to seven they were taken from their mother and placed with a group of boys similar in age. The state required that they live in barracks until age thirty and eat together until age sixty. Spartan education placed its emphasis upon physical training, and those males considered weak were exposed to the elements and left to die. Although known for their seductiveness, Spartan women had no legal rights, were required to have gymnastic training and shouldered the responsibility of running the economy and their lands when the men were fighting. As can be noted, Sparta had little concern for intellectual and artistic pursuits. The ideal for these two areas was achieved in Athens.

Standing roughly three miles from the sea, Athens' early history was one of economic woes, harsh rule, indebted farmers, slavery, feuding among the oligarchy, and a near civil war. Led by Solon's (c. 640-c. 558 B.C.) reforms in 594 B.C., Athens moved from the shadow of disaster to one of stability. One of the key reforms instituted by Solon was the recognition of the rights of the individual: a basic principle upon which western government is based.

Despite Solon's reforms, government control was still vested with the rich families. Fractionalism occurred between these groups and as a result, in 546 B.C. the aristocrat Peisistratus (d. 527 B.C.) seized power. Although considered a tyrant, Peisistratus did not change Solon's reforms and did not govern with a heavy hand. Under his rule and that of his two sons, Hipparchus and Hippas, Athens' power and prestige began to emerge. To accommodate Athens' growing reputation, Peisistratus encouraged the arts, literature and religious cults, such as that of Dionysus. With his death in 527 B.C., his sons assumed leadership. Called the Peisistratidae, the two sons' reign ended tragically. Hipparchus' disappointment in his love affair with a young man eventually led to his assassination (514 B.C.), and his brother's harsh rule led to his being deposed in 510 B.C. With the demise of the Peisistratidae, the oligarchy was somewhat restored. But dissension erupted among the clans which paved the way for Cleisthenes to seize power in 508 B.C. Under his rule, Athenian democracy was founded.

At the beginning of the fifth century, Athens emerged as a powerful state. As a great commercial and industrial center, Athens was the only Greek state with a navy capable of protecting Greece against a Persian attack. Thus, its defeat of the Persians in 490 B.C. at Marathon (Aeschylus fought in the war), and ten years later, the Athenian victory against the second Persian invasion made Athens the acknowledged leader of all the Ionian Greeks, and for that matter, all of Greece. Under the leadership of Cimon (d. 449 B.C.) and Pericles (c. 500 B.C.-429 B.C.), Athens became an imperial power as well as a mecca for poetry, drama, theatre, philosophy, mathematics, music and politics.

The Polis and the Theatre

The Greeks were the first to take theatre and drama from the ritual stage to its present form. As to why the Greeks were the first to formalize theatre and drama, this remains a mystery. Many sophisticated civilizations existed prior to that of the Greeks, yet these did not develop theatre past the ritual level. A key to understanding Athenian society and perhaps a reason for the Athenians' ability to formalize theatre and drama is the concept of the *polis*, which was unique to Greece.

A geographical concept, the polis equates to a county. Thus, every polis was different, just as every county is different. Within that area was located one major town (often walled), a fortified citadel called the acropolis, and a marketplace called the agora. For example, Attica was a polis whose major town was Athens. The citizens comprising the polis were the ruling class, whether a democracy, aristocracy, or oligarchy. In addition to the citizens, other social classes such as slaves and foreigners existed. Since the Greeks believed the polis was descended from a common male, women were not considered real citizens. In fact, they were not considered at all. As Thucydides indicates, it was a woman's duty "to be spoken of as little as possible among men, whether for good or ill." Each polis was comprised of the entire citizen body, and loyalty to the polis was first and foremost to the Greek citizen. This loyalty meant being involved in the daily operations of government. Inasmuch as the citizens made up the state, the name of the state came from the citizens, not the territory. Therefore, the Greek state of Athens is referred to as Athenians, which identifies the people of that state and, in this case, the geographical area. As Thucydides states, "Men are the polis and not the walls or ships without men in them."

The polis affected every part of Greek society and hence directly affected Greek culture. In sixth century B.C. Athens, the tyrant Peisistratus (who ruled Athens continuously from c. 560 to 527 B.C.) reorganized public programs, such as festivals, to encourage patriotism and loyalty among the people to the polis. Thus the people of Attica attached their loyalties to the polis and its functions as a whole rather than to the power of the four ruling tribes who were seeking to depose Peisistratus and regain power.

In 508 B.C. clan or tribe power was finally dissolved under Cleisthenes, who reorganized the four existing tribes into ten tribes, based upon residency rather than loyalty or kinship. The political basis of this reorganization was the *deme*— the smallest unit of the polis. Much like our modern wards, these demes, scattered throughout Attica, were self-governing and were organized into *trittyes* (thirds). Alhough the number of demes in trittyes varied, three trittyes made up one of the new tribes; thirty trittyes made up the ten tribes. Inasmuch as the new tribes were composed of citizens from various parts of Attica, loyalty to the demes and new tribes superseded that to the old tribes. At various demes, theatrical productions were organized and it seems likely that the motive in part was to encourage loyalty to the polis as a whole and the deme specifically.

Greek Religion and Theatre

Although Greek religion had no real authority, no priestly caste, no orthodoxy, no sacred book, or real dogma, it was extremely complex. Based largely on imagination and, hence, subject to interpretation, Greek religion derived a large portion of its beliefs from primitive man's impersonation of natural forces. Also, it stems in part from the primitive idea of ritual as a means to communicate with those forces. In keeping with its complexity, taboo affected Greek religion— that is, certain things were held sacred, clean, and pure. For example, the blood and flesh of a bull or goat were consumed in a sacred communion with the god Dionysus. The worship of this particular god involved also dramatic performances.

The fact that Greek theatre and drama emerged at a religious festival honoring the god Dionysus has created speculation as to the theatre's relationship to Dionysus. In turn, theorists have focused on that relationship in an effort to evolve a theory as to the origin of theatre and drama; namely, that Greek religion influenced the formation of theatre and drama.

About the ninth century, Greek religion became anthropomorphic; that is, the powers of nature were conceived as gods and goddesses who had the same needs, desires and faults of man. These deities lived on Mt. Olympus ruled by Zeus, and they controlled man's affairs. This control was subject, however, to that quality in Greek religion termed fate—destiny, which was determined by Zeus, the will of the gods, or that person's birth-spirits *(parcae)*. God worship became basic to Greek religion in the ninth century.

By the eighth century, the concepts of morality, mysticism, and justice became important, and hence, the notion of retribution, atonement, and guilt came into prominence. These latter ideas dominate Greek tragedy. During the fifth century, these Greek religious beliefs and myths were undermined by the Sophists and, in the Hellenistic period (fourth century) these beliefs were replaced with philosophical thought among the educated classes. For those looking for non-traditional answers, "Tyche" (the god of luck-chance, magic and astrology), provided a choice. During the second century B.C., astrology was to gain a strong following, especially when it was coupled with mathematics. Added to all these different forms of worship was that of king worship, which was traceable to the hero cults of the fifth century. This notion stemmed from the belief that the dead exerted an influence upon the living and thus when offered prayers, offerings, and festivals, that hero would provide and protect. For example, Alexander wanted to be worshipped as a god, and though the Greeks rebuffed this notion, Ptolemy I stole Alexander's corpse and brought it back to Egypt where a cult to Alexander was established. Despite its guise, king worship was in reality worship of the state and, hence, political. Then too, the worshipping of one individual must have had

some influence in laying the foundation for monotheism.

Although the Greeks were not singular in their worship of a deity, they were unified in their pursuit of the ideal. The constant striving for "excellence" was a dominant force to the Greeks. Thus, in this world of magic, myth, king-worship, and other beliefs, the Greeks labored to separate the rational from the irrational, to bring order where chaos existed. This religious pursuit of the ideal manifested itself in the theatre where the Greeks took ritual and formalized it into drama. Drama was one of the ways that the Greeks defined their theology: man seeking the truth. The Greek drama echoes this search for definition.

The Cult of Dionysus

Dionysian worship is traceable to the Minoan (6000-2600 B.C.) and Mycenaean (c. 2200-c. 1100 B.C.) periods. The research of Michael Ventris established in 1952 that the Mycenaeans (who were literate) were the ancestors of the Greeks. Classicist Martin Nilson implied this same point in 1936 when he noted that many of the Greek myths originated in Mycenaean cities. There are additional arguments indicating that Mycenaean myths were the legacy of the Greeks Hesiod and Homer, and that the gods in these myths were part of the Mycenaean religion. As a cult, then, the worship of Dionysus probably made its way from the Minoans to the Mycenaeans who then brought it from Asia Minor to Crete where it was transferred to the Greeks by Archilochus about the mid-seventh century, and later entered Athens.

Initially, the Greeks are said to have rebuffed the cult. When the men became sterile, however, the Delphic Oracle told them to pay homage to Dionysus in order to end their plight. The homage ended their plight giving rise to Dionysian worship. Once the cult was allowed to enter Greece, it gained wide support, and under the tyrant Peisistratus, the cult was encouraged as can be noted in the City Dionysia.

As a myth, Dionysus is said to have been the son of Zeus and his daughter Persephone. Initially called Zagreus, Dionysus was his father's favorite and, consequently, incurred the hatred of Hera, Zeus's wife. Hera got the Titans to kill him, but in an effort to hide him, Zeus changed him to a goat and then to a bull. As a bull, he was captured, whereupon the Titans dismembered and boiled him in a caldron. Athena saved his heart which the mortal Semele impregnated, thus giving him a second birth and the new name, Dionysus.

Dionysus was worshipped for fertility, wine and vegetation. The cult was composed of women overseen by a male priest who ritualized the suffering, death, and resurrection of Dionysus. Known as Maenads (Bacchantes), these women left the cities in spring and went into the hills to meet and worship the reborn god. For two days they drank unrestrained and danced themselves into a frenzy pulling out their hair. After two days, they seized a victim (goat, bull, or man) whom they tore to pieces. The victim's blood and flesh were consumed as a sacred communion in which they believed the god would enter into their body and soul, giving them life eternal. When this cult was accepted into Athens, the rulers humanized Dionysus and, as a result, the worship became less chaotic and more structured. Thus, instead of wild revelry and the tearing apart of a victim, Athens changed the ritual to stately procession, songs, and dramatic performances.

Dionysian Festivals and Drama

To honor Dionysus, the Greeks held five festivals yearly: the *Haloa* (December), the *Anthesteria* (February-March), the *Lenaia* (January-February), the *Rural Dionysia* (December); and the *City* or *Great Dionysia* (March-April). All were held in Athens except the Rural Dionysia, which was held in the various demes outside of Athens. During these festivals the Greeks punctuated their worship with drinking, dancing, wild processions, listening to the story about the life, death and resurrection of Dionysus, and other ritualistic activities.

Epidaurus festival. *Courtesy Greek Embassy.*

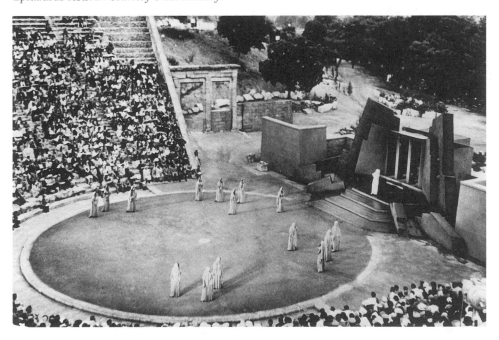

The Haloa Festival occurred in the sixth month of the Attic calendar and was dedicated to Poseidon. Whether a festival was held in this month dedicated to Poseidon is seriously questioned. Parke contends that Poseidon's title in the Mycenean period was "the lord of the earth" and, in this sense, he was worshipped. On the 26th of this month, however, the festival of *Haloa* took place and was held in honor of Demeter and Dionysus. Commentary by Lucian suggests that women believers held a secret fertility ceremony at Eleusis, at which the male magistrates prepared a banquet and then left. The women came to the secret spot carrying male and female genitals, drank excessively, took female lovers, and ate cake shaped in the form of sexual organs of both sexes. Originally considered a fertility festival, this rite evolved into an all-night orgy and tended to become connected with prostitutes.

Also celebrated in this month was the *Rural* or *Country Dionysia*. It was a religious ceremony and like the *Haloa* was originally a fertility festival. Held in villages (demes) outside of Athens, this festival was supervised by the Demarchos, a position filled from a list of names drawn up by the local government and consisted of a parade and in some demes, dramatic contests. The introduction of drama to this festival is uncertain, but performances are noted after 460 B.C. Those festivals which used drama served as a tryout for new plays, a revival for old plays, and to present plays rejected for the *City Dionysia*. The plays were performed by companies that toured the villages. For example, Aeschines, Simykas, and Socrates formed a touring team called the "Deep-Groaners" [Barnstormers?]. The oldest extant remains of a theatre that held dramatic performances for the Rural Dionysia seems to be those at Thorikos which might well be the oldest theatre in Attica.

The *Lenaian* Festival was held in the month of Gamelion (month of marriage) and was organized by the archon *Basileus* (the king) who was originally the chief religious and civil authority. During the fifth century, Eleusinian priests joined with the *Basileus* to oversee the festival whose name seems to be derived from the female worshippers of Dionysus Lenaios. Considered the original Dionysia festival, it predates the entry of Dionysus Eleuthereus and the establishment of the *City Dionysia*.

Dramatic contests were added in 440 B.C. and were held in the Lenaion, which was a place in the city of Athens with an extensive enclosure and in it the sanctuary of Dionysus Lenaios. Inasmuch as the seas were considered unnavigable, the festival became a local celebration in which there was more freedom and less censorship. Thus, Old Comedy with its licentious and satiric format thrived here. Contests for tragedy were added in 400 B.C.

The *Anthesteria* was the oldest festival and like the *Haloa* seems to have little or no connection with the development of drama during the fifth century. It was celebrated in the month Anthesterion (meaning flowers) and lasted three days.

Drama was seemingly begun formally, therefore, as part of a religious ceremony worshipping the god Dionysus. The fact that drama was attached to these ceremonies has led to the conclusion that drama originated out of Dionysian worship—a point that is seriously questioned.

City Dionysia

In spring during the ninth to the thirteenth days of the Athenian month, Elaphebalian, the *City* or *Great Dionysia* was celebrated under the direction of the archon *Eponymous* (chief civil magistrate). The name of the month stemmed from a title given to Artemis—shooter of the deer (elaphebalios). Although the City Dionysia was the last of the Athenian festivals to be instituted, it was the most important and the most representative of the Greek world.

Held at a time when the seas were navigable, citizens and foreigners from all parts of the Hellenic world attended this festival. More people were assembled for this event than for any other. Thus, Athens declared it a national holiday which meant, among other things, that prisoners were freed on bail (some tried to escape), no business was transacted, and honors were conferred to those whose service to Athens was above and beyond the call of duty. In addition, the City Dionysia served as a vehicle whereby allies brought their tribute to Athens. The money was presented in sacks of coins before the assembled audience by placing it in the orchestra. The tribute was used in part to support the orphan sons whose fathers were killed in battle. When the sons became of age, they marched in a "passing out parade" dressed in full Hoplite armour, after which they were invited to sit in front row seats of the theatre to watch the performances.

Preliminary to the festival was a processional reenactment of Dionysus coming from Eleutherai to Athens. Eleutherai was a small community on the border between Athens and Boeotia. About the middle of the sixth century, Eleutherai annexed itself to Athens in order the escape the rule of the Boeotians. With this alignment, it is thought that the transfer of the Dionysian cult was brought to Athens by a missionary named Pegasos.

The procession consisted of terra-cotta phalli carried on poles as a symbol of fertility, and was accompanied by a wooden likeness of the god Dionysus that had been taken from the temple in Athens to a sanctuary (Academy) outside the city walls on the road to Boeotia. Symbolically, this ritual indicated Dionysus's release from winter. After the statue was placed in the sanctuary, sacrifices were made, and then the epheboi (young soldiers) led a torchlight parade in which the statue was escorted back to the theatre. Whether the statue remained in the theatre for the entire festival or was placed back in the original temple is not known. Called "bringing in from the sacrificial hearth," this procession is not to be confused with the *pompe*.

Next came a preview of the performances and the selection of the judges took place. Called the *proagon*, this preliminary event involved the poets with their choregoi, choruses, actors (without masks or costumes) who mounted a temporary platform from which they announced the subjects of their plays. Later that day, the selection of the judges took place. (See Management section for selection process.)

The *pompe* or main procession was essentially a religious holiday and was held on the tenth day of the month. The term *pompe* means "a sending" as in sending Dionysus an offering, and thus, sacrifices were part of this procession. Tradition required the sacrificing of bulls and in 333 B.C. it was reported that as many as 240 bulls were slaughtered. In addition, the tradition had all the social classes colorfully dressed represented in the procession. For example, resident aliens (metoikoi) wore purple robes and carried trays of offerings, and thus, they were known as "tray bearers." Citizens wore whatever they wished and carried leather bottles of wine on their shoulders. They were called "bottle-carriers." A maiden of high social status was chosen as the kanephoros, whose job required her to carry a basket of fruit (no doubt grapes for Dionysus) in the procession. As the procession proceeded with its phalli on poles, it stopped at various religious altars of the twelve gods in Agora, and at each one songs and dances were held commemorating the respective deity. The parade ended at the altar in the theatre where additional sacrifices were made and libations poured. That night a large dinner was held and no doubt the bulls served as the main course.

The number of days given over for the dithyramb, comedy and tragedy contests cannot be fixed. It has been argued that the day after the *pompe* was inactive in order to prepare for the contests. It is widely held that during the Peloponnesian War, three days were given to three tragedies, a satyr play, and a comedy. Other than this, the evidence for the arrangement of the contests is not clear.

Two days after the festival ended, the *ecclesia* was held in the theatre. The function of the council was to investigate the conduct of festival officials such as the archon. Next came complaints of misconduct or injuries received. Although the hearing had no legal jurisdiction, if the Assembly found in favor of the complainer, it would add weight should that individual decide in favor of formal legal action.

Management

The Great or City Dionysia was under the direct authority of Peisistratus who controlled the nominations of the magistrates, particularly the Archon Eponymous, the main official of the festival. The archon's responsibilities were to organize the festival around the principle of competition. One of these areas was selecting the dramatists for the tragedy contests. Probably the archon interviewed each poet, which involved reading specimens of their work, after which he selected three writers to present three tragedies each. In 501 B.C., a fourth play was required—the satyr play. Two points need to be made about the selection process: first, there seems to be no age limit for the poet, and second, the poet did not read his plays for the archon in the theatre.

Comedy contests were introduced in 486 B.C. and this consisted of five writers presenting one play each. During the Peloponnesian War (431-404 B.C.), the number was reduced to three which saved time and money. In the late third and into the second centuries B.C. evidence indicates the number of plays was increased to six, but as the second century wore on the performances of comedy became irregular.

Once the dramatists were selected, the archon's next responsibility was obtaining a choregos for the writers of comedy, tragedy, and dithyrambs. The choregos was much like a modern day "angel" in that his function was to provide most of the financing for the production. How the choregoi were chosen is unknown, but the choice was usually assigned to a wealthy citizen who was obligated by law to fulfill that position and could be excused only by challenging that he was involved in another civic duty, that another citizen was richer, or some other legitimate excuse. For tragedy three choregoi were chosen from three different tribes. When five comedies were presented, five choregoi were needed. Dithyrambs required that two choregoi be assigned from each of the ten tribes: ten for the men choruses, ten for the boys. The choregoi for the dithyrambs were selected one month after the festival ended. In the fourth century two facts emerge: for the boys' chorus one had to be over forty years old and the choosing of the choregoi was assigned to the tribes.

The success or a failure of a production was to a large extent related to the amount of money the choregos spent. His cost included such items as masks, costumes, a flute or aulos player, a chorus trainer, extras (mute actors), the chorus salaries, any special effects and leasing the theatre from the state. He did not have to bear any expense in connection with the main actors' salaries or costumes. Rehearsal appears to have lasted a year and was left to the author who served also as director, choreographer, composer and, at times, actor.

In addition to the proscribed expenditures, the choregos had to select a chorus trainer and a chorus, the latter of which by the fourth century B.C. consisted of professional singers for both tragedy and comedy. Initially, the training of the chorus fell to the dramatists such as Aeschylus who is credited with inventing and choreographing dance routines. Eventually, chorus trainers replaced the writers but when this became the rule is not certain. Further, the state elected certain officials whose offices were to discipline the chorus should they, for example, drink too much as some were known to do.

In the fourth century B. C. (317-307 B.C.) the choregos was abolished and was replaced by an agonthetes. Elected yearly and paid by the state, the agonthetes appears to have been under the authority of archon. At this time, the state enlarged the festival to include the performance of an old tragedy and an old comedy both of which were outside of the competition. Thus, Aeschylus's plays were allowed to be produced at the City Dionysia as were those of Sophocles, Euripides and Aristophanes. As a rule, however, most of the revivals were done at the Lenaia or the Rural Dionysia.

To insure that the contest's outcome was impartial, the state took elaborate procedures in selecting the judges. Before the festival, a list of names selected from the ten tribes was generated. Most likely the choregos had some say in the names selected. At times politics, violence or other pressures were brought to bear to insure that certain names appeared on the list. The names were placed into ten urns which were sealed and placed in the Acropolis. Although it was a crime to tamper with these urns, it was done. At the beginning of the contest, the ten urns were placed in the theatre, and the archon drew one name from each urn. These ten judges were given an oath to be fair in their verdict. Upon the contest's conclusion, the judges placed their votes into one urn from which the archon randomly drew five ballots. Because the judges' votes were made known, it is possible that they were influenced by the audience or some influential person. The herald announced the winner whom the archon crowned with a wreath of ivy.

Audience

During the fifth century, the theatre audience for the City Dionysia numbered 17,000 and consisted of citizens (ten percent of the population), resident aliens (metoikai), foreigners and slaves (about thirty-three percent of the population) if accompanied by their master. The Lenai differed in that only citizens were admitted. Although Aristotle would not have allowed boys, doubt exists about women. There is some indication that women were present at tragedies but not comedies during the fifth and fourth centuries. If women were admitted to the theatre, evidence is unclear.

Women's status with respect to the theatre was clearly a reflection of their position in society. Classicist K. J. Dover observed that "the inadequacy of women as fighters promoted a general devaluation of the intellectual and emotional stability of women." Greek biological theory believed that a woman's function with relationship to the fetus was one of a "greenhouse" role, and that women had no genetic influence. Aristotle asserted that the "female state is one, so to speak, of deformity . . ." A consequence of this perception was the acceptance of infanticide or, if the father chose, placing the baby with a trainer of prostitutes. Death or prostitution were the options for weak female babies. The theory of contraception was taught in the late fourth century, but the lack of contraceptive devices made the theory impractical.

Admittedly, women were considered physically and morally inferior to men, leading to the belief that the polis and its citizens were descended from a common male ancestor. Aristophanes' *Lysistrata* focuses on this inferiority by presenting a situation in which women withhold sex from the men until they stop fighting. The women are unable, however, to carry through on their plan until the Spartan woman, Lampito, shames them into abstention. Lampito is characterized as being mannish and thus serves to contrast the strength of men to the moral weakness of women. Although *Lysistrata* stresses heterosexual relationships, the truth of the matter was that homosexuality was not only a "conspicuous feature of Greek life," but it was more satisfying. Greece's political fragmentation, the constant struggle of the polis to survive war, made the adult male citizen the most valued member of society. As a consequence, Dover sees homosexuality satisfying a need for an intense personal bonding that could not be found in a marriage or in a parent-child relationship. While allowing homosexuality and pederasty, Athenian lawmakers carefully defined their practice. Men procuring boys for sodomy or male prostitution was considered illegal and, in some instances, the death penalty was imposed. A gentleman of wealth or status who had a relationship with a 15-19 year adolescent was considered the most acceptable situation. Yet, any Athenian citizen who was a catamite (boy kept for sexual pleasure) was not allowed to hold governmental offices but (unlike women) they were allowed to attend the festivals.

Although the use and price of tickets is questioned, most historians believe that admission was two obals, which equates to a minimum day's wage in the fifth century. It is known that seats were a premium because foreigners and citizens bought as many as possible. This left the poor without any seats. As a consequence, Pericles devised a *Theoric Fund* (welfare fund) designed to raise money which was given to the poor to buy a seat, although the rich seem to have used it and abused it. The money for the tickets went to the lessee whom the state had granted a contract for maintaining the theatre. Later, it is believed that the two obals were split between the lessee and the provider of refreshments.

Although all seats bore the same price, certain classes sat in certain sections, women (if admitted) apart from men, and prostitutes apart from other women. The priest of Dionysus held the center seat in the front row. Similar seats of honor were taken by the archons, generals, other priests, sons of soldiers killed in battle, and foreign ambassadors (but only on a Council vote). Inasmuch as the theatre was divided into wedge-shaped blocks, a block of seats was provided for each of the ten tribes. Other seat assignments included a section in the middle for the Council and Epheboi (soldiers in training), and a place for foreigners.

The theatre seats were hard and, as with our football games, cushions were used. With the performances beginning at dawn and ending in the evening, refreshments were available; some may have even gone home for food. The refreshments consisted of wines, dried fruits (to throw at the actors), and candies. Aristotle proposed measuring the amount of food eaten during a performance to determine the success or failure of a play. In some ways, Greek audiences resembled audiences of today. They slept during a performance, were rude, were drunk, applauded that which they liked, and made a great commotion about that which they disliked—such as hissing and kicking their heels against the seats. Some audiences made enough noise to prevent a play from continuing. Theophastus had a habit, for example,

of belching when the rest of the audience was silent. To control such crowds, comic actors are said to have bribed the audience by throwing nuts to them.

Costumes and Masks

That masks were worn from the beginning may have been a continuation of drama's ritualistic origins. Then too, the Greeks had no programs and the actors, being roughly sixty feet from the front row and three hundred feet from the back of the auditorium, needed to be identified and their facial expression seen. The mask was the most important item of the costume and was worn by all the performers except the flute player.

The lexicon or encyclopedia assembled about the tenth century, called the *Suidas*, held that Thespis was the first to disguise his face when he used white lead and then hung a garland of flowers (perhaps purslane) on his head. His next effort was the invention of linen masks which were artificially stiffened and had a strap of some sort in order to carry them or secure them to the head. As Phrynichos is said to have introduced the female masks, it appears that Thespis confined his masks to males. As to adding color to the masks and creating "terrifying" expressions, Aeschylus is given the credit. During the fifth and fourth centuries, most likely masks were made of linen, cork, or wood and were very naturalistic.

The earliest examples of tragic masks are to be seen in Basle on a "crater" vase. These paintings indicate that the masks covered the entire head, had eye openings, facial hair, and a small opening for the mouth, which gets larger in the period of Euripides. The suggestion that the masks were constructed to produce a "megaphone-effect" seems unlikely, especially when one considers the material of which the masks were made. The use of a headdress or very high forehead called an onkos is not found on masks in the fifth century but does seem to be characteristic of tragic masks early in the fourth century. The addition of the onkos is said to have been influenced by Lycurgus whose rebuilding of the theatre in stone (c. 338 to 330 B.C.) adorned it with statues of Aeschylus, Sophocles and Euripides. This seemingly inspired the creation of new masks to go with the new theatre.

Julius Pollux in his *Onomastican* (second century) lists 28 masks for tragedy: 6 for old men, 8 for young men, 3 for servants and 11 for women of all ages. Also, he lists special masks of a Giant, a River, a Triton, a Fury, Death, a Titan, Muses, Nymphs, Horns, Blindness, Argos with his many eyes, Thamyras with one dark eye and one blue, as well as other personification and personality masks.

As to comedy, Pollux makes a distinction between *Old* and *New Comedy*. In order to parody living persons such as Agathon, Euripides, Pericles, and Socrates, portrait masks were used. Socrates is said to have stood up in the theatre so that all would recognize the mask burlesquing him. These types of masks are not found, however, in *Middle* and *New Comedy*, which tended to exaggerate facial features. Like tragedy, Old Comedy used special masks such as animal masks for the choruses, slaves, old men, and young women. As to *New Comedy*, Pollux's listing serves more as a source. Many of these examples are categories with a variety of different types under each heading. Young women, for example, contain fourteen different masks, and there are three types of "parasite" characters.

As to the garments of the satyr play, most likely chorus costumes consisted of goatskin loincloth (sometimes made of linen) with a phallus (disappears in the Hellenistic period) attached in the front and a horse-like tail in the rear. Then too, the chorus appeared as hunters, shepherds, etc., and wore the appropriate dress. Further, it is thought that the actor's appearance consisted of a beard and a bald pate in the front of his head, and that the satyr leader, Silenus, was distinguished by his fleecy or shaggy fur or hide tights which are said to appear first early in the fifth century. As to the footwear for the satyrs, they went barefooted. Many satyr costumes were probably variations of the tragic dress as satyr drama tended to satirize tragedy.

Tragic costume is thought to be Aeschylus's creation. Although this is questioned, he is credited with developing "distinguished" costumes for certain characters in tragedy. The basic costume for the tragic actor and chorus was a decorated sleeved garment called a *chiton*, which varied in length and used a belt. At times it was worn with two types of cloaks: a *himation* (a long cloak) or a *chalmus* (a short cloak). The chiton's decoration during the fifth century has raised some questions. Some critics suggest that only the borders and cuffs of the sleeves were decorated. As to the use of the fitted sleeve for the chiton, its first appearance is dated with the flute player about 480 B.C. The fact that the long sleeves could disguise the arms of the male actor playing female parts as well as keep the actors warm seem ample reasons for their use. The footwear raises less questions. Fifth century performers wore a soft-sole shoe or a decorated laced boot (some of which were cuffed) reaching to the calf. In the Hellenistic period the shoe was given a thick sole and called a *cothornus*. It is likely at this time that the tragic actors added padding to their costumes to make them look bigger to go with the thick sole. Perhaps the advent of the raised stage required an actor to appear larger than life.

Comic costumes were based on everyday garments. In parodying tragedy, comic choruses were costumed according to their occupation or nationality. In Old Comedy they appeared as animals, birds, etc., but appeared as ordinary people in Middle and New Comedy. In both, a long robe and a chiton were used. The chiton, however, was extremely short in order that the attached phallus was visible. To add to their sexuality, the actors' tights were padded, flesh color, and very tight. This costume seems to have been standard for Old Comedy. New Comedy utilized everyday dress and a plain white tunic, which was unseamed on the left side. Called an exomis, this garment became the standard for old and young men. Old men added a long white cloak (himation), whereas young men of good families wore a red or purple himation. Other characters like the parasites wore a black or gray himation, and slaves added a short white cloak over their exomis. Young women and priestesses dressed in white and old women were seen in green or light blue garments.

Tragic choruses were costumed according to the part that they played. The leader of the chorus was distinguished, however, by decorated robes. In the fourth century and the Hellenistic period nothing can be determined about the costume of the chorus. Certainly as their function diminished, they sang mainly interludes. Hence, they may not have needed to be costumed.

Stage Machinery

Stage machinery was limited and simple enough to be operated by no more than three people. Besides the *ekkyklema* and the *mechane*, Pollux cites the *hemikyklion* which was located in the orchestra and served to show either a remote area or people swimming. Also mentioned is the stropheion which Arnott places in the Hellenistic period and which seems to have been used to show men dying in battle or being transformed into gods.

Usually assigned to the fifth century is the mechane. Aristophanes states that it was raised like a finger which suggests a counterweight machine. The location of this device is thought to have been behind the skene where the actor could be rigged to it and at the right moment hoisted above the skena or stage area. Other machines used in this period were a thunder machine consisting of a jar full of pebbles and the ekkyklema whose operation is uncertain but whose function was to show interior scenes.

Music and Dance

In the classical period music functioned in the theatre in many of the same ways as modern music functions in film, television, and the stage. It was designed to accompany various passages, to be an integral part of the choral odes, and to evoke and intensify the play's emotional and ethical qualities.

The instrumentation used to accompany the actor and the chorus was played by a flute player who preceded the chorus and whose position on the stage or in the orchestra is unclear. It is known, however, that for the dithyramb the flute player stood in the middle of the circular chorus. The instruments consisted of strings—the lyre and kithara, both of which were used predominantly in lyric poetry; and wind instruments—aulos and syrinx, both of which were flute-type instruments. The syrinx was invented by Ctesibius of Alexandria in the third century B.C., and was considered more of a flute than was the aulos. The latter was related to the clarinet or oboe in that it used a reed, and was the chief instrument for dithyrambs and

The lower frieze on this vase represents satyrs dancing. Note the musician at center; he is playing the double aulos, a reed instrument which is one of three musical instruments commonly used in Greek tragedy. The upper frieze shows the gods bringing gifts to Pandora. *Krater, London, British Museum.*

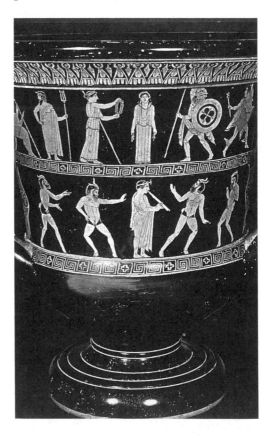

dramatic pieces. Additionally, there were brass-type instruments that functioned like a tuba and a trumpet; and percussion instruments such as the tambourine, cymbals, and castanets (krotala), the latter being used by the chorus leader to mark the chorus beat.

All music demonstrated a strong relationship to oriental music and consisted of various modes (a mode equals eight diatonic tones of an octave and no chromatics). The principal modes were *Dorian, Aeolian, Ionian, Lydian,* and *Phrygian* (which Aristotle describes as orgiastic and passionate). Other variations included the *Mixolydian, Syntono-lydian, Hypodorian, Hypophrygian,* and *Hypolydian.* Based upon Aristides, the various sequence of intervals, and the tones which were not of equal value were arranged as follows:

Lydian:	e f a b b c e e
Dorian:	d e e f a b b c e
Phrygian:	d e e f a b b c d
Ionian:	B B c e g a
Mixolydian:	B B c d e e f b
Syntonolydian:	B B c e g

Dancing was important to the Greeks as it was regarded as expressive of ethical and moral qualities. Its importance to drama can be noted in the orchestra (dancing place) being the focal point of the Greek theatre. Drama is thought to have evolved, a point that is still questioned. As a form, however, dance emphasized two basic characteristics: the gestural *(schemata)* and the rhythmic movements *(phorai).* The latter consisted of three elements: indication (pointing to a person or thing), motions (gestures associated with movements), and postures which are indicative of later acting theories in that they were standardized and given names. Thus, tragedy and comedy had distinctively different postures.

Little information exists as to the exact movements of the chorus. Probably when they delivered the *strophe* (a stanza of the tragic choral ode) or the *antistrophe* (the stanza that followed), they performed the *Emmeleia,* the standard dance of tragedy which was performed in a slow, deliberate, and formal manner. That the movements in the strophe and antistrophe were the same is uncertain, although the music seems to have been repeated in each stanza. Comic dances were less dignified and livelier. The *Kordax,* a crude, vulgar, obscene dance was the standard for comedy. The round dance of the dithyramb called the *Tyrbasia* was a wild, spirited affair in which the chorus moved in a circular motion. That of the satyr play was a dance called the *Sikinnis* derived from the *eponymous Sikinnos* (barbarian) and was a mimetic dance involving animal masks, leaping, pantomime, and wild antics.

Acting

All the actors were men, and the great roles of Electra, Antigone, Medea, Phaedra, etc., were performed by such male actors as Herakleides, Polus, Theodorus, or Thettalus. Before the advent of these actors, the dramatist acted in his own plays. With the introduction of the second and third actors, the poet began to select and hire his actors. Under this system, writers, such as Sophocles, developed a preference for certain actors and even wrote plays with their favorite actors in mind.

About 449 B.C., the state specified that the archon would assign each tragic writer a protagonist. This coincides with the award given to the best protagonist in this same year. The first winner was Herakleides and, as with all winners, he was chosen on his ability and not on the basis of the winning play. Often the winning actor did not come from the best play. Being voted the best actor meant among other things an automatic selection for next year's festival. Under this system, the protagonist acted in all four of the same writer's plays.

The system was changed in the fourth century (Hellenistic period). Acting was more professional and tended to overshadow the writer in terms of importance. Thus, good actors were in demand, and by 350 B.C., leading actors (protagonists) were chosen by lot and required to appear in one play of each writer—to insure fairness.

Vase, early fourth century B.C., depicting actors. *Metropolitan Museum of Art, Fletcher Fund, 1924.*

In the fifth century B. C. the Greek actor was paid by the state, who rated the actors by their ability to sing, gesture, move, and above all, to have a strong resonant voice for enunciation and for projection. Aristotle speaks of the actor learning to adapt his voice to the personality of the character through vocal inflection and when this is accomplished, characterization is achieved. Thus, the better actors not only had excellent voices, but knew how to use the voice in terms of tone and adaptability to the character.

The actor's delivery made use of speech, recitative, and song and each had its own metrical pattern. Prose unaccompanied by music was written normally in iambic trimeters, whereas accompanied prose (recitative) used tetrameters and anapestic dimeters. Song employed various meters. As discussed in music, when instrumentation was required, a flute and lyre were used. During the fifth century the emphasis was upon the word. In the fourth century, however, musical portions were increased and rivalled the words for emphasis.

Clearly required of the fifth century actor was the ability to gesture (use of hands) and move. Actors were required to move rapidly, kneel, and at times prostrate themselves. In addition, they had to be adept at changing their masks quickly if the scene required a change of emotion or facial expression. Where and how often tragic actors changed masks is uncertain. In comedy the actor wore a two-sided mask and simply turned the appropriate side to the audience.

Actors were classified into three categories. A first-rate actor was a *protagonist;* a second-rate, a *deuteragonist;* and a third-rate was termed a *tritagonist.* The classification system provided a method for dividing up the speaking parts. Although there were extras, there were only three speaking actors. This allowance of only three speaking actors was a rule imposed by the state and became known as *"The Three Actor Rule."* Once the poet had a protagonist, it is thought that the poet along with the protagonist chose the second and third actors. On the other hand, comedy required anywhere from three to five performers. How they were assigned is not known but by 442 B.C. the comic actor was given recognition when the Lenaia Festival introduced a contest for the best actor of comedy.

Artists of Dionysus

During the Hellenistic period, the rapid expansion of festivals plus the rise of professionalism in the theatre created a need for the guild known as the *Artists of Dionysus.* Aristotle states that they called themselves Technitai, and they do seem to be in existence by 279-78 B.C. The members of the guild included actors, poets, chorus members, musicians, costumers, oral readers, and trainers. Mime actors were not allowed membership. The chief official was usually a priest of Dionysus who was elected annually by the membership. By 133 B.C., the priest was replaced by a performing artist (epimeletes) who was elected and also could be re-elected. It appears that the members were free to make their own bookings and thus did not have to rely on the guild. Although the guild was not responsible for the members' conduct, once a contract was entered into, failure to comply brought a fine and prosecution by city officials. One of the procedures that is not clear is how each festival hired sufficient "artists." It is known that in some cases the guild appointed contractors. In other situations the various festivals contacted the various branches of the guild. Whatever the arrangement, it does not seem to be uniform.

There were three major branches: the Athenian (headquarters at Athens), the Ionian-Hellespontine (headquarters at Teos in Asia Minor), and the Nemean-Isthmian (headquarters at Corinth). The possibility of a fourth branch at Alexander exists. The Athenian and the Nemean-Isthmian guilds seem to have been created first and at about the same time. The Nemean-Isthmian guild was to dominate Athens from c. 268 B.C. until 130 B.C. at which time the Delphic officials shifted their favor to Athens. In retaliation, the Nemean-Isthmian guild barred Athenian members from certain festivals. This precipitated a feud between the two guilds which eventually required Roman intervention. After a series of legal battles, the Athenian guild was made the central organization in c. 112 B.C.

About 235 B.C., the Aetolian League granted membership privileges to the Ionian-Hellespontine guild. This guild was held in such high esteem by the people of Teos that they bought land for the "artists" in order that they wouldn't have to pay city taxes. A later rift, however, between the "artists" and the people forced the guild to move to the city of Lebedos.

Inasmuch as the artists needed to protect themselves in the unstable times and because rulers wanted the festivals celebrated properly, members were granted certain privileges: immunity from arrest, military exemption, and, in some cases, freedom from taxation. As the artists were guaranteed safety, some members were appointed ambassadors.

Thespis and the Chorus

Evidence indicates that Thespis was a professional actor from Icaria in Attica, who won the first tragedy contest in 534 B.C. and is thought to have performed at the City Dionysia as early as 560 B.C. His name is thought by some scholars to be an aberration, possibly derived from the *Odyssey* or to be a shortened name. His major contributions include coloring his face with white lead, introducing linen masks, and creating a single actor (himself) who was distinct from the chorus. Pollux contends, however, that Thespis may not have been the first to introduce an actor and that there were performances before Thespis involving an actor distinct from the chorus. It does seem clear, however, that his innovation of moving to the spoken element, and away from the lyrical and musical, enabled Thespis to emerge as the best actor of tragedy in 534 B.C.

During the first period or one actor period, plays were lyric rather than dramatic, and thus the focus was on the chorus and the single actor such as Thespis. When the dramatic interest in the play began to outweigh the lyric, the role of the chorus started to diminish. This led to the classical or second period. In this era writers sought to combine the dramatic and choral elements into a unified whole. In the last period, the period of decline, the attempt at unification was abandoned and the chorus was gradually withdrawn as a direct participant in the story.

Although the chorus became obsolete, it made a distinct contribution to the drama. As an agent, it participated directly in the action giving advice, asking questions, providing exposition, contributing to the theatrical spectacle with its song, dance and general movement. It served as the ideal spectator reacting to events and characters as the author anticipated the audience would do. It provided time for costume changes and it set the overall mood.

On the other hand, the chorus posed problems. Its presence created credibility about confidential and eavesdropping scenes as well as monologues and asides. Also, once unity of time and place was established, the chorus being present hindered it. In *The Choephoroi*, for example, we are first at Agamemnon's tomb and then the scene switches to the royal palace. During both scenes, the chorus never moves.

The tragic chorus in the fifth century B.C. appears to have numbered twelve until Sophocles raised it to fifteen. Inasmuch as Aristotle stated that it developed from the dithyrambic chorus, some scholars argue a fifty-member chorus. They draw support from the *Suppliants,* in which the chorus is composed of the daughters of Danaus who, according to legend, numbered fifty. The redating of the *Suppliants* plus newer scholarship appears to make the fifty number untenable.

As for comedy and the satyr choruses, the number twenty-four is agreed upon for comedy but in the third century, the number was reduced to seven. The satyr play had a twelve-member chorus which seems to have been reduced possibly to four in the second century.

Dramatic Origins: Dithyramb, Tragedy, and Comedy

The fact that Greek tragedy was presented at a festival honoring the god Dionysus has influenced theorists to focus on that relationship in an effort to evolve a theory as to its origin. Although scholars have evolved different theories, they have agreed that theatre emerged from ritual. Reliable evidence is lacking, however, and thus the following theories must be accepted only in their theoretical framework.

The term tragedy means goat song, perhaps implying that either a goat was sacrificed or that a goat was given as a prize for the best chorus performers. Aristotle states that tragedy originated out of the mimic representations by the leaders (*exarchon*) of the dithyrambic chorus, who performed a story about the suffering and death of Dionysus. The *dithyramb* is thought to have been developed in Phrygria and to have come to Greece with the cult of Dionysus. Arion (c. 625-585 B.C.) is credited with changing *dithyrambs* into literary compositions at Corinth by creating a stationary chorus who sang a titled poem on a well-defined subject. As a form, the *dithyramb* developed fully in Athens at the City Dionysia, where the first dithyrambic contests were held about 509 B.C., the first winner being Hypodicus of Chalcis.

At the City Dionysia, the *dithyramb* was danced and sung by a chorus representing each of the ten tribes. There were ten choruses for men and ten for boys each composed of one hundred members. Arranging themselves in a circle, with the flute player in the middle, the chorus danced the Tyrbasia unadorned by masks and crowned with ivy.

Chosen by the tribe and appointed by the archon, each tribe had a chorus whose responsibilities entailed hiring the flute player and poet. In determining each tribe's order of each tribe, the archon drew lots. For the winning tribe, the chorogos erected a monument to house the tripod awarded to first place. The winning poet received a bull and it appears that the second and third place writers received, respectively, a vessel of wine and a goat smeared with wine sediment. If Lysias' information is correct, then a men's chorus cost more than a boys or a tragic chorus, and everything was more expensive at the City Dionysia as opposed to other festivals.

In the late fifth and fourth centuries B.C., the *dithyramb* changed. Melanippides introduced lyric solos (anabolic) whose function was to create more emotional intensity. Consequently, the importance of music over the word increased, and hence that of the flute player. In the fourth century, the flute-player's importance is attested to by his name being placed on monuments along with that of the poet and choregos. With the increased importance of music, the *dithyramb* as a religious ceremony diminished and the dithyramb as a secular oratorio was evolved.

As to the origins of Greek comedy, there is less speculation. Francis Cornford in his *The Origin of*

Statuettes of Greek actors. *Metropolitan Museum of Art, Rogers Fund, 1913.*

Attic Comedy (1914) believed that comedy "sprang up and took shape in connection with Dionysiac or phallic ritual." His observations were based largely upon Aristotle who credits the origins of Greek comedy with "those who led the phallic procession." How a sexual ritual was transformed into formal comedy is not known, but Epicharmus of Sicily is credited with making the transformation about 480 B.C. It is asserted also that another influence was the mime from which the Athenians borrowed certain elements which they combined with their phallic choruses to develop comedy. Whatever the development, Greek comedy was given official recognition in 486 B.C., when contests for writers of comedy were instituted at the City Dionysia, the first winner being Chionides.

Aeschylus (525-456 B.C.)

Aeschylus's addition of the second actor to drama marks him as the creator of tragedy. By shifting the dramatic action away from the chorus, Aeschylus made greater development of plot pos-

sible, especially character and dialogue which was his strength. Altogether he wrote ninety plays (some argue seventy or eighty); only seven remain: *The Persae* (472 B.C.); *Seven Against Thebes* (467 B.C.); *Agamemnon, Libation Bearers,* and *Eumenides,* which are grouped under the title *The Oresteia* (458 B.C.), which represents the only complete extant trilogy, a form Aeschylus is said to have favored; *The Suppliants* (c. 468 B.C.); and *Prometheus Bound* (c. 468 B.C.).

He won his first prize in 484 B.C. and was again successful in 472 B.C. with *The Persae.* Sophocles defeated him in 468 B.C. Of this defeat, Cimon, the Athenian ruler and later foe of Pericles, was said to favor Sophocles, in which case Aeschylus could have been the victim of politics. He did rebound, however, with his victory with *The Oresteia* and the satyr play (a form at which Aeschylus was considered unequalled), *Proteus* (now lost), in 458 B.C.

Said to be the "finest achievement in Greek drama," *The Oresteia* was greatly influenced by Pericles' (500-429 B.C.) ascension to power and his ousting of Cimon in 461 B.C. Conditioned by war,

THE ORESTEIA (The Story of Orestes)
AESCHYLUS

CHARACTERS

AGAMEMNON, the King
CLYTEMNESTRA, his Queen
AEGISTHUS, Clymnestra's lover
CASSANDRA, A Trojan captive
ORESTES, son of Agamemnon and Clytemnestra
ELECTRA, Orestes's sister
PYLADES, close friend of Orestes
CILASSO, the old nurse
THE EUMENIDES, the chorus
MINERVA (ATHENA), Roman goddess of wisdom. In Greece she is called Athena.
APOLLO
FURIES, also called Eumenides ("the kindly ones"). They are represented as winged women with snakes about them and are considered primeval beings.

SETTING

A palace serves as the background for the first play, *Agamemnon*, and the second play, *The Choephori* or *Libation Bearers*. In the second play, the tomb of Agamemnon is placed in the foreground and then the scene shifts to the palace. In the last play, *The Eumenides* or *The Kindly Ones*, the scene is Athena's Temple.

BACKGROUND

The Oresteia is a trilogy, that is, three plays forming one entire work. Although each play represents separate events, all three stories concern Orestes. The first play focuses on the death of Agamemnon, the second on Orestes' return and his revenge, and the third is Orestes' trial for the murder of his mother. *The Oresteia* is sometimes titled *The House of Atreus*. Atreus, the tyrant, killed the children of Thyestes and served them to their father at a royal banquet. Agamemnon and Menelaus are sons of Atreus and have gone to Troy to seek the return of Helen, Menelaus's wife who was kidnapped by Paris.

AGAMEMNON

The play opens with a Watchman resting on the outer wall of the palace. He has been keeping watch for ten years and although weary, he continues his vigil, looking toward Troy for King Agamemnon's signal of a beaconfire to indicate Troy's fall. As he laments his lonely watch, he spots the beaconfire and rushes off to Argos to tell the Queen, Clytemnestra.

With the exit of the Watchman, the Chorus of Argive Senators marches in to give exposition as to why Agamemnon went to Troy. They narrate how Paris abducted Helen, the wife of Menelaus, and ran off to Troy. Inasmuch as Menelaus and Agamemnon are brothers, Agamemnon demands revenge. On their way to Troy, however, the wind ceases. In order to get enough wind for his fleet, Agamemnon sacrifices his daughter, Iphigenia—an act which causes Clytemnestra to plot revenge upon her husband. She gives her son Orestes into the care of the King of Phocis. Nursing her hate, she is joined by Aegisthus, Thyestes' remaining son. Together they lay a plan and, joined in common cause, become lovers.

A herald arrives announcing the coming of the King. In a great procession, Agamemnon enters bringing with him his mistress, Cassandra, the prophet whom he has captured at Troy. Amid the pomp and ceremony, the King enters and Clytemnestra is there to greet him. She tells Cassandra to enter the palace as a slave and not to seek any higher station. In a moment of frenzy, Cassandra predicts the murder of Agamemnon, her death and the return of the King's son, Orestes. Further, she foresees Orestes avenging his father's death. Nobody believes Cassandra, for that is her destiny—to predict the future and have her warnings ignored. Agamemnon enters the palace but Cassandra refuses to enter. Clytemnestra returns and orders Cassandra to enter. Again, she refuses. Clytemnestra declares that she will not demean herself by arguing with a common slave and re-enters the palace. After much lamenting and reiterating her prophecy of Agamemnon's death, Cassandra goes into the palace to meet her fate.

The Chorus considers the proceedings during which a cry from the palace of "I'm stabbed with a mortal blow" is heard. The skene doors open revealing Clytemnestra with the bloody axe in her hands standing over her husband's body! She declares that she has killed Agamemnon and Cassandra. With Chorus waiting in the background for Orestes to revenge his father, Clytemnestra justifies her crime. Her lover, Aegisthus, appears and exchanges threats with the Chorus and asserts that he intends to rule. The intervention of Clytemnestra prevents violence. The two lovers return to the palace leaving the Chorus on stage as the first play of the trilogy comes to an end.

THE CHOEPHORI
OR *THE LIBATION BEARERS*

The question as to whether the death of Agamemnon would be avenged closed the first play. If the answer is yes then who would be the avenger? We now learn that Orestes has been in exile, and thus has grown up in a distant land. Learning of his mother's treachery, he goes to Delphi to consult with Apollo for advice. Apollo bids him to return to Argos and avenge his father's death by killing his mother and her lover, Aegisthus. If he refuses tragedy will beset him throughout his life. He must therefore obey the Oracle, and he returns to Argos to carry out Apollo's edict.

The Choephori begins with the entrance of Orestes and his companion, Pylades. Orestes goes to his father's tomb where he offers two locks of his hair as a sign of gratitude. The first lock goes to the river-god, Inachus, and the second lock is given to his father for the love Orestes could not display at the time of the funeral. The palace doors open and a procession of black-robed women led by Electra, Orestes's sister, come forth carrying libations of mixed meal, oil, and honey to be poured on the king's tomb. The queen has sent this chorus of mourners to the tomb as she is fearful of revenge and seeks to appease the wrath of her murdered husband. The Chorus asserts that the murder cannot be washed away. There will be revenge!

On the one hand, the offerings Electra gives are those of her mother, and on the other hand, she wants her father's death avenged—all of which causes Electra to be perplexed. The Chorus suggests that she pray for pity for herself, that Orestes be brought home from exile, and that Clytemnestra be slain. Electra pours the libations over the tomb, and then discovers Orestes' locks of hair. Although the Chorus is puzzled, Electra believes that Orestes has returned. To confirm her belief, she finds footprints leading to the tomb which match hers. Orestes reveals himself to Electra who does not recognize her brother. Thus, she is unconvinced that this stranger is Orestes. Orestes convinces her

and recounts the command of Apollo and what would happen should he not follow Apollo's wishes. Orestes questions as to why Clytemnestra has sent offerings to the tomb. The Chorus replies that she had a dream in which she gave birth to a dragon who fed at her breast. Orestes sees himself as the dragon and predicts "Myself shall slay her." With a firm resolve, he unfolds his plans for revenge. Using his faithful servant, Pylades, Orestes will present himself as a stranger at the palace gates in order to gain admission to see Aegisthus. Once he meets Aegisthus, Orestes will kill him. He does not mention how he intends to slay his mother. His silence is "touching and dreadful."

As Electra returns to the palace, Orestes and Pylades leave. Allowing time for Orestes and Pylades to change into their disguises, the Chorus sings an ode of apprehension, human guilt, and of the past crimes of women. They finish with the cry that justice is always served no matter what the crime or who commits it.

Orestes and Pylades reappear. Walking straight to the palace gate, Orestes knocks and is greeted by a servant who in turn fetches the Queen, Clytemnestra. Disguised as a messenger, Orestes is admitted and here relates his tale. Using a Phocian dialect, Orestes tells her that he (Orestes) is dead. Clytemnestra leaves to relate the news to Aegisthus who now appears to question the Chorus, after which he re-enters the palace to check the veracity of the messenger's tale. A repeated cry is heard and then a servant rushes out, shouting that Aegisthus is dead. Banging the door at the women's part of the palace, the servant yells for Clytemnestra. She reappears with an axe in her hand, the same one she used to kill Agamemnon. On seeing Orestes, however, she tries a different tact and pretends to be tender and loving. Orestes wavers but Pylades reminds him of Apollo's command. After her repeated attempts to dissuade Orestes from killing her, Clytemnestra enters the palace where Orestes slays her. While the murder is occurring, the Chorus sings a hymn of exaltation.

The next scene displays Orestes, sword in hand, standing over his mother's body. Although Apollo's justice has been served, Orestes faces now the Furies of his mother. As he leaves for Delphi to seek the protection of Apollo, the "Gorgon-like" Furies "vested in sable stoles, and their locks entertwined with clustering snakes,"

THE ORESTEIA, continued

attack Orestes driving him to frenzy and madness as he seeks to run away. But there is no escape.

THE EUMENIDES (THE KINDLY LOVERS)

At the time that *The Eumenides* was written, the leaders of the ruling political party, Pericles and Ephialtes, had proposed reforming and/or eliminating the high court of the Areopagus (a council of nobles who governed the state and whose name was derived from the hill where the sessions were held). Considered the highest court in cases of murder, the Aeropagus was considered outdated by some and with reverence by others—such as Aeschylus. By having the Areopagus serve as the setting for *The Eumenides*, Aeschylus intended to make a political statement as well as resolve the Orestes conflict.

Relentlessly pursued by the Furies, a tormented Orestes arrives at Apollo's shrine in Delphi and enters the temple. As the scene begins, the Priestess of the temple is seen praying to the various deities. At the conclusion of her prayers, she enters the temple where very few men have entered. She rushes out screaming that she has seen a man (Orestes) — "His hands still dripping gore, his sword new-drawn" surrounded by sleeping women whose breath, hideous faces, and filthiness of dress make their "presence a pollution to the temple or even to the roofs of men."

The next scene reveals the inner-temple and Orestes sitting on the Omphalos (a navel stone considered the center of the earth) with Apollo standing beside him. Behind them, standing in a semicircle are the sleeping Furies and behind them stands Mercury (Hermes), the escorter of the dead. Apollo declares that he will never desert Orestes, and then he has Mercury escort Orestes to Athens.

Orestes is gone, and the Furies continue to sleep. Clytemnestra appears in dark robes with her bare neck showing the wound inflicted by Orestes. She approaches the Furies who are slow to awaken but once aroused, they seek to renew their vengeance upon Orestes. They confront Apollo whose response is to tell them to leave his temple. They accuse Apollo of being responsible for the murder of Clytemnestra and Aegisthus and for Orestes's punishment. He responds that he had demanded revenge, to which he is told that by his demands he has caused an even greater crime—matricide. Apollo declares that Athena should decide who is right. Fearful of Apollo's silver bow and arrows, they leave.

The scene switches to Minerva's (Athena) temple on the Acropolis in Athens where Orestes is seen begging for protection. The Furies enter exhorting one another to revenge Clytemnestra's death and here encounter Minerva who has come to defend Orestes. She listens as the Furies claim that Orestes belongs to them but she rebukes them for denying Orestes any defense. Whereupon, she turns to hear Orestes's argument. Hearing both sides, Minerva declines to make a decision; instead, she convenes a court.

The scene is now Mars Hill where the Areopagus holds court. Minerva enters at the head of the eleven Athenian citizens who compose the Areopagus. She is the twelfth member. Together, they will decide the issue. A trumpet sounds to convene the court. The Furies begin by examining Orestes who admits the crime but justifies it in the name of Apollo. The next witness to appear is Apollo, who pleads the case for Orestes and in so doing, argues that inasmuch as a man can be born without a mother he is closer to his father than to his mother. For example, Minerva was "sprang full-armed from the head of Olympian Zeus." With all the testimony finished, the judges began to vote one by one. The count is taken and the verdict is five in favor and six against. Minerva votes that "Orestes has escaped the doom of blood." Even though Minerva's ballot makes the vote equal, under Athenian law a deadlock means an acquittal verdict. The deciding vote by Minerva was given on the side of mercy, and historically came to be known as the "Minerva's Pebble."

The Furies are angry but Minerva appeases them, and they agree to convert to kind deities. Henceforth, they are known as the Eumenides and not the Furies.

Aeschylus

Aeschylus's plays underlie his metaphysical views and in *The Oresteia* his questions on original sin (hybris: pride), God's vengeance, justice, and morality are in evidence. He ran into conflict with the traditional views of polytheism when he articulated his position of one god. Further problems occurred when he questioned the seeming contradiction of God allowing the innocent to suffer and to permit the presence of evil, all of which branded him a rebel.

Not only in *The Oresteia* but in all his plays, Aeschylus set down what was to be a major theme not only for the fifth century but for the twentieth century as well—the struggle of man against fate, an idea that influenced Shakespeare, Ibsen, O'Neill, Goethe and Shelley as well. It is central to tragedy, and Aeschylus could only conclude that man's suffering comes from sin—be it his or another generation. No poet spoke more to man's tragic condition than did Aeschylus.

A religious man, Aeschylus belonged to a cult—the Eleusinian Order—and was brought to trial for revealing its secrets. Although he was acquitted, he was unhappy in Athens and left for Sicily where he had been invited by Hieron I of Syracuse. Reportedly he died in Gela, Sicily, when an eagle dropped a tortoise on his head, mistaking it for a stone. Even in death, however, Aeschylus was held in great esteem by the Greeks. In restaging his father's plays, Euphorion was able to claim four victories in his father's name. Further testimony of this esteem was given in the fourth century B.C. when a statue of Aeschylus was erected in the Theatre of Dionysus.

Despite his accomplishments as a writer, the developer of the crane, distegia (balcony), ekkyklema, theologeion, and winning the prize for his plays twelve times, Aeschylus considered his accomplishments secondary to his contributions to the state. His epitaph (supposedly composed by him) reads "Aeschylus, Euphorion's son, Athenian, lies in this tomb, perished in wheat-bearing Gela. Of his valour and fair-fame the sacred grove of Marathon can tell, and the long-haired Persian who learned it there." Aeschylus's pride in being a member of the polis and making a contribution to the same marked him as a loyal Athenian first, and a dramatist second.

Satyr Drama

In addition to the three tragedies, playwrights were required in 501 B.C. to write a play about the Satyrs who were the half-beast, half-man followers of Dionysus. Using obscene language, gestures, and costumes (see section on costumes), the chorus and their leader (Silenus) mocked heroes, legends, and most often the tragedy that it accom-

Vase from fifth century B.C., depicting satyrs dancing. *Metropolitan Museum of Art, Fletcher Fund, 1924.*

THE TRACKERS OR THE SEARCHING SATYRS
SOPHOCLES

CHARACTERS
PHOEBUS APOLLO
HERMES, son of Zeus and the numph, Maria; little
    brother to Apollo
KYLLENE, nymph of the mountain
SILENUS, satyr leader
CHORUS OF SATYRS

SETTING
    Arcadia, southern Greece. On the mountain,
Kyllene. In front of the cave of the nymph Kyllene.

BACKGROUND
    This particular satyr drama was discovered in
Egypt on an archeological expedition in 1912. The
play has been translated into rhyming couplets. It
should be noted that there are sections of this play
missing.

STORY
    Alone in front of Kyllene's cave, an angry Apollo
offers a reward to anyone who can find his cows.
In addition, he threatens harm to anyone who
deceives him. Silenus enters and says that he will
send his sons in search of the missing herd. Apollo
responds with a promise of gold and "freedom
from toil for you and your sons." The chorus of
sons appears and with their leader, Silenus, set off
on their search. During their expedition, they hear
the sound of Hermes's lyre which completely un-
nerves them. Kyllene encounters the Satyrs and
questions them as to their mission. In turn, they
ask her about the music's origin. Swearing the
Satyrs to secrecy, Kyllene reveals that she is a
nurse and mother for Hermes because her real
mother (Maria) did not want the job. As to the
music, it comes from a musical instrument called
a lyre which Hermes invented when he was six
days old. In describing this instrument, Kyllene
states that it has a gut string and an "ox-hide newly
flayed" to cover it. The Satyrs conclude that Hermes
is the thief and convey their suspicions to Kyllene.
A confrontation scene ensues between Hermes
and the Satyrs. Hermes denies the charge. Meanwhile Apollo has found a witness to the theft who
asserts that a youth took the cows. The Satyrs
return to Apollo with their information. Hermes
begins to play the lyre which drives the Satyrs to
dance uncontrollably. Although Apollo finds the
music enchanting and almost spellbinding, he confronts Hermes. Under pressure Hermes admits his
guilt. Promising to reform, Hermes gives Apollo
the lyre as a repayment for the dead cows. The
Satyrs receive the gold and are set free. When
Apollo plays the lyre, however, he is able to hyp-
notically capture the Satyrs who then follow
Apollo's bidding.

panied. The only extant examples are *The Cyclops*
(Euripides) which exists in its entirety, and *The
Trackers* (Sophocles) of which a large portion re-
mains.

Sophocles

    Sophocles (c. 496 B.C.-406 B.C.) came from
Colonus, a suburb of Attica, and was the son of a
sword manufacturer. Thus in times of war, when
others were impoverished, Sophocles' family was
wealthy. Said to be charming, handsome, and
athletic, Sophocles held a variety of political offices under his friend, Pericles. He was a general in
the battle against Samos, and being a religious
man, on occasion filled in the office of priest. In his
youth he favored "money and boys," and in old
age, prostitutes and mistresses were his choice.

    His innovations to Greek tragedy include the
addition of the third actor, the first use of scene
painting, discontinuing the use of connected trilo-
gies, and increasing the size of the chorus from
twelve to fifteen. Sophocles wrote 123 dramas of
which seven are extant—*Oedipus Rex* (c. 430-425
B.C.), *Antigone* (c. 441 B.C.), *Ajax* (c. 450-440 B.C.),
Electra (c. 418-410 B.C.), *Philoctetes* (409 B.C.), *Women*

Sophocles

of Trachis (c. 413 B.C.) and *Oedipus at Colonus* (406 B.C.). In addition, a portion of a satyr play which he wrote, *The Trackers,* is extant. He won twenty-four contests and never finished lower than second.

Whereas Aeschylus preferred the trilogy and focused on the cosmos, Sophocles wrote individual works and looked into the psychological nature of man. In *Women of Trachis* Sophocles examined jealousy; *Ajax* focused on madness; *Electra* was obsessed with hatred, and *Oedipus Rex* looked at incest and madness. Rejecting Aeschylus' viewpoint of resignation in the hands of fate, Sophocles opted for life to be lived vigorously and with dignity. Man may not be the captain of his fate but he is the master of his soul. As Sophocles states in *Oedipus at Colonus,* "The honor of life lies not in words but in deeds."

A conservative upholder of the established order, Sophocles epitomized traditional Greece. He wanted structure, and like Aristophanes, opposed radical change. Thus, freedom was chaos, hence bad, and law was order, hence good. It followed, therefore, that life needed limits in order to have any meaningful purpose. As he became older, Sophocles lamented the decay of Athens, and his outlook became pessimistic. The best thing that could happen to man, he observed, was not to be born. The second best was to die in infancy.

He was a master of technique, the ultimate craftsman. No writer delineated character better or fashioned his plays so solidly. "I draw men as they ought to be drawn," said Sophocles;

"Euripides draws them as they are." Although his characterization and well-made play inspired Aristotle's treatise, *The Poetics,* Sophocles stands below Aeschylus as a poet. His name means "the Wise and Honored One," and upon his death he was worshipped as a hero. Many historians consider Sophocles the finest of Greek tragic dramatists, and his esteem held by future generations can be noted in the poet Shelley (1792-1822), who had a volume of Sophocles in his pocket when he drowned.

Euripides

Named after the strait, Euripus, which separates Euboea from Boeotia, Euripides (c. 480-406 B.C.) was born in Salamis, an island near the coast of Attica. He grew up in an age of skepticism in which he came under the influence of such Sophists as Anaxygoras, Prodicus, and Protagoras. His father wanted him to be an athlete, but Euripides had a loathing for the games, favoring instead painting and books. Painting was in fact his first career choice, but at eighteen he turned to playwriting. Not until age twenty-four were his plays (one of which was *The Daughter of Pelias)* accepted for competition. He won third prize and it would take him fourteen years to win first place (he won first only 5 times). His outspoken opposition to the wealthy, to war, to the subjection of women, and Athens' imperialism, made Euripides unpopular and he left Athens in 408 B.C. He settled

Euripides

at the court of Archelaus in Macedon, where he died accidentally, reportedly torn to pieces by hunting dogs.

The number of plays Euripides wrote is in question as is the authorship of the extant works attributed to him. Of the 92 or 98 plays he is said to have written, 23 were tetralogies, and nineteen plays are extant. *(Rhesus* is questionable as to authorship.) His satyr play, *The Cyclops* (date unknown) is the only complete extant satyr drama; the rest are tragedies.

As a playwright, Euripides remains then as now the most popular, the most quoted, and the most contemporary. His rejection of the standard religious viewpoint in favor of the suggestion that "chance rather than the gods hold sway" (see *The Trojan Women:* 884), and that "The mind within us—that is our god," as well as his lifestyle of living in a cave, wearing a beard, being antisocial, cynical, and his views on peace, war and society mark Euripides as a poet of the 1960s. His characterization is said to be second only to Shakespeare and Ibsen, and his use of psychological realism with its network of complex emotional responses demonstrated a clear advance in this area. His use of children and women as heroes are of particular interest. (See *Medea:* 431 B.C., *The Children of Hercules:* 427 B.C., or *Electra:* c. 413 B.C., for example.) His later works *(Electra* and *Hippolytus:* 428 B.C.) demonstrate a turn toward melodrama.

Melodrama is a moralistic form and Euripides was a moralist; socially he was on the side of the underdog. As a writer he was able to effect this moralistic viewpoint with a contrived ending which is a characteristic of melodrama. His innovation of the deus ex machina (god from the machine) at the play's end effectively allowed the appearance of a god atop the stage building to provide miraculous endings. His use of four minute rescues, the triumph of right over wrong, unexpected discoveries to solve a problem anticipates twentieth century melodrama. Further, his technical advances in the use of the prologue, rhetoric, music, scenic devices, the reduction of the chorus's function, and the use of realistic costumes mark the culmination of Greek drama.

Despite his social unpopularity, Euripides the writer was revered. Plutarch (c. 46 B.C.-120 A.D.) contends that on three separate occasions Euripides' popularity saved the day. Once was when Athenian prisoners at Syracuse were set free because they could recite passages from Euripides. On another occasion, a ship pursued by pirates was unable to enter a Sicilian port for safety until a crew member could recite from Euripides. Plutarch's third event focused on 404 B.C. when Sparta conquered Athens. The Spartan generals reportedly were so moved by a Phoenician singing the first chorus from Euripides's *Electra* that the city was saved from destruction. Although an Athenian delegation was sent to retrieve Euripides' body, the king of Macedonia refused to give it over and thus Euripides was buried there.

Throughout the ages, poets have attested to Euripides' greatness but Goethe in 1831 summarized those thoughts best when he wrote "Have all the nations of the world since his time produced one dramatist who was worthy to hand him his slippers?"

Aristophanes: Old and Middle Comedy

The central dramatist for *Old* and *Middle comedy* was Aristophanes (c. 448-380 B.C.). *Old Comedy* abounds with social satire (society, politics, literature, and war) and is organized around a concept known as "the happy idea." The happy idea is an absurd solution which never really succeeds; for example, a sex strike to end war. The idea is proposed in the first part of the play. Next comes the agon or debate as to the merits of the idea. The decision of the debate always favors putting the happy idea into practice. The action of the play now stops, and the chorus directly addresses the audience, in the name of the writer, about some particular problem. This is called the *parabasis*, which finds its modern sequel in the term *raisonneur* (a character speaking for the author). Structurally, the parabasis divides the play into two parts. The first part is the conception of the happy idea and

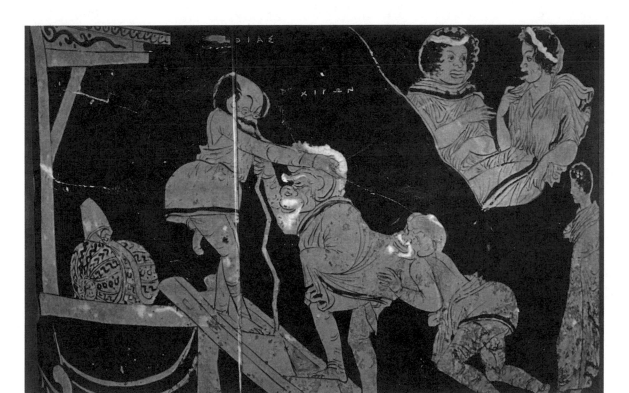

Chiron being pushed up the stairs. This scene from a Phlyakes vase of the fourth century B.C. shows a raised stage. *London, British Museum.*

the debate as to its merits. The second part of the play puts the happy idea into practice to demonstrate its ridiculous nature. It consists of roughly four episodes which are unified through thought— the happy idea. A *komos*, or a final scene of reconciliation, ends the play and all characters gather together for feasting and dancing. This last feature has led some historians to see a direct relationship between the phallic processionals connected to the worship of Dionysus and Aristophanic comedy.

Middle Comedy is transitional comedy. The structure is similar in many ways to Old Comedy except mythology replaces comments make on society's social, political, and economic institutions, personal satire disappears, and the function of the chorus as an integral part of the play is eliminated. Middle Comedy continued until roughly 336 B.C., at which time New Comedy took over.

Our complete knowledge of Greek Old and Middle Comedy is based upon the plays of Aristophanes. Only eleven of these plays exist out of the forty he is thought to have written. Nine of these plays make up Old Comedy—*The Acharnians* (425 B.C.), *The Knights* (424 B.C.), *The Clouds* (423 B.C.), *The Wasps* (422 B.C.), *Peace* (421 B.C.), *The Birds* (414 B.C.), *Lysistrata* (411 B.C.), *The Thesmophoriazusae* (411 B.C.), and *The Frogs* (405 B.C.), whereas *Plutus* (388 B.C.) and *Ecclesiazusae* (392-391 B.C.) constitute Middle Comedy. With only nine plays, it is difficult to determine if Aristophanes' plays are typical of Greek Old and Middle Comedy. Thus, like Greek tragedy, the conclusions made about Greek Old Comedy are far from absolute.

Aristophanes came from a cultured, prosperous family, and his name meaning "the best made manifest" gives an indication of that nobility. Writing at the time that Pericles was in power, strongly opposing the radical changes inherent in democracy, Aristophanes advocated a return to the Athens of old.

A historian and political critic, Aristophanes used satire and invective to argue against two basic evils: democracy and religion. *The Wasps* (422 B.C.) and *The Knights* (424 B.C.) ridicule politics and politicians, and the intrusion of rational philosophy into the religious arena is burlesqued in *The Clouds* (423 B.C.). According to Plato, Socrates indicated that the manner in which he was characterized in *The Clouds* prejudiced the jury against him in his trial (399 B.C.). It was this type of characterization used by Aristophanes that was responsible in part for the 440 B.C. law banning personal satire. Repealed three years later, Aristophanes turned his invective to Euripides in *The Frogs* (405 B.C.) and *The Thesmophoriazusae* (411 B.C.) for promoting individualism. In 426 his satire of Cleon who succeeded Pericles resulted in charges of treason and a heavy fine. Two years later, Aristophanes gained revenge in his allegory *The Knights*. The satire was so sharp that no actor would perform the leading role, which Aristophanes was thus forced to assume. Other objects of Aristophanes' pen were war (*Lysistrata:* 411 B.C., and *The Archarnians:* 425 B.C.), the political movement in general (*The Ecclesiazusae:* 393 B.C.) and education (*The Clouds*).

Menander: New Comedy

The most noted dramatist of Greek New Comedy (330-150 B.C.) was Menander (c. 342-291 B.C.), who was described as handsome and rich. Of the more than 100 plays which he wrote, we possess fragments of about 85 plays and portions of four: *The Girl from Samos, Arbitration, The Shorn Girl,* and *Heroes.* The only complete extant work of Menander is *The Grouch,* which was produced in 317 B.C. at the Lenaian Festival where it was awarded first prize. The only known script of *The Grouch* is a third century A.D. papyrus, which was found in an antique shop in Cairo, Egypt, by a Swiss banker who subsequently kept the script in his private library until 1959; at that time the first translation was made. Based upon this scanty information plus commentaries, historians have evolved some

Menander

characteristics of Menander and, hence, Greek New Comedy:

1. The setting is usually a street in or near Athens.
2. Emphasis is upon domestic affairs of middle class Athenians.
3. A conventional recognition scene serves to solve the problems of the characters. For example, a lost daughter is reunited with her family. There are mistaken identities and twins are used to create situations.
4. Language is everyday speech.
5. The chorus serves the function of entertainment between the episodes. The use of commercials between episodes on television is, in a sense, a continuation of that function.

Menander proved to be an influence upon the Roman dramatists Plautus and Terence, who influenced our modern situation comedy in film, television, and theatre. Ancient commentary has it that at age fifty-two, Menander drowned of a cramp while swimming in the harbor of Piraeus.

Architecture of the Theatre

The Theatre of Dionysus was excavated in the nineteenth century and is one of the few remaining theatres left for modern study. Although the best preserved Greek theatre is at Epidaurus, the Theatre of Dionysus commands the most attention for all the extant Greek tragedies and comedies were first presented here during the City Dionysia. Built in Athens at the beginning of the fifth century, the Theatre of Dionysus was probably a temporary wooden structure at first; however, by 330 B.C. it became a permanent stone theatre. It should be noted, however, that new excavations and information as well as reevaluation of older ideas have brought into question the traditional perception of the structure of the Greek theatre. This new information strongly suggests that the Greek theatre in the sixth century and before was most likely semi-rectangular, square or rectangular, and not circular.

Being outdoor people the Greeks, who were primarily involved in agriculture, built outdoor theatres. Inasmuch as the plays were presented at different times of the year and in order to aid the actors' projection, the theatres were constructed on a hillside in accordance with either the prevailing sea breeze or land breeze and designed so that the air currents would move toward the audience. The first theatre was nothing more than a raised circle called an *orchestra* (dancing place), and the fact that it was in a circle indicates that some kind of circular dancing was done. Homer (if such a person existed) compared the dancers' movement with the turning of the potter's wheel. Indeed, the dithyramb was described as a "circular dance," whereas dance in tragedy and comedy and satyr plays is described as rectangular. According to Dorpfeld's excavations, the orchestra's size was almost 66 feet in diameter for the sixth century and contained an altar *(thymele)* large enough to accommodate the slaughtering of a bull. Surrounding two-thirds of the orchestra was an outer wall · made of stone. Between the orchestra and the first row of seats was a draining ditch for the rain from the sloping hillside, as well as for the orchestra. The middle seat of the front row was occupied by the high priest and beside him sat other priests and dignitaries. Today we consider the seating area the auditorium, but to the Greeks it was the *theatron*, the watching place, whereas to the Romans, it was the auditorium, which means listening place.

Behind the orchestra was a building called the *skene* (a hut or tent) where the actors dressed.

During the fifth century, it most likely was temporary and thus was erected, and then taken down with the beginning and ending of each festival. In addition, the *skene* served as a permanent scenic device. It has been definitely established that painted panels *(pinakes)* were in use during the fifth century but the practice of changing the *pinakes* for each play has not been proven. Supposedly, the *pinakes* were attached to the skene and were painted in perspective. Aeschylus is known to have used pinakes, whereas others suggest that Sophocles introduced the perspective painting at least by 460 B.C. By the end of the fifth century, the *skene* had three doors for stage usage; although Pollux indicates that in a tragedy the left hand door remained closed, which indicates only two real doors. The central door served for use of the *ekkyklema* (thing wheeled out). This was a platform on wheels which either was turned, rolled out, or revolved in order to reveal characters killed offstage, or as in the case of *Prometheus* was part of the physical action. Another scenic device affecting the structure of the *skene* was the *mechane* (Latin, machina) or "crane-like flying machine." Used for characters in flight or for the appearance of a god, the presence of the crane suggests a second level to the *skene* called the *theologeion* (no relationship to the word theology, a high platform) where the gods appeared. It appears to have been used by Aeschylus and especially by Euripides to resolve his plays. As to whether the *skene* had *paraskenia* (side projecting wings to the skene) in the fifth century is debated but strongly urged by Margarete Bieber.

Access to the orchestra area was via passageways called the *parados*, located to the right and left of the orchestra. In Greek drama, the chorus as well as the actors used the *parados* for entrances and exits. It has been stated that the horses and chariots indicated in the scripts utilized the *parados*. Such statements, however, are not easily documented. The Greeks did not have stirrups, and the rock terrain of Greece made chariot warfare difficult if not useless. Further, the entrances to the *parados* seem too narrow for chariots, especially if

Top: Theatre at Dionysus. All the surviving Greek plays were presented at this theatre. *Bottom:* Theatre at Epidaurus. This is the best preserved of all the ancient Greek theatres.

a fast exit was required. In many cases, a ninety-degree turn would be required to prevent the exiting charioteer from having an accident. The orchestra, *skene, theatron, episkenion, theologeion,* and *parados* represent the basic architectural elements of the fifth century Greek theatre. Beginning in the fourth century, Greek theatre and drama underwent changes in which consolidation and extension occurred.

Fourth Century and Hellenistic Period

In the fourth century, which includes the Hellenistic Era (336-323 B.C.), the auditorium was remodeled into stone and completed between 338-326 B.C. This involved the wooden seats being replaced by stone, as well as the seat for the high priest being made into a throne decorated with winged cherubs urging cocks into battle. There were at least fifty rows of seats which were spread into a fan-like arrangement and were sectioned off into wedge-shaped areas by radial flights of steps. As indicated by the *diazomas* (girdle), there were three main seating areas. It is suggested that during the Hellenistic period, a raised stage *(logeion)* was added, whose height is estimated between eight and thirteen feet and 140 feet long and 6 1/2 to 14 feet deep. *Paraskenia* (added by this time) were eliminated and ramps were added in some theatres and stairs in others. Not all theatrical renovations were uniform. A facade was added to the lower level called the *proskenion* and to the upper level *(episkenion)*. The proskenion consisted of one to three doors and pillars which were notched for the use of *pinakes*. In the second century, the space occupied by the three doors was enlarged into wide openings called *thyromata* (big doors) and it is thought that there were as many as seven of these spaces ranging in width of 10-12 feet with height up to the roof. Vitruvius stated that *periaktoi* (triangular prisms which rotated to reveal a different scene—one each for tragedy, comedy, and satyr plays) were placed in the *thyromata* and were painted in perspective. By the time the physical theatre had acquired its permanence, the great age of classical drama had passed.

Selected Readings

Kitto, H. D. F. *Greek Tragedy*, 2nd ed. London, 1950.

Pickard-Cambridge, A. W. *Dithyramb, Tragedy, and Comedy*. 2nd ed. revised by T. B. L. Webster. Oxford, 1962.

_____. *The Dramatic Festivals of Athens*. 2nd. ed. revised by John Gould and D. M. Lewis. Oxford, 1968.

_____. *The Theatre of Dionysus in Athens*. Oxford, 1946

Vince, Ronald. *Ancient and Medieval Theatre: A Historiographical Handbook*. Westport, CT, 1984.

Vocabulary

1.	polis	PAW luhs
2.	Aeschylus	E skuh luhs
3.	Sophocles	SAW fuh kleez
4.	Antigone	an TI guh nee
5.	Oedipus	E duh puhs
6.	Iphigenia in Tauris	i fi ji NIGH uh in TAH ris
7.	Agamemnon	a guh MEM nuhn
8.	phallic	FA lik
9.	Epicharmus	e pi KAHR muhs
10.	Chionides	kigh awn IGH dees
11.	Anthesteria	an thes TAIR ee uh
12.	Lenia	luh NEE uh
13.	Peisistratus	pigh SIS truh tuhs
14.	theorikon	thee OHR ik awn
15.	archon	AHR kawn
16.	satyr	SA ter
17.	Pratinas	PRAH ti nuhs
18.	Silenus	sigh LEE nuhs
19.	choregos	kawr AY guhs
20.	aulos	AW luhs
21.	protagonist	proh TA guh nist
22.	deuteragonist	doo: ter A guh nist
23.	tritagonist	trigh TA guh nist
24.	Menander	muh NAN der
25.	Eumenides	yoo: ME nuh deez
26.	Philoctetes	fil uhk TEE teez
27.	Euripides	yoo RI puh deez
28.	deus ex machina	DAY uhs eks MAH ki nah
29.	Andromeda	an DRAW mi duh
30.	Aristophanes	a ri STAW fuh neez
31.	parabasis	pa RAH buh sis
32.	raisonneur	ray zaw NER
33.	Plutus	PLOO: tuhs
34.	Ecclesiazusae	ek KLAY zee ahd zoo sigh
35.	Thespis	THE spis
36.	chiton	KIGH tawn
37.	himation	him AHT ee awn
38.	thymele	thigh ME lay
39.	diazoma	dee AHD zoh muh
40.	skene	SKEE nee
41.	pinakes	pin AH kayz
42.	thyromata	thigh ROH mah tuh
43.	episkenion	e pi SKEE nee awn
44.	periaktoi	pair ee AHK toy
45.	ekkyklema	ek KIK lay muh
46.	theologeion	thee uh LOH gee on
47.	mechane	may kuh NAY
48.	parados	PAHR uh daws
49.	paradoi	PAHR uh doy
50.	cothurnus	koh THER nuhs
51.	onkos	AWN kuhs

CHAPTER FIVE

❧

Rome:
Wheat Doles and Public Shows

Roman Theatre at Sabratha (Libya). Note the three rows of columns on the scaenae frons. *Roger Wood, London.*

The heritage of Rome is the heritage of western civilization. Political institutions, many western languages, religion, architecture, philosophy and mythology like the proverbial roads to Rome are traced to this eternal city. Traditionally, the founding of Rome is placed at 753 B.C., a date that modern scholars question. That date was set by the writer Varro (116-26 B.C.) in the first century B.C., and according to scholars was chosen arbitrarily. The collapse of the western Roman empire is placed at A.D. 476 and was determined by the forced abdication of Romulus, making him the last Augustus. Between these dates, Roman history is divided into parts: the Republic (509-27 B.C.) and the Empire (27 B.C.-A.D. 476).

Early Rome was settled about 1600 B.C. by members of the Apennine culture: those who lived north in the Po Valley and those who settled in the south in Etruria. The Etrurian culture seems to have developed quicker than that of the Po Valley, and it is likely that Etruscans were speaking a language that evolved into Latin and Italian. This culture gained strength and flourished during the seventh and sixth centuries B.C. Now known respectively as Southern Tuscany and Northern Fazio, this area covered two hundred miles from the Arno to the Tiber Rivers and as far inland as the Apennies. Etruria began colonizing neighboring territories resulting in additional settlements near the Tiber River. These settlements were city-states that were politically, socially, and culturally independent of each other. Rome was not influenced, therefore, by Etruria as a whole but most likely by these Etruscan city-states settled in the south near the Tiber River. Although Rome was at one time an Etruscan city, it, like Greece, came under an oriental influence that can be seen in Etruscan art. In part, this oriental influence resulted from the Greeks whose trade ships brought objects from the east back to their homeland and colonies. It is through the Greek colonies in southern Italy and through the Corinthian craftsmen employed by the Etruscans that this oriental influence came to Etruria. The oriental influence made its way, therefore, from Greece, to Etruria, and then to Rome.

Etruria was, in fact, a chief market for Greek goods, an influence that should not be underestimated in terms of Etruria's influence on Roman theatre.

What attracted the Etruscans to Rome was the Campanian Plain just south of Rome. Extremely fertile, this area had the potential to be an agricultural benefit. The Greeks reached Campania before the Etruscans, however, and consequently placed colonists in this area in the eighth century B.C. Migrating to what is now known as the Bay of Naples, the Greeks settled in Cumae on the coast. It was the farthest Greek outpost in Italy but it became a center for selling grain as well as for the spreading of Greek culture over southern Italy and Sicily. For this reason, this area became known as Magna Graecia.

Although the Greeks were located in one area of Campania, the Etruscans controlled the land routes and harbors between themselves and the Campanian Plain. In this area controlled by the Etruscans was Latium, thus many of the Latin towns came under the domination of Etruscan city-states. Included in these Latium towns ruled by Etruscans was Rome, which was located on Etruria's borders. An important geographical area, Rome was close to the salt basins (Etruria's only source of salt), and access to the Campanian Plain required crossing Rome's Tiber River. As a consequence, Rome came under Etrurian domination and influence. The cultural and economic exchanges between Etruria and Magna Graecia proved to be an influence upon Rome.

Rome's emergence as an entity and a power began with their expelling the Etruscan monarchy in 509 B.C. Although the menace of Etruria had diminished, Rome was victimized by hostile neighbors as well as Etruscan mercenaries. The major confrontation between Etruria and Rome occurred in a war with the Etruscan city-state Veii, which was located twelve miles away. Not only was Rome uneasy by the threat of Veii but Veii recognized in Rome a competitor for the salt basins, markets, land, and ultimately control of the Tiber. In 396 B.C. Rome defeated Veii, making it the first Etruscan city to fall to the Romans. This proved to be a turning point for Rome: it paved the way for their expansion and doubled the size of their territory.

As a result of Roman territorial expansion, the Roman theatre was developed. About 272 B.C., Roman armies conquered the town of Tarentum in the province of Calabria. If you look at a map of Italy, Calabria is located in the heel of the Italian boot. Tarentum was populated by many Greek citizens and, consequently, those not killed by the Romans were brought to Rome as slaves. Inasmuch as teachers were usually slaves, some Greek captives became teachers for the children of their Roman masters. One such Greek was Livius Andronicus (c. 284-204 B.C.), who is considered the father of Latin literature. He taught Latin and Greek and also translated Greek literature into Latin. In 240 B.C. he was requested to translate a tragedy and a comedy for the Roman games *(ludi)*. These ludi were equivalent to the Greek Dionysian festivals. Basing the plays on Greek models, Livius Andronicus wrote a tragedy probably fashioned after Sophocles or Euripides and a comedy modeled on the work of Menander. These translations mark the beginning of regular tragedy and comedy in Roman theatre.

Religion

Religion played an important part in the daily lives of Romans. Not only did the homes have shrines but the state adopted an official cult on behalf of the Roman people. Roman religion was political and the Senate in its political capacity served as a mediator between the people and the gods. Politicians were viewed, therefore, as being favored by the gods. As long as the Romans performed their prayers, sacrifices, auguries, and festivals, the gods were at peace and the people felt assured that they would be rewarded, protected, and supported for doing their duty. Consequently, religion was not considered only from an emotional or personal perspective but a practical one as well. As social and political conditions changed, so did the religious practices of the Roman people.

Roman religion was highly ritualistic and detail oriented. The ceremonies *(ludi)* were scrupulously followed and had to be repeated—if, for example, a priest's hat fell off his head or a rat squeaked. The ritual was viewed as being more important than the deity worshipped. An important aspect of the ritual was that of vows. The Romans maintained a business-like relationship with their gods and did not consider morality. They simply made a vow to give the gods a temple, an offering, institute games in their honor, or some other pledge if that god would fulfill their request.

A dominating influence on Roman religion was that of the Etruscans. Initially, the Romans believed that their lives were under the influence of unseen spirits and that it was important to remain on good relations with these forces. The Etruscans created the idea of transforming the spirits into gods who had human qualities (anthropomorphism). In addition, the Etruscans influenced the Romans creating statues to represent the various gods and placing them in a temple. J. A. Hansen in *Roman Theatre—Temples* argues that the theatrical performances of the festivals *(ludi scaenici)* were connected with these temples and were performed in front of them—the idea being that the performances were done for a god and thus performed in that god's presence.

Under the Etruscan influence gladiatorial contests *(munera)* were developed as part of the religious worship to the dead. Believing that a blood sacrifice was needed for the dead man's spirit, the Etruscans held these combats at the tomb of the dead. Introduced into Rome c. 264 B.C., gladiatorial contests did not become officially recognized until 105 B.C. Up to this time gladiatorial contests were staged by private citizens. In 65 B.C. Julius Caesar honored his father's memory with gladiatorial contests involving 320 pairs of gladiators (from the Latin *gladius* meaning "sword"). In 42 B.C. these contests became financed by the state but were not part of the official ludi festivals and were held therefore on special occasions—such as honoring the dead.

During the second century A.D., there was a vast increase in religious feeling. Past ideas were replaced by a concern for salvation and a belief in divine forces; hence, a turn to magic, miracles, astrology and general mysticism. Concomitant with this change came a dissatisfaction with polytheism which was being undermined by the mystery religions. The two most important of these religions were Christianity and Mithraism. In belief and practice Christianity was viewed as subversive to the Roman Empire. Seeking a new religion for the Roman state, the Emperor Aurelian (200-275 B.C.) established the sun as the supreme God of the Roman Empire. December 25 was set aside to celebrate the birthday of the sun-god, and Sunday was declared that god's sacred day for worship.

Like the Greeks, the Romans kept religion and politics together. Oftentimes, Roman leaders told the people or other politicians that they had consulted the gods in order to implement their own ideas. The fact that church and state were not separate greatly aided Roman society. The business-like attitude and the exact fulfillment of religion promoted discipline and obedience to the state. In turn, the government held annual state festivals honoring the gods which strengthened patriotism to Rome through religious sanctification. It was in these state festivals that theatre and drama were first offered to the Romans in A.D. 240, and it was through theatre and drama that in the third century B.C. religious beliefs were undermined.

Spectacles and Politics

The word spectacle derives from the Latin *spectare* meaning "to look at." Indeed the Roman public had much to look at beside dramas. Chariot races, gladiatorial combats, pantomime, and mime were other forms of entertainment which amused the Roman masses. All of these forms (also drama) were free of charge and provided by the wealthy politicians. Thus, the government was the primary

The Flavian Amphitheatre, commonly called the Colosseum. Animals are pictured coming from their dens into cages, which are then lifted to the floor of the Colosseum. This lifting system is an early example of what we know as the counterweight system. From *The Flavian Amphitheatre*, 1876.

source of entertainment, and the politicians used this source as a political tool to win votes and retain public support. An irony of these spectacles was that the politicians used the entertainment to manipulate the masses but the masses used the games as a means to manipulate if not intimidate the politicians. At these events the Roman people expressed their opinions, and if the politician wished to stay in power he had to attend the event and listen to the complaints. Yet the politician's attendance threatened his security and it was often with great trepidation that he attended these events.

Under Augustus (63 B.C.-A.D. 14), sponsorship of the games was relegated to the imperial family. Although the financing changed, the games did not. In fact, the number of games increased during the imperial period because the emperors recognized that sponsoring the games provided them with great political advantages. Emperor Marcus Aurelius summarized the situation when he wrote "The Roman people is held together by two things: wheat doles and public shows." This observation was supported by the satirist Juvenal who used the phrase "bread and circuses" to indicate that food and entertainment were the pillars of Roman society. For the masses the entertainment sites were the only public forum they had to voice their concerns. For the emperor this presented a method of keeping power; that is, by attending, listening, taking action or promising to take action, the masses were appeased and the threat of an uprising reduced.

Ludi

Like the Greek Dionysian festivals, the ludi were official religious festivals. Rather than honor one god at the festivals, the Romans honored many gods. Some of these gods were Greek gods; Dionysus, for example. To be effective, the ceremony worshipping the gods had to be performed with exact precision. Any mistake meant that the ritual or the festival had to be repeated (see Religion). Records indicate that some rituals at the festivals were repeated as many as thirty times; the entire festival of the ludi Romani was repeated eleven times between the years 214-200 B.C., and that of the ludi Plebii seven times in one year. The concept of repetition carried over into the dramatic performances that were connected to the religious festivals and therefore required precision. This concept of repetition of the ludi, including dramatic performances, was termed *instauratio*.

Although there were a number of festivals, only certain festivals contained dramatic performances. The oldest festival presenting plays *(ludi scaenici)* was the ludi Romani (4-18 September, given in honor of Jupiter) established in the sixth century B.C. Although it had pantomime in 364 B.C., the ludi Romani did not have regular drama until 240 B.C., at which time the plays of Livius Andronicus were presented. Initially, one day of the festival was devoted to dramatic performances but by the time of Augustus (63 B.C.-A.D. 14), seventy-seven days were devoted to the ludi. Of these, fifty-seven were given over to theatrical entertainments such as Atellan farce, mime, pantomime, tragedy and comedy.

As other festivals developed, the concept of dramatic performances was instituted. For example, the ludi Florales (28 April-3 May, given in honor of Flora) was inaugurated in 238 B.C., and added dramatic performances in 173 B.C., devoting five out of six festival day to plays (basically mime). Other festivals included the ludi Apollinaires (5-13 July) which was instituted in 212 B.C. and added dramatic performances in 179, devoting eight out of nine days to these performances. The ludi Megalenses (4-10 April, given in honor of the Great Mother) began in 204 B.C. and added regular performances in 194 B.C. Six out of seven days were devoted to drama. The ludi Cereales (12-19 April, given for Ceres) started in 202 B.C. and, of the eight festival days, seven were given to plays. The ludi Plebeii (4-17 November, given in honor of Jupiter) was instituted c. 220 B.C and added plays c. 200 B.C. Although it originated during the Republic (509-27 B.C.), the ludi Saecufares came into prominence during the Empire (27 B.C.-c. A.D. 476). Its origin is unknown, but it is known that this festival was to be held at intervals of a saeculum (100-110 years). Octavian Augustus in 17 B.C. (31 May-2 June) celebrated the games that included performances of plays. According to the historian Zosimus, a stage was erected in the Campus Martius—the area in which the Theatre of Pompey was constructed (see Physical Theatre).

Atellan Farce, Mime and Pantomime

The Roman theatre is comparable to American television in that it included everything: tragedy, comedy, acrobatics, juggling, trained animal acts, athletic events, violence, and sex. The Roman public was fickle and, much like our television switchers, they left one event for another and demanded diversions. Consequently, the regular forms of tragedy and comedy flourished for a time and then declined. The best period in Roman drama was during the Republic, specifically 240-86 B.C. By 100 B.C. comedy ceased to be a form that could attract or sustain the interest of the audience and by 22 B.C. tragedy seems to have faded. The last writer known to have his plays acted was the Consular, P. Pomponius Secundus. With the demise of tragedy and comedy, minor forms ascended in popularity.

Atellan Farce

Atellan farce *(fabula Atellanae)* was one of the minor forms replacing comedy. Developed during the period of Italy's unification, Atellan farce originated in the town of Atella in the Oscan region (nine miles from Capua near Naples). Essentially a "Punch and Judy show," it was a short afterpiece and was originally nonliterary. During the first century B.C., Pomponius Bononiensis and Novius are said to have turned Atellan farce into a literary form. By the first century A.D., it reverted back to its nonliterary form. With the stock characters of Bucco (a braggart), Pappus (comic old man), Maccus (gluttonous, stupid fool), Dossennus-Mandugus (a hunchback with terrifying facial features), its rustic settings, its witty language, its references to sex and other bodily functions, and its stock situations of intrigues of everyday life, Atellan farce is thought to have a relationship to sixteenth century Commedia dell'arte. Its similarity to mime leads some historians to conclude that it was nothing more than masked mime.

Mime and Pantomime

Writing in 55 B.C., Cicero stated that the Atellan farce had been usurped in its popularity by mime *(fabula Riciniata)*. In that it replaced the Atellan farce, it was performed at the end of the play or what is termed the "exodium." This meant that it was a short afterpiece and that the mime actor would then be called "exodiarius." In addition to being an afterpiece, the mime functioned as a filler to entertain the audience while the main production was being readied.

Mime means "imitation" and as a form, its content focused on an imitation of daily life. A combination of recitation, song, dance, and acrobatics, mime was elaborate, obscene, spectacular, and was associated particularly with the ludi Florales. Although there was a great deal of improvisation, many of the mimes had a written story line. As a nonliterary (impromptu) form, our first evidence is 211 B.C. In the first century B.C., mime was temporarily transformed into a literary composition by Decimus Laberius (c. 106 B.C.-43 B.C.) and Publius Syrus. Under the Empire, however, it reverted to its original concept.

Mime was unique; it was the only form which allowed women to act and in which they stripped off their clothes at the audience's request. The low opinion held of the theatre plus the stripping led to labeling mime actresses as prostitutes. The stock themes of adultery and love affairs were realistically enacted along with other sexual (such as sodomy) and violent acts. Domitian, the Emperor (A.D. 81-96) for example, ordered that a real crucifixion be inserted into a performance along with real executions and sundry sexual acts. As no masks were worn, the sexual emphasis of mime affected how actors were chosen. Those who were handsome would be most desired in a performance involving sexual activity; whereas those who were ugly were used for comedy or violence. In addition to looks, the mime actors had to have good voices and know how to dance. Mime actors were barefooted, which was quite different from actors in tragedy and comedy. Those in tragedy wore a high soled boot called a *cothurnus* and those in comedy wore a low shoe or sock called a *soccus*. Additionally, actors of tragedy and comedy wore linen masks called *persona*, and the parts of the play were labeled according to the masks—*dramatis persona* ("masks of the play"). In both the Eastern and Western Roman Empire, mimes satirized the Christians, public events, and emperors. The emperors were not so forgiving, however; Caligula had one writer burned alive in the arena. Domitian had the actor, Helvidius Priscus, the younger, executed for satirizing the emperor's divorce. Mime remained a dominant form until the sixth century A.D., at which time the theatres were closed.

Whereas farce replaced comedy, pantomime (*fabula saltica*) replaced tragedy. Phylades and Bathyllus are credited with introducing this form in 22 B.C. As noted by the Greek term for it— "Italian dance"—pantomime was a distinctly Latin form. It is thought that the performance took place on stage with scenery and that its primary attraction was the dancers' movements. Although some female dancers appeared on stage, the central figures were male dancers. Generally, the dancers were masked, did not speak, doubled in a number of parts and were accompanied by some sort of musical instrument. In addition, a chorus sang specially written dialogue that centered on a mythological story. With its emphasis upon ballet performances, Roman pantomime could be considered a forerunner to our modern ballet.

Social Status of the Actor

The social status of actors in Rome is not entirely clear. On the one hand, slaves such as Aesopus and Roscius rose to prominence, influence, and wealth. Still others were accorded membership in the *Colleqium Poetarum* (207 B.C.), an association of writers and actors founded in 207 B.C., and as such were given full civil rights. In addition, Tacitus records in his *Dialogues* that "a partiality toward actors and a passion for gladiators and horses— seem almost to be conceived in the mother's womb." On the other hand, Cicero and the historian Cornelius Nepos commented that Roman society had a low estimate of theatre in general and actors in particular. This disdain was written into the Code of Justinian which stated that acting on stage marked one with *infamia*. This meant that most actors would not be entitled to the same rights as Roman citizens. In addition, the actor's descendents could not marry into the upper ranks. This singling out of actors suggests that actors had to be on their best behavior lest they be flogged publicly or if caught with another man's wife— executed. Under the Julian Laws actors and prostitutes were socially grouped together.

For the most part, actors were male and bore

Shelves filled with masks. This tenth century painting of masks from Roman comedy is believed to have been copied from a second century A.D. original and may provide some evidence about imperial Roman theatre (second and third centuries A.D.). *Courtesy Bibliotec Vaticana.*

the title of *histriones* or *cantores* (declaimers). Mime was the exception which allowed women on the stage, and whose performers were labeled *mimus*, *saltator* (dancer or acrobat) or *planipes* (with bare feet). During the Empire, mime became a dominant form of entertainment, and all actors were classified as histriones. Generally speaking, more actors than not were slaves or freedmen, lived in poverty, and were at the bottom of the social scale. Being slaves they were rented to the state by their owners. Acting companies could be owned by a man or a woman, and when the owners died, the acting company could be bequeathed to an heir. Then too, the fans in the theatre might demand a popular actor's freedom for which the emperor had to compensate the owner if the emperor chose to free the actor. Under Nero's reign, the social boundaries between mime actors became obscure, and thus, they had the opportunity to mingle with their masters. For example, Empress Domitia took Paris, a mime actor, for her lover and Nero shocked society by appearing on stage. However, if actors took liberties that might offend, the actor took the risk of punishment. Nero banished an actor from Italy, Caligula had one burned alive, and Heliogabulus had the actor Lauredus crucified on stage. Actors had to walk a fine line. Although they were generally held in low esteem, under the Empire, the opportunity existed for their freedom and should they choose they could continue acting as a freed person.

Audience

Although the dramatic festivals were religious, they were also a signal for the populace to enjoy themselves. The noted Roman dramatist Plautus phrased it best when he wrote: "You may eat what you like, go where you like . . . and love whom you like, provided you abstain from wives, widows, virgins, and free boys."

Admission to the theatre was free and all classes and ethnic groups attended. The populace was made up of Greeks (some slaves and some freedmen), Frenchmen (Gauls), Jews, Egyptians, Syrians, Spaniards, Ethiopians from Africa, "tattooed savages from Britain," "barbarians" from Germany, Persians, Scythians from Russia, and a host of other ethnic groups from Europe and Asia. This heterogeneous group composing the theatre audience included married women, nurses with children, gentlemen, slaves, and (if allowed) prostitutes, who would sit on the stage. As sitting in the theatre was considered tantamount to corrupting one's morals, it seems that prior to 145 B.C., the audience stood. In one Roman play, a character referring to the standing audience asserts, "Cut it short: the stalls are thirsty." In 194 B.C., reserved seats were set aside for senators. After this time, seating for the masses was determined on a first come basis although some seating was segregated. For example, vestal virgins and women of the Imperial family sat in the front rows; all other

Amphitheatre at Pozzuoli, near Naples. Note the traps—those at the edge are for animals, the others are for men and dogs. Also note that each trap has a groove for a cover. This was probably used to make the arena watertight for sea battles (naumachia). The limestone or tufa wall in the background indicates that there was an awning over the galleries. From *The Flavian Amphitheatre, 1876.*

women were restricted to the top rows. Additionally, the audience was usually unruly and actors had a difficult time sustaining the audience's interest, which forced them at times to extremes. At the ludi Florales, for example, the audience wanted and got the female actors to remove all their clothes. Eventually, audience demands required more than tragedy and comedy could provide and encouraged the rise of spectacle-oriented forms.

Physical Theatre

With the spoils from the Mithridatic War, Pompey built the first permanent Roman theatre in 55 B.C. against senate opposition. Inasmuch as the Theatre of Pompey, as it was called, held 10,000, the senate feared that bringing this many people together in a closed structure would invite political discontent and this would lead to civil war (see Spectacles). Prior to the building of this theatre, ludi were presented in an open area fronting the temple of the deity being honored. If any seats were available, they were wood benches. Audiences came and went at their pleasure or displeasure. If unhappy with the production they could move to other entertainments being given at the same time. Although the Theatre of Pompey was intended for theatrical productions, the audiences demanded that other forms such as dancing bears, boxers, and acrobats be presented

Entertainments were held in both the theatre and amphitheater and it appears that these terms were often interchanged. Parallels exist between the two types of structures. They produced similar entertainments and raised stages existed in both structures for usage by actors who sang, danced, and recited odes. Additionally, the area beneath the stages in the theatre and amphitheatre was used for housing stage machinery such as the amphitheatre built by Statilius Taurus in 29 B.C. Of particular interest is the machinery used for those entertainments known as spectacles and performed mainly at amphitheatres—sea battles

Amphitheatre at Pompeii as depicted in a fresco painting. Note the awning, a wine shop in front of the amphitheatre, and another entertainment center next to the amphitheatre. From *The Flavian Amphitheatre, 1876.*

Theatre at Orange, built in the first or second century A.D. in France. It is the best preserved Roman theatre in France and is now being used again for theatrical performances. *Courtesy French Cultural Services.*

(*naumachia*), gladiatorial contests, wild animal hunts, athletic contests, and other events which exploited sex and violence.

The amphitheatre floor was covered with sand (*arena* in Latin) to absorb the blood, was removable and had trap doors. These traps were equipped with counterweight elevators, which raised and lowered the wild beast cages to and from the stage area. The traps were operated from below and gave the effect of surprise when they were opened and the animals sprang from the seemingly solid earth. Wooden frames (much like modern-day flats) with scenes on them, as well as three-dimensional scenery, were located beneath the cavernous stage area and were also sent up through the traps. When the traps were not used, the arena could be flooded for a sea battle—ships and all—and then quickly drained so the arena could be used for the next event. Windlasses were attached to a cradle-type device that was used to drag the vessels. This device was similar to that utilized by Torelli to shift scenery in the Italian Renaissance. The use of a crane and ropes to raise and lower scenery and to fly actors, although used by the Romans, was probably a carryover from the Greeks. A last type of machinery used by the Romans was for rotating the stage area (not the entire building). As a result, they could exhibit plays in the afternoon and by rotating the structure make an amphitheatre for spectacles in the evening.

The basic feature of the Roman theatre was its wooden stage (*pulpitum*). Plautus termed it a scaena (stage, scene building) or proscaenium. It was about five feet high, twenty to forty feet deep, and between one to three hundred feet in length. In front of the stage was the orchestra area, which had varying uses. Movable seats could be placed here for special visitors, the area could be flooded for sea battles or water ballets and sometimes it was used for gladiatorial contests. The orchestra area was a semicircle directly attached to the auditorium (*cavea*), whose seating capacity ranged from 8,000 to 14,000. Prior to the building of the Theatre of Pompey, the Roman theatres were temporary, and thus were constructed and dismantled for the different ludi (at least five) that were given each year. One source indicates that in 58 B.C. a theatre was built with a temporary stage three stories high, with the first story made of marble, the second of glass, and the third of wood inlaid with gold. It had 360 columns, 3,000 bronze statues, and held 80,000 spectators.

Unlike the Greek theatre, the Roman theatre was one complete unit. Thus the auditorium was attached to the stage house (*scaena frons*). Like the skene of the Greek theatre, the front walls of the scaena frons were the basic scenic unit for the Roman theatre. The stage house thus served as a scenic unit, a dressing area for the actors and, with its multiple door openings, represented entrances and exits to designated areas. In comedy, for example, the doors represented houses on a city street; in tragedy the doors represented entrances to a palace or temple. The scene was changed primarily through dialogue. If the actors stated they were in the country, the Roman staging convention was such that the stage and stage house represented the country. This idea of the stage house facade representing the basic scenic background was carried on into the Medieval and Elizabethan periods.

In addition to this scenic convention, the Romans developed a type of air conditioning (air blown over water); an awning that stretched over the audience to protect it from the sun; and types of curtains—the front curtain (*auleum*) and the back curtain (*siparium*). The front curtain was a Roman invention and is said to have been introduced in 133 B.C. Cicero refers to it in 56 B.C. as being raised at the end of a mime. The curtain appears to have been a type of drop curtain that could be lowered into a slot located near the front of the stage. This slot was actually a recessed area under the stage where the curtain could be stored. Raising and lowering it was accomplished via telescopic poles. After the second century A.D., the curtain was operated by a series of overhead ropes.

The back curtain was probably introduced to the theatre through the mimes. It seems to have been a scenic drop as well as a curtain behind which mime actors could hide until their entrance. The actors made their entrance through a part in the curtain that represented a door.

Dramatists

The Romans tended to categorize their drama according to whether the drama was based on Greek life or on Roman life. Roman comedy which focused on Greek life was termed *fabula palliata* and, traditionally, those Roman tragedies modeled after Greek life were called *fabula crepidata.* These two forms were distinguished by what the Romans believed to be typical Greek dress. The crepida was an everyday shoe similar to a sandal and was worn in comedy. There is speculation that crepidata should not be thought of as tragedy but solely comedy, and that the term for derivative Greek tragedy is lost. The pallium, however, was considered the characteristic everyday Greek dress, and inasmuch as comedy dealt with everyday affairs, the pallium was appropriate for comedy. Traditionally, fabula palliata refers to comedy and fabula crepidata to tragedy.

Roman comedy based upon Roman settings, dress, manners, and characters, but structurally based upon Greek New Comedy, is called *fabula togata.* The form flourished in the second century B.C. and the chief writer was Afranius (c. 150 B.C.?). The name togata is derived from the toga, which is thought to be the everyday dress for Romans. This derivation has caused some concern among some historians, however, who believe that the ceremonial toga was not typical everyday dress of the peasants, who dominated this form of comedy. Inasmuch as tabernaria refers to the private houses of the poor, and Roman comedy deals with everyday humble life, *fabula tabernaria* is thought to be a more precise term. Fabula togata, however, is the traditional term. Both forms of comedy existed and were confined to Roman comedy based on Roman life. The only togata comedy recorded as being acted was *Fire,* in which a real

house was built on stage, equipped, and then burned.

Seneca

Born at Cordoba, Spain, Lucius Annaeus Seneca (c. 4 B.C.-65 A.D.), the philosopher, was educated at Rome in rhetoric and philosophy. He became a senator, quaestor (in charge of the state treasury), and a rhetorician in the courts. Caligula's jealousy of Seneca almost cost Seneca his life. In A.D. 41 he was accused of a romantic intrigue for which he was banished to Corsica where he remained until 49 A.D. whereupon he was recalled to serve as young Nero's tutor. As Emperor, Nero listened to Seneca's advice, which kept Nero's reign from becoming worse than it was. In A.D. 65 Seneca was accused of conspiracy and ordered to take his life. He did so calmly and with dignity.

Only ten Roman tragedies are extant. Nine of those are the work of Seneca. He is mistakenly assigned the authorship of *Octavia.* The plays which survive are *The Trojan Women, Medea, Oedipus, Agamemnon, The Phoenician Women, The Mad Hercules, Hercules on Oeta, Phaedra,* and *Thyestes.* These nine tragedies, whose dates are uncertain, are based on Greek originals (fabula crepidata), and were probably not produced in the Roman public theatres. They seem to have been written for a single reciter with the idea of demonstrating certain elements of rhetoric. Plays such as those by Seneca, which were read but never produced, have become known as closet drama.

Seneca flourished during the Empire and, though his plays were apparently never produced, he was nonetheless a major influence on Shakespeare and his contemporaries. That Seneca's plays were read, imitated, and even acted at the English universities during the sixteenth century is a matter of record. His tragedies were translated into English in 1581, and some were acted at Cambridge before this date. The first English tragedy was *Gorboduc,* which was modeled after Seneca's work and presented in 1562 before Queen Elizabeth. Seneca's influence came through the

Elizabethans' interpretation of his plays which in turn led to his influencing the modern theatre. The following characteristics are attributed to Seneca's influence:

1. The structuring of plays into five acts.
2. The use of violence and horror.
3. The use of magic, death, and supernatural events, such as ghosts.
4. Characters obsessed by a single emotion (e.g., Hamlet's revenge or Macbeth's ambition).
5. Interest in morality as noted in characters whose unchecked emotions destroy them (e.g., Othello), and in sententiae (short, pithy statements about the human condition).
6. The use of soliloquies, asides, and confidants (a neoclassical device whereby, in a love affair, servants act as go-betweens for their masters who have confided in them).
7. The employment of rhetorical devices such as forensic speeches (e.g., *Julius Caesar*).

In addition to Seneca, two other writers of tragedy should be noted. The first is Lucius Varius Rufus, whose play *Thyestes* was produced most likely at the ludi Romani in 29 B.C. and represents the last record we possess of a new Latin play being produced. The other writer of tragedy was Gnaeus Naevius (c. 270 B.C.-c. 201 B.C.). Born in Campania, Naevius was the first native-born dramatist of significance. He began writing about 235 B.C. and for the next thirty years produced about forty plays, seven of which were tragedies. In 206-205 B.C. Naevius wrote a comedy that satirized certain senators and their families that resulted in imprisonment and banishment. This case against Naevius is the only recorded conviction against a Roman citizen for political abuse on the stage. Its significance is that it stopped other writers from political satire and, as a consequence, seriously hampered the growth of Roman drama.

Plautus

The immediate successor to Naevius in comedy was Titus Maccius Plautus (c. 254 B.C.-184 B.C.), which translated means Titus, the flat-footed clown. Considered the playwright of the people, Plautus earned his living initially as a stage carpenter as well as working in a flour mill. When not working, he wrote plays based on Greek New Comedy. Naevius' case ruled out the use of Old Comedy that abounded in political satire. On the other hand, coarseness and obscenity were allowed and Plautus was a master at broad humor. Although Plautus's works cannot be dated definitely, he wrote his 130 plays roughly between 205-184 B.C. Of the twenty-one plays that survive, his most important were *The Menaechmi* (an influence on Shakespeare's *Comedy of Errors)*, *The Pot of Gold* (which influenced Molière's *The Miser);* and *Amphitryon* (which served as an influence on Dryden's *Amphitryon or The Two Sosias).*

Characteristic of Plautus was his emphasis upon farcical elements, eavesdropping scenes, improbable events, slaves with more brains than their masters, reversals of fortune, overheard conversations, mistaken identities, colloquial speech, elimination of the Greek chorus, an expository prologue, and his extensive use of music. One of the prominent characteristics of Plautine comedy is the extensive use of song. Plautus' plays were in fact, musicals; one-third was dialogue and two-thirds was sung. Whereas his successor Terence used twenty-five lines, Plautus used over three thousand lines or over sixty songs. For Plautus this averages to about three songs per play. However, *Miles Gloriosus* has no song; *Curculio* has one, as does the *Asinaria*. Plautus' heavy use of song and dance anticipates the musical revue of the nineteenth and twentieth centuries.

Terence

Whereas Plautus wrote for his audience, Publius Terentius Afer (c. 195/185 B.C.-159 B.C.) wrote more for a literary coterie that supported him. Born in Carthage, Terence probably belonged to an African tribe. A slave of Terentius Lucanus in Rome, Terence took his former master's name

THE CAPTIVES
TITUS MACCIUS PLAUTUS

CHARACTERS

HEGIO, a wealthy Aetolian gentleman

PHILOCRATES, an Elian prisoner of war

TYNDARUS, a slave and companion to Philocrates, also Hegio's lost son

PHILOPOLEMUS, Hegio's elder son

ARISTOPHONTES, another prisoner from Elias and friend to Philocrates

ERGASILUS, the parasite character who is dependent on Philopolemus

STALAGMUS, a former slave of Hegio who ran away with Philocrates

SETTING: The town of Aetolia in Greece, outside the house of Hegio

BACKGROUND: This play is different from the general works of Plautus in that the emphasis is placed more on how "to improve the minds of decent men" rather than sex and slapstick humor. The story is thought to have been based on an unknown work by the Greek dramatist Menander and the sensitive handling of a relationship between a master and his slave is said to have made this one of the best of the Plautine comedies. The German poet Lessing considered this to be the most perfect play to appear on the stage. Given this accolade, it should be pointed out that the play has many inconsistencies. Lastly, this play, so different from typical Plautine comedies filled with sex, secret love affairs, and generally farcical in nature, derives its humanity from the parasite character who was a staple of Roman comedy.

The names of the characters have special meaning and are related to the roles they play: Hegio means leading citizen and suggests a gentleman. Ergasilus's name translates as "working for a living" with the connotation of a prostitute. Philocrates ("Lover of master"), Aristophontes ("beastslayer"), and Philopolemus ("lover of war") all suggest names dealing with war and ironically all have been captured. Stalagmus means "Drop" and refers to the slave's lowly status. Tyndarus probably refers to Tyndareos, the father of Helen and hence considered a slave's name.

SUMMARY: A prologue is spoken by an unnamed character who provides the exposition for the play. The character reveals that Hegio has two sons: Tyndarus and Philopolemus. Also it is learned that years before, Hegio's slave, Stalagmus, ran away with Hegio's son, Tyndarus, when the son was four years old. Now there is a war between Hegio's country, Aetolia, and the country of Elias. Unfortunately in this war Hegio's elder son, Philopolemus is taken prisoner. In an effort to free the elder son, Hegio buys Elian prisoners captured by the Aetolian army. His hope is to find a wealthy Elian whom he can exchange for his son. By chance, Hegio buys two prisoners who (unbeknownst to him) include his kidnapped son Tyndarus, who is presently the slave of Philocrates, a wealthy Elian. While captive, Philocrates and Tyndarus secretly exchange clothes and names in order to set Philocrates free. In order to arrange an exchange, Hegio sends Philocrates, who he believes to be the slave, back to Elian. In the meantime, Hegio visits his brother's house where he meets another slave, Aristophontes, who knows Philocrates. Hegio takes this slave back home where the switch is revealed. Hegio, angered by the ruse and still unaware that Tyndarus is his son, sends Tyndarus to the stone quarry.

In the meantime, Philocrates arranges for the exchange of Tyndarus for Hegio's elder son, Philopolemus. Philocrates is an honest man and makes the exchange without any thought of deception. In addition, he goes back to Aetolia to regain his slave, Tyndarus, with whom he has grown up and for whom he has great affection. Upon their return, Hegio has Tyndarus released to his master, Philocrates. While awaiting Tyndarus's return, Hegio begins to question his former slave, Stalagmus, who had been recaptured at Elias, as to the whereabouts of his first son. Stalagmus explains that he sold the son to Philocrates's father. Philocrates then relates how the boy had been given to him as a companion and had become his servant. It is now known that Tyndarus is the kidnapped son. When Tyndarus returns and learns the news, he is overjoyed. Seeking to punish Stalagmus for the kidnapping, Hegio gives him to Tyndarus to be punished. Philocrates suggests having a blacksmith take off the heavy chains on Tyndarus and put them on Stalagmus. Stalagmus accepts his fate as the play ends.

Roman theatre at Leptis Magna, Libya, built about A.D. 1-2 by Annobal Rufus. This theatre is similar to other Roman theatres in its architectural layout. From Cohen's *Le Théâtre en France au Moyen Age.*

when Lucanus freed him. The reception to Terence's first play, *The Andria* (166 B.C.), enabled him to pursue a career as a dramatist. He wrote only six plays, all of which survive. These six plays, plus the twenty-one of Plautus, constitute the complete extant works of Roman comedy. Held in esteem, Horace and Cicero quoted him and Caesar considered him a dimidiate Menander. Terence placed his emphasis upon more thoughtful comedy rather than farce, an emphasis that did not endear him to the public audiences. But Terence seems to have been more concerned with a romantic treatment of his characters. Unlike Plautus, he characterized his females as being sentimental and tender; even prostitutes demonstrated a willingness toward virtue. Structurally, Terence dropped the expository prologue used by Plautus, did not deal with Roman life to the extent that Plautus did, used little obscenity, employed psychological changes in characters, shied away from farce, and wrote well-constructed plots that demonstrated surprise, irony, and a contrast in a character's behavior. Terence's influence can be seen in plays of the seventeenth and eighteenth centuries, such as Wycherley's *The Country Wife* (1675), and in modern plays such as Thornton Wilder's *The Woman of Andros* (1930).

Closing of Theatres

Biological factors seem to have been a fundamental reason for Rome's fall. Granted morals, failing trade, despotism by the rulers, taxes, church opposition, and wars were all strong factors. But a serious decline in the population along with the importation of non-Roman citizens into Rome to serve in the army or to be used in various other capacities were overriding factors. Although credit is given to the Church, Christianity's growth was "more an effect than a cause of Rome's decay." The internal decay of Rome made it too weak to resist the invading barbarians who pillaged Rome in A.D. 410 and A.D. 455. The Roman empire continued in the east until 1453, but its empire in the west ended in about A.D. 476. With the decline and fall of Rome in the west, Roman theatre came to an end. The last record of a performance in Rome is A.D. 533. Theatre continued in the east (Byzantine theatre) but in the west it was relegated to nomadic actors until about A.D. 900, at which time the church resurrected theatre and drama for its own use.

Selected Readings

Beare, William. *The Roman Stage: A Short History of Latin Drama in the Time of the Republic.* 3rd ed. London, 1963.

Duckworth, George E. *The Nature of Roman Comedy.* Princeton, NJ, 1952.

Hanson, J. A. *Roman Theatre—Temples.* Princeton, NJ, 1959.

Vince, Ronald W. *Ancient and Medieval Theatre. A Historiographical Handbook.* Westport, CT, 1987.

Vocabulary

1. Tarentum	tah REN tuhm		21. scaena frons	SKIGH nuh frawns
2. Calabria	kah LAH bree uh		22. proscaenium	pruh SKIGH nee uhm
3. Livius Andronicus	LI vee uhs an DRAW ni kuhs		23. pulpitum	POOL pi tuhm
4. ludi Romani	LOO: dee roh MAH nee		24. naumachia	naw MAY kee uh
5. ludi Plebeii	LOO: dee PLAY bee ee		25. cavea	KAH wee ah
6. ludi scaenici	SKIGH ni kee		26. Pompey	PAWM pee
7. ludi megalenses	me guh LEN sayz		27. auleum	OW lee uhm
8. ludi florales	floh RAY layz		28. siparium	si PAHR ee uhm
9. ludi cereales	kayr ee AH layz		29. fabula palliata	FAH boo luh pah lee AY tuh
10. ludi Apollinares	uh paw luh NAY rayz		30. fabula togata	toh GAH tuh
11. fabula riciniata	FAH boo luh ri kee nee AH tuh		31. fabula crepidata	cre pi DAH tuh
12. Atellan	ah TEL uhn		32. fabula praetexta	prigh tex tuh
13. soccus	SAW kuhs		33. fabula tabernaria	ta ber NAIR ee uh
14. dramatis personae	druh MAH tis per SOH nigh		34. Seneca	SE ni kuh
15. Pylades	PIL ah deez		35. Afranius	ah FRAY nee uhs
16. Bathyllus	bah THIL uhs		36. Hercules on Oeta	HER kyoo leez on OY tah
17. Statilius Taurus	stuh TIL lee uhs TAW ruhs		37. Gnaeus Naevius	GNIGH uhs NIGH wee uhs
18. Titus Maccius Plautus	TIGH tus MAK ee uhs PLOW tuhs		38. fabula saltica	SAWL ti kuh
19. Publius Terentius	POOB lee uhs ter EN tee uhs		39. Diphilmus	digh FIL muhs
20. Terence	TER uhnts		40. Philemon	FIL ay mawn

CHAPTER SIX

❧

The Middle Ages: Between Vices and Virtues

The Martyrdom of Saint Apollonia, a miniature from the *Hours of Etienne Chevalier* by Jean Fouquet. Note the mansions illustrating the various stages of the saint's life. The actors and spectators seem to be intermingled. *Musée Condé.*

The Middle Ages encompass nearly a thousand years of European civilization, and it should be considered in three periods: the rise of the Middle Ages A.D. 313-1050; the High Middle Ages, 1050-1350; and the late Middle Ages, 1350-1500. It is commonplace to state that in this period Christianity became the dominant religion in the western world. In point of fact, throughout the fourth century Christianity was favored by the state and by the end of the century it became the official religion. In one sense, the Church had been a factor in determining theatre's demise. Yet, under the church's guidance, theatre and drama were reborn, flowered, and then secularized. Like modern society, which inherited a legacy of religion, economics, law, scholarship, literature, science, and morality from the Middle Ages, modern drama equally owes a debt to the Middle Ages.

Guided by the church, the medieval period held life to be a preparation for eternity; thus man was not to be concerned with worldly notions but was to prepare himself spiritually. The idea that life was insignificant and that heaven was the goal pervaded the institutions of the Middle Ages. Thus, theological ideas dominated medieval life. A prime characteristic of medieval society was its reliance on authority, particularly earlier Latin writers. These Latin writers and their manuscripts provided a chief method by which the Church could impart its message to medieval society. The Church, and this society, relied heavily on books for authority, and this reliance reveals a society that was organized, rigid, and orderly.

The use of books was a way to provide a logical explanation about man and his universe. The resulting logic was the notion of a fixed universe in which earth was the lowest point, and one advances from here upward through the finite universe. Because the universe is finite, it has shape—the perfect spherical shape—and everything within that shape is ordered. The universe is like a tall building and movement to the earth is down. You thus have absolute up and down, with earth being the very bottom. Because of original sin, man has fallen from heaven to the earth where he remains imprisoned within his body atoning for his sin.

This concept affected also the medieval concept of history which viewed life as a continuum from Genesis to the present day. History was a story based upon the creation, fall, redemption and judgment. As a consequence, medieval society lacked historical perspective, making the need for costumes to be historically accurate insignificant in medieval drama. The past was Adam naked until he fell from grace; after that, the past was in terms of their own age. Classical influence was used only insofar as it reinforced Christian concepts; any other information that did not concur with this notion of history was rejected.

Spiritually then, the past was better than the present, for as the world continued, the sins of mankind became worse. Medieval man felt pleasure therefore in the past; it was a time when man's sins were not so grave and he gloried in the future for it brought him closer to judgment.

Reemergence of Drama

Medieval drama was didactic. Its main function was to teach and enforce the Christian religion. Beginning with the Council of Nicaea in A.D. 325 to the Fourth Latern Council in 1215, the Church articulated the need to teach and enforce Church doctrine. For some historians the Council of Nicaea marks the beginning of the Middle Ages. At this Council the Church fixed its doctrine and its basic beliefs, and hence gave the medieval church its name—Catholic (uniform). This fixity established Christianity as the chief religion and with its support by the Roman Empire, a new civilization replaced the old one based on paganism. Between A.D. 325 and 1215, the Church found itself constantly struggling to maintain its power. Pope Innocent III recognized the need to shore up the Church when he stated that "the corruption of the people had its chief source in the clergy." As a result, he decreed that Jews and heretics had to wear yellow patches and horned caps. Additionally, he defined the doctrine of transubstantion and required all Christians to have communion and confession once a year. It was his efforts that enabled the Church to assume greater organization and hence greater power.

With the rise of the Christian Church and the collapse of the Roman Empire, theatre dissipated. From the sixth century to about the tenth century, western theatrical activity went into a period akin to the Dark Ages. Although theatre continued to flourish in China, India, and Asia Minor, western actors were relegated to wandering the countryside telling stories, juggling, rope dancing, and other such feats. By the tenth century, the Church, which had tried so hard to suppress drama, was responsible for resurrecting it in liturgical or church drama. This rebirth marks the beginning of medieval drama.

Monasteries

The early phase of the Middle Ages overlaps with the final days of the western Roman empire and thus is marked with the barbaric invasions of Rome, political chaos, and a general decay of life in general. This was not true of the eastern Roman empire in Constantinople that survived until 1453. The fortunes of theatre were equally chaotic as can be noted in its attempts to survive which were continually thwarted by the Church. Theodoric, King of the Ostrogoths (493-526) who ruled Italy, permitted entertainers before supper as long as his guests did not have to endure anything indecent. Theatrical entertainment did not even measure up to barbarian standards—tough critics. In 679 the English clergy was warned at the Council of Rome not to maintain the services of musicians or permit plays. In 749 a church canon published at Cloesho alerted bishops to beware that monasteries do not become the home of traveling troupes of entertainers. In 789 a Carolingian statute notified players to not put on church clothing or else they would be punished and exiled. Edgar, the reformist king, complained that English monasteries were so decadent that mime troupes were allowed to mock the

Church in song and dance in the marketplace. Despite the Church's rejoinder against the theatre and the monasteries, when Rome collapsed the medieval society that emerged was disjointed and had no central or effective secular authority. Only the Church offered organization and it was the monasteries, in particular, that provided the basis for the church's stability.

One of the consistent influences affecting the survival of theatre as well as its reemergence was the Benedictine monasteries. All western monasticism is founded upon the Benedictine order, created by Benedict (480-543?) of Nursia in Italy in 529. He brought uniformity and regularity to the monastic order with a constitution that he designed. The monasteries were the only social group in the early medieval period to have a written, carefully constructed constitution. The written constitution was a reflection of the emphasis that monasteries placed on education. Inasmuch as monks were the only group that could read and write, they created schools to teach others.

The ability to read and write enabled the monks to organize what is known as the *scriptoria* (writing offices) where manuscripts for education and church services were copied. It was here that Latin literary works (pagan and Christian) were preserved. In addition, the monks were the most continuous force for education, organization, and social improvement between the sixth and twelfth centuries. They could cope better than anyone and thus with the help of the Papacy, they were able to save the Church from extinction. Inasmuch as the monasteries were a main source of organization and inasmuch as the theatre had no commercial support in the west, the monasteries proved to be a primary influence on the theatre's development in the Middle Ages.

The Benedictine monasteries are known to have played a major role in the use and development of drama. In the first period of the Middle Ages, the religious ritual of the eighth, ninth, and tenth centuries made up the liturgical drama, and out of liturgical drama, secular drama emerged. Religious worship or ritual was divided into two parts:

Mass and Hours. The service began with the Hours. Benedict of Nursia divided the day into "canonical Hours," which were hours of prayer established by rule. The monks rose at 2:00 A.M., went to the chapel, recited or sang scriptural readings, prayers, and psalms. At dawn they gathered for "matins," at six for "prime" (the first hour), at nine for the third, at noon for the sixth, at three for the ninth, and sunset for vespers (the evening hour) and bedtime for the completion. These Hours in the church service were similar in that they consisted of prayers, readings, songs, sermons, and devotional readings. Inasmuch as Hours varied from day to day based on the church calendar, scholars have noted that the eventual development of church playlets occurred in this section of the service.

The second part of the church worship was the Mass. Unlike the Hours which were dynamic, the Mass was static and thus unlikely to include dramatic additions. It should be noted, however, that some scholars such as O. B. Hardison view the mass as a dramatic presentation. To support this position, the manuscript of Amalarius, a ninth century Bishop of Metz (c. 780-850) indicates that the priests who participated in the Mass enacted the life, death, and resurrection of Christ and that a priest (celebrant) represented Christ (not impersonated), while the congregation added a supporting part.

That the Mass was used as drama seems to be further indicated in the use of a *trope* written in England for Easter Mass. The trope called the *Quem Quaeritis* (c. 920-950), which is the trope's opening words—"Whom do you seek?"—was in essence the text of a little scene played out between the angel and the three Marys called the *Visitatio.* The Benedictine monasteries in St. Gallen (Switzerland) and St. Martial (Limoges, France) are noted for having made extensive use of the trope. The first use or composer of a trope is attributed to a monk at St. Gallen named Notker Balbulus ("the Little Stammer," c. 840-912), although he claims to have taken it from the Jumièges Abbey (Normandy) service-book which was brought to St. Gallen.

The term *trope* has two meanings. The first is its literary application. In this sense, it refers to the words and/or music added to the introit (musical composition at the beginning of the service). Translated from the Greek, trope means turn, and therefore its second application relates to a memory device which helped choirs associate the words of the service with their turns or movements. Although the *Quem Quaeritis* exemplified Mass as drama, evidence is missing to confirm that the clergy singing the trope were actors, impersonating characters. Consequently, historians consider the *Quem Quaeritis* an example of liturgical drama and not a play in and of itself.

The earliest extant evidence of the liturgical unit, the *Visitatio,* plus the *Quem Quaeritis* trope is found in the *Regularis Concordia.* Compiled by the Benedictine St. Ethelwold, Bishop of Winchester (fl. 963-984), the *Regularis Concordia* (965-975, "harmony of the rule") is considered the earliest extant medieval drama. The playlet is complete with directions clearly indicating that the piece was to be acted. For example: "While the third lesson is being chanted, let four brothers dress themselves, of whom one, clothed in an alb, enter as if to take part in the service." The *Regularis Concordia* was designed to fortify the faith of the uneducated as well as to establish a uniform practice and purpose in the English churches and monasteries.

Another Benedictine influence upon the development of medieval drama is the Passion Plays discovered in the monasteries. A prime example is *The Carmina Burana* (Beuern Poems) dated from the thirteenth century and printed in 1847. Discovered at Benediktbeuern (Germany) monastery, this manuscript of plays and poems contains two versions of a Passion Play as well as an incomplete text of another Passion Play from a Benedictine monastery in Montecassino (Italy) dated c. 1150. These two Passion Plays plus the *Origny Ludus Paschalis* are significant for containing both Latin and vernacular passages.

In addition to the influences already cited in the tenth century, a Saxon nun, Hrotsvitha, a Benedictine Abbess of Gandersheim (c. 935-c. 1002), wrote six religious dramas that were influenced by the Latin comedies of Terence. Inasmuch as Hrosvitha did not enter the convent until age twenty-five, these plays, in rhymed Latin prose, display a worldly view of human nature—for example, virginity is extolled. Although the plays do not seem to have been acted, they possibly could have been performed for and by the nuns of the convent as well as for the Saxon princesses who were in charge of the convent.

By 1284 religious plays in the vernacular were well established and were an important link towards the development of secular drama. Again, the Benedictine monastery was involved in this development. The first religious drama performed in the vernacular was composed in c. 1155 by Hildegard of Bingen, an abbess like Hrosvitha.

The piece was called *Ordo Virtutum.*

Analogous to the changes that characterize the three periods of the Middle Ages, medieval drama was resurrected in the first period. In the second period, it flourished in the Church, and in the third period became secularized. Whereas the early Middle Ages, or first period, was marked by an agrarian society and political disintegration, the second period evidenced the beginnings of the modern bureaucratic state. During this second period liturgical drama flourished extensively within the church and by the end of the tenth century had spread throughout Europe and into Russia. However, as staging became more elaborate the Church relinquished its hold. Therefore the second phase of the Middle Ages is a transitional period for drama: liturgical drama flour-

Massacre of the Innocents and the Flight Into Egypt, taken from a frieze above the porch of the north transept to Notre Dame Cathedral, c. 1250. Note the medieval costumes. *Courtesy Martial Rose.*

ished to its fullest potential and then gave way to the impending secular drama.

Mystery Plays and Their Staging

When the Church moved outdoors, dramatic production became a joint effort of the Church and State. Although the Church and State were considered as one in the early Middle Ages, that concept was destroyed by the beginning of the twelfth century. With the separation of Church and State came the growth of secular power bringing with it cultural change. Although the specific reasons for moving drama outdoors are unclear, the attempts of the Church to counteract a growing secular power and to reassert its control might be a part of the answer. Two changes support this idea: first, the language of the drama was changed from the Latin to the vernacular; second, in 1264 Pope Urban IV instituted the Feast of Corpus Christi to make the church more meaningful to the common man.

The Feast of Corpus Christi was created through the efforts of Sr. Juliana (c. 1193-c. 1258), a Belgian prioress. In 1264 Pope Urban IV ordered all churches to observe the Feast of Corpus Christi, but his death in 1264 delayed his decree being carried out. In 1311-12 at the Council of Vienna Pope Clement V ratified Urban's decree and by 1318 the Feast of Corpus Christi was widespread. The celebration took place on the Thursday after Trinity Sunday, which meant it varied from May 23 to June 24. This feast is significant because it was fundamental to the advent of secular drama. The presentation of plays with this feast indicates also a change from clerical to lay actors. With the advent of the Feast of Corpus Christi, mystery or, as they were known in England, cycle plays were created. Inasmuch as cycle plays were usually performed on the Feast of Corpus Christi, these plays are sometimes referred to as Corpus Christi plays.

Our knowledge of the cycle plays is based upon the four extant English cycles:

1. The Chester plays established c. 1375, consisted of twenty-four plays.
2. The York plays, 1378 (forty-eight plays) had over fifty guilds.
3. The Wakefield Cycle, 1403 (thirty-two plays). A revision of the first York cycle is also called the Towneley Cycle, after the name of the manuscript's owner who was a nineteenth century Lancashire squire.

General layout of the stage used for Valenciennes Passion Play; miniature from the *Mystere de la Passion. Paris Bibliotheque Nationale.*

4. The Ludus Coventriae, 1392, known as N-town or Hegge Cycle. The N may stand for nomen (name) indicating that the blank was to be filled in by the town where the play was to be presented. For example:

> A Sunday next yf that we may
> At vi of the belle we gin oure play
> In Ntowne.

The towne of Lincoln has been suggested.

Of these four, the York Cycle is the longest, most complete, and best known. Since 1951, a version lasting less than three hours has been regularly performed in York. The original version lasted all day.

The trade guilds responsible for producing these cycle dramas were trade or craft unions (consider the present-day union for motion picture actors, Screen Actors Guild), and in the thirteenth century nearly every major English town had one or more guilds. Being of a religious nature, the guilds had a patron saint, a chaplain, and a chapel. Thus they were likely choices for staging the mystery cycles. The use of the term mystery for these plays is two-fold. First, there was the religious connotation that represented the mystery of Christ's Passion. Second, mystery comes from the French word métier meaning art or craft, and the production of these plays was performed by craft unions. The guilds were important to a city's successful presentation of these plays. They arranged for performances, storage and maintenance of carts, rehearsals, and (under the Church's influence) maintaining the texts. The text recounted Christianity from creation to doomsday with the plays of the nativity and the Passion of Christ considered the two most important parts. Originally written between the twelfth and fourteenth centuries, these texts were both original and were translations of liturgical plays. Further, they were rewritten in keeping with the Reformation, the changes in religious doctrine, and the instability of the guilds—new ones were formed, old ones declined, and others amalgamated.

Every cycle had individual plays, each of which was from twenty-five to fifty minutes in length. Further, it is thought that if violence or crudity was to be presented, children, pregnant women, and the aged were not allowed admission. The plays were produced every two to ten years and started at sunrise and finished at night. The larger guilds would each perform one play of the cycle, and the smaller ones (up to as many as six) would combine to do one play of the cycle. These cycle plays were performed on a wheeled wagon with scenery (called a pageant wagon). Either the wagons were fixed and the plays of the cycle were performed on or in front of them, or the wagons moved in a procession (much like our modern-day parades) with the actors on them, and stopped at a designated spot for the performance. The arrangement is unclear. From the thirteenth century on guilds were assigned particular images or "tableau vivants" (living statues) to produce for the procession. It is thought that these three-dimensional images mounted on wagons would make as many as ten to fifteen stops, at which time communion, worship or a speech occurred. When the plays were presented, they were done in verse making it easier to memorize. This was important for the actors who were the laity and who worked a regular job. The number of actors varied with each cycle (anybody could try out), and once cast, actors were allowed two weeks to refuse their part, after which they *had* to sign a binding contract. A statement from the York cycle indicates that an actor could not perform over two parts.

Town councils and trade officials were in charge of production. They would assign individual plays to particular guilds, regulate the text to make sure it was followed, choose playing sites, and levy fines on actors and the guilds in general for poor production quality. Other aspects of production included a stage director who organized the workers, the staging, supervised the artisans building the scenery, maintained costumes, and secured the musicians, ushers, technicians, and choir boys who played the women's parts. Some directors acquired a reputation and were thus invited to various towns in this capacity.

These plays were called mystery or cycle plays in England; in France they were termed "mystères"; in Germany, "Geistliche Spiele"; in Spain, "Auto

Rustic stage comedy. Note the portable stage and the drawing on the curtain as well as the torches, which were used either for stage effects or possibly to ward off insects. From Cohen's *Le Théâtre en France au Moyen Age.*

Sacramentale"; and in Italy, "Sacre Rappresenta-zioni" or "laudi," which contained choral elements. Because these plays were contrary to the Reformation they were suppressed. As the Protestants gained control, Catholic drama began its demise. This demise created a greater distinction between liturgical and secular drama. Secular topics appeared, natural history replaced Church history, and new secular forms arose, bringing with them the rise of the professional actor. The last completed English cycle on record was in Coventry in 1580 and in France, the last reference was the 1548 act of Parliament suppressing mystery plays.

Latin to the Vernacular

During the period 1066-1300, an economic revolution took place that affected the Church's control of society. Medieval society appeared always on the brink of chaos and it was the Church and its structure that was able to give order to disorder. As such, the Church rose to power and in its position maintained order and unity in western society. In part this unity was maintained through language. Before the thirteenth century, Latin was the international language that the educated (literate) populace of Europe used for correspondence, business, law, science, diplomacy, literature, government and philosophy. The language was spoken daily and new words and phrases were added constantly. At this time Latin was the Esperanto of Europe and it facilitated the exchange of knowledge between countries as well as enabling students to attend different universities without the problem of language. Inasmuch as the Church maintained Latin in its services and in its use of liturgical drama, a great portion of the uneducated public was excluded from understanding or participating in the church services and liturgical drama. It was a barrier that was maintained as long as Latin was the primary language.

During the so-called Dark Ages (500-1000), plague, famine, poverty, barbarianism, and war created chaos in the western world. Especially affected were communications (roads, etc.), commerce, literature and art. In turn, this disorder forced towns to become insular and tended to create nationalism among nations. In addition to the influx of different nationalities into various countries, these disruptions created a change in Latin—new words, new sentence structure, and new speech rhythms—in order to create uniformity of pronunciation. Although Latin was still used by the Church and the educated, the changing of Latin into a vernacular language started with the chaos created in the early Middle Ages. The Church, and particularly Italy, were the last to alter spoken Latin.

The changes in Latin can be noted in Spain, France, and Germany whose vernacular language was rooted in Latin. The influx of the Normans to England brought French to the English language. In terms of ideas and language, this was a profound influence because for three hundred years English literature was basically half French. Linguistically, France and England were one from c. 1050 to 1350. With the loss of her French possessions, England came under another linguistic influence: the Teutonic Angles, Saxons, and Jutes.

The English language is therefore a language of French, German, and English. By the early thirteenth century, the demise of Latin forced the Church to resort to the vernacular in order to maintain its power and in order to reach the people.

Additionally, books aided the rise of the vernacular. All books were written on parchment, papyrus, vellum or paper. It was done with a quill or reed pens using black or colored inks. Paper had been invented in China by Ts'ai Lun about A.D. 105 and was imported to the west from Islam. In 1190 paper mills were erected in western Europe and in the thirteenth century, paper was made from linen. The manuscripts were copied either by monks or scribes who were paid by monasteries, rich men wishing a library, or booksellers. Books were expensive and by today's standards (1993-94), the average book was roughly $800 - $1000. The price of books limited the number of booksellers and hindered literacy as well. Furthermore, the device of punctuation, which was known to the Hellenistic Greeks but lost with the barbarian invasions, was resurrected in the thirteenth century and was established in the fifteenth century with the advent of printing. Books were exchanged between countries, friends, families, and monasteries. Additionally, libraries were started. The use of books aided the transmission of language and knowledge which revolutionized Europe's intellectual life.

It was through Islam that the west was greatly influenced in all areas of society. Greek manuscripts, such as Aristotle's *Poetics*, were translated into Arabic for Islam but had to be translated in Latin for the west, and subsequently into the vernacular. Further, these translations created new developments in grammar and philology. Additionally, these translations brought new knowledge to the West from Islam: algebra, the zero, the decimal system, the theory and practice of medicine, astronomy, and theology. With this knowledge, the medieval system collapsed giving way to the Renaissance.

The Crusades and Industrialism

Although the Crusades ("marked with the cross") were ostensibly a religious war, one of its underlying causes was commercialism—basically, the desire of Pisa, Genoa, Venice, and Amalfi to expand their markets in the near east. Often called "the holy war," the Crusades lasted from 1095 to 1291 and resulted in, among other things, a weakening of Christianity. The Crusaders discovered that those who were non-Christians were civilized, humane, and as honest as themselves, casting doubt on the Church's claim that all non-Christians were barbarians. In addition, the Crusades opened up markets that created commercialism which proved to be a key factor in the demise of liturgical drama. By its contact with the east, western society profited. Commerce and industry increased, bringing with it the growth of towns and the middle class. What had started as an economic venture of feudalistic lords faced with religious fervor ended with an economic revolution that provided the foundation for the Renaissance.

In the thirteenth century under the influence of Islam (near east) Europe began to pave the roads and cities began paving their streets. Prior to this, roads were avenues of dirt, mud, filled with water and holes with very few bridges to connect roads. Roads were so inadequate that travel by water was preferred. With the improvement of roads, trade and transportation of goods and people became the means by which commerce aided the growth of towns. Textile industries arose along with a money system and in turn created the development of interest, bringing the rise of money lenders, bonding and the basic seeds of capitalism. The growth of industry and commerce, the development of a money economy over a land-based economy, the growth of an urban population and the need for labor in towns were all factors in Europe's economic revolution.

Industrialism gave rise to new classes in society who gained economic and political power. Up to the advent of industrialism (c. thirteenth century) only three classes existed: the nobles, the clergy, and the peasants. Before that there were only two: the conquerors and the conquered. The nobles ruled and lived in the country disdaining any association with towns or cities. The development of commerce and industry created a new social class (the bourgeois) and by the eighteenth century money and power had shifted to this class.

The growth of the mercantile class can be noted in the creation of communes—political organizations consisting of merchants and the citizens. The communes were in essence the business class. As a group they fought for and achieved freedom from the feudal lords. By the end of the twelfth century these communes in western Europe had achieved freedom for the cities, gained self-government, and limited the rights of the Church. Municipal and economic life was dominated by this merchant class.

Another complex organization that rose with the communes and were a product of industrial growth was the trade guilds. In the eleventh century the guilds were merchant organizations and included only merchants and master workmen; all others were excluded. Inasmuch as the craftsmen were excluded from the merchant guilds, each trade or craft industry in each town formed their own guilds. Thus, by the twelfth century, guilds changed from merchant to trade/craft unions. By the thirteenth century communes had recognized guilds as self-governing. In some cases, the communes and guilds were one and the same. Furthermore, the strength of the guilds had grown, enabling them to become a factor in controlling a city's economic and political life. In London, for example, the city guilds chose the Lord Mayor.

Typical of an industry that reflected economic growth and subsequently affected the beginning of secular drama was the building of cathedrals. Cathedrals were part of the romantic upsurge that seized Europe from the eleventh century forward. Built by professional architects called "master builders" or "master masons," the cathedrals were modeled initially on the Roman basilica which came to be known as Romanesque architecture and in the middle of the twelfth century evolved to Gothic architecture. Structurally, a church was built so that the head or apse pointed eastward toward Jerusalem and the west door or main entrance would receive the setting sun. The cost of building Gothic cathedrals was so great that the guilds and the communes lost their wealth and with it their power and independence. As a consequence, most of the cathedrals built in the twelfth and thirteenth centuries were left unfinished, and it was not until the early nineteenth century that Gothic architecture returned.

With the advent of commercialism, liturgical drama was altered radically. Production moved outdoors, the language changed from Latin to the vernacular and trade guilds and communes took over theatrical production. All of these factors created more secularism and in turn promoted the rise of secular forms and professionalism in theatre.

Secular Forms

During the twelfth century, a revival in classical theatre occurred. Primarily, the Latin comedies were written in the schools of England and northern France which in turn inspired the development of new secular forms. The rise of new secular forms marks a break with church-drama, and subsequently Church control.

These new Latin comedies were called *elegiac comedies* and included elements from the mime. Although they were called "comoediae," they were not plays but poems that had a mixture of dialogue and narrative. One of the best known is *Geta* by Vitalis of Blois. The poem comprises comic routines, a theme of adultery, a narrative framework and appears to have been influenced by Plautus's *Amphitruo*. In addition, this same period produced the "Comoediae Horatianae," consisting of sexual farces such as *Babio* and *Pamphilus* which were

Hercules Furens. Classical works were rarely, if ever, produced during the Middle Ages. Hence the graphic artist attempted to portray various performances. Note the characters in the tragedy with Hercules in his lion skin in the upper portion of the miniature. The chorus is depicted at the bottom with the audience at upper and lower right. At center is the poet who, according to Middle Age thought, read the dialogue as the actors mimed the action. Miniature from the codex Vaticanus Urbinas 355. *Biblioteca Vaticana.*

influenced by Plautus and Ovid. That a classical stage emerged concurrent with the liturgical stage has prompted some scholars to argue that liturgical and secular drama developed simultaneously rather than the older view of seeing secular drama as a product of cultural Darwinism.

Arguments for a thriving outdoor vernacular theatre are based on the French writer Adam de la Halle's (c. 1238-1800) *Le Jeu de la Feuillée* (c. 1275: *The Play of the Greenwood*, sometimes translated *The Play of the Leafy Bower*). Whereas this work is cited as the oldest extant medieval secular drama, Halle's *The Play of Robin and Marion* (c. 1283) is a folk-pastoral drama and is considered the oldest secular music-drama in France. In addition to these plays, other secular forms developed steadily from the thirteenth century forward: farces, moralities, chambers of rhetoric plays, interludes, mummings and disguisings, royal entries, and tournaments.

The Morality Play and Stage Censorship

Developed in the fourteenth century, the English morality play is important in aiding the transition from medieval to Elizabethan drama. The immediate ancestor of the morality play is the "Pater Noster" prayers (The Lord's Prayer) which the Church divided into seven parts. Each part was devoted to combating one of the seven deadly sins and thus, the purpose of these plays was to improve human behavior through teaching moral lessons (cf. melodrama's purpose). The plays were like sermons in dramatic context, which led one individual to assert that "their very name is like a yawn." In keeping with the symbolism the characters were represented dramatically in the form of an allegory. Allegorical characters such as Sloth, Gluttony, Usury, Anger, Avarice, and a host of others can be classified as either vice or virtue.

The basic differences between the morality and mystery plays are as follows:

1. Generally, the mystery plays did not tend toward allegory whereas morality plays did.
2. The mystery plays became meaningful only in terms of the complete cycle. The morality plays were unattached and individually could render a meaning.
3. Characters of the mystery plays were drawn from the Bible. Those of the morality plays were personifications of vice and virtue and concerned the common man.
4. Conflict in mystery plays was in terms of Biblical stories, whereas conflict in morality plays arose from the battle between vice and virtue over man's soul.
5. The emphasis in mystery plays was on the theological aspects of the Bible. In morality plays the emphasis was on molding human behavior through teaching about life via the example of the characters.
6. The mystery play tended toward the liturgical, and the morality play lent itself to the secular.
7. The mystery plays were performed by amateur actors, and the morality plays eventually became vehicles for professional actors.

As a form the morality play was most popular in England and France. The oldest extant morality play is a fragment from *The Pride of Life* (c. 1400) and the earliest complete extant play is *The Castle of Perseverance* (c. 1425). The latter play is said to be modeled on the *Pas d'Armes*, a form of tournament entertainment involving combat (see Chivalry and Tournaments). In both the *Pas d'Armes* and *The Castle of Perseverance* the besieged castle is located in the middle of the circular arena surrounded by five scaffolds located outside the circle. Scaffolds housed the assailants and God who acts in the capacity of judge. Two additional morality plays of note are *Mankind* (c. 1470-1497) and *Everyman* (c. 1500). Only one part exists of *Mankind* but what exists describes the action being interrupted to allow the actors to collect money from the audience—an indication that this play was performed or certainly adapted by professional actors. *Everyman* is the best known of the morality plays and is said to have been a version of the Dutch play, *Elckerlijk*. Controversy centers, however, around which came first.

One of the most controversial morality plays is John Bale's (1495-1563) *King John* (1538). Bale, an ex-Carmelite monk, wrote this play as an anti-Catholic attack. In it an English king fights against the evil Pope. This and other anti-Catholic plays by Bale provoked Parliament to pass a censorship act in 1543 banning "interpretations of Scriptures . . contrary to the doctrine set forth, or to be set forth, by the King's majesty." This act demonstrated that the government acted as a censor of plays and intended to rival the Church in this area.

EVERYMAN (c. 1485)

CHARACTERS
MESSENGER
GOD
DEATH
EVERYMAN
FELLOWSHIP
KINDRED
COUSIN
GOODS
DOCTOR
GOOD DEEDS
KNOWLEDGE
CONFESSION
BEAUTY
DISCRETION
FIVE WITS
ANGEL

BACKGROUND

The medieval period was more concerned about death than it was about life. This preoccupation took precedent over everything. *Everyman* is a manifestation of that concern. To the average person, this play represented a parable about how one should live life in order to gain heaven. The story was not new and the idea of death and redemption can be found in oriental literature dating to the fifth century B.C.

Everyman is a morality play and its focus on vanity, death, and virtue has proved to be an influence on twentieth century drama. Samuel Beckett's *Endgame* serves as one example, and certainly the term "everyman" has become associated with the universal concept of sin, dying and salvation. Every human being (everyman) must accept the reality of death and thus this play in emphasizing this point, describes how one must come to grips with this eventuality.

SUMMARY

God sends Death to inform Everyman that "in my name, A pilgrimage he must on him take, Which he is no wise may escape; And that he bring with him a sure reckoning." When Everyman encounters Death, he wants more time to put things in order before going. Death refuses. Death tells him that he cannot be bribed and that there is no way that he can escape this pilgrimage. Everyman begs for mercy and asks for company on his journey. Death replies that anybody who wishes to accompany him may do so. In addition, he reminds Everyman that his life and his worldly goods were only lent to him. Death exists leaving Everyman in torment as to not having led a virtuous life.

Seeking companionship for his journey, Everyman encounters Fellowship, Cousin, and Goods, all of whom promise initially to do anything for Everyman. But when he asks for their companionship on his trip, they all refuse. Good Deeds will go with him but he cannot stand because Everyman has not supported him. Responding to Everyman's plea for mercy, Good Deeds sends his sister Knowledge. Knowledge leads Everyman to Confession. After this encounter, Good Deeds is able to rise off the ground and accompany Everyman. Discretion, Strength, Five Wits, and Beauty enter together to aid in completing his redemption. As the Doctor notes, "Remember Beauty, Five Wits, Strength, and Discretion, They all at the last do Everyman forsake. Save his Good Deeds there doth he take." Having made amends, Everyman and Good Deeds enter the grave together.

The City of London entered the fray in 1546 when it claimed the right to regulate actors, the theatres and playing times within the city limits. This began a struggle that would continue throughout the sixteenth century between the Church, the City, the Court, and Parliament.

The morality plays are significant for they mark a departure from liturgical to secular drama. Furthermore, their use and adaptation by professional actors indicate the growth of the common player. Lastly, morality plays contained a diversity of elements and subjects that reflected the political, economic, and cultural changes in society.

Farce

The earliest extant farce, *The Boy and the Blind Man,* is dated in the thirteenth century and gives evidence that farce did not really thrive in France, Germany, and England until the fifteenth and sixteenth centuries. It was strongest, however, in France and Germany and did not fully emerge in England until the sixteenth century with the work of John Heywood (c. 1497-c. 1580).

In France farces were short, in verse, and were concerned with sex and other bodily functions. The best known of the French farces is *Pierre Pathelin* (c. 1470). Two variants on French farce were the *sermon joyeuse,* a burlesque sermon, and the *sottie,* a short religious, political and social satirical piece. The sotties were especially successful and were performed by secular guilds known as the sociétés joyeuses. In Paris the two best known sociétés acting companies were the les Enfants sans Souci, and the Basoche du Palais (a society of lawyers). Of the French writers and actors who were successful in sotties, Pierre Gringare (1475-c. 1539) is noted as the most successful.

In Germany farce was labeled Shrovetide plays and appears to find its roots in pre-Lenten folk festivals. Of the surviving German farces, those from Nuremberg are the most extensive, and were associated with the apprentice revels known as *Schembartlaufen.* The best remembered writer of these German farces was Hans Sachs (1494-1576). In a century of hate his was a voice of cheer. His plays focused on simple people and through them he praised such virtues as affection, duty, marital fidelity, piety, parental and filial love. Sachs is considered "the bard of the Reformation," and in his position he satirized the Catholics and Lutherans. He mourned the immorality and commercialism of his age, which could make him a spokesman for the twentieth century. A man of many skills, Sachs was a shoemaker but became a poet, a musician, playwright, acquired and used a large library, learned Greek literature and philosophy, wrote 6000 poems, 1198 plays, and died at the age of 82 surviving two wives. By taking the Shrovetide plays out of the *Schembartlaufen* (apprentices' revels), Sachs began to present plays regularly with a company of actors. It has been noted that had not political and religious wars interfered, Sachs' work which might have provided Germany with a strong national tradition.

Mummings or Disguisings

Mummings were closely associated with disguisings and dance during the Middle Ages. In fact, disguisings came out of mummings and in turn produced the English Masque, Spanish Momeries, French Ballet de Cour, and Italian Intermezzo. The form consisted of masked actors (guests) bearing gifts who proceeded in a silent procession to a private house, usually during the winter. The silent aspect was to surprise the host, and it also gives the form its name. Mumming seems to derive from the German, mumme; the Danish, mom (meaning closed or sealed lips, silence); or the French word muette (meaning to play in silence). The guests were announced and requested permission to enter. Once inside, they danced (not with the hosts), played dice, drank, left their gifts and then departed. It would seem that this type of entertainment was attached to a special social occasion such as a wedding. When professionals performed or became part of this

Scenes from *Pierre Pathelin* (c. 1470), a French farce which was so popular it went through thirty editions. From the 1500 Edition. *Top left:* The lawyer Pathelin buying his cloth from Madame Guillaume; *Top right,* Pathelin, who pretends to be sick, and his wife Guillemette; *Bottom left,* Pathelin pleading his case before the judge and his son, Greffier.

entertainment is not known. It is known, however, that professionals and Court members participated jointly but that the Court members danced separately from the mummers. This joint participation began, no doubt, when the element of surprise was eliminated and the visitors were expected.

Mummings are noted in 1347 and seem to continue into the fifteenth century. However, the use of masks provided opportunity for crime and, as a consequence, acts were issued prohibiting people wearing masks. At court though and in some nobles' houses mummings continued but in a changed form. It is the changes that led to "disguisings."

Disguisings came out of mummings and are very much like a masquerade ball. They differ from mummings in that gifts are not presented. Additionally, the identity of the players and their arrival time are known. The actors continue to remain silent and their mimed action is narrated. Evidence indicates that both mummings and disguisings made use of scenic devices, costumes, and were composed for presentation at Court or for the mayor and other London officials.

Chambers of Rhetoric

During the fourteenth century in Holland, the guilds that presented mystery plays began to call themselves *Rederykers* or members of the Chambers of Rhetoric. These societies were widespread and by the sixteenth century every town in the Netherlands had one or more Chambers. The members wrote poetry, music, plays, acted, and produced plays, presented pageants, and had playwriting contests. In 1485 *The Mirror of the Salvation of Everyman*—which in the English version is called *Everyman*—won first prize at Antwerp. The plays ranged from farces to tragedies and like morality plays were concerned with teaching or criticizing a religious, political or moral idea. The Catholic church was a favorite target when it was in power, and when Calvinism became the state religion it too became prime subject matter. The government intervened, however, preventing continued satirization of Calvinism. The Chambers were especially effective in the Dutch rebellion against Spain and, as a consequence, in 1539 Catholic church officials passed an edict requiring all plays to be approved by the Church. This forced writers toward more secular topics.

The Chambers began to decline early in the seventeenth century as evidenced in Amsterdam where their number was reduced to two—the Sweet Briar and the White Lavender Tree. Competition was so fierce between the two that a poet-physician Samuel Coster brought them together into the First Academy of Netherlands. Initially, the idea was to create a university, but when the City of Amsterdam gave the society a theatre, the idea was abandoned in favor of play production. The new theatre, called Schouwburg (meaning playhouse) opened in 1618 and was Holland's first municipal theatre. Similarly, in Belgium the Ghent Chamber of Rhetoric (The Fountain) developed into the Flemish National Theatre.

Chamber plays were heavily allegorical and were first presented in churches before moving outdoors as early as 1539. These outdoor performances were on temporary stages described as having two levels. Both levels had three openings with a curtain to reveal interior scenes. On the top of the stage was placed a throne reserved for the figure in whose honor the festival was held. When contests were held, this figure was lowered to stage level to hand out prizes.

Interludes and the Dual Tradition in Acting

Although a variety of dramatic forms existed during the Middle Ages, the only other form (except possibly the disguising, which in seventeenth century England Ben Jonson turned into a Court Masque) to have impact upon succeeding generations was the interlude. The term itself appears to be derived from the Latin *ludus,* meaning play, and *inter* meaning between, among, or during. The definition suggests that the interlude was a short play or plays placed between the intervals of a longer play, such as a mystery play, or perhaps it was a short play placed between the courses of a banquet. In actuality, however, the interlude was any type of play presented during the Middle Ages, especially those plays first presented indoors in the "great hall" as after-dinner entertainment for the nobles.

Historically, the oldest extant English interlude is Henry Medwall's *Fulgens and Lucrece* (c. 1497). Like the morality play, the interlude was performed by professionals, and thus was associated with the rise of professional acting. By having a troupe of professional actors always available, the nobles could have an interlude performed at their discretion. For the professional actor, being attached to a household meant a steady income. When not performing for their employer, acting troupes toured to make extra money. This attachment of actors to households proved to be of vital importance for the professional actor.

From approximately 1500 to 1572, the professional actor in western Europe was denied official recognition by the Church and State, and was therefore hard-pressed to earn a livelihood. Consequently, the support rendered by individual noblemen or rich merchants enabled actors to survive. Also in this interim period religious drama became prohibited, which consequently led writers to choose other subjects. On one hand, this choice of different subject matter for plays marked the decline of medieval drama, and on the other hand, it gave rise to Renaissance drama. Finally, the fact that actors performed indoors as well as outdoors established a dual tradition in acting. This tradition continued in the Elizabethan period where actors made use of outdoor and indoor theatres: specifically, the public theatres (outdoors) and the private theatres (indoors).

Chivalry and Tournaments

Chivalry was a combination of Germanic, Islamic and Christian ideas. Its chief focus was the knight, a person of aristocratic birth who had been formally inducted into the order of knighthood. Once inducted into the order, the knight could now risk his life in tournaments where he would be praised for his skill, endurance and bravery.

Tournaments *(pas d'Armes)* began in the tenth century as an exercise for war and thrived in France. They were utilized to celebrate a marriage, a visit of a sovereign, or of an equally special event. Those knights who offered to take part in the tournament came to the town where the tournament was held. Here they procured their guest rooms from which they hung their armor from the windows of their rooms. In addition, they affixed their coat of arms to castles, monasteries, and other public buildings. In addition to the knights, horse dealers to equip the knight, haberdashers to clothe the knight and his horse, moneylenders, fortune tellers, acrobats, mimes, troubadours, poets, prostitutes, wandering scholars, and noble ladies were also present. In essence, it was a festival.

The tournament lasted anywhere from one day to a week. The field of battle was the town square or an open area partially enclosed by stands for the wealthy to watch. Commoners stood around the field. The stands were decorated and musicians played music before and during the tournament. Between the contests, the wealthy would scatter coins among the commoners.

Sunday was considered the assembly and festival day. Monday and Tuesday were the jousts in which knights rode against each other in single combat. Wednesday was a day of rest and Thursday was the tournament, the climax of the festival. The tournament consisted of the knight fighting an actual battle wherein he tried to capture various mansions which were symbolic representations of woods, castles, ships, etc. Those who were taken prisoners were ransomed (as in war); their horses and armor belonged to their captors to keep or sell. At the end of the contest, whoever was still alive joined the noble spectators for an evening of song, dance, and merry-making. The winning knights were entitled to kiss the women, and heard songs and poems composed about them by the minstrels.

Theatrically, the tournaments are noted for the costumes of the knights that helped identify them, the use of scenic devices (mansions) and properties to determine the locale of the tournament battle, the allegorical representations, and the stadium called "lists" with seating for the spectators. Whereas mumming was primarily the province of the commoners, tournaments belonged to the nobility.

Street Theatre and Royal Entries

Royal Entries were street pageants whose cost and planning was undertaken jointly by the trade guilds and the city council. These pageants were to celebrate a special event such as a visit of royalty, a wedding or other similar events. The pattern was as follows: At a prearranged spot outside the city, the visiting dignitary was met by city officials, clergy, and members of the trade guilds who then escorted the visitor along a designated route which led to the church. After this the visitor was taken to his accommodations. We practice a somewhat similar ceremony with our ticker-tape parades or when we give the keys of the city to an honored person.

Along the parade route the escorted visitor saw allegorical tableaux and other scenic devices. The procession would halt at each tableaux or stage play and then move on to the next. Evidence indicates that when they stopped an articulate representative of the community would explain the tableaux or the "mystery mimes" as they were known. The idea of using lavish tableaux was for flattery and respect but their placement was reminiscent of the use of the nave in churches and pageant wagons. Sometimes the sets conveyed a political or economic message for the visitor. Gradually, scaffolds and stage plays were added and were in definite use by 1298, though evidence suggests their usage by the early thirteenth century.

Liturgical and Vernacular Staging

Liturgical indoor drama was staged in churches whose rectangular structure was based upon the Roman basilica. The church's ground plan consisted of a long nave (note the use of thoroughfares in street pageants) with the apse (head) facing east. In the middle of the church were two side aisles (which were extensions off the nave) called the transepts. The altar was in the apse where the tomb was established for Easter productions.

Movement was a key feature in liturgical drama and to approximate the journeys *(journeés)* separate areas of the church were used. This led to the development of a scenic device called *mansions*. The essential feature of mansion staging (for both indoor and outdoor productions) was the simultaneous appearance *(décor simultané)* on the playing site of a number of scenic locations that were located side by side or in close proximity to each other as in the Valencienne Passion Play. The open area in front of the mansions, between them, or surrounding them was called the *platea* (place) and inasmuch as it was neutral, the space was defined by the dialogue. The actual mansion, that is, its specific location, was called the *locus* and was defined by the structure or the character in the play. In actual construction a mansion may be a house or a single platform. Additionally, benches were mounted on platforms (French: *puy*; English: *pew*; Latin: *podium)* for the audience and were known to have collapsed. Then too, actors were

Décor simultané. Setting by Laurent Mahelot for Théophile de Viau's *Pyrame et Thisbé.* From *Histoire Illustrée de la Littérature Française.*

Terence Stages. It has been suggested that these stages were eventually enlarged to permit playing within the openings and that these openings gradually came together into one large opening or single arch. From Cohen's *Le Théâtre en France au Moyen Age.*

placed on benches distributed throughout the church such as the choir entrance, west door, or parts of the nave.

When plays moved out of the Church is unknown. This move precipitated the rise of vernacular drama but whether the vernacular and liturgical stage developed gradually or whether vernacular drama developed independently is the subject of debate. The traditional view favors the gradual evolution. This is based upon *The Mystery of Adam* (c. 1150), a play with detailed stage directions that indicate an outdoor production adjacent to a church, has dialogue in French and Latin, and has the Latin paraphrased into the vernacular.

Vernacular outdoor plays made use of both fixed and moveable staging. The moveable stages were called pageant wagons (in Spain, *carros*) and were used primarily in cycle plays. The nature of how they were used is open to question; that is, were they used for simultaneous staging or as a separate entity. It is known that the wagons proceeded in a processional manner with each wagon carrying a scenic unit (mansion) and that at least one hundred mansions were used for each cycle play.

Fixed stages were used in Roman amphitheaters, cemeteries adjoining churches, courtyards, monasteries, and public squares. The stage had Hell on one end and Heaven on the other. If circular staging was used, then Hell was in the west and Heaven in the east. The use of scenic devices to represent Heaven and Hell served to represent the dual nature of man (good-evil) and his struggle on earth between vices and virtues. Whereas the mansion of Heaven might be slightly elevated, that of Hell would be lower than the other mansions. In the actual production, the staging was done realistically with the action presented as if it were part of the present; it was a telescoping of time. The ability to create miracles and other special effects (known as *secrets)* was done by the machinist who was second in importance to the director. One of the better known machinist-set designers was Italian architect Filippo Brunelleschi (1377-1446). In his capacity as machinist, Brunelleschi was known to have developed "secrets" for the Italian *Sacre Rappresentazioni.* As a designer, Brunelleschi is credited with developing linear perspective.

Dominated by ceremony and ritual, the Middle Ages evidenced a strong need for structure. It was a period that struggled to impose order on chaos and at the core of the struggle was medieval man, who battled between vices and virtue—the church and worldly pleasures. The theatre of this time exemplifies the ceremony, ritual, and the struggle. In a period where illiteracy was dominant, visual imagery was highly praised and an oral tradition the standard. These two concepts enabled the theatre to thrive.

Selected Readings

Chambers, E. K. *The Medieval Stage,* 2 Vols. Oxford, 1903.

Harris, John W. *Medieval Theatre in Context.* London, 1992.

Tyndeman, William. *The Theatre of the Middle Ages.* New York, 1979.

Wickham, Glynne. *Early English Stages: 1300-1600.* 3 Vols. New York, 1959-1980.

Young, Karl. *The Drama of the Medieval Church.* 2 Vols. Oxford, 1933.

Vocabulary

1.	Ostragoth	OS tra goth
2.	Carolingian	KA ra lin jee an
3.	Amalarius	ah muh LAHR ee uhs
4.	Trope	Troph
5.	Quem Quaeritis	KWEM KWIGH ri tis
6.	Regularis Concordia	re goo: LAH ruhs kuhn KAWR de uh
7.	Hrosvitha of Gandersheim	rahs VI thuh of GAN der shighm
8.	*Fulgens and Lucrece*	FOHL jens and loo: KREES
9.	Ludus Coventriae	LOO duhs kuh VEN tree igh
10.	Valenciennes	yah Len see ENZ
11.	tableau vivants	ta BLOH vee VAHN
12.	elegiac	El a JIAK

CHAPTER SEVEN

❧

Italian Renaissance:
The Age of Scenes and Machines

Seventeenth or early eighteenth century stage setting by Ferninando Galli-Bibiena (1657-1743), known as the "First architect and painter of Festivals and Theatres of Vienna."

In some ways the Italian Renaissance theatre was a continuation of the Middle Ages. First, plays in the vernacular were born in the Middle Ages and were carried over into the Renaissance where they were fully developed. Second, the use of stage machinery, called "secrets" in the Medieval period, was also carried over and made more sophisticated by the Italians. Third, many of the Latin manuscripts preserved throughout the Middle Ages contributed significantly to the development of the theatre of the Italian Renaissance. Fourth, the major forms of Renaissance drama were derived in part from the Middle Ages. Fifth, the medieval novella was continued into the Renaissance.

In other ways, however, the Italian Renaissance represents a departure from the Middle Ages. Painting, sculpture, architecture, and the use of creative literature represent four areas in which the Renaissance departed. Underlying all shifts away from the Middle Ages was the fundamental thought of the Renaissance.

During the Renaissance, unlike the Middle Ages, life was viewed as something to be enjoyed. The Renaissance ideal, much like that of the Greeks, was to balance life within one's self as well as society. The Renaissance desire to imitate antiquity altered the lifestyle and, consequently, affected theatrical development.

Humanism

To the Italians the resurrection of the classical world was called "la Rinascita" (rebirth). This rebirth, or Renaissance as it was later termed, marked a change from the medieval mind to the modern one. "Money is the root of all civilization" and the Renaissance is a prime example. This revival of antiquity required the money of bankers, merchants, the Church, and nobles to pay for the Greek and Roman manuscripts that inspired this rebirth and to support those scholars who devoted their lives to spreading these classical

texts throughout the world. In addition, it took secularism that came with a rising middle class, the advent of universities, new knowledge and philosophy, and a skepticism about church dogma. Under these influences, Italy went from a period of restraint to one of freedom. The domination of the Church was broken and man turned his attention to earth and away from heaven. He was taught to love life and not brood about death. It wasn't that they were atheists but that they conceived that Christianity should not be taken seriously and that, by and large, it was a "myth conformable to the needs of popular imagination and morality."

That the Renaissance began in Italy stems from a number of factors. Roman civilization had left constant reminders in its art, law, architecture, and language (Latin). In addition Italy's commerce and industry made it the richest area in the Christian world. Bolstered by its trade, Italian traders made contact with a variety of races, creeds, and faiths that they brought back from their travels. Finally, the corruption of the papacy afforded secular influences to assert themselves. With the papal seat being moved to Avignon, France, in 1305, rulers from the Italian states competed with one another for power and prestige. One way was to support the scholars, writers, and artists, and it was this patronage that aided the growth of the Renaissance.

The Italian ruler most influential in developing the Renaissance was Cosimo de' Medici (1380-1464) who ruled Florence. This city was one of the two richest states in Italy (Venice was the other), and under the leadership of Cosimo, Florence became known as the "Athens of Italy." In 1439 Cosimo de' Medici offered the resources of Florence to those prelates and scholars from the East and West who gathered together in a conference seeking to reunite Christianity. Known as the Conference of Florence, the theological gathering did more to inspire an interest in Greek civilization than it did to develop Christian unity. This conference brought individuals knowledgeable in Greek literature, philosophy, and language to Florence where their lectures created a passion for antiq-

A Renaissance view of the Roman theatre. From Bapst, *Essai sur l'Histoire du Théâtre*, 1893.

they called the study of antiquity "umanita" (humanities). Initially, the humanists spent their energies on Greece but as more and more Roman classics were revived their interest changed to Rome. They revived Latin, Latinized their names, translated the Greek classics into Latin, and created academies devoted to the study of Roman ideas and authors. The study of Vitruvius, for example, led to an architectural interest in the physical theatre and the interest in Plato led to the developmental of dramatic criticism. During the sixteenth century, the Renaissance began to fade in Italy but it began to blossom in the rest of Europe who based their concept of theatre and drama on the ideas developed in the Italy Renaissance.

With this new emphasis, theatrical productions moved away from the pure didactic of the Middle Ages to pure spectacle. As a result, the Italian Renaissance contributed significantly to many scenic innovations which ultimately influenced modern theatre. The most significant contributions of this period were scenic innovations, the formation of literary principles, and the commedia dell'arte.

Formation of Italian Renaissance Theatre

Two institutions contributed to the development of the Italian Renaissance theatre—the academies and the royal courts. The academies were half literary clubs and half academic societies and were composed of humanists who gathered together to hear speeches and work out common problems. Each of the academies was devoted to the study of a particular subject. Of importance to the Renaissance theatre was the Roman Academy, which was organized about 1460 under the leadership of Julio Pomponio Leto (1425-1498), who Latinized his name to Pomponius Laetus. The academy focused upon Roman life and staged plays by Plautus. Members of the Academy also wrote plays modeled after the Roman dramatists

uity. Fourteen years later with the fall of Constantinople (1453), many of those who attended the conference permanently returned to Florence bringing with them classical manuscripts. In addition to these manuscripts many others were discovered "rotting in dust, mutilated to make psalters or amulets," and were found in some "foul dark dungeon," in tombs, or private chests. In some way or other these texts were doomed to oblivion but managed to be salvaged by those men who placed their value above even food. Among the works saved were the plays of Aeschylus, Sophocles, seven dramas of Euripides and works of Aristotle.

These manuscripts were the underpinnings in turning Italy from heaven to earth. The men who translated and devoted their lives to these classical texts were called "umanisti" (humanists) because

Terence and Seneca. Under this academy's influence, *De Architectura* by Vitruvius (c. 50-26 B.C.) was published in 1486. Vitruvius was an architect who served in the army under Julius and Augustus Caesar. *De Architectura* was a treatise in ten books on Roman architecture. The manuscript was lost until 1414 when it was unearthed by Poggio Bracciolini (1380-1459) at a monastery in St. Gall. *De Architectura*, written about the first century, had twenty-three editions by 1600 and remained an unquestioned authority as a source for Roman architecture for many years. The importance of Vitruvius can be noted in the formation in 1526 of the Academy Della Virtu, which was devoted to the study of his works.

The second institution to have an influence on the Italian Renaissance theatre was the royal court.

Italy was divided into independent city-states, each with its own capital city and court. These courts vied with each other politically and artistically in an effort to demonstrate that their city-state was superior. The man who epitomized the Italian political theory was Niccolò Machiavelli (1649-1527) whose work, *The Prince,* describes the common methods by which one rises to power. In addition to his political writings, Machiavelli is considered to have written perhaps the best comedy of the Renaissance: *La Mandragola* (1520).

In competing with each other, these courts staged the most spectacular productions. Within the palaces were indoor theatres at which were developed many of the scenic innovations to emerge from the period. By 1500, every court had a temporary or a permanent stage. The character-

---

MANDRAGOLA
NICCOLÒ MACHIAVELLI

CHARACTERS

CALLIMACO, in love with Lucrezia
SIRO, Callimaco's servant
NICA, Lucrezia's husband
LIGURIO, a parasite
SOSTRATA, Lucrezia's mother
TIMOTEO, a Friar
LUCREZIA, wife of Nica

SETTING: The action occurs on a street in Florence. To the right is Nica's house, Callimaco's is to the left, and between the two are the church and one or two other buildings. This setting approximates the setting for Roman comedy.

BACKGROUND: *The Mandragola* (The Mandrake) takes its title from the potion that is administered to Lucrezia in order to make her fertile. A satire on the corruption in the church, *The Mandragola* is concerned also with the vices and follies in society. Historians have acknowledged that this play may well be the best comedy written in the Italian language, and serves as a good example of the influence of Roman comedy.

SUMMARY:

Act I. Callimaco reveals to his servant, Siro, that while in Paris he got into a heated discussion with Cammillo Calfucci as to whether the most beautiful women were found in Italy or France. Cammillo said that even if all Italian women were "gorgons," there was a girl in his family, Madonna Lucrezia, who would win the competition for Italy by herself. Calfucci talked about her so much that Callimaco had to see her. He went back to Florence to see her and fell in love with her. In addition to Siro, Callimaco has also told Liguria of his love for Lucrezia and Ligurio has promised to help him. The problem is that Lucrezia is married to the lawyer, Nica, who though older than his wife, still has her loyalty. Ligurio comes to dinner and reveals that he has a plan. Part of it requires that Callimaco pretend he is a doctor of medicine. Ligurio leaves promising to return with details of the rest of the plan.

Act II. Nica wants a son but Lucrezia cannot conceive. Ligurio convinces Nica that Dr. Callimaco can solve his problem. When Nica meets Callimaco,

istic form of entertainment to be presented at the court theatre was the *intermezzi*.

Intermezzi and Opera

The intermezzi were lavish entertainments similar to the English masques and were used to honor births, weddings, royalty, or other such engagements. They were inserted between the acts of the tragedy or comedy being presented, which meant that there would be as many intermezzi as acts in the play; thus, a five-act play would have five intermezzi. By the 1570s, when intermezzi became more popular than the plays being presented, the five intermezzi were combined together like a play. In terms of subject matter, the intermezzi emphasized spectacle and were not related to the tragedy or comedy being staged.

About 1580, intermezzi were absorbed by opera, which was developed by a group of musicians and literary individuals interested in music. This group included Vincenzo Galilei (the father of Galileo), Jacopo Peri, Guilio Caccini, and Ottavio Rinuccini (a poet). These individuals formed an organization known as the Florentine Camerata. (*Camerata* is a term used to designate a club of students.) Believing that Greek tragedies were sung in their entirety, the Camerata set about resurrecting the music of the ancient Greeks. Seeking to conform to what they believed was the Greek concept, they devised a style of music known as recitative, which emphasized solo voices intermittently singing and speaking. Vincenzo Galilei wrote the first compositions about 1590; unfortu-

---

MANDRAGOLA, continued

Callimaco spouts phrases in Latin which impresses Nica. He believes that Callimaco is great. Callimaco prescribes a potion of mandragola (mandrake) for Lucrezia to drink. He tells Nica also that whoever is the first to have sexual relations with Lucrezia after she has drunk the potion will die. She is safe thereafter. Therefore, they tell Nica that they must find a victim. In reality, Callimaco will be the one to sleep with Lucrezia. Nica resists at first but he is convinced by Callimaco and Ligurio. Their problem is to convince Lucrezia to drink the potion and then have sex with a stranger. They hit upon a scheme whereby Lucrezia's mother will have her daughter go to Friar Timoteo for confirmation that she may have sex with a stranger. For this plan to work, they bribe Friar Timoteo, who is all too eager for the right price to say or do anything. Hence, the author is able to make his point about corruption in the church.

Act III. After convincing Lucrezia's mother of the potion and its effectiveness, Ligurio and Nica go to the church to bribe the Friar. With the bribe in place, Lucrezia and her mother go to the church where the Friar tells Lucrezia that she is not breaking any church vows and therefore she may carry out Dr. Callimaco's prescription. Lucrezia agrees, especially when her mother encourages her to "have a night's pleasure without it being a sin."

Act IV. It is agreed to go out that night and capture an unsuspecting victim. Unbeknownst to Nica, Callimaco will disguise himself and pretend to be drunk and thus seem to be the perfect victim. Nica expects Callimaco to be with them, however, when they kidnap the victim. Ligurio solves this aspect of the scheme by telling everyone that they must be disguised. Again, Lugurio goes to the Friar and for a price, the Friar agrees to disguise himself as Callimaco. Thus, Callimaco is free to be the victim. The act ends with Callimaco being captured and led off to Lucrezia's bed.

Act V. The plan works perfectly. Callimaco reveals his love to Lucrezia who, after being with a younger man, agrees to be Callimaco's mistress. Lucrezia convinces Nica that Dr. Callimaco is a man whose friendship he should cultivate. Therefore, Nica invites Callimaco to come to dinner, tells him to come over anytime, and even gives him a key to the house whereby he can come and go at his leisure. This works perfectly for Callimaco, who now has the woman of his dreams.

nately, they are now lost. The first short play was *Dafne* in 1594. Until 1637, operas were given only at court or under the auspices of the academies; in Venice the public was admitted to the performances. Due to the patronage of the Barberini family, opera gained in popularity. Through the intermezzi and the operas given at court theatres, perspective scenery, rapid changes of scenery, lighting devices, and stage machines were developed.

Sebastiano Serlio

Sebastiano Serlio (1475-1554) wrote *Architectura* between 1527 and 1547. Although there are five books, only a small section concerns the theatre. The second book, published in 1545, is considered the first Renaissance work to deal with the theatre. In this section on theatre, Serlio discusses perspective, how to construct scenery, a stage, and how to develop lights.

Perspective was the fundamental principle of the court theatre. The concept was rediscovered and developed by Filippo Brunelleschi (1377-1446),

and seems to have been first used in 1486 in Ferrara for *The Menaechmi* by Plautus. The first treatise on perspective is *Della Pittura* by Leon Battista Alberti (1404-1472), who built one of the earliest, if not the earliest, court theatres, when he constructed a stage in the Vatican for Nicholas V. The best example of a Renaissance theatre utilizing perspective is the Teatro Olimpico at Vicenza, begun by Andrea Palladio (1518-1580) in 1580, and finished in 1584 by his student Vincenzo Scamozzi (1552-1616). It is the oldest surviving Renaissance theatre. Its characteristic feature is its five doorways with a perspective scene behind each door. The limitation, however, was the fact that the scenes could not be shifted.

The changing or shifting of scenery occurred first in 1637 at the public opera house, Teatro di San Cassiano, Venice. The major step toward the construction of a theatre suitable for changing scenery, however, was the Teatro Farnese, built at Parma by Giovan Battista Aleotti (1546-1636) in 1618-1619 at the request of Ranuccio I. Farnese. The significance of this theatre is that it is the first theatre known to have a permanent proscenium

Serlio's tragic scene, from Serlio's *Architectura*, Book 2, 1569 edition. *Courtesy Fine Arts Library, Indiana University.*

Serlio's comic scene (top) and pastoral scene (bottom). From Serlio's *Architectura*, Book 2, 1569 edition. *Courtesy Fine Arts Library, Indiana University.*

arch (a picture frame stage), which also served to hide a complex rigging system above the stage proper.

The basic unit of perspective was the house. Each house had to be equal distance from one another and wide enough to prevent the audience from seeing backstage. The first houses were to be opposite each other and parallel to the stage front; they were to be built against the stage left and stage right proscenium walls. At a predetermined ratio, a series of houses would be placed next to those of the first houses and would continue to progress on a raked (sloping) stage toward a vanishing point at the back wall.

Serlio recommended three types of houses, one per dramatic form. For tragedy, he stated that the houses must be of great persons because all the violence, death, and accidents which occurred in ancient and modern tragedies happened in the houses of kings and other royalty. For comedy, the houses should be of private citizens—middle and lower classes. In addition, three of the houses should be a tavern, a church, and a house of prostitution. For the satyric or pastoral play, Serlio recommended outdoor scenery, and huts in which rustics lived.

The use of houses and scenes painted on canvas-covered wooden frames (flats) marked the beginning of the "wing system." The problem of transferring a perspective picture to flat wings was solved in 1600 by Guido Ubaldus. The first application of Ubaldus' principles belongs to Giovan Battista Aleotti. He began using them as early as 1606 in the Teatro dei Intrepidi in Ferrara, but they were not fully developed until 1619 when Aleotti used them in Parma at the Teatro

Farnese. Today we use the term wings to refer to the offstage area, but wings were originally painted scenery.

In the Renaissance there were three types of wings:

1. The angle wing: a three-dimensional reproduction of a house which showed only two sides—a front and a side. Today the angle wing persists as a "return" and a "tormentor," which are contemporary names for specific types of standing units of scenery (also termed "flats").

2. The periaktoi or triangular wing: revolving triangular prism with a different scene on each side.

3. The flat wing: a series of flats placed at the back of the stage, parallel to the audience. Eventually, flat wings replaced angle wings as the scenery for the seventeenth century stage. The dominance of the flat wings marks the victory of the stage painter over the stage architecture.

Nicola Sabbattini

The standard work on stage practices used at the Italian ducal courts in the late sixteenth and early seventeenth centuries was Nicola Sabbattini's (1574-1654) *Manual For Constructing Theatrical Scenes and Machines* (1638). In the second book of the *Manual*, Sabbattini turns his attention to the intermezzi, and a discussion of such devices as traps in the stage floor in which characters as well as scenery were raised and lowered, cylinders for dimming lights, ships moving on a rolling sea, a rainbow, clouds, lightning, wind, fire, flying actors, and the rapid shifting of scenery. Sabbattini recommends that when the scenery is to be shifted, someone be sent to the rear of the auditorium and, at the proper time, create a commotion or sound an instrument. In this way, the audience's attention will be drawn away from the stage, and they will not see the scenery changed.

As to the shifting of scenery, Sabbattini discusses four methods:

1. Dropping painted cloths over the scene.
2. Building grooves on the stage floor as well as overhead, and then sliding the desired flat in

front of the old one, or pulling the old flat offstage revealing the new flat behind it. The grooves and edges of the flats are soaped and two men per flat are needed for the shift.

3. Using periaktoi. The rotation of the periaktoi is accomplished by using two windlasses.

4. The fourth method relates to the flat wings and the shifting is similar to that in the second method. Flat wings eventually triumphed over the other scenic devices. For changing flat wings, Sabbattini suggested sliding a flat onstage or pulling one off by using a groove system. The back float wings could be changed by opening and shutting the flats like a door, or they could be bolted together as one unit and raised and lowered like a curtain.

In addition to the flat wings, Sabbattini suggested the use of a painted drop and borders to help mask out the backstage area. Wings, borders, and drops continued into the twentieth century as the dominant means of scenic representation. They are the forerunner to the present day "box-set."

Giacomo Torelli

The complete shifting of the wings, drops, and borders required a coordination of movement which could not be achieved manually. At the Teatro Novissimo in 1641, Giacomo Torelli (1608-1678), a pupil of Aleotti, perfected the "chariot and pole system," which is still in use at the Drottningholm and Gripsholm theatres in Sweden, and at Cesky Krumlov, a court theatre in Czechoslovakia. The system involved cutting slots into the stage floor. Underneath these slots, which were placed parallel to the stage, were tracks for carriages (chariots). The carriages were frames, constructed out of poles, with wheels attached. Torelli conceived the idea of connecting all the wings, drops, and borders to a central winching system which one man could operate by cranking a handle. By 1650 this rapid change of scenery became the standard for public theatres throughout most of Europe except in England, the Netherlands, and some parts of Germany. These countries retained the "groove system," which

Sabbattini discusses as his second suggestion for shifting scenery.

Torelli did most of his work between 1641-1645 in the public opera houses, which were the focal point of many of the new scenic ideas developed in the Italian Renaissance. Inasmuch as intermezzi were absorbed by opera, the intermezzi's emphasis on spectacle was also absorbed into opera.

One of the unique devices developed at opera houses was the cloud machine for creating various formations. Another device was the "glory," which was designed especially for lowering heavenly figures from the clouds. The figure could be suspended on a horse, sitting on a cloud, or riding in a chariot.

Joseph Furttenbach

Joseph Furttenbach (1591-1667) was a German who, like the English set designer Inigo Jones, studied in Italy and then took back to his native land the concept of Italianate scenery. Furttenbach's treatise, *The Noble Mirror of Art* (1663), is the only detailed account of stage lighting in the Renaissance. He discusses both the lighting equipment as well as where to place lamps on stage. For example, the discussion focuses on using individual candles with a reflector or grouping the candles in a chandelier. Although the candles smoked, the wax didn't smell of foul odors like oil, and they emitted better light. Furttenbach asserts there is a problem of wax falling on the audience members and ruining their clothes. He then suggests putting a plate or a bowl beneath each candle to catch the drippings. For aesthetic purposes, he recommends hanging the chandeliers at the sides of the stage so that they will not obstruct the audience's view of the stage machines and their effects.

In addition to candles, Furttenbach suggests using about one-fourth pound of olive oil with a wick. The latter will last twelve hours. One of the problems with this type of lighting is the bad smell given off by the burning oil. No matter what system is used, Furttenbach states that water in tubs and jars should be available beneath the stage, as well as above, for emergencies.

Literary Criticism

The literary principles formulated by Renaissance scholars formed the basis for French neo-classicism and English classicism. These principles were derived out of the Renaissance desires to justify creative literature, which the Middle Ages considered morally, aesthetically, and didactically unsound.

The medieval objections to creative literature were a reassertion of those stated by Plato in *The Republic*. Basically, Plato had three objections. Creative literature, he contended, arouses man's emotions, some of which are better not aroused. The ratings of movies today is a distant spin-off of this idea. Secondly, Plato objected to creative literature on the grounds of morality. This objection was based on Plato's assertion that Homer's work contained untruths, obscenity, and religious blasphemy. A third objection was the concept of reality. Literature is three times removed from reality (truth), contended Plato. The truth is in the mind of God, which is formed in life, and which in turn is imitated by the artist. In other words, the artist imitates life which imitates an idea in the mind of God. In addition to these ideas, the medievalist added a fourth—the value of creative literature in society. It was deemed to have no real function and, consequently, "the righteous man" was discouraged from engaging in such an occupation.

In an attempt to create a literature which could not be criticized on the basis of these objections, medievalists resorted to a fundamental concept of the age—symbolism. In interpreting literature, allegory was used. It was first popularized in the Middle Ages by Fulgentius in his *Mythologicon* during the first half of the sixth century. Liturgical and secular literature was thus interpreted and reinterpreted in terms of the allegorical method. Adam and Eve became symbols of virtue as well as of the moral struggle within man's soul. *The Aeneid* is treated like *Pilgrim's Progress* in that the travels of Aeneid symbolize the progress of the human soul from the beginning to final happiness. In the

Middle Ages, therefore, literature was justified as an extension of theology. It was not an independent creative form and, therefore, there could be no literary criticism of it.

Aristotle's *The Poetics* (c. 335-323 B.C.) was responsible for instituting literary criticism. *The Poetics* appears to have been lost until about the thirteenth century, at which time an oriental version of *The Poetics* was translated into Latin. The next important translation was Alessandro de Pazzi's Latin version in 1536, which established Aristotle's influence. In 1549 Bernardo Segni translated *The Poetics* into the vernacular (Italian), paving the way for the innumerable versions which have transcended into the twentieth century. One of these versions was particularly influential, that of Castelvetro in 1570. His misinterpretation of Aristotle was responsible for many of the "rules" by which the French and English of the sixteenth, seventeenth, and eighteenth centuries wrote drama.

In addition to *The Poetics*, Horace's *The Art of Poetry* (first century B.C.) played a part in the Renaissance justification of literature. The treatises of *Daniello* in 1536, *Minturno* in 1559, and Sidney's *The Defense of Poesie* (1595) display a justification of literature in terms of Horace. By combining Aristotle's *The Poetics* and Horace's *The Art of Poetry*, the Renaissance justified literature as a reputable, independent art form. Eventually, theories about what constitutes a good play, based on the concepts of imitation of Aristotle and Horace, resulted in firm rules which were the basis of French and English classicism. These rules established criteria for judging plays, and thus mark the beginning of literary criticism.

Commedia Dell'Arte

Commedia dell'arte means comedy of the profession, indicating that it was performed by professional actors. It was developed in opposition to the commedia erudita (learned comedy), which was performed by amateurs at the courts and academies.

Origins of the commedia dell'arte are unknown. Historians have variously linked it to the Atellan farce of the third century B.C., the wandering mime actors in the Middle Ages, and to the plays of Plautus and Terence. Complicating its history is the fact that it was known also as *commedia a soggetto* (comedy by subject), *commedia improvisa* (improvised comedy), *commedia a braccio* (comedy "off the cuff"), comedy of masks, and Italian comedy. Although it was being performed as early as 1545, the earliest description of a commedia dell'arte performance is that written by Orlando di Lasso in 1568.

There were three standard groups of characters: lovers, servants, and old men. These groups were the mainstays and were supported by other individual types. Unlike the learned or scripted comedy, the commedia dell'arte used no finished script. The actors of the commedia had an outlined story (scenario) which was posted offstage and they simply improvised the action and dialogue around the scenario. The lovers (men and women) were cast according to their looks and youth. They wore no masks, and their costumes represented the latest upperclass fashion. Servants were divided not only by male and female, but also as first and second servants. The female servants were *zagne;* later they were called *fantesche* (maids) or *servette* (soubrettes). They wore no masks, and were noted for the variety of costumes they wore. Zagne were specialists in quick changes and disguises. Their male counterparts were the *zanni*. *Harlequin* (the second zanni) is perhaps the most noted of all the commedia characters. The earliest example of a harlequin is dated about 1570 in a picture painted by Prolius the Elder. Brighella was the first zanni who functioned as the clever servant. The zanni wore masks and supplied much of the comedy through what was known as *lazzi* (stage business). For example, one actor would slap the other's mouth.

The last group was the old men. *Pantalone* was the first old man and the doctor was the second.

Seventeenth century French and Italian comic actors: the upper two and bottom left are French; the bottom right is Italian. From *Histoire Illustrée de la Littérature Française.*

Italian commedia dell'arte actors. From *Histoire Illustrée de la Littérature Française.*

Like the zanni, they wore masks, were generally in their sixties, fathers of families, and looking for a romantic escapade which led them to end up looking foolish.

Although commedia dell'arte continued into the eighteenth century, its peak of popularity was between 1570 and 1650. During that time there were numerous troupes, the most famous of which was the Gelosi company (1568-1604), which derived its name from *virtu fama ed honor ne fer gelosi* (zealous to please their audiences). Despite its decline, the influence of the commedia dell'arte on subsequent generations can be noted in the works of Molière and Shakespeare. In addition to the writers, modern comic actors owe much to the commedia dell'arte. The antics and slapstick comedy of Laurel and Hardy, Abbott and Costello, and the Marx Brothers echo the comedy of the commedia dell'arte

Selected Readings

Artz, Frederick B. *Renaissance Humanism 1300-1500.* Oberlin, OH, 1966.

Campbell, Lily Bess. *Scenes and Machines on the English Stage During the Renaissance.* Cambridge, 1923.

Hewitt, Barnard, ed. *The Renaissance Stage: Documents of Serlio, Sabbattini, and Furttenbach.* Coral Gables, FL, 1958.

Weinberg, Bernard. *A History of Literary Criticism in the Italian Renaissance.* 2 vols. Chicago, 1961.

Vocabulary

1. commedia dell'arte   koh MAY dyuh del AHR tay
2. De Architectura   day ahr ki tek TOOR uh
3. Vitruvius   vi TROO: vee uhs
4. intermezzi   in ter MET zee
5. Vincenzo Galilei   vin CHEN zoh gah li LAY ee
6. Jacopo Peri   JAH cuh poh PAIR ee
7. Giulio Caccini   JOOL: yoh cah CHEE nee
8. Ottavio Rinuccini   aw TAHV yoh ri noo: CHEE nee
9. Camerata   kah muh RAH tuh
10. recitative   re si tah TEEV
11. *Dafne*   DAHF nee
12. Sebastiano Serlio   se bah STYAH noh SAIR lee oh
13. Filippo Brunelleschi   fi LEE poh broo ne LES kee
14. Della Pittura   DEL lah pi TOOR uh
15. Leon Battista Alberti   lay AWN buh TEE stuh ahl BAIR tee
16. Teatro Olimpico   tay AHT roh oh LIM pee koh
17. Vicenza   vee CHEN zah
18. Andrea Palladio   ahn DRAY uh pah LAY dyoh
19. Vincenzo Scamozzi   vin CHEN zoh skuh MAWT zee
20. Teatro di San Cassiano   dee sahn kay SYAH noh
21. Teatro Farnese   fahr NAY zah
22. Giovan Battista Aleotti   joh VAHN buh TEE stuh ah lay AW tee
23. Guido Ubaldus   GWEE doh oo BAHL duhs
24. Teatro dei Intrepidi   in TRE pee dee
25. Nicola Sabbattini   NEE koh luh sah buh TEE nee
26. Giacomo Torelli   JAH kuh moh tawr REL ee
27. Teatro Novissimo   noh VI see moh
28. Drottningholm   DRAWT ning hawlm
29. Gripsholm   GRIPS hawlm
30. Cesky Krumlov   CHE skuh KROOM luf
31. Furttenbach   FOOR ten bahk
32. Mythologicon   mi thoh LAW gi kawn
33.. Daniello   dah NYEL loh
34. Minturno   min TOOR noh
35. commedia erudita   koh MAY dyuh e roo DEE tuh
36. commedia a soggetto   ah saw JET toh
37. commedia all 'improvisa   ahl eem proh VEE zah
39. zagne   ZAHN yee
40. fantesche   fahn TES kay
41. servette   ser VET
42. soubrettes   soo: BRETS
43. zanni   ZAHN yee
44. Harlequin   HAHR luh kwin
45. Prolius   proh LEE uhs
46. Grighella   gri GEL luh
47. lazzi   LAHT zee
48. Pantalone   pahn tah LOH nee
49. Geolosi   Je LOH zee
50. Machiavelli   MAK ee a VEL ee

CHAPTER EIGHT

&

The City and the Crown: English Theatre and Drama to 1642

The Globe Theatre about 1612. From *Londina Illustrata, 18′*

Historically, the Elizabethan period (1558-1603) represents a transition from medieval theatre and drama to modern theatre and drama. Its drama was a merging of two distinct forces: the classical drama as resurrected and developed by the Italian Renaissance, and the popular entertainments which were continued from the Middle Ages. At the beginning of the 1580s, these two forces came together to form what is now regarded as the Elizabethan theatre/drama represented by Shakespeare, Marlowe, and others. With regard to this period, the most outstanding contributions of the Elizabethan period were the development of significant dramatists and drama and the establishment of the profession of acting.

The death of Elizabeth in 1603 technically ends the Elizabethan period. James I (who reigned from 1603-1625) ushered in the Jacobean period. This period is characterized by the works most notably of John Fletcher (1579-1625) and Francis Beaumont (c. 1584-1616). Also significant in this period is the Stuart masque, so named because James I was of the House of Stuart. These dramatic performances were popularized at his court and later at the court of his son, Charles I, who reigned from 1625-1649. Upon the death of James I, Charles I succeeded to the throne and the period became known historically as the Caroline period. During the reign of Charles I, the theatres were closed in 1642 and were not to reopen until 1660.

The interior of Gray's Inn Hall.

Universities and Inns of Court

Humanism, or "new learning," which began in Italy about the fourteenth century, was an important development in Europe; it established the educational system and the cultural tastes of the upperclasses during the sixteenth and seventeenth centuries. Thus education and refinement were the hallmarks of a person belonging to the elite class; money or inherited status were considered insufficient for a person to belong to this select group. Although the Italians borrowed this concept of what makes a superior person from the French aristocracy of the thirteenth century, they changed it enough so that in countries such as England, one wishing to become a truly Renaissance individual had to take lessons from the Italian humanists. Under Henry VII, a Tudor who reigned from 1485-1509, Italian humanists came to England to teach classical arts, literature, and philosophy. The effect was noted in the imitations and revivals of Roman drama at universities. The plays were written and performed in Latin as well as English, and their main subject matter focused on Roman life and literature. Two plays written at the universities are outstanding demonstrations of the influence of Plautus and Terence—Nicholas

Howell's View of London, 1620. From Wilkinson's *Londina Illustrata*, 1825.

Udall's *Ralph Roister Doister* (c. 1534-41) and a composition by "Mr. S" (perhaps William Stevenson) entitled *Gammer Gurton's Needle* (c. 1552-1563).

The universities were not the only institutions to be affected by humanism. Closely related to the universities were Inns of Court, which were schools to train upper-class gentlemen as lawyers as well as to instruct them in all the social graces, music, and dancing. The first English tragedy, *Gorboduc* or *Ferrex and Porrex* (1561), was written by two students, Thomas Sackville and Thomas Norton, of Inner Temple, and displays an influence of the Roman dramatist Seneca. In addition to writing tragedy modeled after Seneca, the Inns presented contemporary Italian drama and staged court masques, which later flourished under James I.

The Merging of Forces

Two forces contributed to the development of Elizabethan drama. The first was the native or popular drama performed by professional actors for the public theatre; it represented a continuation of the morality plays and interludes developed in the Middle Ages. In order to attract as many people as possible, the actors added to the popular drama diverse elements from romantic stories, classical myths, history, and the Bible, and also inserted comic scenes.

On the other end of the spectrum was the second force which, unlike the public theatre, tended to be for a select audience. The actors were amateurs and the plays, written by teachers and students, were a result of the "new learning."

About 1585, the native tradition (popular entertainment) and the classical influence began to merge. This blending of the two dominant forces into Elizabethan drama was due to the efforts of a group of young playwrights known as the University Wits.

University Wits

Apparently the University Wits were so-called because all were associated with the university and all possessed the faculty of wit, which in the Elizabethan period was defined as "smart knowing," repartee, joking, or invention. The outstanding members were Thomas Kyd (1558-1594), Christopher Marlowe (1564-1593), John Lyly (1554-1606), and Robert Greene (1558-1592). William Shakespeare was not a member of "the University Wits."

Thomas Kyd is best remembered for his play *The Spanish Tragedy* (c. 1587), which popularized tragedy for the public theatre. Before Kyd, tragedy was confined to the upper classes, but with *The Spanish Tragedy*, tragedy crossed the boundaries from the classical to popular entertainment. The play's success was due to the fact that it contained classical (Senecan) elements and was also popular entertainment. Kyd's use of a ghost demanding revenge and a play within a play indicates an influence on Shakespeare's *Hamlet*. Although Kyd was the only member of the University Wits not to graduate from a university, he was, nonetheless, extremely well-educated.

The oldest member of the group was John Lyly. Lyly catered to the court, which favored love as a subject for dramatization. Consequently, the central theme of most of his plays is courtly love. His prose novel *Euphues* (1578) introduced the term *euphuism*, which is characterized by flowery prose based on mythology or nature, carefully balanced blending of elements, similes, alliterations, and antithesis. Antithesis is contrasting ideas; for example: "Extremism in pursuit of justice is no vir-

tue, and moderation in pursuit of liberty is no vice." This use of flowery or euphuistic language is a chief characteristic of Lyly. His romantic comedies proved to be an influence on Shakespeare's *A Midsummer Night's Dream* and *As You Like It*.

Robert Greene disliked Shakespeare and indicated this in his pamphlet *A Groatsworth of Wit Bought with a Million of Repentance* (1592), in which he called Shakespeare an "upstart crow." As a dramatist, Greene wrote primarily pastorals and romantic comedy, the best known romantic comedy being *Friar Bacon and Friar Bungay* (c. 1580). His masterpiece, *James IV* (c. 1591), is said to have been a forerunner to the development of English tragi-comedy.

Christopher Marlowe has been called by scholars the "most brilliant and interesting of the University Wits." His life and death are shrouded somewhat in mystery. His best known play is *The Tragicall History of Doctor Faustus* (c. 1588), and his *Edward II* (c. 1592) is considered the model for the chronicle play. Although other writers used blank verse, Marlowe perfected it as a medium for drama. Marlowe's work also emphasizes the construction of a play around a single character. The titles of some of his plays testify to this: *Doctor Faustus, Edward II, Tamburlaine, Parts I and II,* and *The Jew of Malta.* Christopher Marlowe's work represents, more than any of the University Wits, the culmination of classical and native traditions being blended. As a group the University Wits are to be credited for aiding the transitional period between medieval and Elizabethan drama as well as paving the way for the work of William Shakespeare.

William Shakespeare

William Shakespeare (1564-1616) is considered in most quarters the greatest dramatist of all time. In addition to being a writer, he was an actor, owned shares in the Lord Chamberlain's Company, and was part owner of several theatre buildings. He is one of the few figures of the Elizabethan stage not indebted to Phillip Henslowe, a pawn-

William Shakespeare

broker, theatre owner, and general businessman.

Shakespeare's writing career spans the years 1591 to 1611, during which time he wrote thirty-eight plays. As a dramatist, he borrowed extensively, using titles, plots, and sometimes lines. His general education was not extensive and his plays indicate his lack of knowledge. He put a clock in *Julius Caesar*, gave Bohemia a seacoast, placed Aristotle in the third century B.C., and made numerous other errors. As a psychologist, he was first rate, however. His insights about life and human nature are as true today as they were then.

Shakespeare's masterful use of language is unsurpassed. His colleagues testified that Shakespeare never blotted a line, to which Ben Jonson quipped that he "wished to God [Shakespeare] blotted a thousand." His dialogue was not only poetic but particularly abounds with dramatic imagery. Perhaps his only match in the use of imagery was Aeschylus. Shakespeare's plays demonstrate wit, inventiveness, sensitivity, and thoughtfulness. He did not confine himself to one form, but wrote tragedies, comedies, chronicles, and melodramas. These dramas display characters from all walks of life; indeed, his plays imitate life. Perhaps one reason for Shakespeare's greatness is his range in stories, language, and characters, and his ability to relate them to his audience. For Shakespeare these audiences have been of every generation since he penned his work. His plays are timeless; they speak to everyone.

Shakespeare's plays were first published in 1623 by two of his fellow actors, John Heming and Henry Condell, whose intentions were "only to keep the memory of so worthy a friend." This first publication of thirty-six of Shakespeare's plays is known as the First Folio. The First Folio sold at the time for one pound; today there are 200 extant copies, each conservatively valued at more the 20,000 pounds. Only the Gutenberg Bible demands a higher price.

Despite the high regard we hold for Shakespeare, he was not always considered great. His reputation fluctuated throughout the ages. Milton, the poet, praised him in 1630, but when the theatres closed in 1642, his fame ceased. Later, seventeenth century English writers revived his work but were forced to revise it because society considered it too immoral for the age. Seventeenth century France cared little for Shakespeare, whereas eighteenth century German romantics praised him. In eighteenth century England, Shakespeare's reputation became established with a return to his original works. The first critical edition of his work and the first biography were published in 1709 by Nicholas Rowe. The nineteenth century romantics cemented Shakespeare's reputation in England and France. Although Shakespeare reigns supreme today, it was Ben Jonson who was considered the best dramatist while Shakespeare was alive.

Government Regulation

The political and religious struggle between the Church of Rome and England, and between the local and national governments which began in the reign of Henry VIII, continued during the reign of Elizabeth. How Elizabeth attempted to solve these struggles directly affected the rise of the professional actor.

One of the first edicts to affect actors was an order on May 16, 1559, banning all religious or political plays, presentation of unlicensed plays, and making all local officials responsible for performances in their areas. Two points should be noted here. First, the act was designed to curtail possible riot and rebellion against the government through the misuse of drama and to make sure that the heretofore uncertain enforcement of the Crown's policies by the local officials was corrected. Second, Elizabeth was constantly in need of money and loyal servants. The use of monopolies served to accomplish these aims best, since she could show favor and reward services at little cost by granting a license. The licensing of actors was such a favor.

Despite the 1559 act, London officials continued to suppress performances, citing reasons of health. The city was within its rights, since an act of Parliament had granted London officials the power to compel each house-owner to keep his premises clean. In actuality, the Lord Mayor of London believed himself to be the guardian of the city's morals. Moreover, city officials were concerned about the city's industry. The problem of plays drawing citizens from their jobs led officials to use the plague as an excuse to ban plays and actors.

The political-religious struggle was intensified in 1570 when the Pope excommunicated Queen Elizabeth. Concerned about the actor and his ability to spread sedition and heresy through drama, the government issued the 1572 Licensing Act. This act paved the way for the recognition of acting as a profession. The ordinance allowed actors a choice of two licenses: (1) they could belong to any Baron of the realm or "other honorable personage of greater degree"; (2) they could obtain a license from two justices of the peace in each town they played. As a result of the 1572 Licensing Act, religious plays were suppressed and the number of acting companies became lim-

ited; thus the keeping of actors became a status symbol. As for the justices of peace, it appeared that actors had to buy licenses from these local officials. The licensing system could therefore be used as a financial reward as well as a safeguard against the use of drama for antigovernment purposes. The licensing system was revised in 1574, 1584-1585, 1597-1598, and 1604. After 1604, only members of the royal family were allowed to keep acting companies.

Inasmuch as the 1572 act threatened the existence of those actors not attached to a household, a group of actors headed by James Burbage appealed to the Earl of Leicester to form a company. What resulted was the 1574 Licensing Act which granted to the Earl of Leicester the first royal patent. The act itself gave Leicester's company complete freedom to perform when and where they liked without interference except during time of "common prayer" or plague. The only stipulation was that the Master of Revels, an official of the Crown, approve the plays. This gave the Crown complete authority over plays and actors.

Public and Private Theatres: The Dual Tradition

During the Elizabethan period, actors were guided by two traditions: the indoor and the outdoor. Since the late Middle Ages, these two traditions existed simultaneously, for while actors performed within halls, town houses, inns, and churches, they also presented plays in various outdoor areas—for example, inn yards, streets, or village greens. To conclude that the actors adhered to playing solely indoors or outdoors is not warranted by the available evidence. Further, the assumption that inn yards, baiting rings, or other theatre building were prototypes for the Elizabethan theatre is also untenable. The simultaneous tradition of outdoor and indoor performances led to the use of indoor and outdoor theatres, which is demonstrated in the public and private theatres.

Private Theatres

Private theatres were indoor theatres. They were roofed, charged more than the public theatres, had an audience capacity which was roughly one-half of the public theatres, provided seats for all spectators, used candles, catered to an aristocratic audience, and were located within the city of London. Although the theatres were located within the city limits, they were not subject to the legal injunctions that the city officials imposed upon other playing areas. These theatres were situated within the "liberties," which means a self-governing community. The "liberties" belonged to monastic orders, but when Henry VIII broke with Rome he confiscated all church property and placed it under the control of the Crown. Thus these private theatres were protected by the royal government.

The private theatres were known by the monastic order which controlled the liberty wherein they performed. Thus, the first private theatre was known as the First Blackfriars, after the Dominican monks or Black Friars. The private theatre opened in 1606, called the Whitefriars, was named after the Carmelites or White Friars. The first Blackfriar's theatre opened in 1576 under the direction of William Farrant.

The next private theatre was the second Blackfriars which James Burbage built in 1596. This theatre is considered the most important private theatre because, up to that time, private theatres had been the domain of boys' companies, and Burbage intended his theatre as a winter home for his adult company—the Lord Chamberlain's Men. Although local residents of the liberty prevented Burbage from opening by citing his use of adult actors rather than children, the concept of adult troupes performing at private theatres was eventually sanctioned by James I in 1608. At this time, the King's Men performed successfully at the Second Blackfriars. The success of an adult company (the King's Men) prompted others to build private or indoor theatres; about 1610 these theatres became the primary winter homes of the adult companies. While the adult companies used the private theatres from roughly mid-October to mid-May, they performed at public or outdoor theatres for the other five months.

The Old Tabard Inn, sketched shortly before its demolition. Actors possibly performed in inn yards similar to this one. Thornbury, *Old and New London.*

Theatre Structure

Public Theatres

With new discoveries pertaining to the Elizabethan theatre being made, scholars have had to revise their thinking about certain aspects of its structure. Yet on some areas they are still in accord. Most accept that the stage extended into the yard—how far is questioned. The stage was raised four to six feet and the audience viewed the action on three sides. The height of the stage provided an under area (termed "the hell") which could be used as a trapdoor and for storage space. A roof covered the stage (called "the shadow" or "the heavens") to protect the stage from inclement weather and to house machinery such as wenches to raise and lower people and scenery. In some cases, the roof was painted on the underside with astrological signs of the zodiac, and was permanent except at the Hope where the roof was removable to accommodate other events.

At the rear of the stage were at least two doors used for entrances, exits, removing properties and scenic pieces. The use of an inner-stage located on the stage level has divided scholars as to its size, location and actual use. Most agree, however, that some sort of discovery space or spaces existed. Another controversy centers on the second level of the stage as to the amount of acting that occurred here. As to a third level, if it existed, scholars theorize that this was the "musicians' gallery," although acting could have taken place here.

As to the auditorium, it surrounded an open area called the yard, which was paved and sloped towards the stage. There were three galleries.

Private Theatres

Private theatres like the Blackfriars were constructed within large rooms. (The Blackfriars measured 46 feet wide by 66 feet long.) There were two or three galleries, a pit with seats, some private boxes, a raised stage ranging from three feet to four feet, six inches, which was open and without a front curtain or proscenium. Based upon the plans conjecturally identified as those by Inigo Jones, the Cockpit in Drury Lane had a raised stage, three doors on the stage level, one large opening on the second level, an elliptical-shaped auditorium with two galleries extending to the stage on either side.

The Swan Theatre as it appeared in 1614. From *Londina Illustrata*, 1825.

Model of the original stage for Stratford, England. *Courtesy British Tourist Authority.*

were primarily choirboys who were at court chapels and cathedrals. Although these boys were given a good education, they were exploited by the choirmasters who charged admission to the children's plays. In the seventeenth century the use of schoolboys took the place of the choirboys and their popularity continued until about 1610. The children's companies were very sophisticated, had the best dramatists of the period write for them (except Shakespeare), and played to the more educated audiences. Their decline is attributed in part to taking over the theatres and the plays which had been associated with the child troupes.

The adult companies were composed of three types of members: shareholders, "hired men," and boys. For an actor to be a shareholder required two things: that the actor put up a large sum of money and that the actor be invited to be a sharer. Not all the actors were shareholders and not all the shares were equal. As a shareholder, an actor participated in selecting and producing the plays, was accorded special privileges by the royal patron, and played the major roles. The nonsharing adult members were called the "hired men," and most worked under a weekly contract. Their job description included being janitor, prompter, stagehand, and other menial positions. They were paid by the shareholders and thus were not considered actors. The last group consisted of boys who probably played the women's roles, and every company had four to six (ages six to fourteen) who were apprenticed to the company for a period lasting from three to twelve years. During that time, the boys lived with their masters who trained and provided for them. In return, the masters were paid by the company.

The procurement and production of a play were usually done as follows: a playwright read a part or all of his play to the shareholders. If the company bought the play, it belonged to the company. Inasmuch as these troupes changed their bills frequently, they were constantly looking for new plays. This is a major reason as to why some dramatists were under contract to a specific acting troupe. Writers were paid a fee plus the receipts

Another private theatre, the Cockpit in Court, was a theatre used by professional companies when they played at court. The significance of this theatre is that it appears not to have had an inner stage and its second level had only one opening to be used for acting. Inasmuch as the plays performed at this theatre came from the public and private theatres and were performed by the professional companies, the stage must have been similar to the stages in other theatres. Thus, a strong argument has been forwarded that the plans from this theatre plus the excavations of the Rose indicate that the Elizabethan theatre did *not* have an "inner-stage" or a sizeable acting area on either the first or second level.

Acting Companies

Between the years 1558 and 1642, there were two types of acting companies: adult and children. In the sixteenth century the children's companies

Fac-similes of the title-page of Maroccus Extaticus, 1595, and of the rare engraving which represents Banks exhibiting the feats of his celebrated Dancing-horse, in the yard of the Bel-Savage.

Maroccus Extaticus.
Or,

B A N K E S

BAY HORSE IN

a Trance.

A Difcourfe fet downe in a merry Dialogue, between Bankes and his beaft: Anatomizing fome abufes and bad trickes of this age.

Written and intituled to mine Hoft of the Belfauage, and all his honeft Guefts.

By Iohn Dando the wierdrawer of Hadley, and Harrie Runt, head Oftler of Bofomes Inne.

Printed for Cuthbert Burby.
1 5 9 5.

A rare print of an entertainment at an Elizabethan inn yard. Cuthbert Burbage, who was responsible for the construction of the Globe Theatre in 1599, was the son of James Burbage, builder of the first public theatre, The Theatre, in England.

(minus expenses) of the second performance. Once the arrangement with the writer was clear, the play was submitted to the Master of Revels (see government regulations) for licensing. If approved and performed, the play's receipts (minus expenses) were divided between the sharers according to the number of shares each actor had. "Hired men" were considered part of the expenses and thus had to be paid first. When the companies played at court, they were paid a fee and they received a yearly fee plus an allowance for food, light and fuel from their royal patron.

Although there were many companies, the most important were the Earl of Leicester's Men (1530-1597), headed by James Burbage, the Queen's Men (1583-1593), the Lord Admiral's Men, headed by Edward Alleyn, and the Lord Chamberlain's Men for whom Shakespeare wrote. In 1603 the Lord Chamberlain's company became known as the King's Men in honor of James I and subsequently his son, Charles I. Many adult troupes had their names changed during the reign of James I and all were under the patronage of a member of the royal family.

Ben Jonson and the Court Masques

Ben Jonson (1572-1637) was England's first poet laureate in 1616. His first success was *Everyman in*

His Humour (1598), a play in which Shakespeare acted. Humours referred to yellow bile, black bile, green phlegm, and red blood. These four fluids were thought to be within the body, and the predominance of one element over the others determined a person's behavior. By the end of the sixteenth century, the term came to mean whim of fancy. Jonson, however, used the term to denote an imbalance of the fluids; hence, his play *Everyman Out of His Humour* (1599). Should a person become ill, display emotional outbursts or any unusual behavior, the humours were considered out of balance and a purging or bloodletting was required to keep everyman in his humour. *Valpone or The Fox* (1606) rates as Jonson's best comedy and has been produced frequently. In 1977 it was on Broadway as *The Sly Fox*. His major efforts in writing, however, were the court masques.

The English word masque with this spelling was first used in Edward Hall's *Chronicle* in 1548, but the history of masques is traceable to the pageantry of the Middle Ages. The court masques were introduced into England by Henry VIII, but under Elizabeth they were relegated to occasional performances at the Inns of Court. During the reign of James I, however, one a year was produced, mostly at the Banqueting Hall at Whitehead Palace, and this was increased to two under Charles I, who built a special room for the masques. A favorite of James I, Jonson was responsible for writing the majority of scripts and Inigo Jones (1573-1652), England's first important set designer) undertook the design of the scenery.

The court masque placed its emphasis upon the courtier dances. Because nobility did not wish to be labeled actors, they confined their theatrical activities to dancing and left the singing and dialogue to the court musicians, and the comic roles to the professional actors. (Note the twelve nobles who performed in *The Hue and Cry After Cupid.*). As a form, the court masque consisted of lords and ladies who were masked and dressed as mythological characters, shepherds, or other figures. An entrance dance was performed by these nobles and then they went into the audience to dance

many of the well-known dances of the day, called revels. There was also a "going out" dance. By wearing masks and costumes and dancing as the character they represented, the nobles were taking roles in a play. The masque consisted at first of disguised nobles acting out a role, not with dialogue but through the dances, which were symbolic of events or characters. As the masque developed and became more elaborate, dramatists developed allegorical stories into which were interwoven the dances as well as lines spoken by professional actors. In 1608 Jonson added another dimension to the masque when he introduced a comic dance with characters speaking satiric humor. This new form was known as the anti-masque. The anti-masque contrasted sharply with the formal masque and was probably performed by professional actors.

Scenery was considered a "special display" feature of the masque. For some plays, it was a special feature and, for others, an extra adornment. In the Caroline period, some masques did not use scenery. The scenic work of Inigo Jones, however, proved to be an influence on the development of scenery in the English public theatre. Jones went to Italy in 1600 and returned in 1604. When he came back, he brought with him the principles of Italianate scenery, which he used in his designs for court masques. His designs for the court masques included perspective scenery, a proscenium arch, rapid shifting of scenery, and machines. Despite their successes, Jonson and Jones quarreled, apparently over the importance of scenery with respect to the script. Ben Jonson apparently viewed the masque as "an entertainment of moral and intellectual profit," whereas Inigo Jones regarded it as a "mere spectacular amusement." As a result, Jonson lost his patronage with the king and was forced to return to the public theatre. The last masque, *Salmacida Spolia*, was staged in 1640.

Not only did masques prove influential to the public theatre, they also exerted a part in the political fortunes of Charles I. Court masques were extravagantly produced by James I as well as Charles I. The money spent for these productions

A MASQUE
THE HUE AND CRY AFTER CUPID (1608)
BEN JONSON

CHARACTERS

CUPID
VULCAN
HYMEN
VENUS
PYRACMON: cyclop
BRONTES: cyclop
STEROPES: cyclop
GRACES 1, 2, AND 3

SETTING: A high steep cliff ascending toward the clouds. On the two sides of the cliff, Jonson calls for two pilasters to be erected "charged with spoils and trophies of Love, and his mother, consecrate to marriage; amongst which were old and young persons figured, bound with roses, the wedding garments, rocks and spindles, hearts transfixed with arrows, others flaming, virgins' girdles, girlonds [garlands], and worlds of suchlike, all wrought around and bold; overhead two personages, Triumph and Victory, in flying postures, and twice so big as life, in place of the arch, and holding a girlond of myrtle for the key—all which with the pillars seemed to be of burnished gold, and embossed out of the metal." Behind the cliff are thick clouds which break revealing Venus in a chariot being drawn by two swans in silver trappings. Beneath her are the three Graces (Aglaia, Thalia, Euphrosyne). She gets out of her chariot and descends down the cliff on foot, the Graces strewing garlands as she descends.

BACKGROUND: The title of this masque in the 1616 folio reads: "The Description of the Masque with the Nuptial Songs at the Lord Viscount Haddington's Marriage at Court on the Shrove Tuesday at Night 1608." The bride was Lady Elizabeth Radcliffe and inasmuch as Radcliffe refers to red cliff, Jonson used a red cliff as his setting. The Haddington Masque was given the title *The Hue and the Cry After Cupid* by William Gifford (1816 ed. of Jonson's work) and was presented at Court on February 9, 1608, for the Haddington-Radcliffe marriage. As noted in the section on masques, nobles did not wish to be identified as actors, and therefore only danced. To participate in this masque

cost the five English and seven Scottish gentlemen £300 each. Haddington was a favorite of King James and the King drank a toast to their health in a solid gold cup which he later sent to them with as grant of £600 pension a year to them and their survivors. Although short, this masque is representative of Jonson's work. As to Inigo Jones' set designs for this masque, they have been lost.

SUMMARY: Venus opens the masque by querying the Graces of her son Cupid's whereabouts. The Graces do not know where he is and thus Venus offers a reward to the woman that reveals where Cupid is hiding. The Graces begin their search by asking all the women (presumably in the audience) if they have seen Cupid. They give a physical description of him and warn women to "Trust him not; his words, though sweet, Seldom with his heart do meet. All his practice is deceit, Every gift it is a bait, Not a kiss but poison bears, And most treason is his tears." They end by asking the "beauties" (a term for the women in the audience) not to hide him as he is "Venus' runaway."

Cupid appears from behind the trophies. He is armed and attended by twelve boys that represent "the Sports and pretty Lightnesses that accompany Love." Cupid tells the Sports to "Advance your light. With your revel fill the room." The twelve boys each carrying two torches begin to dance, incorporating in this dance a variety of ridiculous gestures and generally adding to the merriment of the audience. The dance ends and Cupid comes forward to speak. His speech is short as his mother Venus grabs him. She confronts him as to what kind of mischief he has been engaged in but he slips away before she receives an answer.

In order to extoll the virtues of the bride and groom, Jonson has Hymen, the God of Marriage, enter. He informs Venus that Cupid has been doing his work as noted by the groom, whose virtues are praised and the bride, who is cited as the model of purity. Now Vulcan enters, dressed in a "cassock girt to him, with bare arms, his hair and beard rough, his hat of blue and ending in a cone, in his hand a hammer and tongs, as coming

THE HUE AND CRY AFTER CUPID, continued

from the forge." He notes how he has forged his best work for this wedding. At this juncture and with "loud and full music," the cliff parts and reveals a brilliantly lighted "concave, filled with an ample and glistering light, in which an artificial sphere" made of silver measuring eighteen feet in diameter "that turns perpetually." The effect is heightened with parts of the globe and the zodiac being colored in gold. Vulcan then describes his creation in the following speech. Under each sign of the zodiac, a masquer is presented (the five Englishmen and seven Scotchmen who paid 300 pounds) who physically represents the astrological sign. As the sphere turns, the masquers dressed in "carnation and silver, enriched both with embroidery and lace; the dressing of their heads, feathers and jewels" are given individual atten-

tion by Vulcan who makes a comment about each sign.

Venus returns to her chariot with the Graces. As she does, Vulcan is calling for the Priests of Hymen who are represented by the musicians. He is interrupted by the Cyclops requesting that the musicians come forward and dance. "Attired in yellow, with wreaths of marjoram, and veils" the musicians dance four dances interspersed with song with the masquers who are lauded for their excellent work. The masque ends with a speech praising both the bride and groom as well as emphasizing the sexual union that is about to occur out of which will be born "a babe t' uphold the fame of Radcliffe's blood and Ramsey's [family name of Viscount Haddington] name."

was a luxury Charles I could not afford. About 1640, when he was broke, he asked Parliament for additional funds which they refused. Civil war ensued. Inasmuch as the majority of the enemies of Charles I were Puritans who were also antitheatre, they used the civil war as an excuse for closing the theatres in 1642 for five years. In 1647 the Puritans gained control of the government and in 1649 Charles I was beheaded. With the Puritans in control, the public theatres remained closed until 1660 when Charles II was restored to the throne.

Selected Readings

Chambers, E. K. *The Elizabethan Stage.* 4 vols. London, 1923.

Eccles, Christine. *The Rose Theatre.* New York, 1990.

Gurr, Andrew. *Playgoing in Shakespeare's London.* Cambridge, 1987.

Orrell, John. *The Human Stage: English Theatre Design, 1567-1640.* New York, 1988.

"Shakespeare: An Annotated Bibliography," *Shakespeare Quarterly* (1924-present).

Vocabulary

1. Jacobean   ja kuh BEE uhn
2. *Ralph Roister Doister*   ralf ROY ster DOY ster
3. *Gorboduc*   GAWR buh duhk
4. masque   mask
5. Thomas Kyd   kid
6. John Lyly   LIL ee
7. Euphues   YOO: fyoo eez
8. euphuism   YOO: fyoo iz uhm
9. *Doctor Faustus*   FOW stuhs
10. *Tamburlaine*   TAM buhr layn
11. James Burbage   BER bij
12. Earl of Leicester   LE ster
13. phlegm   flem
14. *Volpone*   vawl POH nee
15. Inigo Jones   IN i goh

CHAPTER 9

❧

The Transformation:
Birth of the Bourgeois Theatre

François-Joseph Talma (1763-1826) as Manlius in a revival of *Manlius Capitolinus* (1806). Talma, a favorite of Napoleon and considered by many to rival Molière as the greatest French actor, was the first French actor to play Roman parts in historically accurate costume.

Diastrophism is a geological term describing severe folding of the earth's crust. Yet, it is a word that might well describe the convulsions in the structure of aristocratic European society from the middle of the seventeenth century to late eighteenth century. In a sense, it was a progression from the relatively logical or seemingly logical approach to life to a new and, in some ways, revolutionary redefinition of the Western European value system. The philosophical evolution from the writings of Newton, Locke and Rousseau to the innovations of François-Marie Arouet de Voltaire and the Age of Reason were to give rise to a new middle class and a new order. The visual arts were producing some of the great works of all time through the genius of Rubens, Vandyck, Rembrandt, El Greco and Vélazquez. But most of all, the seventeenth century produced the birth of the neoclassical ideal which was to set the standard for drama during the entire period. It was a period of change, which saw the focus of power move from Spain to France, but not before the Spanish drama reached its apogee between the years 1580 and 1680, a period which has been designated the Golden Age of Spanish literature.

Spain's Golden Age

The Golden Age produced two outstanding playwrights, Lope Félix de Vega Carpio, known as Lope de Vega (1562-1635), and Pedro Calderón de la Barca (1600-1681), called Calderón. Voltaire has placed Lope beside Shakespeare in the measure of his work. He does not deserve such an honor, qualitatively perhaps, but if quantity is any measure, Lope must rate high. He was one of the most prolific playwrights of all time, writing over 1800 plays of which more than 450 are extant.

Born in Madrid, Lope de Vega had an eventful, not always exemplary, life. His ability to turn out plays was phenomenal, to say the least. Cervantes is reported to have called him "monster of nature."

Tradition has it that he composed ten plays in one week. Evidences does suggest that he wrote at least two a week during the latter part of his career. There is no question that Lope de Vega was the idol of Madrid. Crowds followed him and it is said that women and children asked for his blessing (he was an ordained priest). As with today's idols, his name was given to objects considered the best of their kind. There were Lope horses, Lope melons, and Lope cigars.

Lope's plays are difficult to translate because they are written in rhymed poetry. For that reason, his fame is confined primarily to Spain. His most popular work for modern audiences is *The Sheep Well (Fuente Ovejuna,* c. 1614). *The Star of Seville (La Estrella de Sevilla)* remains his most famous play in Spain.

Lope's most challenging rival was Pedro Calderón de la Barca. Son of a finance minister under Phillip I and III, he was schooled at Salamanca by the Jesuits who, by the way, were the only religious order allowed to use drama in their teachings. While Lope was primarily associated with the public theatre, Calderón wrote for the court. His most famous secular play is *Life Is a Dream (La Vida es Sueno,* c. 1636), which is a philosophical allegory about the mystery of life.

Perhaps more than anything else, Calderón is noted for his religious plays called *autos sacramentales.* These plays were similar to morality plays in which human and supernatural characters met allegorical figures such as Sin, Grace, Pleasure, etc. The plays always demonstrated the validity of church dogma.

The theatres of seventeenth century Spain were called *corrales*. The corrales were not uniform in design, but there were many common features. Most were constructed around rectangular courtyards. The balconies of surrounding buildings were used to seat spectators, while standing room was provided in the courtyard or *patio* for men only; the women were forced to sit in a gallery called the *cazuela*. The stage was at the end of the yard.

The Birth of the New France

Beginning at the turn of the seventeenth century, France quickly achieved cultural dominance over Western Europe. Certainly by 1650, writers, painters, sculptors and architects made Paris the creative capital of the world. The new movements in art as well as fashion were nurtured in the cafes and byways of Paris and its environs. More, perhaps, than at any other time in history, social trends were given either approval or disapproval by a government, or rather by the courtiers of that government. Names such as Richelieu, Mazarin and Louis XIV became famous as adjudicators for the world of the arts. France rapidly became the most powerful nation in Western Europe and probably in all of Christendom. The period was one of unprecedented glory for France. Moreover, France was to become the birthplace of several new theatrical genres which underscored changes in the social system.

Alexandre Hardy

The first French professional playwright was Alexandre Hardy (c. 1572-1632). Hardy's plays were first produced around 1597, primarily at the Hôtel de Bourgogne by a troupe called the King's Players (les Comédiéns du Roi), the most important company in Paris, headed by Valleran LeComte (1592-1615). The plays are significant because they encouraged later writers to become playwrights.

In staging Hardy's plays several scenes were shown on stage at the same time. This type of setting was called *decor simultane,* or simultaneous

Hôtel de Bourgogne. The print on the left depicts a doorkeeper; to his left is a public crier (the drummer) and behind him is the Harlequin character. The public crier and Harlequin will use their drum and tambourine to announce the play in the public square. The print itself is the frontispiece for Georges de Scudery's (1601-1667) *La Comédie des Comédians* (1632), which was a defense written in behalf of the acting profession. At the top of the print is the stage for the Hôtel de Bourgogne theatre. The print on the right is a pastoral setting at the Hôtel de Bourgogne for Jean de Mairet's *Silvanire* (1625). Mairet created a vogue for pastorals in the years 1625-1628.

Qu'ce Theatre eft magnifique!
Que ces Acteurs font inuentifs!
Et qu'ils ont de preferuatifs
Contre l'humeur melancolique!

Icy d'une pofture drolle
Ils nazardent le mauuais temps,
Et charment tous les Efcoutans,
Auec vne feule parolle

Icy l'ingenieux Guillaume,
Contrefaifant l'homme de Cour,
Se plaift à gourmander l'Amour,
Trouffé comme vn ioueur de paume

Icy d'une façon hazarde,
Turlupin veut faire l'éfvreq,
Et l'efpagnol de peur du cheg,
Fuit le Françoisqui le regarde.

Mais le vray Gautier les furpaffe,
Et malgré la rigueur du fort,
Il nous fait rire apres fa mort,
Aufoiuenir de fa grimaffe

A representation of the Italian farce comedians at the Hôtel de Bourgogne around 1630. The male figures are the Frenchman (extreme left) looking at the Spaniard (extreme right) who has fled from fear of the Frenchman. Turpulin (second from left), whose name means "unlucky," steals from Gaultier-Garguille, whose name means "great greedy mouth." Gros-Guillaume (second from right), whose name means "big Bill," is dressed as a tennis player and is acting the lover. *French Cultural Services.*

setting. Several of these designs by LeComte's designer Laurent Mahelot are extant. This type of staging allowed the actor to stand in a common acting area called the *platea*, and refer through dialogue to the specific scenic background relevant to the scene. While essentially a medieval technique, Mahelot's sets became the accepted method at the Hôtel de Bourgogne until Italian designers were imported.

The Age of Richelieu

Probably the Frenchman most influential on the arts during what might be called the Golden Age of France was a cardinal named Richelieu.

Henri IV was assassinated in 1610, bringing nine-year-old Louis XIII to the throne. The policies followed by his mother and her ministers spawned civil war. Shortly after the war Cardinal Richelieu (1586-1642) quickly became the power behind the throne by seizing control of the nation from the Protestants and nobles.

Striving to create a new center for the European arts community with himself as its chief patron and titular head, Cardinal Richelieu was able to bring in the most important scenic designers of the period from Italy. With the importation of such set designers as Tomaso Francini, Richelieu brought Italian scenic practices to the French stage. Thus the concepts of perspective scenery, angled wings, raked stage, unified sets, scene shifting and

Cardinal Richelieu as portrayed by Edwin Booth. From *Dramatic Portrait Gallery*, 1880.

the proscenium arch became staples in the French theatre by 1620. To facilitate his new artists, Richelieu built a new theatre located within the Royal Palace called the Palais-Royal. Considered the first theatre outside of Italy to have a proscenium arch, the Palais-Royal was constructed so as to adequately house the Italianated scenery. It was also destined to become the home of Molière. Richelieu's successor, Mazarin, continued to import Italian designers. The arrival of Torelli to stage opera and the construction in 1644 of the Theâtre du Marais continued the Italian influence on French theatre. Torelli, one of the most famous scene designers in Italy, converted the Petite Bourbon to house the opera *La Finta*. He installed his *chariot and pole system* and enlarged the stage. The opera was a huge success and many historians cite 1645 as the beginning of the Italian ideal in France. Later Torelli remodeled the Palais Royal to accommodate the chariot and pole system.

To consolidate power over the arts, Richelieu encouraged the gathering of several hand-picked scholars at the home of Valentin Conrart, a secretary to the king. The group met to discuss literary matters and to debate questions of language. Richelieu saw in the group a methodology by

Louis XIII *(right)* and Molière *(left)* at the Petit Bourbon Palace built by Cardinal Richelieu and renamed the Palais Royal after Richelieu's death in 1641. From *Histoire Illustrée de la Littérature Française.*

A meeting of the French Academy which Cardinal Richelieu created in 1635. From *Histoire de la Littérature Française.*

which control could be exercised on the very foundations of French cultural life. In 1635 Richelieu constituted the group as a state-recognized public body called L'Académie Française. The French Academy made up of "the immortal forty" is still considered one of the most prestigious literary groups in the world. It is the French Academy, for example, which determines the gender of any new word added to the French language. It was from this group that the standards of French drama were postulated from the writings of Italians, Lodovico Castelvetro (1501-1571), Antonio Minturno (?-1574) and Julius Caesar Scaliger (1494-1558). These standards have come to be called neoclassicism.

With the addition of the L'Académie Royale de Peinure et de Sculpture instituted in 1648 by Louis XIV, art became an instrument of the government. In many ways, it was similar to the control over the arts exercised by the communist government over the Russian society except that meoclassicism had a better intellectual base. Nevertheless, individuality and originality were suppressed to create a grandiose theatrical style that in many ways matched French imperial designs. This grand combination of church and state in the form of the French Academy established arbitrary rules that were violated at the individual artist's peril.

Neoclassicism

The neoclassical doctrine had at is core verisimilitude or the appearance of truth. Verisimilitude is made up of three basic concepts: reality, morality, and generality or abstraction. Reality simply meant that characters in the play would have to be from real life as it was perceived at that time in France. Writers were discouraged from writing about supernatural or mythical persons and each character in the play must be portrayed realistically. But the concept of portraying characters realistically was modified by the idea of morality. Dramatic characters must be consistent with the moral standards of the time. Since the seventeenth century concept of God suggested that goodness would be rewarded and evil punished, playwrights were forced to confine themselves to incidents and characters demonstrating this premise. Further, the neoclassicist believed that all these three concepts must be modified by their view of universality.

The neoclassicist believed that no two things were exactly alike. On the other hand, all classes of things may be identified by certain characteristics which all members of a class share. For example, while there are many different kinds and varieties of dogs, they all share elements in their makeup which classifies them as dogs. Those common elements were called universals or essences. The neoclassicist believed that it was possible to find the essence of all things or the truth of that particular thing. One could find, through careful analysis, the truth or essence of male, female, dramatic literature, or human society. In dramatic literature the essence of each genre had to be discovered and identified so that it might be presented in its purest form. Tragedy, for example, could not be adulterated with comic breaks or interludes and, conversely, comedy could not contain serious elements. As to human society, it was believed that all societies had permanent aspects that identified

that society's uniqueness. So all studies should aim to identify those truths rather than the irrelevancies of historical trappings. Historical accuracy was, therefore, considered irrelevant—a factor eliminating the need for historically accurate costumes or scenery. Neoclassicists, then, were concerned with those universal aspects of character and situation. Each character portrayed must be appropriate in terms of the universal standard of the norm that was being depicted. This rule was called *decorum,* which evolved from the Academy's misinterpretation of Aristotle's *The Poetics.*

Additionally, it was decreed that a play should be unified in terms of time, place, and action. Most good drama is unified by action, but to impose a

Engraving by Stefano della Bella of a scene from *Mirame,* 1641. This tragi-comedy, by Desmaret de Saint-Sorlin, was performed for the inauguration of the Théâtre du Palais Cardinal. The engraving stresses the ceremonious and static quality of the performance and the elegant symmetry of the groups which harmonizes with the setting. *Courtesy French Cultural Services.*

limit as to time and place was not what Aristotle had intended. The neoclassical ideal called for an action which could take place within twenty-four hours and in one place, or two if the other could be reached in twenty-four hours. Most writers, if they were to maintain any kind of relationship with the Academy or their peers, wrote in accordance with the rules of neoclassicism.

The neoclassical ideal, then, was the purity of tragedy and comedy; strict adherence to verisimilitude and decorum; the observance of the unities of time, place and action; and that the function of drama was to teach and to entertain. The influence of these principles in France was immediate and significant. Under Richelieu's control French writers attempted to follow the tenets of neoclassicism as rigidly as possible for fear of incurring the wrath of the cardinal or the displeasure of the Academy.

Pierre Corneille

Despite the rigidity of the neoclassical formula, France produced three significant playwrights: Pierre Corneille, Jean Racine and Jean-Baptiste Poquelin III. Pierre Corneille (1606-1684), a Jesuit trained lawyer, wrote one of the most controversial and famous plays in French literature, *Le Cid.* Based on Guillén de Castro's *Youthful Adventures of the Cid (Las Mocedades del Cid)*, Corneille's play became at the time a popular hit and a highly controversial cause célèbre.

While *Le Cid* may seem mundane from a modern vantage, the controversy surrounding it was of major significance for several reasons. First, it encouraged Corneille to write critical observations on his art; second, it furnished the historian with

Below left: Portrait of Pierre Corneille. *Below right:* Frontispiece of Corneille's *Le Cid.* The costumes were of the period and the set was a Palais a volonté. The scene is Chiméne and Don Diègue before the king. From *Histoire Illustré de la Littérature Française.*

LE CID

CHARACTERS

DON FERNANDO, first king of Castile

DON DIEGUE, a hero, and father of Rodrigo

DON GOMEZ, count of Gormas, father of Chimene

DON RODRIGUE, lover of Chimene

DON SANCHO, a soldier in love with Chimene

DONNA URRACA, the infanta of Castile

CHIMENE, daughter of Don Gomez

SETTING: Seville

BACKGROUND

Le Cid provoked an interesting controversy. Given classical standards, many critics felt that the play had a number of faults. Richelieu joined in the battle although his interests were probably more political then literary. After an exchange of pamphlets between Corneille and his enemies, the French Academy was asked to render an opinion on how well the play followed the neoclassical ideal. In December of 1637, the Academy published the "sentiments" called *The Views of the Academy on the Tragedy-Comedy of the Cid (Les Sentiments de L'Academie sur la Tragi-Comédie du Cid).* The pamphlet was written by the acknowledged leader of the Academy, Jean Chapelain, and edited, according to some scholars, by Richelieu. The Academy admitted that there was beauty in the play and praised certain qualities. However, Chapelain felt that the play was weak because it contained neither ordinary nor extraordinary verisimilitude. The characters did not behave satisfactorily in terms of norms. In addition, he felt that there were perhaps too many events crowded into twenty-four hours, an observation with which many would heartily agree. The primary disagreement was an ethical one. There was objection to the apparent exaltation of romantic love, and Chimene's words to Roderigue as he went to fight Sancho were thought to be indecent. They were, "Come victor from a combat of which Chimene is the prize."

PLOT

The play is based on the life of Rodrigo Diaz, the half-legendary hero called El Cid by the Moors. Chimene and Roderigue are desperately in love. Act I reveals Chimene's love for Roderigue through the technique of a confidant. Chimene confides her love to Elvise. Before the love can be revealed, Chimene's father, Don Gomez, quarrels with and insults Roderigue's elderly father, Don Diegue. Corneille's dramatic theme is primarily based on the ancient Spanish code of honor which demanded a death for every insult or seduction. Therefore, Roderigue was bound by his code of honor to avenge his father. He then challenges, fights, and kills Gomez. Chimene, who is still deeply in love with Roderigue, feels that she must avenge her father and asks King Fernando to behead or banish Roderigue. Roderigue, upon hearing of Chimene's request, goes to her and in a stirring scene gives her his sword and invites her to slay him. Chimene cannot bring herself to run him through. Don Diegue persuades Roderigue to fight the Moors, who were converging by sea to capture Seville. Roderigue battles the Moors, defeats them, and returns to Seville in glory. All of Seville praises the hero Roderigue, save Chimene, who still demands his death. King Fernand refuses to order the execution of the man who defeated the Moors, so Chimene offers her hand in marriage to anyone who will challenge and kill the man with whom she is deeply in love. Sancho accepts and immediately challenges Roderigue. Roderigue decides to allow Chimene her revenge by letting Sancho kill him. When Chimene learns of the plan, she repents of her revenge and begs Roderigue to defend himself. In the ensuing battle, Roderigue overcomes Sancho but refuses to kill him. According to the code of honor, Roderigue's decision to spare Sancho satisfies Chimene's honor. Chimene, seeing Sancho come to her, believes Roderigue is dead. But King Fernand tells her the truth and Chimene is overjoyed. Roderigue and Chimene meet and agree to marry after a year's mourning period has passed.

invaluable information about Corneille and other playwrights of the period. Certainly the controversy established neoclassicism as the standard because playwrights recognized the futility of challenging the Academy. Corneille never again challenged the concept of the Cardinal's Academy in his later works and was voted acceptance as a member in 1647.

Jean Racine

Although the work of Corneille is outstanding, French tragedy reached its apex with the work of Jean Racine (1639-1699). Born at La Ferté-Milon, Jean Racine's father was the controller of the state's salt monopoly at La Ferté-Milon, and his mother was the daughter of an attorney at Viller-Cotterets. Both of Racine's parents died when he was young and Jean was raised by paternal grandparents. Because of the family's Jansenist bent (a religious order believing in predestination), Racine studied at the petite ecole in Port-Royal (1649-1653) run by the Solitaries, to prepare for a religious life. He received intensive religious training studying both Greek and Latin. At the College d'Harcourt in Paris, Jean became fascinated with the plays of Euripides and Sophocles, philosophy and young women, in that order. During this period, Racine wrote his first play, which was presented to Molière. Although the play was never produced, Molière gave the young poet a small stipend and encouraged him to try again. Racine's inclination to the theatre and women, both an anathema to the preparation and education of a priest, prompted his grandparents to remove him from Paris. Racine traveled to Uzes in southern France, ostensibly to study for the priesthood. It was there that Racine commented in a letter to Jean de la Fontaine that the women of Uzes were "corpus solidum et succi plenum" ("flesh firm and succulent"). By 1663 Racine had determined that his future did not lie with the priesthood and returned to Paris, where (much to the horror of his pious relatives) he turned back to the theatre. An aunt who was a

Jean Racine, as sketched by his eldest son. *Courtesy French Cultural Services.*

member of the sisterhood at Port-Royal-des-Champs admonished the young man, stating: "I have learned with sorrow that you frequent, more than ever, people whose name is an abomination to all who have any measure of piety, and with reason, since they are forbidden entry to the church, or access to the sacrament." All entreaties were to little avail, however, as Racine wrote his second play *The Thebans (La Thébaide)*, which was produced in 1664 by Molière. With this production Racine embarked upon his career as a dramatist. *The Thebans* was followed by *Andromaque* (1667), which was recognized immediately as a masterpiece. *The Litigants (Les Plaideurs)*, a comedy, followed in 1668 and one year later, *Britannicus*,

PHÈDRE
JEAN RACINE

CHARACTERS (Partial List)
THESEUS
PHÈDRE.
HIPPOLYTE
ARICIE
OENONE
APHRODITE

SETTING
Troezen, in Ancient Greece

BACKGROUND

In the long history of dramatic literature there has been a handful of roles that seem to attract actors. Referring to this phenomenon in English and American actors, Carl Sandburg once observed: "They all want to play Hamlet." But if you are female and you are French, the role that is most coveted of them all is Phèdre. Based on *Hippolytus*, by Euripides, the Racine play made many significant changes to adhere to the neoclassical rules. Racine attempted to show only those occurrences which could happen in real life, thereby complying with rules of verisimilitude. Only the sea monster, a part of the original myth, deviated from reality. The character of Hippolytus, as created by Racine, is not the chaste woman-hating, shining paragon of virtue as was the Euripidean original, but a normal seventeenth century Frenchman with a girlfriend. Phèdre, while falling victim to almost uncontrollable love, still has a great capacity for moral feeling. She suffers her fate with great remorse which, for the most part, redeems her in the minds of the audience. Racine is primarily concerned with the universal in character, and therefore, bothers little with delving into idiosyncrasies. Racine was interested in the essence, only those things which focus on the emotions of a woman caught between desire and her own morality. There is no question that in Phèdre Racine turned the prescribed restrictions of form to elo-

quent advantage by the manner in which he focused his drama through careful structure with a singular action and clarity of tone. Racine brought neoclassical tragedy to perfection and must rank among the great writers of all time.

PLOT

After his first wife dies, Theseus remarries the much younger Phèdre. She is a descendant of gods and monsters and is also a helpless victim of Aphrodite's hate. As a consequence, Aphrodite implants in Phèdre a passion for Theseus's son, Hippolytus. Phèdre falls in love with Hippolytus but keeps her feelings to herself. Phèdre feigns dislike for Hippolyte in a futile attempt to avoid the discovery of her love. Hippolyte leaves Troezen in search of his father. Phèdre confesses her true feelings to her nurse, Oenone. News comes back that Theseus is dead. While the struggle for power ensues, Phèdre reveals her feelings to Hippolyte, who is disgusted. He is known to be in love with Aricie. Phèdre threatens suicide. Theseus then returns alive. Oenone suggests that Phèdre tell Theseus that Hippolyte tried to take advantage of her. When Theseus enters, he is told by Phèdre that she isn't worthy to be his wife and that Hippolyte wants permission to leave immediately. Oenone then tells Theseus herself that Hippolyte tried to take advantage of Phèdre. Theseus is enraged and banishes his son from the kingdom and calls down the vengeance of Neptune. Aricie and Hippolyte agree to leave together. Aricie is stopped by Theseus and questioned. He then sends for Oenone. Oenone swallows poison, convinced she has been caught. Hippolyte is killed by a beast from the sea sent by Neptune. Phèdre, when she hears the news, tells her husband the truth and kills herself, leaving Theseus in grief.

which Racine always considered his most careful work. Among Racine's most famous works are *Bérénice* (1670), *Bajazet* (1762), and *Iphigénie* (1674).

Of all Racine's works, *Phèdre* (1677) is considered by most critics to be the crowning achievement of the neoclassical style.

Mlle. Champmeslé (1642-1698), considered to be the finest tragic actress of her time. She was very close to Racine and created the role of Phèdre. When she left the Bourgogne company, the motivation for the formation of the Comédie Française was created.

French Manners

With artistic control of the arts in the hands of the aristocracy, the great tragic characters of the age were drawn from the ranks of the nobility while the comic characters were usually middle class. There was a great deal wrong with French society of the period. Corruption and oppression were prevalent in the ruling class. Since the aristocracy and the church paid no taxes, the middle class grew tired of paying for the extravagances of the monarchy. Indeed, while a growing number of citizens worked long and arduous hours to create the splendors of France, the nobility became increasingly decadent. Yet their praises were continually sung on the stages of the theatre. The theatre, then, was a microcosm of its society.

The disparity between the aristocracy and the working class was apparent in all facets of life. French fashion as well as French manners and morals were duplicated throughout Europe as trend-setting among the aristocracy. Whereas the middle-class clothing usually consisted of a plain black coat covering most of the body, clothing for the elite became a signpost of status. Perhaps no other period in history produced the lushness of costume for both men and women.

The seventeenth and early eighteenth century produced some of history's most colorful male costumes: large brimmed hats covering wigs of long curls down to the knees; trousers, ribboned and ending at the knees, were covered with a long coat with huge cuffs trimmed in lace. Silk stockings were worn along with boots on all occasions. Lace handkerchiefs were sometimes pulled from the sleeve and used to gesture during conversations.

Dresses for women were richly embroidered and gaily colored with laced bodices cut extremely low. Their hair was beautifully ribboned, jeweled, perfumed and curled. Women were encouraged to become educated and witty and to participate in the salon where aristocrats could meet to discuss philosophy and the arts, and flirt.

Flirting was especially important among the aristocracy because of a rather bizarre tradition in France, as well as Europe, concerning marriage. Aristocratic marriages were usually arranged by parents on the basis of property. The result was that young women who were married off to elderly men frequently indulged in affairs of passion. Almost every male aristocrat who could afford it had a mistress, and the number of affairs over a given period was almost as important an indicator of masculinity as the number of battles fought. Indeed, women found the number of admirers in pursuit of their charms a measure of their femininity and openly encouraged many dangerous liaisons. These idiosyncrasies of French life fell under the satirical eye of one of the greatest playwrights of all time, Jean-Baptiste Poquelin, better known as Molière.

Molière

Molière was born in Paris on January 15, 1622, to Jean-Baptiste Poquelin III and his wife Marie Cresse. The elder Poquelin was superintendent of the royal upholstery and was charged with, among other things, the making of the royal bed. Jean IV was schooled at the Collège de Clermont under the Jesuits, who were the only religious group permitted to use drama as a teaching device. Poquelin studied law for a time before turning his attention to the theatre. He formed a liaison with the actress Madeleine Béjart and her two brothers, which resulted in the creation of the Théâtre Illustré in Paris on June 30, 1643. Eventually, the Théâtre Illustré evolved into the Comédie Française, the longest continuing theatrical company in the world, and hence, it regards this date as its beginning. The opposition of the church to any kind of theatrical

This scene shows a crowd protesting against a production and is similar to the protest Molière received for his production of *The School for Wives* (1662). The protest against *The School for Wives* and Molière's ensuing reply are referred to as "The Comic War."

Molière, France's renowned actor and dramatist. *Courtesy French Cultural Services.*

activity forced most actors to take stage names to protect their families from scorn. At this point in time, Jean-Baptiste Poquelin became Molière.

The Théâtre Illustré was hardly illustrious and Molière was arrested at least three times for debt before departing with his company for the provinces. For twelve years Molière learned the art of the theatre both in acting and in writing before returning to Paris in 1658. On October 24, 1658, Molière's troupe presented before Louis XIV Corneille's tragedy *Nicomede*. Voltaire maintains that Molière suffered from chronic hiccough, which often enhanced a comic character but spelled doom to tragedy. Whatever the cause, the tragedy was not well received by the king. The company would have been dismissed and sent back to the country, were it not for an afterpiece (*Le Docteur Amoureux*) written by Molière that so delighted the king that he let the company share a theatre with an Italian group.

Success came to Molière's company in 1659 with his production of *Les Précieuses Ridicules (The Affected Ladies)*. Always interested in the fashions and morals of the salons, Molière was particularly amused by men and women making so much over delicate manners and perfumed speech. With this play he began to chronicle the foibles of his age.

When the Petit Bourbon was torn down, the king aided Molière by assigning his troupe to the Palais-Royal, which Richelieu had built and Torelli had remodeled. Molière and the Troup de Monsieur remained at the Palais-Royal from 1660 to 1673. Although Molière wrote different types of comedy, his most admired works were his comedies of character and manners. His cannon includes *The School for Husbands* (1662), *The School for Wives* (1662), *Tartuffe* (1664), *The Misanthrope* (1666), *The Miser* (1668), *The Learned Ladies* (1672), and *The Imaginary Invalid* (1673).

Satirizing the foibles of an age is not always appreciated. *School for Wives* was attacked by the more conservative members of court. The king himself was young enough to enjoy its levity but others were shocked. Prince de Conti denounced the play as the most scandalous thing ever staged. Some magistrates advocated that the play be banned as an affront to morality and religion. Molière turned his pen on his critics, publishing on June 1, 1663, *The School for Wives Criticized (La Critique de l'Ecole des Femmes)*. The play allows the critics to voice their criticisms but ridicules them through the exaggeration of their own arguments. The rival troupe at the Hôtel de Bourgogne continued the attack with the *Counter Critic*, to which Molière replied with *Versailles Impromptu (L'Impromtu de Versailles)* on October 18, 1663. Throughout all the point-counterpoint, Louis supported Molière, as indicated by the annual pension of a thousand livres he was granted.

After the first performance of perhaps his greatest play, *Tartuffe*, the most heated criticism of Molière surfaced. Père Roullé, vicar of St. Barthelemy, suggested that for writing *Tartuffe* Molière "should be burned at the stake as a foretaste of the fires of hell." Louis did withhold permission for the play to be presented to the public of Paris, but soothed his friend's hurt pride by increasing his annual pension to six thousand livres and taking the troupe under his protection, calling it Troupe du Roi (King's Company).

Tartuffe is a study in religious hypocrisy but was interpreted by many to be a condemnation of

Armande Béjart (1642-1700), wife of Molière, as the heroine in *The Princess of Elide* (1664). *Courtesy French Cultural Services.*

all religion. Molière added lines to the script pointing out that the satire was not of the faithful. He rewrote the play twice, once in 1667 and once in 1669, before Louis would allow it to be produced. On February 5, 1669, *Tartuffe* began a run of twenty-eight consecutive performances. Of all French classic plays, it is perhaps the most frequently produced.

There is a curious paradox in Molière's plays. While they satirize human foibles, there is always a touch of bitterness in them because there was a touch of sadness in the man. By the age of fifty, Molière had lost two of his three children, had contracted tuberculosis, and was involved in a tumultuous marriage. He became sharp-tempered, melancholy and fatigued. Despite his increasing cough, Molière decided to play the leading role in his final play, *The Imaginary Invalid*. On February 17, 1673, Molière's company saw that he was dangerously ill and pleaded with him to close his

LES PRÉCIEUSES RIDICULES
MOLIÈRE

CHARACTERS (Partial list)

MAGDELON, a ridiculous précieuse, daughter of Gorgibus

CATHOS, a ridiculous précieuse, neice of Gorgibus

THE MARQUIS DE MASCARILLE, valet of La Grange

THE VISCOUNT DE JODELET, valet of Du Croisy

LA GRANGE, a rebuffed suitor

GORGIBUS, head of a good bourgeois family

SETTING

Seventeenth-century Paris, France

BACKGROUND

Les Precieuses Ridicules (The Affected Ladies) was produced on November 18, 1659, at the Salle du Petit Bourbon. The play was an instant hit, but more than that, it marked the real beginning of one of the most beloved playwrights the world has ever known. Louis XIV commanded three performances the first year and the play was performed forty-four times.

PLOT

The story begins with the two suitors, La Grange and Du Croisy, discussing the rude, pretentious behavior of the two ridiculous young ladies. Recognizing the women's attempt to be perceived as above their class, they devise a plan to humiliate them. When their father runs into the gentlemen on their way out and learns what has happened, he is livid. He calls down the two women and reprimands them, but they turn around and scold him for trying to match them with such persons. They go on to a long-winded explanation about the trials one is supposed to go through to attain the briefest consideration. Gorgibus, totally confused, leaves in a huff. It is then that a servant announces the arrival of the Marquis de Mascarille. He enters with a flourish, and proceeds to talk himself up to be a "wit," and a regular of the court. When joined by the Viscount de Jodelet, the young women are smugly pleased that the court has finally found its way to them. As the two noblemen charm the ladies, they also prove themselves to be outrageous fops. They quote pathetic poetry and stories of intrigue from the court. They persuade the ladies to have a dance, and invite all the neighbors. When the violinist arrives with the guests, La Grange and Du Croisy reappear and beat Mascarille and Jodelet, identifying them as their valets, and humiliating the women in front of all their neighbors.

Right: Les Delices du Genre Humain, oil on canvas, French school, 1670, Paris. The painting shows leading French actors, including Jodelet and Molière (extreme left), and several commedia dell'arte characters including Harlequin at left center. *Comédie Française.*

theatre and rest. Molière refused to cancel a performance and proceeded with the play. During the performance, he was taken with a fit of coughing and was barely able to finish. A young actor, Michael Baron, and Molière's wife rushed him home. Sensing death approaching, Molière asked for a priest, but none came in time. The coughing continued and he began to hemorrhage, dying shortly thereafter. The failure of a priest to arrive in time caused a rather distasteful event in history to take place. In 398 A.D. the Council of Carthage decreed that actors be forbidden the sacraments unless they forswore their profession. After Molière's death Harley de Champvallon, Archbishop of Paris, ruled that since Molière had not repented his profession, he could not be buried in consecrated ground. Armande, his wife, pleaded with the king at Versaille to intercede. Harley received a message from the King and decreed that the body not be taken into a church for rites but be quietly buried in a remote corner of the cemetery of St. Joseph in the Rue Montmartre. In spite of an attempt to find and move Molière's remains to the present marker in Père La Chaise Cemetery, no one knows the exact location of the body of one of the truly great dramatists of all time.

Comédie Française

After Molière's death, Louis ordered the acting troupe at the Marais and the Molière troupe to combine at a new theatre in the Rue Guénégaud. Jean-Baptiste Lulley's French Opera then moved to the Palais-Royal. This now meant that there were companies in Rue Guénégaud, the Hôtel de Bourgogne and the Palais-Royal. In 1679 Mlle. Champmeslé, the Bourgogne's principal tragic actress, bolted her company to join the troupe at the Guénégaud, precipitating a crisis between the two troupes. Louis issued an order joining the two companies into the Comédie Française which opened on August 25, 1680, at the theatre in the Rue Guénégaud. The Comédie Française is still in operation today.

When first formed, the Comédie Française was given a monopoly on the performance of all spoken drama in France. This monopoly was to produce a chain reaction in the eighteenth century which would have a lasting effect on western theatre.

The extravagances of the French court were manifested in a number of ways but none more infuriating to the average French taxpayer than the subsidies extended to foreign noblemen. In 1650 when Charles II escaped the Civil War in

England he went directly to Paris where he was received warmly by Louis XIV in the form of a pension amounting to six thousand francs. Charles' mother, Henrietta Maria, and sister, Henrietta Anne, had already taken up residence under the protection of Louis. Charles, fluent in French, loved Paris and the theatre wherein he became particularly enamored of the Italianated scenery which had already been imported to England by William Davenant before the closing of the Theatres. With the defeat of the Puritans and the election of a royalist majority on May 8, 1660, the Stuart line was returned to the throne in England.

The English Restoration

As soon as it became evident that Charles was to be returned to the throne, activity began in theatrical circles. Sir Henry Hubert resumed his position as Master of Revels, a member of the Lord Chamberlain's staff, and licensed three companies without the knowledge of the king. Charles, on the other hand, granted William Davenant and Thomas Killigrew, who had both been with the royal family for most of the exile, a monopoly over theatrical productions in London. It was evident from his irresponsible action that Charles intended to make the theatre his royal property in much the same way as the French monarchy had done. The French had no alternative; the English Parliament, however, could have challenged the edict but they were too busy debating whom they should hang for the death of Charles I. They finally arrived at twenty-three men including Cromwell, whose body was exhumed from Westminster Abbey, hanged, and decapitated. The ramifications of these and subsequent acts were to influence the nature of theatre throughout the next three hundred years.

During his exile in France Charles spent considerable time at the theatre but, even more than that, Charles was essentially French in both parentage and education. His mother was French and his father was the great-great-grandson of Mary of Lorraine. He lived in France or on the continent for

Dorset Garden Theatre (also known as the second Duke's Theatre). Depicted is a scene from Settle's *The Empress of Morocco* (1673). From *Londina Illustrata*, 1825.

The inside of the Red Bull Playhouse. The characters probably represent the leading figures in a form known as a droll—a short farcical work from a larger play. The droll was the primary form of entertainment during the years 1642-1660. (Frontispiece to Francis Kirkman's *The Wits: or Sport Upon Sport*, 1672). From *Londina Illustrata*, 1825.

fourteen years and was thoroughly indoctrinated with French manners and morals. It is no coincidence, then, that during the Restoration period the English court embraced, to some degree, French manners and morals. As a result, early Restoration theatre showed a pronounced French influence.

The first type of serious play written during the early Restoration Period was called "heroic" tragedy. These plays frequently deal with two beautiful star-crossed lovers who strive to fulfill their love but are prevented from doing so by circumstances which will bring on dishonor to themselves or their families. The happy endings and bombastic language now seem outrageously overdone and the plays are rarely performed today. Roger Boyle (1621-1679) is remembered for *The Tragedy of Mustapha* (1663) which became a

classic example of this style. Other writers of heroic tragedy included Elkanah Settle (1648-1724) who wrote *Cambyses, King of Persia* (1671); Nathanial Lee (1653-1692), author of *The Rival Queens* (1677); and John Dryden (1631-1700) with *The Indian Queen* (1664).

Dryden's *All for Love* (1677), an adaptation of Shakespeare's *Antony and Cleopatra*, changed the nature of English tragedy by adopting French neoclassical rules to some degree. The work of Thomas Otway (1652-1685) combined neoclassicism and Shakespeare to produce perhaps the best serious plays of the period. *The Orphan* (1680) and *Venice Preserv'd* (1682) are produced occasionally today.

Probably the most important contribution of the English Restoration was its comedy. There was comedy of "humours," comedy of intrigue and comedy of manners. Thomas Shadwell (1642-1692) wrote perhaps the most successful of the "humours" comedies with his *The Sullen Lovers* (1668). The best example of comedy of intrigue was written by Aphra Behn (1640-1689).

Aphra Behn

Aphra Behn is the first woman to have made her living as a playwright. She is also one of the first women to speak out against the loveless unhappy marriages which were arranged by families during this period. In her first play, *The Forced Marriage* (1670), she concerned herself with the plight of women who could not hope to marry if they were not virgins. Once a woman did marry, her property as well as her legal identity became her husband's. She was at her spouse's mercy and had no recourse in law no matter what his excesses were. Behn seemed to express deep concern about the welfare of her sex. The theme of rape and seduction is also prevalent in her plays. Whereas most male writers made the seduction of woman a theme for comedy, Behn was the first to expose the damage to a woman's psyche by such practices. Her most famous play is *The Rover* written in 1677.

Comedy of Manners

Comedy of manners, which usually satirized the foibles of a society, is said to have been fully developed by Sir George Etherege (c. 1634-1691). Restoration comedy of manners was some of the finest if not the bawdiest comedy ever produced. Etherege's plays such as *Love in a Tub* (1664), *The Man of Mode* (1676), and *She Would If She Could* (1668) are still banned on some stages. No theatrical genre prior to the twentieth century seems to have outraged critics more than Restoration com-

edy. The play that most epitomizes Restoration style was *The Country Wife* written by William Wycherley (1640-1715).

Another important Restoration comedy, *The Way of the World* by William Congreve (1670-1729), is still frequently produced and is considered by most critics to be a bona fide masterpiece.

Charles' reign ended on February 4, 1685. He renounced the Anglican Church, called for a priest, professed his Catholicism, and died. The manners and morals of England began a slow movement away from the French through the rule of James II, who reigned from 1685-1688, and William and Mary, who co-ruled from 1689 to 1702. By the end of the seventeenth century, England was evolving a new drama and a different theatre.

The dominance and influence of France during the seventeenth century were manifold: first, Italian theatre architecture and scenic conventions were adopted by the French and copied by the English; second, French neoclassicism became the dominant philosophy of the English theatre; third, the comedies of Molière set a standard for Restoration comedy; and fourth, Louis XIV, granting a monopoly to Comédie Française, may have influenced Charles to grant his monopoly. Certainly granting of monopolies in both countries was destined to create havoc in the eighteenth century. The rise of the middle class continued to exert influence on the theatre as well.

Eighteenth Century Developments

The eighteenth century ushered in many changes in the world of theatre. The first of these was sentimental drama. In many ways the development of sentimental drama was a reaction against the rigidity of neoclassicism. The philosophical core of sentimentalism can be found, among others, in the writings of Jean-Jacques Rousseau (1712-1778) and David Hume (1711-1776). Both Rousseau and Hume believed that human beings are basically good and that if one follows the dictates of the

THE COUNTRY WIFE
WILLIAM WYCHERLEY

CHARACTERS (Partial list)
MR. HORNER, a supposedly impotent woman-
izer
MR. PINCHWIFE, a jealous husband
MRS. PINCHWIFE, his unhappy country wife
ALITHEA, sister to Mr. Pinchwife
HARCOURT, a young man in love with Alithea

SETTING
London, in the seventeenth century

BACKGROUND
Wycherley was born to a royalist family of some wealth. When Cromwell came to power, young Wycherly was sent to France for his education. When he returned to England, he was sent to Oxford; however, he left without a degree to become a playwright. His first success was *Love in a Wood* (1671), which he dedicated to Lady Castlemaine, a mistress of Charles II. After going to war in 1672, he returned to write *The Country Wife* (1675). The play premiered in 1673 in London and is still considered a Restoration classic. While Molière's *School for Wives* probably influenced the play, there is something decidedly original about *The Country Wife*.

PLOT
The story beings with the notorious Mr. Horner having had his quack doctor announce through rumor that he is impotent. The result is immediate; husbands now trust him implicitly with their wives. One of his visitors that day is Jack Pinchwife, a jealous older man who has just married a beautiful country woman in the hopes that her naiveté will keep her from being unfaithful. Horner has noticed this new woman at the theatre and mentions her beauty, saying he would like to meet her. Pinchwife, not knowing of the new rumors about Horner, becomes angry and leaves. At home, he forbids his wife from going out to the theatre again and reprimands Alithea, his sister, for "corrupting" her. When she asks why, he foolishly piques her interest by telling her that he knows of a man who is in love with her. Enter Harcourt and Sparkish, a fool who is engaged to Alithea. Harcourt is immediately smitten with Alithea. Sparkish encourages his interest in Alithea, to her amazement, and they leave for the theatre. A group of women come to bring Mrs. Pinchwife to the theatre, and Pinchwife locks her away, saying that she has smallpox. Horner then shows up. The women are urged by their husbands to go with Horner. They refuse, disgusted, until Horner whispers to the ladies that the rumor of his impotence is just that—a rumor. They depart, without a second thought for Mrs. Pinchwife. After much complaining, Mr. Pinchwife agrees to bring his wife to the theatre if she dresses as a man. Once at the theatre, Horner makes advances on Mrs. Pinchwife, who he immediately recognizes in spite of the disguise, by giving her kisses for "his sister," telling "him" that he was in love with her. The next day, Alithea's marriage is delayed by Harcourt, Mrs. Pinchwife is locked away yet again, and Harcourt is receiving many lady guests. Mr. Pinchwife decides to try to marry Alithea off to Harcourt. Mrs. Pinchwife dresses up as Alithea, and her husband takes her to Horner. Leaving her there to fetch a clergyman, he is confused by meeting Sparkish and then Alithea. Three women show up to see Horner, and discover that they have all been seduced by him. He ushers them out and eventually gets rid of Mrs. Pinchwife, who wanted to live with him. All show up again to confront Horner, including a crowd of angry husbands. The doctor suddenly appears to swear again that Horner is impotent, settling the angered husbands. Alithea's servant takes the blame for lying, leaving all guilty parties innocent and the potential for more intrigue ever present.

heart right actions will result. Plays were written to arouse a sympathetic response from the audience. Middle-class characters were placed in oppressing situations which they bore with admi-

rable valor until they were eventually rescued. Sentimental drama reached its full formulation in *The Conscious Lovers* by Richard Steele (1672-1729). Steele's play deals with a penniless heroine, Indiana, who bravely undergoes suffering and humiliation, only to discover that she is the daughter of a rich merchant.

The second important development during the eighteenth century was the use of a middle-class protagonist in tragedy. While this phenomenon had occurred in isolated dramas as early as the sixteenth century, it was not widespread. George Lillo's (1693-1739) *The London Merchant*, Denis Diderot's (1713-1784) *The Illegitimate Son*, and Gotthold Ephraim Lessing's (1729-1781) *Miss Sara Sampson*, are all classic examples of the innovation.

The third development was the phenomenal growth of the German theatre. Johann Gottsched (1700-1766) and Caroline Neuber (1697-1760) combined to reform what had been a theatre of no consequence specializing in farce into one of the finest theatres in Europe.

Gotthold Ephraim Lessing, considered Germany's first significant dramatist, is best remembered for breaking the neoclassical tradition with his plays and criticism. *Courtesy German Information Center.*

Fourth, Italy's scenic technique continued its evolution from developments of the Renaissance. In addition, Italian commedia dell'arte became a literary form under the pen of Carlo Goldoni (1707-1793).

Fifth, the acting profession produced many of the world's most famous actors. In Germany, F. L. Schröder (1774-1816) began his acting career with the Ackerman Troupe, one of the most popular acting companies in Germany. He is generally considered to have been the greatest German actor of the eighteenth century and, according to some, perhaps of all time. England produced David Garrick (1717-1779), James Quin (1692-1766), and Charles Macklin (1699-1777). Garrick, the foremost actor in England between 1741 and 1776, is credited with elevating the English stage to a position of international esteem. Garrick made reforms in acting techniques, management, and scenic design and was an innovative forerunner to the modern director. He is considered by the British theatrical community to be one of the greatest English actors of all time. Macklin, who acted for seventy years, is most famous for his innovative interpretation of Shylock. This character from Shakespeare's *Merchant of Venice* had been played as a clown complete with red wig until Macklin played him sympathetically.

The seeds of melodrama lay in sentimentalism. There was, however, a great deal of resistance to the new movement. The rigidity of neoclassicism promoted by the courtiers had not only manifested itself in the kind of drama which could be produced, but the way in which it was to be produced.

English Pantomime and the French Fair Theatres

When the Comédie Française was created by Louis XIV, it was given a monopoly to produce legitimate drama which was, for the most part, neoclassical. By 1705 the company was feeling the competition of little theatres in Paris which were

David Garrick, pictured above, was not only a great actor but inaugurated such innovations as concealing stage lighting from the audience and abolishing the audience from the stage. On the right he is depicted as between tragedy and comedy.

Charles Macklin as Shylock in Shakespeare's *The Merchant of Venice*. From *Dramatic Portrait Gallery*, 1880.

located in various districts of Paris called fairs (foire). Foire Saint-Germain and Foire Saint-Laurent, for example, each had thriving theatres which were playing to full houses. To avoid violating Louis' proclamation, the fair theatres produced everything but neoclassical drama. The Comédie Française requested and obtained a new proclamation from the king extending the restriction to any entertainment with spoken dialogue. With their license to perform spoken drama voided by the edict, the fair managers devised various forms of subterfuge to satisfy the demands of their largely middle-class audiences. The first was pantomime *(pièces a la muette)*. The pantomime became successful and once again the houses were full and once again the Comédie Française protested. A new edict was issued and pantomime was banned from the fair theatres. The fair managers, faced with idle companies and dark theatres, reasoned that if they could not do pantomime of the spoken drama perhaps they could do unspoken drama by singing the material. Eventually, three unique dramatic forms evolved from these travesties: *comédies-en-vaudeville*, *opéra comique*, and *melodrama*. Again the major theatres protested and the government

Une parade de foire. Shown are characters at a fair theatre upon the Pont-Neuf. From *Histoire Illustré de la Littérature Française.*

once again restricted all forms of music theatre at the fair theatres. Some of the managers of the fair troupes began to open theatres on the Boulevard du Temple and once again they turned to pantomime. The most important of the new theatres were those of Nicolas Medard Audinot (c. 1728-1796) and of Jean Baptist Nicolet (c. 1728-1796), the *Théâtre des Associés,* and the *Variétés Amusantes.* The new pantomime gradually assumed all of the characteristic traits of melodrama. The stories presented persecuted innocence, a villain, and the eventual triumph of good over evil. Music underscored the emotional qualities of scenes and accompanied the dances. By 1780, dialogue was reintroduced. The restrictions on the theatres were lifted shortly after the French Revolution and in 1800 René Charles Guilbert de Pixérécourt's plays fixed the form of melodrama.

There can be little doubt as to the significance of the fair theatres as a catalyst in the development of dramatic forms. Although there were other forces involved, they must be assigned an important role in the break from neoclassical traditions. More than this, however, the fair theatres represented a reemergence of the popular theatre. The lower class was never welcome at the major theatres even if they could afford them. It is a credit to

the French people that the theatre was not permitted to remain in the hands of the few appointed ones and that the freshness and ingenuity of the fair managers were rewarded with admiration and loyalty. Thus, under the restraint of the French government and under the protective malleability of the Opéra Comique, the seeds of melodrama and romantic drama were planted.

Oddly enough, a similar development was taking place in England. By the turn of the century, the English theatrical monopoly was in trouble. Legitimate drama had been de-emphasized by the public's demand for novelty and imported dancers and singers. By 1708 some of the Italian harlequins of the French fairs had arrived in London, where their performances were billed as "Italian Night Scenes." These pieces were later to form the basis for English pantomimes which, under the direction of John Rich (1692-1761), were destined to become one of the most popular theatrical entertainments of eighteenth century London. The importation of Italian Opéra Serio (serious opera) gradually changed the nature of native English opera. This influence reached a peak in the late 1720s with the works of George Frideric Handel (1685-1759). The reaction against Handel's adaptation of the Italian form culminated in 1728 with

John Gay, poet, playwright, and author of *The Beggar's Opera*, the most successful eighteenth century musical.

the production of John Gay's ballad opera, *The Beggar's Opera*.

The success of the new form not only spawned Gay's own sequel, *Polly*, but also the *Cobbler's Opera* by Thomas Walker, *Mormus Turn'd Fabulist* or *Vulcan's Wedding* by Ebeneezer Forest, and *The Highland Fair* or *Union of the Clans* by Joseph Mitchell. The political satire of *The Beggar's Opera* in some ways set the pattern for minor theatre for some time to come. Although it was indeed amusing to the masses, Robert Walpole found it less than amusing.

Robert Walpole

With the death of William in 1702, Queen Anne became the unwilling sovereign. Anne's own moral fibre helped produce a change in the character of the English court. Her avoidance of the theatre had some influence in improving the very nature of the legitimate drama. But perhaps

the most far-reaching consequences of Anne's reign was the power she allowed her ministers to appropriate. From this time on, political battles were fought between Parliament and the ministers rather than Parliament and the sovereign. In order to prevent the restoration of the Stuarts at Anne's death, Parliament crowned George I of Germany as King of England. Robert Walpole initially assumed power under George I. When the king died in 1727, George II eventually re-hired the minister. Walpole used whatever means necessary to buy members of Parliament, thus becoming one of the most corrupt ministers England has ever had. Still, there was a curious paradox about the man. Although forbidding the publication of Parliamentary debates, he was tolerant, for the most part, of the many attacks on him in print. Such historic magazines as *The Craftsman* (1726), *The Grub Street Journal* (1730-1737), and *The Gentleman's Magazine* (1731) all waged a journalistic war against his policies. To all this he remained relatively calm. But when the ridicule of the Prime Minister moved from the bookstore to the stage, Walpole was provoked. *The Beggar's Opera* did much to infuriate the Prime Minister, but it took the pen of the great satirist Henry Fielding to provide the proverbial straw.

Few aspects of English life were safe from Fielding's pen. Rich's pantomimes, for example, were satirized, as was the Poet Laureate, Colly Cibber. One of Fielding's favorite targets was Robert Walpole. Whenever possible, Fielding lampooned either Walpole or the Walpole administration. Some say that the whole object of Fielding's theatrical management (he was the manager of a bizarre theatre company in the Haymarket) was to embarrass the Walpole regime. Walpole was furious and waited for the opportunity to put an end to political satire in the theatre. In 1737 Walpole came into possession of a playlet entitled *The Golden Rump*, ostensibly written by Fielding. Walpole read portions of the piece to Parliament as a prelude to the introduction of a new law called 10 George II, cap. 28, better known as the Licensing Act of 1737.

THE BEGGAR'S OPERA
JOHN GAY

CHARACTERS (Partial list):
CAPTAIN MACHEATH
POLLY PEACHUM
MR. PEACHUM
MRS. PEACHUM
LUCY LOCKIT
MR. LOCKIT
ASSORTED GANG MEMBERS

BACKGROUND

The Beggar's Opera is important in the development of the theatre in England for two reasons: first, it adapted the French comédies-en-vaudeville style; second, it provided a method by which the little theatres of London would break the monopoly of the legitimate or patent theatres. In The *Beggar's Opera*, Gay made fun of the people he knew best. The people of eighteenth century England were a very tough breed as anyone who has studied Hogarth sketches would surmise. Great fortunes were derived from smuggling, piracy, and even from capturing and selling slaves. English, French, Dutch, and Portuguese ships competed for the privilege of selling Africans to Americans. Gin drinking became a passion to the English, with some retailers promising to make their customers drunk for a pence, and even offering free beds of straw in the cellar. Robbery was rampant. Many eighteenth century playbills included reassurances that "there will be an armed guard on horseback to patrol the roads." If caught, thieves were punished with brutality seldom equaled since. Gallows were raised in virtually every district of London, and on many of them corpses were left to decompose or furnish a macabre morsel for the birds. Hangings frequently had the character of a festival and crowds would line the road to watch the condemned ride the cart to Tyburn. Peddlers sold gin, nuts and apples to the crowd as a kind of bizarre last tribute. Thieves who became successful were frequently made heroes by the public. Jack Sheppard, "Rob Roy" (Robert Macgregor), Dick Turpin, Jonathan Wild, all became legends in their own time. Many writers, including Henry Fielding, were to capitalize on the highwayman craze, but none so well as Gay. *The Beggar's Opera* was first produced by John Rich at Lincoln's Inn Fields in 1728. It ran for sixty-three consecutive nights, a record for that period. The popularity of the piece is still strong, as it played on Broadway as late as 1972 and was recently produced at the National Theatre in London.

PLOT

Mr. Peachum, head of thieves, is going over lists of those thieves that are to be thrown in jail, and those who will escape. Mrs. Peachum recognizes one of the names, Macheath, as the man their daughter, Polly, is in love with. This upsets Mr. Peachum and while they are discussing what to do about it, Polly enters and announces that they have been married. Mr. Peachum becomes very concerned that Macheath will try to take over his business through Polly, and sets about to have him arrested. Polly hears her parents discussing this and warns her husband, who goes into hiding. He is betrayed by some prostitutes and pickpockets, though, and brought to jail. There he faces Lucy Lockit, daughter of the jailer and one of his many women. She has heard about Polly and is livid. After agreeing to marry, Macheath persuades her to try to speak to her father. Just as she is about to go, Polly shows up. Macheath retains Lucy's aid by disowning Polly. Lucy steals her father's keys, and Macheath is free. He is caught again at a brothel. Polly and Lucy beg their fathers to let him go, but to no avail. Macheath resigns himself to death. With the audience of four more of his wives, and many other thieves watching, he goes to hang. However, he is spared death when the crowd insists that the poor be allowed their vices like the rich. A free man finally, he chooses Polly to be his actual wife.

Colley Cibber (1671-1757), poet laureate, actor, and one of the managers of Drury Lane Theatre. Cibber was famous for the plays *The Careless Husband* (1704) and *Love's Last Shift* (1796).

The Licensing Act of 1737

The Licensing Act of 1737 declared that no persons should perform or cause to be performed any play unless their managers had been licensed by the Lord Chamberlain or Letters Patent. This, in effect, was an authorization by Parliament for censorship. It provided that every stage play to be produced must first be sent to the Lord Chamberlain for his inspection and approval, and it gave him the power to prohibit the performance of plays of which he did not approve.

So it came to be that the Lord Chamberlain, an unelected servant of the king, was given the power of life and death over theatrical production on the English stage. Furthermore, the Chamberlain usually appointed an examiner with little or no expe-

rience in dramatic literature to read the plays. At one point in history, a former bank teller had control over the drama in the English-speaking world, since banned plays were rarely, if ever, produced elsewhere in the eighteenth century.

In much the same way as the French monopoly, the English patent theatres were continually threatened by the emergence of small theatres throughout the West End. The patent theatres were constantly bringing charges against these companies. It was not long before a loophole in the law was discovered. In 1751 Henry Fielding, who had turned from the theatre to a judgeship, issued a temporary law called "An Act for the Better Preventing Thefts and Robberies, and for Regulating Places of Public Entertainment, and Punish Persons Keeping Disorderly Houses." The act failed to define precisely what was included in "public entertainment and the like."

It was just this kind of loophole contained in the phrase "the like" that permitted the spirit of the fair theatres in the form of comédies-en-vaudeville or, as it was called in England, the *burletta*.

Burletta

The first burletta was produced in the late 1740s at one of the legitimate houses. After the passing of the licensing act there were only two legitimate theatres in London operating throughout the year—Drury Lane and Covent Garden. At first the unlicensed theatres attempted to get around the law by various liberal interpretations. Henry Gifford charged admission at his Goodman's Fields Theatre only for the concert; the play was free. Some of these ruses were tolerated for a while, but eventually performances were forbidden. It was the ability to license public entertainments under the Fielding Law and the arrival of the burletta that eventually undermined the licensing act.

Whereas some minor theatre companies were forced to close with some moving off to the colonies, others faced the problem of circumventing

Hogarth's *Gin Lane*, picturing the shop of pawnbroker S. Gripe, which is flourishing as is the gin cellar below and the distillery to the right. Above the entrance to the gin cellar is written: "Drunk for a penny, dead drunk for twopence, clean straw for nothing." A barber has hanged himself (upper right) because the people can no longer afford his services. The working class is beset by murder, suicide, starvation, disease, and poverty, and Hogarth indicates that children are the worst victims. Note the mother feeding her child gin (extreme right center). *Courtesy Fine Arts Library, Indiana University.*

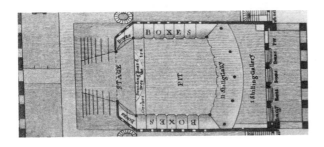

The Haymarket Theatre, originally built in 1720 by John Potter. Henry Fielding took over this theatre, called "The Little Theatre in the Hay," in 1730, but gave it up because of licensing problems. Pictured here is the interior of the Haymarket (rebuilt by John Nash), as it appeared on opening night July 4, 1821, for Sheridan's *The Rivals*. From *Londina Illustrata,* 1825.

the law as an interesting challenge just as it had the fair managers. In 1787 Phillip Astley, proprietor of Astley's Circus, where horse shows and musical entertainments were performed, asked for and received permission to add the term burletta to his amphitheatre license. By adding the title burletta to his equestrian dramas, Astley was able to add plot and music to his shows.

The proprietor of the Sans Pareil Theatre in Bullen Court applied to the Lord Chamberlain's office, asking and receiving permission to add to his license the word burletta. This request was brought up before the privy council and lawyers were called in to decide the meaning of the term and state the law regulating it. The results were indecisive and provided no real legal definition of burletta. The indecision of the privy council lawyers in defining the term created a new opening for the proprietors of the minor theatres. Soon a plethora of burlettas appeared all over London. Robert Elliston, for example, opened a burletta melodrama founded on *The Beggar's Opera*. Later he produced the burletta *Macbeth*. Soon a multitude of famous English tragedies, comedies, and melodramas were performed under the general description of burletta.

The inability of the patent theatres to combat the minor theatres eventually led to the defeat of

Hogarth's *Strolling Actresses Dressing in a Barn* (1738) demonstrates how the 1737 Licensing Act was evaded. The Act (on the crown, left foreground) specified actors; the country company depicted thus used a cast of women and children. The playbill on the bed reveals that the company intended to present *The Devil to Pay in Heaven. Courtesy Fine Arts Library, Indiana University.*

Examples of dress for the opera in 1784.

the monopoly. In 1843 the Theatre Regulations Act restored the spoken dialogue to the minor theatres and their victory was complete.

Summary

The influences on the theatre by governmental restrictions, then, created some rather important changes. First, the fact that both the minor theatres in England and the fair theatres in France were forced to experiment with new genres in effect released them from the rigidity of neoclassicism. In France these experiments led directly to the emergence of melodrama, which in turn was the greatest single influence on the romantic technique of Dumas père and Hugo. In England the growth of the ballad opera and political satire were seriously restricted by the Licensing Act of 1737. The importation of burletta, however, as well as the antisuppression techniques of the fair

theatres, enabled the English minor theatres to continue to search for new means of expression.

Second, both the fair theatres and the English minor theatres catered more to the common clientele who could not always afford to attend the legitimate theatres.

Third, besides the development and popularization of melodrama and romantic comedy, new genres in the form of comic opera in France and operetta in England evolved.

Fourth, in France and England the minor theatres played a major role in the development of social drama both in form and sympathy to the commoner.

Fifth, the 1737 act led to the beginning of professional theatre in America as many companies, including the Hallam Company, had to leave England to find work.

Change was certainly in the air and it was not long before the rise of the romantic ideal and the American and French revolutionary cries of equality, fraternity, and brotherhood began to reshape the world. The bourgeois theatre had, indeed, been born.

Selected Readings

Lancaster, H. C. *A History of French Dramatic Literature in the Seventeenth Century*, 5 vols. in 9. Baltimore, 1929-1942.

Lawrenson, T. E. *The French Stage in the XVIIth Century: A Study in the Advent of the Italian Order.* Rev. ed. Manchester, 1984.

Lynch, James. *Box, Pit and Gallery: Stage and Society in Johnson's London.* Berkeley, 1953.

McKendrick, Melveena. *Theatre in Spain 1490-1700.* Cambridge, 1989.

Mongredien, Georges. *Daily Life in the French Theatre at the Time of Molière..* London, 1969.

Nicoll, Allardyce. *History of English Drama 1660-1900.* 6 vols. London, 1955-1959.

Shergold, N. D. A *History of the Spanish Stage from Medieval Times until the End of the 17th Century.* Oxford, 1967.

Vocabulary

1.	Lope de Vega	LOH puh de VAY gah
2.	Calderón	kahl de ROHN
3.	auto sacramentales	AW toh sah crah men TAH lis
4.	corrales	kaw RAH lis
5.	cazuela	kah ZWAY luh
6.	Richelieu	ree shuh LOO:
7.	Mazarin	MA zah rin
8.	Hôtel de Bourgogne	oh TEL de boor GOH nyuh
9.	Palais-Royale	PA lay roy YAHL
10.	Marais	may RAY
11.	verisimilitude	vai ruh si MI luh tood
12.	Pierre Corneille	pyair kawr NAY
13.	Le Cid	luh SID
14.	Jean Racine	zhaw rah SEEN
15.	La Thébaide	luh tay bah EED
16.	Les Plaideurs	lay play DER
17.	*Phèdre*	FAY druh
18.	Hippolytus	hi PAW li tuhs
19.	Molière	MAWL yair
20.	Jean-Baptiste Poquelin	zhaw bah TIST poh kuh LIN
21.	Madelaine Béjart	mahd LAYN bay JAHR
22.	Les Précieuses Ridicules	lay pray SYERZ ree dee KYOOL
23.	Théâtre Illustré	tay AH truh i lus TRAY
24.	Comédie Française	koh may DEE frahn SAYS
25.	Rue Guénégaud	roo gay nay GOH
26.	Mlle. Champmeslé	shaw may LAY
27.	Denis Diderot	duh NEE DEE duh roh
28.	piéce a écriteaux	pyes ah ay kree TOH
29.	opéra comique	OH PAY RUH CAW MEEK
30.	Foire Saint-Germain	fwawr sanb zhair MEN
31.	Foire Saint-Laurent	fwawr san loh RAHN
32.	William Davenant	DA vuh nuhnt
33.	querelle des bouffons	ke REL day boo FAWN
34.	Jean Vade	zhaw VAHD
35.	Antoine Auvergne	ahn TWUHN oh VAIRN
36.	Les Troquers	lay troh KER
37.	Théâtre des Associés	tay AHT ruh dayz ah soh SYAY
38.	variétiés amusantes	vah ree ay TAYZ ah moo ZAHNT
39.	Pixérécourt	peez ay ray Koor
40.	sans pareil	saw pah RAH
41.	Aphra Behn	A fra Bayn

CHAPTER TEN

❧

Revolution:
The Romantic Ideal

James Henry Hackett (1800-1871), American actor noted for his Yankee characters and the first American to appear in London as a star. In this photo he is playing Falstaff in *Henry IV* in London, 1833. Hackett was also manager of the Astor Place Opera House at the time of the Astor Place Riot. From *Dramatic Portrait Gallery*, 1880.

Rise of Romanticism

In many ways the whole concept of romanticism is based on a longing for a better, more equitable life. Those individuals not fortunate enough to be born aristocratic began to ask the age old question about life—"Is this all there is?" That question was rooted in several factors prevalent throughout Europe in the eighteenth and nineteenth centuries. First, there was a revolt against the old neoclassical ideal and its reliance on cold hard reasoning. Second, there was a questioning of the fairness of the existing social order. Both ideas seem to suggest a breakdown in human values as a determining factor in existence. As early as the seventeenth century, writers such as John Locke (1632-1704) were questioning a status quo that denied God-given rights to all people. In the *Second Treatise of Civil Government,* Locke wrote: "To understand political power aright, and derive it from its original, we must consider what state all men are naturally in, and that is a state of perfected freedom to order their actions and dispose of their possessions and persons as they think fit."

Burke, Rousseau, and others, though not necessarily endorsing the concept of democracy, certainly contributed to the growing demand for equality and liberty from aristocratic governments. Burke defined natural society as "society founded in natural appetites and instincts, and not in any positive institution." In many ways, the idea of natural instincts and the better society was a cry of revolt against artificially applied restrictions against the common man, which created doubt among the middle and lower classes as to the morality of existing political hierarchy. Throughout Europe dissatisfaction against an aristocratic tradition that defied the concept of equality was increasingly evident. In England, for example, the census of 1801 estimated a population of some nine million people, divided into roughly seven different classes. First, there were the princes, dukes, marquises, earls, viscounts and barons, a total of some 7000 persons. Second, there were the spiritual lords, numbering about twenty-six bishops. The bishops along with the peers were entitled to sit in the House of Lords. Third were some 540 baronets and their wives who were entitled to add "Sir" and "Lady" to their names and to transmit their titles. The fourth group included knights and their wives, who were allowed the same prefix as baronets but were unable to transmit the title. Fifth were the approximately 6,000 squires or the gentry, as they were sometimes called. This group included the landowners and, along with the baronets, knights, squires and their wives, were considered lesser nobility. All of the above represented the English aristocracy.

In addition to the aristocracy, there were some 20,000 "gentlemen" or "ladies" living on income without manual work, having a coat of arms, and assumed to be of gentle birth (born into old and accepted families). These groups were followed by the rest of the English population. Considering that the 287 peers received twenty-nine percent of the national income in 1801, the skepticism about the fairness of the existing social order seems justified. Thus a skeptical middle class began to trace the development of unfair political and social structures and, in doing so, tended to idealize primitive society—a society which was free and equal and able to follow the dictates of its own conscience.

In Europe as well as in the United States, these same forces generated revolution. The French Revolution created fear in other European governments that it would spread to their own countries. War was declared against France and a bloodbath ensued. The rise of Napoleon Bonaparte (1769-1821) in 1799 brought order out of chaos but instituted an empire in place of democracy. With Napoleon's final defeat in 1815, however, regimes even more repressive than before were instituted. These developments, coupled with a dramatic rise in the urbanization of Europe, created almost unbearable living conditions. Industrialization, accelerated by the invention of the steam engine and its applications in the form of the power loom and the locomotive, among others, intensified the domination of the factory system over the artisan. It is no small wonder that the common European worker yearned for the freedom of a democratic society already taking root in America. Thus a longing for the ideal to replace the pain of reality fueled the romantic movement in literature and in the theatre.

Philosophical Concepts

Beginning in Germany, romanticism evolved into a series of complex philosophical tenets reaching its apogee about 1830. First, the prevalent idea that repressive governments were a product of modern society created a new interest in the past in an attempt to locate the pure society untouched by modern corruption. Germane to the rise of antiquarianism was the concept that beyond reality was a higher plane of existence created by a supreme spirit embodying eternal truth. Since all things have as their origin the truth of the creator, one must look to the infinite variety of creation to find truth. Inasmuch as this idea was in direct opposition to the neoclassical concept of truth through the observation of observable norms, a search was conducted to find these ultimate truths. First, it was postulated that if everything has a common origin, then a careful observation of any part would give insights to the totality of truth, leading to the assumption that the more unspoiled a thing was the better it would embody a fundamental truth. To know truth, then, it was possible to study a skylark, a cloud, daffodils or even the wind to discover nature's secrets. Nature was considered to be the great unspoiled. Back to nature, then, became almost a rallying cry to the romanticists. To some, only in nature could one find the ultimate lessons in life. The more the artificially created products of society were exposed, the better chance of grasping truth. As Wordsworth wrote: "The world is too much with us. Getting and spending, we lay waste all our powers. Little we see in nature which is ours."

Thus, the romanticist rebelled against a highly structured bureaucratic society that instituted restraints on its people.

Second, the contrast between reality and spirituality was represented in the duality of being—that we, as humans, live in a physical world while our spiritual self tries to transcend it. In a sense, there was an attempt to transcend the physical limitations through a number of alternative methods such as intoxicants and eastern philosophy. The most important method of freeing humanity from the pain of reality, however, was art wherein universal truths could be given apprehensible form. The artistic perception of truth led the romanticist to place the artist-interpreter and the philosopher in the enviable position of spiritual gurus. These gifted individuals or geniuses as they were called were then faced with the impossible task of embodying a truth that can only be found in the spiritual realm. But it was those glimpses into the spiritual provided by the genius that enabled the romantics to rise above mundane reality.

For the playwright, grasping the spiritual became an almost impossible task. The physical limitations of the stage became a barrier to success and some playwrights disregarded them in favor of impossible stage flights of fancy. All restrictions imposed by neoclassical rules were discarded in favor of absolute freedom. Shakespeare's plays became the model because they had never followed those artificially imposed limitations. In their ardent zeal to idealize the freedom of Shakespeare's form, romanticists neglected to understand his discipline. Many of their plays, then, became exercises in disorganization and chaos.

While the political ramifications of romanticism were manifest, its influence on the theatre was even more convoluted. Since the concept of liberty and equality as well as adherence to natural law and values were basic premises of the movement, the theatre became the chief source of these ideas. In a sense, the theatre became a sounding board for the ideal rather than the real. The ideal of equality was staunchly upheld and painted in

Giovanni Battista Piranesi (1720-1778) through his stage settings and engravings of Roman ruins stirred a new interest in the use of light and shadow, which contributed to the eerie mood effects of romantic dramas. These engravings (1765) depict the Forum of Nerva. *Courtesy Lilly Library, Indiana University.*

glowing terms on the stage but the reality was that slavery was running rampant. The ideal of liberty was sung across the footlights of every theatre, but the common worker was held in bondage throughout Europe. The natural values developed in such plays as *The Lady of Lyons* were, in reality, a simplistic paradigm used to create artificial standards.

Concept of Women

Consistent with this viewpoint was the romantic or idealistic concept of women. At first, there was a gradual change in the depiction of women, and for that matter, morals in general. During the period of Louis XIV and the Restoration, reactions against the aggressiveness of women were epitomized in Rousseau's work, *Emile,* wherein he stated that the woman's place was in the home. "She should accept her husband as a master, but in the home she should be supreme. In that way, the health of the race would be preserved." Additionally, Rousseau believed that the education of girls should aim to produce such women. "Girls should be educated at home by their mothers; they should learn all the arts of the home from cooking to embroidery. They should get much religion and as early as possible, for this would help them to achieve modesty, virtue and obedience. In any case, a girl should avoid philosophy and scorn to be *salonnière.* However, a girl should not be suppressed into dull timidity; she should be lively, merry, and eager; sing and dance to her heart's content. Let her go to balls, even to the theatre—under proper supervision and in good company. Her mind should be kept active and alert if she would ever be a fit wife for a thinking man. Further, she should be allowed a certain amount of coquetry as a part of a complex game by which she might test her suitors and choose her mate. The proper study of womankind should be man."

Whatever the present-day reaction to these general thoughts, several points can be made. First, the idea of equality did not necessarily include women, although many free-thinking women did evolve from the movement. Second, the literary concept of women became idealized or romanticized and that ideal was to set an artificial standard of morality for some time to come. Third, the artificial standard of morality was to affect the content of the English drama throughout the nineteenth century. Artificial standards of morality are best understood in the Victorian period.

The Victorians

Perhaps in no age have people been so concerned about the appearance of respectability as were the Victorians, and perhaps in no other age have people been so hypocritical. At the center of this hypocrisy was the middle class, who modeled their behavior and thought after the upper classes, or what they perceived was upper-class behavior and thought. Politically, the Victorians were chauvinistic and imperialistic. The men professed manliness to a fault, honoring the wearing of the uniform above all else. Their sense of duty to country was almost messianic and, in many ways, based on the reality of their world. Yet their treatment of women was based on a romantic concept of ideal femininity. In some ways, the Victorians emancipated women; in other ways, they took from women a vital place in society. Sexually, they were inhibited to the point of almost denying the existence of physical love.

Sexual intercourse and matters related to physical desires were treated as deeds of darkness, as matters which well-bred men and women never discussed. Gentility was thought antipathetic to the physical relationships between the sexes, a view which the medical profession and the clergy constantly reinforced. Doctors proclaimed the inevitability of cancer for those who overindulged in sex. Leading medical authorities cautioned women, in particular, never to indulge in sexual enjoyment. "The ideal English mother," according to Dr. William Acton (1818-1875), one of the most famous doctors in nineteenth century England, "knows little or nothing of sexual indulgences. Love of home, children and domestic duties are the only passion she feels." Forbidden by these unwritten laws of the middle class to indulge in sex or to enjoy it when available, many women found themselves in the unenviable position of becoming child-rearing vehicles, while their husbands shelved their guilt and made use of the vast array of prostitutes, reputed to number 120,000 in London alone. It is small wonder that the middle class found the whole subject of sex taboo. Because of the repressive restraint on the subject, it became confused, even diffused, into other manifestations. The shape of a grand piano, for example, became indecent and piano legs were frequently draped to avoid the possibility of offending young ladies.

Ostensibly, the protection of young ladies or the desire to sustain the romantic conception of sexuality became the prime justification for the English theatrical censor. The real reason was probably political but the English were so caught up in romantic philosophy that its perpetuation became almost an English ambiance. With the romantic idealization of the virtuous woman and honorable man, the English language was subjected to an expurgation of words with even the slightest hint of sexuality. Hence *breast* became *bosom* and even *naked necks. Legs* became *limbs* and the word *thigh* was removed from polite conversation altogether. Any article of underwear was referred to as *unmentionable.* When sex ceased to be talked about openly, it went underground. Probably no society, with the possible exception of our own and the Romans, has been as eager to welcome pornography and indecent engravings as were the Victorians. Since pornography was available through underground book sales and since literature was free from any kind of pre-censorship, the burden of dramatizing middle class standards fell to the theatre. For that reason the censorship of drama reached its apogee during the Victorian period.

Romanticism in Germany

The term romanticism was first used in the descriptive sense in the German literary journal *Das Athenaeum* (1798-1800). The writers were German romantics who were strongly influenced by the Storm and Stress (Sturm und Drang) movement (1767-1787) led by Friedrich Schiller (1759-1805) and Johann Wolfgang von Goethe (1749-1832). The Storm and Stress movement revolted against rationalism and in so doing created what has been described as irrational plays. Their efforts, however, plus those of Gotthold Lessing (1729-1781) before them, paved the way for reform in German drama.

Johann Wolfgang von Goethe, Germany's greatest literary figure. A dramatist, novelist, and director, Goethe did most of his work at the Court Theatre, Weimar (1796-1817). He and Schiller were initially members of a romantic movement known as the Sturm and Drang (Storm and Stress). *Courtesy German Information Center.*

FAUST PART I AND II
JOHANN WOLFGANG VON GOETHE

CHARACTERS (Partial List)
FAUST, a faithful man with a thirst for knowledge
GRETCHEN, a maiden
MEPHISTOPHELES, himself
WAGNER, Faust's servant
HELEN OF TROY, herself
HOMUNCULUS, a spirit

SETTING: The Earth, at an unnamed time

BACKGROUND
Goethe is sometimes called the German Shakespeare and is generally considered to be the greatest of the German writers. He was a universal genius equally proficient in the arts, philosophy, and science. His work in botany is still considered valid. *Faust* epitomizes the romantic philosophy in its search to find truth through the infinite variety of human existence and the impossibility of that search. It is considered by many to be one of the greatest plays ever written by a German writer and certainly one of the greatest if not the greatest play of the romantic era.

PLOT
Part I
God and Mephistopheles make a bet that Faust cannot be tempted away from his faithfulness. Mephistopheles finds Faust in the middle of a philosophical discussion with Wagner. Faust is very tired of his limitations, and wants to do something great. When Mephistopheles tempts him, though, he easily turns him down. Mephistopheles returns later and tries again. This time they talk of how Faust could be happy if he gave in to sensual things. Faust says that if Mephistopheles ever introduced him to something that he wished would never end, then he would cease to exist. After making Faust young again, Mephistopheles introduces him to Gretchen, a pure and wonderful woman. Faust is touched by her, and doesn't wish to hurt her. However, he does eventually go to her. She is completely in love with him, and they make love. She becomes pregnant, and her brother convinces her that what she did was wrong. Faust kills him in a rage. Mephistopheles was confident that Faust would want his time with Gretchen to last forever, but Faust realizes that that wouldn't fulfill the longing in him. When he does return to Gretchen, he finds that she has killed their baby and insisted on dying.

Part II
Mephistopheles brings Faust to the emperor, who asks to see the most beautiful man and woman ever. When he conjures up Paris and Helen of Troy, Faust faints with desire at the sight of Helen. Later, Mephistopheles makes a spirit, Homunculus, to see into Faust's mind. Mephistopheles hopes this will help him understand Faust. Mephistopheles then brings Faust a Helen, but he turns her away, knowing that beauty isn't lasting. Faust returns to his home and gives up his powers to turn a stretch of swamp into a productive piece of land. In his old age, he sees the land he cultivated as having many productive people living on it. Realizing the magnitude of what he has finally accomplished, he wishes for the moment to never end. Mephistopheles appears to claim Faust's soul, but is prevented by angels, because Faust has grown beyond his selfish desires, and has, in giving, remained in God's service.

Although Goethe later renounced romanticism, his *Faust* is considered to be the most important of the romantic plays. The play is divided into two parts (Part I, 1808; Part II, 1831). It epitomizes the romantic philosophy in its search to find truth through the infinite variety of human existence and the impossibility of that search.

Two other German writers were deeply connected with German romanticism, Schlegel and Tieck. August Wilhelm Schlegel (1767-1845) was

Two leading figures in the German romantic movement: *Left:* Johann Gottfried Herder (1744-1783).*Right:* Heinrich von Kleist(1777-1811). *Photos courtesy German Information Center.*

Friedrich von Schiller, another of Germany's great dramatists. Schiller and Goethe formed artistic vews which came to be labeled "Weimar Classicism." *Courtesy German Information Center.*

deeply influential in spreading the romantic movement outside of Germany, particularly in France and England. Like other romanticists, Schlegel preferred to concentrate on the philosophical ideals taught by the play rather than dramatic structure and therefore proclaimed Shakespeare's plays as the romantic ideal.

Schlegel's ideas were put into practice by Ludwig Tieck (1773-1853), who was responsible for disseminating Shakespeare's works throughout Germany. Tieck was a playwright of some distinction, known primarily for *Kaiser Octavianus* written in 1802 and his fantastic comedies based on fairy tales, such as *Little Red Riding Hood* and *Puss in Boots.*

The most important non-romantic writers of the period were Heinrich von Kleist (1777-1811) and Friedrich von Schiller (1759-1805). Kleist, known for his plays, *The Broken Jug* (1806), *Penthesilea* (1808) and *The Prince of Homburg* (1811), was probably the most popular German play-

wright of the early nineteenth century. Schiller, recognized for his plays *The Robbers* (1782), *Don Carlos* (1787), *Maria Stuart* (1800) and *William Tell* (1804), wrote in the romantic style but denied being a romantic.

Most famous of the German actors and actresses were Sophie Schröeder (1781-1868), considered the greatest tragic actress of the period; Ludwig Costenoble (1769-1837), a character actor, and Heinrich Anschütz (1785-1865), probably the greatest German actor of heroic roles.

French Romanticism

Germaine Necker or Mme. de Staël (1766-1817) is generally credited with introducing romanticism to France and Italy when she published *Of Germany* (1810). The book was suppressed by Napoleon but was republished after his downfall.

Although Napoleon had a preference for neoclassical drama and attempted to nullify minor theatres, the development of the romantic theatre not only evolved from the minor theatres but was a reaction to neoclassicism. Out of the romantic theatre emerged the creation of minor forms such as melodrama. René Charles Guilbert de

Pixérécourt (1773-1844) established the form of melodrama which was to become the dominant dramatic type of the nineteenth century. It is important to note Pixérécourt's works were still considered a minor form and were not played by the Comédie Française. It was not until romanticism arrived in France that melodrama became a legitimate form.

Under the influence of Schlegel in Germany and Wordsworth and Coleridge in England, romanticism with its sentimental emotion and its penchant for spectacle was to hold sway in France during the 1830s and 40s. By the 1840s it began to decline and by 1850 it was dead. It was preserved in part by the boulevard theatres where melodrama was dominant. In the major theatres, however, it would give way to realism, especially the "ecole de bon sens" (school of good sense) out of which would come the drama of the Second Empire (Napoleon III: 1808-1873).

In 1822 the English introduced romanticism to France, which was disinclined to accept anything English. Due to the efforts of England's Prime Minister, George Canning's liberal policies towards France, tensions between France and England eased. As a consequence, the French were receptive when an English company visited the Porte-Saint-Martin in 1827. These visits were influential in bringing romanticism to France as well as influencing Victor Hugo (1802-1885), Alfred Givny (1797-1863), and Alexandre Dumas *pére,* who gave literary respectability to melodrama, thereby creating romantic drama.

French romanticism is considered to have begun with Hugo's play, *Hernani* (1830), produced by the Comédie Française. Although this is true to some extent, it should be pointed out that such plays as Frederick Soulie's *Roméo and Juliette,* Hugo's *Amy Robsart* and Dumas *pére's Christine* (1830), which was produced one month after *Hernani* and was also the subject of the classicists' attack, paved the way for romanticism. By the time *Hernani* was presented, neoclassicism was for all intent and purposes dead. The attack against *Hernani* was simply a culmination of events that preceded it and its triumph indicated that roman-

Portrait of Mme. de Staël, whose book *Of Germany* popularized August Wilhelm Schlegel's romanticism and classicism throughout Italy and France. From *Histoire Illustreé de la Littérature Française*

Victor Hugo, French writer whose drama *Hernani* (1830) precipitated a riot between the romantics and the classicists that lasted for forty-five nights. The eventual victory of the romantics signaled the beginning of romanticism in France. From *Histoire Illustreé de la Littérature Française*

Some scholars date the beginning of French romanticism to the production of *Hernani* by Victor Hugo in 1830. This sketch for the set is by J. B. Lavestre from the *Livre de régie. Comédie Française.*

Alexandre Dumas *pére* in his youth.

(1843) and *Columbe's Birthday* (1853). Percy Bysshe Shelley (1792-1822) produced *Prometheus Unbound* and *The Cenci* in 1819. The most popular of the romantic poets to write for the theatre was George Gordon, Lord Byron (1788-1824), whose work *Werner* (1830) became a long-running theatrical vehicle for the well-known actor William Charles Macready (1793-1873). Oddly enough, the most popular dramatist of the day did not belong to the elite school of poets. His name was Edward George Bulwer-Lytton, best known today for his novel, *The Last Days of Pompeii* (1834). As a reform member of Parliament, his influence on the English theatre is exceptional. Bulwer-Lytton joined forces with Macready to produce what was called "gentlemanly melodrama." Their collaboration produced, among others, *The Lady of Lyons* (1838), *Richelieu* (1839) and *Money* (1840), which held the stage for most of the nineteenth century. All of these plays tended to idealize women and the pure of spirit and none better than *The Lady of Lyons*.

Edward George Bulwer-Lytton, the most popular English dramatist of the nineteenth century. From *Dramatic Portrait Gallery*, 1880.

ticism would be a force with which to contend. The play violated every neoclassical rule and was essentially a melodrama with a happy ending, characteristic of most romantic plays.

English Romanticism

The romantic period in England produced some of the finest poets in the English-speaking world, although their theatrical labor was not as successful. Most followed the Shakespearean model and wrote in blank verse. William Wordsworth (1770-1850) wrote *The Borderers* in 1795. John Keats (1795-1821) contributed *Otho the Great* (1819). Samuel Taylor Coleridge published *Remorse* (1813). Robert Browning, one of the more successful of the group, wrote *Strafford* (1837), *A Blot on the Scutcheon*

THE LADY OF LYONS
EDWARD BULWER-LYTTON

CHARACTERS (Partial List)
PAULINE, the Lady of Lyons
COLONEL DAMAS, Pauline's cousin
BEAUSEANT, a wealthy rebuffed suitor to Pauline
GLAVIS, another rebuffed suitor, friend of Beauseant
CLAUDE MELNOTTE, a poor man educated well beyond his station, he is in love with Pauline

SETTING
Lyons, France, Mid-nineteenth century

BACKGROUND
Based on the French tale "The Bellows-Mender." First produced in February of 1838 at the Covent Garden Theatre.

PLOT
The play opens with Pauline turning down her latest suitor, Beauseant, because she hopes to marry into royalty. Enraged that a woman beneath his class should refuse him, Beauseant plots with Glavis, another would-be suitor, for revenge. They decide to finance Claude Melnotte, a gardener's son, to impersonate a prince and ask for her hand. Claude had been infatuated with Pauline and had written her love poems. Her rejection and ridicule angers Claude to the point that he readily accepts the terms of Beauseant and Glavis. Claude courts and wins Pauline's heart and the approval of her parents. Pauline's cousin, Colonel Damas, suspects Melnotte and challenges him to a duel which is won by Claude. Because Claude refuses to kill Damas, he gains his respect. Meanwhile Claude is gradually feeling great guilt for what he has done and pleads with Beauseant and Glavis to be released from the oath to marry Pauline. They refuse and the ceremony takes place with Claude and Pauline retiring to his mother's house. Claude's guilt becomes overwhelming and he admits the truth to both Pauline and his mother. Both women are shocked. Claude resolves not to consummate the marriage to allow Pauline an annulment. Claude sets off to confess to Pauline's parents. While he is gone, Beauseant arrives and once again proposes to Pauline, only to be refused. Enraged, Beauseant draws his pistol and threatens Pauline, but she is saved by the return of Melnotte. Pauline is moved by Claude's bravery and offers to forgive him. He refuses her offer, stating that his actions have made him unworthy of her. Pauline's parents arrive with Damas and are outraged at Claude's conduct. They attempt to take Pauline home but she balks electing to stay with Claude's mother. Damas convinces Claude that the only way to regain his honor is to join the army which is leaving for battle that night. Claude accepts and leaves, vowing to return with honor to Pauline. Two and one-half years pass. Damas returns with the celebrated hero "Colonel Morier" (Claude's alias) from the war. They find that Pauline has been betrothed to Beauseant. Thinking that she had abandoned him, Claude goes to her in disguise. He learns that Pauline's father is bankrupt and will lose his home if Pauline does not marry Beauseant. Claude as Colonel Morier questions Pauline, telling her that he was a friend of Melnotte. She confesses that she is deeply in love with Claude Melnotte and longs for him. Claude, in tears, removes the disguise and they embrace. He pays off Beauseant, thereby saving Pauline's father. They vow never to part again in presence of Pauline's now approving parents. Claude and Pauline slowly, lovingly stare into each other's eyes as the curtain closes.

One of the most important actor managers of the nineteenth century, Macready was also instrumental in imposing stage movement on his actors, thereby laying the groundwork for the modern director. He is also noted for the restoration of many of Shakespeare's altered texts.

Another important actor-manager was John Philip Kemble (1757-1817). Considered one of the most financially successful managers of the time. Kemble made Covent Garden the leading theatre in the English-speaking world. The entire Kemble family achieved notoriety. The most important

Sarah Siddons (1755-1831), considered the greatest tragic actress of the English stage. Along with her brother, John Philip Kemble, she established the "classical" style of acting, so named because of its emphasis upon dignity, grace, and nobility. From *The Kembles and Their Contemporaries, 1892.*

John Fawcett as Captain Copp and Charles Kemble as Charles II in John Howard Payne's *Charles II,* May 27, 1824, at Covent Garden.

members of the family were Charles Kemble (1775-1854) and Sarah Kemble Siddons (1755-1831). Charles is credited with the first major step toward antiquarianism in the theatre. In 1823 he used historically accurate costumes designed by James Robinson Planché (1796-1880) in his production of Shakespeare's play *King John.* Mrs. Siddons became one of the great tragic actresses of the century with her emotional intensity. She is still known in England for her portrayal of Lady Macbeth. Other important actors and actresses of the period were Charles Maye Young (1777-1856), J. W. Wallack (1791-1864), Eliza O'Neill (1791-1827), and Edmund Kean. After Kemble's retirement, Kean became the foremost actor of his day and is generally considered to be the person responsible for the beginning of the "star system."

The romantic period not only established the legitimacy of the actress, it also produced one of the first great female managers in the person of Lucia Elizabetta Vestris (1797-1856), better known as Madame Vestris. Mme. Vestris is noted for her management of the Olympic Theatre, where she is credited with introducing the box set and the extensive use of properties in her productions. Mme. Vestris is also known for simplifying the evening's entertainment to get the audience out of the theatre at a reasonable hour as opposed to the normal 2:00 A.M. closing. This brought even more respectability to the theatre. Still, to understand the difficulties faced by an English manager, it is necessary to look at the political pressure that had to be faced in the form of censorship. While de facto censorship had begun in 1545 with the Master of Revels, the Theatre Regulations Act of 1843 legitimized it. Ostensibly enacted to free the minor theatres from domination from the patent houses, the act of 1843 deeply influenced the English stage for well over a hundred years.

Edmund Kean (1787-1833) as Gloucester in *Richard III*. Kean was a major influence upon the establishment of the "star" system. From *The Kembles and Their Contemporaries*, 1890.

J. R. Planché's costume design for Charles Kemble's *King Henry IV*, 1824. This production marked the first use of both historically accurate costumes and sets. The first use of historically accurate costumes appears to have been Kemble's 1823 production of *King John*, with Planché the costume designer. *Courtesy Lilly Library, Indiana University.*

Censorship in England

The significant second section of the 1843 act gave the Lord Chamberlain the power to license theatres; that is, to license theatre buildings rather than producers, players, or plays. Further, while the justices of the peace had the right to license theatres outside of London proper, the Lord Chamberlain could close them without trial anywhere the sovereign happened to be in residence. In addition, the Lord Chamberlain was given the power to close any theatre in England for misbehavior if an unlicensed play were produced, and to fine any manager in London for breach of the rules. Allowing the Lord Chamberlain to set his own rules gave him legislative and judicial authority, as well as the right to define what constituted a theatre. In addition, actors could now be penalized for performing anywhere except in a licensed theatre. But the most important of all sections was section fourteen which said in effect that "whenever he shall be of the opinion that it is fitting for preservation of good manners, Decorum, or of the public Peace so to do, to forbid the acting or presenting any Stage Play anywhere in Great Britain." This gave the Lord Chamberlain control over the content of English drama.

The actual task of censoring plays was given to a play examiner appointed by the Lord Chamberlain with no literary expertise required. If the examiner wished a word or paragraph changed to fit the ideal conception of British society and its women, the playwright would be obligated to follow instructions or have the license refused. Once refused, the playwright had no right to appeal.

The Victorian gentlemen who became play examiners were particularly alert to the sensibilities of young ladies. One of the nineteenth century examiners, William Bodham Donne, always changed the word God to heaven. The word lord was also changed to heaven on occasion. The phrase "fit for a lord" in W. S. Gilbert's version of *Great Expectations* was changed to "chambers fit for heaven." Donne's replacement, Edward F. Smyth Piggott, banned, among other things, *The Oberammergau Passion Play* and Shelley's *The Cenci*. Piggott was particularly watchful of French pieces, and he censored far more French adaptations than English plays. In one instance related by George Bernard Shaw, Piggott refused to license a translation of a French play on the ground that the heroine, a married woman, had been guilty of an indiscretion in early life. The actress cast for the part visited Piggott and naturally used all her powers of persuasion to induce him to revoke his decision. Finally he consented on condition that the words, "I sinned but in intention," were added into her part. According to Shaw, "every night, during the burst of welcome which hailed her first entrance in the piece, the actress remarked confidentially to the conductor of the band, 'I sinned but in intention,' and thereby rescued her country from demoralization by French levity." Perhaps the most famous or infamous of the play examiners was George Alexander Redford, who had the dubious distinction of refusing a license to Sophocles' *Oedipus Rex*, Maeterlinck's *Monna Vanna*, Ibsen's *Ghosts*, Shaw's *Mrs. Warren's Profession*, and Gilbert & Sullivan's *The Mikado*, to name but a few. *Oedipus Rex* was banned outright because of the incest. The ban prompted the playwright Henry Arthur Jones to comment in his book, *The Foundations of a National Drama*, "If after the production of *Oedipus*, it is found that Englishmen are developing the habit of marrying their mothers, even if there is any noticeable tendency

Astley's Amphitheatre about 1815. Dramatic presentations were staged both in the ring and on stage; the theatre was especially noted for its equestrian melodramas. From *Londina Illustrata*, 1825.

that way, then the censorship must be held to have justified itself, and in this instance to have shown a sagacity and foresight which none of its other actions would lead us to imagine it possessed."

Theatre in America to 1850

There are many arguments both pro and con on the role of the censor on the English stage. Most scholars agree, however, that government control over the theatre and the content of drama influenced the nature of the English stage and, by default, the American stage for many years. Theatre in North America began probably in 1606 with the first play ever written in North America, called *The Theatre of Neptune in New France* by Marc Lescarbot performed in Nova Scotia. The earliest record of a performance in what is now the United States was recorded in 1665 when three men were hauled into court for performing a playlet called

Ye Bear and Ye Cub in Virginia. The beginning of professional theatre can be traced to a company from England headed by Lewis Hallam (1714-1756) first performing in Williamsburg, Virginia, in September 1752. The Hallam company joined forces with David Douglass (?- 1786) and his company who had already constructed the Southwark Theatre in Philadelphia and the John Street Theater in New York. Douglas has been credited with producing the first American play, *The Prince of Parthia* (1767) by Thomas Godfrey, Jr. (1736-1763). The Revolution temporarily halted all professional theatre.

The Hallam Company resumed soon after the war with the addition of some native American playwrights. Among these playwrights was Royall Tyler (1757-1826), who wrote the first American comedy to be performed professionally. Tyler was born in the vicinity of Faneuil Hall, Boston. His father, Royall Tyler the elder, was a graduate of Harvard and a prosperous merchant. At fifteen,

Wood engraving of the John Street Theatre, which opened December 7, 1767, and remained the leading theatre in New York until the turn of the century. *Courtesy Museum of the City of New York.*

Tyler followed his father's footsteps and enrolled in Harvard. He was handsome, had a beautiful voice, a volatile wit, great friendliness, and a gift of laughter. Tyler graduated in 1776 with an A.B. degree from Harvard and an A.B. simultaneously from Yale.

In 1779 Tyler was admitted to the bar and began his practice in Maine and Boston. He courted Abigail Adams, who was the daughter of John Adams, only to lose her to Colonel Smith of the American Legation in London. During Shay's Rebellion of 1787, Tyler was called up with the rank of major to pursue the rebels into Vermont. He continued to negotiate with the rebels both in Vermont and New York. While in New York City, Tyler saw a production of Sheridan's *School for Scandal* at the little red wooden playhouse on John Street. The performance made a great impression on the young lawyer and, in less than a month, Tyler wrote *The Contrast*. The John Street Theatre was occupied at that time by the American Company under the tutelage of Lewis Hallam. Apparently Tyler gave the play to Thomas Wignell (1753-1803), the principal low comedian of the company. The play was first performed on April 16, 1787, with Wignall playing the part of Jonathan.

Napoleon's need for money greatly extended America's territorial limits when he sold France's lands west of the Mississippi. The Louisiana Purchase, the acquisition of Florida, Texas, Arizona, New Mexico and California extended the nation from the Mississippi River to the Pacific Ocean. The demand for theatrical activity increased proportionately. American playwrights were on the increase and along with them, the actors.

The first native-born actress to be internationally acclaimed was Charlotte Cushman (1816-1876). Originally an opera singer, she was to be considered the finest tragic actress of the English-speaking world during the nineteenth century. Cushman made her debut as an actress at the Bowery Theatre in New York in 1836. Between 1842 and 1843, she was the leading lady at the Walnut Theatre in Philadelphia. She was also its manager, which made her one of the first female theatre managers in America.

Charlotte Cushman, first American actress to be internationally acclaimed. Like Edwin Forrest, she relied heavily on her energy and her physical appearance to give her a commanding stage presence. From *Dramatic Portrait Gallery*, 1880.

William Charles Macready was so impressed with her acting that he urged her to go to London. She made her debut at the Princess in 1844 and became an overnight star. When she returned to the United States her reputation was established. Some critics called her a female counterpart of Edwin Forrest because of the physical and emotional power of her characterization, and others called her the "female Macready" because of the similarity in style. However, comparisons with her male counterparts are unnecessary because she was in her own right one of the greatest performers of her period.

In addition to the work of Cushman, Macready and others, the American theatre presented plays that emphasized specialty performers. Prior to 1850, there emerged in the American drama a number of nature types: the African-American character, the Indian, the Irish politician, the city boy, and the Yankee. Most represented a geographical area of the country. Two of these were a direct reflection of the average man: the stage Yankee and the city boy. Initially, the city boy was not well received—he was a symbol of urban life and was a result of the increasing population in the cities. However, with the emergence of Mose, the Bowery Boy, in Benjamin Baker's *A Glance at New*

THE CONTRAST
ROYALL TYLER

CHARACTERS
COLONEL MANLY, an honorable soldier
DIMPLE, a womanizing swine, engaged to Maria
CHARLOTTE, sister to Manly, a debutante
LETTIA, Charlotte's friend
MARIA, a romantic woman, engaged to Dimple
VAN ROUGH, Maria's father

SETTING: Eighteenth Century New York

BACKGROUND
First performed at the John Street Theatre April 16, 1787. The character of Jonathan became an immediate hit. In a sense, the play is a contrast between decadent England with its aristocracy and the romantic America represented by Jonathan. The first stage Yankee, Jonathan, represents the noble savage, the common man, the primitive. His unspoiled nature, in contrast to the polished decadence of Dimple, allows him to speak from the heart in romantic truths. Every American viewer could see in Jonathan a raison d'être for the revolution. Romanticism had arrived in the American theatre.

PLOT
The play opens with Charlotte and Lettia discussing fashion and the unhappy engagement of Dimple and Maria. As the conversation goes on, we discover that the two were engaged very young, and then he went away to Europe. Dimple returned a changed, unpleasant man, while Maria became a very romantic, honorable individual. Still, she can not break off the engagement, or she would dishonor her family. This, it turns out, is exactly what Dimple wants her to do. He has promised the wealthy Lettia that he wants to marry her, while also making advances to Charlotte. All of this, of course, is known only to him. Charlotte's brother, Manly, is coming to visit her. Manly is an incredibly polite, formal, honorable soldier. In short, he is everything that Maria could want. Charlotte and Lettia speculate what it would be like to get Manly and Maria together. Dimple has, in the meantime, accrued many debts that he cannot pay, making it all the more important that he marry Lettia. The next day, Maria and Lettia are visiting Charlotte when Dimple and Manly enter. Charlotte quickly maneuvers Manly into walking Maria home, and the sparks begin to fly. Back at Maria's house, Van Rough has learned of Dimple's gambling debts. Hearing Maria's approach, he hides in the closet. At Maria's home, they talk and recognize the person they have longed for in each other. In spite of this, they realize that they cannot break the engagement, for the love of Maria's father. Manly, back at Charlotte's, mourns his loss, and enters a closet, mistaking it for a library. Dimple and Lettia enter and discuss how they don't want Dimple to marry Maria. When Charlotte enters, she gets Lettia to leave. Actually Lettia remains behind in order to eavesdrop on Dimple and Charlotte. Dimple tries to seduce her. When she refuses, he starts to insist. Manly enters and challenges him to a duel. Van Rough enters then and stops the fight. When he asks for an explanation, Lettia enters and all comes out. Dimple is disgraced, Charlotte and Lettia are changed, and Manly and Maria are to be married. Throughout the play Jonathan is the only character who sees Dimple as he really is.

York (1848), the popularity of the city boy changed. The good-natured roughneck Mose was played by Frank Chanfrau, whose success was overwhelming and led to sequels for the Mose character. After the 1860s, the changes brought about by the Civil War contributed to the disappearance of the Mose character.

Another popular type was the Yankee who made his introduction in *The Contrast* (1787). Simple, naive on the surface, patriotic, faithful, honest, the Yankee character became a symbol of the American common man.

George Handel Hill (1809-1849), considered the best of those portraying the Yankee character.

Frank Chanfrau (1824-1884), American actor whose portrayal of Mose, the Bowery Boy, the New York fireman in Baker's *A Glance at New York*, made Chanfrau's name synonymous with the Mose character. From *The Interviewer's Album*, 1881-1882.

Lithograph made in the 1850s of the stage Yankee, G.E. Locke.

Forrest-Macready Rivalry

The first true star of the American stage among the native-born actors was Edwin Forrest (1806-1872). He was a man of imposing physical strength and he disliked what he called the "repressed" acting of Macready. Forrest's rivalry of Macready led to one of the most bizarre incidents ever to occur in theatre. Forrest had gone to London with the idea of booking into Paris. After encountering abnormal difficulties in meeting with the Paris booking agent, Forrest immediately suspected that Macready had caused the problem. Later as Forrest performed *Macbeth* in London, with Charlotte Cushman as his leading lady, he detected noises in the audience. Enraged at what he thought was prearranged by Macready, he vowed to revenge himself. While Macready performed *Hamlet* at Edinburgh, Forrest, who had taken the week off, purchased a box seat in order to watch his rival perform. During a quiet scene Macready was unnerved by a rather loud hiss from Forrest's box. Forrest never attempted to hide his identity, thus infuriating his English rival.

The next collision occurred as Macready made a series of farewell performances in America. Macready was booked into the Astor Place Opera House and was set to open with *Macbeth*. The story of the feud between the two national idols was well publicized. The situation was further complicated by the engagement of Forrest to open a simultaneous *Macbeth*. Newspapers added fuel to the fire by making the two performances a fight to the finish for theatrical supremacy. Most papers sided with Forrest, certain that the "unsophisticated energy of the daring child of nature" would win out over the "glossy polish" of the Britisher. Any good American preferred "the tomahawk" to the "toga." In a sense, it was a battle between romanticism and neoclassicism.

Macready's opening night audience was infiltrated by Forrest's supporters, particularly in the gallery. The first two scenes were enthusiastically applauded as the American actor, C. W. Clarke, who played Macduff, dominated the stage. At Macready's entrance, however, the "Bowery B'hoys" in the gallery went wild with hisses and catcalls. Macready was pelted with rotten eggs, potatoes, and copper coins. When these were exhausted, the gallery began throwing chairs. The curtain was brought down and Macready was allowed to return to his hotel, resolving to leave for England on the next boat. A steady stream of visitors, including such literary figures as Washington Irving and Herman Melville, apologized for their fellow citizens and urged Macready to continue his run. Macready, the gentleman, was flattered by the response and agreed to continue, a decision he would live to regret.

The Forrest contingents were outraged and began to flood the city with handbills reading:
Workingmen!
shall
Americans or English Rule
in this city
Workingmen! Freemen!
stand by your
lawful rights.

The city was up in arms. The affair was taking on the dimensions of a revolt, pitting the true-hearted American primitive romantic against an English blue-blooded aristocrat which, of course, Macready was not. The police chief G. W. Matsell informed Mayor Caleb S. Woodhull that a riot might occur and the major urged the managers to cancel the performance. William Niblo (1789-1878) and James Henry Hackett (1800-1871), the managers, refused, citing the public's right to see and hear Macready. The major ordered Matsell to position a full police detail at the theatre, and a military force under General Sanford was to be held in readiness.

At curtain there were 1,800 spectators in the building, about 200 policemen inside the theatre, 50 police on the Eighth Street side of the building, and 75 at the main entrance. In addition, there were 200 members of the Seventh Infantry Regiment, two troops of horses, plus a standby unit of hussars.

The first scene went as before with the American actor being cheered, but when Macready entered, the galleries went wild. The police, in an attempt to restore order, arrested three of the most flagrant rowdies. Word of the arrests was passed

William C. Macready   Edwin Forrest

The Astor Place Riot, May 10, 1849.

to the angry crowd outside, and they began throwing sticks and bottles. The army was called and the cavalry unit attempted to clear the area. When they were forced to retreat by a hail of bricks, the infantry moved in with fixed bayonets but was driven back. The order was then given to fire over the heads of the rioters. The crowd moved back temporarily, but thinking that the troops were using blanks, soon returned with renewed hostility. The field commander, General Hall, ordered his troops to fire a second round at the legs of the rioters. Half of the troops balked at shooting Americans and the other half fired, dropping about a dozen people. The crowd charged again with the General ordering his men to fire at will. The cries of the wounded finally broke the spirit of the rioters.

Macready escaped the theatre, spent the night with a friend, took the train to Boston, and on Tuesday, May 22, 1849, sailed for home, never to return.

As for the rioters, thirty-one lay dead in the streets and forty-eight were injured badly enough to be hospitalized. Forrest had won, protesting that he was not responsible for the riot. He was flooded with congratulatory letters, for the most part, saying that the time was at hand when American actors would do American acting.

Selected Readings

Durham, Weldon B., Ed. *American Theatre Companies, 1749-1887.* Westport, CT, 1986.

Herold, J. Christopher. *Mistress to an Age: A Life of Madame De Staël.* Indianapolis, IN, 1958.

Lacey, Alexander. *Pixérécourt and the French Romantic Drama.* Toronto, 1928.

Moody, Richard. *America Takes the Stage,1750-1900.* Bloomington, IN, 1955.

Odell, George C. D. *Shakespeare from Betterton to Irving.* 2 vols. New York, 1920.

Planché, J. R. *The Recollections and Reflections of James Robinson Planché.* 2 vols. London, 1872.

Summary

There is no doubt that America became the bastion of romanticism and there is no doubt that by the end of the century the world was already in the throes of a new revolution. The romantic era as a literary movement had expired. But romantic concepts of the primitive were ingrained into Americans just as romantic concepts of morality were ingrained in the English and, to some extent, the French as well. In many ways, Victoria was the last vestige of a dying era. The Victorians really did not practice equality, fraternity, or brotherhood nor did they really believe in the essential goodness of humanity. Yet, they always claimed to believe. They talked a great deal about virtue, so much so that for a while the middle class almost did believe. But the realities of the world have a sobering effect and the dichotomy between what was being said and what was happening became too evident to be ignored. Sadly, the romantic ideal was seen in Europe for what it was—an ideal. When the truth was recognized, a new and exciting theatre began to take shape.

Vocabulary

1.	Sophie Schröeder	SOH fee SHROH der
2.	August Wilhelm Schlegel	ow goost VIL helm SHLAAY guhl
3.	Johann Wolfgang von Goethe	YOH hahn VAWLF gahng fawn GER tuh
4.	Heinrich von Kleist	HIGHN rik fawn KLIGHST
5.	Germaine Necker	zher MAYN ne KAIR
6.	Mme. de Staël	duh STAHL
7.	Alexandre Dumas *père*	ah leg ZAHND ruh doo: MAH pair
8.	Alfred de Vigny	duh vee NYEE
9.	Heinrich Anschütz	HIGHN rik AN Shoo:tz
10.	James Robinson Planché	plahn SHAY
11.	William Charles Macready	muh KREED ee
12.	*A Blot on the Scutcheon*	SKUH chuhn
13.	*The Cenci*	CHEN chee
14.	Bulwer-Lytton	BOOPL wer LI tuhn
15.	Covent Garden	KUH vent
16.	Smyth Pigott	SMIGHTH PIG uht

CHAPTER ELEVEN

❧

From the Static to the Dynamic:
The Rise of Realism and Naturalism
in France

Concerned about the detrimental effect environment had on the working class, Emile Zola wrote his naturalistic novel, *L'Assommoir*, in 1877. Its success encouraged Zola to write for the stage once again. Aided by William Burnach, a veteran writer of melodrama, Zola adapted *L'Assommoir* into a successful stage play in 1879.

In the intellectual and cultural life of Europe, the eighteenth century was a transitional period. Considered an age of "Enlightenment," the eighteenth century intellectuals built on the ideas of the seventeenth century. Specifically, they espoused the belief that the human condition, i.e., man's behavior and institutions, could be analyzed in a scientific (logical) manner to make man more educated and with that more understanding. Three "philosophies" served to aid this shift in thought: Voltaire (François-Marie Arouet, 1694-1778), Denis Diderot (1713-1784), and John Locke (1632-1704). From Locke, the participants in the movement took the argument that human nature was not fixed; from Voltaire came the philosophy of deism; and from Diderot evolved a strong voice for "the natural man" and the role of passion in the human personality. This reevaluation of traditional concepts affected the French theatre, which between 1720 and 1760 began to demonstrate signs of change.

Denis Diderot, a French writer and philosopher whose essays in the *Encyclopédia* (28 vols.:1748-1772) which he edited, argued against neoclassicism and in so doing advocated ideas in staging and acting that anticipated "the fourth wall" and other aspects of realism. From *Histoire de la Littérature Française.*

Human Nature and the Eighteenth Century Stage

One of the basic shifts to affect the theatre was the conception of human nature. In order to observe the unities, the traditional school determined that human nature ought to be definable and classifiable. Characters were considered types and were listed in books of characters which dramatists consulted. Consisting of a series of sketches, this reference would categorize different social positions, ages, emotions, and other seemingly definable character traits. Characters were thus expected to behave in a set or typical pattern. Typical characters made typical speeches about typical topics such as love, death, and so on. Plays were speech making and not ordinary conversation which made the characters and the action in this "Drama of Declamation" static.

Consistent with static characters was a static setting: the *Palais à volonté* (palace with a portical)

for tragedy, and *Chambre à quatre portes* (room with four doors) for comedy. Furniture was sparse, if at all, as it would give a definiteness to the set. Thus, no use was made of the setting which was basically a decor. As a result, time and place are alluded to vaguely, and characters simply enter, proceed to the front of the stage to declaim their speeches.

Believing that human nature was not muted, and that man's existence varied by experience, French dramatists began a slow but perceptible change toward realism in drama. Initially, playwrights focused on local color and antiquity in the drama which in turn was demonstrated in the sets, costumes, and then the acting. This departure marked a shift from a static theatre to a dynamic one. Influencing this shift were the works and ideas of Voltaire.

The Rise of Historical Accuracy

As early as 1732, Voltaire's *Zaire* made use of historically accurate costumes. Again, in 1755, Voltaire took advantage of the interest created by the missionaries returning from the Orient when he wrote *The Orphan of China*. In keeping with the interest in local color and history, Voltaire insisted upon a faithful reproduction of the Chinese and Tartar interior and exterior sets; that all furniture, properties, and costumes be specifically constructed to fit the period and place; and that the actors replace the traditional declamatory style with a natural one. The Comédie Italienne also began to capitalize on the public's interest in local color by wearing Spanish costumes in its production, *L'Amour Castillan* (1747). In keeping with the change to authentic costumes, writers reasoned that other changes needed to be made. Thus, poetry was changed to prose (natural conversation); this in turn led to naturalness of acting, changes in diction (accents, dialects, etc.), and changes in thought. All of these affected characterization and hence, action. Characters were chosen from the common man, and the action became one of psychological struggles.

Henri-Louis Lekain (1729-1778) in Voltaire's *L'Orphelin de la Chine.* Lekain overcame vocal and physical shortcomings to be admitted to the Comédie Française in 1750. A friend of Voltaire, he became one of the finest tragic actors of the eighteenth century.

Voltaire

Le Kain dans Gengiskhan
(Orphelin de la Chine).

Strengthening this trend in acting was Adrienne Lecouvreur (1692-1730), and especially Michel Baron (1653-1729). At the age of sixty-six, Baron returned to acting at the Comédie Française where he worked toward a more natural presentation in his character. Despite this effort, in which Baron even conversed with actors during a scene, his critics accused him of eventually falling back into the traditional declamatory style.

The Departure from Theatrical Neoclassicism

At the fair theatres, the departure from the neoclassical strictures was more pronounced. Contributing significantly to this undermining of neoclassism was Charles Simon-Favart (1710-1792), who with his wife Mlle. Chantilly (Marie Justine-Benoite Duronceray, 1727-1772) departed from the traditional methods while working toward realistic ones. Up to the time of the Favarts, peasant girls carried large baskets, "wore diamonds in their hair, and gloves up the elbow." In *The Loves of Bastien and Bastienne* (1753), Mme. Favart appeared in peasant clothes wearing a woolen dress, a single gold cross, wooden shoes, no hair decorations, and her arms bare. For *The Chinese* (1756) the cast was costumed in Chinese dress, and reportedly the Turkish costumes for the Favarts production of *The Three Sultans* (1761) were imported from Constantinople.

As a director, Charles Favart demanded concentrated rehearsals to create realistic scenes and characters. His concern for realism extended to properties and scenery which was for Favart a way of explaining and reinforcing the action. In *The Three Sultans*, Favart sought a Turkish set, furniture and properties. He served dinner with Turkish dinnerware which the actors had to handle like a native. Thus, actors could not go to the front of the stage to give their dialogue, and hence, new lighting had to be created for the actors at the back of the stage. The history of French stage directing

begins with Favart, whose break with traditional methods eventually proved influential to the Comédie Française.

A bastion of the traditional neoclassical doctrine, the Comédie Française resisted change toward realism that was occurring at the minor theatres. Favart's influence on Mlle. Clairon (Claire-Josèph-Hippolyte Léris de la Tude, 1723-1803) and Henri-Louis LeKain (1729-1778), however, signified a break in that attitude. Cited by Diderot as the ideal artist, Mlle. Clairon sought a more conversational style in her acting as opposed to the traditional one of declaiming. As a result, Clairon determined that "the truth of declamation requires that of dress." Consequently, Mlle. Clairon sought greater realism in portrayals. Her *Electra* created a sensation when she appeared in a classical dress, arm bracelets, and dishevelled hair. Mlle. Clairon's efforts toward realism were shared by Henri LeKain. In his day he was considered the greatest of tragic actors, and like Clairon, he worked toward greater realism in costume. LeKain shocked his audiences in *Semiramis* (1756) by appearing

Mlle. Clairon à Ferney. Mlle. Clairon was a visiting artist at Voltaire's Théâtre de Ferney. In 1769 under Madame Denis's guidance, the theatre deviated from neoclassicism towards realism. The audience ridiculed these efforts and, despite Mlle. Clairon's secretary, Wagniere, the theatre failed. From *Histoire Illustrée de la Littérature Française.*

with bare arms, bloody hands and his hair in disarray.

Like Clairon and LeKain, François-Joseph Talma (1736-1826) continued the trend toward realistic acting and costume. Said to have attached a great price to realism, Talma spent much time in historically researching the correct garments to wear for the roles he undertook. He is noted, for example, as appearing in Voltaire's *Brutus* (1791) with bare arms, legs, a shaved head, and the classic toga. During the nineteenth century, Talma's acting method and style is said to have approached psychological realism. Although he asserted that he had moments of living a part, he believed that this was due to a lack of control, and therefore gave an uneven performance. To overcome this, Talma developed a system whereby he memorized the inflections as he conceived they should be delivered.

When Baron Taylor took over in 1825 as the head of the Comédie Française, he sought to continue scenic accuracy as well as Talma's ideas with respect to historically accurate dress. Although tragic costume made gains, comic costume remained essentially that of traditional dress. A change was attempted in the plays of Molière, but the comic actress, Mlle. Mars (Anne Boutet, 1779-1847) refused and continued in the fashions of the day. In fact, she opposed the use of gas lighting at the Comédie Française in 1843 because she claimed it was detrimental to her dress. Not until Edouard Thierry became director of the Comédie Française in 1859 was the battle won.

Industrialism

During the years 1830 to 1900, western society was transformed from a rural society to an urban one. In exchanging the garden for the machine, western society sacrificed a benevolent society for an impersonal one, which was symbolized by the city. Industrialism made its chief impact on the city and as a consequence, the city became a metaphor for the change in western society.

Mythologically speaking, this achievement was a Janus. One face presented a social and cultural community with factories, railroads, financial institutions, and vast accumulations in wealth and people. In this society the city was tangible proof that the agrarian community was a thing of the past. The other face appeared within that same city. Although the city provided a lure for the masses from the countryside, it was unprepared for the great numbers and therefore was literally compressed with humanity. Consequently, the industrial magnate who had fostered the city's growth by building factories which in turn encouraged migration to the city, found himself in a paradoxical position. On the one hand, he needed the masses to operate the factories, but on the other hand, their great numbers had accelerated urbanization so rapidly that he sacrificed those democratic principles which were responsible for his rise to power. Under the influence of the corporations, government became very informal with its improverished planning and disregard for the middle and lower classes.

Inasmuch as the industrial magnate was willing to sacrifice democratic government for his own vested interest, he evidenced little concern for the poverty, distrust, immorality, lack of religion, and privation he had created among the urban poor. Consequently, the urban poor starved, while the middle class sought avenues for social position and political influence. Success and respectability were measured in terms of money, and thus, the middle class remained for the most part unsympathetic to the plight of the poor.

Although this social, cultural, and political unevenness made governments fearful of rebellion, the notion of reform was viewed as contradictory to the belief that poverty was the result of laziness or lack of ability. In desperation the lower classes staged a series of generally unsuccessful revolts between 1830 and 1850. If nothing else, the cry of the lower classes heralded need for social and economic reform.

Auguste Comte and the Rise of Realism

A basic response to the need for reform was the abandonment of the romantic notion that God would provide. Instead, the disenchanted romantics opted for science as the savior of mankind. Championing this belief was Auguste Comte (1798-1857). Claiming that science rather than religion was the basis for morality, he labeled his philosophy "positivism." Setting down his principles in a five volume series entitled *Positive Philosophy* (1830-1842), Comte turned away from the metaphysics of the romantics to a study of the natural and physical phenomena found in the sciences. Classifying the sciences according to their simplicity, Comte reasoned that mathematics was the most precise and thus the simpler, and sociology (a term he coined) was the least precise and thus the most complex. Further, Comte believed that the determinant for moral action could be discovered only through scientifically investigating society. Later in this century, Hippolyte Taine (1828-1893) would take Comte's philosophy and apply it to literature and history. His four volume work, *History of English Literature* (1863-64) stressed that all literature was determined by the writer's race, milieu, and moment. A deterministic philosopher, Taine's ideas complemented Comte's in that he sought to explain literature as a product of heredity and environment. The scientific approach advocated by Comte and Taine greatly influenced the development of social drama.

Under Comte's influence, scientific observation became more important to human progress than the romantic notion of imagination. Romantic ideology was replaced by that of the naturalists who believed that heredity and environment were the primary factors in determining human progress. For the writer, as Taine demonstrated, the application of this new philosophy meant a dispassionate investigation of society (i.e., the scientific method). Thus, society became a case study

Portrait of Auguste Comte

Hippolyte Taine was a French critic, philosopher, and historian. He influenced the theories of the naturalists with his deterministic theories on the effect of heredity and environment on humans.

under the writer's pen, and urban conditions became suitable dramatic fare. Whereas the romantics saw life through "rose-colored glasses" the realists were interested in an untinted view.

Alexandre Dumas *fils* and His Contemporaries

As a "school," realism was recognized first in painting; many of the objections to realism in literature had their basis in objections to realism in art. Although philosophically the term realism had long been known, it was during the nineteenth century that the term was added to the vocabulary of painting and literature. One of the earliest uses on record of the term was in 1834 when Hippolyte Fortoul wrote that "M. (Antony) Thouret has written his work with a realistic exaggeration which assumes the manner of M. Hugo." In 1835 and 1837 Gustave Planché defined realism as an objective imitation of nature as opposed to a glorification of nature—a viewpoint the romanticists and the classicists held. To the realists, only "the true, the observable, the verifiable" was the appropriate subject for their work. After 1846, the word became prominent and with the publishing of Duranty's review, *Realism* (1856) and Champfleury's volume of essays entitled *The Realism* (1857), the term became current.

Realism in French drama and hence throughout the world owes its establishment to the work of Alexandre Dumas *fils* (1824-1895). Using the techniques of Eugène Scribe (1791-1861) for his structure and the workings of contemporary society for his content, Dumas *fils* developed realism in the French theatre. His first play, *Camille* (1848) was based on his affair with Marie Duplessis, which he had depicted in his novel *The Lady of the Camillias*. Dumas had hoped to turn the novel into a successful play, but the censorship board considered his work immoral and denied it a production license. The political ambition of Louis Napoleon, however, worked to Dumas' favor. In 1851 Louis Napoleon overthrew the Second Empire to make himself Napoleon III and hence the autocratic ruler of France. The new government made Dumas' friend, the Duc de Morny, head of censorship. Three days after his appointment, *Camille* was

Alexandre Dumas *fils*

authorized for production which occurred February 2, 1852.

The tendency today is to view *Camille* as a romantic melodrama but its detailed focus on contemporary French society, and the story about a prostitute "with a heart of gold" created a stir. *Camille* marks a transition in the French theatre from romanticism to realism, and its author certainly considered himself a realist whose "duty" was to influence the betterment of his society.

Although the courtesan is treated sympathetically in *Camille*, she is treated unsympathetically in Dumas *fils The Demi-Monde* (1855). The author takes a conscious stand in this play against immoral love, and in so doing inaugurated his social problem or "thesis" plays. *The Natural Son* (1858) was written to demonstrate that the laws and conventions concerning the illegitimate child are unjust and needed changing. In these "thesis" plays, Dumas *fils* made use of Scribe's well-made play formula for suspense, entertainment, and a raissoneur (author's spokesperson) who utters the play's message, a message that seems to defend the family against undue passion and immoral love. In all likelihood this "puritan stand" of Dumas *fils* is a carryover from his childhood relationship with his father.

Another writer whose works like those of Dumas *fils* were realistic yet tinged with romanticism was Victorien Sardou (1831-1908). It was Sardou who carried romantic-realism to its zenith at the traditional theatres. Although considered a successor to the romantic Eugène Scribe, Sardou's plays were realistic to the extent that they focused on contemporary subject matter and made use of historical accuracy in the sets, costumes and properties. *Patrie* (1869), *Hatred* (1874), and *Theodora* (1884) are three examples demonstrating Sardou's focus on historical accuracy, which incidentally drew praise from Zola and later Antoine. As a romantic-realist, Sardou wrote a number of plays for the actress Sarah Bernhardt (1845-1923), a collaboration that would prove enormously successful for both. *Fédora* (1882), and *Tosca* (1887) were among the best. In defending *Tosca* against the critic, Sarcey, Sardou summed up his passion for historical research when he stated, "It is therefore surprising that he [Sarcey] should be not only indifferent, but even hostile to any attempt to reproduce the scenes, costumes, or customs of the past." Sardou's concern with realism extended to subject matter as well. *Daniel Rochat* (1880), and *Let's Get a Divorce* (1880) serve as examples of Sardou delving into contemporary subject matter such as politics and morality. *L'Affaire des Poisons* (1907) was Sardou's last success, and affirmed the author's faithfulness to historical accuracy.

Emile Augier (1820-1889) was a contemporary of Sardou, Dumas *fils*, and Montigny and his work can be classified as social drama. Beginning his career in 1844 as a follower of François Ponsard's "Theatre of Common Sense," Augier's plays can

Victorien Sardou wrote seventy plays which included melodrama, comedies, vaudevilles, and historical dramas. In the historical dramas unified production was fully realized in France.

be earmarked as providing a transition between the romantics and the realists. As such, after having written seven romantic verse plays, Augier adopted the realistic school. His first realistic work was *Mr. Poirier's Son-in-Law* (1854). The argument of the play focuses on the uniting of social classes—the nobility and the middle class. His best play was *Olympe's Marriage* (1855), which was intended as a reply to *Camille*. It is an indignant protest against the rehabilitation of the courtesan and her admission into a respectable family. In technique, Augier like Dumas *fils* utilized Scribe's well-made play formula. His constant themes are the power of money and the influence of the Church in politics and marriage. Augier's plays seem quieter in ex-

Eugène Scribe was known for his "well-made plays" (pièce bien fait). Such plays as *The Glass of Water* and *Adrienne Lecouvreur* (1849) are samples of his formula.

pression, and more natural than those of Dumas *fils*. He relies on good sense and tempers his logic by a rational approach based on experience. Thus, his plays seem better motivated but somewhat less exciting than those of Dumas *fils*.

Emile Zola and Naturalism

Emile Zola (1840-1902) is considered the primary spokesman for naturalism—a term he claims to have invented. The movement was active during the 1870s, and was largely influenced by Darwin and Comte. The single strongest influence on Zola was Claude Bernard's (1813-1878) *Introduction to Experimental Medicine* (1865) which studies the effects of heredity and environment. Using this work as his model, Zola sought to apply the same ideas to literature. Stressing that the writer was

Emile Augier

Emile Zola

OLYMPE'S MARRIAGE
EMILE AUGIER

CHARACTERS
MARQUIS DE PUYGIRON
BARON DE MONTRICHARD
BAUDEL DE BEAUSÉJOUR
MARQUISE DE PUYGIRON
GENEVIÈVE DE WURZEN
PAULINE, COUNTESS DE PUYRIRON
   ("OLYMPE TAVERNY")
HENRI, COUNT DE PUYGIRON
IRMA, PAULINE'S MOTHER
ADOLPHE, a comedian

SETTING: Pilnitz (near Dresden, Germany) and Vienna. Time 1854.

BACKGROUND: This play was written as a reply to Dumas *fils' La Dame aux Camélias* but failed because the subject matter was exhausted in the Paris theatre and Augier's treatment was too didactic. Augier objected to Dumas *fils'* seeming condoning of illicit love and the idea that a courtesan is capable of true everlasting love, like Marguerite in *Camille.* The play opened July 17, 1885 and was not well received, but the play is Augier's best example of the well-made play to social drama and his most didactic.

SUMMARY

Act I: At a restaurant in Pilnitz, Montrichard learns that Olympe Taverny, "one of the most luxuriously and frequently kept women in Paris," died in San Francisco. Baudel engages Montrichard in conversation. He knows that Montrichard is a man of the world, an excellent swordsman, and is well received in the best circles of society. He knows also that Montrichard is broke. He tells Montrichard that he will loan him 50,000 francs if Montrichard will wound him with a sword. Although Baudel has a lot of money, he is not received into society and this wound by a man of renown will help him. They agree and set up a

phony argument to precipitate a duel. Baudel exits and Pauline enters. Montrichard recognizes her as Olympe Taverny. Initially, she denies it but confides in Montrichard whom she has known before. She has married Henri, Count de Puygiron, in order to get into upper society and thus is trying to hide her past. Montrichard agrees to keep her secret if she will introduce Montrichard to Puygiron's granddaughter. Enter the Marquis and Marquise de Puygiron, Henri's uncle and aunt who have not seen Henri for three years. This chance meeting is a pleasant surprise for all until it is learned that Henri has secretly married Pauline. As head of the family, the Marquis is shocked and angered that Henri has married beneath his station and as a result, the Marquis refuses to accept Pauline. In an effort to win acceptance Pauline concocts a story that she is a farmer's daughter and was given an education above her social position. In addition her father was a Vendéen who died in the counterrevolution in western France during the French Revolution. This little lie changes the Marquis's attitude toward her and he accepts her into the family. Henri is upset by the lie but says nothing.

Act II: The scene opens in the home of the Marquis in Vienna. Pauline, Geneviève, the Marquis and Marquise are engaged in conversation. It is learned that the Marquise (Geneviève's grandmother) was wounded in a battle at the Château of Péniscière. The Marquis and Marquise exit after revealing this piece of information. Pauline and Geneviève are left alone. Pauline tries unsuccessfully to plead Montrichard's love to Geneviève. She tells Pauline that she is not interested in Montrichard and that at one time she loved a man who was supposed to be her husband. He, however, married another and now Geneviève has little interest in the world and desires to enter a convent. Pauline surmises that the man is Henri, but does not reveal her

OLYMPE'S MARRIAGE, continued

guess. Baudel enters and in the following exchange with Pauline, he reveals that he and Olympe knew each other and that she was madly in love with him. In fact, he asserts that he was the reason Olympe ran away to California. Although she resembles Olympe, Pauline has completely fooled Baudel, and she is amused by his comments. In fact, it is later learned that Baudel has "belonged to the number of those who" were not her lover. Like the duel in the first act, Baudel is constantly seeking ways to elevate his social standing. His ploy this time is to give Pauline a pearl attached to a necklace of diamonds in an attempt to become a lover of a countess. She refuses just as her husband Henri enters. In a clever strategy Baudel tells her husband that Pauline was trying to convince him that the necklace was paste. To which Henri asks his wife if she bought the necklace. Trapped, she says that she bought it and must now keep Baudel's gift. Baudel exits. Alone with Henri, Pauline is disturbed by his attitude. He reveals that he is still suspicious of her intentions in marrying him. She tries to dispel his fears by confessing that she knew Henri's uncle would be at Pilnitz and that she engineered the seemingly chance meeting between Henri and his uncle. Henri is not appeased, however, and in the ensuing scene Henri confronts her by asserting that she has cleverly disguised her real motives and that everything she has said or done was a ruse. She confesses that he is correct and suggests that they separate. He refuses on the grounds that he will not allow the name of his family to be dragged through the gutter. Pauline exits. Henri then is met with the entrance of Irma, Pauline's mother. It is enough for Henri to have married Pauline but to have to endure the mother forces him to get rid of her with a bribe. Inasmuch as she is broke, she accepts. In reality this is the only reason she has appeared at the Marquis' home pretending to be the devoted mother. The Marquis, Marquise, Henri and Geneviève depart for dinner leaving Pauline, her mother, and Montrichard, who has entered. Adolphe, a comedian, enters hoping to sell tickets to his benefit performance. Adolphe is made welcome and is asked to sing. After much drinking and singing, he reveals that he has a wife and three children and no money to support them. Pauline tries to give him money which he refuses. She then gives him the pearl from the necklace Baudel gave her. Although everybody except Adolphe believes it to be paste, Pauline reveals to her mother that the pearl is real. Adolphe departs and Pauline believes that giving the pearl away will bring her luck.

Act III: The setting is the same as Act II. Pauline tells Montrichard that she plans to run away with Baudel. Baudel has left for Nice but Pauline has stayed behind to negotiate a separation. Pauline considers Baudel the "prince of fools," but at the present he will serve for her needs. Pauline believes that she has complete control and that the Puygirons will negotiate anything in order to save their family honor. Geneviève believes that Pauline is dying of consumption and convinces her grandparents that the entire family should take a trip to Italy. In the meantime Adolphe enters and returns the pearl. The Marquis is so taken with his honesty that he buys the pearl from Adolphe in order to give it back to Pauline. Henri enters and then Pauline. In a heated exchange between Henri and Pauline as to how she got the necklace, Henri reveals Pauline's true identity and begs forgiveness from his uncle for dishonoring the family name. Pauline has taken Geneviève's diary in which she divulges that Henri made love to her. Shocked that Henri made love to his cousin, the Marquis and Marquise are willing to bargain with Pauline. She wants an amicable separation and she plans to continue using the family name for which she will return the diary. They despise her and in his anger, the Marquis takes his pistol and shoots Pauline.

simply a "recorder" of human events, Zola railed against the realists for their "desire for legislation, preaching, and conversion." In other words, the writer no longer "makes use of human observation" which was at the core of naturalism. Contrary to public opinion, Zola found that the realists were simply continuing "conventionalities," and that unless the dramatist searched for truth, "the stage will become flat and more and more inferior."

Basically, Zola wanted the stage to be a copy of life in all manner, shape, and form. This uncensored, unfiltered reproduction of life was designed to illustrate the laws of heredity and environment. He wanted the writer to display his work like a scientist, a researcher. He was to be detached (impersonal) and, like the scientist looking for a cure for a disease, the dramatist would examine social problems in order to find a relationship between their cause and effect. It was a way for Zola to investigate and seek a remedy for societal ills. Zola's major work on this subject was the dramatization of his novel, Thérèse *Raquin* (1873). His other works were *Madeleine* (written 1865 but produced 1889), *The Rabourdin Heirs* (1874), *The Red Button* (1878), and *Renée* (1887).

Claude Bernard influenced Emile Zola's ideas about art.

Eighteenth Century French Stage Production

During the 1850s, the French theatre moved toward the concept of specialization. Although the idea of synthesis was not as yet an overriding principle, the attention to detail, and need for specialist to create that detail was recognized. In costume, for example, the actor Etienne Melingue had Eugene Delacroix do costumes for him. Also during this same period, the practice of handing a production over to a director was standard. The director would consult with the writer, and then give the scenic requirements to the carpenters. Cardboard models were then made and after approval, the set was built. Once constructed, the sets were then jobbed out to a scenic studio for painting.

Two designers significant in contributing to realistic stage production were Louis-Jacques Daguerre (1787-1851), and Pierre-Luc-Charles Ciceri (1782-1868). Although Daguerre was later noted for his work with photography (Daguerreotype, 1839), his scenic efforts with dioramas and panoramas did much to establish scenic illusionism on the French stage. His first diorama (1822) involved seating the spectators on a platform which revolved every fifteen minutes. As the platform turned, the audience viewed on proscenium-like stages two illusionistic paintings which were displayed one at a time. The illusion of assimilating sunsets, moonrises and other weather conditions as well as time of day was accomplished by the shifting of natural light through shutters and screens. As a scenic illusion, the diorama was effective but inasmuch as it depended upon a rotation platform, and the manipulation of natural light, it could not be used in a theatre. It was, however, the panorama which was effectively employed in the theatre beginning in 1821.

Invented prior to Daguerre's diorama, the panorama was a large illusionistic painting which surrounded the audience. The panorama could be reduced, however, and assume the shape of a diorama. When reduced, it was attached to an overhead track, and at both ends to a spool-like mechanism. The spools turned much like film in a camera revealing a continuous scene which could serve as a scenic background. The panorama allowed set designers to discard sky-borders which hindered illusion, and eventually led to the development of the modern day neutral cyclorama.

Since 1800 Parisian theatres had been lighted by Argand lamps. This changed, however, in 1822 when Daguerre and Ciceri, working together as set designers at the Opera, used gas lighting on stage in *Aladdin and the Wonderful Lamp* and the ballet *Alfred the Great*. Despite his success with Daguerre, Ciceri's work individually was in great demand. He was hired by Baron Taylor, director of the Comédie Française to do sets for the Comédie. Additional demands led him to open a scenic studio where he trained scenic artists such as Charles Sechan and J. P. M. Dieterle. This enabled Ciceri's work to be continued after he retired. Working primarily at the opera in the 1820s, Ciceri designed sets for Dr. Paul Veron who like Baron Taylor realized the need for realistic spectacle to attract audiences. Encouraged by Veron, Ciceri created for the first time on a stage precipices, ravines, storms on a lake and bridges between mountains, all of which required more than a quick scene change. Ciceri was responsible, therefore, for inaugurating at the opera the trend of lowering the curtain between acts.

The illusion of reality on stage continued to be motivated and developed by the work of Adolph

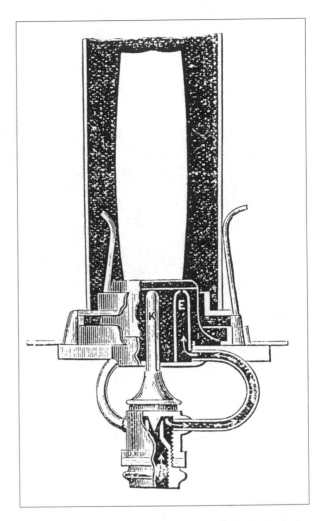

The Argand lamp created the principle upon which the Argand burner or round flame burner is based. The Argand burner was invented in 1780 by Amie Argand. Its features were less smoke, less oil, more heat, and more light. It is considered the first major innovation in lighting since candles. The Argand burner prompted interest in stage lighting and was a primary reason for the new technology in nineteenth century lighting.

Montigny (1805-1880), the director of the Gymnase. As a director, Montigny clearly anticipated Antoine by use of the box set depicting a realistic interior. Additionally, his strict attention to detail, longer rehearsals than had been the custom, having the actors look at each other rather than the audience when they conversed, pieces of business to make the dialogue realistic, real properties such as tea and sugar, and natural movement indicates that

PHEDRE

Mlle. Dumesnil (Marie-Françoise Marchand, 1713-1803) portraying Phèdre. She was probably the most famous French actress of the eighteenth century. Note the costume—French actresses wore the latest fashions regardless of the role. *Comédie Française*

Henri Becque

Montigny anticipated the modern period. His efforts must be credited in part, however to writers such as Dumas *fils* who had written plays with everyday dialogue, contemporary settings, and contemporary social issues.

From 1870 to 1900, Emile Augier, Victorien Sardou, and Alexandre Dumas *fils* monopolized the French theatre. Because they were proven dramatists, other writers found it difficult to have their plays staged. More specifically, the naturalistic works of such writers as Henri Becque (1837-1899) were slow in being produced. Unlike Dumas *fils*, Augier and others of the Second Empire whose realistic plays were tinged with romanticism, Becque's dramas were considered too brutal with their candor, and thus were deemed failures. Even his masterpiece, *The Vultures* (1882), produced by the Comédie Française was not well received.

Although history recognizes in Henri Becque's work a real spokesman for naturalism, he was basically a failure to his contemporaries. His last play, *The Puppets*, was never completed and after 1855 Becque ceased to be a productive dramatist. Instead, he devoted himself to writing for journals and trying to get revivals of his earlier works staged.

Becque was symptomatic of the stagnation besetting the French theatre of the 1880s. Subtle changes were being implemented, however, that eventually would enable new writers, actors, and directors to emerge and develop. One of the most important of these changes was the "classic matinees" of Hilarion Ballande. These matinees were instituted in 1867, and orginally were designed to present lesser works of known authors. Ballande's success at the Gaîté and Porte-Saint-Martin encourged all the major theatres in Paris to start a similar program. In 1876 at Ballande's Troisieme Théâtre Français new authors became part of the matinee program. Thus it was Ballande's pioneer effort that motivated other theatres to follow suit, especially in developing matinees to introduce new authors. Among those so motivated was the director Tallien, whose "matinées inédites" in 1879 at the Cluny introduced Eugène Brieux (1858-1932). Although Brieux's work would earn him world-wide recognition by 1911, his success was slow and can in great part be attributed to André Antoine and the Théâtre-Libre.

André Antoine

Influenced by the experiments of Ballande and Tallien, André Antoine (1858-1943) began in 1887 to produce the works of new realistic writers. Beginning his career at Le Cercle Gaulois in 1886, Antoine within a year formed his own theatre. Taking Paul Alexis's (novelist, theatre critic) suggestion to call his venture the Théâtre-Libre, Antoine opened March 30, 1887. To circumvent the censor as well as to finance his theatre, Antoine employed the subscription method. As a subscription theatre, Antoine's theatre was essentially an "independent theatre," which meant that he was outside the jurisdiction of the policies governing traditional theatres and their productions. Thus, Antoine moved from a traditional posture in his choice of plays and production methods to new and innovative ones. Under Antoine's guidance, the Théâtre-Libre became synonymous with all that was new in theatre. It was "the mother of them all," and experimental theatres throughout the world, especially the American little theatres, the off-Broadway, off-off-Broadway, regional, and the anti-traditional theatres of the 1960s are the direct descendants of the Théâtre-Libre. Not only does this theatre's influence extend to America, but also to Germany's Freie Bühne, Russia's Moscow Art Theatre, Ireland's Abbey Theatre, and England's Independent Theatre.

One of the writers to emerge from the Théâtre-Libre who also articulated Antoine's obsession for naturalistic acting, sets, and properties, was Jean Jullien (1854-1919). Echoing the phrases of Zola and Diderot, Jullien demanded that plays be "a slice of life," and that set designers, directors, and actors recognize that a "fourth wall" exists between the stage and the audience. As a dramatist, Jullien wrote what was labeled "comédie rosse." This term was used to describe naturalistic plays that presented life in a harsh cynical manner and depicted characters who exemplified man's baser instinct. As Jullien phrased it, "A play is a slice of life *(tranche de vie)* put on the stage with art." Thus, the subject manner was shocking to many of the audiences. Jullien, however, provided Antoine not only with new plays but ones with which Antoine could artistically experiment in terms of acting, sets, lights, props and directing.

André Antoine lecturing at the Théâtre-Libre.

Although Comédie Rosse became a dominant genre at the Théâtre-Libre, it was not the only form presented. In addition to presenting the works of Ibsen, Strindberg, and Hauptmann, Antoine produced the plays of other French dramatists who were more conservative than Jullien in their depiction of man, but nevertheless can be classified as realistic-naturalistic. One of the most gifted of Antoine's discoveries was Georges de Porto-Riche (1849-1930) whose work delved into the psychological nuances of love and its conflicts. The first of these works was *Francoise's Luck* (1888). His most powerful play was *Infatuated* (1891) which deals with a physician and his sexually frustrated wife. The psychological realism of the play drew great reviews even from such moderate critics as Sarcey who praised Rejane and Lucien Guitry in the leading roles.

The strongest rival to Jullien and other Antoine discoveries was Eugène Brieux (1858-1932). His first work *Household of Artists* (1890) drew little attention, but his second effort, *Blanchette* (originally *Bichette,* 1892) "triumphed with every line." Concerned with such social problems as arranged marriages, gambling, divorce, birth control (or lack of it), premarital sex, and veneral disease, Brieux surpassed Jullien in boldness, and by 1911 was considered one of the major dramatists in the western world. His best work, *The Red Robe* (1900) indicts the French judicial system charging that the system creates victims rather than justice.

François de Curel (1854-1929) was another talented dramatist discovered by Antoine. Curel submitted his play, *The Other Side of a Saint* to Antoine under the name Charles Watterneau. Antoine decided to produce it, because it was "the most important and the most likely to survive the great demands placed on new authors at the Théâtre-Libre." As a writer, Curel's strength resided in his psychological depictions. Antoine considered *The Other Side of a Saint* "so new, so completely internal, that it is extremely difficult to interpret." The critics were mixed in their opinions but this would be the standard reception given to Curel's work

Eugène Brieux

throughout his life. His most noted play, *The Fossils* (1892), "created a sensation" and established him as a dramatist. As with Chekhov's *The Cherry Orchard* (1904), Curel depicts a dying aristocracy through the psychological conflicts of his protagonist, Robert de Cantermelle.

In addition to developing new drama, Antoine reshaped the French theatre in other ways. He demanded that the set be considered an environment which was to be changed with each play and each act if necessary; that the properties be real objects (not artificial) as in his use of real carcasses of beef in *The Butchers* (1888); that the lights be natural as possible in terms of trying to approximate the direction of the source such as the sun, moon, etc., or as in *The Death of the Duc d'Enghien* (1888), using real lanterns to light the scene; and that the actors create a real life on stage and disregard the audience. Antoine opposed artifice on stage and wanted his actors to "live" the life of the character.

Clearly Antoine's ideas and staging methods helped usher in the modern theatre of the twentieth century. Although Antoine left for South America in 1894 the Théâtre-Libre continued under the guidance of Paul Larochelle until 1896 when it closed. Returning in 1897 to Paris, Antoine opened the Théâtre Antoine where he remained until 1906. He moved then to the Odeon where he was named director. The fact that Antoine was placed at the head of a state theatre signifies the acceptance of realism and naturalism in the French theatre. Just as Hugo championed the romantics against the neoclassicists, Antoine waged the fight for the realists and naturalists. By his influence and example, André Antoine ushered the realistic theatre throughout the world into the twentieth century.

Suggested Readings

Antoine, André. *Memoires of the Théâtre-Libre.* Trans. by Marvin Carlson. Coral Gables, FL, 1964.

Matthews, Brander. *French Dramatists of the Nineteenth Century.* 5th Ed. New York, 1914.

Moynet, Jean-Pierre. *French Theatrical Production in the Nineteenth Century (L'Envers du Theatre).* Trans. and Augmented by Allan S. Jackson with M. Glen Wilson, Binghamton, NY, 1976.

Weinberg, Bernard. *French Realism: The Critical Reaction, 1830-1870.* Chicago, 1937.

Vocabulary

François-Marie Arouet	Frahn swah Mah ree Ah roo a	Adolph Montigny	Ah doe lf Moan tea gnee
Voltaire	vohl tair	Gymnase	Gee m nahz
Denis Diderot	Dee na Dee d roh	André Antoine	Ahn dray Ahn twuhn
Zaïre	Zah ir	Sardou	Sahr doo
L'Amour Castillan	Lah moo ur Kah stee yahn	*Patrie*	Pah tree
Adrienne LeCouvreur	ah dree ehnn Leh coo vrurr	Sarcey	Sorr see
Michel Baron	Me shell bah row hn	*Daniel Rochat*	Dah knee eh Row shah
Comédie Française	Koh may dee Frahn says	*L'Affair des Poisons*	Lah fair day Pwa zone
Charles Simon-Favart	Shar ul see moan fah var	Emile Augier	Ay meel Ah zhyay
Mlle Chantilly	Shahn tee yee	Ponsard	Pon sar
Marie Justine-Benoite	Mah ree Juice teen Beh nwa teh	Poirier	Pwa ree ay
Duronceray	Do row n she ray	Robert de Cantermelle	Row bear duh Kahn tair mell
Bastien	Bah stee yen	*Olympe*	O leem puh
Bastienne	Bah stee yen	Henri Becque	Ahn ree Bek
Claire Josèph Hippolyte	Clay air Joe say f Epo leet	Hilarion Ballande	Ee lahr trr own Bah lahn duh
Léris de la Tude	Leh ree duh lah Tood	Gâité	Gah ee tay
Henri-Louis Lekain	Hhn ree Loo ee leh Kan	Porte-Saint Martin	Port San Mahr tan
Talma	Towel mah	Troisieme Théâtre	Twa zee m Tay aht
Semiramis	Si mir mis	Français	Frahn say
Anne Boutet	Ahnn Boo tay	Tallien	Tah lee yen
Edouard Thierry	A do whar Tea a ree	matinées inédites	mah tea nay een a deet
Auguste Comte	Aw too st Kohnt	Cluny	Kloo nee
Hippolyte Fortoul	E po leet For tool	Brieux	Bree uh
Hippolyte Taine	E po leet Tany	Théâtre Libre	Tay aht Leehb ruh
Thouret	Tour a	Le Cercle Gaulois	Leh Sair kluh Gall wah
Gustave Planché	Goo stah veh plahn shay	Freie Bühne	Frigh uh Byoo nuh
Champfleury	Shaun flurry	Jean Jullien	Jawn Jew lee ehn
Dumas *fils*	Doo mah fees	Comédie Rosse	Koh may dee Row su
Scribe	Skreeb	Georges de Porto-Riche	Gorge duh Port o Ree shuh
Camille	Ka mheel	Rejane	Reh jahn
Marie Duplessis	Mah ree Do pleh see	Lucien Guitry	Loo see n Guee tree
Duc de Morny	Do kuh duh Morn ee	Blanchette	Blan shet
Demi-Monde, Le	Dem ee mond leh	Bichette	Bee shet
Etienne Mélinigue	A tea n Muh lahn guh	Curel	Cure l
Eugène Delacroix	U jene Dell lah krwah	Watterneau	Vater no
Louis-Jacques Daguerre	Loo ee Jah kuh Dah gair	Chekhov	Che kawf
Pierre-Luc-Charles Ciceri	Pea air Loo kuh Shar ul Sea suh ree	Duc d' Enghien	Do kuh dawn Gee enn
Veron	Vuh row hn		

CHAPTER TWELVE

❦

Exporting Enlightenment: Realism and Naturalism in Europe and America

Henrik Ibsen, considered the "Father of Modern Drama."

The idea that all men were created equal was not only a great rallying cry but probably a great theoretical truth—that is, if equality means that everyone has the right to pursue happiness. The sad reality during the later part of the nineteenth century and the first part of the twentieth was that not everyone did have the right to pursue happiness. While the middle class was indeed growing, the aristocratic system still exerted abnormal influence upon thought. The middle class itself became guilty of reinforcing the existing class system by establishing its own hierarchy. This anomaly exacerbated an already deepening chasm between the "haves" and the "have nots." In effect, the middle class aspired to be considered genteel without truly understanding why. Non-hereditary titles were awarded to successful middle-class families to defuse resentment toward the upperclass. The result was the rise of extreme poverty coupled with a growing feeling of hopelessness in the lower classes. This malaise became universal throughout the poor of Europe. Therein lies the seeds of the realistic movement.

As in France, the chief catalyst of ferment was ingrained in the industrial revolution which had begun during the latter half of the eighteenth century. The entire world had begun to open up to trade. Competition required an increase in the speed of transportation and communication. With each new market came a demand for new and efficient means of manufacture and delivery. In England, for example, the Seven Years War insured supremacy of the sea and new and lucrative markets throughout the world, which in turn required bigger and faster merchant ships. Ships that could easily make the long voyages to Indian and China as well as new world markets began to be manufactured. Larger ships demanded larger ship-building facilities, thereby moving industry out of homes and into factories, creating a private enterprise system unlike any before it. With the construction of expanded facilities usually located at ports to insure easy transportation, communities around them expanded at abnormal rates to house the influx of workers from the country. The factory system began to dominate the economy as well as the landscape as smokestacks rose over the new industrial centers of Europe.

Capitalism

Capitalism exists on the principle of supply and demand. Thus as increasing numbers of farmers poured into the cities of Europe, there was less demand for workers. The increased competition for jobs meant that less salary was necessary to guarantee workers. Thus the areas around the factories became more and more depressed as more workers emigrated, only to find that there were no jobs for them and less money for those fortunate to have them. Employers, in an effort to increase profits, hired the cheapest labor possible, frequently in the form of women and children. Little children were hired and exploited in such jobs as chimney sweeps, where they rarely reached puberty before succumbing to lung disease. Compounding the almost unbearable living conditions was the frequent outbreak of disease caused, in part, from severely strained and already inadequate sanitation facilities. Cholera, contracted from the grossly-polluted drinking water in most cities, took a horrifying toll. The disease raged throughout Europe until John Snow (1813-1858), general practitioner, published in 1849 the suggestion that cholera was spread by the practice of dumping raw sewage into the rivers which were the main source of drinking water. Only then, were steps taken to relieve this condition.

Writers throughout Europe used these appalling conditions as inspiration for a variety of publications—literary, scientific, and political. The playwright Henrik Ibsen immortalized the cholera epidemic in his play *Enemy of the People.* Charles Dickens used the frightful living conditions apparent during the nineteenth century in England as a basis for many of his novels and short stories. In Germany a young Karl Marx wrote about working conditions in the Rhineland and the insensitive Prussian royal house. For his trouble, Marx was expelled from the Rhineland to France, where he wrote in support of French workers. He was ordered to leave France in 1844 moving to Brussels where he supported a series of strikes, was arrested, deported and settled in London. It was in London at the British Museum, at a desk still used and duly noted, that he wrote *Das Kapital*. His attack on the capitalistic system found ample negative documentation in the industrial quagmire of Europe in general and London in particular.

Marx was not the only one to realize that the workers' lot needed improvement. Reformers like Robert Owen warned Parliament that violence would be forthcoming if factory conditions were not improved. Intolerable social conditions eventually led to revolt. Following the Silesian weavers uprising, later dramatized in Gerhardt Hauptmann's *The Weavers*, there were several uprisings in 1830 and still larger ones between 1845 and 1850. It became more and more evident that the workers would play a part in their own government.

Since new technology requires scientific expertise, it is no small wonder that more and more thinkers began to turn to science as a way of solving the problems threatening the world. Science and more specifically the scientific method which, by its very nature was a reaction against the nebulosity of romanticism, became the methodology of change.

Darwin

Auguste Comte's theories of positivism in France were reinforced by the publication of one of the most remarkable and controversial books ever written. Published in 1859 by Charles Robert Darwin (1809-1882), *The Origin of the Species* still provokes heated debate today. Few books have had the impact on the entire world's concept of itself than this book. Written after a long voyage to various islands, Darwin postulated two basic premises. First, all forms of life have evolved from a common ancestry. His second postulate was that there is a process of natural selection which operates in nature to strive toward perfection. He writes:

> All the living forms of life are the lineal descendants of those which lived long before the Cambrian epoch, we may feel certain that the ordinary succession by generation has never once been broken, and that no cataclysm has desolated the whole world. Hence we may look with some confidence to a secure future of great length. And as natural selection works solely by and for the good of each being, all corporeal and mental endowments will tend to progress towards perfection.

While cataclysmic theory has recently been questioned, most of what Darwin said here is still valid. It is important to note, however, that Darwin never intended to apply his theory to societies. Nevertheless, the concept of progress had an enormous influence on the thinking of the nineteenth century. England had already expanded her empire to a great degree. The concept of progress gave colonization a new raison d'etre. The idea that western society was at a higher stage of evolution gave British imperialism an almost messianic fervor. If we accept the premise that one society is in a higher state of evolution than another, then the higher society may attempt to "civilize" the other. This idea has come back to haunt the British more than any other country. The idea of progress, however, in spite of its unfortunate interpretations, was one of the more important Darwinian theories.

The concept that all forms of life evolved from a common origin had even more impact on world thinking. While Darwin never intended to question religious thought, his ideas were interpreted as casting considerable doubt about the existence of God, or at least God as conceived by the major religions. This factor seriously questioned the concept of immortality and therefore underlined the importance of fulfillment in one's lifetime. It thus became important to improve the conditions of the present life, and science seemed to offer the best means of doing so.

Darwin's strong emphasis on heredity and environment as the most important factors in natural selection strongly influenced later thinkers. First, while little could be done to alter it at that time, heredity was recognized as being responsible for certain character traits and actions. Second, the importance of environment as a controlling force in the development of the individual was postulated. The theory suggested a need for society to recognize the influence of an inadequate environment and work to improve it.

Perhaps the most far-reaching ramification of the Darwinian theory was the reevaluation of the human species. For the first time in the history of western civilization, humans were viewed as animals. Human status as a god-like creature was lost. The impact of this concept caused the western world to begin to rethink its whole moral structure. Prior to this time, humanity enjoyed a status superior to all other creatures. All things on this earth were thought to have been created by God for the exclusive use of humans. Darwin's theory first suggested that incredible idea that other life forms might have a right to exist. In some ways, the modern environmentalist was born with the publication of *The Origin of the Species*.

There is no question that the scientific revolution had been launched. The effect of these developments on the arts, particularly the theatre, was not immediate. Yet with so much emphasis being placed on the observation of life in terms of the five senses it was only a matter of time before new dramatic styles were to evolve. What seemed to be necessary were styles that would allow dramatic action to develop logically in a cause-effect manner. These new styles were called realism and naturalism.

The use of realism and naturalism in drama spread throughout the world. The best of these works occurred in eastern rather than western Europe. Science was less important in the east than it was in the west, and the west had tied its naturalism to Zola, who in turn coupled natural-

ism and science so closely that artistic creativity was limited. Dramatists in Germany, Russia, and Scandinavia were especially successful but those in France and England came under the sway of French and Scandinavian realism in advocating social reform in their plays. In Germany Gerhart Hauptmann's early plays exemplify best eastern naturalism. Chekhov, Ibsen and Strindberg are excellent models from Russia, Norway, and Sweden.

The Freie Bühne and German Realism

In Germany Otto Brahm (1856-1912) became the first president of the Freie Bühne (Free Theatre) founded in Berlin in 1889. To avoid censorship, the Freie Bühne was organized along the lines of the Théâtre Libre as a private institution. Among its initial works were *Ghosts*, Tolstoi's *The Power of Darkness*, Zola's *Thérèse Raquin*, Becque's *The Vultures*, and several of Strindberg's plays including *The Father*.

Perhaps the most significant discovery by the Freie Bühne was the playwright Gerhart Hauptmann (1862-1946), one of Germany's most respected writers and recipient of the Nobel Prize in Literature in 1912. The production of his *Before Sunrise* by the Freie Bühne in 1889 is considered by many scholars to mark the birth of modern German drama.

Hauptmann used the deterministic theory advocated by the naturalists throughout his work. In 1886 Hauptmann, Johannes Schlaf, and Arno Halz organized a group called Durch, which was designed to put into practice the naturalistic theories advocated by Bleibtren in his pamphlet *The Revolution in Literature* (1886). Hauptmann's masterpiece, *The Weavers* (1891-1892), was created to demonstrate the group's theories. In addition, it also draws inspiration from Tolstoi's *The Power of Darkness* (1886), and an economic study done on the Silesian linen industry in 1885. *The Weavers*

THE WEAVERS
GERHART HAUPTMANN

CHARACTERS
PFEIFER, a manager
DREISSIGER, a merchant who sells the weavers' work
OLD BAUMERT, a weaver
BECKER, a young, angry weaver
MORITZ JAEGER, a soldier
OLD HILSE, a weaver
GOTTLIEB HILSE, his son
LUISE HILSE, his wife

SETTING
Germany in the 1840s

BACKGROUND
Instead of emphasizing the individual, Hauptmann emphasizes the masses and creates a collective hero, making the play a drama of the group. Stultified horribly by their environment, the weavers rise up against forces which they cannot control. The play reaches a startling climax as the weavers seek to destroy the machines which have become a symbol of the fate that has oppressed them.

STORY
The weavers have come to Dreissiger's house to have Pfeifer buy their work. Pfeifer is merciless in how low he pays the starving weavers. When Becker objects to the ridiculous amount he is offered, Dreissiger comes in and announces that he is hiring two hundred more weavers, and that will mean even lower payment. Later, at the Baumert home, Old Baumert arrives with his small dog slaughtered for meat, and Jaeger, the soldier. They cook up the dog meat, but Old Baumert can't hold it down because he has been starving so long. Jaeger is sickened at the weaver's plight, knowing that there was no help in sight, which he tells them. He reads them the news, where the politicians have said that there is no hunger in their country. He then reads them an angry marching song about the misery of the weavers, inflaming them. The weavers start to openly talk about how abused they are, which starts to build to a frenzy. A policeman comes by and tells them they can't sing their song anymore, which just makes them sing it the louder. Dreissiger tries to have Becker arrested, but the mob attacks the policemen and frees him. A pastor tried to talk the crowd down to no avail. Livid, the weavers sack Dreissiger's house and take to the streets. The next town over, Old Hilse and family hear of the violence and are divided in their opinions. Old Hilse thinks it is wrong that the weavers are breaking the laws, while Luise believes it is time to rebel. Luise goes out and joins the riot. When the police come, Gottlieb joins his wife. Old Hilse is struck by a stray bullet. As he dies, the rioters overwhelm the police and go on.

was produced at the Freie Bühne in 1893 and in May of that year at Antoine's Théâtre Libre. It is based on the revolt of the linen weavers in Silesia and is structurally unique in its depiction of the protagonist.

Henrik Ibsen

Whereas Hauptmann championed naturalism. Henrik Ibsen (1828-1906) was realism's defender and, as such, is considered the father of modern drama.

Henrik Johann Ibsen was born March 20, 1828, in Skien, Norway, where he lived in luxury until 1836 when his father fell into bankruptcy. The disgrace of his father's failure turned the sensitive boy into a near recluse. In 1844 Ibsen left home to become an apothecary's apprentice in the town of Grimstadt. While there, the young apprentice read every book available to him and quickly acquired a good education. Ibsen remained at Grimstadt until 1850. Deeply influenced by the romanticists, Ibsen wrote his first finished play, *Cataline,* which was transported to Christiania by a close friend Ole Schulerud in the hope of publication. When all hopes failed, Schulerud had the scripts printed at his own expense and sent for Ibsen, who spent the next two years in the capital city. Despite, the failure of *Cataline* in Christiania, Ole Bull, a national hero and world famous violinist, became interested in the young poet, and employed him to assist in creating a national theatre in Bergen. This position eventually led to Ibsen's first grant for study outside Norway. The playwright received 140 pounds for studying the theatre in Denmark and Germany, with the prospect of later becoming stage manager or director of the Bergen Theatre.

Upon his return to Norway, Ibsen continued to experiment with romanticism. In 1857 he became artistic manager of the National Norwegian Theatre in Christiania and wrote the epic *The Vikings at Helgeland.* Another romantic play, *Love's Comedy,* was written in 1862. In 1863 he was granted his second travel stipend by the government. This grant was later augmented by private contributions collected by Bjørnstjerne Bjørnson, Johan Sveredaup, and other literary friends of Ibsen. *The Pretenders* (1864) was completed before Ibsen left Christiania for Copenhagen. He then departed for Rome, where he wrote his great poetic masterpiece *Brand* (1866). This romantic drama eliminated most of the financial problems that had plagued Ibsen. Shortly after the success of *Brand,* he was granted a stipend by the Trondheim Scientific Association and a new travel grant by the Norwegian government. Beginning in 1866, Ibsen received an annual stipend from the government that made him financially solvent for the rest of his life. Between the years 1867 and 1874, Ibsen completed three plays, including his romantic masterpiece *Peer Gynt* (1867). *Peer Gynt* was later immortalized by Grieg's famous *Peer Gynt Suite.* Ibsen continued to travel, and was one of the first to pass through the newly constructed Suez Canal in 1869. After the publication of *Emperor and Gallilean* (1873), Ibsen was made a knight of St. Olaf by King Oscar II.

Janet Achurch (1864-1916), English actress who in 1889 presented the first unadapted version of Ibsen's *A Doll's House.* A champion of Ibsen's work, she was called by George Bernard Shaw "the only tragic actress of genius we now possess." From Dirck's *Players of Today,* 1892.

Despite the honors showered on him, Ibsen was unhappy. His peers had attacked his poetry and had been highly critical of his last few poetic plays, including *Peer Gynt.* When the most famous poet of Norway, Bjørnstjerne Bjørnson, downgraded the quality of his poetry, Ibsen remarked: "If I am not a poet, then I have nothing to lose. I will try my hand as a photographer." Four years later in 1877 Ibsen published *Pillars of Society,* the first of his realistic plays. This play shows the influence of Scribe in terms of dramatic structure and established a structural technique that Ibsen generally followed throughout the rest of his career. It was not until the publication of three highly controversial plays, *A Doll's House* 1879), *Ghosts* (1881), and *An Enemy of the People* (1882), that Ibsen established the reputation of social dramatist, which was to earn him the label "father of modern drama."

A DOLL'S HOUSE
HENRIK IBSEN

CHARACTERS

TORVALD HELMER, a newly promoted manager of a bank
NORA HELMER, his wife
CHRISTINA LINDE, her old friend
KROGSTAD, a moneylender and an employee at Torvald's bank

BACKGROUND

With the outcry that followed the production of *A Doll's House*, Ibsen was linked with a new controversial movement which sprung up shortly after the publication of John Stuart Mill's book *The Subjection of Women*. The book set off controversy in Norway as it did throughout their world as most men in general opposed the idea of more freedom for women on the basis that it would destroy the family as well as the idealized status that women enjoyed under romanticism. On the other hand, the suffragists objected to what they termed the "white slavery of women." In 1874, Aasta Hansteen, a pioneer suffragist in Norway, lashed out against the existing inequality of women. Although initially irritated at this outbreak, Ibsen believed in individual as well as national freedom and eventually extended his demand of individual freedom to include women whom he considered to be oppressed in their efforts at self-realization. In *A Doll's House*, the suffragist movement found what it hoped to be a spokesman for the cause. Ibsen objected throughout his life to being categorized and felt that he was a spokesman for all and not an evangelist for the few.

Ibsen made public his views on this subject in an address to the Women's Rights League in 1898.

I am not a member of the Women's Rights League. Whatever I have written, has been without any conscious thought of making propaganda. I have been more poet and less social philosopher than people generally seem inclined to believe. I thank you for the toast, but must disdain the honor of having consciously worked for the Women's Rights Movement. I am not quite clear as to just what the Woman's Rights Movement really is. And if you read my books carefully, you will understand this. True enough, it is desirable to solve the problem of Women's Rights along with the others; but that has not been the whole purpose. My task has been the description of humanity.

STORY

Nora is bustling around the house, having just got back from Christmas shopping. Torvald enters and the two have a discussion over money that defines their relationship: he is allowed to be a grave adult and she a silly child. He returns to his work and Mrs. Linde pays a visit. Nora has not seen her in years. They discuss Mrs. Linde being a lonely widower of three years. It is here that Nora reveals a very adult, competent side of her personality by telling Mrs. Linde a story about Torvald. The story explains a period of time when Torvald became quite ill and was in danger of dying if they could not go abroad. They had just had their first child and did not have extra money for the trip. Torvald refused to borrow money. Nora's father was terminally ill and unable to help her so she tried the only thing that she could to save her husband's life. She took out a loan from a man named Krogstad, who is an employee of the bank. To secure the loan, it was necessary for her to forge her father's name as co-signer. The trip was made and Torvald's life saved. Since that time Nora has been scrimping and saving to pay off the loan without Torvald's knowledge. It is also revealed that Mrs. Linde is in need of work, and Nora offers to speak to Torvald for her. Krogstad intrudes upon their discussion to speak with Torvald. Mrs. Linde and Nora move into the kitchen where they are later joined by Torvald. Nora makes her pitch for Mrs. Linde and Torvald agrees. Everyone leaves, and Nora is alone with the children when Krogstad returns. He tells her that he is to be fired, and that Nora must prevent that, or he will reveal everything to Torvald and the town. Nora tries in vain to persuade her husband. When Krogstad receives a

A DOLL'S HOUSE, *continued*

letter formally firing him, he writes his letter in return, and drops it in the mailbox. Nora does everything she can to keep Torvald away from the mailbox, because she doesn't have the key. Mrs. Linde persuades Krogstad to not ruin the Helmers by promising to marry him. However, it is too late—Torvald has read the letter. He rails savagely at Nora, and announces that though she can stay for the sake of appearances, she is no longer his wife and her children's mother. A complete turnaround then occurs when Torvald receives a letter saying that Krogstad will do nothing. Suddenly, he is the loving husband, and she the perfect wife. However, Nora has finally seen Torvald as he is, and cannot bear to play his child-wife any longer. Though he begs her to stay, she leaves to make a life for herself, to become the woman she has never been allowed to be.

Ibsen was disturbed by the criticism that *A Doll's House* had received because of what he called "ecclesiastical narrow-mindedness" in Norway. Partly as an answer to his critics, Ibsen wrote his third social play, *Ghosts*, in which the central character, Mrs. Alving, unlike Nora, does not leave her husband but stays and is brought to tragedy because of that decision. Her son Oswald goes mad from syphilis ostensibly inherited from his father.

The worldwide reaction to *Ghosts* was tumultuous. Some hailed the play and Ibsen with almost messianic fervor while others called him a lunatic and pervert. Edward F. Smyth Pigott, the British play examiner between 1874 and 1895, was quoted as saying:

> I have studied Ibsen's plays pretty carefully, and all the characters in Ibsen's plays appear to me morally deranged. All the heroines are dissatisfied married women in a chronic state of rebellion against not only the conditions which nature has imposed on their sex, but against all duties and obligations of mothers and wives: and as for the men they are all rascals or imbeciles.

Ghosts was banned from the legitimate stage in England; however, it was given a performance at the Independent Theatre in London founded for the productions of new plays by J.T. Grein. The reaction to *Ghosts* in London was varied depending upon the reviewer. George Bernard Shaw and William Archer, among others, hailed it as a masterpiece; other Victorian critics were outraged. Clement Scott, a popular critic of the day was particularly bitter. After viewing *Ghosts* he called it "a play that if presented to the general public would, if not hissed off the stage the first night, close the doors of any London theatre in a fortnight." He went on to say: "If it is desirable to drive decent minded women from the playhouse, and to use the auditorium as a hospital ward or dissecting-room, let it be so . . . But in our hurry to dramatize the Contagious Diseases Act let us first set about writing a good play." But the reaction of the play did not deter Ibsen from attacking social idols. Although Ibsen gradually became more mystical in his later plays, turning against realism, his plays set the model for the modern realistic play that is still recognized today.

Anton Chekhov

While Ibsen was attacking society's problems in Norway, Anton Chekhov (1860-1904) was advocating reform in Russia. Chekhov's success is closely associated with Stanislavski and the Moscow Art Theatre, although he had artistic differ-

Maxim Gorky and Anton Chekhov in 1900. *Courtesy Tass from Sovfoto.*

ences with the group. In analyzing Chekhov's work (that is, his technique), contemporary critics tried to categorize his plays according to established norms. But Chekhov's plays defied strict categorization as Chekhov, the artist, was searching for a new form. From a style perspective, Chekhov is a realist in content and intent (basically his search for reality), but whether the form of his plays is tragedy, comedy, or a mixture of the two, has been the crux of the controversy.

As a medical student, Chekhov turned to writing out of financial necessity. His theatrical career is said to have begun with *Platonov* (1881), a play that was neither published nor performed and was discovered in his papers about 1920. The significance of this work is that it marks the beginning of his development as a writer. *Ivanov* (1884)

was his next major effort and was written the same year he received his medical degree. Chekhov is most remembered for four plays: *The Sea Gull* (1896), whose eventual success with the Moscow Art Theatre established Chekhov, the dramatist, Stanislavski, the actor, and the Moscow Art Theatre, whose symbol became the sea gull; *Uncle Vanya* (1889), a rewrite of his earlier work, *The Woed Demon; The Three Sisters* (1901); and *The Cherry Orchard* (1904).

Chekhov was ill throughout his life and died of consumption in 1904. A key to understanding Chekhovian drama is the silences: it is not what is said but what is *not* said. The scene between Varya and Lopakhin (Act Four) in *The Cherry Orchard* serves as an excellent example. Chekhov radically altered the traditional perception of drama and in so doing, prepared the way for Brecht, Pirandello, and the absurdists. He showed how drama could be relevant to the life experience through the great use of irony. As Chekhov indicated, we do not live our lives in extremes but we spend it simply— talking, eating, and sleeping.

Scenic Ideals

With plays from both the realistic and naturalistic schools of thought being written, it became necessary to alter techniques of the theatre itself in order to produce them. The new styles demanded several drastic changes. First, new scenic approaches utilizing more photographic reproduction to deal with the slice-of-life techniques were needed. Second, if the plays attempted to reproduce life as it is, new acting styles were needed. Third, to make all elements unified, an overseer, in the form of the Regisseur or director, was needed. Fourth, new theatres were needed because, as we have seen in England, the old theatres would not always produce the new plays and, in many cases, were too large for plays demanding intimacy.

Realistic scenery had begun to evolve as early as the last of the eighteenth century with Phillippe Jacques DeLoutherberg's experiments in local color. Madame Vestris continued the evolution with the first use of the box set in England around 1832. Charles Kean (1811-1868), more than any other English producer, developed historical research in designing scenery. Beginning with *Macbeth* in 1853, Kean provided his audiences with a printed list of authorities he had consulted in striving for historical accuracy. His productions at the Princess Theatre did much to bring fashionable audiences back to the theatre as well as to refine the gentlemanly melodrama originally begun by Macready and Lytton.

Scenic development continued with the Bancrofts at the Prince of Wales. Mrs Bancroft, born Marie Wilton (1838-1921), and her actor husband, Squire Bancroft (1841-1926), were famous for refining the use of the box set and utilizing many small realistic properties. Henry Irving (1838-1905), the first actor in English history to be knighted, is famous for his development of three-dimensional stage pieces and what has been called pictorial realism.

In America David Belasco created sets with absolute fidelity to the original. In *The Governor's Lady* (1912) Belasco re-created New York's Child's Restaurant on stage, complete with restaurant apparatus and the food stocked daily by Child's for consumption during the performance. For his production of *The Easiest Way* (1909), an entire room from a boardinghouse (wallpaper and all) was transferred to the stage.

Naturalism as scenic design, while still used in contemporary theatre, is more frequently used to describe what has occurred in cinema. As a matter of fact, naturalistic design has been the prevalent style until the more recent cinematographic experimentation in special effects. Selective realism, in which enough realistic scenic devices are utilized to give the impression of realism, is more prevalent on the stage. When a stage or theatrical environment is real to life, then the environment requires actors to function realistically within that environment. The illusion of reality in acting is not exclusively a nineteenth century phenomenon. Greek actors were frequently judged and compared as to their realistic styles. In many ways the conception of realism through the ages is directly related to the kind of scenic environment within which, or in front of which, the actor moved. Hence, idealized scenic background, along with other factors such as theatre size and shape, produced a particular style of acting. When the theatre turned toward realistic literature, a new acting style became necessary. The rise of the director greatly influenced the evolution of acting styles. One of the more important groups evolved to handle the new realism was the Moscow Art Theatre of Russia.

The Moscow Art Theatre and Its Influence

On June 21, 1897, Konstantin Stanislavski (1863-1938) and Vladimir Nemirovich-Danchenko (1858-1943) drafted the general artistic principles and managerial procedures of the Moscow Art Theatre. Among the procedures set down was the stipulation that Nemirovich-Danchenko exercise authority over all literary matters and Stanislavski over matters of production. Nemirovich-Danchenko had veto rights in questions concerning content, Stanislavski in questions concerning form. Although Stanislavski and Nemirovich-Danchenko were heralded as the guiding forces of the Moscow Art Theatre, Savva Morozov was the chief financial supporter as well as the actual owner of the Moscow Art Theatre. His control enabled him to have as much artistic and managerial control as he desired and he was constantly a thorn to Nemirovich-Danchenko, who detested him. As time went by, Stanislavski became more and more interested in the actor. His theories on acting, particularly those theories concerned with reaching an intense psychological realism, became for some the ideal method of producing the needed acting style. Stanislavski's influence on the theatre has been monumental, particularly after the Art theatre's world tour in 1923. Many American directors were influenced by the Stanislavski technique and several acting companies and schools were set up. The Group Theatre, the most distinguished troupe of the 1930s, was founded by several students of the Stanislavski system, including Lee Strasberg and Harold Clurman. The system was taught in the United States by two Moscow Art Theatre members, Richard Boleslavsky (1889-1937) and Maria Ouspenskaya (1881-1949), who elected to stay in the United States and were co-directors of the American Laboratory Theatre between 1923-1930.

Above: Konstantin Sergeivich Stanislavski (nee Alexeyev), Russian actor, director, and teacher, shown on the occasion of the fiftieth anniversary of the Moscow Art Theatre. *Below:* Vladimir Nemirovich-Danchenko who, along with Stanislavski, founded the Moscow Art Theatre. *Photos Courtesy Embassy of the Union of Soviet Socialist Republics.*

Maria Ouspenskaya (1881-1949) toured America in 1923 with the Moscow Art Theatre. She and Richard Boleslavsky remained in America to head the American Laboratory Theatre, where they introduced the Stanislavski system of acting. Ms. Ouspenskaya is pictured here in her role as Baronness von Obersdorf in Sidney Howard's *Dodsworth* (1934: Starring Walter Huston and Fay Bainter). She was rarely without her monacle handging from her neck. *Courtesy Joseph "Mac" Dixon.*

Richard Boleslavsky (1889-1937), right, shown here with a student, Ruth Nelson, and Robert Edmond Jones, was a noted teacher of acting. A member of Stanislavski's Moscow Art Theatre, Boleslavsky joined Maria Ouspenskaya in heading the American Laboratory Theatre. His text, *Acting:The First Six Lessons*, is still widely used today. Robert Edmond Jones (1887-1954) is generally credited with introducing the "new stagecraft" in America with his design for *The Man Who Married a Dumb Wife* (1915). *Courtesy Joseph "Mac" Dixon.*

The Actor's Studio, founded by director Elia Kazan, Strasberg, and Cheryl Crawford in 1947, used a variation of the Stanislavski system. The Actor's Studio utilized exercises derived from Stanislavski in an effort to free actors from psychological inhibitions and to encourage imagination through emotion memory. Much of the Studio seemed to be geared toward encounter session and self-understanding by the actor.

The Actor's Studio was often criticized for fostering the negligence of theatrical techniques and

for encouraging self-indulgence of its actors. The success of Marlon Brando (b. 1924) as Stanley Kowalski, in Tennessee Williams' *A Streetcar Named Desire* directed by Kazan in 1947, placed the work of the studio in public light. Brando's lifestyle and the novelty of a serious actor mumbling lines created, fairly or unfairly, an image of the school not altogether flattering. Nevertheless, actors competed for acceptance to the school and many graduates went on to fame, fortune and, in some cases, disaster. Graduates include Marlon Brando, James

The Moscow Art Theatre in 1899. In the center (with hand on lapel) is Stanislavski; to his left is Nemirovich-Danchenko. In the second row (third from left) is Olga Knipper, Chekov's wife; in the first row (far right) is Ivan Moskrin. *Courtesy Embassy of the Union of Soviet Socialist Republics.*

Dean, Marilyn Monroe, Lee J. Cobb, Geraldine Page, Rip Torn, Paul Newman, Jane Fonda, Joanne Woodward and Susan Strasberg, among others. Many actors who attempted to imitate what they thought to be the new style by mumbling lines and inventing endless amounts of inconsequential stage business, in spite of Strasberg's objections, were thought to be perpetrators of the Studio style. Strasberg's techniques, real or imagined, generated endless debates as to whether they were actually Stanislavski's methods. An interesting paradox is that no one actually knows what Stanislavski's method was, probably not even Stanislavski. In truth, his "system" was the result of years of evolution and testing and was compartmentalized by later writers and theorists.

The Independent Theatre (England)

Because of the theatrical monopoly in England, the legitimate houses had grown tremendously in size. Both Covent Garden and Drury Lane could seat as many as 8,000 people. Playing without sound amplification and with some of the audience considerable distance from the stage, an exaggerated acting style was necessary. Moreover, actors from the old school were not overly anxious to sanction legitimate drama in a small theatre. Charles Kemble (1775-1854), an actor-manager of some fame, commented in 1833 that "regular"

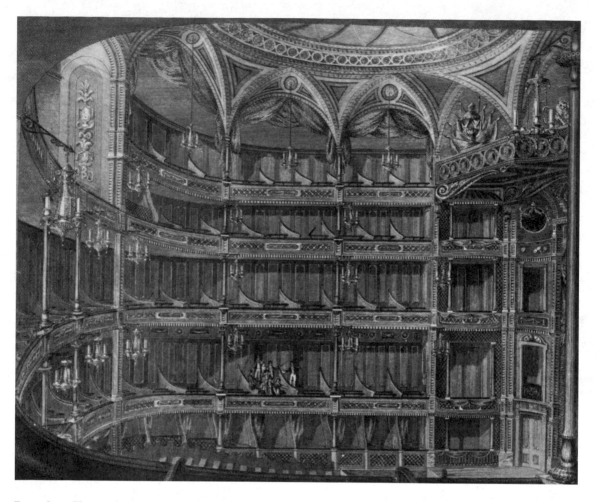

Drury Lane Theatre, built in 1794 by Henry Holland. From *Londina Illustrata*, 1825.

drama can only be presented in theatres of certain dimensions. "I assure you a very small theatre is destructive of good acting; instead of being favorable to an actor, it brings him so near the audience that he cannot abstract his mind from the audience." Kemble maintained that anyone could hear in a major theatre. The fault, he commented, was with the audience, not the theatre. Edmund Kean (1787-1833), also an actor of great popularity, agreed with Kemble that anyone could see from any part of the theatre. "I think the intellect becomes confined by the size of the theatre," he states. "The larger the stage the better the actor, and the less observable are his faults."

The Theatre Regulations Act of 1843 officially ended the theatrical monopoly and with it the large theatres. Smaller theatres, such as the Prince of Wales and the Princess, moved toward ensemble acting. These theatres were subject to theatrical censorship and would not or could not perform the new drama, even though the new theatrical techniques and scenery were utilized in the performance of the old. This phenomenon was also true in other countries. Since the new drama was considered offensively immoral, theatres attempting productions were frequently denied licenses to perform. In an effort to provide a space for these new dramas, the independent theatre movement was formed. The most successful English theatre to emerge from this movement was The Independent Theatre.

On March 13, 1891, J. T. Grein (1862-1935), a

Dutchman residing in London, created a group called The Independent Theatre. Their first production was *Ghosts*, which had been banned by the Lord Chamberlain. (A portion of Clement Scott's review of that performance was quoted earlier.) The Independent Theatre became the second English group to produce plays by means of private subscriptions. The Shelley Society had produced *The Cenci* by that means in 1887. Grein primarily produced continental drama because for obvious reasons, English playwrights were not writing controversial plays in the new style. Grein appealed to a young Irish critic and novelist to fill the void. In 1892 at the urging of Grein, George Bernard Shaw (1856-1950) began his long career as a playwright with the Independent Theatre's production of *Widower's House.*

Considered one of the preeminent dramatists in the history of literature, George Bernard Shaw wrote primarily in the comic form. This form enabled him to dramatize his real concerns for social reform, social problems, the influence of heredity and environment upon individual choices, the perfectability of the human race, and the misconceptions about historical figures and events.

Like the Freie Bühne, the Independent Theatre's production of Shaw's plays merits this theatre a place in history. More than that, however, it provided an outlet for English playwrights for a number of years. The Independent Theatre was replaced by the Incorporated Stage Society in 1899. The Stage Society, by providing an outlet for young English writers whose works might otherwise have been emasculated by the stage censor, also provided a continuing service to the theatre. While the Independent Stage Society no longer exists, the theatre it founded, The Royal Court, continues producing new plays.

Realism, both in scenic technique and dramatic literature, had established itself in the theatre by the turn of the century. It remains one of the most popular styles of the twentieth century on both stage and television. Scenic naturalism has become, more or less, a province of the cinema and has been, until recent times, the prevalent style. But realism was not the only style to come out of

George Frederick Cooke (1756-1812) as Richard III. An English actor, Cooke's career and reputation were ruined by alcoholism. When sober, however, he was considered one of the finest actors of his generation. A coarse, yet powerful actor, he was given to playing his roles intuitively rather than studying them. On tour in the United States, he remarked that President James Madison was "the contemptible King of the Yankee Doodles." From *The Kembles and Their Contemporaries,* 1890.

the latter part of the nineteenth century. Several new styles were to come forward that questioned the relevancy of the five senses as the only instrument in the search for truth.

Many important changes were occurring in the United States which were to fashion the nature of an emerging American theatre. There was a great deal of territorial expansion during the last half of the nineteenth century. The westward movement, spawned by tales of great mining wealth, was instrumental in the formation of a railway system culminating in the first transcontinental railroad completed in 1869. With the great emigration to the west came a young, highly mobile, struggling, yet dynamic theatre.

The American Theatre to 1930

The American theatre which had begun in the colonies spread westward across the Alleghenies, crossing the Missouri by boat and the plains by covered wagon. Poor but proud theatrical companies found themselves in Colorado mining camps, sweating with the silver prospectors in Death Valley, and involved in gun fights in California during the gold rush. A theatre was established in Sacramento, California, as early as 1849. Such actors as Junius Brutus Booth, Frank Chanfrau, J. W. Wallack, Jr., and the first western performer, Lotta Crabtree (1847-1924), braved the long journey west. Other early western theatres were opened in San Francisco in 1850, Nevada City, Nevada in 1860, and in Salt Lake City in 1865.

During the last half of the nineteenth century, theatre in America became a thriving business, and for that reason it demanded a strong box office return. America had no long tradition of theatre, as had England, for example, so its audiences had to be nurtured. Since Americans as a whole were working people, the theatre was geared primarily to the public's taste. This was not bad nor unique, as most of what was popular in England was popular in the United States. But what did make a difference was that in England there were enough theatre lovers to allow a variety of theatres to survive. Not so in America, where the audience preferred to see stars and their vehicles. The fact that America could import a quality product from England made it difficult for American-born playwrights and actors to survive in the beginning. Playwrights, actors, and designers did develop in America but, for most of the nineteenth century, their work was primarily in the commercial mainstream.

One of the most successful dramatists was Bronson Howard (1842-1908), who is considered America's first professional playwright. He began his career in 1864 and had his first success in 1870 with *Saratoga*. As a writer he was the first American dramatist to receive royalty payments

Bronson Howard, America's first professional playwright.

and he was responsible for creating the Society of American Dramatists and Composers, a forerunner to the Dramatist's Guild.

Principles of economics had a great deal to do with shaping the American theatre. Because of the difficulties in traveling during the early part of the nineteenth century, most American cities had resident stock companies producing a number of plays in repertory. It was not long, however, before producers began to realize that it was cheaper to mount a single production and run it for as long as it made money, than to produce several plays for a short period of time. The length of runs at the Boston museum increased from an average of fourteen days in the 1860s to seventy-five in the 1880s.

Producers also found that the public would pay more to see a "star" than they would to see local professionals; hence, stars were frequently booked in to play major roles. This practice was not unusual as foreign stars had been doing it for years.

Above: Engraving of the first Bowery Theatre, New York, which opened October 23, 1826, but was destroyed by fire May 26, 1828. *Bottom:* McVicker's Theatre, which opened November 5, 1857, in Chicago. This photograph appeared in the *Chicago Illustrated*, October 1866.

American reaction to a "star," Edmund Kean's performance as Richard III in 1825. There was a great disapproval to Kean who, after his initial triumphant tour in 1821, returned to Boston to smaller than expected houses. After two nights, Kean refused to perform for small houses. Audience dissatisfaction found voice in scathing denunciations in the Boston newspapers. It was four years before Kean attempted a return, but this time he was contrite.

They came into a city, performed, and left. The resident company then went on as before. Soon, however, one star was followed by another and the resident company became merely a support team. Then the idea of traveling a single show to various cities was initiated with success.

Once traveling companies became popular with producers, it is not surprising that a tour base was needed. Even less surprising is the fact that New York was the most likely center for this activity. New York had held a leading position in the theatre business since 1830. It had the largest concentration of theatres in the United States and a population that was growing at a faster rate than the total population of the country. Because for-eign stars usually landed in New York, managers were accustomed to booking out of Manhattan. Since the booking machinery for stars was already there, it was an easy matter to extend it to shows. By 1880 New York became the base for a large percentage of theatrical tours. In addition, if a producer expected to make money on the road, it became essential that the play be a New York success. Managers of various theatres throughout the country journeyed to New York to arrange for the tours. Because of the centralization of the theatre and the difficulties involved with the enormous number of producers, monopolization of theatrical production in America became possible.

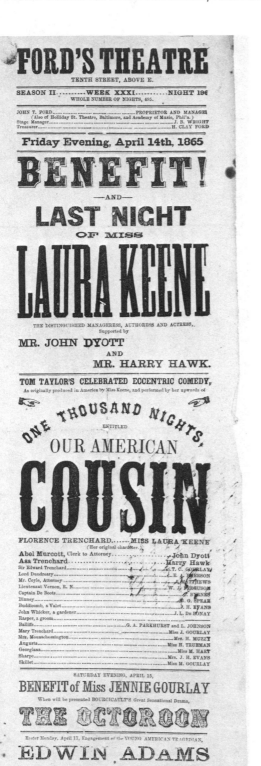

Left: Playbill for Ford's Theatre the night President Abraham Lincoln was assassinated. This playbill was printed before it was known that Lincoln would attend; after his plans were known, the playbill was reprinted to include a patriotic song and chorus to the soldiers

Below: The frontiersman was another native type which became popular in American theatre. Frank Mayo (1839-1896), American actor, achieved his greatest success in Frank Murdoch's *Davy Crockett*. Mayo played the role from 1872 until his death; after 2000 performances, he stopped counting. From *Dramatic Portrait Gallery*, 1880.

The Arch Street Theatre, Philadelphia, which opened October 1, 1828, under the management of William B. Wood (1779-1861).

The new Chestnut Street Theatre, Philadelphia. The original Chestnut Street Theatre opened February 17, 1794, but burned in 1820; the new theatre opened December 2, 1822.

Charlotte (Lotte) Crabtree (1847-1924), American actress who began her career at age eight by performing in mining camps. In 1864 she became a major star in New York. She was a versatile performer who could sing, dance, play the banjo, and act. She is pictured here in one of her most memorable roles, Musette. From *Dramatic Portrait Gallery*, 1880.

Clara Morris (1846-1925) as Evadne. An American actress, her realistic acting and emotional outbursts gained her the label of "Queen of Spasms." Few actresses have possessed such personal magnetism; it is said she hypnotized her audience. Miss Morris never rehearsed, preferring instead to rely on her instincts and intuition. By 1880, she was billed as "America's greatest living actress." From *Dramatic Portrait Gallery*, 1880.

The Theatrical Syndicate

In 1896 Sam Nixon, Fred Zimmerman, Charles Frohman, Al Hayman, Mark Claw, and Abraham Erlanger formed what was called the "Theatrical Syndicate." Basically, the Syndicate connected key routes between the large cities in the United States by building theatres or by forcing existing theatres into signing exclusive contracts. New York producers who refused to cooperate were denied bookings and noncomplying actors were punished by being blackballed from all tours. The American theatre fell under the complete control of the Syndicate by 1900. Because the Syndicate was primarily concerned with the commercial aspects of the theatre, scripts considered unlikely to appeal to a mass audience were not performed. The Syndicate, therefore, held what might be called de facto censorship over the American stage between the years 1900-1915.

Several stars, whose names are still mentioned with respect in the theatrical profession, emerged during this period. Among them were John Drew II (1853-1927) and Otis Skinner (1858-1942), Ethel Barrymore (1879-1959), E.A. Sothern (1859-1933), and the lovely Maude Adams (1872-1958), who gained theatrical fame by her performance in *Peter Pan*.

Some actors and directors held out against the Syndicate: Mrs. Fiske (1865-1932), who was the first American to produce the new realistic drama; James O'Neill (1847-1920) who became forever identified with the leading role in *The Count of Monte Cristo*; and David Belasco (1854-1931), who became the father of naturalistic staging in America. Belasco's productions were so much in demand that he was able to dictate his own terms to the Syndicate, which was the first crack in its power.

Belasco and the Shuberts

Belasco joined forces with Lee, Sam and J. J. Shubert, who had started in the theatre in Syracuse, New York. Their plan was to book shows into their own theatres. They initiated what was called the "open door" policy by allowing any production the right to play in a Shubert house. Because this practice appeared so liberal in comparison to the heavy-handed policy of the Syndicate, the Shuberts were called the saviors of the American theatre. The Syndicate fought back in several ways. First, they tried to persuade the Shuberts to limit the number of productions and the construction of new theatres. Second, they insisted on the exclusive rights to book all Shubert theatres. Third, they eventually closed all Syndicate theatres to Shubert productions.

In January 1907, Belasco and the Shuberts took the Syndicate to court for criminal conspiracy in restraint of trade. The Syndicate won the case, but the decision of Judge Otto A. Rosalsky set a legal precedent that was to enable the Shuberts to hold control over the theatre for years to come. The decision included several interesting points. First, Judge Rosalsky ruled that the Syndicate had the right to exclude a business rival from the use of their premises. Second, the Shuberts and Belasco were not being prevented from practicing their trade. Third, and most important, the judge ruled that theatrical amusements could not be considered as "articles of trade and commerce" and, therefore, were not subject to the antitrust laws.

The Syndicate suffered a severe blow when their knowledgeable colleague, Charles Frohman, was killed with the sinking of the *Lusitania* in 1915. From that time forward, the Shuberts became the power controlling the legitimate stage. The stock market crash in 1929 put them temporarily in bankruptcy, but in 1933 they were able to buy themselves out of bankruptcy. The last of the Syndicate members, A. L. Erlanger, died in 1930, leaving the Shuberts with a monopoly that, by virtue of judge Rosalsky's decision, was nearly unchallenged.

The rule of the Shuberts was every bit as dictatorial as that of the Syndicate. The choice of productions was geared primarily toward fattening the box office and not the mind. Their control

David Belasco (1853-1931), sometimes called the "Bishop of Broadway," is noted for his naturalistic staging, his battle against the syndicate, and his lighting innovations.

lasted until the Rosalsky decision was overturned in a federal antitrust suit in 1950. The Shuberts were forced to dispose of several of their theatres and the monopoly was broken by 1956. Although neither of the three Shubert brothers is living today, Shubert Theatre Enterprise is still a large legitimate theatre chain.

The commercialization of the American stage followed a relatively common pattern of industrial development. First, small local units were replaced by a large central unit. Second, the business aspects of the theatre were separated from the production element. Third, the products were standardized, as each play was produced by only one company or a number of duplicate companies. Fourth, theatre came under the control of big business. While the control over the theatre did little to improve the legitimate stage, the state of the theatre was not as vacuous as one might believe.

The power of the Shubert monopoly was, in many ways, similar to the governmental restrictions which had influenced the theatre in England and France. With the so-called legitimate stage effectively controlled, those who, for one reason or another, refused or were denied participation in the monopoly began to look elsewhere for a chance to make their livelihood in the theatre. Once again dissenters were to contribute an important new creative force to the American theatre, in particular, and the theatre in general.

The first of these creative forces began in American colleges and universities. For the first time courses were being offered in the drama. The most important course, known as English 47, was taught by George Pierce Baker (1866-1935), beginning at Radcliffe College in 1903 and then at Harvard in 1913. In 1925 Yale enticed Baker to move with a promise of a new theatre, a promise Harvard would not make. The first degree program was established in 1914 at Carnegie Institute of Technology by Thomas Wood Stevens (1880-1942). In 1918 Frederick Koch (1877-1942) established the Carolina Playmakers at Chapel Hill, North Carolina, listing playwright Paul Green, novelist-playwright Thomas Wolfe, and perhaps the greatest American theatre teacher to date, Hubert C. Heffner, as members

Little Theatre Movement

The second creative force was the "little" theatre movement. Following the pattern of the independent theatres in Europe, several little theatres were established as an American laboratory for the innovations that were being developed in Europe. Some of the most important were the Toy Theatre, founded by Mrs. Lyman Gale in Boston in 1912; Maurice Brown's Little Theatre, opening in Chicago in 1912; New York's Neighborhood Playhouse, formed by Irene and Alice Lewisohn in 1915; the Washington Square Players, established in New York in 1915; and the Provincetown Players, organized in Provincetown, Massachusetts.

The Provincetown Players began as a group in the summer of 1915. They were not professionals of the theatre per se, but were journalists, painters, sculptors, teachers, and the like. These were restless individuals raised under Victorian morality who questioned why Strindberg was condemned and Ibsen was considered immoral. Values were being questioned and the commercialism in the American theatre further reinforced the concept that the older generation was essentially corrupt. Many of these young rebels from Greenwich Vil-

lage spent their summers at Provincetown, a small Cape Cod settlement not far from Plymouth, Massachusetts. The group included, among others, John Reed, Mary Heaton Vorse, George Cram Cook, Susan Glaspell, Hutchins Hapgood, and Robert Edmond Jones. The first plays were given at Hutchins Hapgood's house and consisted of *Suppressed Desire* by Susan Glaspell (1882-1948) and George Cram Cook (1873-1924) and *Constancy* by Neith Boyce. The productions were designed by Robert Edmond Jones (1887-1954), who was to become one of the premier set designers of the American stage and a leading advocate of the "new stagecraft." Jones used the veranda with the ocean in the background for the first play, and then asked the audience to turn their seats around in order to view the set design for the second play which was a broad doorway at the opposite end of the room. As might be imagined, the Hapgood house was quite crowded for the first production. Consequently, a deserted fish house on the wharf, owned by Mary Heaton Vorse, was renovated with fish nets and circus benches for the next performances. The theatre was named "The Wharf Theatre," and interest in the colony reached a responsive note.

At a meeting called to discuss several new plays for production consideration, a member casually mentioned the name of a young man who was rooming with the vagabond philosopher, Terence Carlin. Carlin later introduced a shy, dark boy and read one of his plays called *Bound East for Cardiff*. The play was produced immediately, and the young Eugene O'Neill was made a member of the Provincetown Players.

Eugene Gladstone O'Neill (1888-1953) was born in a Times Square hotel. His father was James O'Neill, one of the more popular actors of his day. Eugene's early education was as fragmentary as his home life. He attended Princeton before signing on as a seaman and making several voyages throughout the world. After a brief spell in a sanitarium in 1912, O'Neill developed an interest in playwriting. In 1914 he enrolled in George Pierce Baker's playwriting class (English 47) at

THE EMPEROR JONES
EUGENE O'NEILL

CHARACTERS
BRUTUS JONES, Emperor of the island and an ex-con
HENRY SMITHERS, a trader
LEM, a native

SETTING
The West Indies, Nineteenth Century

BACKGROUND
When George Cram Cook read the play he already knew that it was going to take something special to capture the play scenically. He decided to build a dome of plaster and concrete. Starring as the Emperor in the play was Charles Gilpin (1878-1930), who as the first professional actor was paid the only salary among the cast, a stately sum of $50.00. Gilpin performed Brutus Jones 240 times throughout his career but was passed over during the 1924 revival of the play in favor of Paul Robeson. O'Neill did not want Gilpin to continue in the role because of a drinking problem. Although O'Neill later admitted: "As I look back on all my work, I can honestly say there was only one actor who carried out every notion of a character I had in mind, that actor was Charles Gilpin."

STORY
Smithers gives Jones word that the natives of the island he has ruled are going to rebel. Jones had ruled there by convincing the natives he was a magician. He then taxed and abused them to the point that they were now ready to kill him. Jones leaves immediately and heads into the jungle, giving Smithers the palace and bringing a gun with a silver bullet. The sound of drums follows him. On the way, he tries to find some food he had stored, but can't. As it turns dark and the moon comes out, he sees a man he had killed throwing dice. When the figure doesn't respond to him, he shoots at it, and it disappears. Terrified, he runs on with the drums still sounding. He reaches a road, where a chain gang is working. The guard tells him to get back to work, whipping him. He shoots at the guard, and the chain gang disappears. The sound of drums gets louder. He starts to another clearing, and is put up for slave auction. Once again, he shoots, this time at the auctioneer and someone else, and they all disappear. The drums get closer still. He next finds himself a slave on a ship. He just runs away, because he knows he only has one more bullet: the silver one. He then comes to an altar, which he kneels before. A witch doctor comes out and tells him he must sacrifice himself. A crocodile comes out of the woods then, and he shoots it. They all disappear, but Jones is in a near catatonic state with his fear. Lem's men come upon him, and fire a silver bullet especially made for him. Smithers believes that the bullet isn't what killed Jones, but his own fear.

Harvard, but left that spring (1915) for New York. While living in New York's Greenwich Village, he met Carlin.

For some, the founding of the Provincetown Players marks the birth of American drama. The players moved to 139 Macdougal Street in Greenwich Village in 1916. During the next two years at this location, six new plays by O'Neill were produced. The group moved to a larger place at 133

Macdougal and gained substantial notoriety considering that they were still an amateur group. A milestone was reached on November 1, 1920, with the opening of O'Neill's *The Emperor Jones*.

The Emperor Jones was also significant in that it marked a change in the nature of the Provincetown Players. The success of the play provided an opportunity to move to a Broadway theatre. At first there was a division of opinion among the players,

Eugene O'Neill's *The Emperor Jones,* as produced at Western Kentucky University. Directed by Loren K. Ruff; set design by James Brown.

but the possibility of making money for new plays overcame theoretical objections and the play opened at the Selwyn Theatre on December 28, 1920.

After 1923 O'Neill, Kenneth Macgowan, and Robert Edmond Jones formed a branch of the players to perform period plays—foreign and non-commercial. The other branch continued in the old manner. Provincetown playhouse closed in 1929, finally succumbing to financial pressures. The discovery of O'Neill alone justified its existence, but others launched through its efforts read like a *Who's Who.* Susan Glaspell, Paul Green, E. E. Cummings, Norman Bel Geddes, Edna St. Vincent Millay, Robert Edmond Jones, Paul Robeson, Frank Wilson, Water Abel, and Charles Gilpin, among others, went on to contribute significantly to the American theatre.

The American little theatre movement culminated in the formation of the Theatre Guild. This organization was the most respected theatre group in the United States between 1920 and 1930. Its artistic director was Philip Moeller (1880-1958) and its principal designers were Lee Simonson, Robert Edmund Jones, and Norman Bel Geddes (1893-1958), all advocates of "new stagecraft." Basically the "new stagecraft" was the result of a trend started by Swiss-born Adolph Appia (1862-

1928) and the Englishman Gordon Craig (1872-1966). Appia is noted for his innovation in lighting theory and Craig in theatre design. Another Englishman, William Poel (1852-1834), is credited with being one of the forerunners of theatrical eclecticism. Poel founded the Elizabethan Stage Society in 1894 and attempted to perform Shakespeare's plays on a stage similar to the Elizabethans. Up until this time, Shakespeare's plays were produced according to the style popular at the time of their production. If the prevalent theatrical style was wing and drop, pictorial realism, or realism, that was the way the play was produced.

Poel's ideas were reinforced by Max Reinhardt (1873-1943) in Germany. Reinhardt believed that each play should be approached differently and that theatre architecture and dramatic styles are related. Reinhardt's work was called "eclecticism" or "artistic realism." The new approach freed design from the rigidity of a particular style. All elements of theatre, and conventions of all periods, could be utilized in the design of the production.

The constructivism of Meyerhold, the distortions of the expressionists, the dream atmosphere of the symbolists, the epic staging techniques of Brecht, could be combined in production with actors utilizing the acting techniques of Stanislavski. The artist was given the freedom to use any device to enhance the artistic signature of the twentieth century theatre.

The new stagecraft designers opted to create a specific statement by utilizing all aspects of technical theatre to enhance the play. The design of Norman Bel Geddes for Dante's *The Divine Comedy* in 1921 remains one of the classic examples of the new school.

While it is true that Americans had been writing plays for some time, the plays were based on European models. With the discovery of Eugene O'Neill at the Provincetown Playhouse, America began to establish itself to the world as a theatrical power. In Europe, however, still another artistic movement was already breaking away from the dominant realistic revolution. This movement or movements was to redefine the modern theatre.

Selected Readings

Brockett, Oscar G. and Findlay, Robert. *Century of Innovation: A History of European and American Theatre and Drama Since the Late 19th Century.* 2nd ed. Boston, 1991.

Jackson, Holbrook. *The Eighteen Nineties.* New York, 1913.

Meyer Michael. *Ibsen.* New York, 1971.

Miller, Anne Irene. *The Independent Theatre in Europe.* New York, 1931.

Valency, Maurice. *The Flower and the Castle.* New York, 1963.

Vocabulary

1. Auguste Comte — oh GOO:ST KOHNT
2. Eugene Scribe — yoo ZHAYN SKREEB
3. Henrik Ibsen — HEN rik IB suhn
4. Bjørnstjerne Bjørnson — BYAWRN styern BYAWRN suhn
5. André Antoine — ahn DRAY ahn TWUHN
6. Konstantin Stanislavski — kawn stahn TEEN sta ni SLAHF skee
7. Vladimir Nemirovich-Danchenko — VLA duh mir nuh MEER uh veech dahn CHEN koh
8. Richard Boleslavsky — boh luh SLAHF skee
9. Maria Ouspenskaya — MAHR ee uh oo spen SKIGH uh
10. Elia Kazan — EE li uh kuh ZAHN
11. Freie Bühne — FIRGH uh BYOO: nuh
12. J. T. Grein — GREEN

CHAPTER THIRTEEN

❧

Idealism and the Spirit:
The Antirealist and
The American Renaissance

A scene from Ntozake Shange's *For Colored Girls Who Have Considered Suicide When the Rainbow is Enuf*. Pictured are (left to right): Beverly Anne, Barbara Alston, Candy Brown, Trazana Beverley, Alfre Woodard, Marilyn Coleman, and Jonelle Allen. *Courtesy Mark Taper Forum.*

The industrial revolution of the nineteenth century was instrumental in producing the growing perception that the mechanization of western culture was, in effect, dehumanizing people. As a consequence, there arose a dissatisfaction with the use of science as the guiding force in determining societal values and human destiny. Realism only exacerbated the situation. Self-doubt and a desperate need to reaffirm, or at least to establish, a new set of values led to a challenge of science. The reaction against realism was slow in growing but once established in intellectual circles, several groups were spawned that were to influence the direction of the theatre. The antirealists were aesthetically united only in the theory that there is more to life than what meets the eye (objective reality). To some, realism's emphasis on the scientific method, which tended to reject, ignore, or overlook the metaphysical, denied the very basis of art. To draw upon a Biblical analogy, for some artists the Philistines had won the day. Again, almost analogous to the Biblical warning that "man cannot live by bread alone," groups of detractors formed to reject out of hand the scientific view of human destiny. These artists were not necessarily ready to return to religious orthodoxy, but were ready to address the vacuum that scientific realism had created by rejecting transcendental alternatives.

In short, life without the fourth dimension had proven difficult and the antirealists began to experiment with ways to deal with what might be called scientific myopia. First, there were those who believed that a dramatist should be a mythmaker and should portray the ideal. This group included those who felt that art exists for its own sake and those who felt that the creation of art is intuitive and not logical. Second, there were those who attempted to justify the metaphysical by giving it scientific legitimacy. Third, some artists maintained that reality was not logical and could not be universally defined. This group tended to be almost messianic in their attempt to show a personal view of reality. Fourth, some artists asserted that science with its precision and order was

destroying the world and that true art can be found in antiorder or chaos. Finally, there was the rise of eclecticism that began in the independent theatre movements and gradually redefined mainstream theatre throughout the world.

Richard Wagner

An early antirealist whose work gave evidence of change in the world of theatre was Richard Wagner (1813-1883). Born in Leipzig, Wagner initially wanted to be a poet but later became fascinated with music and studied composition. Unhappy with contemporary theatre, he began to formulate a theory that was to plant the seeds of modern theatre. Wagner was disgusted with the trend to show sordid affairs on the stage, and became determined to lift the theatre above domesticity and into the realm of mythmaker. Fundamentally, he wanted to portray life as it should be, not as it is, by finding binding truths locked within the mythology of a people. He would later call this racial consciousness. Wagner felt that a common thread existed in all cultures that united them as "folk." Later the Nazi party elevated Wagner to hero status for his ideas by misinterpreting his intent. This has led some to call Wagner a Nazi sympathizer, although he died six years before Hitler was born.

Wagner believed that spoken dialogue alone could not always reach the ideal. He postulated that drama should be "rinsed in the magic fountain of music." Although respectful of the genius of Shakespeare, he felt that if Shakespeare were combined with Beethoven, a new and powerful voice would be created. Further, he argued that the dramatist's works are frequently violated by the actors' interpretation. Thus the accurateness of interpretation demanded that high drama is only possible with the help of music. To Wagner, music would allow the dramatist to control every nuance of sound that the actor makes, and thus would assure a work of art performed as it was intended by the dramatist-composer. He argued:

What was not practically possible for Shakespeare—to be himself the actor of each one of his roles — is practicable for the musical composer, and this with great definiteness — since he speaks to us directly through each one of the musicians who executes his works.

Wagner theorized that the author-composer should work to fashion all aspects of the drama into a unified work of art *(Gesamtkunstswerk)*. His ideas were best conceptualized in his great tetralogy, *Der Ring des Nibelugen,* and in *Tristan und Isolde.* His opera house at Bayreuth was designed to create a "mystic chasm" between the real world and ideal. The theatre, opened in 1876, featured a hidden orchestra pit, a steam curtain to mask scene changes, and a double proscenium arch. The main part of the auditorium was shaped like a fan, insuring superb sight lines. Wagner was the first to turn out the lights in the theatre; he would not allow musicians to tune up once the audience entered. By attempting to create an ideal environment on the stage, Wagner paved the way not only for Appia's experiments in lighting but modern scenery as well.

Gordon Craig

Adolphe Appia and Gordon Craig

Adolphe Appia (1862-1928), born in Switzerland, became impressed by Wagner's theories of artistic unity. To achieve unity, Appia proposed the elimination of two-dimensional settings replaced by three-dimensional units to provide a transition from the horizontal to upright scenery. Since he considered light as a visual counterpart to music, Appia emphasized the need for light to be a fusing element. He also argued that to achieve artistic unity, one person must control all elements of production. Appia's ideas not only strengthened the concept of a director, but laid the foundation for modern stage lighting.

His ideas were reinforced and publicized by Gordon Craig (1872-1966), who established the model for modern scenic designers. For Craig, the theatre was an independent art form and was best realized when words, line, color, action and rhythm were blended into a whole. Overseeing this theatre would be the master artist whose responsibility included every area of production—much like today's notion of director. In addition, he favored the visual over the aural and, therefore, suggested "a theatre of silence" in which the visual would take precedence over the word. Craig's opinion of the actor, like that of the dramatist, was suspect and thus he conceived of the "übermarionette" (superpuppet), a concept still open to interpretation. The idea was that the puppets would be without ego and would subject themselves totally to the director. Thus, the actor's ego and the actor's tendency to inject personal ideas into the script would be eliminated. Only the master artist's (director's) view would remain.

The work of Appia and Craig was considered irrational before World War I but thereafter their theories were to dominate. Their ideas constitute what is termed in America as "new stagecraft."

Friedrich Nietzsche

Perhaps the greatest articulator of the Wagnerian theories was the nineteenth century philosopher Friedrich Nietzsche (1844-1900). Nietzsche was born in Rocker, Germany, and studied in Bonn and Leipzig. He met Wagner in 1870 and became engrossed in the composer's theories and operas. His obsessions culminated in the publication of *The Birth of Tragedy from the Spirit of Music* in 1872, which was dedicated to Wagner.

Nietzsche attempted to reinforce the idea that ritual and myth are at the very heart of the dramatic phenomenon. Knowing that contemporary theory postulated that tragedy arose from the dithyrambic hymns to Dionysus, Nietzsche used the Greek theatre as a metaphor.

> I have borrowed my adjectives from the Greeks who developed their mystical doctrines of art through plausible embodiments, not through purely conceptual means. It is by those two art-sponsoring deities, Apollo and Dionysus, that we are made to recognize the tremendous split, as regards both origins and objectives, between the plastic, Apollonian arts and the non-visual art of music inspired by Dionysus.

Nietzsche viewed the Apollonian as representing the dream world of clarity and order and the Dionysian as intoxication or irrational disorder. The Apollonian world of the dream where "nothing seems indifferent or redundant" tends to protect humanity against the terrors of reality. According to Nietzsche, it was the Apollonian spirit that demanded the creation of Olympian Gods as a way of giving meaning to human life. The Apollonian spirit thus provides the necessary illusions to fuel the human spirit. The myth of perfection which centers on human superiority and individuality over nature is fostered by the Apollonian. The Dionysian spirit, on the other hand, fills the mind with the intoxicating joy of primal nature.

> Man now expresses himself through song and dance as the member of a higher community; he has forgotten how to walk, how to speak, and is on the brink of taking wings as he dances. Each of his gestures betokens enchantment; through him sounds a supernatural power, the same power which makes the animal speak and the earth render up milk and honey. He feels himself to be godlike and strides with the same elation and ecstasy as the gods he has seen in his dreams.

The almost orgiastic Dionysian spirit, then, shatters all illusion of human superiority, strips individuality, and makes us one with nature.

Accordingly, tragedy arose from the conflict between the desire for clarity and order and the wild primitive urge toward disorder. Tragedy exists as a "symbolizing of Dionysian wisdom by means of the expedients of Apollonian art." It reaffirms the value of life itself through the death of an individual because life will go on seeking perfection in any case. In a sense, the spirit of all is reaffirmed through the death of one. Nietzsche believed that in order to have great art, a balance between the Dionysian and Apollonian elements was necessary. He deplored realistic drama because he held that realism (science and the Darwinian theory of progress) had blocked out the Dionysian vision. Yet, others believed that a balance was not necessary at all—that true art existed in the Dionysian vision. The idea of the Dionysian vision manifested itself in the arts in many ways but the most important early example was that of the symbolists.

The Symbolists

The inspiration for the symbolist movement stemmed primarily from the American poet Edgar Allen Poe (1809-1849). Poe's works were read throughout Europe and he was considered a visionary by such writers as Baudelaire. Baudelaire was the first to draw attention to Wagner's theories. Stephane Mallarmé (1842-1898) was the acknowledged leader of the movement by writing poetic drama but was not a significant dramatist. Mallarmé was anti-spectacle and wanted "detheatricalization of the theatre" and "dematerialization" of the stage. The stage was to be reduced to

Three leading figures in the symbolist movement: *Left to right:* Mallarmé, Maeterlinck, and Claudel.

the bare essentials to support the written word. Poe's poetry and stories explore the Dionysian. His works delve into the unknown and the mysterious and are filled with symbolic overtones. Seeking to create emotional impressions through suggestion, Poe used color to render an almost psychedelic beauty which bombards the senses and creates a feeling of horrified fascination. Symbolists postulated that art must be an expression of the inner voices if it is to be an expression of truth. In many ways, symbolism was similar to romanticism in its reflection of the concept that the ultimate truth may be found only in rational thought processes. For that reason, the movement is sometimes called neoromanticism. But the symbolist believed that truth can be grasped only by intuition. Since ultimate truth cannot be understood logically, it cannot be expressed in logical language. Therefore, ultimate truth can only be suggested through symbols which evoke in the minds of the audience those feelings which are similar to the dramatist's intuition of reality. Through a series of carefully selected symbols, the dramatist attempts to intoxicate the audience by linking them with primal forces, or at least the

artist's intuition of those forces. Actually, the audience may reach a state of grace or ecstasy through the feelings evoked through the suggestiveness of the symbols. The symbolists argued that it was not necessary for drama to teach, because beauty was an end in itself. The most important dramatists of the symbolist school were Maurice Maeterlinck (1862-1949) and Paul Claudel (1868-1955).

Maeterlinck was a Belgian-born lawyer who became influenced by the symbolist movement while living in Paris. During the Nineties, Maeterlinck became a spokesman for the group. He wrote three plays that became indicative of the symbolic ideals: *The Intruder* (1890), *The Blind* (1890), and *Palléas and Mélisande* (1892). Maeterlinck maintained that the dramatist must be a poet.

 The dramatist must show us how, under what form and conditions, according to what laws, to what end, the superior powers act upon our destinies, the unintelligible influences, the infinite principles of which he as a poet is convinced the universe is full.

Paul Claudel (1868-1955) was perhaps the strongest of the symbolic dramatists after

PELLÉAS AND MÉLISANDE
MAURICE MAETERLINCK

CHARACTERS (Partial list):
PELLÉAS, Grandson of King Arkel
GOLAUD, his brother
MÉLISANDE, Golaud's child-like wife

SETTING: Allemonde during the Middle Ages

BACKGROUND
Maeterlinck's most successful play in his battle against realism; it is a retelling of Dante's *Paolo and Francesca*. It was first presented in 1892.

STORY
Golaud is lost while hunting in the woods. While wandering, he comes across the weeping Mélisande. Her clothes are torn and her crown is in the spring. When he offers, she refuses to allow him to get her crown. They fall in love, marry and go to the castle. Pelléas shows Mélisande Blind Man's Spring while Golaud is out hunting. When Pelléas questioned her on where she came from, her wedding band that she had been playing with fell into the spring. When it fell, the clock struck twelve. At exactly the same time, Golaud's horse ran into a tree and threw him to the ground. Mélisande comes to tell him that she wants to leave the gloomy place. He notices her ring is missing and she lied and said she lost it while picking up seashells by the ocean. Pelléas later takes her to such a place so that she could describe it if she had

to. Pelléas and Mélisande spend more and more time together. Golaud scolds them for what he refers to as their childish flirtation, especially since Mélisande is pregnant. As time goes on, however, he starts to understand that the flirtation isn't so childish. Pelléas announces that he is going on a journey, and he asks Mélisande to meet him at Blind Man's Spring that night. They make love under the stars, and are caught up in each other when they realize that they have been locked outside the gate. Just then, Golaud appears and slays Pelléas in the midst of a kiss. The next morning, Golaud and Mélisande return to the city. Mélisande has a small cut under her breast, and gives birth prematurely to a girl. Golaud tries to kill himself, but fails. Mélisande is dying, even though she isn't hurt. On her deathbed, ostensibly with no recollection of what happened, he questions her fidelity, and she claims that she is innocent. The child was brought in and she said that she felt sorry for the baby because it looked sad. She then died.

NOTES ON THE PLAY
Pelléas and Mélisande is perhaps the most famous of Maeterlinck's symbolic plays. It is delicate in its rendering, weaving loosely-defined symbols throughout. Water, light, and darkness are recurring motifs in the play.

Maeterlinck. His three most famous plays are *The Tidings Brought to Mary* (1912), *Break of Noon* (1915), and *The Satin Slipper* (1919-1924). Claudel's plays are difficult to produce but have enjoyed a resurgence in post World War II theatre.

The symbolists found a champion in Aurélien-Marie Lugné-Poë (1869-1940). Lugné-Poë had worked with Antoine but quickly became intrigued with the symbolists. On May 17, 1893 Paul Fort (1872-1962) and Lugné-Poë opened the Théâtre de l'Oeuvre with the premiere production of *Palléas*

and Mélisande.

Supporting Mallarmé's ideas, no properties or furniture were used and the stage was semidark with a gauze curtain hung between the actors and the audience, creating an air of mystery. Costumed in vaguely medieval style, the actors chanted their lines and, according to some critics, behaved like sleepwalkers. Lugné-Poë followed the motto of "the word creates the decor" and simplified his scenery a great deal. He used settings by such artists as Toulouse-Lautrec, Denis, Vuillard,

Paul Fort, who at age seventeen, founded theThéâtre d'Art (1890). He left in 1892 and joined the Théâtre de l'Oeuvre.

Bonnard, and Odilon Redon. The Théâtre de l'Oeuvre was to become to the antirealist what the Théâtre Libre had become to the realist.

Art-for-Art's-Sake

Another variation of symbolism was found in the "Art-for-Art's-Sake" movement whose chief spokesman was Theophile Gautier (1811-1872). Gautier maintained that art and beauty need not exist for practical reasons, they exist for their own sake. He perhaps expressed it best in his manifesto:

Nothing that is beautiful is indispensable to life. One could suppress the flowers, and the world would not suffer materially from it, and yet who would be willing for there to be no flowers? I should sooner give up potatoes than roses, and I suspect that there is not more than one utilitarian in the world capable of digging up a tulip bed to plant cabbages.

Of what use is the beauty of women? Provided that a woman is medically normal, in a condition to receive a man and to a have children, she will always be good enough for the economists.

Oscar Wilde (1856-1900), a leading member of the "Art-for-Art's-Sake" movement in England—a movement similar to the French symbolist and German neoromantic movements. As a dramatist, Wilde is best remembered for *The Importance of Being Earnest* (1895), *Salomé* (1893), and *Lady Windermere's Fan* (1892). From Dirck's *Players of Today*, 1892.

What good is music? Or painting? Who would be so mad as to prefer Mozart to a republican politician like M. Carel, or Michelangelo to the inventor of white mustard?

There is nothing truly beautiful except what is no use; everything useful is ugly, for it is the expression of some need, and man's needs are ignoble and disgusting, like his poor, infirm nature. The most useful spot in the house is the bathroom.

Gautier found a following in England with Oscar Wilde (1856-1900). Wilde wanted to turn life into art rather than art into life. *Salomé*, written

Above: Cyrano de Bergerac, the hero of Edmond Rostand's best known play. Above right is a portrait of Edmond Rostand.

in 1893, is probably the best example of English symbolism. Still his immensely popular *The Importance of Being Earnest* (1895) is the crowning achievement of the movement. The play is delightfully funny by making its point almost through the sheer brilliance of its diction. Social commentary it is not, but it is a wonderful example of how language itself can be an art form.

On the fringe of the symbolist writers but nevertheless important was Edmond Rostand (1868-1918). His *Cyrano de Bergerac* (1897), a classic example of neoromanticism, is still performed on the stage and was recently made into a highly successful movie. Rostand's *Romancers,* a delightful satire on young love, is the story upon which the popular 1960s musical, *The Fantasticks,* is based.

The symbolist movement left its mark by influencing other antirealist schools of thought.

Sigmund Freud

Science was feeling the pressure to investigate the concept of the unknown, of powerful forces existing outside the five senses. Science needed a way to explain the unexplained. In 1900 Sigmund Freud (1856-1939) published his *The Interpretation of Dreams,* which was to have a profound influence on modern drama. Since that time, Freud has been known as the "father of psychoanalysis." Although his theories are undergoing considerable re-evaluation and are no longer widely accepted, Sigmund

Freud's ideas were revolutionary and immensely influential on early twentieth century life. Freud postulated that there are three aspects of personality: the id, the ego, and the superego. The id, which may be loosely defined as the primitive uncensored impulse, is roughly analogous to Nietzsche's Dionysian spirit. The ego and the superego are similar to the Apollonian in that they represent the ordered element of character. Freud's ideas have affected both the realistic and the nonrealistic theatre. The idea that dreams might well be expressions from the id, and therefore inner truths, was fascinating to the nonrealistic dramatist. Actually, Freud considered the unconscious as the "real psyche." He argued: "Its inner nature is just as imperfectly reported to us through the data of consciousness as the external reported to us through indications of our sensory organs."

Freud found that through dreams the id finds expression. Since neurosis occurs when there is imbalance between the conscious and the unconscious, Freud found it necessary to identify repressions or drives locked into the id. The analysis of dreams became a diagnostic tool in bringing repressed desires and memories to the surface. He observed that fears and desires were rarely expressed logically. They were expressed in terms of symbols and were extremely difficult to interpret. To the Freudian, a dream of flying, for example, is sometimes interpreted as an indication of sexual frustration.

The whole concept of repression of the id by the superego was, according to Freud, manifested in society. He maintained that people fear the licentiousness of nature and its psychic components; culture tends to defend us against nature. A community is in itself a safeguard against individual license. Some societies, such as the Victorian, were constructed on the renunciation of instinctual gratification. All of this suggests difficulty in identifying the nature of moral truth since values seem to be dependent on public opinion. The question of the lack of universal morality has become a major theme in some of our more recent drama.

August Strindberg

The popularity of *The Interpretation of Dreams* and a later book called *Three Contributions to the Theory of Sex* (1905) underscored the interest and acceptance of the later works of the Swedish dramatist August Strindberg (1849-1912). Strindberg began his career as a naturalist and had gained world-wide notoriety with *The Father* (1887) and *Miss Julie* (1888). After a bout of mental illness, Strindberg began to study the philosophies of Schopenhauer and Nietzsche under whose influence *To Damascus* (1898-1901) and *The Dream Play* (1902), were written. In the preface he wrote:

> The author has tried to imitate the disconnected but seemingly logical form of a dream. Anything may happen; everything is possible and probable. Time and space do not exist. On an insignificant background of reality, imagination designs and embroiders novel patterns, free fancies, absurdities and improvisations. The characters split, double, multiply, vanish, solidify, blur, classify. But one consciousness reigns above them all—that of the dreamer; and before it there are no secrets, no incongruities, no scruples, no laws.

August Strindberg, shown in his study about 1900.

THE DREAM PLAY
AUGUST STRINDBERG

CHARACTERS

THE DAUGHTER, the daughter of Indra, god of
   the heavens
THE OFFICER
THE PORTRESS
THE LAWYER
THE POET

BACKGROUND

The play deals with our incapability of resolving the conflict between the spirit and flesh. It has an ethereal beauty about it and has recently become extremely popular in the United States. The central character is probably Strindberg, or at least a revelation of his unconscious mind. Certainly Strindberg's sense of the contradictions of life are readily apparent. The Dreamer says:

> Why are we born like animals?
> We who stem from God and man,
> Whose souls are longing to be clothed
> In other than this blood and filth.
> Must God's image cut in truth?

STORY

The Daughter expresses curiosity at the Earth and its people. She leaves her father to walk amongst them. She is led to the Officer, who is a prisoner. She sets him free, and they speak of how life has wronged him. They come upon a Father and Mother. The Mother is dying, and Father brings her a silk mantilla, which she lets the servant girl use to go to baptism. When the Father is offended, and the servant girl feels guilty, the Mother dies of frustration. The Daughter then ends up at a theatre, where the Soldier is waiting for his fiancee to come down after a performance. The Soldier waits and waits and becomes old, without his fiancee ever coming down. When they try to open the door that has never been opened, a Policeman forbids them, so they go to a Lawyer. The Lawyer is an honest, but miserable man. The Daughter and he get married. Married life shows the Daughter much of the frustrations life offers. Their daughter pastes holes in the walls all day. In spite of their attempts to accommodate each other, the marriage is a very unhappy one, fraught with tensions. They recognize the only way they can get along together is to suffer in silence. The Officer comes and offers to take the Daughter away. She goes with him, unable to bear it any longer. They see more scenes of misery, until they meet the Poet. The Lawyer returns, though, to introduce her to another one of life's most miserable things: repentance. To retrace your steps, to return to the marriage she abandoned. She refuses, and goes out to the wilderness with the Poet. They go to a cave by the sea and contemplate justice, and the poetry of the winds. The Daughter says that the human race is to be pitied. The Poet tells the Daughter a prayer he has written that he wishes her to bring to her Father. The scene returns to the Officer waiting for his fiancee to descend. They try to open the door again, but are prevented by the Deans of Theology, Philosophy, Medicine, Faculties, and Jurisprudence. When they finally open the door and a philosophical argument ensues, the crowd turns on the Daughter. The Lawyer makes another attempt to get the Daughter to return to him, and she again refuses. For the first time, the Daughter feels remorse. The Daughter and the Poet leave and set fire to the castle. All of the people from the show come through, and throw something into the fire. Finally, the Daughter walks into the fire, and we are left with miserable faces of the living.

Strindberg's vision of man as a tortured soul and his techniques of externalizing psychological concepts were to influence still another group of antirealists who called themselves expressionists. Strindberg's ideas later adapted by the expressionists were: (1) the destruction of the limitations of time, place and logical sequence by adopting the viewpoint of the dream; (2) flowing one event into another without any logical explanation; (3) characters who are dissolved and transformed into other characters; and (4) blending time and place together.

Expressionism

The term *expressionism* came from France and was coined by the French artist Hervé to create a commonality between the works of Van Gogh, Cézanne and Matisse. Their work seemed to project a personal view of reality while the other impressionists seemed to capture the appearance of objects under a particular kind of light at a given moment—one was eye oriented, the other mind-oriented. Julien Auguste Hervé initiated the movement in 1901 when he exhibited his paintings in Paris under the title "Expressionismes." Worringer, the art historian, introduced it into Germany (1911) and Herman Bahr (critic and dramatist) popularized it. It burgeoned in Germany under the theorist Kasimir Edschmid.

Reinhard Johannes Sorge (1892-1916) wrote *The Beggar* (1912) and produced it in 1917. Sorge's play is considered by some to be the first truly expressionistic drama. For the expressionists truth existed within the subjective realm. This led them to be almost messianic in their desire to show the spiritual qualities of humanity. Therefore all things, even inanimate objects, must be viewed anthropomorphically so that the myth of external reality as truth would be debunked. In some ways they were fighting against materialism by trying to look inside humanity and rediscover what they considered significant values. They wanted to show how current ideals have distorted human spirit and

created a machine through false values.

The expressionistic movement in the theatre is divided into two basic groups: the activists and the mystics. The mystics were concerned with making their audiences aware that an almost primal values system exists within us all. The activists, on the other hand, tried to show how industrialism, chauvinism and politics were conspiring to destroy the human spirit and create a mechanized, emotionless, mindless and unhappy robot. The activists argued that realism tends to reinforce the idea that human beings are machines because it focuses on our outward state alone, our external reality, without attempting to study our souls. The expressionist argued that if man and the world are to be saved, we must understand man's soul. We must view society from the perspective of the soul instead of interpreting the soul from the perspective of a corrupt society. In many ways, the expressionists were the most messianic theatre movement of the period. For that reason, much of their drama was concerned with the salvation of the world and is message-centered. Frequently the central characters are Christ-like figures searching for truth, only to be martyred by a materialistic society. The two most respected expressionistic playwrights were Georg Kaiser (1878-1945) and Ernst Toller (1893-1939). Kaiser's first important expressionistic play was *From Morn to Midnight* (1916).

Toller, a staunch antiwar activist, wrote his first play, *Transfiguration*, in 1918. His most influential work, *Man and the Masses* (1921), is the story of a woman who dedicates her life to help the downtrodden, only to be beaten by those who place artificial political values above humanitarian principles.

The expressionistic movement, with its hope for reformation of society, reacted strongly to the disaster of World War I. The very idea of a world at war was an anathema to the group, although some supported their country and even died in battle. During the latter half of 1914, many of the expressionists met in Weimar to oppose the war. Some of the group became more disillusioned after the war during the peace settlement, when it

FROM MORN TO MIDNIGHT
GEORG KAISER

CHARACTERS (Partial list)
CLERK, a clerk at a bank
LADY, a beautiful Italian
SALVATION LASS, woman begging for alms

BACKGROUND
From Morn to Midnight was one of a series of works beginning with *Coral* in 1917, followed by *Gas I* in 1918 and *Gas II* in 1919. The first two plays are more optimistic than *From Morn to Midnight* but *Gas II* ends in the world's cataclysmic destruction.

STORY
A Lady enters a bank. She is Italian and has come to withdraw money with a note that her bank sent with her. Apparently, the notice has not arrived at the bank, so she cannot get anything. She leaves and the Manager and a customer make comments suggesting that she is a whore, and they will never see her again. She returns to offer her diamonds as collateral. They turn her away again, but she catches the attention of the Clerk. When she is gone, he convinces the others to leave the room for a moment, and steals sixty thousand dollars. After he is gone, notice from the bank in Italy comes in, verifying the Lady's story. The Clerk goes to the Lady at her hotel, thinking that she is for sale. She sets him straight, and he runs out. He goes to see his family, filled with triumphant feelings that he has freed himself. He sees them go about their business, and cannot stay. After he leaves, his Manager enters, telling the family what happened. He goes

to a racetrack, where he puts up a high sum of one thousand dollars to be won. The race happens, but he watches the crowd get excited and start to lose control. He then announces that he will offer a prize of fifty thousand dollars. It is announced and the crowd goes insane. Just before the race is to start, His Royal Highness enters, and the crowd becomes contained and quiet. Disgusted, the Clerk leaves, saying that he will not support groveling dogs. A Salvation Lass asks for ten pfennings, and he turns her down, saying that he only has gold. He goes to a private cabaret supper room, setting up an expensive dinner. He has guests come that are all masked. He tries to seduce one, and she falls asleep. He tries to get two of them to remove their dominoes, and when they do, he is repulsed. The Salvation Lass re-enters, still calling for money and he turns her down. He then goes to a Salvation Army meeting and hears confessions from people. After each confession, the Salvation Lass asks him if he wants to speak yet. Finally he does. He confesses all, and talks of how the money didn't make him happy. He tosses all the money out, and all the people scramble and fight to get it. Only the Salvation Lass doesn't join them. The Clerk is elated by this until she brings in the police, asking them for the reward. The policeman shoot him, after they shut off the lights. He dies, saying the words of Pilot before Christ was crucified. When he dies, all the lights explode. The last words are uttered by the Policeman, who says "There must be a short circuit in the main." The lights go to black.

became obvious that the terms of agreement would probably be a factor in sparking another war. For some, the belief in the nobility of humankind and its potential for greatness turned to a belief in the inevitability of its destruction.

From Morn to Midnight by Georg Kaiser. A contemporary production by the University of Southern Maine with lighting and scene design by Michael Roderick; directed by Walter R. Stump.

Vsevelod Meyerhold

Along with the revolt of the antirealists, another somewhat different movement was developed in Russia by Vsevelod Meyerhold (1874-1940). Meyerhold began his career as an actor with Stanislavsky's company in 1905. He left the Art theatre because he disagreed with the realistic style, but by a quirk of fate, Meyerhold became the nominal head of Russian theatre after the revolution. His work did not please the communist authorities, however, and in February, 1921, he resigned his position as head of the theatre section of the party. He was then appointed director of the State Higher Theatrical Workshop, which trained young directors. He used this opportunity to engage in a series of experiments dealing with what he termed biomechanics, theatricalism, and constructivism, all of which underlie his "theatre of social action." Meyerhold's basic premise was that in order to serve the socialist revolution best, he must also create a revolution in the theatre.

Since realism was the basic philosophy of the revolution, he proposed to treat realistic social problems with completely nonrealistic means. Meyerhold believed that the stage, the actor, the scenery, the lighting, the costumes, and even the script, were a single complexity to be used by the director in interpreting society. To achieve his controlled machine, Meyerhold devised biomechanics as a system to train his actors.

Biomechanics was simply a method by which the actors trained their bodies so that they might respond as machines to anything demanded of them. They trained in gymnastics, dancing, fencing, and other physical disciplines which eliminated the superfluous from movement. This method of training allowed the actor to maintain the theatricalism necessary to Meyerhold's concept.

Theatricalism was a method by which the audience was made aware that it was in a theatre and that it was seeing a theatrical representation. Trapezes were hung from above, the curtain was removed, and lights were placed in full view.

Since the audience was never allowed to confuse the action on stage with real life, Meyerhold hoped to focus their individual attention on isolating social problems. His hope was that the audience would leave the theatre with the goal of solving problems existing in the outside world.

While he did not originate the art form, Meyerhold's theatrical work has come to be associated with the term *constructivism*. He felt that the stage setting should be practical rather than decorative, and he stripped the stage of any identifiable decor and used platforms, intersecting planes, and other structural devices. In effect, the stage was a machine for the director to run. Meyerhold's legacy may well be the way in which he inspired others. Sergei Eisenstein (1898-1948) utilized Meyerhold's ideas by bringing biomechanics and other techniques to the People's Theatre in Moscow when he became director in 1922. Eisenstein

first used the concept of montage with this group when he juxtapositioned unrelated scenes to point up contrasts, a technique he utilized in his career as a filmmaker.

Bertolt Brecht

Meyerhold's ideas were further refined in Germany through the works of Bertolt Brecht (1898-1956) and his Epic Theatre. Brecht agreed with the expressionists that the then contemporary theatre was corrupt in that it had reduced the spectator to passivity. To stir the audience to an active or

Meyerhold State Theatre, Moscow, during V. Mayakovsky's *The Hot Bath*, Act VI, produced by Meyerhold, 1930. *Courtesy Novosti from Sovfoto.*

Vsevolod Meyerhold in 1922-23. *Courtesy Novosti from Sovfoto.*

Second scene, "Near the gate of Velikograd," from *Les Soirs,* as staged by Meyerhold and Bebutov. The play, written by Emile Verhaeren, premiered November 7, 1920. *Courtesy Novosti from Sovfoto.*

dynamic state, Brecht created a new theatre, out of which emerged three key terms to describe the dramatic change he intended: historification, epic and defamiliarization or alienation.

Brecht wanted to achieve what he called entfrendung, which can be translated as alienation, a word which has become central to Brechtian theory. Actually Brecht more often used the coined term verfremdungseffekt, which could mean defamiliarization or, as it is sometimes translated, to make strange. Historification is a part of the defamiliarization process. Brecht argued that the theatre should attempt to remove past events from the present. For example, in many of the old Hollywood historical epics, history was viewed from a contemporary viewpoint. Characters were evaluated in terms of their morals and values as if they existed in the present. If the characters did not live in a manner acceptable to contemporary society, they did not receive a sympathetic response from an audience. Brecht felt that this kind of a viewpoint perpetuated the myth that values were universal and cannot be altered, thereby making it useless to advocate change.

Defamiliarization was also a process of awakening the audience from its passivity. Brecht wanted to make the audience aware that it was in the theatre. Lights and other technical devices were in plain view and, in some instances, were utilized to make a point to the audience. Songs, filmed sequences and narrative passages kept the audience from becoming too empathically involved in the story. Brecht wanted his audiences to watch productively. Each element of the production served as a focusing device, forcing the audience to be intellectually aware of what was said. Each independent aspect of the play contributed to the overall effect, which aimed to awaken the spectator to his sense of social responsibility. Brecht wanted his audience to state: "If I had lived this, I would have done something."

To differentiate his theatre from the old, Brecht used the term *epic,* because he felt that his theatre resembled the epic poem more than it did the traditional stage. Brecht's drama moved over a great span of time just as the epic poem, bridging gaps with narrative sequences. Brecht's best-known works are *The Three-Penny Opera* (1928), which was written with Kurt Weill, *Mother Courage and Her Children* (1938-1939), *The Good Woman of Setzuan* (1938-1940), and *The Caucasian Chalk Circle* (1944-1945).

Bertolt Brecht (1898-1956). *Courtesy German Information Center.*

To clarify his own theory, Brecht made the following comparison of his theatre with what he called the dramatic form:

DRAMATIC FORM	EPIC FORM
1. The stage "incarnates" an event.	1. Relates the event
2. Involves the audience in an action; uses up its activity.	2. Makes the audience an observer but arouses its activity.
3. Helps it to feel.	3. Compels it to make decisions.
4. Communicates experiences.	4. Communicates insights with an event.
5. The audience is projected into an event.	5. The audience is confronted.
6. Suggestion is used.	6. Arguments are used.
7. Sensations are preserved.	7. Impelled to the level of perceptions investigation.
8. The character is a known quality.	8. The character is subjected to changes.
9. Man unchangeable.	9. Man who can change and make changes.
10. His drives.	10. His motives.
11. Events move in a straight line.	11. Events move in "irregular" curves.
12. The world as it is.	12. The world as it is beginning.

Futurists

One of the earliest movements to excoriate the past was the futurist movement, a highly aggressive group concerned with the creation of a masculine fighter driving forth the creation of a new society based on the giver of the future. "We wish to glorify war—the only health giver of the world—militarism, patriotism, the destructive arm of the anarchist, the beautiful ideas that kill, the contempt of women." Founded by the Italian poet Filippo Tommaso Marinetti (1876-1944) before the war, it found redemption in the acceptance of the future and the rejection of the past. It set forth the kind of mentality that became rampant at the time. The futurists wanted the creation of a new world in which machinery would be deified. They saw the race car, for example, as a modern equivalent of the winged horse of ancient mythology. Marinetti and his followers called the theatre a museum and equated it with the old and dying. He wanted youth (whom he categorized as anyone under forty) to rise up and take over the world. He states: "When we are forty let others, younger and more valiant, throw us into the wastebasket like useless manuscripts." There is evidence that Marinetti later modified this view when he became forty-one.

Based on the style of production found in the music halls of Europe, the futurists called for a more vital theatre. They liked the idea of performers mingling with the audience and the use of modern technology to create multimedia productions. They were essentially antiliterary and even antiactor, creating actor lights and even actor gasses.

Dadism

Another movement to come out of the post-war psychosis was dadaism, which rejected the futurists' glorification of war. The name *dada* was coined for its meaninglessness and was chosen randomly from the dictionary by a group of artists residing in Zurich in 1916. It is baby talk for anything to do with horses. The leader of the movement was an eccentric thirty-year-old German poet named Hugo Ball (1886-1927). Ball started the cabaret Voltaire at a bar called the Meierei where dada began. Generally, the dadaists wanted to free the imagination from its traditional structure and thus created a program of surprises, shocks, and brutality, and experimented with mosaics, dance and costumes. It ended as a conscious movement in 1924. Like the expressionists, the dadaists were appalled at the sheer insanity of war in a scientific age. They reasoned that the logic and precision of science had produced logical and precise weapons to methodically destroy the world. The Apollonian vision had created a new god of war and perhaps it was time for the Dionysian world of discord and chaos to rebel. They reasoned that perhaps truth might be found in the absence of logic and precision, in complete freedom to study the absurd. Since the values of the past were considered destructive by the dadaists, society must give the individual freedom to be spontaneous in the future.

The movement produced antiartistic paintings and poems, illogical works and innovative ways of doing art. The dadaists were the first to use garbage as the means of art, creating rubbish collage and sculptures. Music was composed using nontraditional instruments crafted out of junk. They were probably the first school of art to use what is now called performance art. The group had moved to Paris where Tristan Tzara (1896-1963) became their principal spokesman. Tzara wrote seven manifestoes between 1916 and 1920. Their first theatrical presentations were done on March 20, 1920, at the Théâtre de l'Oeuvre. The performances included *The First Celestial Adventure of Mr. Fire Extinguisher* by Tzara and *The Silent Canary* by George Ribemone-Dessaignes. *The Silent Canary* deals with a megalomaniac who thinks himself to be Gounod and who teaches a canary to sing *Faust,* silently. Among the entr'actes was a *Cannibal Manifesto* read entirely in the dark. The performances concluded with the actors and the audience interchanging insults to the general merriment of all. Another performance featured *You*

Would Have Forgotten Me by André Breton and Philippe Soupault and a musical piece by Tzara called *Vaseline Symphonique,* which provoked the audience to lob eggs at the performers, thus relieving their hostilities.

Surrealism

Dada was gradually absorbed into surrealism, which was influenced by the works of Alfred Jarry (1873-1907) and Guillaume Apollinaire (1880-1918). Jarry's *Ubu Roi* (1896) has been called the first absurdist drama. Apollinaire's *The Breasts of Tiresias* (1917) is ostensibly a plea for the repopulation of France after the horrors of war. This work totally rejects traditional logic and combines all the dramatic forms as well as fantasy, acrobatics, music, dance, color and lighting effects and did, in effect, become a performing art.

Surrealism is probably the best known of the new movements and several manifestoes were published by the group's spokesman André Breton (1896-1966). Breton was highly influenced by the works of Freud, particularly after meeting him in 1921. Breton agreed with Freud that within the subconscious, one might discover essential truths. For that reason, he attempted to neutralize the censorship of the superego and the logic of the ego. He described surrealism in his manifesto as:

> . . . pure psychic automatism, by which is intended to express, verbally, in writing, or by other means, the real process of thought. Thought's dictation, in the absence of all control exercised by the reason and outside all aesthetic or moral preoccupation.

Breton, then, turned to Freud's world of the dream to find truth. In 1926, he converted to communism and tried to make the movement into a proselytizing tool. As a viable artistic movement surrealism faded quickly, although it received a great deal of notoriety in 1938 when Salvador Dali and other surrealist painters received recognition at an international exhibition. Dali's paintings of everyday objects, usually in a dream background, intertwined the familiar with the strange, thus visualizing the metaphor.

The influence of the movement on the theatre was more subtle but certainly obtained respect with Jean Cocteau's (1892-1963) production of *Parade* in 1917. The music for the ballet was written by Erik Satie, the scenery designed by Pablo Picasso, with choreography by Leonid Massine. Cocteau's *Orpheus* (1926) and *The Infernal Machine* (1934) are considered the best examples of the use of surrealistic techniques in the theatre.

Antonin Artaud

Another former surrealist who was to have a great deal of impact on the theatre was Antonin Artaud (1896-1948). His influence on the theatre of the 1960s was paramount. Artaud's approach to the theatre was on the one hand original, but on the other hand influenced by the movements before him. His basic theory was that the theatre in the western world was bankrupt in that it limited its concern to a narrow range of the human experience. It did not probe into the inner recesses of the mind wherein lies the real problem of existence. The present theatre, he argued, was a preserver of a culture that lulls the mind. He proposed a theatre which will not "numb us with ideas for the intellect but stirs us to feeling by stirring up pain." Artaud called his new theatre the "theatre of cruelty." He believed that spectacle would act as a catharsis, almost a religious experience, removing violence from the spectator.

> The theatre will never find itself again, i.e., constitute a means of true illusion except by furnishing the spectator with the truthful precipitates of his dreams, in which his taste for crime, his erotic obsessions, his savagery, his charisma, his utopian sense of life and matter, even his cannibalism, pour out, on a level not counterfeit and illusory, but interior.

Artaud proposes to place the spectator in the center of the theatrical space surrounded by the action, a complete break from traditional theatre but very similar to dada and surrealistic staging techniques. For Artaud, theatre was the pulse of

Antonin Artaud

not concerned with physical cruelty, but moral cruelty which "goes to the extremity of instinct and forces the actor to plunge right to the roots of his being so that he leaves the stage exhausted." Artaud felt that poetry and language had become opiates in the western theatre. He wanted the drama taken out of theatres and placed into barns, factories, or even old airplane hangars. The theatre, he says, which is in no thing, but makes use of everything—gestures, sounds, words, screams, light, darkness—rediscovers itself at precisely the point where the mind requires a language to express its manifestations. He employed electronic devices along with what he called nonverbal sounds. In this way, he sought to break down the audience and force them to cleanse themselves through catharsis down to their inner reaches where the true person exists. Then and only then, he felt, can man exist in harmony with others.

civilization. He hypothesized that one of the signs of the decay of western civilization was that it had enshrined such lazy, unserviceable notions as art. "Art," he asserted, "is the expression of one man, while culture is the expression of all." Artaud wanted the theatre to investigate myth and ritual but not the old myths. New myths must be created, according to Artaud, out of severe disaster like the plague. For him, the beauty of the plague was its destruction of repressive social forms. He writes: "Order collapses, authority evaporates, anarchy prevails and man gives vent to all the disordered impulses which lie buried in his soul." Artaud wanted to hammer the conscious mind until it gave up its secrets. The truth, he felt, lay in the subconscious mind and must be explored. He was

Antirealistic Summation

Thus the antirealistic theatre had established itself well into the twentieth century. Contributions and ideas of the antirealists were quite substantial. First, they all revolted against the concept that science will be the savior of humanity. Second, they agreed that ultimate truth cannot be found in external reality. Third, most felt that modern society tended to dehumanize and was wasting away basic goodness. Fourth, as a means of studying true human feelings and desires, there was a general movement to either the subconscious or myth and ritual. Fifth, the subconscious provided the key to truth and could be penetrated against the opposition of the logical mind. Sixth, the language in the theatre must be altered in order to reach the subconscious. Seventh, they all agreed that new theatrical techniques should shatter the world of the familiar. Eighth, their ultimate goal was the destruction of repressive social, cultural and mental controls. There is no question that the antirealist revolution seems to have coalesced into a new and exciting driving force of creative energy.

The New Theatre

In France Jacques Copeau (1879-1949) at the Théâtre du Vieux Colombier formed the Cartel des Quartre, dedicated to placing a new emphasis on the playwright and setting a new standard in the performance of Shakespeare. Copeau's work deeply influenced the French theatre through the work of Louis Jouvet (1887-1951), Charles Dullin (1885-1949) and Georges Pitoëff (1884-1939). The most celebrated playwright during the period between the wars in France was Jean Giraudoux (1882-1944). One of Giraudoux' most successful plays was *Ondine* written in 1939.

Italy produced one of the greatest playwrights of the period Luigi Pirandello (1867-1936). Pirandello began his career as a novelist of considerable fame turning to playwriting in 1910. He headed the Art Theatre of Rome between 1924 and 1928. His most respected plays are *Right You Are— If You Think You Are* (1916), *Six Characters in Search of an Author* (1916), *Henry IV* (1922), *Each in His Own Way* (1924), *Tonight We Improvise* (1930), and *As You Desire Me* (1930). Pirandello took issue in his plays to reality as truth or, better, the scientific conception of reality as truth. He constantly championed truth as necessarily personal and subjective.

Spain's second republic fostered the career of Federico Garcia Lorca (1899-1936). Working with a troupe of university students subsidized by the government called La Barraca, Lorca wrote some of the finest Spanish dramas since Calderón and Lope de Vega. His *Blood Wedding* (1933), *Yerma* (1934) and *The House of Bernarda Alba* (1935) are considered to be bona fide masterpieces of the twentieth century.

The emergence of the Old Vic as the principal producer of classics stimulated a renaissance in the English theatre. Led by Tyrone Guthrie (1900-1971) the Old Vic became the most respected theatre in England by 1939. The Birmingham Repertory Company under Barry Jackson (1879-1961), The Gate Theatre directed by Peter Godfrey (1899-1971), The Oxford Repertory Company led by J. B. Fagan (1873-1933) and The Stratford-on-Avon Theatre under W. Bridges-Adams (1889-1965) and B. Iden Payne (1881-1976) led to the development of some of the finest actors and directors in England's history. Such actresses as Sybil Thorndike (1882-1976), still remembered for her portrayal of Shaw's *Saint Joan* and her work at the Old Vic, and Peggy Ashcroft (1907-1991) are highly respected and honored for their individual contributions. This period also produced John Gielgud (b. 1904), Alec Guinness (b. 1914) and Byam Shaw (b.1904).

Playwrights such as Somerset Maugham (1874-1965) and Noel Coward (1899-1973) contributed sophisticated comedies such as *The Circle* (1921) and *Private Lives* (1930), which established the norm for English drawing room comedies. Serious writers included J. B. Priestly (1894-1984), *Time and the Conways* (1937); Emyln Williams (1905-1987), *The Corn Is Green* (1938); and T.S. Eliot, *Murder in the Cathedral* (1935).

Ireland's most important playwright was Sean O'Casey (1884-1964). O'Casey started his career as a realist with such plays as *The Shadow of a Gunman* (1923), *Juno and the Paycock* (1924), and *The Plough and the Stars* (1926). Later he changed from a realistic style to expressionism with such works as *The Silver Tassie* (1928) and *Red Roses for Me* (1943).

ONDINE
JEAN GIRAUDOUX

CHARACTERS (Partial list)
AUGUSTE, a peasant fisherman
EUGENIE, his wife
ONDINE, their remarkable adopted daughter
HANS, a knight
THE OLD ONE, King of the Sea
BERTHA , Hans' fiancee
BERTRAM, a poet

NOTES ON THE PLAY
Girardoux rebelled against the onslaught to abolish language by some of the antirealistic schools of theatre. His plays were written in a prose filled with poetic imagery and elevated language and reflected his deep faith in the ultimate goodness of humanity.

STORY
Auguste and Eugenie are discussing how their "daughter" can control the storms, the lake, the fish, when Hans enters. He has been on a mission set to him by his beloved, Bertha, and is in need of food. Ondine enters and immediately says how handsome he is, and that she is in love with him. After talking with her, Hans falls desperately in love with her, forgetting Bertha completely. All of Ondine's friends, especially The Old One, warn her not to love him, because he will betray her. But it is too late, she already loves him. She agrees to a pact he doesn't know about, that if he betrays her, he will die. She bids good-bye to all of her friends, and leaves the waters with her not-too-bright fiancee the next day.

At the King's hall, the story is controlled by "The Illusionist," who is really The Old One. He shows when Bertha and Hans meet, and how Bertha tries everything that she can to get him back. Finally, right before the wedding, there is a confrontation between Ondine and Bertha in front of the King. Ondine already knows all that will happen, and accuses Bertha. Hans defends Bertha. The King removes everyone, and speaks to Ondine alone. He speaks kindly to her, and advises her to leave Hans, because he believes that Hans will betray her too. She refuses, and decides to be nice to Bertha, so that Hans will lose interest in her. She invites Bertha to live with them. Hans has trouble with the lake by his castle, and the rain that falls and such because the water hates him, knowing he will betray Ondine. Some time elapses and Bertha and Hans are to be married. He betrayed Ondine, and he has heard from everywhere that Ondine betrayed him back with Bertram. Hans knows that this is the day of his death. He has had people searching for Ondine, and finally someone has caught her. She is tried by two judges. Hans accuses her of loving him beyond human endurance, understanding, and limitations—of loving him too completely. She doesn't deny it, but there is the matter of her betrayal with Bertram. Bertram is summoned, and it is proven that they never had anything, even though Bertram was desperately in love with her. Ondine is found guilty and sentenced to death. All leave, and The Old One tells Ondine that she will forget Hans shortly, at the same time Hans dies. Hans shows up, having gone insane, and now understanding all. They talk and forgive each other. Hans laments that now he must die when, for the first time, he could love her. Hans dies, and Ondine forgets him. Seeing his dead body, she remarks to The Old One that she could have loved so handsome a man as they exit.

JUNO AND THE PAYCOCK
SEAN O'CASEY

CHARACTERS
"CAPTAIN" JACK BOYLE, a lazy, drunken man
JUNO BOYLE, his wife
JOHNNY BOYLE, their son, a former soldier for
    Ireland
MARY BOYLE, their daughter
JOXER, Boyle's drinking buddy
JERRY DEVINE, Mary's would-be fiancee
CHARLIE BENTHEM, a school teacher/lawyer

SETTING: Dublin, Ireland 1922

BACKGROUND
This play is universally regarded for its poetic language. It and many of O'Casey's early plays reveal the effects of the Irish rebellion on the lives of the common people.

STORY
Juno and Mary are sitting about, discussing the recent murder of Robbie Tancred, an Irish Republican. Johnny leaves, not able to take their talk, having lost an arm and damaged a hip fighting for Ireland. The ladies then discuss how poor they are. Jerry enters with a message that there is a job for Boyle. Boyle and Joxer enter drunk. Juno commands her husband to go and take the job, and then leaves for work. Jerry proposes to Mary again, who turns him down again. Boyle and Joxer sit down and ramble for a while when Charlie Benthem enters to tell Boyle that he has been left two thousand pounds. The family buys a new gramophone, new furniture, and Boyle a new suit. Benthem and Mary are now engaged. Johnny, in the middle of tea, thinks that he sees Robbie Tancred's ghost. Shortly after, Robbie's funeral procession goes by, and a man comes in and yells at Johnny for not going to the funeral. Johnny is ordered to attend an investigation of Robbie's death. Two months elapse. Benthem has deserted Mary, and Mary has to see the doctor. News has gotten out that the inheritance has fallen through. All of the furniture is repossessed, along with Boyle's suit. A neighbor takes the gramophone in lieu of the three pounds she is owed. Jerry Devine once again proposes to Mary, but backs away when told that she is pregnant. Johnny's delusions have gotten even worse when he is dragged off by two men who claim that he informed on Robbie, causing his death. Juno and Mary are later asked down to identify a body. Juno and Mary leave forever. Joxer and Boyle return, drunk again. They ramble about the sad state of the world as the show closes.

American Theatre to 1940

There is no question that the theatre in the United States began to deserve and receive international recognition. Between 1915 and 1940 several American dramatists' work emerged upon the world's stages. Such writers as Eugene O'Neill (1888-1953), Maxwell Anderson (1888-1959), Elmer Rice (1892-1967) and Lillian Hellman (1905-1984) with such plays as *What Price Glory?* (1924), *The Adding Machine* (1923), and *The Little Foxes* (1938), among others, enabled the United States to develop a dramatic base. Phillip Barry (1896-1949), George S. Kaufman (1889-1961), and Moss Hart (1904-1961) wrote some of the most enduring American comedies. Barry's *The Philadelphia Story* (1939), and Kaufman and Hart's *The Man Who Came to Dinner* (1940) are considered American classics.

Other playwrights of exceptional talent were William Saroyan (1900-1981), Clifford Odets (1906-1963), Robert E. Sherwood (1896-1955), and Thornton Wilder (1897-1975). All of these writers are still produced both here and abroad and were instrumental in establishing what may yet be called the golden age of American theatre. Further, the period between 1920 and 1940 saw the popularization in the United States of an English entertainment which was to form the basis of a new strictly American genre, musical comedy.

The latter half of the nineteenth century in England saw a rise in popularity of the English music hall. The music halls specialized in light

---

THE MAN WHO CAME TO DINNER
GEORGE KAUFMAN AND MOSS HART

CHARACTERS (Partial list)

SHERIDAN WHITEHEAD, a famous and tyrannical writer/radio personality, known especially for his true murder stories.

MAGGIE CUTLER, his assistant

BERT JEFFERSON, a local reporter, also a budding playwright

LORRAINE SHELDON, a famous actress, also a vamp

MR. STANLEY, a conservative family man

STORY

Sheridan Whitehead, in the middle of his lecture route, has imposed upon the Stanley family by an unfortunate accident. As he was leaving their house, he slipped on some ice and was thought to have broken his hip. He is now confined to a wheelchair, and is doing his best to make everybody know how miserable he is. His longtime assistant, Maggie, and he are setting up an office in the middle of the Stanley's living room, forbidding guests, and monopolizing the phone. Virtually everybody in show business either stops by to see Whitehead, calls or sends large, ostentatious gifts. In the midst of this, newspaperman Jefferson shows up and charms an interview out of Whitehead. He also charms Maggie and they fall in love. Maggie tells Whitehead this, and also that Jefferson has written a fabulous play that he should look into. The selfish Whitehead won't allow his best assistant to go off and have a life of her own, so he plots against them. He calls up Lorraine Sheldon, saying that there is a part for her in this brilliant new play that he has just read, and she should get down here to convince the playwright. After this call, the doctor informs him that he mixed up the x-rays and his hip was never broken. Whitehead buys some time from the doctor to finish his plans against Maggie. Lorraine arrives, and Whitehead tells her that Jefferson wants another actress to play the part, so she'll have to be *very* persuasive. Maggie makes a counter plot against Lorraine, but it is undone by Whitehead. Lorraine dresses to the nines, and spends all night with Jefferson at a bar, hearing his play. She convinces him to do some small rewrites with her at Lake Placid. When Maggie finds out she is crushed, and she prepares to leave Whitehead anyway. Whitehead finally realizes that she really is in love, and decides he has to undo what he did. Mr. Stanley comes in and informs Whitehead that he has to leave in fifteen minutes, or he will be escorted off the premises by two policemen. A mummy case arrives and, thinking quickly, he locks Lorraine in it, shipping her off to Nova Scotia. Smug with a minute to spare, he gives Jefferson and Maggie his blessing, walks out the door, and promptly slips on the step.

NOTES ON THE PLAY

This play is performed today more frequently than any other comedy from this period. The character of Sheridan Whitehead is modeled after Alexander Woollcott, critic of the New York *Times*.

musical entertainments, short skits sometimes with music and sometimes without, Pose Plastiques, ballets, and burlesques. Pose Plastiques consisted of females in various skimpy attire posing in a manner describing a famous painting. The ballet was divided into two kinds: the ballet divertissement and ballet d'action. The former was primarily a drama-dance with spectacular costumes, scenery, and lightly-clad women.

The Black Crook

The music hall type of entertainment provided the basis for a new development in the United States. A group of ballet dancers in New York to perform the opera *La Biche au Bois* in 1866 were stranded when the Academy of Music burned. The manager of Niblo's Garden, William Wheatley

(1816-1876), conceived the idea of incorporating the ballet troupe into a play called *The Black Crook* by Charles M. Barras (1826-1873). The result was a musical extravaganza similar to those produced in the English music halls. The production included spectacular scenery, scantily-clad ballet girls, and song. Significantly, it grossed over a million dollars at the box office. A reviewer in the New York *Tribune* wrote: "The scenery is magnificent; the ballet is beautiful; the drama is rubbish. There is always a bitter drop in the sweetest cup, a fly in the richest ointment. Mr. Barras' drama is the bitter drop and the superfluous fly in this instance." *The Black Crook* was a product of industrialism spawned by the Civil War. Hence, some of the by-products of urbanism are evident in some of its contributions. First, its sixteen months run initiated the long run into the American theatre.

Canterbury Hall, opened in 1849 by Charles Morton (1819-1904), known as the "father of the halls." At first Morton did not charge admission to what is now considered the first organized music hall in England, relying instead on the drinks sold. Note the wing scenery and the man being beaten in the box.

Second, *The Black Crook* gave the commercial use of sexual exploitation a foothold in America as it was considered the first major "leg" show. Third, it introduced the can-can to the United States. Fourth, its choreographer, David Costos, introduced the chorus line.

Scene from *The Black Crook* by Charles M. Barras. The first New York production opened September 12, 1866, at Niblo's Garden Theatre. *The Black Crook* was a major step toward the development of American musical comedy. *Courtesy Harvard Theatre Collection.*

Burlesque

Although the term *burlesque* has sexual connotations, the term originally suggested satire, parody. Many apologists for the modern day version of burlesque seek to trace its roots back to antiquity. While this suggestion may have merit, the burlesque form found on the American musical stage finds its roots in England. The satirical works of Henry Fielding in the eighteenth century, the burlesque extravaganzas of the 1870s, and the English music halls of the late nineteenth century with their musical travesties—all had a greater bearing on American burlesque than anything else. As a satirical form, burlesque can be found in the works of John Brougham (1810-1880, his most famous work being *Po-ca-hon-tas, or The Gentle Savage* (1855). This conception of burlesque was overshadowed by *The Black Crook* whose female chorus wore tights, which at that time (1866) was considered extremely provocative.

Seizing on the penchant of American audiences for scantily clad women, Lydia Thompson and Michael Leavitt created musical entertainments designed to reveal the female figure. Lydia Thompson and her "British Blondes" made their debut in 1868. The dress and performance of Thompson earned her the title of first queen of burlesque. Although Michael Leavitt gives Thompson the credit for developing modern burlesque, his Rentz-Santley production starring

Niblo's Garden Theatre, New York, 1855. The theatre opened in 1827 as the Sans Souci, was reconstructed in 1828 as Niblo's and continued through 1895. America's first "leg show," *The Black Crook*, was produced here in 1866. From *Ballou's Pictorial,* 1855.

Above: Lydia Thompson (1836-1908), best known for her contribution to striptease. She and her "British Blondes," seizing on the popularity of *The Black Crook*, toured the United States in 1868-1869, introducing the modern concept of burlesque. *Courtesy Lilly Library, Indiana University.*

Below: "A Vaudeville Turn—I'm so glad you've found me. Oh, take me away!" Drawn by William Glackens for *Scribner's Magazine* in 1901.

Mable Santley was the first show to be labeled burlesque. Once the notion of scantily clad women became a marketable product, modern burlesque became established. Between 1900 and 1905, burlesque was marketed on a large scale. Theatre owners and managers became aligned to specific theatres and these theatres were part of a specific circuit, which in burlesque jargon, was called "wheels." The two main wheels in 1900 were the Columbia and the Mutual. The Columbia Wheel desired to keep burlesque clean and wholesome for the entire family. On the other hand, the Mutual Wheel wanted to exploit sex and off-colored jokes. By the 1920s the burlesque circuits (wheels) gave way to stock burlesque. In 1930 the most famous of the stock burlesque companies was Minsky's. Located in New York City, Minsky's ruled burlesque between 1830 and 1940. It was at Minsky's that Ann Corio and Gypsy Rose Lee created the art form known as "striptease," and it was at Minsky's that the runway which is used in all beauty contests was first used. In 1940 the City of New York closed Minsky's and with this closing burlesque fell into disrepute and was relegated to obscurity.

Because of its sexual overtones and the addition of the striptease in 1929, burlesque came to be associated with mostly male audiences. In 1880, however, Tony Pastor (1837-1908) initiated a burlesque form intended for the family. This form, called vaudeville, became one of the most popular types of entertainment to emerge in America. Many famous personalities got their start in show business on the vaudeville stage—Bob Hope, Jack Benny, Milton Berle, Groucho Marx, Jimmy Durante, George Burns and Gracie Allen, among others.

The Development of Musical Comedy

Three forces aided the development of the American musical theatre: the Puritans, who brought music (a cappella); the Cavaliers, who encouraged theatre; and the actors who were forced from England by the 1737 Licensing Act. Initially, the American musical theatre was basically English, using English forms, but eventually its own brand of musical entertainment was created.

Ballad opera was one of the first English forms to appear in the American theatre. Characteristically, the music in a ballad opera is not original, whereas that of another form, comic opera, has original music. The first ballad opera in America was an English import, *Flora* (1735). It was not until 1767 with *The Disappointment* that American audiences saw the first ballad opera created in America. *The Disappointment* is important not only as the earliest example of a native ballad opera but also because it introduces the African-American character and it contains the earliest reference in American literature of the tune "Yankee Doodle." As to the earliest native comic opera, technically *The Temple of Minerva* (1781) by Francis Hopkinson can claim this honor. However, this musical was only a two-act after-dinner entertainment and was not a legitimate musical. Thus, the first original native score appears not to have been until *Evangeline* (1879). In addition to ballad and comic opera, American musicals made use of adaptations or what is termed "musicalization." By definition, this term means losing the content of a musical on a piece of literature. The earliest use of this device is *The Reconciliation* (1791) by Peter Markoe.

From 1800 to 1866, the two major musical forms to emerge were the minstrel show and burlesque. The first minstrel show was the Virginia Minstrels (1843) and, as a form, it is considered by most historians as being the only musical form created in this country. Thomas D. Rice (1808-1860), Dan Emmett (1815-1904), and E. P. Christy (1815-1862) were among the leading names in minstrel shows.

From 1870 to 1900, influences on the development of musical comedy included Edward Harrigan's *The Mulligan Guard's Ball* (1878), Edward Rice's *Evangeline* (1879), and the operettas of Gilbert and Sullivan. *Evangeline*, written by Edward Rice, introduced the term *musical comedy* as well as having the first original score. *The Mulligan Guard's Ball* aided the rise of realism with its emphasis on local color and, in particular, was the first musical to have African-American performers play their respective parts. With Gilbert and Sullivan the vogue for comic opera was established. Also during this period, the initial attempt at synthesis emerged with *The Brook* (1879) by Nate Salsbury. At this time, writers began to provide a framework for the musical; i.e., they wrote a story in attempts to justify the song, dance, etc. But the emphasis was on the parts. This perception did not change until Jerome Kern's *Very Good, Eddy* (1915), wherein the whole is more important than the parts.

The operettas of Victor Herbert (1859-1924), while introducing a new musical form to the Broadway stage, set in motion the argument of what constitutes a comic opera and what is an operetta. Today, musicals labeled operettas in some quarters are referred to as comic operas by others. The reverse is also true. A case in point is *Robin Hood* (1891) by Reginald DeKoven, which is considered by some as America's first native comic opera, yet others see this production as an operetta. The work of Victor Herbert made an important contribution to the American musical by simplifying the score. This provided allowance for the non-operatic voice.

In addition to operettas coming into fashion during the 1880s and 1890s, the musical revue was introduced as well. In 1894 the musical revue came of age with *The Passing Show of 1894*. A French creation, the revue was brought to America by George Lederer. The critics labeled the show a "review," but later changed the spelling consistent with the French. Revue means "survey" and is described as consisting of unrelated songs, dances, sketches, and monologues. When this form came to America, it changed to include

Set for *H.M.S. Pinafore* by W. S. Gilbert (pictured below) and Arthur Sullivan. Minor Rootes, Designer.

ragtime music, which the white community renamed jazz, tap dance (in 1900 tap was known as "buck and wing"), comedy routines and unification by an idea rather than being completely integrated. Revues were very large and spectacular. Synonymous with the *spectacular revues* was *The Ziegfeld Follies*, which started in 1907 and continued until 1931. Originally labeled *The Follies of [Year]*, this revue was renamed *The Ziegfeld Follies* in 1911. In the 1930s, the depression forced this musical form to be reduced in stature. As a result, revues became known as *intimate revues*. These

William Schwenck Gilbert (1836-1911), English dramatist who collaborated with Arthur Sullivan (1842-1900) in writing *Trial by Jury* (1875), *H.M.S. Pinafore* (1878), *The Mikado* (1885), and *The Pirates of Penzance* (1879). Their first work led to a partnership with Richard D'Oyly Carte (1844-1901), who built the Savoy Theatre to present their plays. Gilbert and Sullivan discontinued their collaboration in 1896, perhaps because of Gilbert's temper and rigid disciplinarian attitude. Gilbert was knighted in 1907. From *The Theatre, 1882*.

musicals focused upon the life and works of a composer or entertainer, had small casts, and generally had small sets—all designed to keep the costs down.

From the turn of the century until 1920, the names of George M. Cohan (1878-1942), Jerome Kern (1885-1945), and Joseph Urban (1872-1933) stand out for their contributions. Cohan is considered the "father of the American musical theatre" with his emphasis on native themes, subject matter, characters, and informality. It was Cohan who moved the musical from European formality to American informality. The culmination of his career must have been his being awarded an honorary Congressional Medal of Honor for his sons "Over There" and "You're a Grand Ole Flag," which served to arouse patriotic fervor and support for America's participation in World War I. During this period, Joseph Urban's scenic efforts in *The Ziegfeld Follies of 1915* marked the introduction of the "new stagecraft" (see page 235: Appia and Craig) to the musical theatre. In essence, it meant the integration of scenery into the musical format. Also during this period, the works of Jerome Kern signalled the beginning of interlocking the music, lyrics, and book. Although synthesis had been introduced with *The Brook* (1879), the emphasis had been on the parts. Kern reversed the process by making the whole more important than the parts. In other words, anything presented on the stage had to be justified within the framework of the story. *Very Good , Eddy* (1915) demonstrates Kern's fusion of book, lyrics, and comic routines. By the end of 1917, the integration of the American musical in terms of its parts was firmly established.

During the 1920s, revues featuring African-Americans made a sizeable contribution to the Broadway stage. These musicals are responsible for the introduction of jazz and tap dancing. Of particular note is *Shuffle Along* by Noble Sissle (1889-1975) and Eubie Blake (1883-1983) which had in the cast Paul Robeson and Josephine Baker. This musical was significant for being the first African-American musical to play at a white theatre, creating a demand for musicals by African-

Americans, and developing a craze for tap dancing with such tunes as "I'm Just Wild About Harry" and "Love Will Find a Way." Another musical of importance was *Runnin' Wild* (1923), produced by George White, which introduced the Charleston. This dance was a catalyst for popularizing tap dance with the public and thus it became a necessity for musicals. Its popularity was so great that it became a feature of ballroom dancing.

With the advent of the tap dancer, the role of the dancer took on another dimension. The dancer was not highly regarded until tap became a desired feature of the musical and when George White in his revue, George White's *Scandals of 1919*, elevated the status of the dancer by giving the dancer equal billboard recognition with that of the other performers. As a form, tap dancing is a product of the Irish clog dance and the high step of the minstrel shows (based upon African dances). The African-American performer blended these two dances into its present form and was responsible for introducing and popularizing it in the American musical. Tap became a regular feature in musicals due to the efforts of Bobby Connelly and Charles Davis. No name is more synonymous with tap dancing, however, than that of Bill "Bojangles" Robinson (1878-1949). Achieving his success in *Blackbirds of 1928,* "Bojangles" became a legend and is considered the first African-American dancing star on Broadway. With the demand of tap dancing and jazz, white composers and producers borrowed extensively from those of the African-American, and white revues began to feature rhythms and dance found in African-American musicals. Thus, the public demand for tap, jazz, as well as nudes or scantily clad women, and lavish sets became regular features of revues. Their appeal to the audiences enabled them to dominate the musical stage from 1900 to the 1930s. The exception was *Show Boat.*

On December 27, 1927, at the Ziegfeld Theatre, Florenz Ziegfeld produced *Show Boat* by Jerome Kern (1885-1945) and Oscar Hammerstein II (1895-1960). The show was an outstanding hit. *Show Boat* was innovative in many ways: it was the first musical to successfully do away with the tradi-

"Love Will Find a Way," along with "I'm Just Wild About Harry," were two popular hits from *Shuffle Along* by Noble Sissle and Eubie Blake. *Shuffle Along* helped to establish the form of the American musical comedy. *Courtesy Frank K. Carner.*

tional opening chorus line number; it was the first to deal with a serious subject (miscegenation); it utilized the "new stagecraft" techniques with the designs of Joseph Urban; and it utilized American musical style, including jazz. A reviewer in the *New Republic* wrote: "'Can't Help Lovin' That Man' is an interesting and successful experiment in Negroid forms and inflections by a composer who til now had ignored them."

During the 1930s the American musical matured in two ways: the integration (synthesis) of dance and the use of serious subject matter. *Show Boat* had proved a pioneer in the use of serious subject matter but the idea that musicals could be more than just revues was not fully established until the critics awarded the Pulitzer Prize for the first time to a musical, *Of Thee I Sing* (1931). The book was written by George S. Kaufman (1889-1961), the music by George Gershwin (1898-1937) and the lyrics by his brother, Ira Gershwin (1904-1983). The musical's dimension was increased in 1935 with America's first folk opera, *Porgy and Bess* by George Gershwin. To paraphrase one critic, the musical had been elevated as far as it could go. In addition to the musical developing depth in terms of the book and score, its use of dance added to its maturity. With the introduction of modern dance through the work of Isadore Duncan (1878-1927), Charles Weidman (1900-1975), Martha Graham (1894-1991) and others, the use of ballet by the Russian-born George Balanchine (1904-1983), the American musical was able to integrate dance skillfully into the musical. These two forms spelled the demise of tap; it could no longer carry a musical. Balanchine's jazz ballet "Slaughter on Tenth Avenue" for the musical *On Your Toes (1936)* was the particular ballet sequence cited as ending the reign of tap; it was the first use of ballet for relating a story in a Broadway musical. In addition to *On Your Toes*, Balanchine made contributions that created the basic framework for the integration of dance and story which is a trademark of the present day musical. In *Babes in Arms* (1937) Balanchine unveiled a dream ballet marking the first use of dance to express the subconscious. In order to maintain continuity and to use dance to strengthen the story line, Balanchine had a dancer assume a principal non-dancing role in *I Married an Angel* (1938). He became the first choreographer to direct a musical when he was chosen to direct the African-American musical, *Cabin in the Sky* (1940). If Balanchine's ballet work spelled the death of tap, *Oklahoma* choreographed by Agnes de Mille made any comeback for tap impossible. Hereafter ballet would be the rage. Although tap was to diminish, it was not completely abandoned. During the 1930s, Robert Alton was the first to successfully integrate tap into modern dance and ballet. With the use of modern dance and ballet, as well as tap, dancers had to be trained. The demand that dancers know all three forms led to the opening of dance schools.

African-American Theatre

The contributions to musical theatre by Noble Sissle and Eubie Blake were just some of the many produced by African-Americans. Still, African-Americans in the theatre (as in American society) were not always welcome. James Weldon Johnson (1871-1938) once said that "the Provincetown Playhouse was the initial and greatest force in opening up the way for the Negro on the dramatic stage." Johnson, an African-American poet-novelist, American consul, and former secretary of the National Association for the Advancement of Colored People, was referring to the difficulty the African-Americans had in making a living in the theatre. Part of the problem was that African-American characters were highly stereotyped. They were classified into five basic types: the lovable but ignorant clown; the tragic mulatto or half-breed who cannot find happiness in either the white or African-American society; the religious slave who is the soul of passivity and goodness; the amoral savage who breeds like an animal; and the beast who sets out to become equal so he can destroy white society.

The first type, the lovable clown, was by far the most popular for white audiences. Thomas D.

John Kani (left) and Winston Ntshona enjoy eating oranges as they stagger home after a night on the town in a scene from *Sizwe Banzi Is Dead*, the South African drama devised by Athol Fugard and Kani and Ntshona. *Photo by William L. Smith.*

Rice (1808-1860), a white man, introduced a song and dance character of this type in 1828. He called his character "Jim Crow," creating a new expression in the language. Rice's success with the Jim Crow character helped develop the minstrel show, which was refined by E. P. Christy in 1846 with his "Christy's Minstrels."

The first known company of African-American actors was developed in New York in 1821 by Henry Brown. Brown wrote the first play by an African-American, a play entitled *King Shotaway*. The company performed a repertory which included *Othello* and *Richard III*, with James Hewlett, a West Indies native, in the leading roles. Brown's group was constantly harassed by groups of white rowdies and was disbanded bout 1823. Brown probably provided Ira Aldridge (1807-1867) with his first acting experience.

With the closing of Brown's theatre, Aldridge was unable to find work on the American stage, and in 1825 he traveled to England where he made his debut as Othello. He became immensely popular and was billed as the "African Roscius." Aldridge toured throughout Europe and the British Isles, once playing Othello to Charles Kean's Iago. He received decorations from the rulers of Prussia, Russia and Saxe-Meiningen. He became enormously wealthy and successful in virtually every country save his own.

Outside the minstrel show and Jim Crow dancing, African-Americans in the theatre were relegated to stereotypes. In 1915 Anita Bush organized the All Colored Dramatic Stock Company, which gave African-American actors their first and longest period of stability. Redgeley Torrence's *Three Plays for Negro Theatre* (1917), which marked a movement away from the stereotyped African American character, were the first plays which allowed African-American audiences in Broadway theatres. In addition, *The Emperor Jones*, *Porgy* by DuBose and Dorothy Heyward, and *The Green Pastures* by Marc Connelly provided acting opportunities for the African-American actor. *The Green Pastures*, based on *Ole Man Adam and His Children* by Roark Bradford, a white journalist, created the most impact. Canadian-born Richard B. Harrison, a speech and dramatics professor who played De Lawd, had to be trained by a white actor to speak in the so-called "Negro" dialect. The production had difficulty in finding rehearsal space, as few rehearsal halls in New York would allow African-Americans on the premises. But the play was a hit and African Americans were given the opportunity to earn a decent living in the theatre. *Green Pastures* was also made into a film which marked the debut of several African-Americans, including Eddie Anderson, who was to become a famous radio personality as Jack Benny's chauffeur, Rochester. While these plays may now be considered as racist by some, in their time they were a welcome breakthrough for the African-American community.

The first serious play to be produced on Broadway by an African-American was *The Chipwoman's Fortune,* a one act play by Willis Richardson produced in 1923. The play was performed by the Ethiopian Art Players of Chicago for two weeks on Broadway. Garland Anderson's *Meek,* opening on February 6, 1928, was probably the first full-length play to be produced. Several other African-American playwrights wrote between the years of 1928 and 1935. For example, Langston Hughes's *Mulatto* had the longest Broadway run of an African-American playwright to date.

Several off-Broadway productions by African-Americans were produced before the war, including Langston Hughes' (1902-1967) *Don't You Want to Be Free?* (1938) and Theodore Ward's (1902-1983) *Big White Fog* (1940). *Big White Fog* was perhaps the most vitriolic play about the African-American's condition in America to have been produced to that date. The play contains the character of Marcus Garvey, the founder of the Black Muslim movement in America, and is a stirring drama of despair. But even in the collapse of the Mason family, there was hope that African-Americans and whites would reconcile their differences. Given a boost by the federal theatre project, Ward worked to achieve acceptance of the African-American artist by the theatre community. In spite of the many rebuffs that Ward suffered, he never gave up believing that eventually artists, African-American and white, would be judged by their art alone.

One of the most refreshing achievements of recent years has been the development of an innovative African-American theatre movement, which has paralleled the world theatre in microcosm. It began in 1963 with the Free Southern Theatre, quickly radicalized in 1964 with the Black Arts Repertory Theatre School, headed by Imamu Amiri Baraka (Everett LeRoi Jones). Baraka's (b. 1934) group, influenced by Nietzche's condemnation of western culture, set out to develop a new black culture. Larry Neal, writing about the movement, states: "We advocate a cultural revolution in art

Adolph Caesar and Larry Riley in Charles Fuller's murder-mystery, *A Soldier's Play. Photo by Nancy Hereford.*

and ideas. The cultural values inherent in western history must either be radicalized or destroyed, and we will probably find that even radicalization is impossible." Baraka moved from comparatively mild plays, such as *The Toilet* (1964) and *Dutchman* (1964), to *Slave Ship* (1969), which advocates a total rejection of western society. His most recent play is *Boy and Tarzan Appear in a Clearing* (1983).

The Negro Ensemble Company, founded in 1968 in New York, produced a series of plays which were of concern to African-Americans. It is probably the most prestigious African-American company in America today. Originally directed by Douglas Turner Ward, Robert Hooks, and Gerald S. Krone, the Negro Ensemble has consistently maintained a high quality in their works.

The New Lafayette Theatre of Harlem opened in 1967 with Robert Macbeth as its director. The company lasted until 1973, publishing the *Black*

Theatre Magazine and providing an information service to African-American groups throughout the country.

African-American playwrights, actors, and directors have distinguished themselves on the theatrical scene. Lorraine Hansberry (1930-1965) won considerable acclaim in 1959 with *A Raisin in the Sun*, the most successful play by an African American writer to that date. Her second play, *The Sign in Sidney Brustein's Window* (1964), is still played frequently throughout the country.

Ed Bullins (b. 1935), editor of the *Black Theatre Magazine,* has produced several plays exploring black pride. His best works are *Clara's Old Man* (1965), *The Electronic Nigger* (1968), *The Pig Pen* (1970), *The Taking of Miss Jamie* (1975), and *Daddy* (1977). August Wilson (b. 1945) is perhaps the most successful of the contemporary African American playwrights, having won two Pulitzer Prizes: *Fences* (1985) and *The Piano Lesson* (1990). His first success was *Ma Rainey's Black Bottom* (1984). Charles Fuller (b. 1939) won the Pulitzer in 1982 with his *A Soldier's Play*. He is currently working on a cycle of plays.

The considerable talent of Ntozake Shange (b. 1948) had been displayed on Broadway with *For Colored Girls Who Have Considered Suicide When the Rainbow is Enuf*. Shange, originally from the Bay Area (San Francisco), first produced her "choreopoem" at the Bacchanal, a woman's bar just outside Berkeley, California. The play was brought to New York where it attracted the eye of producer Woody King. It eventually played at the Public Theatre and then traveled to Broadway in September 1976 for a long run. The work, enhanced by dance and music, explores the reality of seven different kinds of women. The language is poetry and the effect is superb. Other African-American playwrights include Lonne Elder III, Joseph Walker, Charles Gordone, Richard Wesley, Ron Milner, Adrienne Kennedy, Philip Hayes Dean, Vinette Carroll, and Leslie Lee. There is no question that African-American playwrights are a compelling force within the American theatre.

Cinema and Theatre

The development of the cinema out of the theatre was another important factor during the early part of the twentieth century. The invention of the motion picture can be divided into three phases: animated pictures, animated photographs, and finally, motion pictures. In 1877 Thomas Edison (1847-1931) joined with W.K.L. Dickson in trying to photograph and project motion. Utilizing the invention of photography on celluloid by William Friese-Greene, George Eastman quickly developed a flexible film. Edison and Dickson then developed the kinetoscope, which used Eastman film with a shutter moving as fast as forty frames per second. The kinetoscope utilized a light source under the film and a magnifying glass through with one looked at the moving picture. Thomas Armat then projected Edison's kinetoscope on a screen with a projector called a vitascope. Edison collaborated with Armat on a improved projector which they called, for reasons only they knew, a kinetoscope. The year 1895, then, marks the birth of the motion picture industry.

Since we are primarily concerned with the theatre and its influence, no attempt will be made to present a detailed history of the cinema. Yet there are factors in the relationship between the cinema and theatre that are important to consider. First, many developments in spectacle in the nineteenth century theatre were utilized in the early cinema. Second, the early cinema came at a time when realism was in vogue. And, third, cinema was effectively able to capture the mass audience market. The theatre had been rapidly moving toward spectacle by the end of the nineteenth century. Three producer-directors had developed styles of production which were to make them exceedingly popular to mass audiences. They were Henry Irving (1838-1905) in London and David Belasco and Steele MacKaye (1842-1894) in America.

Henry Irving took the popularity of melodrama and created spectacular theatrical effects. He spared

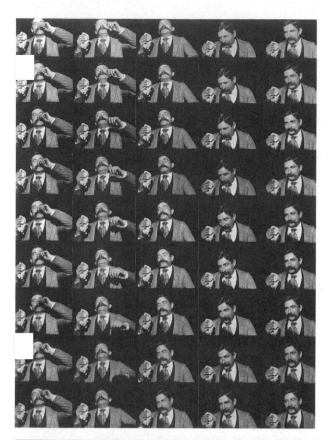

Left: The Sneeze, 1894. Edison's kinetoscope, a forerunner to the vitascope, was introduced April 14, 1894, at 1155 Broadway, New York. Unlike the vitascope, the kinetoscope was perfected at Edison's laboratory in West Orange, New Jersey.

Below: The vitascope was introduced by Edison April 23, 1896, at Koster and Bial's Music Hall, Herald Square, New York, after Edison purchased the manufacturing and marketing rights from Thomas Armat. Such projectors aided Edison in creating the film industry.

little in devising various traps which would make an actor appear or disappear. One of the most famous was the vampire trap which enabled actors to "float" up form beneath the stage. Witches faded in and out of fog and castles dissolved into courtyards. Many of these devices were utilized in the production of Shakespeare as well. Irving used flashback techniques and even crosscutting, all later absorbed into the cinema. In fact, when cinema arrived, Irving's theatre declined.

Belasco concentrated on making his sets and interiors as realistic as possible. Belasco, like Irving, used technical devices to cater to mass audiences. His was the naturalistic stage where drugstore bottles contained real pills. But Belasco, like Irving, found it difficult to survive when the cinema beat him at his own game. Photographic reality was simply more exciting than the illusion of reality.

Steele MacKaye was an important inventor in the America theatre. In addition to the hat holder that used to adorn the bottom of all theatrical seats, MacKay invented several methods of eliminating pauses for scene shifting, thereby allowing scenes to flow in and out of each other. The most important device was the elevator stage which he designed in 1879 for the Madison Square Theatre. The elevator stage consisted of two levels, one built on top of the other, placed in a large elevator shaft. While one scene was playing, the stage crew either shifted to the next scene from below or from above the audience level. He also designed a sliding and floating stage.

MacKaye was interested in controlled spectacle, not necessarily limited to the theatre stage. William Cody ("Buffalo Bill," 1846-1917) once hired him to stage a series of mammoth pictures that were to illustrate the growth and expansion of

A Russian Honeymoon, presented in 1883 at the Madison Square Theatre, incorporated Steele Mackaye's ideas and naturalistic settings.

America. The panorama alone was half a mile long and fifty feet high. The production included a cyclone supplied by four six-feet exhaust fans which entirely destroys a Colorado mining camp. The production was filled with action and scene changes. Scene three, for example reads in the following way: "A cattle ranch, where the cowboys' fun in interrupted by an Indian attack, which is beaten off at last by Buffalo Bill and a party of rescue. . . . "

MacKaye invented what he called the Spectatorium for the Chicago Exposition of 1893. The Spectatorium was a huge building which included twenty-five telescopic stages. The frame of the stages was 150 by 170 feet. They moved over six miles of railroad tracks and their aggregated weight would have been 1,000 tons. A new lighting system capable of reproducing any natural lighting effect and a cyclone system, which would have required over 400 horsepower to run, was to be constructed. MacKay's Spectatorium was similar, at least in concept, to the modern cinema sound stage. Unfortunately, it was never constructed.

Irving's romantic melodrama, Belasco's stage realism, and MacKaye's superspectacle, then, were made to order for the new art form. Many of the first pictures were merely melodrama photographed from a fixed camera, but in 1903 E. S. Porter discovered realism and sensationalism as methods of presenting melodramatic material. His film, *The Great Train Robbery,* was the first step by the cinema in its separation from the theatre. But it was not until the release of D. W. Griffith's *The Birth of a Nation* in 1915 that the cinema reached a position to challenge the theatre. *The Birth of a Nation* surpassed anything the theatre had ever done in terms of spectacle, realism, and melodramatic power. Hence audiences, which to this point had been fed the same formula in the legitimate theatre, logically turned to a media that could do it better. While Irving, Belasco, and MacKaye were cited as specific examples illustrating the kind of theatre being produced, they were by no means the only practitioners. Many affiliated with the commercial stage in America were, for the most part, equally guilty. Therefore, the effect on the American theatre was serious, particularly after the invention of the sound motion pictures in 1927. Certainly, cinema had to be a factor in the change which occurred in the American theatre between 1920 and 1940. There is, perhaps, a certain amount of irony when one listens to contemporary critics of the American movie business: "Too much spectacle, too much realism, and too much melodrama."

World War II and After

World War II was one of the most destructive events that we have ever known, and its resolution the least satisfying. The world was left divided into two potentially hostile camps with the threat of a nuclear holocaust hanging over its head, producing a kind of social paranoia during the 1950s. This paranoia was reflected in the theatre in a number of ways. First, dramatists questioned the moral validity of a generation which had committed such horrors. Second, there were questions about mankind as a whole being able to function in a responsible manner. Third, there were questions about man's ability to survive the anxiety about the future and guilt over the past. Fourth, there were questions about man's corruptibility.

Playwrights throughout the world began to explore these themes. Jean-Paul Sartre (1905-1980) found solace in a new philosophical movement called existentialism. Sartre reasoned that no just God would have allowed the holocaust; therefore, God does not exist. If there is no God, then there is no universal morality and, therefore, no fixed standards of conduct and no verifiable moral codes. Each person, he argued, is free to establish his own values and morals and to live by them if he chooses to do so. Conformity to the code of values of a society that produced the war was considered immoral by Sartre. He expressed his ideas in the French theatre through several plays. The most important of his existential plays were *The Flies* (1943) and *No Exit* (1944). Sartre and Algerian-born Albert Camus (1913-1960) were instrumental in laying the foundations of the Theatre of the Absurd, which will be discussed later.

The postwar French theatre also produced, among others, actor-director Jean-Louis Barrault (b. 1910) and actor-director Jean Vilar (1912-1971). The most important playwrights excluding the Absurdists are Jean Anouilh (1910-1987) and Henry de Montherlant (1896-1972). Anouilh's *Waltz of the Toreadors* (1952) and *Becket* (1960) together with Montherlant's *The Master of Santiago* (1948) are considered masterpieces.

In Germany Rolf Hochhuth (b. 1931) with his *The Deputy* (1963) and Peter Weiss (1916-1982) with *The Persecution and Assassination of Jean-Paul Marat as Performed by the Inmates of the Asylum of Charenton Under the Direction of the Marquis de Sade* (1964) and *The Investigation* (1965) are respected dramas.

The Swiss playwright Friedrich Duerrenmatt (b. 1921) studied the question of the corruptibility of man in many of his works. He is best known for *The Visit* (1956), which was performed on Broadway by one of finest theatrical teams of the American stage, Alfred Lunt and Lynn Fontaine. *The Physicists* (1962), *Play Strindberg* (1969), and *The Collaborator* (1973) have also received critical acclaim.

Postwar English Theatre

The English theatre was in shambles after the war, both literally and figuratively, as only one theatre in London remained open after the German blitz. Terence Rattigan (1911-1977), Christopher Fry (b. 1907), and American expatriot T. S. Eliot were the most important writers on the commercial stage.

The most significant company immediately after the war was the Old Vic. Initially under the direction of Tyrone Guthrie, the management was passed on to Laurence Olivier, Ralph Richardson, and John Burrell. The group declined as Richardson and Olivier turned more and more to other commitments such as the cinema. To fill the void, the Stratford Festival Company with its group of exciting actors, both new and old, became critically acclaimed. The company boasted Peter Brook (b. 1925), Paul Scofield (b. 1922), John Gielgud (b. 1904), Anthony Quayle (b. 1913), Michael Redgrave (b. 1908), Peggy Ashcroft (1907-1991), and Olivier, among others. In spite of these companies, however, the English stage was declining, if not doomed, in the eyes of many critics. The year 1956 marked both the low point and the beginning of a revival which once again would thrust it into favor. During that year, two producing units were formed in London—the English Stage Company and the Theatre Workshop. The Theatre Workshop, operating as a private club, organized in 1945 under the direction of Joan Littlewood. The group was instrumental in the development of Brendan Behan (1923-1965) and Shelagh Delaney (b. 1939).

The English Stage Company (known as the Royal Court because it is housed in the Royal Court Theatre) was started by George Devine (1910-1966), who had taught at Michel Saint-Denis' London Theatre Studio from 1936-1939. Devine's theatre was to have a major effect on the English stage in two ways: first, it introduced several major playwrights; second, it was instrumental in ending the almost ancient struggle for a free stage in London.

By the mid-fifties there were a number of young playwrights who were unable to get their plays produced in the commercial theatre. One of the major reasons for the problem was the Lord Chamberlain's insistence that the scripts be altered. In short, many of the new dramatists refused to be intimidated by the office of the play examiner. As in the past, when the government imposes restriction, theatre people find a way around it. They resorted to the private club ruse as others had done before them. The English Stage Company was a private club and charged a small entrance fee. Card holders were then permitted to purchase tickets and see unlicensed plays. As a result, a kind of symbiotic relationship existed between the commercial stage, the Lord Chamberlain, and the private theatre clubs. The commercial stage had no desire to produce plays by new writers and was not bothered by the loss of audiences, since those who attended the private showing did not necessarily frequent the commercial stage anyway. The Lord Chamberlain tolerated the arrangement because it allowed the playwrights a place to perform and kept them from criticizing the play examiner. The private clubs tolerated it because it was the only way for them to keep open. The only fly in the ointment was that it was illegal to perform an unlicensed play if the actors were paid. It was simply against the law. Yet no one pursued the point, and Royal Court produced John Osborne's (b. 1929) play *Look Back in Anger* (1956). The play attacks the established society with such vehemence that the central character soon became a symbol of England's "angry young men." *Look Back in Anger,* by the way, had been banned on the commercial stage by the Lord Chamberlain. Osborne has since written a number of plays, notably *Luther* (1961) and *Inadmissible Evidence* (1965).

The Royal Court also introduced John Arden (b. 1930), who wrote *Sergeant Musgrave's Dance* (1959), N. F. Simpson (b. 1919), who concentrated on Theatre of the Absurd with such plays as *A Resounding Tinkle* (1956) and *One Way Pendulum* (1959), and Ann Jellico's (b. 1928) *The Knack,* produced in 1961.

The Repeal of Censorship

The Royal Court continued to produce through the sixties, introducing playwrights Joe Orton (1933-1967), David Storey (b. 1933) and probably the most important, Edward Bond (b. 1935). Devine retired from the English Stage Company in 1965. He was replaced by William Gaskill (b. 1930), who maintained two theatre spaces at the Royal Court. The upstairs was devoted entirely to new works and the downstairs to mixture of old and new. In 1965 Gaskill produced a play by the young playwright Edward Bond. The play, called *Saved,* had been banned by the censor as immoral. The scene

in question involves a group of young thugs who abuse a baby by rubbing the baby in its own excrement and then stoning it to death in its carriage. The play deals with the decadence and violence of London's East Side and this scene underscores the point. Gaskill's direction was subtle and intentionally geared to get the idea across without being vulgar. Nevertheless, some members of the press condemned the scene without having seen it performed and supported the censor. Buoyed by unexpected praise from the press, the Lord Chamberlain's office sought to close the play. When a member of the Lord Chamberlain's office was admitted to the play without a membership card by a harried box office ticket seller, the Chamberlain closed the theatre and a court trial followed. The Chamberlain's office maintained that the English Stage Company had violated its status as a private club by selling a ticket to a nonmember. Selling tickets to the general public constituted a public theatre which was subject to the Lord Chamberlain's jurisdiction. The English Stage Company, on the other hand, maintained that the ticket error had been an individual mistake by busy office personnel and not at all the general policy of the organization. The trial aroused a great deal of interest as the great and the near-great of the English theatre came to testify on behalf of the English Stage Company. Sir Laurence Olivier's impassioned plea for the defendants was considered the high point amount the theatrical community. At the end of three months' testimony, the judge rendered his verdict. Gaskill and the English Stage Company were found guilty but not for the reasons cited by either the prosecution or the defense. The judge knew what many scholars of the theatre had known for years—according to the Theatre Regulations Act of 1843, if a theatre paid its actors, it was a public theatre whether or not a membership card was needed.

Both the Chamberlain and the English Stage Company were shocked with the decision. For the Chamberlain, the safety valve allowing for the private showing of new plays was effectively destroyed. For the English Stage Company, its very

Shakespeare Memorial Theatre at Stratford, where the Royal Shakespeare Company performs throughout the year. Adrian Noble, artistic director. *Courtesy British Tourist Authority.*

reason for being, the production of new play-wrights, was now under the control of the Lord Chamberlain who, by the very nature of his charge, must ban them from production. Parliament addressed itself to the situation. A hearing was held featuring testimony from numerous theatre and theatre-related personages. During the latter part of 1968, Parliament abolished censorship, freeing the English stage from the control of the Lord Chamberlain for the first time in almost 300 years.

English theatre has been a product of its environment, socially, psychologically, and physically. Censorship over what could not be seen on the English stage first became a tool of the monarchy to influence the minds of the common man. During the Walpole regime it evolved into a means of controlling political dissent, and with the Act of 1843, censorship became a reflection of the Victorian conscience.

Falsely or not, the Victorian middle class aspired to the morals (or what they thought to the be manners and morals) of the aristocracy and, in many ways, did not desire equality or the breakdown of the English caste system. One cannot help but remember Chrichton's words in Barrie's *The Admirable Chrichton:* "The division into classes, my Lord, are not artificial. They are the natural outcome of a civilized society. There must always be a master and servants in all civilized communities, my Lady, for it is natural, and whatever is natural is right." So it was with the Victorian middle class.

To the middle class, the rise of the lower class was synonymous with the movement toward equality and, with it, permissiveness. A similar development took place after the war when the commercial theatre continued to cater to middle-class values of the past. The new theatre was viewed with a certain amount of fear by the middle class. The battle between the Lord Chamberlain who became the upholder of past values, and the new theatres was symptomatic of this fear. Because of its revolutionary slant, the new theatre was suspected of being a kind of theatrical Frankenstein capable of destroying or undermining the traditional values of English life. But it began to be

Michael Hallifax was stage manager at the formation of the English Stage Company at the Royal Court. He later became company manager of the National Theatre under Sir Laurence Olivier and Sir Peter Hall.

more and more obvious after World War II that the values of the past were not always applicable to today's society. As long as the voice of the new drama was allowed expression, the archaic office of the censor lived on. But when the old threatened to strangle the new, the inevitable battle producing the inevitable conclusion began. As a result, theatrical censorship, one of the last vestiges of Victorian England, was dead.

The modern English theatre is once again one of the world's best. Playwrights such as Peter Shaffer *(The Royal Hunt of the Sun* and *Equus),* Edward Bond *(Lear* and *The Fool),* and Harold Pinter *(The Caretaker* and *The Homecoming),* have gained worldwide fame. The English stage has produced some of the finest actors and directors in the world, such as Laurence Olivier, John Gielgud, Ralph Richardson, Geraldine McEwan, Paul Scofield, Peter Brook, William Gaskill, Nichole Williamson, and Joan Littlewood, to name but a few. It is alive and well today, with a superb system for the training of young actors. Significantly, its policy of reduced-rate tickets for students will build future audiences. Because of the quality of the theatre, many English productions are finding their way to Broadway.

Postwar American Theatre

The American theatre after the war was clearly a product of trends established before the war. Playwrights such as Tennessee Williams (1911-1983) and Arthur Miller (b. 1916) were to achieve fame with primarily realistic plays, although both were to experiment with other styles later in their careers. Williams produced a number of excellent dramas, usually based on the survival of love and beauty in a brutal world. His *The Glass Menagerie* (1945), *A Streetcar Named Desire* (1947), and *The Rose Tattoo* (1951) all had a delicate, almost poetic, quality to them. In 1955 he turned briefly away from realism to expressionism with his *Camino Real*, which failed on Broadway but may yet survive the test of time as one of his best plays. Williams completed *This Is an Entertainment* (1976) and reworked *Summer and Smoke* into an entirely new script called *Eccentricities of a Nightingale* (1977). His last play *Vieux Carré* (1978) was not well received.

Arthur Miller was, like Williams a product of university training. His *Death of a Salesman* (1949) remains one of the classics of American theatre. Miller has been concerned with values in a highly materialistic society. His *The Crucible* (1953) was written during the time of the McCarthy hearings of the House Un-American Activities Committee. The parallel between the Salem witch hunts and this committee are not lost. Miller's more recent plays include *After the Fall* (1964), *Incident at Vichy* (1964), *The Creation of the World and Other Business* (1972), *Archbishop's Ceiling* (1977), and *Ride Down Mt. Morgan* (1990).

Because the New York stage is a business enterprise, the singular most important factor in its survival is that it must make money. This is not new; Shakespeare's theatre had to make money

and so did Garrick's. But the difference is in the amount of money needed before expenses are paid. For Shakespeare, overhead expenses were minute compared to Broadway. Production costs in the theatre today are astronomical and producers are forced to concentrate on plays that will appeal to the tastes of mass audiences. For that reason, New York has once again become the center for commercial theatre. Broadway must leave the work of discovery to either the regional theatres, off-off-Broadway, or the English stage. Neil Simon has been the most successful of the Broadway writers, producing a string of hits: *Barefoot in the Park* (1963), *The Odd Couple* (1965), *The Last of the Red Hot Lovers* (1970), *California Suite* (1976), and *Chapter Two* (1978) have dominated the New York stage. Edward Albee (b. 1928) exploded on Broadway with *Who's Afraid of Virginia Woolf* in 1962. Albee's later works have not been financially successful, but he remains an important American writer whose output is awaited eagerly by the theatre public as well as critics.

Arthur Kopit (b. 1938) gained success with his *Oh Dad, Poor Dad, Mama's Hung You in the Closet and I'm Feeling So Sad* (1960). Kopit's *Indians* (1968) was even more successful and was made into a screen play. Among the more recent writers Sam Shepard (b. 1943), Lanford Wilson (b. 1937), David Rabe (b. 1940), David Mamet (b. 1947), Marsha Norman (b. 1947), Maria Irene Fornes (b. 1930), Wendy Wasserstein (b. 1950) and Beth Henly (b. 1952) have shown outstanding talent.

Musical Theatre to the Present

In the 1940s swing music supplanted the demand for jazz. The demise of jazz was signaled with the death of George Gershwin in 1937. Despite the demand for this new type of music, composers such as Irving Berlin, Cole Porter, and Richard Rodgers wrote in a different vein. In 1940 *Joey* by Rodgers (1902-1979) and Hart, based on John O'Hara's stories from *The New Yorker*, created an antihero (Joey Evans, played by Gene Kelly) as the central character. The fact that this character does not seem to have any redeeming values created negative reviews. Yet, the use of an antihero was a first. In addition, this musical established the concept of musicalization: the use of literature as the basis for a musical. After this musical, the concept became the rule rather than the exception. In 1943 Rodgers teamed with Oscar Hammerstein II (1895-1960) for *Oklahoma*. The show was based on Lynn Rigg's (1899-1954) play *Green Grow the Lilacs*. Although its success was in doubt, after its opening it played for 2,248 performances. It featured all the innovations that had been introduced in the American musical to date. It had total synthesis and the choreography by Agnes de Mille took a page from George Balanchine by totally fusing the dance with the story. At the insistence of Rodgers and Hammerstein, de Mille was the first choreographer to be given the same status as the composer and the lyricist. In addition, she was extremely influential in beginning the Society of Stage Directors and Choreographer's union. In 1947 Kurt Weill's musical *Street Scene* brought up the issue of labeling all musicals as "musical comedy." He stated that he was going to write a musical tragedy. The decade closed with Rodgers and Hammerstein's *South Pacific* (1949), which was the second musical to win the Pulitzer Prize.

Musical theatre in the 1950s was the domain of Rodgers and Hammerstein. But innovation was being created in the new off-Broadway theatres. Of particular interest was *The Golden Apple* (1954) which opened at the off-Broadway Phoenix Theatre. Its success prompted the producers to move it to Broadway, which then made it eligible for the Tony award. Although it closed two weeks after moving, it did win the Tony award and thus became the first off-Broadway musical to win that award. In 1956-1957 came *My Fair Lady* (1956) and *West Side Story* (1957), both of which made history. *My Fair Lady* became the longest running show to date and *West Side Story* (directed and choreographed by Jerome Robbins) was the first musical in which the director and the choreographer were the same person. In addition, it was an example of musical that was built entirely around dance. Some musicals require little or no dance, but this one was

unique in its requirement for dance. In 1959 Elvis Presley was inducted into the army and to commemorate what many thought was the end of rock and roll, the musical *Bye Bye Birdie* (1959) was created. This musical had a chance to become the first truly rock musical but it opted instead to be about rock. This same year *Fiorello*, starring Tom Bosley, opened. It became the third musical to win the Pulitzer Prize.

On May 3, 1960, history was made when *The Fantasticks* opened off-Broadway at the Sullivan Street Playhouse. It is still playing and is the longest running musical in American theatre history. If you're thinking that the honor belongs to *A Chorus Line*, remember that this musical was on Broadway and has since closed. Incidentally, the honor of longest running play belongs to *The Mouse Trap* by Agatha Christie, which opened in 1952 and is still playing in England. In 1961 *How to Succeed in Business Without Really Trying*, starring Bobby Morse, opened and became the fourth musical to win the Pulitzer. The 1960s were a decade that witnessed the demand for rock music. It was evident in *Hair* (1968), which established the rock musical, and a rock version of Shakespeare's *Twelfth Night* called *Your Own Thing* (1968).

From 1970 to the 1990s musicals continued to be innovative and respond to audience demands. In the seventies *Annie* (1977) proved to be the most successful comic strip put on stage, winning a Tony for best musical. After much turmoil and a long out-of-town run, Annie II opened under the name *Annie Warbucks* (1993). In 1975 *A Chorus Line* opened at Joseph Papp's Public Theatre. Initially, it lost $18,000 a week but this was reversed when the production moved to Broadway, where it became the longest running musical in Broadway history. In addition to winning the Tony award, it became the fifth musical to win a Pulitzer Prize. In 1978 *Ain't Misbehavin*, based on the life and works of jazz pianist Fats Waller, became the first all-African-American musical in terms of cast and content to win the Tony award. During the Reagan years (1980s) musicals began to become more lavish. In 1983 *La Cage Aux Folles* was significant for being the first Broadway musical built around the theme of homosexuality; it won a Tony award. It paved the way for such successes as *March of the Falsettos* (1991) and the non-musical *Angels in America* (1993), Part I: *Millennium Approaches* and Part II: *Perestroika.* The 1980s witnessed the opening of *Cats* (1982) and in 1984, *Sunday in the Park with George,* based on the Seurat painting *An Afternoon Picnic on the Isle of Grand Jette,* became the sixth musical to win the Pulitzer Prize. Also opening in this decade was *Les Miserables* (1987), *The Phantom of the Opera* (1988), and *Grand Hotel* (1989). In the 1990s came *The Secret Garden* (1991), *The Will Rogers Follies* (1991) and *Miss Saigon* (1991). The latter created much controversy over what is termed non-traditional casting and almost stopped the production from coming from England to America. In 1993 some of the most successful musicals were revivals: *Guys and Dolls* and *Crazy for You* (from Gershwin's *Girl Crazy:* 1930), *The Who's Tommy,* based on the Who's concept of the rock opera by Peter Townshend, and *Kiss of the Spider Woman,* which won the Tony award in 1993. Of all these musicals, however, the composer whose work dominates at present is Stephen Sondheim: *West Side Story* (1957), *Company* (1970), *A Little Night Music, Pacific Overtures* (1975), *Sunday in the Park with George, Sweeney Todd* (1979), *Song of Singapore* (1991), and *Assassins* (1991), which deals with presidential assassinations throughout the centuries.

The Regional Theatres

The "regional" or nonprofit theatres are a product of the last forty years. The term *regional* is derived from the fact that these theatres are located in various regions throughout the United States. The fare of these theatres is basically noncommercial and thus they must find their support through grants, endowments, or benefactors. These theatres employ resident companies and are considered part of The League of Resident Theatres (LORT). The movement was initiated primarily by three women: In 1947 Margo Jones opened her

Theatre 47 in Dallas; in the same year Nina Vance started the Alley Theatre in Houston; and Zelda Fichandler's Arena Theatre in Washington, D.C., opened in 1950. The Alley and the Arena continue to operate. From these beginnings, the Regional Theatre has expanded to over 235 theatres and has demonstrated that theatre can thrive outside New York City. In fact, the commercial theatre in New York City now looks to these theatres for new plays and talent.

In the New England region, three theatres are particularly outstanding. In Cambridge, Massachusetts, the American Repertory Theatre stands as a noted addition to regional theatres. Known as ART, this company was founded by Robert Brustein in 1980 and operates out of the Loeb Drama Center at Harvard University as well as a smaller facility nearby. Of particular interest is the controversy that director Joanne Akalaitis created with her rendition of *Endgame* by Samuel Beckett, whose protest nearly caused the production to be cancelled. The theatre was recognized in 1980 when it was presented the Tony award for excellence in theatre. In New Haven, Connecticut, the Long Wharf and Yale Repertory Theatre are two other outstanding regional theatres. The Long Wharf was created in 1965 and is under the leadership of Arvin Brown. Many of its productions, such as *Quartermain's Terms, Requiem for a Heavyweight,* and *Long Day's Journey into Night,* have found their way to New York. Yale Repertory Theatre (YRT) was founded in 1966 by Robert Brustein who moved to Harvard. It was under the direction of Lloyd Richards, who assumed his position in 1979, that the YRT gained its reputation. Of note are the plays of South African Athol Fugard and American August Wilson, whose works *Fences* and *The Piano Lesson* have won Pulitzers. The work of these two writers was first staged at the YRT and subsequent efforts will seemingly be staged at this theatre as well.

Another equally excellent regional theatre is the Steppenwolf Theatre Company, whose presentation of Frank Galati's adaptation of *The Grapes of Wrath* won a Tony award for the outstanding

John Rubinstein and Juliane Gold appear in a scene from the world premiere of Mark Medoff's *Children of a Lesser God* at the Mark Taper Forum. *Photo by Jay Thompson.*

whose work has been extended to movies. In addition to Steppenwolf, Chicago also boasts of the Goodman Theatre which is the oldest and largest company in Chicago. Founded in 1925 by the Chicago Art Institute, the Goodman Theatre was named for the playwright, Kenneth Sawyer Goodman, and was designed by Thomas Wood Stevens. David Mamet has been an in-residence playwright and his works of *American Buffalo*, *Glengarry Glen Ross* and *A Life in the Theatre* were premiered here. In 1992 this theatre company won a Tony for outstanding work as a regional theatre.

Another theatre in the midwest is the Guthrie Theatre in Minneapolis. Founded by Tyrone Guthrie (1900-1971) in 1963, the success and publicity given this theatre proved to be a catalyst to the movement in general. With Guthrie's death, the second artistic director was the Romanian, Liviu Ciulei, and at present the theatre's $25 million budget is overseen by the third artistic director, Garland Wright. Its strength has been in doing the classics and it has built its reputation upon such productions as *The Tempest*, *The House of Atreus*, and a variety of Shakespeare and Greek works.

The Actors Theatre in Louisville, Kentucky, (ATL) was a product of the merger between Actors Incorporated and Theatre Louisville in 1964. Ewel Cornett and Dan C. Byck, Jr., headed Actors Incorporated and Richard Block, with the assistance of Barry Bingham, Jr., was at the helm of Theatre Louisville. The organization did not come into prominence, however until Jon Jory assumed the role of artistic director in 1969. With a budget at that time of $234,000, Jory built the theatre into one whose budget is ten times that. The ATL is most noted for its Humana Festival as well as its "Classics in Context." The Humana Festival attracts thousands of would-be writers, from which only five to ten scripts are chosen. Such plays as *Crimes of the Heart*, *The Gin Game*, *Agnes of God*, and most recently, *Marisol*, have been discovered at this festival. The "Classics in Context" is an attempt to weld scholarship, film, and theatre production together. In such programs artists and academi-

production of the year as well as a Tony in 1985 for theatre excellence. Located in Chicago, the Steppenwolf Theatre Company has been a pioneer in choosing to create what is known as the "Chicago style" of acting—a style based upon naturalism and steeped in emotion. Founded in 1976 in Highland Park, Illinois, by Gary Sinese, Jeff Perry, and Terry Kinney with a theatre that held 211 people, the company in 1991 moved closer to midtown Chicago into a multimillion dollar theatre that has a seating capacity of 510. In addition to the work of Gary Sinese, a major talent to emerge from this company is John Malkovich,

cians pool their talent to present a program on such areas as the Moscow Art Theatre, the Victorian Period, and the 1920s.

In the Los Angeles area, the Mark Taper Forum is noted as one of the two most noted regional theatres. Gordon Davidson was responsible for its creation in 1967. Like ATL the Forum specializes in new American works which eventually find a larger market. *Jelly's Last Jam, The Kentucky Cycle* (Pulitzer Prize winner in 1993), *Children of a Lesser God, The Shadow Box, Getting Out,* and *The Trial of the Cantonville Nine* serve as examples of some of the plays developed at the Forum. The other theatre in this area is located forty-five miles south of Los Angeles and, although perhaps not as well known nationally as the Mark Taper, the South Coast Repertory Theatre (SCR) is three years older and has been equally successful. Founded by David Emmes and Martin Benson, who are still the codirectors, the company prides itself on building strong community ties in addition to developing excellent productions. Of note, Craig Lucas's *Prelude to a Kiss* was commissioned by the SCR and *Search and Destroy, Sight Unseen,* and *The Extra Man* were works created at the SCR and seen in New York in the 1991-1992 season. This company received the 1988 Tony award for regional theatres.

In Seattle the theatre with the most noted national reputation is the Seattle Repertory Theatre (SRT). The SRT is a playwright's theatre. Its works of *The Heidi Chronicles, Conversations with My Father,* and *Largely New York* went to New York and were great successes. *The Heidi Chronicles* won the Tony for best play of the year and also a Pulitzer Prize for its author, Wendy Wasserstein. Additionally, the Seattle-based theatre has joined with the New York Circle Repertory Theatre to produce the premiere of Lanford Wilson's *Redwood Curtain.* The Intiman is the other Seattle theatre which is lesser known but whose production of *The Kentucky Cycle* has done much to aid its reputation. This theatre is devoted to doing plays that are unusual and avant-garde.

Of the many theatres to emerge from the New York area, the New York Shakespeare Festival Public Theatre, founded in 1954 by Joseph Papp (1921-1991) is probably the most ambitious in its undertakings. The basic premise behind Papp's theatre is to present free Shakespeare productions. Papp started his endeavor in the basement of a church and since those initial beginnings, the theatre has mushroomed. The company operates the Public Theatre which houses six performance areas; it gives free Shakespeare in the Park performances at the large outdoor Delacorte Theatre in Central Park; and it tours around the city bringing theatre to the masses. Among the theatre's most successful productions are *A Chorus Line, The Pirates of Penzance* (with Kevin Kline and Linda Ronstadt), *The Mystery of Edwin Drood, That Championship Season, Plenty, Talk Radio, For Colored Girls Who Have Considered Suicide When the Rainbow is Enuf, Hair, Hamlet* (with Kevin Kline), *The Three Penny Opera* (with Raul Julia), *The Taming of the Shrew* (with Morgan Freeman and Tracy Ullman), *Tis a Pity She's a Whore* (directed by Joanne Akalaitis and starring Val Kilmer). Additionally, works by Richard Foreman, Gerald Freeman, and the late A. J. Antoon have graced the stages of the Public Theatre. Prior to his death, Papp appointed Joanne Akalaitis as artistic director along with George Wolfe and David Greenspan. In 1993 Akalaitis was dismissed and George Wolfe was placed as the sole artistic director.

Selected Readings

Bentley, Eric. *The Playwright as Thinker: A Study of Drama in Modern Times.* New York, 1946.

Block, Haskell. *Mallarmé and the Symbolist Drama.* Detroit, 1963.

Boardman, Gerald. *Americna Musical Theatre.* New York, 1978.

Brockett, Oscar G. and Findlay, Robert. *Century of Innovation: A History of Euorpean and American Theatre and Drama Since the Late 19th Century.* 2nd ed. Boston, 1991.

Brook, Peter. *The Empty Space.* New York, 1968.

Gordon, Mel. *Dada Performance.* New York, 1987.

Hill, Errol, Ed. *The Theatre of Black Americans.* 2 vols. Englewood Cliffs, NJ, 1980.

Ritchie, J. M. *German Expressionist Drama.* Boston, 1976.

Valency, Maurice. *The Flower and the Castle: An Introduction to Modern Drama.* New York, 1963.

Valency, Maurice. *The End of the World: An Introduction to Contemporary Drama.* New York, 1980.

Ziegler, Ronald. *Regional Theatre.* New York, 1973.

Vocabulary

1.	Richard Wagner	RI kahrt VAHG ner
2.	Bayreuth	bigh ROYT
3.	gesamtkunstwerk	ge ZAHMT koonst vairk
4.	Der Ring des Nibelungen	dair RING des NEE buh loong uhn
5.	Tristan und Isolde	TRI stahn oond iZOHL duh
6.	Friedrich Nietzsche	FREE drik NEE chuh
7.	Apollonian	ap uh LOH nee uhn
8.	Dionysian	digh uh NIZ ee uhn
9.	Théophile Gautier	tay oh FEEL goh TYAY
10.	Maurice Maeterlinck	moh REES MAY ter lingk
11.	Paul Claudel	kloh DEL
12.	Edmond Rostand	RAW stand
13.	*Pelléas and Mélisande*	pe lay AHS me li ZAHND
14.	Aurelien-Marie Lugné-Poë	awr re LYEN muh REE loo NYAY POH
15.	Théâtre de l'Oeuvre	tay AHT ruh duh LER vruh
16.	Schopenhauer	SHOH puhn how er
17.	Georg Kaiser	GAY ohrg KIGH zer
18.	Filippo Tommaso Marinetti	mahr uh NE tee
19.	Tristan Tzara	TRI stan ZAH ruh
20.	André Breton	ahn DRAY bruh TAWN
21.	Philippe Soupault	fee LEEP soo POH
22.	Guillaume Apollinaire	gee YOHM uh paw lee NAIR
23.	Jean Cocteau	zhaw kawk TOH
24.	Antonin Artaud	An tuh NEEN ahr TOH
25.	Vsevelod Meyerhold	vuh SE vohlt MIGH er hohld
26.	verfremdung	fer FREM doong
27.	Jacques Copeau	ZHAHK kah POH

CHAPTER FOURTEEN

❧

The 1960s and Beyond: Changing the Structure

The Moscow Theatre of Drama and Comedy on Taganka Square, better known as Taganka Theatre, is traditionally the most experimental and liberal in Moscow. Founded in 1964, the theatre is under the direction of Yuri Lyubimov, who is shown here congratulating the cast after the production of *Under the Skin of Liberty Statue. Courtesy Tass from Sovfoto.*

The unrest of the 1960s brought unmitigated changes and challenges to the societies and the theatre of the western world. Events and movements such as the civil rights struggle in the United States, opposition to American involvement in Vietnam, sexual liberation, Eastern European resistance to Russian domination and rising feminism jolted theatre practitioners out of the naturalistic mode that had dominated theatre practice for nearly a century. Hearkening back to Brecht's desire for a thinking spectator and Artaud's rejection of "masterpieces," newly politicized theatre artists searched for new forms and methods to displace the passive spectator and to encourage audiences to take active participation in the formation of a new world order. As demonstrations and political protests became common occurrences in everyday life, playwrights, directors and actors reflected the dissatisfactions of society in both the medium and the message of their performances.

Rather than accept the view of society as a series of established, irrevocable assumptions and behaviors, theatre practitioners embraced the work of psychoanalysts such as R. D. Laing (1927-1989), anthropologist Lévi-Strauss (b. 1908), and socialist thinkers such as Herbert Marcuse (1898-1979). R. D. Laing (*The Politics of Experience*, 1967) suggested that, contrary to Freud's theories, society is not the "norm" to which people must adjust; rather, it is the society itself that may need changing. Lévi-Strauss' studies (*Mythologiques*, 1967-1972) of tribal systems argued that myths reveal the structural "grid" of society and that these myths unconsciously affect the way members of the society perceive the world. Herbert Marcuse's *One Dimensional Man* (1964) exposed corporate capitalism as the enemy of the masses through its "repressive tolerance," which satisfies material needs while sacrificing more fundamental freedoms. Politically, revolutionaries such as Che Guevera and Mao Tsetung became the heroes of the disenfranchised youth of many capitalist countries.

Traditional commercial theatre, which embodied a reverence for the "classics," conventional performing spaces, high ticket prices and compla-

cent attitudes, became the enemy of radical theatre groups who supported the ideals of pacifism, solidarity and the rights of individuals to live how and where they choose. Instead of seeking theatre buildings in which to perform, artists began producing in almost any empty space: barns, deserted factories and city streets became the new "theatres." Ensemble work, in the truest sense of the word, was emphasized as actors, directors and playwrights created plays, built sets, sewed costumes, sold tickets and sometimes lived together. The newly created plays were concerned with issues of workers' rights, Third World solidarity, the peace movement and sexual freedom, to name a few. Rather than deliver their message to the wealthy theatre patrons who could afford high-priced Broadway seats, the radical theatre groups often took their plays to heavily populated neighborhoods and rural areas, charging minimal or no admission prices. Spectators were often encouraged to participate directly in the action, or were placed in non-traditional juxtapositions with the actors.

The new shape of 1960s theatre practice confirmed what opponents of the theatre had known for thousands of years: that the theatre is a potent and effective political force. No longer content with commercial plays that presented placebos of contemporary life, theatre during the 1960s became a revolutionary format that articulated the problems, desires and pains of an increasingly large middle class society. Many of the theatre groups that were formed were short-lived; some were unable to survive financially, some suffered from poor artistry or incoherent communication, some simply presented their message and faded away, their company members drifting into other activities. However, a few groups survived well into the 1980s and some continue today. Failing economies, escalating prices, and changing audiences have now forced some survivors to accept monetary assistance from those same governments and corporations they once reviled, often making messages politically impotent. Nevertheless, at their apex these groups and individuals provided a powerful forum for the social changes that shaped the subsequent theatres of the 1970s, 1980s and 1990s.

The Forerunners: The Polish Laboratory Theatre and The Living Theatre

Two theatre groups, Jerzy Grotowski's Polish Laboratory Theatre (formed in 1959) and Julian Beck and Judith Malina's Living Theatre (formed in 1946), provided the groundwork for many of the radical theatre groups established during the 1960s and '70s. Grotowski's (b. 1933) work was popularized primarily through the publication of his collected essays, *Towards a Poor Theatre* (1968). Together, Beck and Malina wrote *Paradise Now: Collective Creation of the Living Theatre* (1972) and with Aldo Rostagno published *We, the Living Theatre* (1970). Both Beck and Malina published their own journals as well. In Beck's journal, *A Life of the Theatre* (1972), he sums up his objection to commercial theatre:

> I do not like the Broadway theatre because it does not know how to say hello. The tone of voice is false, the mannerisms are false, the sex is false, ideal, the Hollywood world of perfection, the clean image, the well pressed clothes, the well scrubbed anus, odorless, inhuman, of the Hollywood actor, the Broadway star. And the terrible false dirt of Broadway, the lower depths in which the dirt is imitated, inaccurate.

Both Beck and Grotowski rejected the theatre of the privileged, modern aristocracy. For Beck, the essence of the performance was the convergence, or communion, of actor and spectator. His Living Theatre (so named because of the group's commitment to topical, contemporary pieces, hence "living" works) productions often removed any barrier between the two so that the action might evolve from the interaction of actor and audience. Grotowski sought what he labeled a "poor theatre," a theatre in which everything but the essential is stripped away. This included the banish-

ment of elaborate lighting effects, makeup, traditional scenery, and costumes. For Grotowski, the heart of the performance was the actor, who must be trained and then encouraged to rely upon his or her own resources rather than on the support mechanisms of the commercial theatre.

Grotowski's work began in 1959 in Opole, Poland, where the Theatre of 13 Rows was formed. Although initially Grotowski's work was largely ignored, even in his native land, his book is one of the most widely read (and widely translated) theatre books of contemporary times. Nevertheless, by the time the company moved to Wroclaw (1965) and adopted the simplified name of Laboratory Theatre, Grotowski's company was beginning to acquire an international reputation, touring and giving workshops in France, England, Sweden, and Denmark. By the 1970s, the group was internationally acclaimed.

As the name Laboratory Theatre implies, Grotowski was more concerned with process than with product. Grotowski's theatre has a strong affinity with the theories of Antonin Artaud *(The Theatre and Its Double),* seeking to expose archetypal experiences and impulses that are a part of the "collective unconscious." Yet, unlike Artaud's writings, Grotowski's work extended far beyond the theoretical. The Polish Laboratory Theatre became simultaneously a training ground for actors, a laboratory for exploring actor-spectator relationships, and a springboard for the director auteur.

Complete dedication to the work was demanded of actors in Grotowski's Lab Theatre. Each day began with an intensive regime of physical training so that they might discover and release these buried impulses: gymnastics, acrobatics, rhythmic dance, yoga, mask composition, pantomime, Oriental theatre exercises.

> The education of an actor in our theatre is not a matter of teaching him something: we attempt to eliminate his organism's resistance to [the] psychic process. The result is freedom from the time lapse between inner impulse and outer reaction in such a way that the impulse is already an outer reaction. Impulse and action are concurrent: the body vanishes,

burns, and the spectator sees a series of invisible impulses. (*Towards a Poor Theatre*)

In order to communicate with the audience, the actor must be able to re-create basic impulses spontaneously by discovering the physical stimuli which give expression to the collective unconscious. Grotowski rejected the actor who "struts across the stage with padded chest, false nose and delicately applied makeup." Rather, Grotowski's training aimed at surpassing the mediocrity of naturalistic or "common" methods of moving and speaking. Communication with the audience involved speaking to the spectator's unconscious, subliminal reactions. Although much of the final product was developed in improvisational work during the rehearsal period, in performance each moment on stage was executed with precision and discipline. Part of the "poor" theatre's impact was due to the exceptional concentration, precision and richness of the performers, rendering naturalistic, representational aspects of production shallow by comparison.

Grotowski was equally demanding of his audience, often restricting attendance at a performance to no more than 100 spectators. Throughout the history of the Laboratory Theatre, Grotowski experimented with audience participation, beginning initially by creating new spatial relationships between actors and spectators and moving gradually to include the audience's physical participation in the creative act. One of his earliest productions, *Kordian* (1962) was set in a psychiatric hospital, in a large room filled with hospital bed, on which the actors performed and which also served as the audience seating area. In his 1963 production of Marlowe's *Tragical History of Doctor Faustus*, the audience sat as Faustus' friends at banqueting tables, while Faustus, from his position at the head of the table, called forth scenes from his past to be played by the actors upon the table tops.

Almost in direct response to Artaud's plea for "No more masterpieces," Grotowski approached each script as an original piece waiting to be discovered. Freely adapting the material he used,

Grotowski used the script as the raw material of his creation, rearranging scenes, displacing action and substituting simplified props for elaborate technical requirements. His masterpiece, *Apocalypsis cum figuris* (1968), was an amalgamation of the Bible, T. S. Eliot and Dostoyevsky and was performed with the barest of essentials: an empty room, six actors, a few candles, a knife and a loaf of bread.

Poster for Grotowski's *Apocalypsis cum figuris*. Lewis Loyd Collection, Harvard Theatre Collection.

Although the Polish Laboratory Theatre did not dissolve until 1984, Grotowski's personal experimentations with theatre lessened his direct involvement with the group. In his "paratheatrical experiments" Grotowski explored the actor/spectator relationship by completely removing the barrier between the two. Setting these "project-events" in various natural surroundings, such as woods, hills, or fields, Grotowski stretched to discover an entrance to man's elemental, primitive relationships between himself, others and the natural world. From these experiments evolved the Theatre of Sources, an attempt to discover the transcultural transmission of ritual and ceremony. During the 1980s, Grotowski traveled the world, studying ritual practices in Mexico, Haiti, Bengal, West Africa, India, Japan, France and elsewhere, seeking to identify the source of the simple truths that resonate in all human beings. Today, Grotowski continues his research and work at the University of California, Irvine, where he has been a professor since 1983.

Though the Polish Laboratory Theatre is not commonly associated with having an overt political purpose (indeed, Grotowski himself denied any political implications of his work, perhaps a necessary strategy in Poland under the Communist regime), the effect it had on the development of other theatre groups, including those with specific political agendas, was profound. The parallels between Grotowski's Lab Theatre and Beck's Living Theatre are undeniable, though there are significant differences as well. Julian Beck was an audience member at Grotowski's *The Constant Prince* in France:

> I was struck by it immediately. I recognized. . . that it was in direct relationship with what we were sketching for our *Antigone* rehearsals . . . I was greatly encouraged, because I saw proof that what we wanted to do could work; it was working. *(The Living Theatre)*

Although the Living Theatre was formed initially to eradicate naturalistic techniques in favor of a poetic, non-realistic theatre, eventually Beck and Malina's political convictions merged with the theatrical enterprise. By the mid-1960s, the Living Theatre's persistent goal was to use theatre as a means of stimulating social change. As the name suggests, members of the company blurred the distinction between life and art, and the company's communal style of living created additional controversy to their already radical politics.

One of the longest surviving theatre groups to emerge from the 1960s, the Living Theatre repeatedly engaged in confrontations with governments, police and irate audience members that led to their arrest, impounding, deportation or flight from several countries, including its native United States. To the many disillusioned and disenfranchised audience members of the 1960s, the Living Theatre and its confrontational style became the symbols of revolution, personal conviction and freedom.

The Living Theatre began in Judith Malina (b. 1926) and Julian Beck's (1925-1985) living room in New York with a series of non-realistic productions of poetic dramas, including the works of Gertrude Stein, T. S. Eliot, Alfred Jarry and Bertoldt Brecht. The 1959 production of Jack Gelber's *The Connection* won them numerous awards, including the Critics Circle Award at the Theatre des Nations. As work continued on such productions as *The Marrying Maiden* and *The Brig,* the group became increasingly improvisational and collective, moving slowly away from single authored texts and relying almost entirely upon improvisations developed from scenarios. In *Mysteries and Smaller Pieces,* improvisation and ritual were interspersed with images that evoked authoritarian repression and freedom. Audience members were then asked to respond by suggesting how repression might be transformed into freedom. Using improvisation in conjunction with an established piece of drama or literature as the base, ensemble creations evolved that were the result of collective scripting.

Many of the Living Theatre pieces were the result of research, discussion and improvisation by the collective company. *Frankenstein* was roughly based on Mary Shelley's novel, interjected with newspaper items, Shakespeare, Karl Marx and Mao Tse-tung. In performance, each

South America and the United States, attracting hangers-on and assorted groupies. Frequently critics wrote of the "amateurish" quality of the acting, and government censors canceled performances because of perceived "anti-social" behavior on the part of individual company members.

Audiences, uninfluenced by the professional critics and government regulations, flocked to performances throughout their tours. Part of the reason for their popularity was the Living Theatre's consistent commitment to confronting social and political issues, often inspiring rage or ectasy amongst audience members, but rarely boredom. Like the Laboratory Theatre, the Living Theatre abandoned elaborate scenery, costumes, props and lighting in favor of a more immediate and anticapitalist, experience. Beck and Malina elaborated on Grotowski's experiments which redefined actor-audience relationship. Frequently separation between the actor and the audience was eliminated; verbally and physically, the audience was invited to join in with the actors during the performance. Behavior between the actors and the audience was totally unrehearsed, dedicated to breaking down the physical, spiritual and emotional barriers between the two. Audience members were insulted, conversed with, touched, and welcomed. *Paradise Now*, the company's most provocative piece, included "The Rite of Universal Intercourse" in which the spectators were invited to join the semi-nude actors by stripping off their clothes and caressing and undulating with the cast. The grande finale of *Paradise Now* was a recessional parade of the audience, led out into the streets, proclaiming "The theatre is in the street. The street belongs to the people. Free the theatre. Free the street. Begin."

Opposed to capitalist society, and advocating peaceful revolution from within, the Living Theatre became a model for other radical theatre troupes. Despite the constant poverty that members of the group endured, the Living Theatre provided a model for theatre artists seeking change in the world and in the theatre. Consequently, other theatre artisans were encouraged to explore

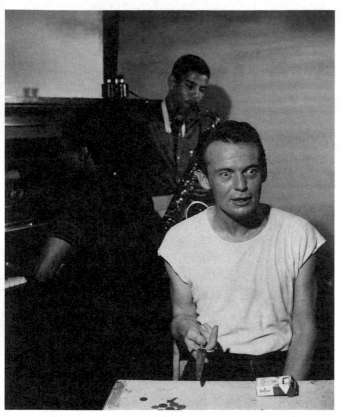

The Living Theatre's production of *The Connection. Alix Jeffry photograph, Harvard Theatre Collection.*

actor created and played multiple roles, some of which were personifications of abstract qualities such as Imagination or Love. The concept for the play was a metaphor, seeking to show the evil that corrupts each person's heart. In rehearsal for the piece, actors were required to "confess" to some evil that they themselves had done.

Malina and Beck's company was made up of an ever-changing group of actors, sometimes numbering up to sixty adults and several children. Unlike Grotowski's highly disciplined actors, the Living Theatre was most often comprised of inexperienced performers, willing to work by day at other jobs, who sought to discover in the theatre a means of expression for their own political leanings and sexual inclinations. The troupe led a nomadic existence, traveling throughout Europe,

alternative methods of rehearsing and performing, as well as to challenge the playwright's lofty position as the creator "god" of the theatre. Grotowski had begun to experiment with the audience's participation during performance; the Living Theatre broke all barriers. Because of the Living Theatre, nudity on stage has slowly become accepted. The company's often controversial communal lifestyle gave new meaning to the word "ensemble;" as an extension of their life together off stage, the pieces that were created were truly the work of a collective.

Until Beck's death in 1985, the Living Theatre continued performing, though less regularly and less rigorously than during previous years. Drawing on the work of Meyerhold, Artaud, Piscator, Brecht, Stanislavski and others, the Polish Lab Theatre and the Living Theatre significantly influenced the growth of alternative theatre throughout the world. As theatre artists continuously seek the means to reflect and influence society's weaknesses, traces of their influence continue today. The effect of these influences may be summarized as follows:

1. A shift from the primacy of the written word, to an emphasis on visual impact;
2. A resistance to the traditional actor/audience relationship (separation);
3. A collective method of developing the script, beginning with a primary idea or concept and evolving to a finished performance, not subject to a single author;
4. A rejection of theatre as a commercial vehicle; rather, it is a testing ground for new aesthetics, new cultural awareness, new political convictions rather than an affirmation of the status quo;
5. A reluctance to speak only to those audiences who make up the bourgeois mentality of societal norms; rather, alternative groups often target specific audiences for their message, usually with the intention of empowering the disempowered to create change outside of the theatre, if only in new ways of thinking.

Hundreds of alternative theatre groups were formed internationally, some more politically radical than others. Few enjoyed the longevity of either the Polish Laboratory Theatre or the Living Theatre. Nevertheless, a significant number of contemporary theatre artists received their apprenticeships, and their craftsmanship, in these theatres. Soon after alternative theatres disbanded or were no longer able to survive financially, a new generation of theatre artists arose, individually committed to giving voice to the issues of the times, by combining the proven techniques of the financially successful commercial theatre with the popularly successful alternative theatres.

The Open Theatre

Though trained as a traditional Method actor, Joseph Chaikin (b. 1935) became a member of the Living Theatre in 1959. Chaikin was interested in the creation of the "inside" of a situation, rather than the realistic, "outside" behavior that one usually sees. Drawing from the work of the Becks, Grotowski, Violin Spolin and others, Chaikin and Peter Feldman formed the Open Theatre in 1963. Though many of the works that emerged from the Open Theatre had a distinctly leftist political point of view, the primary purpose of the group was to experiment with the concept of a performer as a "presence."

To achieve this end, Chaikin developed a series of improvisations and acting exercises through which actors would free themselves to respond instinctively, rather than through carefully constructed artistic representations. Like Grotowski, Chaikin sought to remove the barriers between the actor and his response, advocating a "poor theatre" in which actors appeared in street clothes, and scenery was kept to a minimum. Although direct confrontation with the audience was rarely used, actors of the Open Theatre did not play realistic characters who would maintain a barrier between themselves and the audience. Rather,

Open Theatre pieces concentrated on creating the abstraction of a character, seeking to affect the audience on a "gut level," or using Grotowski's Jungian term, the "collective unconscious."

The first performances of the Open Theatre were based upon improvisations that had been developed by the actors with the aid of play-wrights such as Megan Terry and Jean-Claude van Itallie (b. 1936). These improvisations were structured into short pieces and full length productions such as *Viet Rock* (1966) and *The Serpent* (1969). *Viet Rock* evolved from the strong antiwar sentiments of the group who, working from the theme of violence, gathered newspaper articles and other sources of information about the Vietnamese war. Megan Terry developed these ideas into a loosely structured series of scenes showing young men drafted into the army, trained and then killed in Vietnam. The actors, a group of sixteen men and women, switched roles frequently, using sounds and short phrases to communicate character as well as to portray inanimate objects. *Viet Rock* ends with a communal touching of the heads of audience members. Similarly, *The Serpent* evolved from a series of improvisations but found its basis in the Book of Genesis. As with *Viet Rock*, actors contributed their own ideas and experiences, as well as collecting material on current events, including the assassinations of John Kennedy and Martin Luther King. Jean-Claude van Itallie gave the collected improvisations their non-linear form, and the piece became the signature performance of the Open Theatre on its tour throughout the United States and Europe.

Within the Open Theatre the emphasis was on the process of creation rather than on the finished product. Most of the Open Theatre performances explored cultural beliefs, and used the actor's insights to express these beliefs. Thus, the performer, and not a carefully constructed character, was always the focus of the performance. Though Chaikin did not advocate the breaking of physical barriers between the audience and the performers, the Open Theatre was committed to exploring to the fullest the potential for a real encounter between the two. In 1973, torn between the group's desire to become more politically active, and Chaikin's wish to remain apolitical, the Open Theatre disbanded.

The Performance Group

The concept behind the work of the Performance Group is most completely illustrated by Richard Schechner's (b. 1934) book *Environmental Theatre,* published in 1973. Schechner had previously written his "6 Axioms for Environmental Theatre" (1968) in which he rejected traditional theatre spaces in favor of those places that are either "found" or transformed. Perceiving the spectators as "scene-makers" and "scene-watchers" simultaneously, Schechner's Performance Group chose environments for their productions. Borrowing from Grotowski and the Living Theatre, audience members, performers and location were part of the total picture, which often involved multiple and unequal points of focus, as in real life.

The company was formed in 1968 and almost immediately began work on its first production, *Dionysius in 69.* Using Euripides' *The Bacchae* as the unifying concept for the production, the final piece included some of Euripides' text as well as dialogue developed by the actors during their rehearsal period. Strongly influenced by Grotowski, Schechner wanted his actors to delve beyond the mask of conventional characterization. During the performance, actors made themselves visible and vulnerable to the audience by utilizing exercises and improvisations in which they responded as themselves, rather than as characters, and by performing parts of the play requiring complete nudity. Ironically, it was Grotowski who inspired Schechner's use of nudity.

> Grotowski saw the play in November 1968. He liked the environment we had built in the garage and parts of the *mise-en-scene.* He felt the acting was hysterical, that we confused

Mother Courage by Bertolt Brecht as performed by Richard Schechner's performance group. The performers are singing the song of Mother Courage's Boots in Scene 1. *Courtesy Clem Fiori.*

touching skin with psychic contact. He did not like the costumes. The red chitons and black underpants of the women and the black jockstraps of the men were too much like striptease, he said. He felt that one might either perform naked as a sacred act or let the nakedness come through everyday clothes. I decided a few days later that the performers would do sections of the play naked.

Similar to portions of the Living Theatre's *Paradise Now*, the actors interacted with the audience, at times speaking to them directly, at times choosing individuals to caress and kiss. In this way, the actor's focus was on performance rather than on a specific character.

Each production of the Performance Group was produced in the Performance Garage on Wooster Street in New York. A new environment was created for each, and individual audience members were often unable to see all of the action from where they were sitting. Spectators shared the sometimes cramped space with performers. Rather than representing a specific or single location, the environment was a flexible, integral part of the whole event. Consequently, each audience member had a somewhat different experience of the performance, as some were able to see portions of the piece that others were not.

The Performance Group expanded some of the techniques used by Grotowski, the Living Theatre and others. During the production of *Makbeth* (1969), spectators were allowed to wander around in their stockinged feet throughout the production. In *Commune* (1970), audience interaction began as spectators were asked to place their shoes in a large mound before entering the space. These shoes were later worn by the actors, and returned again to the spectators. Though Schechner withdrew from the group in 1980, his influence continues to be seen and felt in the work of other contemporary artists. The Performance Garage space was taken over by the newly formed Wooster Group in 1980. This group included some members of the disbanded Performance Group such as Spaulding Gray (b. 1941) and Elizabeth LeCompte (b. 1944), who were the main forces of the group.

Agitprop Theatre: The San Francisco Mime Troupe, Bread and Puppet, and El Teatro Campesino

Perhaps the most powerful resonance of the Living Theatre's influence was in the creation of radical theatre groups whose message was inextricably intertwined with politics. Like the Living Theatre, these groups opposed capitalist society, the bourgeois status quo and American involvement in Vietnam. Three of them, the Bread and Puppet Theatre, the San Francisco Mime Troupe, and El Teatro Campesino, continue to operate today. Amongst these three groups there are some significant similarities. They are organized as collectives, though each is headed by a strong leader/

director whose artistic vision guides much of the work; each is dedicated to changing social structures and cultural biases; each began as distinctly non-commercial, performing both in theatres and on the streets, for an audience that was not a typical theatre audience; each uses comedy and elements of contemporary culture to communicate its message; each of them uses "audience friendly" techniques such as circus, puppet, melodrama, parades and vaudeville techniques, to insure both the exhilarating quality of their performances as well as the inescapability of their messages; and each has the fluidity to adapt quickly to insure that the message contained in the work is topical and pertinent.

The San Francisco Mime Troupe was founded in 1959 by Ron Davis, a professional dancer who trained with Etienne Decroux. Early on, the Mime Troupe embraced the techniques of the commedia dell 'arte players, performing stereotyped characters in farcical situations with exaggerated movements and gestures. Between 1962-1970 their works were adaptations of plays by Molière and Goldoni, often with modern twists. Thus, Goldoni's *L'Amant Militaire* (1967) became a protest of the Vietnamese war, with topical references to chemical warfare and an easily recognizable imitation of Lyndon Johnson.

Comedy was a critical element in the success of the San Francisco Mime Troupe and the energy and enthusiasm of the actors often carried into the audience for a post-performance discussion of the issues viewed in the play. Each piece focused on a political problem selected by the group, who collectively contributed to researching and developing the overall shape of the piece. One of the earliest Mime Troupe performances, *A Minstrel Show, or Civil Rights in a Cracker Barrel* (1964), satirized racial prejudice. Others satirized corrupt housing practices (*San Fran Scandals*, 1973), price and wage control policies (*Frozen Wages*, 1972), air pollution (*The Great Air Robbery*, 1974) and unfair minority wages (*Electro-Bucks*, 1978), to name a few.

Despite their longevity, the San Francisco Mime Troupe continues working today under the shadow of poverty. This is due, in part, to their long-standing commitment to bring theatre to society's disenfranchised. The Mime Troupe has toured extensively, and continues to work towards empowering social change.

On the surface, the Bread and Puppet Theatre may appear to be the least radical of the long-surviving groups. The company's outdoor performance generally begins with a parade through the town, involving not only performers but spectators and giant puppets as well. Like the San Francisco Mime Troupe, poverty constantly hovers near its door, despite the respect and admiration the company has gained. Peter Schumann (b. 1934), a sculptor, dancer and puppeteer, and the founder of Bread and Puppet, had his first New York production in 1962. As his concerns moved from the Vietnam war to other issues, he began the practice of distributing his homemade dark bread to the audience following the performance. In this respect, he physically recalls the impetus for his theatre:

> We sometimes give you a piece of bread along with the puppet show because our bread and theatre belong together. For a long time, the theatre arts have been separated from the stomach. Theatre as entertainment was meant for the skin. Bread was meant for the stomach. Theatre is more like bread, more like a necessity.

Bread and Puppet performances are highly visual, with tall oversized puppets (with an actor inside) creating the story in a style that is marked by simplicity. Banners, painted cloths, music, clowns, processions and an informal atmosphere are trademarks of the Bread and Puppet Theatre. This is not to imply a lack of intellectual sophistication, by any means. Despite the accessibility of the Bread and Puppet Theatre performances to all audiences, serious messages about materialism, war, and the dehumanization of the spirit are recurring

Scene from a two-day-long puppet and musical extravaganza entitled *Our Domestic Resurrection Fair and Circus* by the Bread and Puppet Theatre at its home in Glover, Vermont.

themes. Yet the Bread and Puppet Theatre does not preach and does not demand. It is a kinder, gentler political theatre, interested in presenting elemental human conditions, and posing questions about social conditions, that "make sense" to five-year-olds and adults alike.

Initially (1961-1970), the group made its home in New York, and instituted a yearly tour of Europe as part of its program. Bread and Puppet was often in attendance at anti-war demonstrations throughout the United States. In 1970, the group moved to Goddard College in Plainfield, Vermont, where they lived as a theatre-in-residence. By 1974, members of the group agreed to separate, and Schumann moved with his family and puppets to a farm near Glover, Vermont. It is from this location that the Bread and Puppet Theatre continues to operate, performing locally and touring nationally, usually as guest artists at colleges and universities. Performances take place in non-traditional spaces, such as sidewalks or open fields, varying the spatial relationship between the actor and spectator as necessary. Communion with the audience is an essential ingredient in the Bread and Puppet experience, symbolized by the sharing of bread at the conclusion.

Annually, the public is invited to a two-day event at the Schumann's farm to attend the Bread and Puppet Domestic Resurrection Circus. A celebration of life, the event has all the atmosphere of a circus, as spectators move from location to location, viewing simultaneously occurring performances throughout the grassy meadows of the farm. Puppetry combines with crazy clowns, forty foot long dragons, marching bands and the ever energetic Peter Schumann to create a collage of scenes and experiences that leave thousands of spectators joyous and thoughtful. To a large extent, the work of the Bread and Puppet has been formed by the happy assimilation of art and life which marks Peter Schumann's own life.

Perhaps more closely aligned with the San Francisco Mime Troupe than with the Bread and Puppet Theatre, El Teatro Campesino (The Farm Worker's Theatre) got its start in 1965 when Luis Valdez (b. 1941) began performing agitprop skits with the striking Mexican and Chicano grape pickers in the Delano Valley of California. Interested in plays and acting since childhood, Valdez spent a summer as an apprentice with the Mime Troupe, and saw the possibility for the interconnection of art and politics. Beginning with a company of amateur actors, made up of migrant workers and union volunteers, Valdez developed *"actos,"* or short bilingual sketches from the improvisations of the group. Working specifically towards the goal of unionization under Cesar Chavez, these short pieces blatantly conveyed messages of political and human exploitation. Each piece was approximately fifteen minutes long, capable of being performed on the picket lines, and each made a clear point. In *Los Dos Caros del Patronicito (The Two Faces of the Boss,* 1965), the capitalist Boss, wearing an appropriate Pig mask, tries to convince a migrant worker of the joys of grape picking. He succeeds so well that he convinces himself and removes his Pig mask. Placing the mask on the worker, the former Boss takes on the role of a farmhand. When he is harshly awakened to the realities of the farmworker's life, the *Patronicito* demands his old job of Boss back, calling on Cesar Chavez for help.

Humor and satire are essential to El Teatro Campesino. In 1967, the group moved to Del Rey, California, and broadened their political agenda to include other aspects of Chicano life. *Actos* continued to explore social issues, such as in *Vietnam Campesino* (1970) which shows drafted Chicano workers in Vietnam, killing peasants who are similarly exploited by their government. By the early 1970s, the focus of El Teatro Campesino changed from presenting issues of contention to building a sense of unity and brotherhood amongst Chicanos, and, ultimately, a harmony with the wider universe. This move away from radical activist theatre caused severe friction at the Chicano and Latin American Theatre Festival held in Mexico in 1974 between El Teatro Campesino and other radical Latin-American troupes. Many of these progressive troupes had taken El Teatro Campesino as their inspiration and role model, and felt betrayed by Valdez's expanded point of view.

A scene from the world premiere of *Zoot Suit* by Luis Valdez. Pictured are (front) Daniel Valdez and Miguel Delgado and (back) Roberta Delgado Esparza, Paul Mace, Mike Gomez, Enrique Castillo, Edward James Olmos, Vikie Sheckter, and Ronald Linares. *Photo courtesy Mark Taper Forum.*

Two scenes from *Los Dos Caros del Patronicito (The Two Faces of the Boss)*. The Boss is wearing the mask. The scripts are a mixture of English and Mexican slang. To help those in the audience who do not speak English, the actors wear signs to identify the character's name or role. For example: *Patroncito* (grower), *Amelgista* (striker), *Contratista* (contractor).

El Teatro Campesino has metamorphasized slowly into a sophisticated commercial theatre company, particularly through the success of Valdez's *Zoot Suit* (1978), a production which moved to New York after an initial run at the Mark Taper Forum in Los Angeles, and was billed as the first Chicano Broadway production. Despite the fact that *Zoot Suit* is concerned with the historically based 1940 Chicano riots, and the subsequent wrongful convictions of Chicano gang members, critics of Valdez accused him of "selling out" to the establishment. More recently, Valdez's Hollywood success as the screenwriter of *La Bamba* (1987), and El Teatro Campesino's increasingly substantial corporate gifts list, has made the group a target for Chicano scorn. In the 1990s, Valdez's decision to cast an Italian-American in the leading role of his movie about the life of Frida Kahlo was met by outrage from artists in the Hispanic community. Consequently, plans to begin shooting the film have been delayed indefinitely.

Valdez remains committed to voicing the history of Hispanics, and also believes that Chicano theatre arts must compete successfully with the best of professional theatres. In one sense, the voyage from migrant farmworkers to successful commercial production represents the ultimate accomplishment of the radical theatre movement. Both on stage and in film, Valdez's work has and continues to provide employment, artistic success and viability for Chicano theatre. It is sadly ironic that some of his most vociferous detractors are those same artists who generated their own success from the model of El Teatro Campesino.

Theatre of the Absurd

Samuel Beckett (1906-1989), Eugene Ionesco (b. 1912), Arthur Adamov (1908-1989), and Jean Genet (1910-1986) are considered the mainstays of absurdist drama. Although theatre of the absurd is a French phenomenon, Genet is the only native Frenchman. Beckett is Irish; Adamov, Russian; and Ionesco, Rumanian. All came to France, and all wrote their plays in French. All four writers share a similar philosophy which suggests that the

Fernando Arrabal's *The Emperor and The Architect* is an excellent example of an absurdist play. This scene is from a production by Humboldt State University. (See Chapter 18.)

human condition is one of isolation and futility, and that man is at the mercy of unknown forces. These writers have influenced a host of dramatists throughout the world, including Edward Albee (b. 1928), Harold Pinter (b. 1930), Günter Grass (b. 1927), Max Frisch (b. 1911), Slawomir Mrozek (b. 1932), Vacláv Havel (b. 1936), Fernando Arrabal (b. 1932) and Friedrich Duerrenmatt (b. 1921).

The absurdist playwrights believe that life is absurd because it has no "purpose or goal or objective." We are born without asking to be born, and we die without really seeking death. Our entire lives are spent like puppets hanging in limbo. We don't know where we came from, and we don't know where we are going. Taking a cue from Albert Camus' *The Myth of Sisyphus* (1942), who spent eternity rolling a boulder up a hill only to have it roll down again, the absurdists see our lives spent in futile, hopeless labor. We do the same things day in and day out with slight variation. Life seems meaningless because we do not know the answers; we possess only functional knowledge. We therefore invent religion and fill our lives with meaningless devices to rationalize our existence and to keep our minds off the fact that we will one day die. We are not only ignorant of life, but incapable of doing anything about our ignorance. This makes us insecure. Furthermore, in that all things are doomed to death and decay, we cannot create anything of significance. Life is thus a senseless, meaningless concept devoid of purpose of significance—it is absurd.

The classic example of absurdist drama is Samuel Beckett's *Waiting for Godot*, (1953); more properly, the title, *En Attendant Godot*, should be translated *While Waiting for Godot*. Essentially a novelist and poet in the thirties and forties, Beckett turned to the dramatic form in the 1950s and *Godot* represents his first effort. It has been translated in over a dozen languages, has sold over 50,000 copies in French, and over 350,000 copies in Beckett's English translation. For this play as well as his other efforts, Samuel Beckett was awarded the Nobel Prize for literature in 1969.

Existentialistic in philosophy, the play focuses on two tramps, Estragon and Vladimir, who wait on the side of a road for someone name Godot. While waiting, they occupy their time playing games, complaining about life, sleeping, calling each other the nicknames of Didi and Gogo, and generally engaging in various diversions.

Joining Vladimir and Estragon is Pozzo, a tyrant, and his terrified slave, Lucky, who is forced by Pozzo to show his tricks, do a dance, and demonstrate that he can think (which he really cannot). These two disappear into the darkness. Later they return—Pozzo is blind and Lucky, dumb. They are unable to recall who they are, let alone who they were. The entire play focuses not on who the characters are, but what the characters do while waiting. As Estragon reflects, "Nothing happens, nobody comes, nobody goes, it's awful."

The play has two acts, each of which ends with

Eugene Ionesco, a Rumanian by birth, is among the most successful of the absurdists. *The Bald Soprano* (1949), *The Lesson* (1950), *The Chairs* (1952), and *Rhinoceros* (1960) remain classics from the Theatre of the Absurd. *Photo Agnes Varda, courtesy New York Public Library at Lincoln Center.*

a boy delivering the message that Godot cannot come today but maybe tomorrow. Estragon then asks "What shall we do?" to which Vladimir replies, in existentialistic fashion, "Wait for Godot." Like Vladimir and Estragon, mankind occupies itself in a variety of diversions while waiting.

Historically, the term *absurdism* was coined by Martin Esslin in the book *Theatre of the Absurd* (1961). The roots of absurdism are generally traced back to Alfred Jarry's (1873-1907) *Ubu Roi* (1896), which was first produced in Paris. Ubu is the false King of Poland, who personifies human greed, brutality, selfishness and cruelty. The manner in which Ubu was characterized became a trademark of the theatre of the absurd—the external characterization of a character's internal qualities. Rather than infer the character's psychological nature, dramatists of the absurd theatre blatantly express the character's nature. For example, Ubu's human grossness is shown by his enormous belly, mask and exaggerated costume. The character is made larger than life.

Influences upon absurdism come from many sources. In addition to Jarry, Guillaume Appollinaire (1880-1918), Antonin Artaud (1896-1948), August Strindberg (1849-1912), Franz Kafka (1883-1924) and the existentialist Camus (1913-1960), lent their influences. The influences can be noted in some of the outstanding characteristics of the absurdist theatre.

1. Conventional language is degraded. This device is utilized to emphasize that there is a lack of communication between people. The absurdists believe language is empty of substance and thus has fallen into a mere convention of slogans and cliches.

2. The focus of absurd drama lies in the action. No connection exists between what the characters say and what they do.

3. Characters are patterned after Ubu; they are not literary characters, but are cardboard figures who entertain.

4. Conventional logic is rejected.

5. The audience is forced to ask not what will happen next, but what is happening.

Outside the United States

Unlike many earlier artistic movements, the radical theatre movement was ignited primarily in the United States, spreading throughout Europe after international tours by many American companies. The 1960s were globally troubled times and the theatre community was quick to respond, taking its cue from the practices of such troupes as the Living Theatre, the Open Theatre and the Performance Group. France and Italy developed some of the most outspoken groups, many of which have been in existence now for over twenty years.

In France, one of the oldest (and still successful) groups is the Théâtre du Soleil, under the direction

Günter Grass (b. 1927), Germany's best known contemporary author. The majority of his plays belong to the absurdist tradition. As a novelist, he is best known for *The Tin Drum*. Grass was awarded the Georg Buchner Prize in 1965. *Courtesy German Information Center.*

of Ariane Mnouchkine. Founded in 1964 as a worker's cooperative, its first performances were heavily rooted in realistic acting techniques and adherence to established texts. The first overtly political piece to break away from the group's traditional theatre practice was the company's creation of *1789* (1970). By this time, the theatre had taken up residency in an abandoned munitions factory, the *Cartoucherie*, on the outskirts of Paris. *1789* was created collectively, emerging from the group's research into the French Revolution and improvisations developed by the actors. The parallels to the 1968 student riots in Paris were unmistakable. With this production, and its sequel, *1793*, Théâtre du Soleil became recognized as one of the most significant companies in the world.

Productions since then have reflected the company's commitment to social reform, adapting theatre techniques from world theatre, including the commedia dell'arte, Asian theatre and classical Greek. Like many of its American counterparts, Théâtre du Soleil experiments with audience/actor relationships. In *L'Age d'Or (The Age of Gold*, 1975), no seating was provided and audiences moved with the actors from gigantic craters to the valley in between. One of the trademarks of the Théâtre du Soleil is its refusal to separate actors from audience, beginning with the audience's arrival. In 1992, for example, audience members entering the Brooklyn Academy of Music (BAM) for the internationally toured *Les Atrides* first passed through a public area that served as the actors' dressing room. Similarly, the Cartoucheries has no fixed performance area; rather, the entire interior space is redesigned appropriately for each production.

Unlike some political theatre groups who directly address topical issues, the Théâtre du Soleil re-examines historical moments with the intent of commenting on these earlier eras metaphorically. Ariane Mnouchkine, the talented director of the group, views theatre as a means to come to terms with history, and many of the textual/subject choices of the group reflect her vision. Since its early success, the company has moved away from the collective scripting techniques, and has become dedicated to strong, poetical texts that provide the springboard for historical understanding.

Elsewhere in France, Théâtre Populaire du Lorraine (1963) and Teatre de la Carriera (1968) were formed as theatres "of the people." Following the 1968 uprisings in Paris, Théâtre Populaire du Lorraine abandoned the classical canon of theatrical literature and instead created original satires devoted to exploring the cultural and economic problems of the Lorraine region. Similarly, the work of Teatre de la Carriera is geographically and culturally specific, providing themes based on Occitanian socioeconomic problems. Like El Teatro Campesino in the United States (which uses a combination of Spanish and English languages),

plays are performed in a mixture of Occitanian and French dialects to emphasize the distinct regionality of the company.

Although he began his career as a set designer and decorator, Dario Fo (b. 1926) has quickly emerged as one of the finest comic actors in the international theatre, as well as a gifted playwright and director. His work is undeniably political, and has its roots in the agitprop theatre that evolved in the 1960s. Fo began his writing and acting career with a series of cabaret-style skits, which he performed with his wife, the actress Franca Rame. His earliest company, Associazione Nuovo Scena, was operated under the jurisdiction of the Italian Communist Party and worked to bring performances to working-class audiences throughout Italy. The political relationship between Fo's work and the ideology of the party soon erupted in discord, and Fo established Colletivo Teatrale La Commune in 1968. Located in an abandoned vegetable warehouse in the working-class district of Milan, the company incorporated commedia dell'arte techniques, singing, mime, juggling, and a wide range of satirized topics. Since 1986, it has ceased to exist as a production company; Dario Fo and Franca Rame are the only remaining members. However, together the two performers are the most popular international theatre artists of our time. They perform throughout Europe with regularity, and Dario Fo's works are performed throughout the world.

One of Fo's most popular pieces is *Mistero Buffo*, first created in 1969. It is a one man show, Fo's signature piece, and relies heavily on the skill of the performer, who must make lightning speed changes. A "comic mystery play," borrowing from the medieval mysteries performed by wandering players, the piece satirizes the Church's upholding of the status quo by using scriptures to point out the existence of the "haves" and the "have nots." His plays, *Morte Accidentale di un anarchio (Accidental Death of an Anarchist*, 1971), and *Non si paga, non si paga! (We Can't Pay, We Won't Pay!*, 1974), gained Fo popular acclaim by their productions in the United States and England. A series of short feminist pieces, under the title *Female Parts,* was created collectively by Dario and his wife featuring Franca Rame as the performer.

Because of their popularity abroad, Fo and Rame continue to operate their political venue throughout Italy without government subsidy. In addition to presenting powerful satires aimed at illustrating the oppression of women and workers, the performances are enormously entertaining in the hands of these two gifted performers. They continue to set an example for political theatre throughout the world.

With the exception of Colletivo Teatrale La Commune and Peter Schumann's Bread and Puppet Theatre, most political theatres must rely on some form of commercial or government subsidy. This has had the effect of lessening the stridency of their collective political voices. Because each of the groups has a distinct style of performance, their plays are not readily transferable for production by any other group. Frequent fluctuations of performers, writers and directors, as well as changing political conditions, mean that political groups often do not have the stability and longevity that mark establishment theatre companies.

The 1970s and 1980s: New Approaches

Though the revolutionary fervor of the 1960s and early 1970s began to fade, the radical theatre movement had triggered some fundamental questions about the practice and purpose of theatre. Who is theatre for, and what is its purpose? What does it mean to "interpret" a text? To what degree do the interpreters (directors, actors, designers) become authors themselves? Is there any singularly "right" style for a dramatic text?

These theoretical questions were also provoked by the changing intellectual climate of the 1970s and 1980s. The two theories that have had the most profound influence on theatre since the 1960s are postmodernism and poststructuralism (deconstruction). Postmodernists contend that twentieth

century art has evolved beyond "modernism"—the early twentieth century term for contemporary art movements such as expressionism and epic theatre. Within an expressionistic text, for example, all of the elements are unified by their adherence to expressionistic style: action, design, and performance. Oppositely, postmodernists see value in intermingling dramatic styles and forms, as well as different periods and mediums. Acknowledging no difference in value between "high art" and "low art" (popular art), postmodernists often combine the two, resulting in startling new insights. Some artists, such as Charles Ludlam, argued that there are no new ideas. His theatre, the Ridiculous Theatrical Company, "recycled culture," showing us new images of familiar material so that we might view them with renewed and altered significance.

Poststructuralism (deconstruction) supported many of the elements of postmodernism. Jacques Derrida (b. 1930: *Writing and Difference,* 1967; English translation, 1978) is the founding father of deconstructionist thought. Deconstructionists argue that language itself lacks the ability to communicate objectively. Linguistically communicated statements are the result of imbedded ideologies which may be broken down into an infinite number of different meanings. Each statement is accompanied by its unspoken double (or triple, or quadruple); for everything that is expressed (privileged), there is another element that is suppressed (ignored). The impact of this on theatre is profound: there can never be any single "right" reading of a work, for there are always additional readings of which even the author may not have been aware.

Although there are many practitioners of postmodernism and poststructuralism in the contemporary theatre in America, a few groups and individuals will serve to illustrate the practice: Richard Foreman's (b. 1937) Ontological-Hysteric Theatre, Mabou Mines, the Wooster Group and the Ridiculous Theatre Company.

Richard Foreman writes and directs his own pieces for the Ontological-Hysteric Theatre, which he founded in 1968. Some of his earliest works, *Dr.*

Selavy's Magic Theatre (1972), *Pandering to the Masses* (1974), and *Rhoda in Potatoland* (1974), use the theatre as a means to deconstruct the process of thought, and to show, in an obvious and explicit way, that art is being made. Like his plays, Foreman's writing process is non-linear, made up of notes and passages he has written over a period of time. In discussing his own methods, Foreman relates how he spreads all of his jottings out on a couch or table, and then begins to assemble them into a completed "play." Actor's lines are similarly interchangeable. It is not unusual for Foreman to transfer lines from one character to another as the script is formulated. For many of his performances, Foreman sits in the front row of the theatre as an audience member, a director, and a sound board operator. Sound effects, and his own voice amplified over a microphone, direct audience members to focus their attention on certain ideas, moments or characters in the play. Most of Foreman's plays feature the actress Kate Manheim, who, according to Foreman, allowed him to explore much of the erotic material that appears in the plays. The simultaneous existence of eroticism and intellectualism is an awareness that Foreman seeks to make his audience confront:

> The cold, presentational setting made the eroticism more present, palpable, shocking, but at the same time, it was something the spectators had to deal with in an almost clinical manner. If you became empathetically involved in a romantic scene between two actors, you forget you're watching a staged performance and identify with the actors—you become aroused as if you were a part of that erotic scene. But if the eroticism is staged in a detached, presentational manner, you may then be led to ask, Do I feel awkward confronting this? Sexually aroused? What is my attitude towards this? Am I able to function in the way that I want to function, using my head, applying my aesthetic sensibility, or am I swamped by my erotic response? And isn't this an interesting problem—working out the relationship between the variety of feelings this scene arouses in me?
> *(Unbalancing Acts)*

The Ontological-Hysteric Theatre is Richard Foreman's vision of a world in which he controls all of the elements: lights, sound, script and focus.

Because of this, audience members often leave bemused. However, even his more recent, less "theatrical" pieces leave the audience cognizant of their thinking processes, especially as these processes war with their erotic or emotional selves for dominance.

Mabou Mines (named after the mining town in Canada where the group was first formed, though it is now based in New York) was formed as a collaborative structure in 1969. Since its inception, the nine member group has evolved so that various members take control at different times. Perhaps the two most well-known members of the group are Lee Breuer and JoAnne Akalaitis. Their approaches to theatre in some ways typify the collective, though synthesis is hardly an accurate description of the varied interests of Mabou Mines. Lee Breuer (b. 1937) achieved significant fame through his treatment of Sophocles' *Oedipus at Colonus*, renamed *The Gospel at Colonus* (1983) which was set as a modern day black gospel meeting. Within this setting, Breuer created the ecstasy of religious feeling, so essential to the ancient Greek theatre, by using four famous gospel combos, a full choir and Clarence Fountain, a blind gospel singer, as the blind Oedipus. Breuer's later work with *Lear* (1990) was an investigation of power, specifically women with power. Transporting Shakespeare's play to a location in Georgia, Breuer reversed the gender of the characters and transformed the warring nations into rival racial groups.

JoAnne Akalaitis (b. 1937) has achieved an international reputation as a director, but also as a creator of her own works. *Dead End Kids* (1982) is a piece that focuses on the ever-present threat of nuclear destruction, but also explores the quest for knowledge that gave impetus to the discovery of nuclear power. Characters from history (Madame Curie, Albert Einstein, Faust, General Groves) interact with a magician, twentieth century nerds, a sixteenth century alchemist, cub scouts, and ordinary citizens in a collage of theatrical devices, including the use of film and music. Her vision of Samuel Beckett's *Endgame* (1984) at the American Repertory Theatre in Cambridge, Massachusetts, resulted in a highly publicized controversy over the author's rights to dictate, or oversee, the production of his or her scripts. Akalaitis set the play in an abandoned subway tunnel, one of the few places that might provide shelter for inhabitants following a nuclear holocaust. Incidental music composed by Philip Glass was played on high tech electronic instruments. In addition, Akalaitis chose to cast the show interracially, Hamm and his father played by black actors and Hamm's mother played by a white actress. Samuel Beckett brought legal action against the American Repertory Company, arguing that the director's changes distorted the meaning of his play. Although Akalaitis maintained that her casting choices reflected her desire to show that the play could be about anyone, Beckett insisted that the cross-racial casting implied statements about miscegenation. The production was withdrawn.

A similar debate occurred with the Wooster Group's planned production of *L. S. D. (... Only the High Points)* in 1984. The Wooster Group uses deconstructionist techniques in many of its pieces. *L. S. D.* intended to show the similarities between colonial and modern day witch hunts by juxtaposing sections of Arthur Miller's *The Crucible* with readings from Timothy Leary, the self-appointed leader of the "tune in, drop out" generation. Leary is dramatically pitted against Miller's protagonist, John Proctor. The witchcraft of colonial America is juxtaposed with the 1960s persecution of Leary's followers who used hallucinogens. John Proctor stoically awaits his sentence in jail, while Leary, a tarnished hero, "rats" on his followers to secure his own release. Both men stand in opposition to the status quo of societal norms. Arthur Miller contended that the Wooster Group's production would "among other things, tend to inhibit first-class productions" of *The Crucible.* Ten days after *L. S. D.* opened in New York, the Wooster Group received notice to "cease and desist" from including Miller's work in their piece. After a further month of struggle with lawyers and courts, the Wooster Group withdrew the production.

Theatre of the Ridiculous was created by John Vaccaro, Bill Walters, and Harvey and Ron Tavel.

Charles Ludlam (1943-1987), one of the actors of the group, formed the Ridiculous Theatrical Company, a rival company, in 1968. It has been described as:

> an anarchic undermining of political, sexual, psychological and cultural categories, frequently in dramatic structures that parody classical literary forms or re-function American popular entertainments, and always allude to themselves as "performances." A highly self-conscious style, the Ridiculous tends towards camp, kitsch, transvestism, the grotesque, flamboyant visuals, and literary dandyism. It is comedy beyond absurd because it is less intellectual, more earthy, primal, liberated. Not tragi-comedy but metaphysical burlesque, the Ridiculous offers a new version of the "clown." Its dependency on the icons, artifacts and entertainments of mass culture in America—the "stars," old movies, popular songs, television, and advertising—make the Ridiculous a truly indigenous American approach to making theatre. *(Theatre of the Ridiculous)*

The Ridiculous Theatrical Company spoofs many readily recognized plays, movies, and novels in what Ludlam referred to as "recycling culture." By performing established "classics," both popular and literary, in high camp, overblown acting styles, which always includes cross-dressing, the Ridiculous Theatrical Company calls into question some of the most common assumptions of contemporary society. Cross-dressing calls attention to the purely artificial, yet widely accepted, gender constructions that have been imposed upon western civilization. Although Ludlam died in 1988, his lover and fellow company member, Everett Quinton, continues to operate the company with the same focus.

One of the company's most popular pieces, *The Mystery of Irma Vep* (1984), is based loosely on a cross between the Hitchcock thriller, *Rebecca*, and Bronte's *Wuthering Heights* and explores the hackneyed cliches of gothic romance, including hidden passages, a creaking mansion, werewolves and mysterious mummies. It is in the performance of the piece, however, that its significance is most fully revealed, for the entire play is performed by

THE MYSTERY OF IRMA VEP
CHARLES LUDLAM

CHARACTERS
LADY ENID HILLCREST, Lord Edgar's new bride
LORD EDGAR HILLCREST, the lord of Mand-
  acrest
NICODEMUS UNDERWOOD, the outdoor help
JANE TWISDEN, the long-suffering serving maid,
  faithful to her original mistress
AN INTRUDER
ALCAZAR, an excavator (and entrepreneur) of
  Egyptian artifacts
PEV AMRI, a resuscitated Egyptian mummy
IRMA VEP, the true owner of Mandacrest

SETTING
Act I takes place in the library drawing room of
Mandacrest, an estate near Hampstead Heath. Act
II, Scene 1, takes place in various places in Egypt,
specifically the newly uncovered tomb of an Egyptian mummy. Act II, Scenes 2 and 3, returns to the
library drawing room of Mandacrest.

BACKGROUND
The Mystery of Irma Vep is a tour-de-force piece
intended to be performed by two actors who skillfully quick-change and appear in different costumes, genders and character roles from one moment to the next. This type of performance requires great skill and consummate concentration.
In this play Charles Ludlam made use of the many
devices and themes of the "penny-dreadful." When
the play opened, it truly established the Ridiculous Theatre Company as a major artistic entity.

STORY
Act I, Scene 1: The play begins as a stormy
evening is settling in on Hampstead Heath. The
new mistress, Lady Enid has just awaken (it being
her habit to sleep all day and rise at sunset), and,
for the first time, she sees the portrait of her prede-
cessor, the late Lady Hillcrest. Though she feels as
if a cat had walked over her grave when she gazes
at the portrait, she is calmed when Lord Edgar
arrives home from his day of hunting (dragging
the carcass of the wolf he has shot). She persuades
him to have the portrait taken down; satisfied, she
leaves to change for dinner. Both Nicodemus and
Jane have misgivings about the new mistress; Jane,

loyal to her true mistress, refuses to allow the
picture to be removed. When Nicodemus joyfully
shows Jane that the master has killed the wolf at
last, she remarks that it is "the wrong wolf."

Scene 2: Later that evening, Jane and Lady
Enid are settled in before the dying embers of the
fire. Lady Enid persuades Jane to tell her some of
the history of Mandacrest. Jane reveals that the
master had a son, Victor, who died a gruesome
death—his throat was ripped out by Lady Irma's
pet wolf, also named Victor. Jane plants the suspicion that it was no ordinary wolf that killed the boy
in the snow—but a werewolf, for there were human tracks surrounding the body. After Jane re-
tires for the evening, Lady Enid is attacked by a
skeletal intruder, who drags her off through the
double doors, emitting horrible sucking noises
above her terrified screams. Lord Edgar and Jane
enter and begin the search for Lady Enid as
Nicodemus appears, carrying her limp body.
Nicodemus has seen a dog-like skull staring out at
him, and Lord Edgar rushes to get his gun. The
scene ends as the gun goes off, striking the portrait
of Lady Irma, which begins to bleed. Nicodemus
sees visions of the dead woman, a ghost woman
"with ashes on her breath."

Scene 3: Lord Edgar is questioning Lady Enid
about what happened and she tells him of the book
she was reading before the attack. It was a chapter
on Egyptian mummies, specifically the Princess
Pev Amri, "She Who Sleeps but Will One Day
Wake." Lady Enid exits, refusing attention for the
wound on her neck, and Nicodemus and the master confer. Lord Edgar voices the suspicion that
there is one at Mandacrest who will never die—a
vampire. He resolves to go to Egypt to discover the
answer amongst the pyramids and their sacred
mummies.

ACT II, Scene 1: In the company of Alcazar,
Lord Edgar discovers an unopened tomb. Ad-
vancing into the tomb, Lord Edgar finds the mum-
mified body of a woman—Princess Pev Amri. She
awakes, indicating a stiffness in her spine (ex-
claiming "Cairo! Cairo! Practor!") and mysteri-
ously turns into a decomposed corpse. The scene
ends with Lord Edgar vowing to bring her back
again.

THE MYSTERY OF IRMA VEP, continued

Scene 2: Evening of the full moon. Jane and Nicodemus are discussing Lady Enid's insomnia, when Nicodemus, screaming, is transformed into a wolf and runs out the door. Lady Enid appears and confides in Jane that she feels Lord Edgar and she are drifting apart. Jane recommends that Lady Enid appear in Lord Edgar's favorite dress as a special surprise for him. As Jane exits, Lord Edgar arrives, having just returned from purchasing silver bullets. Vowing to kill the werewolf, Nicodemus, at the window, fears the bullets are meant for him. Appearing in the dress that Jane suggested, Lady Enid discovers a secret panel in the fireplace, where she hears a voice that claims to be Lady Irma— a prisoner of the house. Lord Edgar enters and, seeing Lady Enid in the dress, demands she take it off. He tells Lady Enid that he is Irma's prisoner and is immediately choked by some unseen force. Nicodemus comes to the rescue and Lord Edgar goes off in pursuit of the werewolf. Opening the secret panel in the fireplace, Lady Enid is attacked by Irma who announces that "Irma Vep" is "vampire" anagrammatized. Ripping the face off Irma Vep, Lady Enid discovers that she is really Jane, who then attacks Lady Enid with a cleaver. Announcing that she killed Lady Irma the same way, Jane is suddenly grabbed by Nicodemus and dragged outdoors. Lord Edgar enters and shoots Nicodemus, who is transformed into a werewolf. The play ends with Lady Enid and Lord Edgar alone at Mandacrest, Enid confessing that it was she who impersonated Pev Amri in Egypt in order to gain his love.

two male actors who cross-dress and quick change as needed to portray all of the characters. At first glance, the overdone performance of a hairy chested male in a low cut white dress may be a cause for humor. However, as Ludlam showed in his moving interpretation of *Camille* (1973), gender roles, unlike biological determinations of sex, are largely artificial constructions of society. Ludlam deconstructs the notion of "masculine" and "feminine" behavior with hilarity and power.

Deconstruction is an empowering methodology in the rapid growth of feminist theatre. In the midst of the 1960s, feminism was strengthened by the growing civil rights movement and the impetus toward global awareness. The publication of Kate Millett's *Sexual Politics* (1970) brought a clear-sighted vision of the existing gender bias in art and politics, pointing out that historically art and literature have been dominated by men. Women characters have been created from exclusively male points of view. Combined with "New Historicism," feminist theatre scholars and artists were inspired to re-evaluate the images of women in plays, past and present, and to re-create those images free from "the male gaze." Deconstruction is a logical ally in the process of exploring the cultural fictions of womanhood portrayed by male dominated female characters, particularly in texts written by men.

Feminist theatre is an exploration of the exclusion of women from the patriarchal social, economic, cultural and intellectual models. Feminist plays often place women at their center, and explore women's marginalization on the basis of sex. Not all feminists, however, agree with one another on what the goals of a feminist theatre are. Feminist theatre groups began forming in the early 1970s, and have continued to gain power and prestige. The earliest feminist groups in the United States are New York's New Feminist Theatre and the Los Angeles Feminist Theatre, both of which began in 1969 within a few months of each other. Many of the first theatre companies that identified themselves as "feminist" or "women's theatre" were initiated by playwrights, performers and directors who had gotten their professional start with one of the political theatre groups of the 1960s. For many of these women artists, a growing

A scene from *Babes in the Bighouse* by Megan Terry as performed by the Omaha Magic Theater.

awareness of their peripheral positions within the male-dominated theatre structure brought a desire to create a different kind of theatre. Megan Terry (b. 1932), sometimes referred to as "the mother of American feminist theatre" and one of the early members of Chaikin's Open Theatre, moved to join Jo Ann Schmidman and the Omaha Magic Theatre in 1974 to free herself and her writing from patriarchal suffocation. Megan Terry was also instrumental in founding the Women's Theatre Council (1972), along with Julie Bovasso, Rosalyn Drexler, Maia Irene Fornes, Adrienne Kennedy and Rochelle Owens.

Although many of the radical theatre groups of the 1960s allowed women much more freedom in the creative process than traditional theatre, disenchanted women playwrights were moving forces in the growth of feminist theatre. Playwright Martha Boesing of the Firehouse Theatre helped to found At the Foot of the Mountain (1974). The mission statement from the 1976 At the Foot of the Mountain brochure describes the focus of many early feminist theatre companies:

> At the Foot of the Mountain is a women's theatre—emergent, struggling, angry, joyous. Through our own consciousness-raising, workshops in vocal and body awareness, and varied improvisational and Gestalt disciplines, we are now in the process of developing a company voice, a company style. We are asking: What is a woman's space? What is a woman's ritual? How does it differ from the theatre of the patriarchy? We struggle to relinquish traditions such as linear plays, proscenium theatre, non-participatory ritual and seek to reveal theatre that is circular, intuitive, personally involving. We are a theatre of protest, witnesses to the destructiveness of a society which is alienated from itself, and a theatre of celebration, participants in the prophesy of a new world which is emerging through the rebirth of women's consciousness.

Aided by contemporary studies of women's psychology and moral development (Jean Baker Miller, *Towards a New Psychology of Women*, Carol Gilligan, *In a Different Voice*), women's theatre groups saw the necessity of honoring, rather than repressing, traditionally devalued qualities such as nurturing, intuition, emotionality, support and connection. For many women theatre artists, these new perspectives required a new kind of theatre organization, as well as new forms of play structure. Although not every woman's theatre nor every woman playwright definitively follows a proscriptive model, some of the dominant qualities of the emerging feminist theatre can be summarized as follows:

1. Theatres organized as collectives, rather than centered around a primary power figure, or leader;
2. An emphasis on process, as opposed to product;
3. Communication, in the plays, of an inner life as opposed to an emphasis on events;
4. Rejection of the well-made linear play formula in favor of more cyclical, imagistic forms of dramatic structure;
5. Celebration of the ambiguous and questions with no answers;
6. Acknowledgment of women's experience, in its many forms, as valid and important.

One of the most important outcomes of the emergence of feminist theatre groups has been the visibility it has provided for the work of women theatre artists, most notably women playwrights. The feminist theatre movement has been largely responsible for the development of a growing legion of women playwrights. Providing both space and time for the production of works that would be otherwise ignored by the traditional theatre, women's theatres have served an important function by making plays by women accessible to the general public and, most particularly, to women. In England, France and the United States, important women playwrights have been instrumental in transforming the drama: Simone Benmussa, Helene Cixous, Caryl Churchill, Pam Gems, Maria Irene Fornes, Ntozake Shange, Michelene Wandor,

Marsha Norman, Nell Dunn, and Wendy Wasserstein, to name a few.

Though still largely in its infancy, feminist dramatic theory began evolving formally in the 1980s. With the support of academic groups, such as the Association for Theatre in Higher Education (ATHE), which added a Women and Theatre Program (WTP) in 1975, theatre scholars, academicians and theorists have recently added to the growing body of feminist literary theory, expanding into considerations of performance and gender representation on stage. This attention to feminist concerns in the academic arena has led to two major developments: (1) an awakened interest in reconstructing the history of women in theatre and (2) the articulation of a dramatic theory of feminist literature. Early in the women's movement it became clear that not all women who identified themselves as feminists had similar goals and beliefs. In her book, *Feminist Theories for Dramatic Criticism* (1990), Gayle Austin defines three categories of feminist dramatic theory which are useful starting points:

Liberal
1. Minimizes the differences between men and women.
2. Works for success within system; reform, not revolt.
3. Individual more important than group.

Radical
1. Stresses superiority of female attributes and difference between male and female modes.
2. Favors separate female systems.
3. Individual more important than group.

Materialist
1. Minimizes biological differences between men and women.
2. Stresses material conditions of production such as history, race, class, gender.
3. Group more important than individual.

Even given these guidelines, it is difficult to categorize most feminist theatre groups or playwrights as consistently representing only a single viewpoint. In the 1990s, there are hundreds of feminist theatre groups in existence, devoted to

Lisa Mayo, Gloria Miguel and Muriel Miguel of Spiderwoman Theatre in *Winnetou's Snake-Oil Show from Wigwam City. Courtesy New World Theatre, University of Massachusetts.*

creating theatre that speaks to women's issues. Some are organized under the artistic leadership of a single person, while others operate as collectives, rejecting the patriarchal model for group structures and choosing instead to share decision making power collectively. Recognizing both the similarity of experience for all women, and the difference of experience between women of color, women with lesbian-identified orientations, women of disability and white "privileged" women, for example, the scope and variety of feminist theatre groups appear nearly endless. The Split Britches Company, formed by Peggy Shaw, Lois Weaver and Deborah Margolin (1981), concentrates on the history of women who are marginalized by society, particularly lesbian women. Peggy Shaw and Lois Weaver are also the co-founders of the New York WOW cafe, a performance space dedicated to presenting the works of women. Spiderwoman Theatre is one of several groups constructed of Native American women who relate their ethnic-specific experiences. Formed by Lisa Mayo, Gloria Miguel and Muriel Miguel, Spiderwoman Theatre addresses issues and complexities of heritage using satire, musical comedy and poetry. A quick glance at the names of some feminist theatre companies gives an indication of the diversity within the movement: Teatro de la Esperanza, Asian Lesbians of the West Coast, "Ain't I a Woman? Theatre, the Company of

Women, Women's Experimental Theatre. Since 1980, women's theatre festivals have been annual occurrences in both the United States and Great Britain.

A similar diversity of experience can be seen in the global theatre of the 1990s. Sparked perhaps in part by the feminists' recognition of simultaneous sameness and difference within women's issues, as well as changing popular beliefs in nationalism, internationalism and ethnicity, the dominant movement in theatre of the 1990s is towards interculturalism. Led by Peter Brook's *Mahabbarata* and his subsequent pleas for a theatre that is based on a merging of cultural traditions, leading avant-garde directors (such as Lee Breuer, Robert Wilson, Ariane Mnouchkine, Tadashi Suzuki, Peter Sellars, to name a few) are exploring the meanings of culture, concepts of universality and authorship. As the world rapidly becomes a stage for the "global village," experimentation in overlapping and occasionally discordant cultural values becomes increasingly relevant. Multi-language and multi-cultural productions reflect the highly integrated impact of a shrinking world. Balanced between the risk of reducing class, gender and ethnicity to a dull sameness, and the danger of creating greater isolationism, the theatre of the twenty-first century faces challenges on stages that are no longer rooted in single nations.

Selected Readings

Austin, Gayle. *Feminist Theories for Dramatic Criticism.* Ann Arbor: University of Michigan Press, 1990.

Croyden, Margaret. *Lunatics, Lovers, and Poets: The Contemporary Experimental Theatre.* New York, 1974

Derrida, Jacques. "The Theatre of Cruelty and the Closure of Representation," in *Writing Difference,* trans. Alan Bass. Chicago, 1978.

Esslin, Martin. *The Theatre of the Absurd.* Rev. ed. New York, 1969.

Keyssar, Helen. *Feminist Theatre.* (London: Macmillan Publishers, Inc., 1984)

Shank, Theodore. *American Alternative Theatre.* (New York: Grove Press, 1982)

van Erven, Eugene. *Radical People's Theatre.* (Bloomington: Indiana University Press, 1988)

Back issues of: *(TDR) The Drama Review, Women and Performance, American Theatre, Performing Arts Journal, New Theatre Quarterly, Theatre Journal.*

Vocabulary

1.	Jerzy Grotowski	YE zhee gruh TOW skee
2.	Antonin Artaud	An tuh NEEN ahr TOH
3.	Joseph Chaikin	CHAY kin
4.	Richard Schechner	SHEK nuhr
5.	El Teatro Campesino	el tay AHT roh cahm pe see noh
6.	Théâtre du Soleil	Tay ahtr dew so leh y
7.	Ariane Mnouchkine	a ree on ma nush shin
8.	Le Théâtre Populaire du Lorraine	luh tay ahtr pope u lair dew la rayn
9.	Albert Camus	al BAIR ka MUU
10.	Alfred Jarry	jah ree
11.	Arthur Adamov	AH duh maw
12.	Jean Claude van Itallie	Jon Claud von a tal lay
13.	Il Colletivo Teatrale La Commune	el ko let te vo tay ahtr ra lay la ka mune
14.	Jacques Derrida	zh ahk day ree da
15.	JoAnne Akalaitis	ACK o lite tis
16.	Vacláv Havel	vahs LAHF hah VEL
17.	Arrabel	AH rah bahl
18.	Ubu Roi	OO boo rwuh
19.	agitprop	AJ it PROP

CHAPTER FIFTEEN

৯

Oral Interpretation + Reader's Theatre = Performance Art: An Alternate Form

Honors Tour Group in San Diego State University television studios performing in staged Readers Theatre style. *From the Institute for Readers Theatre, William Adams, Director.*

Background

Not long ago a production moved from London's west side to Broadway to become a hit. The fact that this production was so successful in the United States was remarkable for several reasons. First, it was not a dramatic script in the traditional sense of the word; second, it was based on a nineteenth century novel; third, the production was divided into two parts requiring an audience to leave the theatre; fourth, the entire performance of the two parts ran just slightly under eight hours; and finally, good seats cost a little over $100 each. Most theatre goers will recognize that this production was none other than the Royal Shakespeare Company's adaptation of Charles Dickens' *Nicholas Nickelby* directed by Trevor Nunn. Nunn and the company fashioned the production directly from the novel. Although theatrical adaptations from novels are not unusual, the way in which this production was fashioned made it unique. Normally, an adaptation attempts to create a play out of another literary genre. The Royal Shakespeare Company attempted, however, to dramatize the novel without destroying its literary values. Long descriptive passages were woven into the production and were delivered by individual characters as narration. This technique is called Story Theatre.

Story Theatre was developed by Paul Sills and the Second City Company of Chicago founded in 1959. Sills, son of Viola Spolin who wrote the respected *Improvisation for the Theatre,* created a group of actors who improvised theatre pieces, sometimes from famous works of literature. Story theatre is aptly named because stories have long been a part of the total theatre experience.

The art of story telling is probably as old as the human race. Stories in the form of myths existed long before a methodology for transcribing them was formulated. We also know that members of various primitive groups became known as story tellers. In Greece, for example, evidence exists demonstrating that long before 534 B.C., oral storytellers or rhapsodes were reciting the *Iliad* and *Odyssey.* Later the first professional acting organization called the Artists of Dionysus included both poets and interpreters as well as actors among their ranks.

By the nature of its educational system, the medieval period disseminated news and epics primarily through artist interpreters in the form of minstrels, jongleurs, troubadours, scops or gleemen. In many ways these individuals were the historians and educators of their time. Being able to entertain an audience was considered a virtue by contemporaries. The very format of Geoffrey Chaucer's *Canterbury Tales* is a group of storytellers trying to ease the tedium of a long journey.

The Renaissance with Dante's *Divine Comedy* and Boccaccio's *Decameron* had the interpreter as chief disseminator. With the advent of the printing press, oral presentations were no longer the chief method in the dissemination of stories. During the Elizabethan period, the theatre as an institution began to replace the storyteller as the most accessible method of making words come alive. The art of expression was still individually debated as one would gather from Shakespeare's gentle admonition to the artist interpreter in *Hamlet:*

> Speak the speech, I pray you, as I pronounc'd it to you, trippingly off the tongue; but if you mouth it, as many of our players do, I had as lief the towncrier spoke my lines. Nor do not saw the air too much with your hand, thus, but use all gently; for in the very torrent, tempest, and, as I may say, whirlwind of your passion, you must acquire and beget a temperance that may give it smoothness. O, it offends me to the soul to hear a robustious periwigpated fellow tear a passion to tatters, to very rags, to split the ears of the groundlings, who, for the most part, are capable of nothing but inexplicable dumb shows and noise.

Although storytellers were plying their trade, little was written on the subject until the nineteenth and early twentieth century. Many of these works were concerned primarily with the art of speaking. John Bulwer, François Delsart, and James

Rush attempted to establish procedures of speaking. Delsart's work was translated for Americans by actor, playwright, inventor Steele MacKaye (1842-1894). This work formed the basis for what is now called the elocutionist school. Delsart postulated a series of performative gestures designed to reinforce emotional moments. Gestures such as clasped hands for praying, another hand behind the ear to represent a significant sound, and a hand on the forehead to indicate a distant vision are illustrated in his books.

Schools of expression were opened in Boston by two of MacKaye's students, S. S. Curry and Charles Wesley Emerson. Still another school was opened in New York by Leland Powers. Later *Werner's Magazine* became the first journal devoted to articles on vocal and bodily expression. Beginning in 1915 with S. H. Clark's *Interpretation of the Printed Page* and Rollo Anson Tallcott's *The Art of Acting and Public Reading* (1922), the art of storytelling or the public reading of literature was explored. The most important of these new works was the publication of Cornelius Carman Cunningham's monumental *Literature as a Fine Art* (1941), in which a new and exciting performance art form reached full formulation. Cunningham called the new form oral interpretation.

Oral Interpretation

Cunningham postulated a methodology different from any previous analytical theory that literature could be analyzed both for its intellectual and its emotional content. He felt that the artist interpreter must first intellectually understand the text as literature before the material can be analyzed as to its connotative powers. *Literature as a Fine Art* and a later textbook called *Making Words Come Alive* (1951) outlined his techniques. Cunningham identified ten sense stimuli appealed to through the process of association. He defined the oral interpreter as the "sentient instrument through whom words are given vividness and

fullness of meaning." He wanted the interpreter to be aware of certain sensory appeals so that words could be given their full connotations. Noting that psychologists differ as to definition, classification, and relationship of the senses as perceptual media, Cunningham formulated a list of senses which he postulated as being important in the process of interpretation. His list follows:

1. Sight—the *visual* sense
2. Hearing—the *auditory*, aural, or auditive sense
3. Muscular effort or strain of any kind, skeletal, affecting the outer parts of the body—the *kinaesthetic* sense
4. Stimulation of inner organs, the visceral as distinguished from skeletal—the *organic* sense
5. Motion, involving little or no muscle participation—the *kinetic* sense
6. Balance or loss of balance—the sense of *equilibrium*
7. Touch—the tactual or *tactile* sense
8. Smell—the *olfactory* sense
9. Taste—the *gustatory* sense
10. Temperature, cold or heat—the *thermal* or thermic sense

The key to the Cunningham methodology, then, was for the artist interpreter to prepare for performance by understanding the connotative power of words and phrases in a piece of literature being prepared for performance. This necessitated a thorough analysis of the senses appealed to through the process of association. Cunningham established one of the first departments of interpretation at Northwestern University. His pupils included such leaders in the field as Charlotte Lee, Robert Breen, John Edwards and William J. Adams, to name but a few.

Charlotte Lee, now retired, is considered Cunningham's champion in the field. Her text *Oral Interpretation* (1992) written with Timothy Gura is highly respected. Breen is famous for his work in Readers Theatre and his texts on the subject. John Edwards continues to work in the field at the University of New Hampshire and has tutored many excellent practitioners such as Ted Davis.

William J. Adams is currently director for the Institute for Readers Theatre, which sponsors workshops every year in cities throughout the world. The international institute has been highly successful and is open to all students regardless of theatrical experience. Adams has brought in a distinguished faculty and guest lecturers including Ray Bradbury, Sir John Gielgud, Michael Halifax, Mary Martin, Eva Marie Saint, Paul Sills, Tom Stoppard, and John Updike. His Board includes or has included Robert Breen, Charlotte Lee, Norman Corwin and Joanna Maclay. He also maintains the highly respected Readers Theatre Script Service out of his San Diego, California, office.

Readers Theatre

While Adams freely acknowledges the contributions of Cunningham and others to his conception of Readers Theatre, he has evolved a distinctive style of his own. Adams classifies Readers Theatre into four major styles: simple, staged, chamber, and story.

Simple Readers Theatre emphasizes oral interpretation to a greater degree than the other forms. It is essentially presentational in nature in that it does not attempt to re-create events, but rather suggests them in the mind's eye of the audience. In a sense, it is theatre of the imagination in that the audience must share the job of making the words come alive. Normally, Simple Readers Theatre is performed with the use of offstage focus. Offstage focus is rarely used in stage plays. It is a technique in which performers, generally seated in a line facing the audience, never look directly at each other. They visualize the character as being out beyond the audience. This method enables the audience to see every nuance in the face of the interpreters while making the audience feel they are a part of the conversation. Although this approach may seem awkward and artificial, it is surprisingly effective and powerful if done correctly. The following is Adams' method.

Style I: Simple Readers Theatre

The readers are usually arranged in a formal straight line seated on stools or chairs or standing at music stands. The readers are placed in a meaningful relationship to each other; that is, a narrator for a particular character is usually placed by that character. If there is a main character, that reader will probably be placed center.

Focus:

Narrators: Audience Focus. They "see" the characters in offstage focus;

Characters: Offstage focus.

Scripts:

Scripts are used. Even if lines are memorized for public performance, the cast should appear to read from their scripts. They should be controlled so that turning of pages and other physical usages do not distract the audience. Hardbacked folders are helpful to achieve good script handling. Scripts are not used as props in this style.

Actions:

No literal movements are used. Entrances are indicated merely by looking up from the script with an inner surge of psychic energy (called "taking the stage"). Exits are indicated by looking down at the script with a decrease of energy. Discard all pantomime and gestures, but encourage inner responses. Simple Readers Theatre should have the same energy, expressiveness, and involvement as more external styles.

Style II: Staged Readers Theatre

This performance style emphasizes the literature while providing certain theatrical elements that help to bring the text alive for readers and audience. It is particularly suited to beginners in Readers Theatre because the mime and other actions on stools are highly involved, but full stage movements are not required. It both controls and frees the performer. It uses the following techniques:

Set-up of Revolving Stools and Reading Stands.

Revolving stools and stands are usually placed in a straight line to indicate the nonrealistic style.

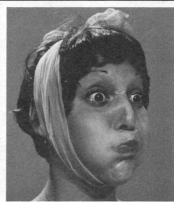

Below: A scene from a production of the Institute for Readers Theatre, William Adams, Director. Closeups above include *top left*, Todd Bittner; *top right*, Janet Breale; *bottom left*, Blake Maas; *bottom right*, Stacey Wein.

Stands are sometimes angled slightly toward each other to show the narrator's relationship to both audience and cast. Characters are placed to indicate characters' importance and relationships. Note: If stools are not available, chairs can be placed profile to the audience permitting 3/4 turns. Wooden stools can be given false revolving tops of plywood or enameled for easy turns.

Focus:

Narrators: Audience focus is used. Also narrators look from time to time at the performers with onstage focus as an added bridge between cast and audience, and because this style is more theatrical than simple Readers Theatre.

Characters: Offstage focus is generally used.

Script Folders:

Scripts are used in this style to prompt the reader, although there is no reason why the words should not be memorized if a polished performance is desired. They also emphasize the importance of the literature in Readers Theatre. Scripts are also used to suggest props (a tray, a fan, a frisbee, etc.).

Actions:

This style uses entrances and exits by characters revolving on stools front and back to audience. Gestures and mimes are also used, but they are highly selective with no attempt to do more than suggest the actions of the text. The mime is also done with offstage focus; that is, the reader hands an imaginary cup of coffee toward the offstage spot where the receiving character is visualized rather than to the actual reader on stage. It is important that the actions are synchronized so that the cup is not taken by the receiver before it is offered by the giver.

Style III: Story Theatre

Story Theatre is a term with two meanings:

1. A technique for arranging a literary text so that the characters speak their own narrations as well as dialogue, and can be performed in any style.

2. A staging form advocated by Paul Sills in which the actions are performed as conventional theatre by actors who speak their own narration and dialogue.

This second type of Story Theatre uses the following techniques:

Set-up:

Provide whatever stools, chairs, steps, tables or platforms the actions and locales of the script require. Realistic scenery is rarely used. If a script calls for several locales, the weight-bearing structures are usually placed simultaneously for the entire time, or cast members rearrange them as the actions dictate. Simplicity is the keynote to Story Theatre.

Children touring in a production of *The Story of Lengthwise* in staged Readers Theatre Style. *Institute for Readers Theatre, William Adams, Director.*

Focus:

Characters: The characters use audience focus for the narrative elements and onstage focus for the dialogue.

Scripts:

No scripts are used because the literature is acted out with full stage movements. Lines are memorized as in conventional theatre so that the performance will not resemble a play rehearsal.

Actions:

The actions are performed with full stage movement as in conventional theatre. There is a basic difference, however, because literature other than plays often telescopes time, requiring extreme compression of movements. Or "real" time stops while the narration comments on a situation. Or there may be abrupt changes of time and locale.

Text:

Narration is an essential element in Readers Theatre based on literature with that ingredient. Do not attempt to drop or minimize the narration to make a "play" of the script.

Style IV: Chamber Theatre

Chamber Theatre is a style advocated by Robert Breen as a theatrical approach to performing narrative literature. It is a still-evolving form, so do not hesitate to experiment to find the most effective and appropriate ways to make the script come alive as theatre. Note: Most of its techniques are the same as those in Story Theatre, since both use the same basic approach to full-stage performance.

Set-up:

Simple weight-bearing structures are used as needed. (See Style III: Story Theatre.) In some Chamber Theatre productions, the full physical resources of theatre (lighting, scenery, costumes, makeup, props, sound) are provided. A general principle of Readers Theatre in any form, however, is to seek the maximum communication of the text with the simplest means.

Scripts:

Scripts are not ordinarily used. (See Style III: Story Theatre.)

Focus:

Narrators: Audience focus is used.

Characters: Onstage focus is used. Sometimes it is meaningful for characters to speak their narrations to other characters on stage.

Action:

Full stage actions are performed as in conventional theatre. (See Style III: Story Theatre.) Since separate narrators are used, unlike Story Theatre it is necessary to integrate them fully into the production. Narrators are alter-egos, confidants, and commentators on the action, as well as the author's storytellers. They must not be shunted to the side as if they were merely to be heard rather than seen. They are the "camera's eye," following the action with wide, medium, or close-up shots, so arrange their stage relationships accordingly.

Text:

Narration is an essential element in Readers Theatre based on literature with that ingredient. Do not attempt to drop or minimize the narration to make a "play" of the script.

Performance Art

Recently there has been considerable new scholarship into the role of performance in communications and behavioral science. Departments of Interpretation have plunged into new and challenging methodologies that go much further than the traditional parameters of oral interpretation and Readers Theatre. Many have felt that the label *performance studies* is more in keeping with the new agendas. Scholars reason that performance incorporates a whole range of activity. Under the umbrella of performance studies the performance phenomenon is being studied in its various manifestations. It is now being argued in academic circles that there are three basic groups of performances: cultural, literary, and performance art.

Cultural performance is used to describe those acts performed in everyday life, such as personal narratives, public display, and public performances that utilize various media such as musical state-

Above: Actors with ACTER frequently use Readers Theatre techniques. *Left to right,* Bernard Lloyd, Lisa Harrow, Patrick Stewart, Tony Church, Associate Directors of ACTER in London.

Below: Reading brought to life. A performance of the Peanut Butter Readers, South Windham, ME. *From left to right,* Pam Jones, Mark Nutial, Richard Green and Andrea Wright. *(Courtesy Peanut Butter Readers)*

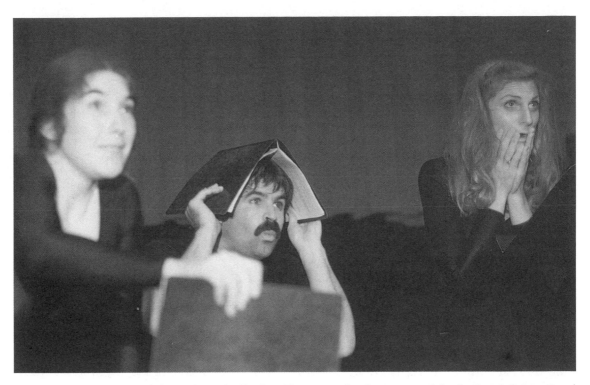

The Honors Tour Group of the Institute for Readers Theatre, performing at one of the Institute's International Workshops. William Adams, Director.

ments, mime, masks, light displays and other visual resources. Communal forms of ceremony such as national political conventions, vigil marches, some street theatre where live bodies take on symbolic meaning are presently considered cultural performances. All of these events tend to affirm, reaffirm or reject value systems. While cultural performances may draw on literary tradition, they tend to be more oral-centered than print-centered.

Literary performance under this new organization would include oral interpretation, Readers Theatre, and traditional theatre. Any performance of literature is placed under this category. Plays, short stories, poetry, novels, essays, humorous literature of all kinds form the text of performances. The artist becomes an interpreter of dramatic literature in a stage play and an oral interpreter if he or she is interpreting a poem. Literary performance, then, embraces the more traditional roles of textural performance.

Performance art is the most controversial of the performance studies because it involves the study of performance artists who create their own texts from eclectic sources such as music, dance, media art, visual art, sculpture and the like, and because it resembles the so-called avant garde theatre of the twentieth century. These performances tend to be antiestablishment, often assaultive, and frequently in opposition to commonly accepted definitions of art. They often incorporate multimedia collages of seemingly incongruous material in an effort to attack traditional value systems. The performance art artist sometimes takes physical risks in an effort to reexamine the boundaries of aesthetics.

Chris Burden, Eleanor Antine, Whoopi Goldberg and Spalding Gray are listed as prominent performers of performance art by Stern and Henderson's book *Performance Texts and Contexts*. They represent a rather wide spectrum of method. Burden and Antine tend to use their bodies as text, while Goldberg and Gray are more concerned with words.

Chris Burden's pieces have involved considerable risk to himself. In *Prelude to 220 or 110* Burden bolted himself to the floor of a studio with copper bands. Close by on the floor were live electrical wires of 220 volts next to buckets filled with water. Should the audience choose, they had but to dump the buckets over and electrocute Burden. A recorded voice taunted the audience but Burden survived to prove his point. Ostensibly, the piece created a new relationship between the audience and the art. In another creation which Burden called *Shoot* (1971) he had himself shot in the arm at close range by a friend.

Eleanor Antine's experiments were concerned with exploring her body through multimedia means. In *Carving: A Traditional Sculpture* (1972) Antine used the idea of traditional Greek marble sculptures as a basis for her work. As she explains it "they would keep carving around and around the figure and whole layers would come off at a time until finally the aesthetic ideal had been reached." In this particular work she had herself photographed naked from several different angles for thirty-six days while she dieted. In viewing the photographs the audience could see the attempt to achieve her self-described aesthetic ideal. It was possible for the audience to see Antine playing a game with time.

Whoopi Goldberg is included as a performance artist by Stern and Henderson because of her one-woman shows in which she challenges society through monologue. Her most famous work is called *The Spook Show.* While Goldberg is much more verbal centered than Antine or Burden, she is nevertheless more the performance art artist than the actress. In one performance of *The Spook Show,* when she did not get the response from the audience that she wanted, she stopped the performance and instructed them as to the proper response. Goldberg's characters are iconoclastic and instructional. From Fontane, the drug-addicted Ph.D. from Columbia, to *Little Girl with the Blond Hair,* Goldberg breaks traditional stereotypes and attacks racism.

Spalding Gray has been called an "auto-performer" by critics. A student of Richard Schechner, Gray is a performance art artist in that he uses himself as text. His longest and most complex as well as most famous autoperformance is *Swimming to Cambodia.* Gray performed a small role in the film *The Killing Fields* and used his experience as a scenario. Ostensibly autobiographical, Gray weaves a kind of fiction that tends to give the piece a different kind of aesthetic as he explores Gray the person, Gray the author, as well as Gray the performer.

Certainly performance studies give us an interesting way of looking at the performance phenomenon. Whatever the label, the rich heritage of interpretation, Readers Theatre, and theatre itself is ever present. Further, underlying the performance aesthetic, whatever it may be, is a determination to communicate and performance is a very exciting way to produce art.

Selected Readings

Cunningham, Carman C. *Literature as a Fine Art: Analysis and Interpretation.* New York, 1941.

Lee, C. I. and Gura, T. *Oral Interpretation.* Boston, 1992.

Pelias, R. J. *Performance Studies: The Interpretation of Aesthetic Texts.* New York, 1992.

Stern, C. S. and Henderson, B. *Performance Texts and Contexts.* White Plains, NY, 1993.

Part III
CREATIVE INSIGHTS

CHAPTER SIXTEEN

❧

Playwriting:
The Art of Imitation

George Bernard Shaw (1856-1950).

The art of playwriting is the one literary form that is specifically created to be performed by an artist interpreter. Similar in that respect to music, plays can exist in notation and can be read for enjoyment and intellectual stimulation for those who can read. But, generally, they realize their full potential only in performance. Plays have a different goal than other forms of literature. As Louis Catron tells us in his book *Playwriting*, a writer can be identified by goals. He states that:

The novelist records life

The essayist seeks to correct life

The Poet responds to life

The Playwright imitates life and the work appears to be life.

Indeed, imitation is a key word in the art of the theatre. No other art form attempts to imitate some facet of human life more than the theatre. A drama or a play is the one literary genre that requires components other than the script itself in order to become fully formulated. A play is written by a playwright or, literally, a skilled constructor, builder or maker of plays to be produced as a theatrical event; it must have a space, possibly scenery, costumes, and some kind of actor or interpreter.

In many ways a playwright creates order out of chaos. A playwright's vision is a personalized formula for the expurgation of bad dreams and the dissemination of good ones. A playwright eventually gropes with the age old questions of life. What does to exist mean? Why must there be suffering? What is the meaning of death? What is the meaning of life? It is through the playwright/artist's vision that we actually experience the universal, the weltschmerz, suffering and its purgation, while at the same time reaffirming the vibrancy of life.

These makers of plays have been with us since the beginning of communication when early man first began to verbalize ideas and tell stories. Plays in literary form have been with us since the fifth century B.C. and possibly earlier. From Aeschylus to Marsha Norman, writers of drama have imitated and are imitating the lifestyles, conflicts, and philosophies of their individual worlds. In some ways dramatists are the great articulators of an era. During the classical Greek period, for example, Aeschylus, Sophocles, Euripides, Aristophanes and Menander left us with insights into the very nerve center of Athenian thinking by imitating the actions of their contemporaries. Seneca, Hrosvitha, Calderon, Molière, Racine, Shakespeare, Goethe, Chikamatsu, Shaw, O'Neill, Sartre, Hare, Wilson, and Fornes, to name but a few, have supplied the various theatres of their day with some of the world's most stimulating literature. In a sense, each work is a record of its maker's life experience and a view of the civilization of which he or she was or is a part. Many of these playwrights have left to posterity masterpieces, written in a manner which makes them accessible to countless generations. Where do the ideas come from and how does one go about writing a play? What is it about a play that makes it different from other kinds of writing? How is the vision manifested? What is the playwriting process?

The Vision

Playwriting is a personal process, and accordingly, writers vary in their approach to their work. Some writers begin the playwriting process out of an idea arising from some sort of personal anxiety or experience. Arthur Laurents (b. 1918), for example, wrote *Home of the Brave* (1945) out of his combat experiences during World War II. He brooded on the discrimination he had suffered as a Jew and finally created his study of religious bigotry. The Drama Critics Circle Award play, *Raisin in the Sun*, was based upon Lorraine Hansberry's memories of her own childhood, when at the age of eight, she moved into an all-white neighborhood. Archibald MacLeish (1892-1982) was tormented by the meaning of suffering after witnessing the results of a Nazi bombing raid on the English town of West Hamm. Some victims had their homes bombed as many as four times. The idea of meaningless suffering and persecution seemed to MacLeish to be the universal theme of war. It was this idea that led to the completion of perhaps his most famous play, *J.B.* (1958). Adrienne Kennedy's plays seem to be an outlet for psychological confusions stemming from her childhood.

Some writers have political agendas and weave those ideas into their scripts. These plays are intentionally didactic but the best political writers allow the ideas to come out of story rather than impose political statements on character. Bertolt Brecht's plays such as *Good Woman of Setzuan, Mother Courage,* and *The Caucasian Chalk Circle* all make political statements on the human instinct for survival. Clifford Odets' masterpiece *Waiting for Lefty* and Hauptmann's *The Weavers* are examples of the common man revolting against a despotic system.

Ideas for a play can be philosophical ones. Jean-Paul Sartre, with messianic fervor, composed his modern version of the Greek myth of Orestes which he called *The Flies*, to define the philosophical idea of existentialism. Eugene Ionesco touted a similar idea in *The Bald Soprano*. Ionesco tells us:

> The non-metaphysical world of today has destroyed all mystery; and the so-called "scientific" theatre of the period, the theatre of politics and propaganda, anti-poetic and academic, had flattened mankind out, alienating the unfathomable third dimension which makes a whole man. The theatre of ideologies and thesis, proposing political solutions and presuming to save humanity—to wish to save it is to kill it—and there are no solutions. To realize that is the only healthy solution.

Some playwrights are concerned with social injustice. Many of Henrik Ibsen's plays tackled the staunch puritanical rigidity of Scandinavian society and by default, western standards. August Wilson (b. 1945) documents changing race relations in many of his plays, as did the late Lorraine Hansberry (1930-1965). Caryl Churchill (b. 1938) frequently explores the use of punishment and discipline by a society afraid of change.

Still other playwrights find their germinal seed in history, newspaper articles, mythology, or stories. One of the great teachers of playwriting,

Anna Cora Mowatt Ritchie (1819-70), actress and playwright who is remembered for her social comedy, *Fashion* (1845), which is considered to have established social comedy in America. From Seilhammer's *The Interviewer's Album,* 1881-1882.

George Pierce Baker, once said: "Undoubtedly he who begins with a story is nearer his goal than he who begins with an idea or character." William Shakespeare himself was a frequent adapter of material. *Plutarch's Lives, The Holinshed Chronicles, Euphues,* and *UR Hamlet* all furnished the basis for such plays as *Julius Caesar, Richard II, As You Like It,* and *Hamlet.* Lillian Hellman's (1905-1984) reading of *The Great Drumsheugh Case* from one of William Roughead's anthologies of criminal law trials was the spark that resulted in *The Children's Hour* (1934). A newspaper story about a mysterious blinding of horses set Peter Shaffer (b. 1926) writing *Equus* in 1973.

Aeschylus, Sophocles, Euripides, Seneca, Racine, Anouilh, Anderson, Giraudoux, and O'Neill are among the many authors who wrote plays based on mythology. Some of Henrik Ibsen's early plays were based on Norse mythology, and *The Black Mass* (1966) by Imamu Baraka (E. Leroy Jones, b.1932) was based on the Muslim myth of Yacub. Folk legends have also been utilized as idea material. The Tevye story of Sholom Aleichem provided Joseph Stein (b.1912) with the background to create the book for the musical *Fiddler on the Roof* (1964). Ibsen's *Peer Gynt* and *The Warrior's Barrow* fall into this category.

Plays based on character have been extremely popular with playwrights. Joseph Keselring (1902-1967), the author of *Arsenic and Old Lace*, admits "I got my idea for *Arsenic* by deliberately selecting my grandmother as a focal point and trying to imagine the most improbable thing she could possibly do." Both *All My Sons* (1947) and *After the Fall* (1964) by Arthur Miller were based on real life people. The main character in *All My Sons* evolved out of Miller's acquaintance with a businessman who was turned in by his own daughter for manufacturing defective machinery during World War II. The character of Maggie in *After the Fall* was patterned after Miller's former wife, Marilyn Monroe.

Sometimes the character is fictitious from the onset and takes the form of a stereotype. Molière's plays frequently used stereotypical characters. George Axelrod (b. 1922), author of *The Seven Year Itch*, describes that play's genesis in this manner: "As everybody who writes down words on paper for a living knows, once in a while you get an idea that's a natural. One that can't miss. As I say, the idea came in one piece. The summer bachelor. The girl upstairs. The wife we only see in the hero's imagination. The whole business."

Sometimes the original germinating idea, be it philosophy, story, personal experience, or character, will become disguised as the playwright begins to formulate the work. In some cases, a playwright may not remember what started the creative process at the onset. Perhaps the work was begun as a philosophical idea and evolved to a character study. Whatever, at a certain point most playwrights begin to select and order the material

Georg Büchner (1813-1873), a major nineteenth century dramatist, was a forerunner of expressionism and naturalism. He wrote three plays: *Danton's Death* (1835), *Leonce and Lena* (1836), and *Woyzeck* (1836: pronounced Voycheck). *Courtesy German Information Service.*

in a way that will cause the audience to react in the desired manner.

The Plan

Some playwrights plan their play in much the same way as an architect develops a set of plans. A plan for a play is sometimes called a scenario. The kind of scenario developed by the playwright varies from a relatively complete narrative or even short story of the play. Sometimes the narrative is broken down into units initiated by the entrance or exit of a character called a *French scene*, and sometimes playwrights like Bertold Brecht resort to a sketchy one page outline.

John Howard Payne (1791-1852), the first American dramatist to win international success, wrote or adapted roughly 50-60 plays. His work is considered to have been instrumental in laying the foundation for native American drama. He also wrote the song "Home Sweet Home." From Coleman's *Players and Playwrights*, 1890.

Henrik Ibsen wrote extremely detailed scenarios that gave character motivational sketches as well as intended impact of the scene. Eugene O'Neill not only wrote a rather complete scenario but also kept a work diary in which he recorded ideas and impressions of the play. Auguste Strindberg, Anton Chekhov, Tennessee Williams, Moss Hart, John Millington Synge, Lillian Hellman, Somerset Maugham and Arthur Wing Pinero are among the writers who worked out an almost excessively complete scenario.

Other playwrights seem to be able to compose the entire play in their heads. Noel Coward was one of the most famous writers who seemed to thrive using this method. In his autobiography, *Present Indicative* (1937), Coward relates how he wrote *Private Lives* (1930). He had promised to write a play for Gertrude Lawrence while on a trip to Yokohama. For quite some time he was unable to produce anything of consequence until one evening in Shanghai after going to bed. "The moment I switched out the light, Gertie appeared in a molyneux dress on the terrace in the south of France and refused to go again until four a. m. by which time *Private Lives*, title and all, had constructed itself."

Writers such as Sam Shepard visualize a character and begin to write letting the character lead where it may. Still others like Victorien Sardou (the most successful of the nineteenth century French dramatists) wrote the climax first and then worked backward. Sometimes a writer will "think on paper," that is, a play is started with a vague idea of its own outcome and is allowed to develop as it will. This technique can be rather painful and, generally, is not recommended by either playwrights or teachers of playwriting. Oddly enough, it is the very method most frequently utilized by inexperienced writers.

The Rewrite

Regardless of what technique is used to develop the play, one thing should be noted: a play is rarely, if ever, produced from a first draft. It has been said that plays are not written, they are rewritten. Lillian Hellman not only spent a great deal of time writing a scenario, but also went through no less than fourteen complete drafts of *The Children's Hour*. Even Sam Shepard, who long refused to revise at all on the grounds that to do so would be like lying since it would deny what he had originally set down, is said to have written dozens of versions of *Fool for Love* (1982). Marsha Norman watches rehearsals until late at night and then works on a computer making whatever revisions are necessary. Every professional playwright knows the agony of creating a work of art; indeed, some playwrights have developed bizarre creative habits. Lord Alfred Douglas writing in *Oscar*

Edward Sheldon (1886-1946), American dramatist whose plays *Salvation Nell* (1908), *The Nigger* (1909), *The Boss (1911)*, and *The High Road* (1912)reflected the progressive reform movement in the United States. *Photo Pirie MacDonald.*

Marsha Norman is among the outstanding women playwrights of contemporary American theatre. Her first big success was *Getting Out* (1978), which premiered at the Actors Theatre of Louisville's Humana Festival. In 1983 she won a Pulitzer Prize for her work *'night Mother*. Her next work, *Traveller in the Dark*, was unsuccessful but she gained a hit with her script for the musical, *The Secret Garden* (1991). *Courtesy Actors Theatre of Louisville.*

Wilde and Myself (1914), tells us that Wilde started drinking around four in the afternoon when he began to write and did not stop either activity until three the next morning; yet he was rarely drunk. Most playwrights, however, are more like Neil Simon, who tends to work on a diet of coffee, cookies, and dry roasted peanuts. Ibsen, Chekhov, Shaw, and Williams almost completely abstained from food while working. Whatever the condition of the body and mind, whatever technique, many playwrights really do not know how they create their plays. Alexander Dumas *fils* once remarked: "I'll own up that I don't know how to write a play. One day a long time ago when I was scarcely out of school, I asked my father the same question. He

answered 'It's very simple; the first act clear, the last act short, and all acts interesting.'"

The Production

After the playwright has taken a germinal idea, made the necessary artistic choices, fashioned a play plan, and written and rewritten the play, a production will probably be desirable. In this situation, a producer is sought to gain finances and to

Jane Anderson, contemporary playwright, began her career as an actress, appearing in *Sexual Perversities* and her one-woman show, *How To Have a Gifted Child.* Her most noted works as a playwright include *Defining Gravity* (1991), for which she won the Susan Blackburn Award; *Food and Shelter* (1991), her series of Lynette plays, the first of which *Lynette at Three A.M.* appeared at the Actors Theatre of Louisville; her Emmy Award-winning HBO film, *The Positively True Adventures of the Alleged Texas Cheerleading Mom* (1993), and her movie scripts, *Cop Gives Witness Two Million Dollar Tip* and *How to Make an American Quilt. Courtesy Actors Theatre of Louisville.*

Suzan-Lori Parks has an impressive career as a playwright. Her work, *Imperceptible Mutabilitics*, won the OBIE Award in 1990 as the "Best New American Play." Among her many plays and films are *The America Play* (1993), *Venus* (1993), *Devotees in the Garden of Love*, produced by the Humana Festival of the Actors Theatre of Louisville in 1992; and *The Death of the Last Black Man in the Whole Entire World* (1990), produced at the Yale Repertory Winterfest in 1992. *Courtesy Actors Theatre of Louisville.*

oversee the agonies and trials of a professional production. For a revealing account of this process, playwrights are advised to consult William Gibson's *SeeSaw Log* (1959). *SeeSaw Log* is a day-by-day description of the evolutionary process needed to take his play *Two for the SeeSaw* (1958) to Broadway. Although most plays do not reach Broadway, a good proportion of them are produced somewhere, somehow. Most playwrights would rather work in regional and off-off Broadway theatres because of their sensitivity to the wishes of the writer. Considering the amounts of money invested in a Broadway production, producers are very reluctant to take chances. It is perhaps best to consider professional resident companies, summer theatres, universities and playwriting contests. A complete list of available markets can be found in such publications as *Writer's Market* and

Simon's Directory of Theatrical Services and Information. Both of these publications can be found in most well stocked libraries.

Such organizations as the Eugene O'Neill Theatre Center in Waterford, Connecticut, Playwrights Horizons, and the Manhattan Theatre Club in New York are set up to help new playwrights. The Actors Theatre of Louisville in Louisville, Kentucky, The Mark Taper Forum in Los Angeles and the Seattle Repertory Company in Seattle, Washington, are organizations that will and do produce new plays. It is best to inquire as to which of these theatres take unsolicited scripts before submission is made.

The problems of finding a producer and a theatre for a production of a new play are so difficult that more and more playwrights are attempting to locate an agent. Agents can be of tremendous value to the playwright as they understand the financial and legal ramifications of the production of a script. Securing an agent can in itself be a difficult process as agents make their living from a percentage of their clients' earnings. It is important, therefore, for agents to accept only those clients that they feel have a better than average potential for success.

The art of playwriting is a unique and exacting process, but the experience of watching the performance of a play fashioned out of a germinal idea can be one of the most rewarding moments of a lifetime.

Selected Readings

Catron, Louis E. *Playwriting: Writing, Producing and Selling Your Play.* Prospect Heights, IL, 1990.

Cooper, Lane. *Aristotle on the Art of Poetry.* Boston, 1913.

Rowe, Kenneth Thorpe. *Write That Play.* New York, 1939.

Smiley, Sam. *Playwriting: The Structure of Action.* Englewood Cliffs, NJ. 1971.

CHAPTER SEVENTEEN

❧

The Director and the Actor

Sarah Bernhardt as Mrs. Clarkson in *The Stranger*.

Theatre is live and about human relationships, otherness, needs, actions, crises, and values. In performance, the actor is the embodiment of the liveness and the humanity of theatre. In rehearsal, the actor and director together search out that liveness and humanity from the text, among and between the actors, in the moment. The most intense collaboration in the theatre is therefore that which occurs between director and actor.

Theatre-goers see and hear what the actor does, even if they don't understand his or her process. That is, the general audience thinks the actor's job is to memorize the lines, speak them clearly and loudly, and pretend to be someone other than himself or herself. They don't know what the director does even on that superficial level. Films and television sit-coms usually portray the director yelling a lot. Probably the only thing the unschooled could agree on is that the director is the boss and that is not necessarily so.

It is the purpose of this chapter to discuss the jobs and processes of the director and actor in the production of a play. Those jobs and processes begin long before the first rehearsal and vary with the style, training, and experience of each individual. They are impacted by the particular level at which the play is being produced, i. e., professional, academic, or community, and available resources in terms of time, personnel, dollars, and technology.

THE DIRECTOR

Each production is different from all other productions. Therefore, the director's chief responsibility and privilege is to articulate the parameters of a unique production between and among particular artists for a particular audience in a particular theatre at a particular moment in time.

Pre-Production

Usually the process begins with the selection of a script. When it does not, it may begin with the

director and a group of actors, actors and dancers, actors and designers, etc., coming together to explore some theme or idea through improvisation or oral history. *A Chorus Line* was birthed that way. A group of Broadway support, as opposed to lead, dancers met to share their own stories, dreams, and pain, with director-choreographer Michael Bennett—and each other—in a series of workshops. Eventually many of those stories were to make up the final show. Some of the dancers were cast in "their own" roles, others were not. In such a process, the director still outlines the parameters of the production by establishing the thread that will tie it together and the rules under which the company will work. He or she stimulates, receives, and shapes what happens among the artists involved. When the process is about the creation of new work, it is exciting because the territory is unexplored and the outcome totally unpredictable.

When the process begins with an already existing script, which is most of the time, the director, if fortunate, is involved in its selection. Sometimes the producer or the institution determines the play and hires or assigns a director for the project. When the director is allowed to choose, he or she looks for a script that says something he or she wants to say; a script with characters about whom one can care; a script with relevance in the world, in this place, at this time; a script with language and ideas that uplift or challenge or excite or move; a script that will fulfill artists and audiences alike; a script that can be done, as Hedda Gabler says, "beautifully," by those who will do the doing.

Needless to say, the director must know a lot of dramatic literature. He or she must also understand the bottom line of a play: that which must finally be on the stage for the play to work. For example, if Hedda is only manipulative and unsatisfied with her life, the audience cannot care about her and their experience in the theatre doesn't matter. If, on the other hand, Hedda is an intelligent and capable woman caught in a patriarchal power structure in which she has no means of self-determination, her struggle and her choices can be understood and therefore have meaning and value.

Research is an important tool for the director. He or she needs to know about the playwright and the body of work of the playwright, the play and its various productions, the social, historical, economic, political, geographical, and religious context of the play. In addition, the director must understand the theatrical genre and the style of the play. That is, he or she has to know what Brecht's Epic Theatre really was before embarking on a production of *Mother Courage and Her Children.* The content of the play or even the characters' physical states may dictate areas of research. For example, plays such as *The Elephant Man* and *Children of a Lesser God* provide impetus to delve into relevant medical data and case studies.

Research, while essential, should not supplant meticulous work on the text. The text itself is the key to the integrity of the director's process and product. The director begins with the text by asking himself or herself myriad questions. Why is this character in the play? Why is this scene in the play? Why is this speech in the play? Why does the character enter at this moment—what changes? Why does the character leave at this moment— what changes? What does each character want or need? What is he or she willing to do to get it? What are the stakes for each character? Which character experiences the most fundamental change in the play? At what moment does that change begin? At what moment is that change complete? What are the major symbols of the play? What are the major images of the play? What are the major ideas of the play? What are the major themes of the play? What are the important words in the play? What is the dynamic of the play? What is the rhythm of the

Scene from *Peer Gynt* by Henrik Ibsen. This production by the University Resident Theatre Company of The Pennsylvania State University was directed by Carole Brandt with associate directors Manuel Duque and Jane Ridley, April 1992. *(Courtesy William Wellman)*

Scene from April 1993 production of *Blood Wedding* by Frederico Garcia Lorca, directed by Manuel Duque, University Resident Theatre Company, The Pennsylvania State University (*Courtesy William Wellman*)

play? How does language provide tension and conflict? What is the single most important moment in the play? What are the inherent traps in the play?

Some directors will formally analyze the script utilizing a structure offered by theoreticians such as Francis Hodge in his book *Play Direction: Analysis, Communication, and Style* or ones they have devised for themselves. Others will read the script over and over and over and let it "speak" to them intuitively. Still others will expect the answers to be found in the rehearsal process. Whatever the system, it is imperative that the director completely understand *and be able to articulate* to other collaborative artists such as designers and actors what the play is finally about and what this production of the play is specifically about. Those are the parameters of the production referred to above.

Parameters may be expressed by the director in the form of a concept. Some directors provide brilliant incisiveness into a play and others muck it up irreparably with concept. When the concept grows out of the text and reveals its specialness, it is the former; when the concept springs from what the director wants to say independent of the text, it is the latter. An example of a concept intrinsic to

a text was Elia Kazan's "butterfly in the jungle" metaphor for his production of *A Streetcar Named Desire*. Examples of concept imposed on text unfortunately abound and range from decisions to turn Shakespeare into Star Wars in order that it be more relevant, to the intertwining of *Pygmalion* and *My Fair Lady* because the director wanted to do *Pygmalion* and the producer advertised *My Fair Lady*.

Conferences between director and designers begin when the director "knows enough" about the parameters of the production and early enough for the production staff to meet all deadlines. Design conferences are creative and collaborative. They are for the director and designers to discover and imagine the world they will put onstage. They are times to share the wildest ideas and images and to check each other so that all of it, including the work the director will do with the actor, *belongs in the same world*. Initial design conferences should not be about how to do it or can we afford it. They should be about what the production feels, smells, tastes, sounds, looks like to each and then to all artists. Often these conferences include sharing research and discussion about texture, line, color, weight. Eventually, they include presentation by the designers of ground plans, thumbnail sketches, models, renderings, plots, swatches, etc. It is during this period that choices are made which are irrevocable. Quality of communication and the spirit of collaboration will inform the experience and end result of the production.

As the production begins to take form for the artistic staff, the director's mind turns to casting, the process by which actors are selected to play specific roles. Casting can be accomplished in various ways: the director can simply ask actors with whom he or she has worked before or about whom he or she knows; the director can identify a casting agent to select the actors for him or her; the director can audition actors himself or herself. Most of the time, directors prefer the latter.

It seems elementary to state that the director must know what he or she is looking for in each role prior to going into auditions. That may mean the physical type of each character. More importantly, it means the essential quality that each character must project. For example, does the role require a hard edge or a darkness to make the play work? Or, do the actors have to all "belong" to a family or in a larger than life world? Auditions are held at designated times and usually by appointment. Sometimes they are limited to certain groups. An Equity call means that only actors belonging to the union, Actors Equity Association, will be seen. A cattle call is the name given to open calls in which anyone, sometimes thousands for a few roles, can audition. One of the most famous cattle call auditions came in the 1960s for a young and unknown *Hair* company.

Directors vary in what they ask actors to prepare for and do in an audition. For musicals, they may want only sixteen bars of two contrasting songs and to see the actor in a dance class. When casting Shakespeare, directors may ask for a soliloquy from the play or monologue from other classical material. When a season of plays is being auditioned, actors will generally be asked to prepare a series of one and two minute pieces from which the director or directors can choose. Some directors want to work improvisationally with actors during the audition to test their imaginations,

Machinal by Sophie Treadwell, directed by Helen Manfull, October 1992 production of the University Resident Theatre company at The Pennsylvania State University. *(Courtesy William Wellman)*

directability, and collaborative skills. Other directors will try to get to know the actors by asking them to tell something about themselves or their work in the theatre. Most directors will ask actors sometime during the process to read from the script with other actors. This helps the director project the actor into the role quite specifically and to put actors together in various combinations to determine workable relationships.

However the director chooses to do it, casting is crucial to both the process and product of theatre. The right actor in the right role can make the process joyful and exciting, the product rich and meaningful. The wrong actor can deaden or sidetrack the process, and even prevent the play from working. So the director who is going to succeed cannot make casting errors. It is interesting to note that the three things that can make or break a director all happen in the pre-production stage:

play selection, creation of the ground plan—which will be discussed below, and casting.

Rehearsal and Production

Rehearsal and production periods vary. When new work is being created, it is often workshopped first to provide time for gestation and rewriting. Most professional productions of existing plays are in rehearsal and production three to four weeks. Summer stock is often an exception, with productions pushed into a week to ten days. Universities and colleges generally spend four to five weeks and high schools five to eight weeks. Community theatres fall into the same patterns as schools since they also work only a portion of each day in rehearsal and production.

The director moves into the rehearsal and production period with a plan for getting to opening night. The first rule he or she abides by is that no matter what, the curtain goes up at 8:00 P.M. on a specific date and he or she is finally accountable for what the paying audience and critics experience in the theatre that night. The director's plan is the rehearsal schedule which is sketched out, usually in conjunction with others such as the production and stage managers, design and technical staff, musical director and choreographer, if appropriate, prior to the first rehearsal.

Rehearsal

More often than not, the rehearsal schedule is fleshed out backwards. Opening night is Day A and the first rehearsal is Day Z. The final week or ten days, depending upon the complexity of the production elements, are reserved for mounting rehearsals: forging all elements of the production into a seamless whole. Scenery, lights, sound, costumes, makeup, properties and orchestra are joined with actors. Rehearsals during that period are devoted to setting and cueing levels, timing, and shifts. Each element must be *ready* to be phased into the production on a pre-determined schedule.

This period, usually referred to as tech and dress rehearsals, is pressure-packed because: this is the first time all the collaborators share the theatre space simultaneously; the realized production may be different from the imagined production; and everyone is exhausted. The dynamic, rhythm, and fluidity of the finished production are outcomes of these rehearsals. Therefore the director must not drop out even when the technical staff needs much of the time to solve problems—How does the actor make the quick change and re-enter from stage right when he left fifteen seconds earlier from stage left? What is the resolution when the color of the lights kill the colors of the sets and costumes? How can the technician pulling the drapery not wipe out the conductor and her music stand at the end of the overture? What can be done to make the floor safe and not slippery for the dancers?—and rehearse the run crew. This period is the most threatening to the director who feels loss of control of the play while others adjust and fix. The play, even if it is in terrific shape going into these rehearsals, usually falls completely apart during them because actors are totally distracted working with props and hoop skirts and follow spotlights and revolving turntables and flying scenery. What the director must remember is that the quicker technical solutions are found, the sooner he or she gets the play back and the rush toward opening night can resume. During the final stages of rehearsal, it is easy to see what is extraneous or doesn't work. The director has both opportunity and responsibility to make hard decisions at this point, i.e., to eliminate a number and its twenty-seven costumes or cut twelve minutes from the run time—if necessary.

Prior to the mounting process, rehearsal and production take place independently of each other. The director with the assistance of the stage manager conducts rehearsals. Most rehearsal periods begin with time set aside for discussing the production concept and design to help actors visualize the world which is going to be created and in which they will exist as characters. This may be a time for sharing research or feelings about the play itself. The way the director intends

Shakespeare's *Comedy of Errors*, directed by Cary Libkin, produced by the University Resident Theatre Company at The Pennsylvania State University, November 1992. *(Courtesy William Wellman)*

to work and his or her expectations in terms of homework, work ethic, and discipline are communicated. These early rehearsals are critical to whatever bonding the company will eventually do. The director assures actors of his or her trust in them and sets a tone for them to take risks. The director can never forget that the actor is the most vulnerable of all artists in the theatre and that it is his or her job to protect that vulnerability.

In productions of complex or unfamiliar language and style, as much as a week may be spent on what is called table work, where actors and director dissect the script, language, and dramatic action, before movement is blocked or anyone is asked to "act." Improvisation is a viable tool in early rehearsals when directors don't want actors picking up bad habits by trying to produce results too soon. If actors have a thorough understanding of the characters they are to play, they can imagine them in scenes not in the text but which impact the dramatic action. For example,

we know that Blanche Dubois' life was never the same after an occurrence at a dance at Moon Lake Casino when she was seventeen. The actress playing Blanche could be helped immeasurably if that scene were improvised. Or, in plays such as *A Delicate Balance*, where a character who never appears haunts the lives of others who do, actors can discover stakes and history that will greatly enrich their performances. Improvisation in rehearsal takes time and needs to be utilized as a tool rather than for its own sake. The director needs to realize that some actors embrace it while others fear and reject it.

Table work and improvisation serve some directors well. Others want the play "on its feet" immediately. Whatever the plan, it has to work not only for the director but for the actors as well. The director's approach to the rehearsal period is influenced by the level of experience and training of the cast. Good professional actors can be expected to do much for themselves. They should know what homework they need to do and do it. They usually bring something into rehearsal to which the director can respond and with which he or she can work. Less experienced and trained actors do not necessarily do that. They may need stronger and more specific direction. Often they need to be taught how to fill out a role. They may not understand transaction or making choices. Particularly challenging to the director is the cast whose range is across the spectrum of experience and training. He or she will have to decide where to put in time and what others, such as movement or voice or acting coaches, might be brought in to help with the rehearsal process.

Directors usually view the rehearsal process as one of layering. That is, they make several passes through the play with each pass resulting in more and deeper layers. The first step in the process has been described above as table work. The second is getting the play "on its feet."

"On its feet" happens basically two ways. First, the director may choose to pre-block. That is, prior to going into a blocking rehearsal, he or she writes down movement patterns and business for each character at specific moments. The rehearsal will then be spent with actors writing down and walking through their own blocking. The advantage of this approach is that it saves rehearsal time and has been carefully thought through in terms of dramatic action and the aesthetic. It also provides the director, actors, and if they are invited, the designers and technical staff, with the shape of the whole very early on. Pre-blocking is particularly helpful with inexperienced and untrained actors. Or, the director may choose to discover the movement patterns and business with the actors in the rehearsal process. Although time-consuming, this may result in blocking that is more organic and natural. It also utilizes actors' imaginations and instincts, making them collaborators from the outset. Some directors want it both ways. They pre-block in order to move through that stage quickly and provide a starting place. Then during the work-through rehearsals, they and the actors find different or other moments. The result is a fast-paced and dynamic process.

Work-throughs are the heart of the rehearsal process. The director and actors work-through each moment of the play in terms of action and choice, in search of its truth and reality. Relationships between and among characters are discovered and explored in these rehearsals. Both the director and actors are looking for clues to get the characters to the end of the play. Work-throughs ask questions like who am I, what do I need, what will it cost, and what am I willing to do to get it. The danger in working in such detail moment by moment is that the director and actors can get wrapped up in the trees and lose the forest. Therefore it is necessary to run-through a whole scene or an act or the play periodically, to keep the forest in focus. A trap that inexperienced directors fall into is trying to do everything at once. Actors cannot assimilate that way. The director therefore has to set specific goals for each rehearsal in terms of layering.

As a rule, the director tries to make three or more passes through the play to accomplish the layering. A typical schedule might be as follows:

Week One: Stumble through show by the end of the week.

Week Two: Work through Act I; run through at end of week.

Week Three: Work through Act II; run through II and show at end of week.

Week Four: Re-work I and II; run each act and show; technical rehearsals at end of week.

Week Five: Dress rehearsals; previews; open at end of week.

Sample rehearsal schedules for *Peer Gynt* and *Crime on Goat Island* are included at the end of the chapter.

Directing musicals is very complicated because vocal, dance, and scene rehearsals must be scheduled. Most of the time, music is learned first with dance rehearsals on big or difficult numbers fed into the process almost immediately. Two weeks may be required before the music and dance is far enough along to get to scene work-throughs. Finally, it all must be seamless as characters burst into song or break into dance because mere speech

Scene from *Children's Hour* by Lillian Hellman, directed by Manuel Duque, produced by the University Resident Theatre Company, The Pennsylvania State University, April 1991.

and movement are no longer enough to express their feelings. Sample rehearsal schedules for *A Little Night Music* and *Carousel* are included at the end of the chapter.

The director's plan for getting to opening night must take into consideration such disparate elements as the size and complexity of the play, technical sophistication of the production, experience and skill level of all collaborators. No time or work is more immediate or important, however, than that between director and actor. It is this relationship that is the most exciting and most difficult.

The director's point of view is from the house to the stage; the actor's point of view is from the stage to the house. In rehearsal, the director serves as audience for the actor—hearing, seeing, and responding to him or her. The actor cannot remain inside the world of the play and monitor what he or she sounds like, looks like, is, in fact, doing. The director then is the actor's mirror and the mirror must never lie. Enormous trust is fundamental in their relationship. The director must be sensitive to the special vulnerability of the actor, recognizing

the actor's only instrument as his or her own body, voice, and essence. Theatre critics review actors individually rather than as the "brass section," personally rather than as a sculpture or painting.

The director sets out not only to create a work of art but to insure that every actor's performance has integrity. Just as the director describes the parameters of the production to other artistic staff, he or she reiterates them to the actors. It is also important at the beginning of rehearsal to establish expectations—what the director expects of, needs from, the actors; what actors in turn can expect, what they need from the director. Sometimes there are things that are negotiable, and others that are not, i.e., strict deadline for being off-book (lines learned). Everyone should know the "rules" from the beginning.

Most directors believe that one of their chief jobs is to build a strong ensemble from individual members of the acting company. Because good actors allow themselves to be vulnerable, they need to feel support from others. In order for them to be good, they have to feel they can take real risk in rehearsal, dare to stretch, to be bad in order to b better in performance. That means they need to feel safe. One way they feel safe is by knowing that the director and other actors are not judging them during their search for character and dramatic action. Another way is by sharing their search with the ensemble rather than in isolation. Many actors are very generous with each other; some are too self-involved. An example of the former is the actor who asks another actor "What do you need from me in this scene?" The actor who is not the focus of a particular moment but who draws attention to himself or herself by moving or mugging, is an example of the latter. In the theatre, pulling inappropriate focus is called upstaging.

All directors and actors set out to have a strong ensemble because it cuts down on tension throughout the process and allows the group to "do battle with the play" instead of each other. Nothing is more rewarding to a company than the sense of community, collectively and collaboratively, creating art. Theatre people are totally dependent upon their ability to work together. When ensemble doesn't happen, whether it is about personal egos or artistic differences, the experience can be so damaging that, even if the product is brilliant, the artists may walk away without fulfillment.

In the early stages of rehearsal, the director may know more about the character than the actor does; by the end of rehearsals, however, the actor should know more about what makes the character tick each moment than the director does. It is sometimes helpful at the outset for the director and actors to discuss traps in the script or characters which they must avoid. For example, the plays of Neil Simon have tricky fight scenes. The characters say terrible things to each other and do a lot of screaming. All of this is supposed to be funny and we are supposed to love people who are being ugly to each other. For the production to work, the director and actors must insure that it is funny rather than distasteful and that these are people about whom we can care. Another trap to be avoided, in Simon plays in particular, is for actors to play the laughs or jokes and not the intentions

and needs of the characters. Traps include such things as trying to act style, i.e., Shakespearean or Greek, instead of finding the dramatic action. Language can be a trap for actors if they fall in love with the beautiful words or their own voices and allow it to be narrative rather than active. Production can be a trap if it becomes so important that the director and actor make choices, not because they are intrinsically right in terms of the text, but to accommodate the costumes or scenery.

One of the primary concerns of the director is the choices actors make. If for example, a character wants to provoke another, he or she may walk away from or toward, may smile or frown, may kiss or slap, etc. Choices made provide unique tensions and make characters strong or weak, compelling or boring. To pour orange juice on the white carpet is a more provocative choice than to stomp around the living room. Literally thousands of choices are made by the director and actors throughout the rehearsal period. It is possible to change the meaning of the play with a wrong choice. For example, the choice to *not* slam the front door at the end of *Doll's House*, leaves the play unresolved because we do not know that Nora left although that is clearly the intention of the playwright.

When choices are uninteresting or do not help clarify character, relationships, or dramatic action, the director and actors need to explore other choices in rehearsal. When a moment "is not working" because it is untruthful, unfocused, or unfilled, the collaborators try to determine if it is a problem that must be solved by the actor or if it could be solved by something as simple as moving a piece of furniture. If, for example, a sofa were placed far from the door, the burglar hiding behind it would be more justified using the window directly behind the sofa rather than trying to get to the door across the room *if the moment* in the play is about escaping. Or, if the moment is about how dangerous it is for the burglar to escape, the choice is for the actor to motivate his or her cross all the way to the door rather than make a quick exit through the window.

The most important thing the director and actors

Scene from *Pirates of Penzance* by Gilbert and Sullivan, directed by Cary Libkin, November 1991. Produced by the University Resident Theatre of The Pennsylvania State University.

do together is remain open to each other and to the process. When it is a power struggle about the director being the boss or who is right, the creative work is endangered. When actors get defensive or are threatened, art rarely happens. Some directors are known as actors' directors because they approach the process primarily as acting coaches, allowing conceptual and technical aspects secondary consideration. That is not good or bad. It is simply a way of identifying style or strengths of individual directors. Some directors are more comfortable working with props than they are with actors so rehearsals are about how and when the props are used by actors. That is somewhat of an exaggeration, of course, but not entirely. The thing to remember is that all directors and actors work differently and they make theatre by seeking ways of working together that stimulate and feed their individual creativity and give everyone ownership in that which is created.

Production

As stated above, the ground plan is an important tool for the director. It is a map of the set (walls, doors, windows, steps, platforms, ramps, etc.) and furniture. It must accommodate dramatic action and facilitate movement patterns. Ground plans evolve from director-scene designer interaction during the design process prior to rehearsal and are only good insofar as they provide the amount and kind of space necessary for actors to make the play work and are aesthetically pleasing. When furniture is placed center stage, the ground plan is probably not a good one because that is the most powerful position onstage and should generally be reserved for actors. When the set for a three or four character play spans a forty foot proscenium opening, the ground plan is probably not a good one because the set can overpower the small cast and make it difficult for them to "fill" the space or even cross it effectively. On the other hand, a play such as *Waiting for Godot* can be about individuals isolated—and of course, waiting—in space. In that case, expanse is essential. When everything is symmetrical or the furniture placed flat against walls or linearly, the ground plan probably is not good because it provides neither visual tension nor physical obstacle. Conflict, which is intrinsic in dramatic literature, is realized onstage, for the audience visually and the actors physically, by irregular angles and shapes, pieces to be surmounted, i.e., stairs, or chase around, i.e., sofas. When all of the "heavy" scenery or furniture is on one side, the ground plan is probably not good because the stage will be out of balance. Directors can create balance by moving actors but if the weight of one side of the stage is greater than the other, he or she is artistically handicapped because choices are limited. Some directors are capable of visualizing the production working with only the ground plan. Others need renderings, elevations, and models. Whatever the method of communication, the director and scene designer must find a way early on to "see" the same production. Ground plans for selected scenes from *Merrily We Roll Along* are included in the fold-out at the back of the book.

During the build process, the director needs to be in close contact and problem-solving mode with the other artistic and technical collaborators. Production meetings discussed above are one avenue. Another is getting set, costume, and prop pieces into rehearsals early enough to identify what needs to be changed or eliminated before it can't be. Stage managers and technical directors often instruct the director and actors on how and when things work. They also are concerned about actor safety; i.e., rough spots on a floor with a cast in bare feet, a lighted torch tossed from a high platform and caught below, a revolving turntable with actors getting on and off in the dark. The crew that runs the show must be integral to the whole. Follow spot operators need to be able to come up on moving targets with subtlety and surety; dressers need to be respectful of the personal contact they have with actors and so efficient with quick changes that they are calming influences

backstage; prop people need to know that the scene doesn't work if the gun doesn't fire or the chair doesn't get onstage. Whatever the job, it matters.

The director is partnered throughout the production process by the stage manager. Professional stage managers, like professional actors, may belong to the union, Actors' Equity Association. For each production they prepare the promptscript in which they record all blocking and cues and from which they call the show in performance; schedule times, rooms, personnel and transportation for all rehearsals, costume fittings, production photos, etc.; run production meetings; serve as liaison with all shops, front of house, marketing and public relations; insure communication through rehearsal, meeting, and performance notes; lay out the ground plan in the rehearsal space; track actors, props, and costume pieces each moment in the play; enforce policies and procedures of the theatre and the union; manage all rehearsals and serve as the director's or producer's surrogate during performances. The stage manager trouble shoots and often serves as a sounding board for the director. Once the show has opened, the stage manager is responsible for maintaining the integrity of the director's work. If the director is not present at the time cast members are replaced during a long run or in case of incapacity, the stage manager rehearses the replacements and puts them into the show. Sample stage management forms are included at the end of the chapter.

The director's job is usually complete opening night. Preview performances prior to the official opening afford him or her opportunity to test the production with audiences and without critics. The actors and audience must interact in real time and space for theatre to occur *between* them. Actors need the audience to laugh or listen or weep or applaud. The director's final responsibility is to help them find the moments where they cannot continue because the audience is laughing too hard; where they are listening so intently with their hearts as well as their ears, that the stillness is sacred; where they are weeping profoundly and,

Scene from *Buried Child* by Sam Shepard as produced by the University Resident Theatre, The Pennsylvania State University, March 1992, directed by Kristin Graham.

as we do in life, need something outrageous to occur; where they are applauding an entrance or an exit so much that the actors must make up something until an audience comes back to the action of the play. The liveness of the audience informs the dynamic and rhythm of the production and makes each performance different. It challenges theatre artists and validates theatre art.

THE ACTOR

In the theatre, actors create fictive characters in real time and space before live audiences. The resulting tension is complex and layered. Because the actor is his or her own instrument, the process of creation begins with the *self* of the actor. Who is he or she? How similar or different is he or she

from the character; how far apart are their values, lifestyles, ages, needs, appearances, languages, families, dreams, etc? The second layer is the character's relationship with other characters in the given circumstances of the play. What do they want/need from one another? What is the degree of conflict between and among them? Who and what are the obstacles with which the characters must do battle? Finally, the audience provides the most spontaneous layer in the actor's creative process. Its participation is prepared for and expected, but not predictable. Because every audience participates differently from every other audience, actors must make adjustments every performance. The aesthetic contract between them is one in which they come together to pretend that the characters are alive and real. The character's relationship to the audience informs the actor's process and performance. Is the character beloved or tolerated by the audience? Do they care about him or her? Do they sit mesmerized or rustle programs and talk back to the stage?

Sometimes, when the actors are major stars or even understudies, the audience has a particular and peculiar response to them that adds another element to the tension referred to above. If the actor is Liza Minnelli, the audience may go to see Liza Minnelli and not the character she plays. They may in fact not be able to ever suspend their disbelief enough to forget they are watching Liza, the Star. If Ms. Minnelli is ill and an understudy performs in her place, the audience, if it stays, grieves throughout, and may even be hostile toward the production and certainly in comparative mode in its relationship with the understudy. On the other hand, if an understudy is in the place of a non-star, often the audience will "root" for the understudy who is getting a chance. All of the above underscores how difficult the actor's job is, how elusive the art of theatre.

Pre-Production

Actor homework, like director homework, begins before auditions. The actor must first find out where the jobs are—who is casting, what they are looking for, what they are paying, where the play will be produced, by whom it will be produced, if it is a tour, etc. If the actor has an agent, he or she may get a call from the agent about a particular role in a forthcoming production. If the actor doesn't have an agent, he or she may read trade papers or call in to a hotline. In academic and community theatre, actors may find notices on call boards or even hear of possible roles through word of mouth.

Actors traditionally get roles by auditioning although the audition process may be by-passed when actors are known or established. Generally, an actor's ability to audition well determines whether or not he or she works most of his or her professional life. Therefore, much actor training is about audition skills and attitudes and actors continue to take audition classes and workshops throughout their careers.

An audition skill essential to all actors is the ability to do cold readings. Cold readings occur when actors are handed material they have not prepared for the audition. They need to be able to create characters and, when reading with other actors, relationships; to find emotional truths, play intentions, choose tactics, and overcome obstacles—during the reading itself. Actors who struggle just to read the words or who lack instinct and imagination or who fear auditioning, find cold readings excruciating.

An audition attitude essential to all actors is a realistic and comfortable sense of self. As stated earlier, actors are incredibly vulnerable, particularly at auditions, when most of them will, by the very nature of the process, be rejected. They cannot, and this is the most difficult, take the rejection personally if they are to survive as actors. The actor has to realize that the person doing the casting may have a tall, thin Native American in mind for the role he or she wants and he or she is short, round, and Irish. Or, he or she may not be the best choice for the role in relationship to the others who will be in the company. Or, the actor may be too frail or too rough or too sophisticated or too down-home to fit into the world of the play.

Before going to the auditions, the actor prepares by reading and studying the script if one is

Ellen Terry (1847-1928), the first actress to be knighted (1925), shown here as Portia in *The Merchant of Venice*. Her greatest fame came as Henry Irving's leading lady at the Lyceum. She is the mother of Gordon Craig and the grandmother of John Gielgud.

available. In the case of a musical, the actor works on at least two contrasting songs (usually, one ballad/one up-tempo) from the show being cast or material that is similar. He or she may work with an acting or voice teacher or take dance classes if there is time. For musical auditions, actors sometimes take their own pianists because they have worked with them and feel more secure.

Before going into an audition, savvy actors know the role or roles in the play for which they will most likely be considered. Therefore, they usually rehearse the speeches and study the qualities of the particular character or characters.

The Booth Brothers, John Wilkes (1839-1865), Edwin (1833-1893), and Junius Brutus, Jr. (1821-1883) at the Winter Garden, New York, November 25, 1864, in *Julius Caesar*. This photo was taken five months before Lincoln's assassination.

They often dress in a way appropriate to or evocative of the character or characters. That is to say, actresses auditioning for *Nunsense* dress and "act" very differently than actresses auditioning for *Ain't Mis-behavin'*. That helps them and often it helps the director who is casting "see" them in the roles. Some actors prepare to audition by doing something nice for themselves, buying a new shirt or indulging in a bubble bath, so they will feel special. Auditioning, like acting, is very personal.

Going into an audition, the actor has to remain as relaxed, focused, and open as possible. That is particularly difficult when the adrenalin is pumping and the need to get work or a role "to die for" is great. When the actor is relaxed, vocal and physical tension is eliminated and emotional connections can occur. The actor should focus on

and be open to the character and the director. A good audition is grounded in actor preparation and released through his or her imagination and energy.

Once cast, the actor must deal with the role which he or she will play. If a major part, responsibility includes leadership within the ensemble as well as delivery of the role. Leadership includes setting the standards of preparation and discipline, being supportive toward all members of the ensemble, and, in some cases, driving the show. Those cast in small roles have responsibility to recognize the importance of their places in the whole. Sometimes actors cast in small roles or roles other than the ones for which they were auditioning, are disappointed. If they are disappointed enough, or even angry, they should not accept the roles offered them. Actors with attitude problems negatively impact the process and, probably, the product. Most actors are happy to have work and to be doing what they love and their disappointment dissipates quickly. Regardless, every actor is a collaborator in the creation of a unique work of art, therefore essential to and inextricable from it.

The research homework for an actor is similar to that of the director. For example, both should have knowledge of the playwright's body of work. The director is concerned with major themes, recurring symbolism; the actor looks at character, i.e., what drives Williams' (Tennessee) women? The director's research spans the wide world of the play; the actor's research focuses on the particular character in particular circumstances at a particular moment in time. Actor research includes observation of people. How do they move? How do they sit? What are their mannerisms? How do they behave when they are threatened? tickled? hurting? If they were animals, what animals would they be?

Actors work with the text in very specific ways. They analyze their characters to discover what the characters want and what they are willing to do to get it. They look at the tactics used by the characters and at the obstacles in their way. They identify change that takes place within their characters throughout the course of the play; what the characters want at the end different from what they wanted at the beginning. They write the above in the script itself, scoring it, indicating where beats change, in order to provide themselves as actors with a road map through it. Actors do such homework prior to going into rehearsal, knowing they will make many more and perhaps different discoveries in the rehearsal process.

Rehearsal

Part of the actor's discipline is to be early for rehearsal, mentally and emotionally ready to begin at the stroke of the appointed time. He or she prepares for each rehearsal by dressing appropriately for whatever might happen; having script, notepad, and pencil in hand; and warming up his or her instrument vocally and physically. Research and relevant homework should be ongoing.

Memorization is one kind of homework. As stated above, many theatre civilians equate acting with learning lines; most consider it the hardest part of being an actor. Indeed there are roles, such as King Lear, Peer Gynt, and Hamlet, where the act of memorizing is itself intimidating. But in fact, and even in these roles, getting the words into the mind is like learning to shift the gears before driving the Grand Prix—one must be able to do it instinctively in order to race. Lines must be so solidly in the memory that they are reflex when cued. What is essential about memorization is that it be perfect. The playwright's words must be what the actor speaks. That protects the integrity of the work and, because of the collaborative nature of theatre, it ensures precise cueing and timing every performance. The actor who does not say the right words may find himself or herself onstage without a phone being rung or another character making an entrance because *the crew member or actor did not get the right cue.*

For aesthetic reasons, actors rarely go into the first rehearsal off-book. If they merely learn words, they may establish patterns that will be difficult to break later, and their acting may be stilted because the process began with the words rather than growing out of character and situation. Also, actors who memorize too soon are in danger of interpreting the script or the character differently than the director and that may eventually prove counterproductive or even damaging. Most actors find it easier to memorize once they know the blocking, i.e., they associate crossing to the table to pick up the coffee cup with a particular line or phrase. Both directors and actors usually want scripts out of hand by the work-through rehearsals because they are physically and psychologically in the way. It is difficult to make discoveries in a love scene with books between actors or to utilize tactics when actors aren't making eye contact because they are reading the script. At any rate,

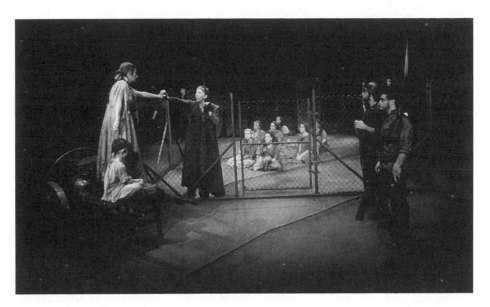

Scene from *Trojan Women* by Euripides. Directed by Cary Libkin, produced by the University Resident Theatre Company, The Pennsylvania State University, November 1991.

memorization must occur early enough that the artists are totally secure with it and can concentrate on acting.

Acting is *Doing.* It is truthful behavior under imaginary circumstances. It grows out of the use of Self and is firmly rooted in instinctual behavior. It involves creativity, discipline, imagination, form, and choice. It hopes for emotional life and talent. In *Respect for Acting,* Uta Hagen defines talent as: ". . . an amalgam of high sensitivity; easy vulnerability; high sensory equipment (seeing, hearing, touching, smelling, tasting—*intensely);* a vivid imagination as well as a grip on reality; the desire to communicate one's own experience and sensations to make one's self heard and seen."

Acting is about imagining, finding out "What If." What if I were the King of Siam? What if my skin were brown? What if I were a victim of abusive behavior? What if my child were dying of AIDS? What if I lost everything but my life in Hurricane Andrew? What if you did this to me? What would I do?

Acting is reciprocal and transactional. It happens between actors and between characters. It is about action and reaction. "A" causes "B."

Acting is about choices. Actors choose their action each moment—to laugh at, to walk away from, to physically crowd—and that results in choices by other actors. Characters make choices that cause other characters to respond in quite specific ways.

Rehearsal is when actors, working with the director, discover the action of the play and build the ensemble. The action of the play is what is really going on. The playwright provides the text—what people say and do. But there is also subtext—the implicit or metaphorical meaning—that must be ferreted out by the director and actors in order that it be understood by the audience. For example, that which is not being said may be more charged with meaning than what is said. When Mark Anthony calls out "For Brutus is an honorable man," we know he means everything but that. Such incongruity between the situation and accompanying words or actions, understood by the audience but not the characters, is known as dramatic irony.

Ensemble means absence of egocentric behavior. No stars. To reiterate what was stated above, everyone's contribution is essential in and important to process and product. Most artists feel safe when they are part of a creative whole. Because they do not have to take risks alone, they are willing to risk more. They have a safety net which they can trust. Trust is required of and by every creative artist in the theatre. Artists have to trust themselves to consistently deliver that which they must deliver. They must trust and be trusted by every person who participates in the collaboration known as theatre. They trust each other to make entrances and not leave them on stage alone; they trust the dresser to be in the wing with their costume change organized when they exit the stage; they trust the flyer to understand he or she has their lives in their hands when they swing Peter and Wendy and Michael out that window into the night; they trust the audience to applaud where they are supposed to and not go to the lobby until the end of the act. Trust both nurtures and charges the creative climate.

Performance

Actors, the most vulnerable theatre artists, are also the most visible and celebrated. In performance, they *do.* They embody the psychic energy and dramatic action of human beings in unique and imaginary circumstances. Actors and audience together create theatre. It happens in their minds and souls. They each reach out for the other, to touch or be touched. Actors act because they need to connect with, make a difference for, be validated by, the audience present at that performance. Audiences go to the theatre because they need to get "outside" themselves, to experience images or ideas or issues essential to their own humanity and heritage, to bond with their community. And, actors and audiences make theatre together because they enjoy it. It feels good.

The actor, in order to create, before and with the audience, surrounded by the technicians and crew needed to make the "magic," functions in a state of public solitude. That means that insofar as possible, the actor onstage shuts out of his or her consciousness, the presence of all those not in the

world of the play, those in other realities. Because the character does not acknowledge the existence of an audience, he or she does not hear them cough; because the front door is real for the character, the doorbell rings because it is pushed by another character, not the sound technician. The actor onstage must also find a mental place that allows him or her to, without embarrassment, display extraordinary or outrageous behavior in public. Such behavior could be seeming to kill or rape someone, to vomit or weep inconsolably.

In performance, the actor must be consistent and in control. As stated above, other actors, the stage manager, and run crew must be able to trust him or her to do the play as it was rehearsed. The very liveness of the event endangers consistency, but the integrity of the production requires it. Part of maintaining consistency is the actor remaining in control. The key word in the preceding paragraph is seeming. The actor is seemingly killing or raping or vomiting or weeping inconsolably. Theatre is dangerous. Someone gets hurt if an actor loses control—a slap to another actor's face in the wrong place or an arrow shot one line too soon. Or, the audience cannot hear or understand the words when the actor loses control of his or her inconsolable weeping.

Audiences too must be able to trust the actor to do the play as rehearsed. Most of the time they believe that everything that happens onstage is supposed to happen because actors are terrific at making it seem that way. But when things are obviously wrong—the door sticks, a line is dropped, the gun doesn't fire, the zipper breaks— audiences, notoriously empathetic, worry. They cannot stay in the world of the play, the world created onstage and in their minds, if, for example, they fear that the actor, rather than the character, is hurt. They may be perfectly comfortable with a drunk character; they are totally uncomfortable with a drunk actor.

If consistency and control describe the craft of the actor, the illusion of the first time prescribes the art of the actor. Simply stated, the illusion of the

God's Country by Steven Dietz, as performed by the University Resident Theatre Company of The Pennsylvania State University, October 1991, directed by Bob Leonard.

first time means that no matter how many times actors rehearse or perform something, it must seem as if this time is the first time they have ever said those words, made those discoveries or decisions, done those actions, thought those thoughts. The illusion of the first time has to do with the fact that although the actor knows how the play ends, the character doesn't. The character has to get to the end, *each time.* Actors are taught they must "stay in the moment," to allow the character to get to the end, each time—one moment at a time. Characters don't know they are tragic heroes. They don't know they will win the lottery. They have to find it onstage. Actors skilled in the illusion of the first time ward off boredom with the repetition and prevent the production from becoming stale.

Generally, actors and audiences are generous with each other. They like and need each other. They are the bottom line magicians in the product called theatre.

Selected Readings

Benedetti, Robert L. *The Actor at Work.* 3rd. ed. Englewood Cliffs, NJ, 1981.

Brook, Peter. *The Shifting Point.* New York, 1987.

Cole, Toby, and Chinoy, Helen K., eds. *Actors in Acting.* Rev. ed. New York, 1970.

Cole, Toby, and Chinoy, Helen K., eds. *Directors on Directing.* Rev. ed. Indianapolis, 1963.

Hagen, Uta. *Respect for Acting.* New York, 1971.

Spolin, Viola. *Improvisation for the Theatre.* Evanston, IL, 1963.

Stanislavski, Constantine. *An Actor Prepares.* Trans. by Elizabeth Reynolds Hapgood. New York, 1936.

PEER GYNT: **Tentative Rehearsal Schedule***
University Resident Theatre Company, Spring 1992
Director—Carole Brandt

WEEK ONE

M M 2	-	7:00 P.M. -	Show and Tell
		8:00 P.M. -	Read-through
T M 2	-	7:00 P.M. -	Discussion/Improv/Sing/Movement Work
W M 4	-	7:00 P.M. -	Block Act I/Wedding Dance Work
T M 5	-	7:00 P.M. -	Troll Dance Work
		8:30 P.M. -	Stumble through Act I
F M 6	-	7:00 P.M. -	Block Act II/Anitra Dance Work
S M 7	-	10:00 A.M. -	Vocal Work
		11:30 A.M. -	Stumble through Act II

WEEK TWO

M M 16	-	7:00 P.M. -	Warm-up and Run Show
T M 17	-	7:00 P.M. -	Work Scenes 1 and 2 (Act I); Wedding Dance Work
		8:30 P.M. -	Troll Dance Work
		10:15 P.M. -	Vocal Work
W M 18	-	7:00 P.M. -	Work Scenes 3, 4 (Act I)
		10:15 P.M. -	Run I - 1-4
T M 19	-	7:00 P.M. -	Work Troll Movement/Dance
		8:15 P.M. -	Work Scenes 5, 6, 7, 8 (Act I) Vocal Work as Scheduled
F M 20	-	7:00 P.M. -	Work Scenes 9, 10, 11, 12 (Act I)
S M 21	-	10:00 A.M. -	Work Scenes 13, 14, 15 (Act I) Wedding Dance Work Troll Movement/Dance
		12:30 P.M. -	Run Act I

WEEK THREE

M M 23	-	7:00 P.M. -	Work Scenes 1, 2, 3, 4, 6, 7 (Act II); Anitra Dance and Vocal Work
T M 24	-	7:00 P.M. -	Work Scenes 5, 8, 9, 14 (Act II): Prison Ensemble Movement
W M 25	-	7:00 P.M. -	Work Scenes 10, 11, 12, 13 (Act II); Congregation Vocal Work
T M 26	-	7:00 P.M. -	Work Scenes 15, 16, 17, 18 (Act II); Churchgoers Vocal Work and Staging
F M 27	-	7:00 P.M. -	Run II; Dance and Vocal Work
S M 28	-	10:00 A.M. -	Run Show

WEEK FOUR

M M 30	-	7:00 P.M. -	Rework I (Scenes 1-5) on Set; Vocal/Movement/Dance Work
T M 31	-	7:00 P.M. -	Rework I (Scenes 6-12) on Set; Vocal/Movement/Dance Work
W A 1	-	7:00 P.M. -	Rework I (Scenes 13-15) on Set; Vocal/Movement/Dance Work
		9:15 P.M. -	Rework II (Scenes 1-2) on Set
T A 2	-	7:00 P.M. -	Rework II (Scenes 3-10) on Set; Vocal/Movement/Dance Work
F A 3	-	7:00 P.M. -	Rework II (Scenes 11-18) on Set; Vocal/Movement/Dance Work
S A 4	-	10:00 A.M. -	Run Show Vocal/Movement/Dance Work

WEEK FIVE

M A 6	-	7:00 P.M. -	Dry Tech with Actors Whatever Needs It Most
T A 7	-	7:00 P.M. -	Dry Tech with Actors
W A 8	-	7:00 P.M. -	Run Show Special Effects
T A 9	-	7:00 P.M. -	Tech Show (4:00 - H.S. Teacher Round Table)
F A 10	-	7:00 P.M. -	Tech Show
S A 11	-	12:00 P.M. -	Tech (10 out of 12)

WEEK SIX

M A 13	-	7:00 P.M. -	First Dress
T A 14	-	7:00 P.M. -	Second Dress
W A 15	-	8:00 P.M. -	First Preview
T A 16	-	8:00 P.M. -	Second Preview
F A 17	-	8:00 P.M. -	Opening Night
S A 18	-	2:00 P.M. -	Matinee
		8:00 P.M. -	Performance

WEEK SEVEN

M A 20	-	8:00 P.M. -	Performance
T A 21	-	8:00 P.M. -	Performance
W A 22	-	10:00 A.M. -	Matinee (High School)
		8:00 P.M. -	Performance
T A 23	-	10:00 A.M. -	Matinee (High School)
		8:00 P.M. -	Performance
F A 24	-	8:00 P.M. -	Performance
S A 25	-	2:00 P.M. -	Matinee
		8:00 P.M. -	Performance

*Schedule subject to change up to 24 hours before each rehearsal. Please be early and prepared. The work is exciting, challenging, and all we can handle in the time we have.

Would the following people make appointments for 30 minute character conferences with me the week of March 2-6: Kirsten Olson, Patricia McLaughlin, Tom Bruno, Jim Sioutis, Paul Stetler, Toni Hood, Kurt Johnson

CRIME ON GOAT ISLAND: Tentative Rehearsal Schedule
University Resident Theatre Company, Fall 1991
Director—Carole Brandt

TS 4	-	7:00 P.M.	-	Show and Tell - Read Through/Discussion
WS 5	-	7:00 P.M.	-	Characterization/Improvization
TS 6	-	7:00 P.M.	-	Block I without Chorus
FS 7	-	7:00 P.M.	-	Block II and III without Chorus
SS 8	-	10:00 A.M.	-	Run Show (Chorus watch)

MS 10 - 7:00 P.M. - Work Unit 1; 7:30 P.M. - Work Unit 2;
9:00 P.M. - Work Unit 3; 7:30 P.M. - Chorus
Characterization/Improvization

TS 11 - 7:00 P.M. - Work Unit 4; 8:30 P.M. - Work Units 5, 6, 7;
9:30 P.M. - Mask and Movement Work

WS 12 - 7:00 P.M. - Chorus Mask and Movement Work;
7:00 P.M. - Run Act I; 8:30 P.M. - Work Units 8, 9;
9:15 P.M. - Work Unit 10

TS 13 - 7:00 P.M. - P.M. - Chorus Mask and Movement Work; 8:30 P.M.
7:00 P.M. - Work Units 11, 12, 13; 8:15 P.M. - Work Units 14, 15, 16, 17, 18; 9:45 P.M. - Run Act II

FS 14 - 7:00 P.M. - Chorus Mask and Movement Work; 8:30 P.M.
7:00 P.M. - Work Units 19, 20, 21; 8:30 P.M. - Work Units 22, 23, 24, 25; 9:30 P.M. - Work Units 26, 27, 28; 10:00 P.M. - Run Act III

SS 15 - 10:00 A.M. - Company Call - Run Show - Work Chorus

MS 17	-	7:00 P.M.	-	Rework I with Chorus
MS 18	-	7:00 P.M.	-	Rework I with Chorus
WS 19	-	7:00 P.M.	-	Run Act I; 9:00 P.M. - Rework II with Chorus
TS 20	-	7:00 P.M.	-	Rework II with Chorus
FS 21	-	7:00 P.M.	-	Run II; 9:00 P.M. - Rework III with Chorus
FS 22	-	10:00 A.M.	-	Rework III with Chorus; Run III; 11:30 A.M.
		2:00 P.M.	-	Run Show

MS 24	-	7:00 P.M.	-	Whatever Needs It Most; Character Conferences
TS 25	-	7:00 P.M.	-	Whatever Needs It Most; Character Conferences
WS 26	-	7:00 P.M.	-	Run Show Onstage
TS 27	-	7:00 P.M.	-	Tech
FS 28	-	7:00 P.M.	-	Tech
SS 29	-	12:00 P.M.	-	Tech Run; 7:00 P.M. - Midnight - Tech Run

MO 1	-	7:00 P.M.	-	1st Dress
TO 2	-	7:00 P.M.	-	2nd Dress
WO 3	-	7:00 P.M.	-	1st Preview
TO 4	-	7:00 P.M.	-	2nd Preview
FO 5	-	8:00 P.M.	-	Open
SO 6	-		-	Performance 2:00 and 8:00 P.M.

MO 8	-	Performance
TO 9	-	Performance and Photo Call?
WO 10	-	Performance
TO 11	-	Performance
FO 12	-	CES Faculty and ACTF Adjudication
SO 13	-	2:00 and 8:00 P.M. - Close

A LITTLE NIGHT MUSIC: **Tentative Rehearsal Schedule**
Illinois Wesleyan University, Fall 1976
Director: Dr. Brandt; Musical Director: Ms. Birden; Choreographer: Ms. Romersberger

WEEK ONE:

Sept.

T11	-	6:30 P.M.	-	Read and sing through show - Company
F12	-	6:30 P.M.	-	Weekend in the Country - vocal
		8:00 P.M.	-	Discussion and improvisation - Company
S13	-	1:00 P.M.	-	Block Act I
		9:00 A.M.	-	Liaisons - Vocal
		9:45 A.M.	-	Miller's Son - Vocal
		10:30 A.M.	-	Later - Vocal
		11:15 A.M.	-	Night Waltz - Vocal
		9:00 A.M.	-	Unit 77 - Staging/Dance
		10:00 A.M.	-	Unit 1 - Staging/Dance
		11:00 A.M.	-	Unit 3 - Staging /Dance

WEEK TWO:

M15	-	6:30 P.M.	-	Now (Vocal), Night Waltz (Dance)
		7:15 P.M.	-	Soon (Vocal), Night Waltz (Dance)
		8:00 P.M.	-	Run Act I
T16	-	6:30 P.M.	-	Glamorous Life (Vocal)
		7:30 P.M.	-	Block Act I
W17	-	6:30 P.M.	-	You Must Meet My Wife (Vocal) Work Units I, 2, 3, 77 (Without Desiree/Frederick)
		7:15 P.M.	-	Now, Soon, Later (Vocal)
		8:00 P.M.	-	Run Act II
T18	-	6:00 P.M.	-	Every Day a Little Death
		6:30 P.M.	-	Remember (Vocal); Now, Soon Later (Stage)
		7:15 P.M.	-	In Praise of Women (Vocal)
		8:00 P.M.	-	Run Show
F19	-	6:00 P.M.	-	Now (6:30 - W; 7:00 - M)
		6:30 P.M.	-	Every Day a Little Death (Vocal)
		7:45 P.M.	-	You Must Meet My Wife (Stage); Improvisation and Characterization
S20	-	9:00 A.M.	-	Act I Music (Vocal)
		9:00 A.M.	-	Stage Glamorous Life
		10:00 A.M.	-	Remember (Stage)

Week Two, cont'd.

11:00 A.M. -	In Praise of Women (Stage)
11:30 A.M. -	Every Day a Little Death (Stage)
1:00 P.M.	-	Run Units 1, 2, 3
1:30 P.M.	-	Work Unit 4
2:00 P.M.	-	Work Unit 5
2:45 P.M.	-	Work Unit 6
3:15 P.M.	-	Work Unit 7
3:45 P.M.	-	Work Unit 8
4:00 P.M.	-	Work Unit 9
4:15 Pl.M.	-	Work Unit 10
4:30 P.M.	-	Run Units 1-10

WEEK THREE:

M22	-	6:30 P.M.	-	The Sun Won't Set - Vocal
		6:30 P.M.	-	Liaisons - Stage
		7:15 P.M.	-	Miller's Son - Stage
		8:00 P.M.	-	Work Unit 11
		8:30 P.M.	-	Work Unit 12
		9:15 P.M.	-	Work Unit 13
T23	-	6:30 P.M.	-	The Sun Won't Set - Stage
		8:00 P.M.	-	Work 14
		8:15 P.M.	-	Work 15
		8:45 P.M.	-	Work 16
		9:00 P.M.	-	Work 17
		9:15 P.M.	-	Work 18
		9:30 P.M.	-	Work 19
		10:00 P.M.	-	Work 21
W24	-	6:30 P.M.	-	Weekend in the Country - Vocal
		7:15 P.M.	-	It Would Have Been Wonderful - Stage
		8:00 P.M.	-	Run I-21
T25	-	6:30 P.M.	-	Send In the Clowns - Vocal; Perpetual Anticipation - Stage
		7:30 P.M.	-	Send in the Clowns - Stage
		8:00 P.M.	-	Work Unit 22
F26	-	4:00 P.M.	-	Work 23
		4:15 P.M.	-	Work 24
		4:30 P.M.	-	Work 25
		4:45 P.M.	-	Work 26
		5:00 P.M.	-	Work 27
		5:30 P.M.	-	Work 28
		6:00 P.M.	-	Review Dance Numbers
S27	-	1:00 - 4:00 P.M.	-	Act II Music Rehearsal

Rehearsal Schedule, *A Little Night Music,* cont'd.

WEEK FOUR

S28	-	7:00 P.M.	- Run Units 22-28
		7:45 P.M.	- Run Units 1-28
M29	-	6:30 P.M.	- Vocal Reharsal - Armfeldt, Petra, Quintet, Charlotte
		6:30 P.M.	- Work Transitions (Waltz/ Scene Changes)
		8:00 P.M.	- Work Units 29, 30
		8:45 P.M.	- Work 31
		9:00 P.M.	- Work 32
		9:30 P.M.	- Work 33
		9:45 P.M.	- Work 34
		10:00 P.M.	- Work 35
T30	-	6:30 P.M.	- Vocal Rehearsals for Henrik, Fredrik, Anne, Desiree, Carl-Magnus
		6:30 P.M.	- Work Transitions (Waltz/ Scene Changes)
		8:00 P.M.	- Work 36
		8:15 P.M.	- Work 37, 38
		8:30 P.M.	- Work 39, 40
		8:45 P.M.	- Work 41, 42
		9:00 P.M.	- Run Units 29-42

Oct

W1	-	6:30 P.M.	- Weekend in the Country - Vocal
		8:00 P.M.	- Run Act I
T2	-	6:30 P.M.	- Vocal and Dance Warmups
		7:00 P.M.	- Work 43
		7:15 P.M.	- Work 44
		7:30 P.M.	- Work 45
		7:45 P.M.	- Work 46
		8:00 P.M.	- Work 47
		8:15 P.M.	- Work 48
		8:30 P.M.	- Work 49
		8:45 P.M.	- Work 50
		9:00 P.M.	- Work 51
		9:15 P.M.	- Work 52
		9:30 P.M.	- Run 43-52
F3	-	6:30 P.M.	- Vocal and Dance Warmups
		7:00 P.M.	- Work 53
		7:15 P.M.	- Work 54
		7:30 P.M.	- Work 55

		8:00 P.M.	- Work 56
		8:15 P.M.	- Work 57
		8:30 P.M.	- Work 58
		8:45 P.M.	- Work 59
		9:15 P.M.	- Work 60
		9:45 P.M.	- Run 53-60
S4	-	9:00 A.M. - 12:00	- Whatever Needs It Most
		1:00 P.M.	- Work 61
		1:30 P.M.	- Work 62
		1:45 P.M.	- Work 63
		2:00 P.M.	- Work 64
		2:15 P.M.	- Work 65
		2:30 P.M.	- Work 66
		3:00 P.M.	- Work 67
		3:10 P.M.	- Work 68
		3:20 P.M.	- Work 69
		3:30 P.M.	- Work 70
		3:40 P.M.	- Work 71
		3:50 P.M.	- Work 72
		4:00 P.M.	- Work 73
		4:45 P.M.	- Work 74
		5:00 P.M.	- Work 75
		5:15 P.M.	- Work 76

WEEK FIVE

S5	-	1:30 P.M.	- Work 77
		2:00 P.M.	- Run II
M6	-	6:30 P.M.	- Warmups
		7:00 P.M.	- Run Show
T7	-	6:30 P.M.	- Rework 1-27
W8	-	6:30 P.M.	- Rework 28-43
T9	-	6:30 P.M.	- Rework 44-77
F10	-	6:30 P.M.	- Run Show
F11	-	1:00 P.M.	- Run Show with Orchestra

WEEK SIX

S12	-	1:00 P.M.	- Tech Show
M13	-	7:00 P.M.	- Run Show
T14	-	7:30 P.M.	- Dress with Orchestra
W15	-	8:00 P.M.	- Dress, Makeup with Orchestra
T16	-	8:00 P.M.	- Open *A Little Night Music*

CAROUSEL: Tentative Rehearsal Schedule
Florida Players, Spring 1987
Director — Carole Brandt

MO6	-	6:30 P.M.	-	Read/Sing Show
TO7	-	6:30 P.M.	-	Block Act I
WO8	-	6:30 P.M.	-	Block Act II
TO9	-	4:30 P.M.	-	Run Show
FO10	-		-	Homecoming - No Rehearsal
SO12	-	6:30 P.M.	-	Characterization/Improvisation
MO13	-	9:00 P.M.	-	Vocal Rehearsal Company #'s
		6:30 P.M.	-	Dance Prologue
TO14	-	6:30 P.M.	-	Vocal Rehearsal Company 3's
		8:00 P.M.	-	Dance June is Busting Out . . ., Finale I
WO15	-	6:30 P.M.	-	Vocal Rehearsal Company #'s
		8:00 P.M.	-	Dance Blow High, Blow Low, Hornpipe
TO16	-		-	Extremities Opening - No Rehearsal
FO17	-	6:30 P.M.	-	Vocal Rehearsal Principals
		8:00 P.M.	-	Dance Clambake, Granniums, Finale II
SO18	-	2:00 - 5:00 P.M.	-	Ballet
SO19	-	2:00 - 5:00 P.M.	-	Work Dance Numbers
MO20	-	6:30 P.M.	-	Mister Snow
		7:00 P.M.	-	Work Units 1-10
TO21	-	6:30 P.M.	-	Soliloquy
	-	6:50 P.M.	-	Mr. Snow Reprise
	-	7:00 P.M.	-	When Children Are Asleep
WO22	-	6:30 P.M.	-	Soliloquy
	-	7:15 P.M.	-	Work Units 21-31
TO23	-	6:30 P.M.	-	Run Vocal/Dance Act I
	-	8:00 P.M.	-	Run Act I
FO24	-	6:30 P.M.	-	Run Vocal/Dance Act I
	-	8:00 P.M.	-	Run Act II
SO26	-	2:00 - 5:00 P.M.	-	Dance Ballet/Prologue
MO27	-	6:30 P.M.	-	What's the Use of Wondering
		6:50 P.M.	-	Work Units 32-41
TO28	-	6:30 P.M.	-	Highest Judge
	-	6:50 P.M.	-	Work Units 42-49
WO29	-	6:30 P.M.	-	Work Units 50-59
TO30	-	6:30 P.M.	-	Run Vocal/Dance Act II
	-	8:00 P.M.	-	Run Act II
FO31	-	6:30 P.M.	-	Run Show
SN2	-	2:00 - 5:00 P.M.	-	Rework Units 1-13 (inc. #s)
MN3	-	6:30 P.M.	-	Rework Units 14-31 (inc. #s)
TN4	-	6:30 P.M.	-	Rework Units 32-44 (inc. #s)
WN5	-	6:30 P.M.	-	Rework Units 45-59 (inc. #s)
TN6	-	6:30 P.M.	-	Vocal/Dance
	-	7:30 P.M.	-	Run Show
FN7	-	6:30 P.M.	-	Dry Tech
SN8	-		-	Run Show
SN9	-		-	Tech
MN10	-		-	Dress with piano
TN11	-		-	Dress with orchestra
WN12	-		-	Dress with orchestra
TN13	-		-	Preview
FN14	-		-	Open 8:15
SN15	-		-	Performance
SN16	-		-	Performance
TN17	-		-	Performance
WN19	-		-	Performance
TN20	-		-	Performance
FN21	-		-	Performance/ACTF Critique
SN22	-		-	Performance

Stage Management Forms

Production Analysis Form

Almost all stage managers do a production analysis of some sort. The way they do it differs from stage manager to stage manager. The following form is something I use when I first get a script. I take time to read the script for enjoyment, then I begin to break the script down into its various elements. This information becomes invaluable when I sit down with the director to discuss the production and prepares me with questions when I hold the first production meeting.

The form is fairly straight forward. It lists the act, scene, and page number, with information on the characters, the setting, the props, the lights, the costumes, and any other special effects and/or considerations that may arise from the script.

Props Tracking Form

The form is something I use to track props that need to move from location to location during the run of the show. Based on these forms I will then create the master preset for the show. In rehearsal where you might not be working Acts and Scenes in show order, this form gives me an immediate double check on whether or not a scene is set and whether we are prepared to start rehearsal.

On the top of the form is the stage furniture and props set onstage as the scene begins. I sometimes include diagrams to be more specific in placement. Below, in the section which divides the stage into right and left, I track individual props that are brought onto the stage by page number, character, the particular prop, and the side of stage it exits. I include under notes if it exits stage under a different character.

Below that I have a small section for notes that will aid me in training the backstage crew on where and when props have to be moved from one side of stage to another.

The form has proven invaluable to me in running rehearsals and for preparing the necessary paperwork required to ready a show for technical rehearsals. It also helps me keep the director informed as to where items end up and their location so impossible situations don't arise (i.e., a prop that exits stage right and would be implausible to enter another side of stage in the scene directly following).

Prepared by Travis DeCastro, The Pennsylvania State University, 1992.

Production Analysis Form   **Production:** _____   **Page #** _____

Act/Scene Page #	Characters	Setting/ Furniture	Props	Lighting	Costumes	Special Considerations

Props Tracking Form   **Act** _____ **Scene** _____

Onstage Props

Stage Right				**Stage Left**			
Pg.	Char.	Props and Notes	Ex	Pg.	Char.	Props and Notes	Ex

Notes on props that have to be tracked

Merrily We Roll Along

Furniture, Hand Props, Flying Pieces

T=transition between scenes

ACT/Scene	Furniture	Hand Props	Flying Pieces
ACT I			
I.1 Graduation	Podium 2 potted palms	Glass of water (podium)	Banner Scrim Drop
I.1-T	1 Three-wheel bicycle		
I.2 Hollywood	Piano Piano bench Umbrella table & 3 chairs 2 louge chairs 4 potted plants Pool fabric	Beach ball Designer Innertube (BUA) 2 Pool towels Cigarette holders, 12 M, 12 W Cigar (J. J.) (Kutos) Lighters? Champagne glasses Champagne bottles 4 trays Breakaways	

I.2-T	4 Tricycles (small) with license plates
	   Rossmer (1979), Raffouf (1978),
	   Skowron (1976), Kreitman (1977)
	1 Tricycle (medium) (Marcus)		

I.3 Restaurant	2 round tables
	2 booths
	Maitre'd podium
		5 drink glasses
		   1 champagne, 1 high ball, 2 martini,
		   1 grasshopper
		Gossip columnist little black notebook
		   and pen (Leberknight)
		Wallet and money (Charley)	

I.3-T	Gurney		
I.4 Studio	2 swivel chairs 2 cameras 2 boom microphones Piano Piano bench	Clipboard (Bisi)	
I.4-T	2 Tandem bicycles		
I.5 Apartment	Step unit Planter	Flashlight (Frank) Bag with two beers Carton of orange juice 3-4 color swatches (Gussie's purse) 1 bottle of Dom Perignon 5 champagne glasses (repeat) Small silver tray Cigar (J.J.) Bottle capper and bottle caps	Ceiling unit
I.5-T	18 Yo-yos 2 Skateboards 3 Paddleboards		
I.6 Courthouse	Step unit Escape platform Escape steps	Hand-held TV camera (Goffredo) Microphone and recorder (Soundman) (Hart) Still cameras (Mackall, Buchanon)	

ACT/Scene	Furniture	Hand Props	Flying Pieces
		Flashbulbs	
		Hand microphone and recorder (Williams)	
		Clipboard and pencil (repeat) (Kreitman)	
		Tacklebox with makeup puff and mirror (Skowron)	
		2 Briefcases	
ACT II			
II.1 Alvin Theatre		12 umbrellas	Marquee sign
		Gussie's umbrella	
		Cigar (J.J.)	
		Tape recorder (Practical)	
II.2 Brownstone	Piano	Cigarette holders?	
	Piano bench	Cigarettes	
	FloWer pots	Cigar (J.J.)	
	Small table	Lighters?	
	Plant stand	Champagne glasses (repeat)	
		Trays (repeat)	
		3 plants	
		Pruning snippers (Gussie)	
		Watering can (Gussie)	
II.3 Nightclub	3 round tables	Cigar (J.J.)	Sign
	9 chairs	Lighter?	
	Piano	Bouquet (Beth)	
	Piano bench	Wallet (J.J.)	
		Money (J.J.)	
		Ring in satin pouch (Mrs. S.)	
		Bouquet and vase	
II.3-T Typewriter	1 rolling typing stand	1 manual typewriter	
	Piano	Manuscript paper	
	Piano bench	Pencils	
	1 Palette (Mary)	Typing paper	
	with rug	Cigar (J.J.)	
	cushions	Audition music paper	
	phone	2 phones (Frank & Charlie)	
	popcorn and bowl	8 pairs of roller skates	
	Rolling chair for J.J.		
II.4 Rooftop	(Trap)	2 scripts	(Drop out)
		1 binoculars	
II.5 Graduation	Podium		Banner in
	2 potted palms		Scrim in

Consumables:
Ginger ale (champagne)
Cigarettes
Flashbulbs
Food coloring (grasshopper, scotch)
Breakaways
Paper bags
Batteries for tape plyer
Cigars
Popcorn
Lighter fluid

Possible rolling items:
1 Three-Wheel Bicycle
Unicycle
5 Tricycles
18 Yo-yos
4 Hula hoops
Small red wagon
Wheelchair
Gurney
Skateboards

Actor Character Breakdown: *Merrily We Roll Along*—Act I

		I.1	I.2	I.3	I.4	I.5	I.6
Bisi	8	Student	Waitress		Prod. Asst.		Photographer
Bua	6	Student	Swim/guest				Ogler
Buchanan	15	Student	Waiter	Hd. Waiter			Photographer
Goffredo	10	Student	Guest		Camera op.		Camera Op.
Gottfeld		?					X
Guichard		?	X	X		X	X
Hart	11	Student	Meg		Boom op.		Boom op.
James	16	Student	Backer				Ogler
Kreitman	14	Student	Movie Star		Boom op.		His staff
Kutos		?				X	X
Leberknig	7	Student	Guest	Gos Column			Ogler
Lewis	13	Student	Waitress				Ogler
Loprete	19	Student	Guest		TV Host		Ogler
Lyon		?		X	X	X	X
Mackall	17	Student	Decorator				Photographer
Marcus	12	Student	Guest				TV Reporter
Nauman	9	Student	Guest		Camera op.		HR Lawyer
Pelusi	2	Student	Attorney				Attorney
Pisarri	20	Student	Swmr/P.A.				HR Staff
Raffauf	3	Student	Swimmer				Ogler
Redmon							
Robinson		X	X	X	X	X	X
Rossmer	18	Student	Guest				HS Cam. Op.
Skowron	4	Valedict.	Waiter	Waiter			HR Staff
White		?	X	X		X	X
Williams	1	Student	Protege				Reporter 2
Withers							
Zimmerman	5	Student	Guest				Ogler

Actor Character Breakdown: *Merrily We Roll Along*—Act II

		II.1	II.2	II.3	II.4	II.5
Bisi	8		Dancer/Guest	1st Girl		Student
Bua	6	Audience	Waiter			Student
Buchanan	15		Dancer/Guest	Skater/Tapper		Student
Goffredo	10		Guest	Skt/Tap/Min		Student
Gottfeld		X	X	X		
Guichard		X	X	X		
Hart	11	Audience	Guest	Skater/Tapper		Student
James	16	Audience	Guest	Audience		Student
Kreitman	14		Mv Str/Danc	Skater/Tapper		Student
Kutos		X	X	X		
Leberknig	7		Photographer	Skater/Tapper		Student
Lewis	13	Audience	Guest			Student
Loprete	19	Audience	Guest			Student
Lyon		X	X	X	X	X
Mackall	17	Audience	Columnist	Skater/Tapper		Student
Marcus	12	Audience	Guest			Student
Nauman	9	Audience	Guest			Student
Pelusi	2	Audienc e	Dancer/Guest	Pianist		Student
Pisarri	20	Audience	Dancer/Guest	Skater/Tapper		Student
Raffauf	3	Audience	Guest			Student
Redmon				X		
Robinson		X	X	X	X	X
Rossmer	18	Audience	Guest	Audience		Student
Skowron	4		Dancer/Guest	Skater/Tapper		Valedictorian
White		X	X	X	X	X
Williams	1	Audienc e	Guest			Student
Withers				X		
Zimmerman	5	Audience	Waitress			Student

Production Calendar

January 1993
Merrily We Roll Along

SUNDAY	MONDAY	TUESDAY	WEDNESDAY	THURSDAY	FRIDAY	SATURDAY
					1	2
3	4	5	6	7	8	9
10	11 7:00 First Full Rehearsal PAV	12	13	14 4:00 Production Meeting- TAPS	15	16
17	18	19	20	21 4:00 Production Meeting- TAPS	22	23
24	25	26	27	28 4:00 Production Meeting- TAPS	29	30 Light Hang 9:00 AM
31 Load-In						

December 1992

S	M	T	W	T	F	S
		1	2	3	4	5
6	7	8	9	10	11	12
13	14	15	16	17	18	19
20	21	22	23	24	25	26
27	28	29	30	31		

February 1993

S	M	T	W	T	F	S
	1	2	3	4	5	6
7	8	9	10	11	12	13
14	15	16	17	18	19	20
21	22	23	24	25	26	27
28						

February 1993
Merrily We Roll Along

SUNDAY	MONDAY	TUESDAY	WEDNESDAY	THURSDAY	FRIDAY	SATURDAY
	1	2	3	4 4:00 Production Meeting- TAPS	5	6 9:00 AM- Light Focus
			Load-In			
7 Light Levels	8 6-11 Light Levels	9 Scenery Dry Tech	10 Dry Tech w/actors, mics, orchestra	11	12	13 Tech.. 10 out of 12
			Tech 7-11			
14	15	16	17 8:00 1st Preview	18 4:00 Production Meeting- TAPS 8:00 2nd Preview	19 8:00 OPEN!!	20 8:00 MERRILY
	7:00 1/2 hour 7:30 Dress w/Orchestra					
21	22	23	24	25	26	27 2:00 MERRILY 8:00 MERRILY: CLOSE!!
			8:00 MERRILY			
28 ***STRIKE ON THE FIRST OF MARCH***						

January

S	M	T	W	T	F	S
					1	2
3	4	5	6	7	8	9
10	11	12	13	14	15	16
17	18	19	20	21	22	23
24	25	26	27	28	29	30
31						

March

S	M	T	W	T	F	S
	1	2	3	4	5	6
7	8	9	10	11	12	13
14	15	16	17	18	19	20
21	22	23	24	25	26	27
28	29	30	31			

Tech Schedule
Merrily We Roll Along

Friday	2/5	
	1:00 - 4:00	Show props delivered to Playhouse
	4:00 - 7:00	Spike furniture
	7:00 - 11:00	Cast on stage, spacing
Saturday	2/6	
	9:00 - 12:00	Morning cast on stage run through /crew called
	12:00 - ??	Afternoon/evening light focus
Sunday	2/7	
		Cast day off
		Light levels, time?? Walkers, scene changers?
Monday	2/8	
		Pit load-in??
	6:00	Light levels
	7:00	Cast Szitsprobe, location t.b.a.
	11:00	Break
Tuesday	2/9	
	7:00 - 11:00	Cast work on stage
Wednesday	2/10	
		Afternoon, tape sound cue levels
	6:00	Crew call
	7:00	Actors into microphones, sound check
	7:15	Begin teching ACT I, lights, sets, sound, with piano
	10:45	Clean-up
	11:00	Break
Thursday	2/11	
	6:00	Crew call
	7:00	Actors into microphones, sound check
	7:15	Continue teching ACT I, lights, sets, sound, with piano
	10:45	Clean-up
	11:00	Break
Friday	2/12	
	6:00	Crew call
	7:00	Actors into microphones, sound check
	7:15	Begin teching ACT II, lights, sets, sound
	10:45	Clean-up
	11:00	Break
Saturday	2/13	
		ten of twelve
	11:00	Crew call
	12:00	Actors into microphones, sound check
	12:15	Continue teching ACT II with piano
	4:45	Clean-up
	5:00	Dinner break
	6:00	Crew call
	7:00	Actors into microphones, sound check
	7:15	Tech run with orchestra? Piano?
	11:45	Clean-up, notes
	12:00	Break
Sunday	2/14	
		Cast day off
		Paint day and technical notes
Monday	2/15	
	6:00	Crew call
	7:00	Actor call - work with dressers on costumes and changes
	7:30	1/2 hour - actors into microphones
	8:00	1st dress with orchestra
	10:45	Clean-up
	11:00	Break
Tuesday	2/16	
	6:00	Crew call
	7:00	Warm-up notes, stage
	7:30	1/2 hour - actors into microphones
	8:00	Final dress rehearsal with orchestra
	10:45	Clean-up
	11:00	Break
Wednesday	2/17	
	6:00	Crew call
	7:00	Warm-up, Room 119
	7:30	1/2 hour - actors into microphones
	8:00	1st Preview
		Notes following performance
Thursday		
	6:00	Crew call
	7:00	Warm-up, Room 119
	7:30	1/2 hour - actors into microphones
	8:00	2nd Preview
		Notes following performance
Friday	2/19	
	6:00	Crew call
	7:00	Warm-up, Room 119
	7:30	1/2 hour - actors into microphones
	8:00	Opening Night
		Opening Night Party, Nittany Lion Inn

Continue the regular performance schedule

List of Rail Cues
Merrily We Roll Along

Scene		Cue #	Action	Scene		Cue #	Action
ACT I				**ACT II**			
Preshow		IN	Scrim (#24)	Preset		IN	Marquee (#4)
			Banner (#19)	II.1 Alvin Theatre			
			Drop#27	II.2 Brownstone		OUT	Marquee (#4)
I.1 Graduation				II.3 Nightclub		IN	Sign (#7)
I.2 Hollywood Party		OUT	Scrim (#24)	II.3-T Typewriter		OUT	Sign (#7)
			Banner (#19)	II.4 Rooftop		OUT	Drop (#27)
		IN	1 (#3), 2 (#10), and			IN	Scrim (#24)
			3 (#20) Portals	II.5 Graduation		OUT	1 (#3), 2 (#10), and
I.3 Restaurant							3 (#20) Portals
I.4 Studio						IN	Banner (#19)
I.5 Apartment		IN	Ceiling (#15)				
I.6 Courthouse		OUT	Ceiling (#15)				

Merrily We Roll Along
Furniture, Hand Props

ACT/Scene		Furniture	Hand Props
ACT I			
I.1	Graduation	Podium	Glass of water (podium)
		2 potted palms	Frank's speech
			Glasses (costumes)
Transition 1		2 scooters	
I.2	Hollywood	Piano	Beach ball
		Piano bench	Designer Innertube (Bua)
		Umbrella table & 3 chairs	2 Pool towels
		2 lounge chairs	Cigar (J.J.) (Kutos)
		4 potted plants	Champagne glasses (3 dozen)
		Pool fabric	4 trays
Transition 2			
I.3	Restaurant	2 round tables	5 drink glasses
		2 booths	1 champagne, 1 high ball, 2 martini, 1 grasshopper
		Maitre'd podium	2 menus (one opens)
			Gossip columnist little black notebook and pen (Leberknight)
Transition 3			
I.4	Studio	2 swivel chairs	Clipboard (Bisi)
		2 cameras	Pipe (Loprete)
		2 boom microphones	
		Piano	
		Piano bench	

Merrily We Roll Along: **Hand Props, Furniture,** *continued*

ACT/Scene	Furniture	Hand Props
Transition 4	3 paddleboards	
I.5 Apartment	Step unit	Flashlight (Frank)
	Planter	Bag with two beers
		Carton of orange juice
		4 color swatches (Gussie's purse)
		1 bottle of Dom Perignon
		5 champagne glasses
		Small silver tray
		Cigar (J.J.)
		Bottle opener
Transition 5		
I.6 Courthouse	Step unit	Hand-held TV camera (Goffredo) with hand microphone and recorder
	Escape platform	Still cameras (Mackall, Buchanan)
	Escape steps	Flashbulbs
		Hand microphone and recorder (Williams)
		Clipboard and pencil (repeat) (Breitman)
		Tackle box with makeup puff and mirror (Skowron)
		2 briefcases
ACT II		
II.1 Alvin Theatre		8 umbrellas
		Cigar (J.J.)
		Tape recorder (practical)
		Whistle (J.J.)
Transition 6		
II.2 Brownstone	Piano	Cigar (J.J.)
	Piano bench	Champagne glasses (repeat)
	Flower pots	Trays (repeat)
	Small table	3 plants
	Plant stand	1 plant (gets thrown)
		Pruning snippers (Gussie)
		Spray bottle (Gussie)
Transition 7		Wheelbarrow
		Red wagon
		Bubble stuff
II.3 Nightclub	3 round tables (with table- cloths and centerpieces)	Shopping bag
		Ashtray (at center table)
	6 chairs	Bible
	Piano	Cigar (J.J.)
	Piano bench	Lighter
		Bouquet (Beth)
		Wallet (J.J.)
		Money (J.J.)
		Ring in satin pouch (Mrs. S.)
		Bouquet and vase
		2 hankies (Spencers) (Costumes)

Merrily We Roll Along: **Hand Props, Furniture,** *continued*

ACT/Scene	Furniture	Hand Props
Transition 8		
II.3-T Typewriter	1 Rolling typing stand	2 manual typewriters
	Piano	Manuscript paper
	Piano stool	Pencils
	1 Palette (Mary)	Typing paper
	with rug	Cigar (J.J.)
	typewriter	Lighter
	phone	Audition music papers
	pens & pencils	2 phones (Frank and Mary
	Coke	
	Rolling chair for J.J.	
Transition 9		
II.4 Rooftop	(Trap)	2 scripts
		1 binoculars
Transition 10		
II.5 Graduation	Podium	

Consumables:
Seltzer (Champagne)
Flashbulbs
Food coloring (grasshopper, scotch)
Paper bags
Batteries for tape player
Cigars
Coca-Cola for Mary

Possible rolling items:
Scooters
5 tricycyles
18 yo-yos
8 hula hoops
Small red wagon
Gurney
Skateboards
Wheelbarrow
Wheelchair

Other:
1 Selectric typewriter for orchestra pit

Scene from *Merrily We Roll Along* by The University of Pennsylvania's University Resident Theatre Company. Music and songs by Stephen Sondheim, book by George Furth, from the play by George S. Kaufman and Moss Hart. Directed by Carole Bandt; scenic design by Daniel Robinson; costume design by Dana Pinkston; and lighting design by Daniel Walker.

| *Funny Girl* | **Stage Manager's Performance Report** |

Day/Date: Thursday, June 17
Curtain Time: 8 P.M.   **Performance #:** Preview 2

Running Times: Act I: 1:26   Inter: 21 min.   Act II: :54   Total: 2:41

Curtain Up: 8:04   Curtain Down: 10:45

House Notes: **House Count:** 287

TECHNICAL NOTES
Scenery/Flies:
—2 casters came off SL wagon
—top of SR rat-tat cut out broke off
—RWB drop slamming into electric and knocking
   fresnels out of focus
—glaze DR
—bar needs touch-up
—coking floor worked!

Lights:
—spots practice picking up Fanny with LQ 179
—LQ 15, 16 combine?

Sound:
—Fanny had mike trouble in Act 1, switched it out
   at intermission
—Fanny is still having a hard time hearing moni-
   tors in her numbers (Don't Rain on My Parade,
   I Want to Be Seen with You)
—Del: can the paging system go to Rm. 6?

Props:
—need more telegrams
—one of the slates on a crate came off
—clean out dressing that is backstage

Costumes:
none

PERFORMANCE NOTES

The first act started out well, but towards the end
it got a little shaky. Lines seemed to be tentative,
and wrong. Act II continued to slide downhill.
Rat-tat tag was off for the first time. Scenically,
things went pretty well, with only a few loud
bangs from backstage at inappropriate times.

Accident/Incident:
—Stephanie Smith slammed her knee into the fly
   rail during the shift out of Rat-tat. An ice pack
   was applied and she stayed off of it for a bit, but
   was limping on her way out. She said she was
   ok.

SM:
—bump elevator top of show
—Eddie tap
—slower on traveller, mike Mrs. B?
—rasp for taps
—light R3 for Mrs. B EX out of II:2
—don't pin wagon UC out of II:6
—glow spikes for Lisa in II:8
—signs for grn room

CHAPTER EIGHTEEN

❧

Mandala:
Scenic Actualization and Set Design

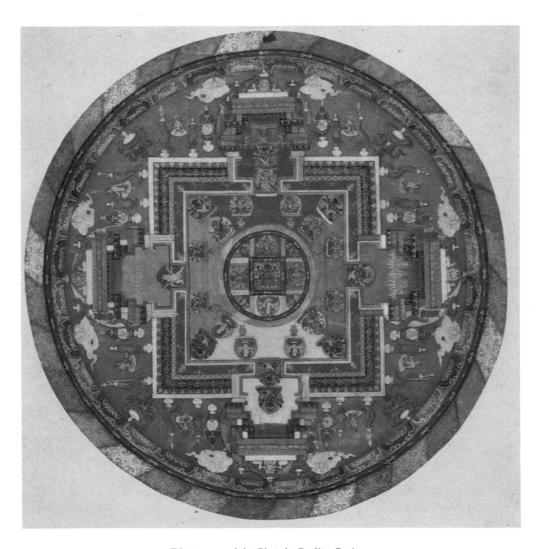

Tibetan mandala. *Photo by Realites Paris*

Theatre as Collaborative Process

Live theatre is unique in terms of the fine arts. By definition, it belies a singular, individual statement and embraces the nature of a group, collaborative process. By virtue of this distinctive process, the products are exceptional in terms of human expression and represent a rare opportunity to explore the nature of creativity and the human condition.

The traditional fine arts (painting, sculpture, music, etc.) often reflect a singular perspective and one frozen perception of the world. The subjects of Van Gogh paintings are rendered solely through his eyes at a particular moment, and we either identify with his perspective, remain neutral, or reject it. In music, it is an artist's singular rhythm and form to which we respond and react. In theatre, the collaborative contributions of playwright, director, designer/technicians and actors combine in a unique effort to make a statement in a particular time and space. The time is *that* moment in the theatre (and is like no other moment). The space is that which *you*, the audience, occupy for that specific performance. What is perceived is both *greater than the individual parts* and *unique to that individual moment*.

To achieve this requires a special state of mind and exceptional cooperation. It means subordinating the "self" to the degree that other opinions, impressions and imaginations have at least equal value. It is a rare moment in both art and the life experience, when the art form itself demands a special openness and vulnerability in order for the artistic statement to be communicated. The basic energy must emanate from a central image and embrace all the creative potential available.

Theatre production requires a radiating pattern of energy (comparable to a pebble thrown into a pond), with the script (central image) tossed into the pool, filtered through the director's interpretation (as if a lens) and subsequently interpreted for production by the actors and designer/technicians for a specific audience, as expressed in Figure 1.

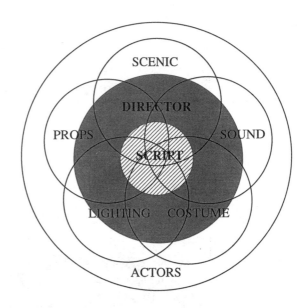

Figure 1. Director/Designer/Actor Mandala

In this context, the flow of energy (concept) is all-inclusive, and can embrace a 360 degree radius of impressions, interpretations, and emotions to provide the greatest possible artistic statement.

The Role of the Designer

Within this paradigm, the designer responds to the script, as orchestrated by the director, for the greatest possible articulation of the concept in relation to the human experience as art. What this means in simple English is that we, as aspiring artists, must search for several levels of meaning and "actualization" (practical realization) to make the theatrical moment the most concentrated and insightful experience for the audience. The definition of these various levels and our success in articulating them onstage will define the success or failure of the theatrical event.

To illustrate what this might mean specifically in terms of theatrical design and production, let us explore the levels or facets of the design/analysis process—the first phase of the script interpretation. A diagrammatic statement of these aspects might appear as in Figure 2.

The three overlapping concepts of this approach essentially embrace all aspects of the nature of theatrical expression and the challenges of visual articulation to the designer. To better understand this challenge, let us analyze each facet individually as well as the implications of their overlapping tendencies and the dynamic design process they foster.

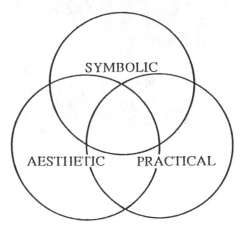

Figure 2. Scenic Paradigm Mandala

The Metaphorical/Symbolic

This realm represents the underlying, universal aspects of the scriptural statement. It assumes that all worthwhile scripts, no matter how specific in terms of context or reference/time, somehow speak to a "universal" condition or question of humanity. They are somehow symbolic, and by implication, represent the universal human spirit.

The challenge here is to visually capture some element of this symbolic aspect in order to kindle the universal subconscious and guide the audience towards a deeper understanding of the dramatic moment. This is often achieved by the use of a *visual metaphor*. A metaphor [pronounced *met-a-*

phor (noun)] is a figure which is transferred from the object it ordinarily designates to an object it may designate only by implicit comparison or analogy.

One of the assumptions implied here is that human beings enjoy experiencing life on several levels simultaneously. On the one hand, we can relate to the mundane, immediate trivialities of daily existence while searching for a greater meaning to our lives. This is part of what theatre can reinforce and part of the commission of the theatre (design) experience.

For instance, in a production of Sophocle's *Oedipus Rex*, the predominant image is of a regal figure (King Oedipus) lording over his subjects. Ultimately, he loses this distinction and is reduced to a blind beggar, banished from his own kingdom. To symbolize this action, the scenic environment could include a prominent, raised area for Oedipus's "regal mode" to graphically (symbolically) represent his initial power. By contrast, some particularly "lowly" space should be considered to represent his ultimate "fall from power."

Based upon the interpretation one wishes to pursue, specific demands are placed upon the scenic elements that must be addressed to effectively translate the play's intent to the stage. Nothing is arbitrary. Ideally, each choice has several levels of meaning and statement.

The Aesthetic/Harmonic

In addition to the underlying symbolic or metaphoric patterns inherent to a given script, certain aesthetic expectations or requirements must be met to effectively articulate the needs of the production. These are usually emotionally based and tend to create an ambiance that reinforces the mood and style of a script. They should be essentially subconscious to an audience, subtly fulfilling the expectations or clarifying the intent of the production. This point of subtlety should be stressed. All too often designers, in an effort to convey meaning to the audience, destroy the process of individual discovery by overstatement or blatant symbolism. A designer should be aware that today's audiences are quite sophisticated and capable of their own visual analysis and interpretation; they need not be "hit over the head." In seeking to establish the ambiance, the designer makes choices that are employed through the basic elements of design. See box below.

One example of an aesthetic design choice is the selection of a specific architectural or fine art style appropriate to the script/production. For instance, in a production of Moliere's *Tartuffe*, the director and production team might elect to use the style of Louis XIV to reflect the decadence and appropriate historical ambiance of the period in which the play was originally produced. This choice would impose certain line and shape qualities indigenous to the architectural period. Accordingly, a color pallet suitable for emphasizing the decadence and sensual aspects of the script might be drawn from a contemporary painter such as Reubens.

The Salon de la Guerre in the Palace of Versaille. *(Hardouin-Mansart, 1678)*

Elements of Design

Line: A dynamic, implied movement of a point in time and space. Often conveys a sense of energy and kinetic potential with an emphasis on character.

Shape: Defined by a "closed line" and suggesting a separate value from the background and an emphasis upon contour. Generally implies a two-dimensional entity, lacking individual details and affecting the symbolic unconscious.

Form: Shape extended to the third-dimension, predominantly through the use of light and shadow. Generally emphasizes weight, mass and scale or proportion.

Texture: The surface quality of a shape or form. Often significantly effective in stimulating emotional response through tactile association.

Color: A portion of the spectrum of white light reflected by an object. Basic properties include hue, value (light to dark) and intensity (brightness). Highly volatile dimension in visual communications, primarily due to the extensive and often contradictory sociological and symbolic associations.

Emphasizing the dark, cold atmosphere of a castle transports the audience to medieval times for this production of Shakespeare's *Hamlet*. (Designer Gerry Beck, Humboldt State University)

A more subjective example might involve scenically reinforcing a specific mood or emotional ambiance appropriate to the style and atmosphere of a given script/production. For instance, in a production of Shakespeare's *Hamlet*, the ensemble might wish to stress the medieval "moodiness" and dark, cold sense of the chambers of a medieval castle. This could entail the textural choice of coarse, crude stone construction and a cool, oppressive color pallet.

In each instance, the design influences the visual impression of the audience and attempts to establish a mood and atmosphere suitable to the conceptual approach to the script. The design should put the audience in an appropriate state of mind, consciously or subconsciously, to best perceive the intent of the production.

The Practical and Technical: Kinetic Design Process

So far, two levels or "layers" of the design statement have been defined—the metaphorical (symbolic) and the aesthetic (emotional). The third realm deals with the more mundane, physical world, yet is critical to the effectiveness of its two preceding more "ethereal" realms. This is the realm of time and space.

A sense of time is effected through the pacing and actual rhythm of movement in the dramatic environment. Space implies composition and balance, and the scale of the production in proportion to the human form. The diagrams in Figure 2 illustrate some of these choices.

This practical level will critically affect our sense of rhythm or harmony in a production and define the options for composition to the director and the acting company. In many respects, it is the most critical area of design, for in this sphere exists the interface between the sculptural (static) form and the critical element of theatre—the live actor (kinetic) form.

Specific examples are numerous and traverse a wide range of choices. They range from such mundane issues as the height of a stair rise to the engineering of an entire scene change. For instance, the difference between a six-inch stair riser and an eight-inch stair riser will have a significant effect upon how we perceive the human form in motion. The former provides a very comfortable and pleasing ratio to movement up or down a staircase. When increased to the latter dimension, movement becomes awkward and harsh. Which would be most appropriate to Cinderella's grand entrance into the ballroom? To Quasimoto's descent from the bell tower of Notre Dame?

A less specific, but even more critical consideration, addresses the rhythm or harmonic ambiance of an entire production. In a French farce (*A Flea in Her Ear*, for example), the placing of entrances and the physical relationships between characters can be critical to maintaining the tempo of the production, and the overall rhythm critical to the comic effect. If a given doorway is too far from another, the tempo is broken and the comic effect compromised. It is the responsibility of the scenic designer to distill the production's critical elements and provide a vehicle (sculpture) capable of facilitating an effective interpretation on behalf of the script, the director and the cast.

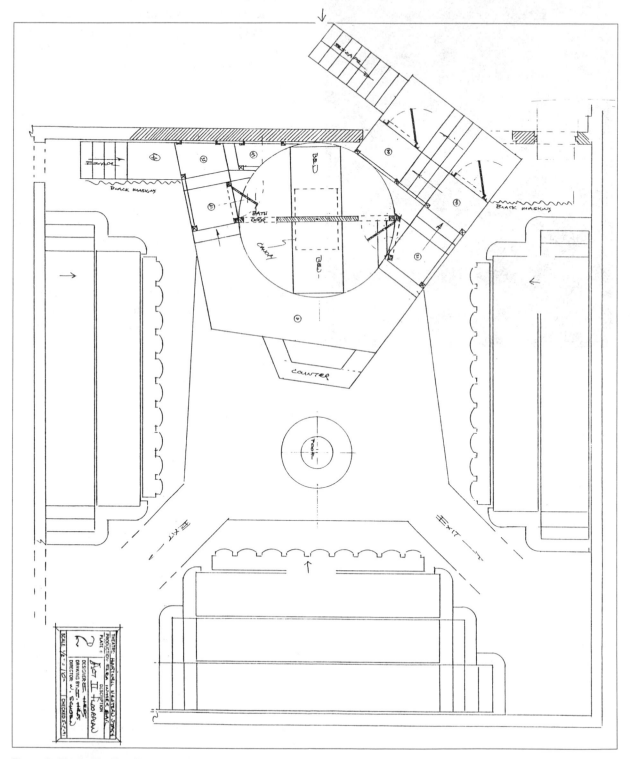

Figure 3. *Flea in Her Ear*, floorplan, option one (*Hartnell Western Stage*)

The evolution of the floorplan is generally the initial phase of this process. Movement patterns, relationships between entrances and objects, and general changes in elevation can be explored on the two-dimensional plan, much in the same way that a football coach might diagram a team's action.

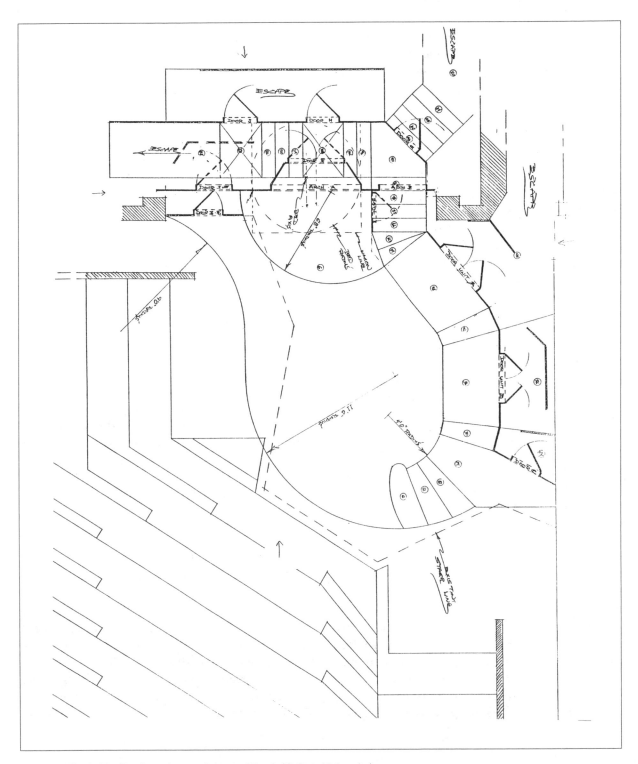

Figure 4. *Flea in Her Ear* floorplan, option two *(Humboldt State University)*

Another example entails the more technical aspects of the scenic change, especially in relationship to the audience's impression of, or reaction to, the overall production. A successful production will be a totally orchestrated experience for the audience; every pause and transition handled so that it has meaning and relevance to the conceptual approach. In other words, the script is "scored," not so much musically but in terms of concept/image.

The familiarity of contemporary audiences with film and television places new demands upon the modern scenic environment. Many contemporary scripts move back and forth between an almost infinite array of environments, and often through time as well. This requires a dramatic space and design imagination much more malleable than previously demanded, and a far greater stretch of the artistic spirit than traditional theatre conventions allow. The "box set" and other conventions are no longer sufficient to accommodate the world of the dramatic imagination.

These new challenges represent one of the true joys of scenic design—to create a resilient, malleable world for the birth and evolution of ideas and emotions. At our disposal is three-dimensional space and the world of time. To achieve this and still equitably address the spectrum of design responsibilities represented in our diagram, requires a fluid and constantly moving pattern through these three spheres of influence.

Fortunately, this process produces a synergistic (cooperative) energy that can ultimately become most productive. For instance, technical problems can often be creatively resolved by simply moving to another "sphere" and addressing the problem from a totally different perspective. In the same context, an aesthetic ambiguity may have its resolution in either the symbolic or the technical realm. The key is to constantly traverse these three realms, compare notes and search for the obvious associations that will lead to a creative solution.

This phenomenon may be referred to as the Kinetic Design Process (see Figure 5) and it is recommended that aspiring designers begin to

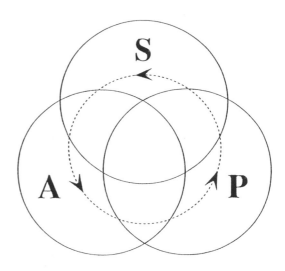

Figure 5. The Kinetic Design Process

develop a sensitivity to the potential of this state of mind. A useful analogy might be to envision oneself among three mountain peaks. When standing on the summit of one peak, you can observe from a distance the details of the other two quite objectively, but the third peak (upon which you stand) evades this analysis from its sheer proximity. If you depart from your present position and scale another peak, this new perspective provides a whole new concept of your initial point of reference. The kinetic design process is consequently the procedure of constantly shifting perspectives; keeping the imagination in motion and constantly shifting the creative point of view.

Script Analysis and Visual Communications

In an effort to understand more clearly the process and aspects of design as outlined above, it might be instructive to analyze a specific script and explore one possible design interpretation.

The Architect and the Emperor of Assyria by Arrabal is a fascinating and rich example of the Theatre of the Absurd. It radically manipulates both space and time and is an exciting example of the challenges of a relatively contemporary script. Although complex in action and style, it requires only a single setting described by the author as a sandy beach, a throne and a small hut on the beach. In addition, numerous props appear "magically" onstage, and at one point the two characters dig a hole in the sand in search of "god."

The story is rather bizarre and involves only two characters: the Architect, initially an "ignorant savage" discovered on the deserted island, and the Emperor, the sole survivor of a plane crash, who has been cast ashore on the island. Throughout the course of the action, the Emperor teaches the Architect to speak, builds a shelter, and begins to reign over his sole subject. The ensuing relationship between the two explores the Emperor's past, his family, his fears and his aspirations, and the two characters assume multiple roles. The scenes range from a mock trial, where the Emperor assumes the character of people in his past, to a macabre "picnic." Ultimately, the Emperor condemns himself to death for his sins and expires in the arms of the Architect, but not before the Emperor extracts a bizarre promise: for the

Architect to eat the Emperor's body and consequently absorb his persona.

However, this is only what the script says on the surface. At this stage, the artistic insight and individuality of the members of the ensemble come into play as they explore what lies beneath the surface—the subtext of what will be *their* production.

This process usually begins with the director's analysis. To review the analogy of the pebble and the pond, the director initially focuses or interprets the energy of the script at the first phase of the production process, attempting to isolate issues inherent in the script that warrant exploration and communication to an audience. In this production of *The Architect and the Emperor of Assyria*, the director shared the following impressions:

1. The structure of the script is cyclical, suggesting a never-ending cycle as opposed to a straight, linear progression. See Figure 6.

2. This cycle tends to suggest a symbolic association with the progression of human life (e.g., birth, adolescence, maturity, old age, death and rebirth). See Figure 7.

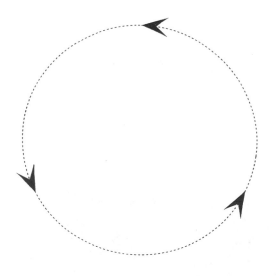

Figure 6. Basic Cyclical Image

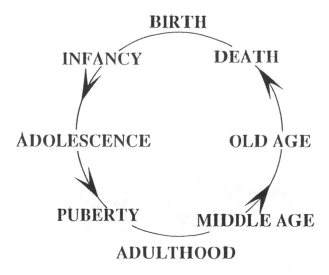

Figure 7. The Lifecycle Image

3. In the course of this cycle, Arrabal seems preoccupied with the nature of "games" people play, both in terms of childhood games and more adult, psychological "games."

Playing Tag

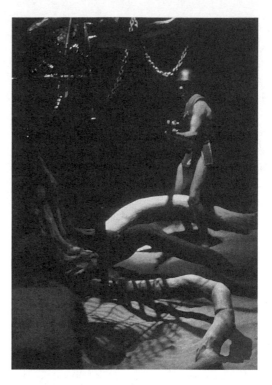

Playing War

4. One possible symbolic interpretation of the two characters is that they might represent the conflict of nature (the Architect) and technological society (the Emperor). In this sense, Nature would have a soft sensuality whereby Society would reflect the harshness of contemporary technology.

Images of the natural world

Images of the technological world

5. It seems important that the energy of the dramatic world (the deserted island) remain singular and intact. Neither character should ever leave the "island" or compromise the "aesthetic distance" between their world and ours.

6. In all its elusive forms, time is somehow a critical element of the piece (here the director used the analogy of the contrast between the first and last three minutes of a basketball game). This becomes more of an exploration than a literal image (although the director initially suggested using a scoreboard clock as part of the actual setting).

With these impressions and the details of the script itself, the design process begins. One approach to this process using the "triad form" described earlier is to take inventory of the three areas of influence: the symbolic, the aesthetic and the practical. The following is a partial inventory based upon *The Architect and the Emperor of Assyria* to illustrate this basic process.

Metaphoric/Symbolic

The metaphorical/symbolic realm deals with universal symbols and associations. Development here often leads to the discovery of recurrent lines or complementary shapes that reinforce the patterns that will evolve between the sculptural scenic space and the dramatic action.

1. The cyclical nature of the script might suggest a curvilinear form to reinforce the fluid flow from scene to scene and the underlying endless cycle suggested by the playwright. Rigid, geometric forms tend to suggest structure and order, conflicting with the amorphous nature of the script and the implied world of the play.

The use of two overlapping circles maintains this curvilinear quality with the added advantage of suggesting the duality/conflict inherent in the script (Architect/Emperor, Nature/Technology, etc.), further developing the metaphorical sphere of the design statement. (See Figures 8, 9 and 10 below.)

2. Just as the script explores the various stages of the life cycle, the scenic environment needs to adapt to and support these shifts in style/reality. The challenge is to create "layers" of meaning/function with specific elements provided by the script (the throne, the hut). These layers are then exposed or defined through the specific actions of the characters in the context of any given scene. For instance, the throne is a "power point" which the Emperor assumes periodically when he feels the need to lord himself over his "subject" (Architect). However, the Emperor also regresses into infancy at times, throwing temper tantrums and acting like a baby. With the simple addition of a flip-over eating tray, the "throne" becomes a "high chair," aiding in the character transformation and the symbolic association.

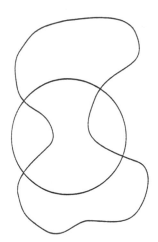

Figure 8. Curvilinear Natural Line Qualities

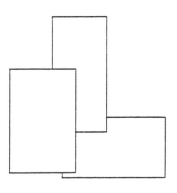

Figure 9. Rectilinear Structured Line Qualities

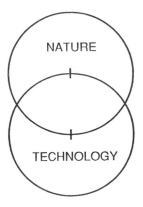

Figure 10. Overlapping Duality of Nature and Technology

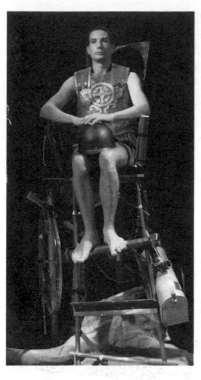

The Emperor's throne becomes a high chair to symbolize his regression from ruler and leader to infant.

The hourglass image reminds the audience of the image of time.

3. As mentioned previously, the director felt that some symbolic reminder of "time" was important to include as a recurrent metaphor throughout the play. In lieu of the distracting literalness of a basketball scoreboard, more subtle possibilities were explored.

The solution offers a clear example of how the overlapping kinetic design process can function. Moving from the symbolic realm to the aesthetic and practical realms provides the objective distance to solve the time mandate. The beach is obviously composed of sand suggesting the cliché the "sands of time." This leads to the hourglass, an ancient and universal image of time which uses sand. Thus, an hourglass becomes one of the omnipresent props for the production, the inversion of which marks the internal divisions of the "games." Also, its repeated use by the actors constantly reminds the audience of the image of time.

The Aesthetic/Harmonic

This is the realm of emotions, where we explore how we feel about the space, relate to the objects and respond to the interrelationship of the human form and the dimensional world we will construct. Often we find the use of textures, colors and three-dimensional forms creates the most effective visual statement.

1. One of the precepts we began with was the conflict/confrontation between nature and humankind as exemplified by technology or man-made objects. One possible visual dichotomy to represent this conflict might be the contrast between a living tree and cold, hard steel—more specifically, the image of a rusted nail driven into a living tree or old barbed wire which has been wrapped around the tree and over the years begins to girdle the living form. These emotive im-

Basic Floor Plan

The hut and throne were built from metallic objects, imposing metal into primitive nature.

ages represent the two main characters as well as support most of the confrontational aspects of the dramatic action.

Subsequently, the Architect's world becomes a living tree, growing from the sand with its roots defining the boundaries of their world. The Emperor's association is the imposition of metal into primitive nature. The hut and throne (symbols of the Emperor's world) were built totally from metallic objects—old rusted metal that might have been salvaged from the wreck of his airplane. The choice of the natural root line quality provided further aesthetic value. The heavily symbolic shape of the hourglass is far too literal. The tree roots provided a means to soften the visual metaphor and create a more subconscious statement.

The kinetic design process developed as the possibilities of the tree and its relationship to the Emperor's hut began to grow. Moving to the sym-

bolic perspective of "games" and childhood, the image of a tree fort comes to mind, once again commenting on the age cycle and the game competition of the dramatic action.

2. Suspended in space and time, the complete isolation of this world was another mandate important to the style and ambiance of the production. Ideally, we desired that Arrabal's world literally float in order to create a magical void between the audience and the world of the play. Another emotive quality dealt with evolving a sense of "sensuality" and intimacy in the production. Textually, human flesh was a recurrent theme (the Architect actually eats the Emperor at the end of Act II, Scene I) and the director wished to use the exposed flesh of the actors as a constant symbol/reminder of human frailty and animal sensuality.

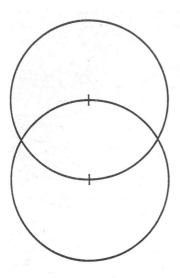
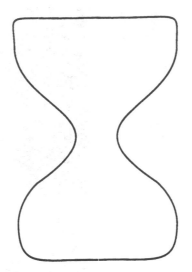
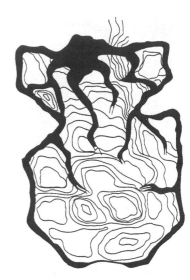

Evolution of the Floor Plan

This led to an intimate studio production, with the audience surrounding the action on three sides in very close proximity to the actors. The set was raised and "floated" with a black chasm between the set and the audience. The organic root structure of the tree contrasted against the black void defined the island. Finally, the bark texture of the tree and roots realistically suggested human flesh, mirroring the human flesh of the actors.

3. Yet another psychological/emotional quality desired for the production dealt with the other-worldliness of "magic." Periodically, objects simply appeared out of nowhere. This quality reinforced the absurd aspects of the style, as well as lending a vague supernatural characteristic to the world of the play. In addition, there are several "leaps in time," where the action moves forward several years in a moment. This convention required devising a special effect consistent with the magical quality we were attempting to define.

Once again the kinetic design process proved reliable in guiding the development of the physical space to a harmonic conclusion. By moving temporarily to the symbolic and technical realm of sand, with all its associated images to time and the hourglass, we found a resolution. First, the objects intended to "magically appear" could simply "rise from the sand." Others were literally built into the set and extracted when required. (The throne sup-

Human flesh was a recurrent theme—the Architect eats the Emperor in one scene; the texture of tree and roots further suggested human flesh.

Floorplan with sand reservoir locations

The Emperor and the Architect: Model photo with audience orientation.

plied many props throughout the action.) Second, the time transitions were borrowed literally from the symbolic image of the hourglass. Reservoirs of sand were built into the lighting grid, ringing the perimeter of the "island." At the moment when a blackout would traditionally occur to symbolize the change of time, the reservoirs were unplugged sequentially from above, forming a growing (moving) curtain of sand, reminiscent of sand falling through the orifice of an hourglass.

Practical/Technical

Many of the practical/technical aspects relative to this production have already been referred to or implied. As no single area is isolated from the other, this overlap is inherent in the graphic diagram and the actual process. As mentioned previously, the technical realm will significantly affect the rhythm and patterns of the production, as well as the options available for character development and directorial options.

This is the area demanding very close associa-

tion between the director and the scenic designer. In many respects, the realms of both individuals significantly overlap and clear lines of communication are imperative. The design decisions made here will define actual blocking patterns and character relationships—issues critical to the directorial approach.

It is not uncommon that this realm reflects a "problem-creative solution" format. A healthy production concept will present many exciting technical problems and artistic challenges—that is what is so exciting about theatre. The joy of design is discovering the solutions inherent in the script. This is a learning process not restricted to design and is intrinsic in the total spectrum of the theatre experience.

The following examples are specific to this production of *The Architect and the Emperor of Assyria*, but are illustrative of common choices in the evolution of a design.

1. To maintain complete isolation of the island in time and space, with the actors never violating the chasm between audience and dramatic space, how does the Emperor actually get onstage? In the original script he simply walks on from offstage. The solution drew from previous "discoveries." The "sand curtain" effect and the development of the tree fort established a vertical precedent in the dramatic space. A simple extension of this precedence allows the Emperor to parachute in from above, never violating the "magic chasm" and reaffirming the vertical development of the dramatic space.

2. The aspect of verticality, in terms of the tree fort, imposed additional technical/practical concerns which significantly (and creatively) affected the overall rhythm of the production. The problem is one of strength and aesthetic expectations. The significant statement of a tree and substantial "fort" will demand creative use and must be strong enough to accommodate extensive physical action without drawing attention to itself. In addition, as the tempo of a given scene changes from another, different types of vertical movement are required. Consequently, throughout the course of rehearsal, various means of developing this scenic element were constantly added and modified to support the physical action that evolved. Various ladders, firepoles, ropes and changing branch configurations of the tree were employed to provide the variety of movement and composition that were discovered by the actors and director.

The fundamental problem or challenge in this instance is how to "build a tree" which does justice to the textural (aesthetic) requirements of the production, while providing a strong and functional superstructure for the dramatic action. The solution presented itself in the relatively obvious form of nature itself. In the course of studying local driftwood for the bark textures and line qualities desired (aesthetic considerations), the inherent structural qualities of the driftwood became obvious. The solution was simply to weld aesthetically pleasing driftwood forms into a composite and structurally sound "tree." The separate pieces were

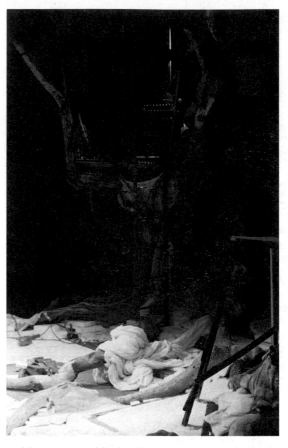

Ladders, ropes and limbs allow movement on the fort.

joined with rigid foam and "skinned" with tissue for a common texture.

3. As mundane as it may sound, the simple placement of objects onstage is often of critical importance to both composition (and subsequently the ambiance of a space) and to the blocking patterns which emerge from the dramatic action. The challenge (or problem) is to establish an appropriate "dynamic tension" as well as motivation for blocking patterns that will reinforce the dramatic action. In the example of *The Architect and the Emperor of Assyria,* the objects are few but critical. The composition is designed to reinforce the asymmetrical, natural world of the Architect as opposed to the structured, symmetrical composition that might better reflect the nature of the Emperor. Consequently, the throne is placed in the lower region, in an extreme stage left position.

Driftwood as a design resource.

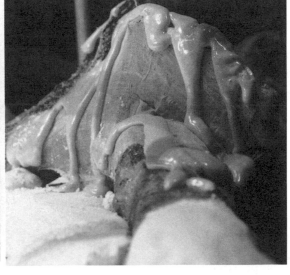

Driftwood tree being assembled.

Model shot with specified objects.

The relationship between the organic shapes of the roots and the body composition of the actors is part of the design process.

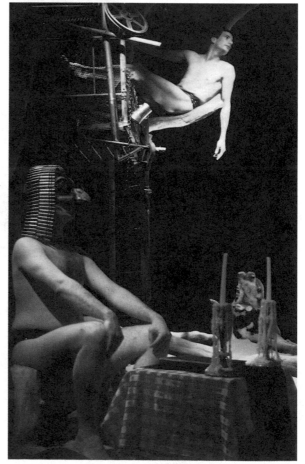

This elevated but small position (Emperor's) is complemented by the large expanse of virgin sand before it (Architect's).

The tree is also asymmetrical and placed off-center in the upper stage area favoring the opposite side of the stage space. The extreme upstage placement of the tree has other practical/technical implications critical to the effective use of the space in performance. The most dynamic (and potentially unsettling) movement takes place on this scenic form. By placing it the maximum distance from the audience (aesthetic distance), the potential distraction of violent movement is minimized.

All these choices, in addition to the specific placement of the roots, were calculated to channel forms of energy (aggressive and passive) throughout the production. Consciously manipulating blocking patterns extracts the greatest dynamic potential from a minimum space. Even the relationship between the organic shapes of the roots and the body composition of the actors is part of the design process calculated for maximum communication and communion with the audience.

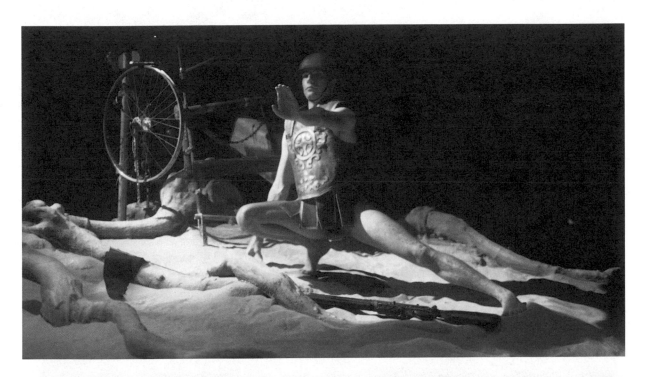

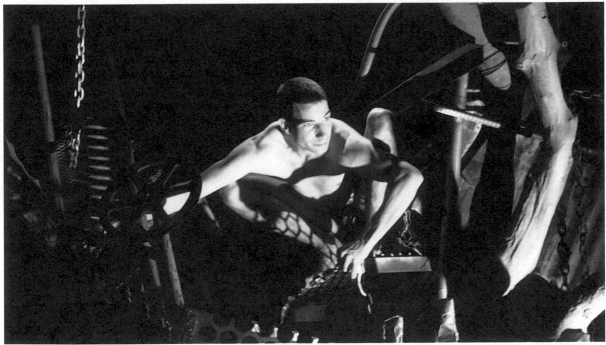

Images and Movement: *Opposite:* Aesthetic distance; *AboveTop:* Root images and the human form; *Bottom:* High energy action and aesthetic distance.

Obviously, there is a great deal more to the design of dramatic space than the relatively simple creation of "a pretty picture." Dramatic space is *alive*, constantly changing and adapting to the ebb and flow of the energy within a given script. The production analyzed here is one example of a small cast, studio-type production. The design process changes in many aspects when the production moves to a large, proscenium space or to an even more intimate arena configuration. However, the basic process and the collaborative nature of theatre remains essentially the same.

In this constant metamorphosis lies the true and challenging art of theatrical design. The process is complex and rewarding. It entails conception, birth, maturation and culmination. Each production can be a microcosm of the life experience and its creative realization can be just as difficult, rewarding and ultimately inspiring.

Selected Readings

Anderson, Donald M. *Elements of Design*. New York: Holt, Rinehart and Winston, 1961

Campbell, Joseph. *The Power of Myth*. New York: Doubleday, 1988.

Jones, Robert E. *The Dramatic Imagination*. New York: Duell, Sloan and Pearce, 1941.

Jung, Carl G. *Man and His Symbols*. New York: Doubleday and Company, 1964.

Lawlor, Robert. *Sacred Geometry: Philosophy and Practice*. New York: Crossroads Pub., 1982.

Payne, Darwin R. *The Scenographic Imagination*. Carbondale: Southern Illinois University Press, 1981.

(The production of The Architect and the Emperor of Assyria *referred to in this chapter was by Humboldt State University, directed by John Heckel, scenic design by Ivan E. Hess, lighting design by Mark Hopkins, costumes/masks by Agnes Delucchi. The photographs were taken by Ivan Hess and Mark Hopkins and diagrams were prepared by Ivan Hess and Klaus Larsen.)*

CHAPTER NINETEEN

❧

The Costume Designer

Engraving of Charles Kean as Hamlet, c. 1860. *From the author's collection.*

Functions of Costume Design

The scene designer provides the environment in which the characters of a play generally appear and enact the dramatic action; the costume designer, however, must provide the specific appearance of each of the characters in order to identify each and to separate the distinct natures of the individuals. It is this specificity of the task of the costume designer that provides the measure of the success of his work. According to the noted writer on the nature of theatre, Robert Edmond Jones in *The Dramatic Imagination,* each costume must be so derived that it is appropriate only for *that character,* at *that moment,* and in *that situation.* A costume appropriate for one character should not be appropriate for another. The individuality of each character in the play must be communicated to the audience, and in designing the unique features of each character, the designer creates individualized costumes.

A specially designed costume also distinguishes itself from an ordinary, manufactured, fashionable garment because it is created for a specific character fulfilling a specific function in a specific environment, as opposed to a dress for any consumer to select in a marketplace. Theatre is not life; it depicts life. Costumes are not created for the masses; they are customized for actors to wear while depicting life in the theatre.

In order to accomplish this vital individuality, the costume designer must have a vast knowledge of many areas: fashion, both modern and historical; social trends, including manners, customs, and mores; cultural and artistic movements; and most importantly, a total understanding of and appreciation for the operation of the art of the theatre. For practical purposes, the costumer must have the utilitarian skills of a visual artist, a seamstress and tailor, a textile manufacturer, and a businessman, as well as a management foreman. He must also be attuned to the particular terminology, as well as needs and functions of his other theatrical coworkers: the director, the scenic and lighting designers, the choreographer, and most importantly, the actors. The costume designer works more personally with more members of the theatrical company than does any other person involved in the production process except the director.

This close relationship allows for the smooth function and integration of the costumes into the unity and artistry of the theatrical production. As an entity, costumes must fulfill a number of important functions. First, the appearance of a costumed actor on stage immediately provides many factual details. Without the actor's uttering a word, the audience can deduce a wide range of specific information: gender and age (perhaps a middle-aged man); the amount and success of his education and occupation (a CEO of a major firm versus a struggling artist); his health and physical condition (a sickly figure in a wheelchair versus a robust, athletic demeanor); the historical period (classical Greek versus contemporary society); plus many other details, such as geographical origins, time of day, social event in progress, climatic conditions, and particular setting.

The second phase of the functions of a costume involves the intangible or interpretative suggestions about a character signalled through what he is wearing. The most significant statement in this regard applies to the *mood and atmosphere.* For example, in *Hamlet* the frenzy and confusion of Ophelia is well communicated through a dishevelled, uncoordinated or incomplete costume, whereas the meticulous attention to detail of the attire of her father Polonius would express his character's precise control and excessive nature. (See Figure 2.) Also, an obvious choice of elements for costumes appropriate to as serious a play as *Hamlet* would be in marked contrast to the choices for a non-serious play like *Twelfth Night.*

In addition to mood and atmosphere, the costumes can be used effectively to establish *character relationships.* An example of this function in *Hamlet* would be the grouping of Hamlet and his closest

Figure 2. Four costume designs for Gertrude and Ophelia by Charles Karl for the 1902 production of *Hamlet* by E. H. Sothern. *From the W. H. Crain Collection, Theatre Arts Collection, Harry Ransom Humanities Research Center, The University of Texas at Austin.*

allies in one distinct and obvious hue and the selection of that hue's complement for his adversaries. Changes of hue can also be used to indicate a realignment, an alteration, or a cessation of antagonism, if this be the case.

Another function of costume design is to establish character importance and emphasis. The designer accomplishes this function by concentrating the design elements with the greatest notice on the character of greatest importance. This focuses the attention of the audience where it should be. For example, Hamlet constantly appears as the point of greatest emphasis if a designer dresses him in dark, sombre colors and stark decor at the time when the remainder of the cast wears elaborate and festive colors, as, for example, at the wedding celebration of Gertrude and Claudius. Another illustration of this function is the practice of placing only the main character in a complement of the colors worn by the remaining cast members. Thus, unquestioned importance is given to the character costumed in royal blue when everyone else appears in attire of variations of orange or rust.

Lastly, the costumes function as *reflections or manifestations of the progress of the dramatic action.* Costumes in particular must mirror the changes, however subtle, that a character undergoes throughout the course of the conflict of the plot. A character's deterioration from a position of composure and control in the beginning of the action to a level of anxiety and desperation at the conclusion is easily communicated to the audience by the changes in the costumes and appearances of the character as the play progresses. The single-minded determination of Hamlet to avenge his father's murder is well illustrated by the constancy of his somber, unchanging costume, illustrating his faithfulness to his goal.

Thus, the multiplicity of the functions of a stage costume as well as the areas with which a designer must be familiar in successfully designing stage costumes becomes obvious. *The definition of costume design can best be stated as the process of selecting and arranging design elements to communicate the personality of characters involved in dramatic action.*

Phases of Costume Design

The designer must proceed through three main sections of the design process in order to complete the costumes: analysis of the play, rendering and construction, and performance.

The *analysis* section composes two distinct divisions of the preparatory work that precedes a production conference between the designers and the director for the purpose of melding of the ideas and conceptions based on the designers' suggestions and the director's interpretation of the play; the first division is devoted to achieving a unifying concept and then preparing to achieve it. Though the director must maintain final control of all artistic decisions, he should avoid the pitfall of stifling the designers' opinions at this early stage and of preventing them from making a creative contribution. Minimally and ideally, a director at this point should present his opinions as to the period of the play, the intended style of the production, a statement of the form of his approach, and ideas about any alterations in such important areas as characters, settings, or scenes. (See Figure 3.) It is a competent designer who is prepared for this initial conference with a significant understanding of the play and characters. He should most definitely be in a position to pose intelligent questions in order to avoid future problems. In addition, he should present his own ideas and be able to make suggestions for a thoughtful approach from his interpretation of the design concept. However, he must also be open to the interpretation of the director and other designers. The most successful designer is one who is adaptable to unifying the artistry of all design areas into a single cohesive production.

No two designers follow the same process, and normally each play dictates some procedural alterations. Because there is no prescribed manner or order to creativity, the means of achieving a

Figure 3. Photograph of Hamlet and the Ghost from a production, *Hamlet Collage*, devised and directed by Eric Voss at the University of Georgia.

design concept are as varied as the number of designers facing the task. There are, however, several purely mechanical steps which a designer may employ in order to fulfill the analytical phase of the process.

The first step involves the creation of a *character distribution chart* (Figure 4). This instrument lists each character in a left-hand column. Across the top of the chart the designer notes the appearance of each character in each major unit of dramatic action (as opposed to the use of broader editorial act-and-scene divisions). Whenever a major character enters or leaves, a unit is created and is noted appropriately on the chart. Often the designer will list notations of scenic and time changes along the bottom of the chart. These can be used as indicators of possible additional costumes necessitated by changes in location and

time. This chart serves the purposes of providing a graphic representation of each character's appearances throughout the play, of indicating the inherent rhythm of the dramatic action of the play, of detailing the physical linear progression and development of characters, of focusing on patterns of character relationships, and of identifying the scenes in which a large number of characters on stage will cause greater attention to coordination of design elements by the designer. Another idea which the designer might employ in this phase is the formation of a *character sociogram* (Figure 5), a device which can be used to establish clearly character relationships. The primary characters are the focal points around which the secondary characters are attached. Usually a pattern of character clusters which can be of benefit to the costume designer appears. Each designer may employ various types of lines to attach specific characters relative to the respective relationships in the play. Another variation on this character sociogram is its use as an aid in color coordination. Coloring individual and/or groups of characters in each of the areas in separate or coordinating costume colors is a preliminary step in this important aspect of design, showing character relationships.

Perhaps the most important step in this phase concerns the preliminary formation of the *costume casebook*. In this device, the designer designates one page per character in the play, and from the very beginning of the project records notes concerning the individual characters. Such information will cover textual references to costumes, notes about quick costume changes, the number of costumes required, notes on manners and movements, topics that will require research, unfamiliar terms, and any other objective data relating to a particular character. The costumer will also want to record any of his subjective reactions to each character, such as descriptive adjectives, initial color impressions, images of the character, or any other clues that will assist in analyzing the specific qualities of each character. He may also want to record line impressions for each character as well.

CHARACTER	ACT ONE															ACT TWO										ACT THREE												
	Sc. 1			Sc. 2				Sc. 3		Sc. 4			Sc. 5			Sc. 1		Sc. 2								Sc. 1			Sc. 2									
Francisco	x																																					
Bernardo	x	x	x																																			
Horatio		x	x							x	x	x			x														x	x	x	x	x	x				
Marcellus		x	x							x	x	x			x																							
Ghost			x								x		x		x																							
King				x	x													x	x	x	x					x		x				x	x					
Queen				x	x													x	x	x	x					x						x	x					
Hamlet				x	x	x	x			x	x		x	x	x							x	x		x		x		x	x	x		x	x	x	x	x	x
Polonius				x	x				x							x	x	x	x	x	x			x		x		x						x				
Laertes				x	x			x	x																													
Voltimand				x															x																			
Cornelius				x															x																			
Court				x	x													x	x	x												x	x					
Ophelia								x	x								x									x	x	x				x	x					
Reynaldo																x																						
Rosencrantz																		x					x	x		x					x					x	x	
Guildenstern																		x					x	x		x					x					x	x	
Osric																																						
Priest																																						
Players																								x			x			x					x			
Grave-digger																																						
Fortinbras																																						
Lucianus																															x							
Soldiers/Sailors																																						
Gentlemen																																						
Location	Elsinore-Before Castle			State Room in Castle				Polonius' Room		Before Castle			Same			Polonius' Room		Room in Castle								Room in Castle			Great Hall									

Figure 4. Character Distribution Chart for *Hamlet*

CHARACTER	Act 3 Sc. 3 (Room in Castle)	Act 3 Sc. 4 (Queen's Closet)	Act 4 S1 (Room in Castle)	Act 4 S2	Act 4 Sc. 3 (Another Room)	Act 4 Sc. 4 (Plain in Denmark)	Act 4 Sc. 5 (Room in Castle)	Act 4 Sc. 6 (Another Room)	Act 5 Sc. 1 (Graveyard)	Act 5 S2 (Great Hall)
Francisco										
Bernardo										
Horatio							x x	x	x x	x
Marcellus										
Ghost		x								
King	x x x		x		x x		x x x x	x	x	x
Queen		x x x	x				x x x x x	x	x	x
Hamlet		x	x x		x x				x x	x
Polonius	x	x x								
Laertes							x x	x	x	
Voltimand										
Cornelius										
Court					x				x	x
Ophelia							x	x		
Reynaldo										
Rosencrantz			x x	x x		x				
Guildenstern			x x	x x		x				
Osric										x
Priest									x	
Players										
Grave-digger									x	
Fortinbras						x				x
Lucianus										
Soldiers/Sailors						x x		x		
Gentlemen							x			

Figure 4. Character Distribution Chart for *Hamlet, continued*

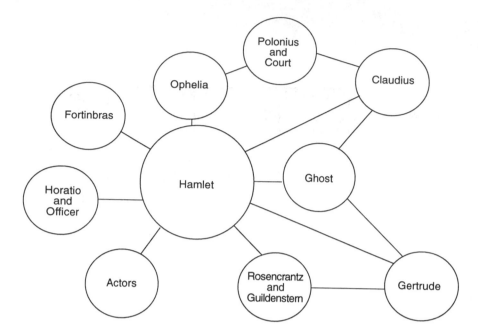

Figure 5. Character Sociogram
for *Hamlet*

Upon the completion of these suggested exercises, the first phase of the analysis section, the costume designer has already formulated concepts, approaches, and interpretations of the characters and of the play. He is now ready to come together with the other designers and the director to reach agreement on the matters that will determine the style of the production. In this sense, *style* is defined as a recognizable pattern created by the repetition of specific elements. The director must establish the parameters of his choice of style and bring about a synthesis of each designer's creativity to communicate the style in a unified and artistic manner.

Within the stylistic limitations, the costume designer focuses on such practical concerns as the actors and roles: the numbers of characters—particularly extras; textual alterations; and, in some cases, construction. This latter concern is usually determined by the level of the producing company: community, educational, regional, or Broadway. At this point, the costume designer has all the necessary information about practical matters, as well as about the stylistic approach to begin the task of actually designing the costumes, the second phase of the overall process.

Designing the Costumes

All designers communicate through the selection and arrangement of four elements: *line, color, texture,* and *shape.* It is the costume designer's challenge to select and arrange the options of the characteristics of each element of design in order to create the desired costume. An examination of each of the elements will illustrate the variety from which selections can be made.

The costume designer views the element of *line* as the edge of a shape. Line can be applied to an external shape like a silhouette or the outline of a skirt. Also, it can be used as an internal line created by the edges of shapes in a fabric design for a paisley print or a floral brocade. Both the external and internal lines are functional in a costume. Every line possesses specific characteristics of direction, length, strength, and speed. The directions of line are vertical, horizontal, and diagonal. Length is a relative measurement of two lines of equal or unequal extension. The characteristic of strength is measured by the width of a line, with a bolder, wider line possessing greater strength than

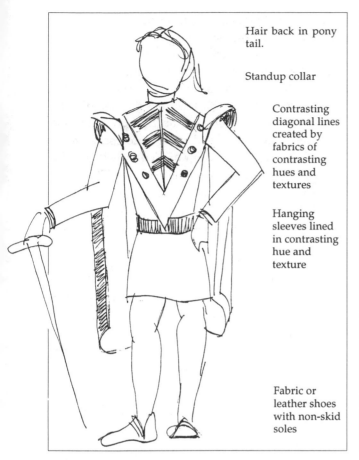

Hair back in pony tail.

Standup collar

Contrasting diagonal lines created by fabrics of contrasting hues and textures

Hanging sleeves lined in contrasting hue and texture

Fabric or leather shoes with non-skid soles

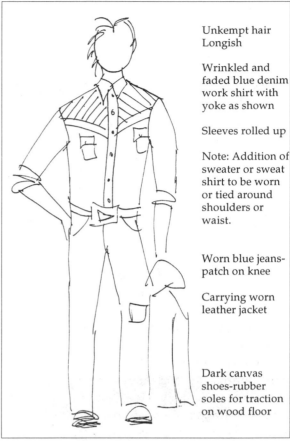

Unkempt hair Longish

Wrinkled and faded blue denim work shirt with yoke as shown

Sleeves rolled up

Note: Addition of sweater or sweat shirt to be worn or tied around shoulders or waist.

Worn blue jeans-patch on knee

Carrying worn leather jacket

Dark canvas shoes-rubber soles for traction on wood floor

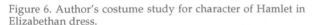

Figure 6. Author's costume study for character of Hamlet in Elizabethan dress.

Figure 7. Author's costume study for character of Hamlet in contemporary dress.

a narrower and delicate line. The characteristic of speed is determined by the amount of curve. It ranges from a straight line with no curve and thus described as static to one with sharp curves described as fast. No one characteristic is isolated, but all interrelate in an endless series of combinations. The designer's task is to choose the most appropriate combination to express each character's individuality.

An examination of the varying uses of lines in Figures 6 and 7 illustrates the manner in which a designer utilizes line within the framework of historical periods. In the Elizabethan costume the appearance of line is more obvious whereas with the contemporary garb the line is more subtle. In both sketches the overall direction of the line is vertical indicating the character's basic strength and firmness of purpose but the contrasting diagonal lines indicate tension and uncertainty in the character's disposition. All the lines are static and indicate stability and directness of purpose. Both sketches convey a linear statement of burdensome accessories with the use of the hanging sleeves in one and the leather jacket in the other.

Whereas the audience reacts to the element of line on a rather passive, subconscious level, it responds to the element of color in a much more active, conscious manner. It is, therefore, an element to which the designer devotes much careful consideration in making choices. In dealing with the elements of color, the designer has three factors to weigh: the specific *hue*, the *saturation* or

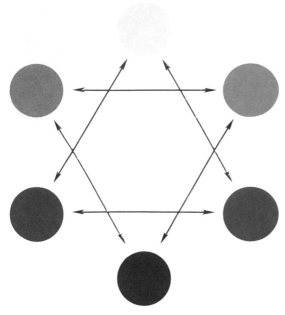

Figure 8. Color Wheel:
Red, Yellow, Blue = Primary
Orange, Green, Purple = Secondary

Figure 9. Hue Saturation Scale illustrating brightness or purity of hue.

Figure 10. Hue Value Scale illustrating the lightness or darkness of a hue.

purity, and the *value* or lightness (tint) or darkness (shade) of the hue. By mixing the three primary hues of pigment (red, yellow, and blue), one creates the three secondary hues (orange, green, and violet). This arrangement is best expressed by the color wheel (Figure 8). The hues that fall directly opposite each other (red and green, blue and orange, and yellow and violet) are complementary hues. The saturation of a color is its brightness, e.g., Chinese red versus brick red. The purity or saturation of a hue can be reduced by the addition of its complementary hue. When a color is bright and pure, it has none of its hue opposite on the color wheel; conversely, the dullness and impurity of a hue is determined by the presence of its complement (Figure 9).

A hue of high value is created by the addition of white to form a tint, or a hue of low value by the addition of black to create a shade. For example, the addition of white to the hue red creates pink; of black, wine. Value is determined separately from saturation, making it possible to have a hue of high saturation and low value or any other possible combination of the two factors. It is the mixing of hues, complements, and black and white that creates the almost endless varieties of hues, saturations, and values. (See Figure 10.)

Each hue with its numerous variations of saturation and value has distinctive communicative potential to an audience. A hue can have realistic occurrences, psychological implications, and symbolic associations. For example, red is found in the gemstone ruby; it communicates a sense of danger psychologically, and it is used to symbolize adulterous behavior. Usually a character's extroverted temperament will be expressed in pure tints of warm analogous hues such as red, orange, and yellow, whereas cool, dull shades of the hues express the opposite sense.

Texture or the contour of the surface is generally expressed in terms of a measure from rough to smooth and is heightened by the amount of light and its reflection on the surface. Costume designers usually use smoother, more reflective textures to express more refined and distinguished characters whereas they depict lower class characters in coarser and duller fabrics. The gamut of textures in *Hamlet* would extend from the rich metallics, furs, and velvets of the King to the loosely woven and uneven tatters of the gravedigger. Texture is a valuable resource for the designer in communicating to an audience the unique qualities of each character.

The shape of the costume is determined by the silhouette of the historical period. The basic shape of the Elizabethan period, for example, is conical or triangular. In the case of the men, the triangle is created by the use of broad shoulders extended by the addition of shoulder crescents and rolls and large leg o'mutton sleeves. The doublet features a V-shaped bodice coming to a point below the waist. The female costume utilizes this same triangular shape in the upper portion of the body; the same shape is evident in the skirt's silhouette, which is either triangular or conical, depending upon which of the three shapes of farthingales or undergarments is being worn. The two other basic shapes of costume, in addition to the conical, are the tubular and the ovoid or bell-shaped.

The designer is now at the point of having completed the first phase and is ready to begin the actual mechanical task of designing of the costumes. He has mastered three preliminary objectives: what each costume must communicate about the character who wears it; how the costumes fit into the total visual aspect of the production; and what elements are at his disposal to accomplish these objectives. At this point, it is impossible to prescribe only one method which each designer should follow, but the designer must review several basic considerations as he begins his character-by-character approach to creating effective costumes, both individually and as a unified ensemble.

A return to the character distribution chart, color sociogram, and costume casebook for a review of the notations for each character will be vital in helping the designer reach specific uses of the four elements. He will choose the specific line, color, texture, and shape impressions for each character. He may choose for Hamlet at the beginning of the dramatic action a weak diagonal line, a dull grey hue, a matte texture, and a rectangular shape to suggest the character's passive ambivalence. This initial combination of choices will obviously change to reflect the progression in the character's attitudes and behavior. As the dramatic action climaxes, the designer might well choose for the character a strong vertical line for decisive authority, a saturated hue of low value for determined will, a more reflective texture for confidence, and a triangular shape for action.

The next step in the design of costumes is illustrated by an examination of the engraving of Charles Kean as Hamlet at the beginning of this chapter which will provide examples of most of the six interrelated components of a total stage costume. It is vital for the designer to consider each of these generic parts to achieve the appearance of a complete costume. These six components are under or foundation garments (the white undershirt for the actor or a corset and farthingale for an actress in an Elizabethan costume), footwear (the square-toed slippers with an arch strap), headwear (none is pictured but an Elizabethan flat cap might be appropriate for the exterior scenes), outergarments (the full-skirted doublet), accessories (the belted sword), and finally makeup and hairstyle (the neck-length uncombed hair). Detailed attention to each area assures that the costume will be complete and will achieve its required specificity of character statement.

The foundation garments are of significance in two areas: they provide the basis for proper historical silhouette of the period and they dictate movement. It would be impossible for an Elizabethan garment to represent properly the latter half of the sixteenth century if an actress were not wearing a suitable corset of the period and the correct farthingale. In addition, these foundation garments also dictate representative movement by placing the proper restrictions and weight distribution on the actor; e. g., in the Elizabethan period, all movements by women, including dance, followed a vertical pattern because the corset totally precluded any forward movement at the waist.

Closely related to the area of movement is the costume component of footwear, which is also a major determinant of movement. This is true because the height of the heel places the tilt of the body forward and controls the muscular tension of the body. These restrictions directly relate to the tempo of the walk and the length of the stride. The absence of a heel allows the body to resort to a state of relaxation and repose that results in a slower pace and a longer stride. The costumer's principle thus becomes apparent: the higher the heel, the quicker and shorter the stride. Similar results can be noted from other variations, among which are the thickness of the soles, the security of the fit of the heel, and the tightness of the lacing. Obviously, a costumer must be aware of all of these factors.

The component of headwear is also an important factor in the movement of the costumed actor. A broad-brimmed hat can carry a considerable amount of weight, which in and of itself presents a balance control problem for the actor and severely restricts all but studied head movement other than side to side. The placement of the center of gravity also determines the position in which an actor must hold his head to maintain a functional operation. (See Figure 11.)

The category of outergarments comprises the attire most obvious to the viewing audience. In some case, the foundation garments can be the outergarments as well, as in the case when an actor appears in less than complete street or public dress. Whatever the case may be, the outergarments are greatly complemented with the addition of carefully chosen accessories. These items cover an extensive range and help to complete the individuality of a character.

An accessory is any item carried or worn by the actor or attached to the outergarment that completes the appearance of the costume. Without accessories, a costume might appear incomplete and would lack the individuality necessary for the

Figure 11. Plate of headgear designs ascribed to Tom Hesselwood for the 1905 H. B. Irving production of *Hamlet* at the Adelphi Theatre. *From B. J. Simmons Collection, Theatre Arts Collection, Harry Ransom Humanities Research Center, The University of Texas at Austin.*

character identification. It is quite easy for two characters costumed in basically similar outergarments to communicate entirely opposite statements to an audience strictly though the use of accessories. For example, an Elizabethan courtier with a meticulously styled ruff, with coordinated gloves, garters and shoe roses, with a tastefully trimmed Valois bonnet, and discreet jewelry will greatly contrast with another character in similar garments with with a wrinkled ruff, with no gloves and with contrasting garters and shoe

Swords—

Scandinavian.

Necklace, Polonius

Figure 12. Plate of sword and jewelry designs ascribed to Tom Hesselwood for the 1905 H. B. Irving production of *Hamlet* at the Adelphi Theatre. *From B. J. Simmons Collection, Theatre Arts Collection, Harry Ransom Humanities Research Center, The University of Texas at Austin.*

roses, with a plain flat cap and with excessive jewelry. In some cases, it may be the costume designer's intention to use the presence or absence of accessories to make a statement. In the case of the character of Hamlet, such may be the case. The obsession of Gertrude and Claudius for power should be quite evident in excessive and opulent accessories. This appearance would be in stark contrast to Hamlet, who would be noticeably lacking in accessories, except perhaps for an article that had belonged to his father, in order to show his single-mindedness in avenging the murder of his father. (See Figure 12.)

The last generic component of a total stage costume, makeup and coiffure, is usually designed by the costumer, though in some cases, separate makeup artists and hairstylists are employed. Regardless, this area is vital to the realization of the main goal of individualizing each character. In the same manner of using costumes to reflect progressions and alterations in dramatic action, makeup can also be used effectively to this same purpose.

As the character of Ophelia, for instance, changes from an initially vibrant and active young lady to a deranged, suicidal person, the makeup can and should make this alteration of temperament visually evident to the audience. (See Figures 13 and 14.)

Figure 13. Plate illustrating three complete costumes for character of Hamlet by Charles Karl for the 1902 producton of *Hamlet. From the W. H. Crain Collection, Theatre Arts Collection, Harry Ransom Humanities Research Center, The University of Texas at Austin.*

Figure 14. 1905 photograph of E. H. Sothern and Julia Marlow as Hamlet and Ophelia in costumes by Charles Karl as published in *Theatre Magazine. From the Theatre Arts Collection, Harry Ransom Humanities Research Center, The University of Texas at Austin.*

After these selections are completed for every character, the designer can begin the task of actually transferring his impressions of the elements and incorporating them into sketches and drawings, a task with much experimentation as the designer reaches the best combination of the elements to capture the essence of each of the characters. The format of the presentation of the final sketches or costume plates, the term used by professionals to describe the completed costume rendering, is a matter of personal choice: some designers will complete the minimum of only a pencil sketch with attached fabrics while others will submit a fully colored painting of minute detail. This latter is time consuming and not always necessary as the costume rendering should not become an end in itself, a situation which often happens with this type of presentation. The focus and emphasis should never be subverted from the ultimate goal of the design process: the completed costume worn by an actor in the stage setting. Each designer develops a style of rendering which most satisfies his requirements.

The next step in the process involves transforming the sketch or costume plate from the designer into a costume worthy of stage appearance. This step depends entirely upon the professional level of the producing theatre. In commercial theatre, the designer must be a member of the union, United Scenic Artists, and the costumes will be built or constructed by specialty costume houses with experience professional staff of union members who can complete the full range of costumes quickly and punctually as dictated by the financial restraints of commercial theatre. These companies also have the resources later to duplicate single costumes or an entire wardrobe as cast members change or if the production's popularity requires touring companies.

Most regional and large educational theatres have an on-site studio that can construct costumes and provide training and experience in costume crafts and techniques. On this level, more time is required for construction, more instruction and supervision are necessary, and the costumes are not constructed as durably as they are for professional theatre. In community and smaller educational theatres, the availability of suitable costumes is a strong factor in play selection, and plays requiring extensive period costumes are usually avoided unless the costumes can be borrowed or rented from costume rental companies. A valuable source of costumes which should not be ignored is the possibility that a garment might be taken from storage and recycled for this production. This process may require restyling, alterations, and changes of ornamentation in the original garment, but it is much quicker and more economical in terms of budget and time than producing an original garment. If this option is not available and it is determined that a new costume will have to be constructed, the process is the same.

Regardless of the level, the costume construction process involves similar steps, the first of which is for the worker to study the costume sketch carefully to make sure that he understands what the designer has intended and to discuss any problems. This step is followed by taking precise measurements of the actor who is to wear the garment. The care with which these measurements are taken will often determine the successful fit of a costume after completion because the actors may not be available for fittings as the costume is being built. The second step is to fit the actor in proper foundation garments. Another set of measurements will have to be taken then because of the changes that these garments will make in the actor's body. Also of great importance is for the designer to supply the actors with rehearsal costumes that will closely approximate the movement limitations of the actual performance costume. These will greatly assist the actors in preparing physically for the roles by adjusting to movement restrictions and to become accustomed to movement in the completed costume.

The next step involves the matter of patterns. Every studio maintains a collection of pattern books and of patterns themselves. It is possible that an Elizabethan pattern, for *Hamlet*, for example, could be adapted from one reprinted in a historical pattern book. The technician may find it

Figure 15. Series of eight photographs illustrating steps in the construction of an Elizabethan costume for the stage.

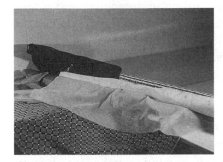

A. Selection of materials

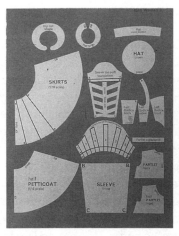

B. Selection of pattern

C. Enlargement of pattern with use of anopaque projector

D. Laying out pattern on muslin

E. Cutting pattern for mock-up

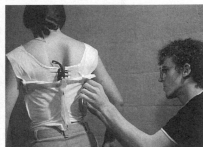

F. Fitting undergarments

G. Fitting mock-up

H. The completed costume

easier, however, to draft or create his own pattern based on the designer's sketch. After the pattern has been drafted on paper, the preliminary garment is cut from muslin, stitched together, and fitted to the actor. This garment is called the mock-up. Following corrections or adjustments to the mock-up, the technician is ready to cut and sew the garment with the outer fabric, using the muslin as the pattern. Eventually, the muslin may be resewn and used as the lining for the finished costume.

The actor must be present for the fitting of the outer garment, the completion of which permits the application of the ornamentation and decoration and the coordination of accessories. This lengthy construction process requires the contributions of many, if not all, of the following functionaries: shoppers, who are familiar with the sources and purchase any goods; drafters or drapers, who derive the initial pattern for the costume; cutters who take the pattern and actually cut the material; pinners, who join the pattern pieces together; tailors and stitchers, who sew the garment; fitters, who adjust the garment to the actor; and painters, who distress or age a costume if the script calls for a well-worn garment as opposed to a brand new one. Most studios will schedule a final fitting with the actor for the benefit of the designer in order to finalize the costume before it leaves the construction phase.

The actual phase of the performance section begins with the dress parade, a portion of a rehearsal period several days before the commencement of dress rehearsals. At this event, the actors appear first one-by-one and then by groups and finally as a cast on the setting and with stage lighting. As the actors parade on stage, the director and designers examine each costume carefully. The purpose here is to anticipate any problems with the costumes and any clashes with other areas of the production. This procedure allows time for any problems to be corrected and any adjustments to be made. With the beginning of dress rehearsals prior to the opening performance, the costumes are placed under the control of the head dresser and a crew of assistants, if the size of the cast is large. These people share the responsibility of keeping the costumes in fit condition for performance, including maintenance and minor repairs. They also assist the actors in quick costume changes backstage throughout the run of the show. At the close of a performance, the dressers carefully check all costume items and prepare them for the next usage.

At the conclusion of the performances of a production, costumes are always cleaned. In professional theatre, as many of them as possible may be used for touring companies, or they may be sold to rental companies or even donated to costume collections for rental/use by non-profit theatres. In regional, educational, and community theatres, available space usually determines whether a costume is to be stored for possible future use. Large wardrobe storage facilities depend upon orderly hanging arrangements and cataloging systems for quick and easy access to the costumes for use at a later date.

Selected Readings

Arnold, Janet. *Patterns of Fashion.* 3 Vols. London: Macmillan London Limited, 1964-85.

Barton, Lucy. *Historic Costume for the Stage.* Boston: Baker, 1961.

Corson, Richard. *Stage Makeup.* 8th ed. Englewood Cliffs, NJ: Prentice-Hall, 1990.

Cunningham, Rebecca. *The Magic Garment: Principles of Costume Design.* New York: Longman, 1989.

Ingham, Rosemary and Elizabeth Covey. *The Costumer's Handbook: How to Make All Kinds of Costumes.* Englewood Cliffs, NJ: Prentice-Hall, 1980.

Warrne, Geoffrey. *Fashion Accessories Since 1500.* New York: Drama Book, 1987.

CHAPTER TWENTY

❧

Lighting:
Fade In — Fade Out

The Women of Troy, produced by the Cumberland County Playhouse, directed by Abigail Crabtree, lighting by Steve Woods, scenery by James Crabtree.

In each chapter of this book the student has seen the building process of theatre. For the lighting designer, collaboration with the designers of scenery, costumes and sound; the playwright and director; and the acting company itself is fundamental. Perhaps no other theatre artist with the exception of the director must juggle the needs of so many, and perhaps, no other theatre artist can in a single-handed fashion destroy the "look" of a show. The lighting designer shapes how the audience perceives the play.

To understand how a designer approaches the lighting of a production, we must first understand the functions of stage lighting.

Functions of Stage Lighting

For purposes of discussion, the functions or objectives of stage lighting can be divided into six parts: (1) selective illumination; (2) establish time and place; (3) assist in creating mood; (4) support the style of production; (5) create visual compositions; and (6) strengthen the central visual image. Most designers agree on these elements, however they may have different ways in which to express them.

Selective Illumination

Selective illumination is a method used by the director and designer to guide the eye of the audience. To achieve this, the designer may simply remove light from the stage, creating areas of shade and shadow. If the audience cannot visually follow the action of the play then an otherwise good production will fail.

The lighting designer must be aware of the moving action of the play. For example, in *A Streetcar Named Desire*, which takes place in a two-room flat, lengthy scenes occur in only one of the rooms at a time. In this play, one room will almost always be somewhat brighter than the other. The brighter room will pull the focus of the audience, while the dim light in the second room will support the action.

Selective illumination is illustrated in this scene from *A Streetcar Named Desire. (Louisiana State University Theatre, directed by John Dennis, lighting by Steve Woods, scenery by Nels Anderson)*

The lighting designer helps establish time and place as in this night scene from *Dracula*. *(Heritage Repertory Theatre, directed by George Black, lighting by Steve Woods, scenery by Ron Keller, costumes by Gwen West)*

In this scene from *The Diviners*, the use of color helps establish the mood. *(Louisiana State University Theatre, directed by Jean Korff, lighting by Steve Woods, scenery by Kevin Hagan)*

Establish Time and Place

The director and designer must choose when and where the action of a play takes place. If an audience is to believe they are watching a scene taking place at sunrise, then the designer must establish how the lighting at sunrise is different from the lighting at sunset. How is the lighting of an apartment in a large city different from that of a small town?

Good lighting provides the audience with helpful clues. These may be abstract and work on a subconscious level or be quite blatant. The lighting designer may be called upon to create a night effect on stage. He must decide how to color night.

Is it a rainy night? How is the lighting of a rainy night different from that of a snowy night? Perhaps, as in *Dracula*, the lighting of the night must convey both seduction and evil.

Assist In Creating Mood

The designer begins to use color to help establish the mood of the play. In comedies, bright, festive lighting is often required. When lighting a tragedy, a designer will frequently choose to work with dark, somber, heavier colors. The lighting should reflect the action and mood of the play. The photo above presents a very "up" moment in *The Diviners*.

In this scene, the lighting designer has created a unique world to support the expressionistic style of the production of *Macbeth*. *(Louisiana State University Theatre, directed by Barry Kyle, lighting by Steve Woods, scenery and costumes by Marina Draghici)*

Intensity and color are used to create a visual composition in this scene from *Oh, What a Lovely War*. *(Louisiana State University Theatre, directed by Barry Kyle, lighting by Steve Woods, scenery by Nels Anderson, costumes by Gerilyn Tandberg)*

The lighting, as in this production of *Taming of the Shrew*, can heighten the conceptual approach to the production and strengthen the central visual image. *(Louisiana State University Theatre, directed by Rita Giomi, lighting by Steve Woods, scenery by Nels Anderson)*

Support the Style of Production

Is the production realistic or nonrealistic? If realistic then the lighting needs to come from obvious sources within the play, such as sunlight through a window, lamps for indoor lighting, the reflection of light from a lake or perhaps the warm glow of a fireplace. For the lighting designer, a realistic play can be one of the most difficult. Abstract plays allow the designer's imagination to explore other lighting possibilites, such as shafts of light, saturated colors or haze and smoke to delineate walls of light. Often the style of the production may be expressionistic. In the above scene from *Macbeth*, the lighting has created a totally unique world for the play.

Create Visual Compositions

One of the most obvious ways to see an example of visual composition at work is to attend a rock concert where moving lights and swirling clouds of smoke create the background for a song. Skillful use of intensity and color can greatly affect depth perception, but its usage must be harmonized with the set designer's work.

Strengthen the Central Visual Image

The director, playwright and members of the design team work from an agreed upon conceptual approach to a production. Unlike scenery or costumes, lighting is the most flexible once the production moves into the theatre. It will highten and strenghthen the central visual image of the play. The production of *Taming of the Shrew* (above) was set at a popular French Canadian circus.

A Brief History of Stage Lighting

Earliest man performed theatre outdoors and relied on the sun for natural illumination. Once

theatre moved indoors an artificial light source was needed. Pine knots in iron cressets and oil lamps with floating wicks were used.

At the beginning of the Renaissance, three light sources were available: oil lamps, the wax candle (the molded candle was introduced in the eighteenth century) and torches (including lanterns). With the theories of Sebastiano Serlio (1475-1554), Leone di Somi (1527-1592), and Joseph Fürtenbach (1591-1667), modern stage lighting is said to have begun.

Fürtenbach in his treatise *Sciena di Comoedia* (1628) is credited for developing footlights—rows of oil lamps at the edge of the stage, out of the audience's sight. These footlights were called "floatlights" and like all early lighting equipment caused fires. Large buckets of water and large sponges attached to sticks were necessary in the theatre.

By the seventeenth century, the major lighting conventions of positioning, coloring, dimming, floodlighting, transluscenies and the darkening of the auditorium were developed. Although the technology was two hundred years away, the Renaissance theorists had conceived of these major lighting principles.

Candles and oil dominated from the Restoration to 1800s until flammable gas came into use in the 1790s. Gas lighting was first used in London by the Lyceum Theatre in 1803, and was put to use on the stage regularly in 1815 at Covent Garden and the Olympic theatres. Gas was first used on the American stage in 1816 at the Chestnut Street Theatre in Philadelphia.

Developed in the 1820s, the limelight was an offshoot developed from the use of gas. Called calcium light, the oxy-hydrogen light, or Drummond light, this instrument was based on the principle of heating a block of compressed quicklime with a flame of oxygen and hydrogen mixed together. Limelight was put to theatrical use between 1826 and 1837. The limelight has survived as a term for being in the spotlight or wanting to be seen.

Once theatres converted to gas light, a measure of safety and controllable illumination was achieved. However, almost overnight, electricity found its way into the theatres. The electric arc was developed by Sir Humphrey Davy in 1808 and first used in 1846 at the Paris Opera House. It was here in 1860 that the first use of the electric spotlight (carbon arc) to "spot" or follow the character was introduced.

Next came the Jablochkoff candle (1876) consisting of two parallel vertical rods separated by insulation. This achievement created a constant burning of the arc. A major breakthrough came in 1879 with Edison's incadescent electric lamp. Again, the Paris Opera in 1880 was the first to use these lamps on stage. With electricity came the invention of modern efficient stage lighting equipment.

Lighting design began to develop into an art form during the twentieth century. Among the first to recognize the importance of lighting and the "new stagecraft" were Gordon Craig (1872-1966) and Adolphe Appia (1862-1928). They were followed by pioneers such as Stanley McCandless, Jean Rosenthal, and Tharon Musser.

Lighting Equipment

Stage lights fall into three categories: spotlights, floodlights, and strip lights.

Spotlights

Two basic groups make up spotlights. The first is *Ellipsoidal Reflector Spotlight (ERS)*, or as it is more commonly known, the *leko*. The ERS has become an indispensable tool for controlling light placement in stage work. If the designer needs a sharp or hard edge of concentrated light then an ellipsoidal is used. An ERS uses an elliptical reflector to direct light through a series of plano convex lenses of different sizes and focal lengths based upon the placement of the light. By moving the lense barrel the light produces either a sharp or

Altman 360Q Ellipsoidal

soft edge. Texture can be added by inserting a pattern holder and template or gobo. The gobo is a metal cutout of a shape that is projected by the light.

The shutter system also controls light coming from the unit. By using the shutters, the beam can be shaped into numerous patterns. The light can then be tightly focused on the stage without ambient spill. Each ERS has four shutters, allowing the designer to cut the beam of light to fit a needed angle on stage. Units were once labeled based on lense size and focal length, i.e., 6 x 9, 6 x 12, and 6 x 16. Currently, the preferred method of identification is field angle such as 40, 30 or 20 degrees.

The second group of spotlights developed in the early 1930s are called *fresnels,* after Augustin Fresnel, who around 1800 developed the unique lense for use in light houses. Sometimes called an *inkie,* a *coffee grinder* or a *junior,* the fresnel comes in

Altman 65Q Fresnel

various sizes from the 150 watt, 3" lense Inkie to the 10,000 watt, 20" lense used in television and film. The fresnel produces a soft diffused beam of light which can either be small (spot focus) or large (flood focus.) Unlike the leko the fresnel has no shutter system but uses an add-on piece of equipment known as a *barndoor* to control the edges of light. In addition, a second device known as a *top hat* or *snoot* can be used. The fresnel is a good unit to be used when ambient light is not a problem.

Altman Scoop #154

Floodlights

Initially, floodlights were called "bunchlights" because electric lamps were manufactured as a unit with 10-12 lights per unit. Floodlights make up a broad grouping of units used for blending and toning. These lights are good for lighting cycloramas, drops, scenery or backings, and unlike spotlights, do not use a lense. Lights or instruments that fall into this category include scoops, olivettes, cyclights and borderlights. The oldest example of a floodlight still in use is the olivette, which first appeared in 1913.

Striplights

Striplights are unique lighting instruments. These lights are made up of a series of lamps mounted into a narrow rectangular metal trough. They may be built in any length; however, the typical unit measures between six and eight feet long and about ten inches wide. These lights often use colored glass filters, known as *roundels*, to add color to the stage.

Striplights may be mounted on the floor (footlights), used to tone scenery (border lights) or placed below and above a cyclorama (ground row, cyc foots/cyc lights) to give a general wash.

Altman Skycyc

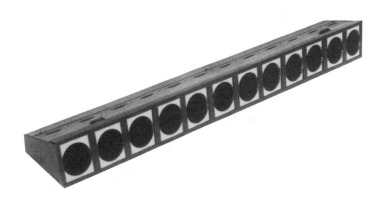

Altman Borderlight #R40

Follow spotlight: Lycian #1278

Altman PAR 64

Miscellaneous Lighting Equipment

PAR 64: A basic light source for concert lighting, the PAR 64, is a metal shell or can which holds a lamp made up of a reflector and lense that drop into place. The lamps are available in a variety of wattages and focal lengths. The name PAR is derived from the lamp, parabolic aluminized reflector. The PAR lamp resembles a car headlight and is cheap, rugged and easily installed. PAR fixtures are commonly found at rock concerts, clubs, and more and more in traditional theatres. Because of the simplicity of the unit, the cost is far less than that of either a ERS or fresnel.

Follow Spotlight: These lights come in a wide variety of throw distances and are commonly used in the theatre, at sporting events, ice shows and at concerts. The lights are operated by stagehands and require a good deal of skill and training. The purpose of the light is to provide a moving special around the stage to highlight action for the audience. These lights are a staple in the Broadway musical, ice shows, circus, and rock and roll con-

certs. Followspots come in various sizes and have a throw distance of 50 feet up to greater than 400 feet.

Color Media

The work of Munroe R. Pevear made possible the manufacturing of color media. He was one of the first to advocate the use of color synthesis—using primary colors with clear tinting. The primary colors used by the lighting designer are red, blue and green. These colors can be mixed to achieve the complementary colors of magenta, yellow and blue-green. This process of additive mixing to create the secondary colors will also create white light when the three primaries overlap. Primary colors cannot be created by blending the secondary colors.

One of the misconceptions about color media or *gels* (translucent colored sheets) is that a particular gel superimposes its color onto the stage. Actually, the main color of the gel blocks all other color in the spectrum. A blue gel, for example, blocks all other color in the spectrum leaving only blue to be seen by the eye. When one light is used on a subject, this method of adding color is known as *subtractive mixing*. When two or more lights are focused onto the stage and their color is mixed in the atmosphere, it is referred to as *additive mixing*. In additive mixing, a blue and red unit are focused at the same spot of stage. The audience will perceive a shade of pink or magenta.

The word *gel* is a derivative of gelatin and refers to a time when gelatin was a principle ingredient in color. The initial gels were fragile and designed to be used with equipment that rarely exceeded 500 watts. Traditional gel can still be purchased. Generally, a sheet of gel is 24" x 24". For a university, light lab work gel is ideal. Extremely low in cost (about $1.00 per sheet), gel permits the student designer to change color easily and inexpensively. Gels, however, have a limited color range and are unsuitable for professional theatre.

Today color media is supplied in plastic sheets. The base material is either polyester or mylar. The new media withstand the bright light and intense heat generated by modern fixtures. Today's designers prefer brand names such as Roscolene, Roscolux, Lee and GAM. The variety of color range is excellent and, because of the modest price (usually under $5.00), color experimentation is the best way for the lighting designer to build his.

Another type of color media often used when primary colors are needed are *Roundels* or glass filters (see striplights). Roundels have an almost indefinite life span, an extremely limited color range (usually available in about a dozen colors), and resist fading.

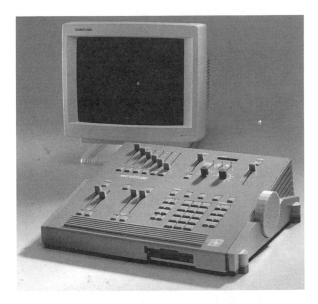

ETC MicroVision$_{FX}$ Lighting Control Console

Lighting Control and Dimming

Once the lighting for a show is "hung" (all lights placed in their proper positions on battens), some way is needed to turn the lights on and off. The lighting control board and the dimmers are used to vary the intensity and time that a light is on. Lighting boards come in a variety of styles; however, they can be grouped into two classifications. The first are *computer boards* which allow the designer to program the rate, intensity and time that a light is on. By using the computer, a complex series of cues may be programmed over

several hours of rehearsal. Once the show is recorded to memory or disc, it can then be recalled by pressing a button. The time spent in recording the show by the lighting board operator is well made up by the ease of operation and revision during technical rehearsal. Also, the computer boards allow for moving from cue to cue very rapidly. Most computer boards can handle the printout of cue sheets, electronic repatching, color changes by electronic scrolling devices mounted onto the lights, and many special effects including the controlling of robotic lights. Computer consoles can cost as little as several thousand dollars and increase up to the price of a modest house. Among the better known manufacturers of computer consoles are Strand Lighting and ETC.

The second classification is *Preset* or *Manual consoles*. These boards require an individual to set the faders (see vocabulary) on the console for each cue to be "run" (operated) during a performance. Preset boards are time-consuming to set up, subject to human error and require a skilled, sensitive operator as the fading of lights is controlled by the human hand. The technical rehearsal (and for that matter, the show) can only move at the pace of the operator. Most manual boards have a two-scene capability so that one cue may be preset while a

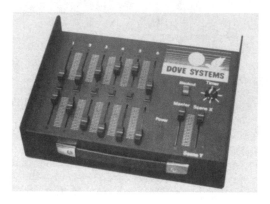

Scenemaster 6

second cue is in operation on stage. Most lighting design teachers agree that student designers should begin with manual boards as they give the beginning designer a sense of how show lighting evolves, its timing and its cue structure. Preset boards are normally found in university black box theatres as a training tool and in smaller community theatres where computers are unnecessary. Most preset boards cost less than a thousand dollars.

Cue sheets are needed for both consoles. These can be either electronic or handwritten records of each cue. Information included on a cue sheet is the running order, the rate at which the lights move, the intensity, the repatches and information on when the cue happens within the action.

Dimmers

A dimmer is basically a switch that turns the electricity on and off at a very fast rate. Depending upon the amount of time the switch is on or off, the light is either bright or dim. This is an overly simplistic description of the dimmer and the student can easily find several books dedicated to how the dimmer works. Like control boards, dimmers come in a variety of price ranges. Most theatres use either 1.2 kw or 2.4 kw dimmers. A 1.2 kw dimmer will power a group of lights that use no more than 1200 watts of power. More wattage will overload the dimmer, resulting in a protective

Strand Dimmer Rack

breaker to trip and shut off the unit. Dimmers are available in a variety of power ranging up to 12,000 watts. They are mounted in metal racks with as few as six units per pack (portable) and up to 200 per rack (permanent installation). The most common dimmer on the market today is the *SCR (Silicon Controlled Rectifier)*.

The Lighting Team

The lighting designer or LD is in charge of the stage lighting. It is this person's responsibility to create and oversee the artistic elements connected with the lighting of a show. Lighting designers, like scenic and costume designers, are often members of U.S.A.A. (United Scenic Artists of America). This union assists with contract negations, labor disputes and other business elements. During the early part of the 20th century, lighting designers were rare; thus, stage lighting was the domain of the scenic designer or stage manager. As lighting became more complex and directors began to understand how lighting could enhance a play, the position of lighting designer became legitimized.

In most cases, the Assistant Lighting Designer (ALD), who works closely with the designer to implement the design, will draft the final plot as per the designer's specification. The ALD will often apprentice with a well known designer in order to break into the business.

Used by the Master Electrician (or ME) to determine how the show is hung, the *light plot* is a scale drawing showing the exact location of each light, its color, focus and often the location of its electrical outlet. Lighting plots are drawn usually in 1/2"=1'0" scale with two drawings being generated: the plan view (which is an overhead view) and the section view (which is a side view). Once the plot is completed, an instrument schedule is required. The instrument schedule is a form used to record all of the technical data about each light used for the production. By using this form, the crew working on the show can readily track equipment, color, circuits and dimming.

The ME, who is often a member of the I.A.T.S.E. (International Alliance of Theatrical Stage Employees), oversees the shop order which must include every item the lighting crew will need. If the theatre does not own lighting equipment, as is the case in most New York theatres, this can be a complex task. A skilled ME or a Production Electrician will therefore order slightly more equipment and supplies than the designer thinks he will need. Several days will be spent in the preparation of a show at a lighting shop. During this time, all of the equipment will be tested and packed for transportation to the theatre.

The ME hires a crew of stage hands called electricians to load the show in and prepare it for the LD to focus. During this time, if the designer is unavailable, the Assistant Lighting Designer will be in the theatre watching the progress of the load in and making decisions. A working designer might easily have two or more projects overlapping and often will not be readily available.

Once all the equipment is in place along with the scenery, the designer will focus each light to the area of the stage it is to illuminate. The process can be long and tiring. Most off-Broadway shows as do LORT (League of Resident Theatres) houses allow about a week for all lighting work to be finished. In contrast, a Broadway show might take several months to complete basically the same job.

Next, the director and actors move into the space and a lighting, or "cue to cue," rehearsal begins. It is during this technical rehearsal that the intensity of each light will be set. The cues of the show will be recorded and entered into the stage manager's prompt book. The prompt book is a copy of the script in which all the cues and stage actions are recorded. During the performance the stage manager then uses the book to determine the placement and execution of lighting cues.

Once the show has opened, it becomes the responsibility of the stage manager and master electrician to maintain the look of the show. If the show is to go on the road, the LD will redesign the show to package it into smaller venues and to streamline the equipment needed for the look of the show. Most road shows will load into a theatre the same day of performance.

The following pages illustrate a sample light plot, instrument schedule and shop order.

The Lighting Designer's Training

Many universities offer Master of Fine Arts programs for the theatre artist. The MFA program is designed to establish a conservatory-like atmosphere where the student can concentrate on be-

Light Plot (left portion)

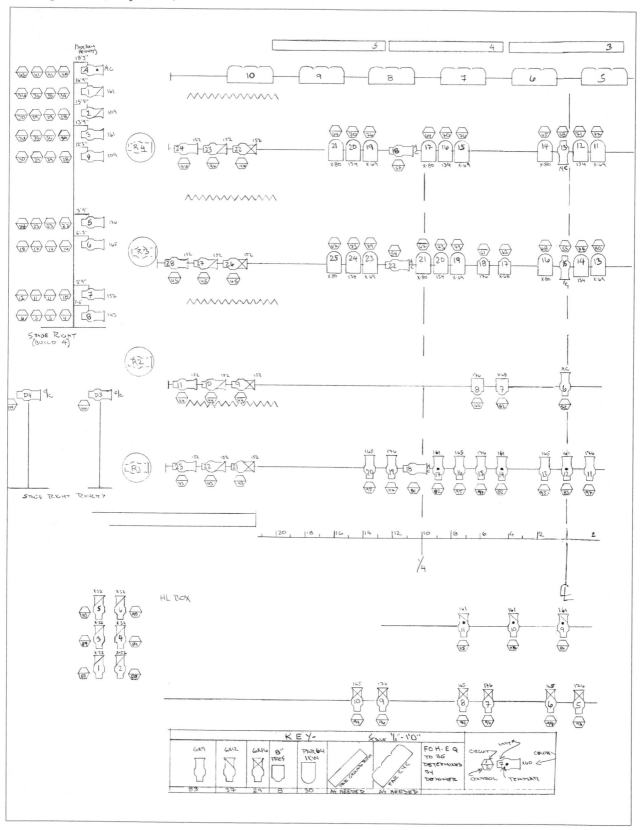

Light Plot (right portion)

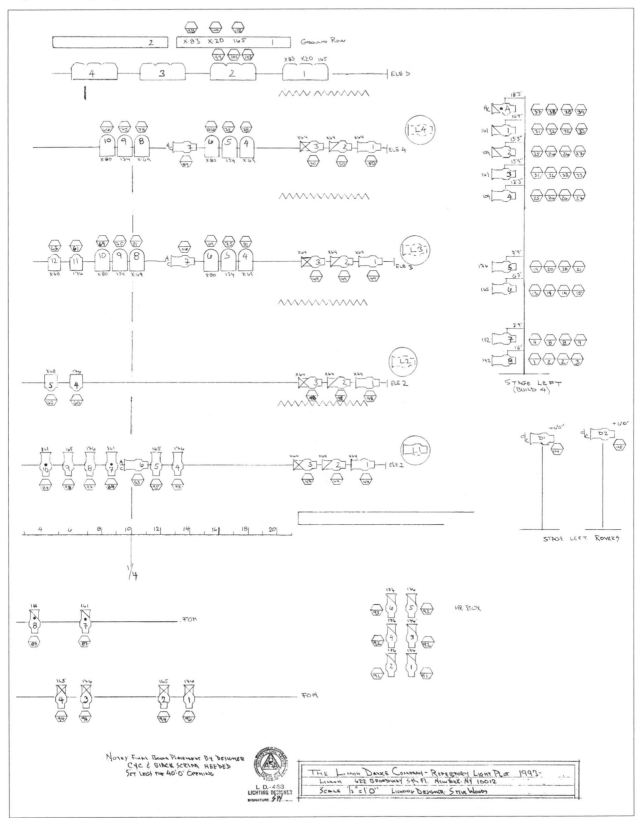

Instrument Schedule (Channel Hookup)

Lighting Design: Steve Woods					Channels (1) through (19)		
Chn	**Position**		**Unit**	**Type**	**Watts**	**Purpose**	**Color**
(1)	L1	BOOM	7	6x9	1kw	KICKER	142
(2)	L2	BOOM	7	6X9	1kw	KICKER	142
	L3	BOOM	7	6X9	1kw	KICKER	142
(3)	L4	BOOM	7	6X9	1kw	KICKER	143
(4)	R1	BOOM	7	6X9	1kw	KICKER	143
(5)	R2	BOOM	7	6X9	1kw	KICKER	143
	R3	BOOM	7	6X9	1kw	KICKER	143
(6)	R4	BOOM	7	6X9	1kw	KICKER	143
(7)	L1	BOOM	6	6x9	1kw	KICKER	152
(8)	L2	BOOM	6	6X9	1kw	KICKER	152
	L3	BOOM	6	6X9	1kw	KICKER	152
(9)	L4	BOOM	6	6X9	1kw	KICKER	152
(10)	R1	BOOM	6	6X9	1kw	KICKER	153
(11)	R2	BOOM	6	6X9	1kw	KICKER	153
	R3	BOOM	6	6X9	1kw	KICKER	153
(12)	R4	BOOM	6	6X9	1kw	KICKER	153
(13)	L1	BOOM	5	6X9	1kw	HEAD HI	CC
(14)	L2	BOOM	5	6X9	1kw	HEAD HI	CC
	L3	BOOM	5	6X9	1kw	HEAD HI	CC
(15)	L4	BOOM	5	6X9	1kw	HEAD HI	CC
(16)	R1	BOOM	5	6X9	1kw	HEAD HI	CC
(17)	R2	BOOM	5	6X9	1kw	HEAD HI	CC
	R3	BOOM	5	6X9	1kw	HEAD HI	CC
(18)	R4	BOOM	5	6X9	1kw	HEAD HI	CC
(19)	L1	BOOM	5	6X9	1kw	HI SIDE	109
	L1	BOOM	5	6X9	1kw	HI SIDE	109

Shop Order

Quantity	Product Description	Quantity	Product Description
6	1 1/2" Heavy Duty Flange	1	35# Base
10	1 1/2" Swivel Cheseboro	4	50# Base
50	1 1/2" Right Angle Cheseboro	1	24 x 1200 Dimmer Pack ETC L86
60	12" Side Arm (Single Tee)	5	12 x 2.4K Pack D-192 Colortran
20	12" Side Arm (No Tee)	1	Microvision FX Console
2	Tall Adjustble Stand	1	Microvision FX Road Case
	Castered Base, Single Unit Top	1	Microvision Monitor Road Case
5	8# Base	5	Colortran D-192 Pack Road Case

coming a designer. During their training, lighting designers must develop a variety of skills. They must be trained as electricians, able to understand how dimmers and control consoles work, how lights distribute illumination, and how to hang, cable, and focus a show. They must also develop the skills of a visual artist, learning about composition, line, form, and mass. As many designers use story boards to lay out the lighting of a show for the director, drawing skills are also important. Directors often discuss lighting by suggesting that the designer study the work of a particular artist or composer; thus, most established designers have a broad range of knowledge in both music and art.

Like an engineer, designers must study drafting so as to provide exacting information on paper for those who install the equipment. If the lighting designer is to work with opera, then the ability to read music will come in handy. Like any artist, designers must be well read and aware of contemporary social and political issues.

Finally, the designer must be able to communicate ideas clearly. In addition to the course work offered by the university, a student designer should consider joining a professional theatre company as an apprentice or intern. Here the student can work with different directors, designers and playwrights to see how commercial theatre operates. Most LORT houses offer summer intern programs that include modest salaries and often housing. A listing of these theatres can be obtained from Theatre Communications Group (TCG), New York City. The training and growth process never stops. For example, during an interview, a designer was asked what foreign languages she spoke. As a result of her foreign language skill, she was invited to join a dance company that toured Europe.

The Design Process

Each designer works in a diverse fashion to develop the lighting for a show. Although designers may disagree on how a show develops, the first step begins with the play itself. All designers begin by studying the script. From the script, basic information about the lighting of a play can be found. The playwright will often give valuable suggestions to how the show should look. Tennessee Williams, for example, often describes the setting, costumes and lighting effects in great detail. By carefully reading the script, the designer will find basic information including the time of day, season, weather and location of a particular scene. The script provides the designer with information that will allow him to make a credible look on stage. Each time the designer reads the play, he may find new information that will be invaluable.

At some point the designer begins research on the project. Research may be as theoretical as studying the quality of light and color at a particular time of day, or as mechanical as finding the right piece of equipment to achieve a special lighting effect. Research helps the designer to put the pieces of the design puzzle together. After becoming familiar with the script, the next step is to meet with the director and other members of the design team to determine the show's concept. This conceptual approach to the production is the vision of the work that will shape the show.

During design meetings the show's final look will be determined. It is essential for all involved to discuss the show in a free and open manner. The director and designers must remain open to new suggestions and ideas that are brought up for consideration. In all things, however, the director has the final word.

As a show is put together, it is important for the designer to be clear on the function of each lighting instrument. What purpose does that particular light serve? Does the equipment add solely to the illumination of the stage or does it assist in creating mood. The lighting of the show should be connected or linked. Each cue should lead to the next. Just like the lighting plot, the design should follow some logical order. Is the story line advanced by the design? Does the lighting assist in guiding the audience around the action area? After attending several rehearsals and seeing how the scenery, props and costumes are coordinated within the production, a light plot will be drawn.

Designing a Dance

First staged in 1971, *Dances For Isadora*, was recently remounted by the Limon Company as part of their active repertory of dances. Many designers have worked with the company since its inception in 1946 by Jose Limon and Doris Humphrey; and though the current designer may put his name on this design, it is difficult not to be influenced by the previous lighting interpretations of the piece. As companies often maintain certain designs throughout their lifespan, it is important to be clear on what is truly new lighting work and what is merely being re-created. The Martha Graham Company is well known for re-creating the work of the late Jean Rosenthal who designed for the company. With *Dances For Isadora*, the artistic director wanted to capture the spirit of the original lighting, as suggested by Limon, while at the same time giving the designer the freedom to create a new environment.

The dance is divided into five sections with each capturing a moment in the life of the dancer Isadora Duncan. These sections are I. Primavera, II. Maenad, III. Niobe, IV. La Patrice and V. Scarf Dance. The design images for each section are:

1. Birth and Joy, a bright spring day.
2. Growth and struggle, still warm but problems and complications arise.
3. Reflection and Sorrow, a rainy day in Paris.
4. Power and Mystery, the pinnacle of success.
5. Despair and Death, alone.

The first step in creating the lighting for a dance is to become familiar with both the movement and music. Just as the playwright's words serve as a roadmap for the designer, so does the choreography. The lighting must reinforce the story being told. In addition, research into the original production, discussion with the dancers performing the work, perhaps looking over the many books about Isadora Duncan, all aid in developing the design.

Because the company is actively touring, a *repertory light plot* is needed to service not only one piece but the needs of a variety of pieces. This type of plot is used when a theatrical company performs several works with no change over time to re-focus or re-color. Repertory plots are common with dance companies, summer stock and some LORT companies.

In dance, basic lighting positions include side light, pipe ends, back light and box positions. These hanging positions permit maximum sculpting of the dancers. Often the side light positions, particularly the *kickers* (lights mounted low, about 2'0" from the floor) are often considered color change units. These units have the color changed between dances to increase the flexibility of the lighting rig.

As with most New York dance companies, the Limon Company has no permanent theatre base for rehearsals. It is a rarity to be able to rent a theatre, hang the lights and work "a cue to cue." The lighting concept and the basic cue placement are developed in the studio under work lights. The beginning, middle, end and the structure that connects all the cues are discussed. Costumes are used and are available for color work with a makeshift light lab consisting of several inkies (three-inch lense Fresnel). A good deal of time is spent in discussion as to what each section of a dance means. Basically, what is the message of the choreography and how will the lighting reinforce that?

Once the company goes on tour, the lighting rig is in place and the lighting rehearsal begins. Because of this arrangement, the lighting for a new piece often develops over several months. As a new dance is added into the repertory, the lighting is slowly refined. *Dances for Isadora* will go through this process. As the tour continues, new areas of the dance are explored to see if additional cues are necessary. In some theatres, a cyclorama is not available, so the piece is danced in front of a black scrim or curtain. Since a dance may be staged to be framed by a dark blue sky, the black background gives the designer a chance to explore lighting the piece in a different way. Perhaps if not for the lack of a cyclorama the designer and direc-

Birth and joy is the design image shown above from
Dances for Isadora. (Limon Dance Company, Emile Plauche)

tor would never consider looking at the piece
against blackness. Although the look for the dance
is set, each house has a different environment for
the performance. Elements that work are added
into what will become the final lighting look, and
failures are cast aside. The dance becomes a little
better each time it is shown. Some of the looks that
do not work for this dance may be tried in the
future on other dances.

The typical day for the lighting designer on
tour usually means long hours and stress. The
designer is always moving forward once the show
is "loaded in." Almost always, time is the greatest
problem facing companies on tour. No matter
what happens during the load in, the stage hands
are always working with the knowledge that in a
few hours an audience will be arriving expecting
a show. With the Limon company, the move into
the theatre is early morning; by lunch between 150
and 200 lights will have been hung and focused.
After lunch break, the cues for the evening will be

recorded. By early afternoon the dance company
will arrive and a spacing and lighting technical
rehearsal begins. By early evening the entire show
will be ready for an 8:00 P.M. performance. The
next day the process repeats. Life goes on.

A Lighting Vocabulary

The following list offers definitions for the
most common lighting terms. Some of these may
be very familiar, some abstract and some may be
known by different names.

Adaptor: A short cable used to plug equipment into an
    outlet having different types of plugs.
Backlight: Light which illuminates the actor from the
    rear, very useful to add plasticity to the stage look.
Barndoor: Metal device made up of hinged flaps re-
    sembling doors. Used commonly on equipment
    that has no shutter system to control light spill. Most
    often used on fresnels or parcans.
Batten: A pipe usually suspended from a grid and on
    which lights can be hung using C-Clamps.
Beam: A term used to describe the light coming from an
    instrument.
Cable: The insulated wire used to conduct electricity.
C-Clamp: A C-shaped metal clamp that attaches to the
    light and then to a mounting position.
Color Frame: A metal frame used to hold gel in front of
    the lenses.
Connector: Another name for an electrical plug.
Dim: To lower the intensity of the lights.
Downlight: Similar to Backlight; however, this light is
    mounted directly over the actor and projects straight
    down.
Faders: Each dimmer is controlled by a fader which is
    a single remote sliding handle on the console.
F.O.H.: Front of House
Gobo: Also known as a cookie or template, this is a
    metal cutout which projects a shadow pattern on
    the stage.
Hot Spot: The brightest spot in the light, usually the
    center.
Instrument: A popular name for lighting fixtures.
Iris: A drop-in accessory to an ERS which allows the
    light to be reduced in aperture. Usually found in
    follow spotlights.
Jumper: A short piece of cable used to connect a light to
    a receptacle.
Key: The principal direction from which the source
    light is coming. Also known as Key Light and used

Rosco Designer Pattern (Gobo)

commonly in television. The light which supports the key is known as the Fill Light.

Kilowatt: A unit of measurement which equal 1,000 watts. Dimmers are rated is kilowatts.

Light Board: A common name for any lighting control console. The light board sends a low voltage signal to the dimmers which in turn adjust the levels of the different lights in use.

Lighting Grid: Used in black box theatres or spaces without a fly system, this is a series of nonmoving battens from which lights can be hung.

Lighting Template: A plastic or metal plate with a cut-out of the different lighting instruments. This in turn is used by the designer to trace the outlines of the lights onto the light plot. These templates come in several scales, however, 1/2"-1'0" is the standard.

Light Tree: A vertical pipe mounted in a base from which lights can be hung. Also known as a boom.

Male Plug: A plugging device from which metal blades project. The male plug connects into the female (load bearing) plug.

Non-Dim: An electrical circuit which is not capable of dimming.

Patch Panel: A system which allows for the manual patching of circuits to dimmers. Most theatres today opt for dimmer per circuit, avoiding the cost of the patch panel. Also known as Interconnecting Panel.

Pigtail: The wire coming from a light.

Raceway: A metal trough in which multiple electrical circuits are mounted. The box itself is mounted onto a batten and supplies power for multiple lights. A batten on which a raceway is mounted is said to be an "electric."

Side Light: In dance, it is the light mounted on booms or light trees positioned in the wings. The light projects the width of the stage.

SO Cable: The rubber-jacketed, insulated wire commonly used in the theatre to supply current to the lights. The most common is 12/3. This cable is 12 gauge (capability 20 amps) and made up of 3 wires: a black or hot, a white or common, and a green or ground.

Shutter: A metal device, used in a grouping of four mounted inside a ERS or "leko." It controls and shapes the beam of light.

Special: Usually a single light used to call attention to specific place or moment on stage.

Spill: Unwanted or misdirected light on the stage.

Step-Lens: The reverse of a fresnel lense. Used in place of a double plano convex lense in an ERS.

Throw: The distance between the light and the subject.

Top Hat: Another name for a snoot. This attachment resembles its namesake and mounts onto the front of a light, usually in ferns, to control spill.

Two-fear: A "Y" cable which allows two lights to be plugged into the some circuit.

Selected Readings

Lighting the Stage: Art and Practice, Willard F. Bellman

Stage Lighting Revealed, Glenn Cunningham

Designing With Light, J. Michael Gillette

Light on the Subject, David Hays

A Method of Lighting the Stage, Stanley McCandless

A Process for Lighting the Stage, Ian McGrath

Concert Lighting: Techniques, Art, and Business, James Moody

The Lighting Art, Richard H. Palmer

Scene Design and Stage Lighting, Oren W. Parker and Harvey Smith

Stage Lighting, Richard Pilbrow

The Stage Lighting Handbook, Francis Reid

Handbook of Scenery, Properties, and Lighting, Volume 2, Harvey Sweet

Handbook of Stage Lighting Graphics, William Warfel

Lighting Design Handbook, Lee Watson

The Magic of Light, Jean Rosenthal and Lael Wertenbaker

The publisher gratefully acknowledges the assistance of Jackie Leiby and the Magnum Companies, 170-A Ottley Drive, Atlanta, GA 30324, telephone 1-800-255-1774; Peter Halsey and Electronic Theatre Controls, Inc., 3030 Laura Lane, Middleton, WI 53562, telephone 608-831-4116; and Strand Lighting, 18111 So. Santa Fe Ave., Rancho Dominguez, CA 90224, telephone 310-637-7500.

Part IV
PRACTICAL CHOICES

CHAPTER TWENTY-ONE

&

Managing the Store:
The Business of Theatre

Actor-manager Henry Irving in the role of Shylock. Irving was the dominant force in English theatre between 1880 and 1900 and was the first performer to be knighted (in 1895) for his achievements. From *The Theatre*, 1880.

The business of the theatre is business. In fact, the theatre has been called the worst-run business in America. Nonetheless it does pay attention to its management. Good management means a well-run organization, and even more importantly, it means money. Management includes a broad spectrum of activities from the box office to backstage. It includes operating, financing, and staging a production from the initial purchase of a script to the final curtain. This chapter is about management. It is not intended to be a handbook for management but simply a statement of what goes into producing a theatrical production. Bear in mind that, due to inflation, the various amounts of money indicated could change, even as this line is being written.

Producing A Play

Let's suppose you are a producer who wants to put a play on Broadway. The first step is to get a property, a play intended for production. You can purchase an original play or perhaps you have found a translation or an adaptation that suits you. You could even produce a play that is in public domain—which means no copyright and therefore no expenditure for the rights. On the other hand, you don't own the rights. Whatever type of property you choose, when you find a script that you want to produce, you take an option on that property; you purchase the right to produce the play. By paying the owner of the script money to produce the script, you are in essence saying, I will pay you money for the exclusive right to produce your play within a designated time—usually six months or one year. This is an option.

The Dramatists Guild

The Dramatists Guild is the union designed primarily to protect the author's rights. The right to produce a play in America or Canada is known as the Dram. Guild Contract, which is short for the Dramatists Guild, Inc. Minimum Basic Protection

Contract. The Guild contract is thus a type of license requiring you to pay the author royalties on his or her script. A royalty is a fixed amount of money paid to the author or owner of the work being produced. The contract also requires that the author's name appear on all programs and advertisements. The contract is lengthy, detailed, and confusing to the layman. For example, the contract provides that the author is entitled to purchase (not comps.—complimentary) a certain number of seats for each performance of the play. Also, prior to the closing or one month after the New York opening (whichever is earlier), the producer must furnish a neat copy of the script to the author. This script includes the information about lighting, costumes, properties, set, sound, and actors' cues. This is the stage manager's script and is called also the prompt script. The Dramatists Guild Basic Production Contract is only one contract which this union uses. There are also a Revue Product Contract, a Collaboration Contract, and Stock Tryout Production Contract, a Dramatic Contract, and a Dramatico-Musical Production Contract.

Financing the Production

Assuming you have an option, you must next decide who will produce the play. Will you do it by yourself or will you seek help? Most producers get help—that is, they get financial assistance rather than pay the cost themselves. A common method used by producers is to form a "limited partnership" with outside investors (sometimes called "Angels," possibly from the guardian angel or from the phrase "Isn't he an angel?" meaning that he is a doll, which a backer certainly is). The investors are considered the limited partners and the producer is the general partner. *Limited* means that the investors are limited in terms of how much input they have in the actual production and, more importantly, it means that they are limited in terms of how much money they have to put into the production. Usually a limited inverstor is liable for a fixed amount plus an overcall, which is additional money ranging from ten to twenty percent of the limited partner's original inverstment. When the investor gives the money to the producer, the producer must put it into a bank until he has enough money to produce the show. He cannot spend it before time, unless the contract so states. When the producer reaches the amount he has estimated is needed to produce the show, he may withdraw the money.

Assuming that a producer chooses to form a limited partnership, his next step is to convince investors to put their money into his production. One method used, though doubt has been raised as to its effectiveness, is the backer's audition. At a backer's audition, prospective investors view a sampling or a condensed version of the play. The presentation can be held in an apartment, dining hall, rehearsal hall, etc.; food and drinks are usually served; questions are answered by the producer; and entire program lasts about an hour.

Regardless of how a producer chooses to raise funds, he must treat the play as he would a stock listed on the stock exchange. For example, if the producer wishes to raise money outside the state of New York (whether by phone or mail or in person), he must file appropriate forms with the Securities and Exchange Commission (SEC). The forms are designed to insure that the investors are protected against "shady" schemes and to aid the SEC in determining whether the producer and his associates are entering into a legal business endeavor. The SEC forms ask for such information as:

1. Where you will be doing business.
2. People with whom you are associated.
3. Pertinent information about you and your associates.
4. The name of your attorney.
5. The state in which you intend to raise money.

Along with the questionnaire, a detailed prospectus must be mailed to all potential investors. The prospectus describes all those involved with the production, the financial arrangements, and a brief summary of the play; it also contains a "risk to the investor clause." This clause requires that the producer, in essence, try to discourage would-

be investors. The clause must therefore contain the following information:

1. The investor should be prepared for total loss.
2. The number of Broadway plays which lost money the prior season.
3. The odds against the play being successful and thus the remote chance of having your investment pay off.

If you, as producer, decide to confine your money-making activities to New York, you also need to file with the New York attorney general. If you raise money outside New York state, you must always file with the attorney general in the particular state. All states have what are known as "blue sky laws." The term stems from the idea that when the individual invests his money, he will have nothing but blue skies—meaning the investment will automatically be successful. All investments are not assured, however, and many producers may be dishonest. To protect the consumer from being literally robbed by a fraudulent scheme, many states require the producer to file with the attorney general or the appropriate officials.

In addition to limited partners who will help you finance the actual production, you will more than likely need help with the pre-production expenses. Even if your show is a hit, it usually takes three to four weeks for the money to begin accumulating so that you can pay expenses as well as the investors. Thus you will need front money—perhaps $20,000. Funds will be needed to post the bonds demanded by various unions. The actors' union, Actors Equity Association, requires a bond of two weeks' salary for each actor plus a bookkeeping charge of $50.00 per week. The Association of Theatrical Press Agents and Stage Managers requires two weeks' salary. A week's salary is demanded by the American Federation of Musicians (that is, if you do a musical or hire musicians), and the theatre owner requires a deposit of three to six weeks for rent plus $1,000 for possible damages. As a producer, you will need money for other pre-production expenses such as buying the option, printing the scripts, advertisements, auditions, rehearsals, payments to a "star" and/or director, and other such items. To assist with these expenses, a producer may choose to have an associate or coproducer in addition to limited partners. This associate may or may not be part of the actual production. His primary function is to assist with pre-production expenses in return for a percentage of the producer's share of the profits.

The Theatre Owner and the Unions

Assuming that you have an option, have satisfied all the unions, have filed with the SEC and attorney general, and have sufficient funds, your next step is to obtain a theatre. A good location is fundamental, and according to some sources, Greenwich Village is the best location for walk-in trade. In obtaining a theatre, a producer must deal with the League of American New York Producers. The League was founded in 1930 and acts as the bargaining agent for theatre owners with producers, theatre owners and producers with the unions, theatre owners with unions, and producers with unions. Initially, the League dealt only with Broadway theatres of which there are thirty-five, but they presently negotiate for all first class theatres and theatre owners throughout the nation. If a theatre is classified as a Broadway theatre the owners of the theatre *must join* the League. This is contrary to the League of Off-Broadway Theatres and Producers, which is a volunteer organization and thus does not require compulsory membership.

Those contracts negotiated between the theatre owners and unions include the Theatrical Protective Union. This union includes electricians to service the electrical equipment and maintain public address systems, carpenters to build sets, a curtain man, a property master, fly men to raise and lower the scenery, soundmen, and "taking in" and "taking out" personnel—those concerned with taking in and taking out of the theatre all equip-

The Bancrofts (Marie Wilton: 1839-1921) and Squire Bancroft (1841-1926). During their career as managers the Bancrofts managed their own theatre, The Princess of Wales, from 1860-1880 and the Haymarket from 1880-1885. They established the "long run" for plays, the "run of the play contract,"abandoned the benefit system, raised actors' salaries, and introduced domestic realism to England. From *The Theatre*, 1885.

ment in front of the house as well as backstage. In addition to this crew, theatre owners must provide ticket sellers and ticket takers, and thus must negotiate a contract with the Legitimate Theatre Employees Union. This Union not only controls the hiring of ticket takers, but has jurisdiction over employing ushers and backstage doormen as well.

The hiring of ticket sellers comes under another union—The Treasurers and Ticket Sellers Union. The personnel involved in this area comprise the box-office staff. The box-office staff usually consists of a box-office treasurer and two assistants who are responsible for handling ticket sales and monies. Inasmuch as a ticket is a legal contract, the implication is that the theatre is liable for the information printed on the ticket.

A collection of theatre tickets used at public theatres during the seventeenth and eighteenth centuries. From Wilkinson's *Londina Illustrata.*

Tickets usually are of two types—general admission and reserved seats. However, theatres sometimes issue special types of tickets known as hardwood. In New York, for example, many commercial establishments handle a hardwood ticket known as a "twofer." The "twofer" is a pass given out free which, on redemption at the box-office, enables the customer to purchase two tickets for (twofer) the price of one. Hardwoods are thus a form of complimentary tickets, or as a free pass is termed in the theatre, "Annie Oakley." The is so known because Annie Oakley, whose real name

was Phoebe Anne Oakley Mozee Butler (1860-1926), gave out free passes with her picture on the ticket. Another explanation is that the holes punched in tickets look as if Annie Oakley used them for target practice.

The issuance of complimentary tickets is part of the contract agreement that theatre owners sign with producers. In fact, the theatre owner has sole control over the box-office and all that goes with it. The producer cannot, for example, "paper the house" (give away tickets without the theatre owner's consent). The idea is to sell all the tickets (go clean) and not have any unsold tickets (deadwood).

Computerized ticket sales have facilitated greatly the job of the box office personnel. Computerizing also helped overcome, to a great extent, the mishandling of ticket sales. Although illegal, box office treasurers have sold tickets above the ticket price, keeping the difference for themselves. Because such activities are illegal as well a difficult to determine, the term ICE (Incidental Company Expenses), which refers to all shady box office activities, is applied. Historically, the term seems to have been used by bookkeepers to account for the shortages which occurred when managers took box-office money or issued free tickets. Computerizing box-office sales, however, has done a great deal to minimize any illegal activities with regard to tickets.

Two additional unions with which theatre owners must negotiate are the Theatre Amusement and Cultural Building Service Employees, and the International Union of Operating Engineers. The latter is the bargaining agent for those employees involved in the operation and maintenance of the theatre's heating and cooling systems. The former bargains for the cleaning personnel, the porters, the elevator operators, and the night watchmen.

The Producer and the Unions

Like the theatre owners, the producers must enter into a series of contractual negotiations with the various employees of a production. The union that most affects the producer and, for that matter, the entire production is Actors Equity Association, known as Equity. Equity represents the entire cast, as well as the stage manager and assistant stage managers. Equity derives its charter from the Associated Actors and Artists of America (the four As) which is a voluntary association governed by the AFL-CIO. Equity is therefore subject to the influence of the labor unions; the actor and the laborer have a common bond.

Initial casting of actors is usually done by the stage manager and the casting director (if there is one). This spares the director, author and producer, who ultimately make the final casting decisions, from having to deal with the many Equity actors who by Equity laws are entitled to an audition. Separate auditions are held for chorus and principal actors. Equity also requires an open call for auditions in order that any Equity member may try out. If auditions require more than two days for a chorus role and four days for a principal part, the actor must be paid. After the initial cuts the remaining actors are called back for final auditions.

The final choices are determined and contracts issued. Equity provides many types of contracts, including a production contract, a resident stock contract, a nonresident stock contract, resident theatre contracts (called LORT), children's theatre contracts, dinner theatre contracts, off-Broadway (this refers solely to the New York area), and the "Hat-Bat" contract (this refers to the Hollywood Area Theatre—Bay Area Theatre. The three "floor" (basic) contracts from which all contracts are drawn are the (1) production, (2) stock, and (3) children's. The actor who is doing a Broadway show would be involved with a Standard Minimum Production Contract for principal actors, a Standard Minimum Production for chorus, and a Standard Run of the Play Production Contract. The Standard Minimum Contract for principal actors provides a good example of some of the provision which Equity requires in its contracts. The actor, for example, is guaranteed salary for two weeks but he is also placed on probation, during which time he may be replaced or leave (Equity permitting). If the contract is signed seven days or less before the first rehearsal, the probationary period is five days for the producer to replace the actor or for the actor to request to be replaced. If the contract is signed seven days or more, then written notice and salary for two weeks are to be given by the person requesting a change. Two weeks' notice is the required period once the production has opened.

Madame Vestris (1797-1856), nee Lucia Elizabetta Bartolozzi, made her major contribution as manager of the Olympic Theatre from 1831-1839. She is credited with introducing (though not originating) the box set into England in 1832. She is shown here in the role of Apollo in *Midas*. From Coleman's *Players and Playwrights*, 1890.

Actress-manager Lillie Langtry (1852-1929), whose beauty and social position created a sensation when she went on stage. Prominent in English society and a friend of Eward VII, she was one of the first women from "society" to become an actress. From *The Theatre*, 1882.

In terms of actual parts to be cast, directors, writers, and producers are primarily concerned about the "star" and other principal roles. A star is defined as a performer whose name appears above the title or whose name carries the phrase *starring* or *also starring*. Stars, however, are generally excluded from auditions and are approached through friends or agents, whose function is to get jobs for actors and entertainers in their respective media. The agent in return receives a commission. The agent was proverbially known as the ten percenter, since this was his commission, but inflation has increased the percentage. Stars will usually be cast as hired. This means they perform a specific role and do no other parts. Other principal actors, however, may be cast as hired or understudy as cast, which means they play one part and understudy other parts.

In addition to the rules for stars and principal actors, Equity has rules for other cast members. If a part requires a juvenile actor, then the juvenile must be fourteen years old or younger. Equity also requires that if extras are used, they cannot be a definite character, cannot sing, dance, understudy, speak lines except in omnes (in a group), and cannot rehearse until two weeks before the show's opening. They are to be used for atmosphere and background only. Supernumeraries, known as "supers" or "supes," must be mute on stage, cannot travel with the company, and can rehearse only on the day they are to appear. In a musical chorus members are hired not only as dancers and singers, but may be contracted to understudy a role, play a part or be hired as a swing (a non-performing member of the chorus who "swings chorus members performing chorus numbers").

Laura Keene (c. 1820-1873), nee Mary Moss, was one of the first female theatrical managers in America. She was acting the part of Florence Trenchard in *Our American Counsin* at Ford's Theatre the night Lincoln was assassinated. Her theatre, interior pictured below, opened November 18, 1856, in New York City. The theatre held 1800 persons. (Photo from *Leslie's Magazine*, 1856).

Creator of "The Greatest Show on Earth," Phineas Taylor Barnum (1810-1891). Barnum was noted for his showmanship and his circus, which he created in 1871. From Seilhamer's *The Interviewer's Album*, 1881-1882.

musical), regulations govern additional monies for extended rehearsals. Ten days, however, is the maximum additional rehearsal allowed before the producer must begin to pay the actor his regular performance salary as opposed to the rehearsal salary. To hold down costs, rehearsals are held in a hall or rented studio until the final week before opening, and thus, the producer is conscious about adhering to a strict rehearsal schedule.

Equity is not the only union with which the producer must deal. He is also responsible for negotiating a contract with the director, who belongs to the Society of Stage Directors and Choreographers if the production is a first class theatrical production. Nightclubs, concerts, theatre restaurants (except Las Vegas), or readings are not considered first class. Should the production require dancers, then the producer must hire a choreographer, a person who composes the dance movements. Choreographers have the privilege of naming a dance captain whose duties are to call dance rehearsals in order to "maintain the quality of the dancers' performance."

Unions for Wardrobe Costumer, Lighting, and Scenic Designers

The Theatrical Wardrobe Attendants Union is another union with whom the producer must negotiate a contract. The personnel protected by this union are the wardrobe supervisors, assistants, and dressers. The rules are very strict with regard to the duties of these employees. The wardrobe supervisors and assistants may not help the actors change costumes nor may another performer help. This function belongs to the dresser. Conversely, the dresser may not perform the duties of the wardrobe supervisors except in an emergency. The duties of the wardrobe supervisors include making, cleaning, repairing, and remodeling costumes.

The lighting, scenic, and costume designers are

Once the cast is assembled, one of the members is chosen by a cast vote to be a deputy. The deputy is the designated representative for Equity members in dealing with the producer should a problem arise.

Because Equity has jurisdiction over the actor, it controls the rehearsal and performance schedule as well. Only eight performances are allowed per week and, according to Equity, a week is six days. This means that two matinees are given on two days of the week and on one day the theatre is dark—no performance is scheduled. Furthermore, when rehearsals are ongoing, they can only be for eight and one-half hours, of which one and one-half hours must be given for breaks. In other words, Equity allows only seven hours for rehearsal. The exception is the final week before production. During that time, a company may rehearse ten out of twelve hours.

Although rehearsal pay for a dramatic presentation is limited to four weeks (five weeks for a

all members of the United Scenic Artists of America (USAA). The minimum salary for a scene designer is presently $1,500; $750 for a lighting designer; and costumers are paid $75 per costume for stars or featured players, $35 per costume for the first fifty costumes for supporting players, and $25 for each costume over fifty.

The scenic or set designer must construct, color, and provide working sketches (to scale) of the set for the construction carpenter to build and paint the set; get estimates for materials; design, select, and approve properties, including furniture and draperies; attend the first out-of-town and New York openings and dress rehearsals; and perform all of these functions for road companies. Unlike the professional theatre, in colleges and universities, high schools, and community theatres, the set designer will also double as the technical director (TD). This position focuses on building, setting up, and striking (removing) the scenery.

The lighting designer must provide a list of all equipment and light plot, which is a ground plan of all the lights drawn to scale showing position, color, media, and type of all instruments. In addition, the lighting designer needs to provide all information requested by the contract electrician; supervise special effects as well as get estimates on their cost; supervise hanging and focusing of all instruments, and set up the light cues; attend first out-of-town and New York openings and dress rehearsals and conduct the lighting rehearsals for these performances; and perform all of these functions for road companies.

The costumer must submit complete costume sketches with color samples for all characters; provide a costume plot, which itemizes all costume changes for each character scene by scene; get estimates of materials from three costume shops; select all costumes, including those used by an actor from his personal wardrobe; be responsible for all accessories, footwear, and headwear (wigs, beards, and moustaches included); approve hair styling and supervise all necessary fittings and alterations (wardrobe makes the costumes); and attend the same rehearsals and

The most famous actor-manager from 1900-1914, Sir Herbert Beerbohm Tree (1853-1917). Tree developed an acting school which later became known as the Royal Academy of Dramatic Arts. From Dirck's *Players of Today*, 1892.

performances required of the set and lighting designers.

The Theatre Owner-Producer and the Unions

The remaining series of contracts to be negotiated are between the theatre owner and producer as an entity and the unions. The Association of Theatrical Press Agents and Managers, known as ATPAM, is one such union. ATPAM covers the employment of press agents, house managers, and company managers. Each area covered is considered a specialized position; doubling is not allowed. A house manager, for example, may not also be a company manager.

The duties of a press agent begin four weeks before the first paid New York performance. His

Charles Fechter (1824-1879), English actor-manager, pictured here in the role of Hamlet. Fechter is credited with popularizing realistic acting, reviving interest in the box-set, and aiding the vogue of "gentlemanly" melodrama. He also wrote several dramatizations of novels. From *Dramatic Portrait Gallery*, 1880.

function is to publicize the production; the object is SRO—standing room only. He also functions as advance man. In this capacity, he goes out on the road in advance of the production and will publicize the show, set up interviews for cast members, check on housing, transportation, and the theatre facilities for the technical crews. The press agent also works with an advertising agency which the producer has hired to do all the paid ads, such as those that appear in the trades (theatre papers) or the dailies (New York newspapers which are published daily).

The individual responsible for managing the front of the house (auditorium and lobby) is the house manager. The house manager functions as the representative of the theatre owner; he works for the house. He oversees the ushers, ticket-takers, box-office personnel and doormen, and checks the box-office statement. The house manager functions primarily in front of the house and keeps things running orderly. Before the curtain goes up, the house manager and stage manager are in contact with each other should something be askew either backstage or in the front of the house.

Whereas the house manager attends to the front of the house, the stage manager supervises the backstage area. He must be a member of Equity, but he is not permitted to act. During the rehearsals he assists the director, but once the production begins, he is in charge of the entire backstage as well as the stage area.

Inasmuch as the house manager attends to a particular theatre building, he will not tour with the company as does the company manager. The company manager handles the company's administrative problems and is the producer's representative. This explains why in reality one person could not be a house manager and a company manager for the same production.

The last union with whom the theatre owners and producers must negotiate is the American Federation of Musicians. The ATPAM and the musicians' contract are the only two which the producer and theatre owners enter into jointly. Some theatres decide at the start of each season not to enter into a contract with AFM for the forthcoming year. In one way this is advantageous as the owner is not required to hire any musicians unless needed. A signed contract between the AFM and the theatre owner at the beginning of the year obligates the theatre owner to hire a set number of musicians for each production whether he needs them or not. If a production requires musicians, however, and the theatre owner has not entered into an agreement, he then must pay more for the musicians than if he had entered into a contract. In other words, he is penalized. Noncontracted theatres are known as penalty houses. When musicians are needed, they are selected by a contractor, much as a casting director is used to select actors. It should be pointed out that musicians who invest in a production cannot be hired for that production or vice-versa. Also, if a cast album is made, the musicians in the production must be used for recording the album. This is also true for actors and the stage manager.

Pre-Broadway Tryout

Having cast the show, rehearsed, and negotiated with the various unions, the producer is now ready to try out the show before opening on Broadway. Cost is an important factor in determining whether to attempt a pre-Broadway run. The purpose behind the tryout is to test the production on an audience as well as out-of-town critics, and based on their reaction, adjust the production or rewrite if necessary. If rewriting is required, a play doctor is sometimes hired. He might be a writer or a director and his job is to reshape the script in order to save the show. There is the story about Kermit Bloomingdale, owner of the famous department store, who had a production requiring a play doctor. He called in the well-known playwright and director, George Kaufmann, to doctor the show. After Kaufmann viewed the show, Bloomingdale asked him for advice on how to save the show. Kaufmann suggested that Bloomingdale keep the store open late and close the show.

Pre-Broadway tryouts are designed to have the show in the best condition possible so that it can be ready for the Broadway critics. Often a producer will discover through a pre-Broadway tryout that the production will not survive and will, therefore, close the show before it ever opens in New York. The expense of trying a show out of town first, say in New Haven, Boston, or Philadelphia, or if a musical, the O'Keefe in Toronto or the Fisher Theatre in Detroit, has become extremely expensive. In addition to the major cities many productions will try out at universities or smaller towns such as Winston-Salem, North Carolina, where

Frank Benson (1858-1939), English actor-manager whose Shakespearian productions contributed to a nonrealistic approach in staging. Benson, an athlete at Oxford, subjected his company, The Bensonians, to rigorous physical training. From Dirck's *Players of Today*, 1892.

Neil Simon's *Lost in Yonkers* played before moving to Broadway. Consequently, a producer may have a Broadway preview. This means the play will stay on Broadway for one to three weeks before officially opening. One the other hand, if the production is toured first before opening on Broadway, then the show will probably remain on tour anywhere from four to six weeks if a drama, and six to ten weeks if a musical. The production would then spend a few days in New York before opening.

Broadway

Once a producer determines that the production is ready for Broadway, he must negotiate a

CHARLES KEAN.

Charles Kean (1811-1868), famous for his management of the Princess Theatre from 1850-1859. Among his many contributions were the development of historical accuracy in his 1852 production of *King John* and his 1853 *Macbeth* (the audience was given a list of authorities he had consulted); efforts to establish the director as the main artist of the theatre; elimination of the afterpiece, which he placed before the main production; and the elimination of variety acts which led to specialization acts. From Coleman's *Players and Playwrights*, 1890.

license agreement with the theatre owner. The license of theatre agreement is issued by the New York City Department of Licenses. The license varies with each theatre but contains such items as:

1. The date the show is to open.
2. The date the producer may occupy the theatre.
3. What the theatre owner is to provide (see contract negotiations required for the theatre owners and for the producers).
4. What the producer is to provide (perhaps that a particular staff is to be provided by the producer).

5. The percentage of the box-office receipts against a guaranteed payment which the theatre owner is to receive.
6. A stop clause. If gross box-office receipts fall below a specified mark for two weeks, the producer or the theatre owner may break the agreement. The producer or theater owner may not purchase tickets to increase the gross weekly receipts.
7. That a producer must "strike" (remove) the set and be out of the theatre within anywhere from twelve to forty-eight hours.
8. Provisions for free seats for the press as well a specifying the number of seats the theatre may purchase as well as get free.

There are numerous other provisions relating to expenses and who is responsible for these expenses. This agreement is similar with slight variations to the out-of-town agreement which is also used for pre-Broadway tryouts. If the license agreement is not used, then a form is furnished by the Independent Booking Office. This agency is designed to supply out-of-town bookings for pre-Broadway shows.

The cost for a dramatic show or a musical is a minimum of $75,000. According to available statistics, a dramatic show grosses between $45,000-$75,000 and a musical $70,000-$100,000. Of course, these figures fluctuate according to the size of the theatre and inflation. With so much money invested, a producer has to weigh carefully the reviews his show receives. The reviews come out in the early morning after the opening. After reading the reviews, the producer meets with members of his staff (company manager, press agent) to determine, in essence, what to do—close or stay open. This decision will be based upon review, advance ticket sales, and other potential income. If the show is a success, then the producer plans the advertising campaign. A big hit in New York will probably result in the formation of another company for touring. The stage manager will put the touring show together while he proceeds with rehearsals. This is a relatively easy task because the stage manager will duplicate (using

Augustin Daly (1838-1899), manager, director, and playwright whose efforts contributed to the establishment of the *regisseur* as a major component in the theatre. Daly had absolute control over every aspect of his theatre; he successfully encouraged ensemble acting with no "stars," natural acting, and historically accurate sets, costumes, and properties. These marked his company as one of the most progressive in the world and a pioneer in American theatre annals. Daly is pictured here in his office at the Daly Theatre located between 39th and 30th Streets in New York, *From author's private collection.*

his stage manager's script) the Broadway production. During the last week of rehearsal for the touring company, the original director takes over and continues with the show through opening night. Often before a production goes on tour or closes, it will be staged about midnight for members of the profession who couldn't see it because they were working at the same time the production was playing. This particular performance is called a "Gypsy Run-Thru," and is usually done without benefit of sets, costumes, or the other elements of spectacle used to stage the production.

From option to closing, producing a show requires good business practices. To enter into the producer's role for the so-called glamour of the entertainment world should be a minor consideration. The business of show business is to make money, and this means sound management.

Selected Readings

Bennett, Susan. *Theatre Audiences.* London, 1990.

DiMaggio, Paul. *Managers of the Arts.* Washington, DC, 1988.

Faber, Donald. *From Option to Opening.* New York, 1968.

Langley, Stephen and Abruzzo, James. *Jobs in Arts and Media Management.* New York, 1986.

Langley, Stephen. *Theatre Management in America.* Rev. ed. New York, 1980.

Lydon, Michael. *How to Succeed in Show Business by Really Trying.* New York, 1985.

CHAPTER TWENTY-TWO

&

Dependency:
Careers in Theatre

How I Got That Story by Amlin Gray. *Courtesy Amlin Gray. Photo by Mark Avery.*

Theatre is a business that breeds dependency. If you cannot take rejection, do not like waiting, do not like being dependent upon someone else for your job, then the best way to get into theatre is to buy a ticket. Better yet, do it anyway and save a lot of grief and anguish. If you are determined, however, then the first thing you need is training.

University Training

Uta Hagen asserted that the reason acting does not have respect is that everybody has the opinion that they can do it. Unfortunately, the vast wasteland of film and television continues to reinforce this general notion. Just as lawyers, doctors, or engineers train for their respective fields, so too must actors, if they wish to be competent.

There are a variety of ways for an actor to obtain training. One is through a university. Accredited college and universities provide excellent facilities and staff for the novice and experienced actor. Classes ranging from acting technique, diction, scene study to theatre history and dramatic literature enable the would-be actor to gain a solid foundation upon which to build.

Acting is not, however, the only field for the theatre student. Granted it has the most visibility and thus is usually the student's first career choice; but not everybody can act, let alone make a living at it. Therefore, if a person wants a career in the theatre, that individual should examine other areas—just in case.

Career opportunities as a director, set designer, costumer, stage manager or teacher, are a few of the many jobs that exist in theatre. In a well-rounded university program, students are exposed and trained in many diverse areas. Such diversity gives the student background training which will probably provide a job somewhere down the road. In many cases this job may evolve into a life-long career, even though it was not the student's first choice. Whatever the choice, the university programs offer the prospective theatre student excellent training and contracts.

Participation in university productions provides excellent training. Below is Anna Cora Ritchie's *Fashion* (1845) as produced at the University of Georegia. Directed by Fay Head; costume design by Jackson Kesler. *Courtesy Jackson Kesler.*

Commercial Training

There are a variety of schools and teachers in cities throughout the United States, especially in Los Angeles and New York, that offer commercial training in the theatre. Many of these school and teachers are not reputable, so beware! You should check the unions and other actors to determine the good schools and teachers. Whether you attend a university or not, an actor should continue to study at a reputable commercial school. Programs offered at H.B. Studios (New York), Weiss-Barron-Hill (camera training), Los Angeles and other large cities, and Film Actors' Workshop (Los Angeles) are examples of programs which provide the actor with professional training and professional atmosphere. A good commercial program will give you what you need to survive and "make it."

Agents

No matter which theatrical career you choose, at some point you will encounter the services of an agent, especially if you are an actor. Getting a good agent is sometimes as difficult as getting a part. Many beginning actors decide that agents are unnecessary and thus try to find work on their own. In regional areas such as Atlanta, Nashville, Dallas, etc., an actor can do this and be moderately successful. But whether in New York or Atlanta, the good agents have the contacts and in the long run, they can get an actor more auditions and work than the actor can get on his own. In other words, if and when this same actor gets the part (the national averages are for every 112 parts for which you audition, you get 9), the actor then must negotiate for his salary and then make sure he's paid and, moreover, paid correctly. Without an agent, inexperienced actors are so excited about getting a part that they may sign a contract for less than they should be paid. (Remember that acting is a business.) Perhaps the contract will be a "buyout." This means for a flat fee ($200 for example),

the actor agrees to do the commercial without any further compensation. The commercial may air for six months or longer, but the actor will not get any more money. The basic fee, or what is termed a session fee, for a thirty- or sixty-second commercial on camera (in New York) is $414.25; off-camera (voice-overs) for two hours recording, $311.50 plus residuals. This means that the actor has lost the potential of earning a great deal more than the $200.00 because he did not know his options. Get an experienced and reputable agent.

Obtaining an agent who is reputable can pose a problem. One good way is by word of mouth. Another is to check to see if an agent is *franchised*—that is licensed by the respective unions such as Screen Actors Guild (SAG), Actors Equity Association (AEA), and American Federation of Radio and Television Artists (AFTRA). If an agent is franchised, then check with the union offices to see if any complaints or problems have occurred with that agent. Also, bear in mind that just because an agency is large does not necessarily mean that the agent will be the best representative for you. Many smaller agencies often do an excellent job of getting work for their talent; whereas, many large agents are often indiscriminate, only giving the work to those few whom they like or who have been successful in the past. The others are filed away and only occasionally, if ever, are called by that agent for an audition. Additionally, a large agency will add new talent only after the talent has established credentials or achieved great success. Then they offer the reputation of their agency as a means to hire the proven talent. Choosing an agent is, as James Kirkwood (coauthor of *A Chorus Line)* states, a matter of "chemistry" between you and the agent, and not the size of the agency.

Once you have chosen an agent, if all goes well and they want you, you may have to sign an exclusive contract. This means you cannot work for another agent or even respond to another agent's call for an audition. Professional agents have contracts specifically designed by SAG, AFTRA, and AEA which spell out the agent's obligations as well as provide the actor with an escape clause in the contract. For example, for a SAG or AFTRA contract, if you do not earn $2000 in 15 days or get 15 days work within 91 days in Los Angeles, and 120 days in New York, you can break the contract. Remember the agent makes a living for two people. Also, you can request in writing from the agent a monthly report of (1) what the agent has done to get you work and (2) how many of your type are in the agency. If there are too many like your type then the chances for audition or selection are reduced by that number. Choose an agent in which your type is extremely low. Once you are committed to an agency, you should check in with your agent once a week—Wednesday is a good time. Be nice but do hustle your hustler. As mentioned earlier, theatre is a dependent profession.

Unions

To work in a professional theatre you must belong to the union or unions that govern you career choice. To join a union you must serve some sort of apprenticeship period in practically all areas. As an actor, you are faced with the "cycle of impossibility." This means you cannot join a union without a job, and you cannot get a job without belonging to a union. There are options however:

1. Join SAG by starting your film career in a "right to work" state (Texas, Georgia, Tennessee are examples). As a non-union actor, you may audition, as well as work in film and television productions in these states. When you are cast in your first union part, you will have the option to join SAG. Should you decide not to belong to SAG on your first "shoot" (actual filming), you are classified as Taft-Hartley. There is no option for your second union part; you must join!

2. Join AFTRA. Anybody can belong. After one year in AFTRA, plus having performed one major role, you are eligible to apply to SAG, and/or "Equity" (AEA). SAG and Equity have reciprocal agreements whereby a member of one union may join the other. If you prefer to join AEA and not SAG then after one year in AFTRA, plus a principal part of three days work "comparable to that of an Extra Performer" (that is, on stage), you may then apply to Equity.

a. SAG: Screen Actors Guild is the national union whose jurisdiction covers film as well as television (live or taped—*The Tonight Show* is SAG, but *The Arsenio Hall Show* is AFTRA). To join, you must have a principal part or a speaking part under a SAG contract, belong to a "sister union" (AEA, ACTRA, AGMA, AGVA, AFTRA) for one year in "good standing" plus during that year you work three days in an extra role at SAG rates ($65.00 per day). If you meet these requirements, SAG requires a cashiers check or cash in the amount of $974.50. Unlike Equity, SAG will *not* deduct the membership fee from your check.

b. AEA: Actors Equity Association, better known as *Equity*, is the national union for stage actors and stage managers. To join you must be a member of a "sister union" (see SAG) in good standing for one year and have worked under that union's jurisdiction. The national rate to join is $800 and the membership can be deducted from your check. Once you are a member in good standing, you are eligible to "buy" into another union through what is termed the "open doors admission policy." In fact, eligibility to buy into another union is true of all closed shop unions. If you are cast in an Equity show and that show closes within thirty days, you do not have to join Equity. You will become what is termed "Taft-Hartley." Another way to join Equity is through the EMC Program (Equity Membership Candidate).

c. The *EMC* program offered by Equity is administered through the LORT (League of Resident Theatres). You pay a $100 membership to enroll in the program. After an

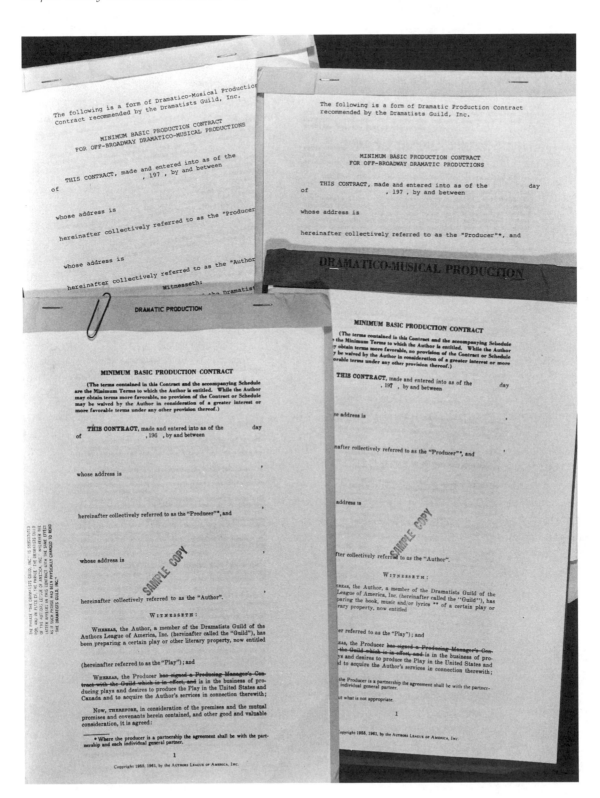

Samples of contracts issued by the Dramatists Guild, Inc.

accumulation of fifty weeks of work (also termed fifty points) at any LORT theatre, you automatically qualify for your *Eligible Performers Card*. With this card, you may audition for an Equity show and if you are cast, you will get your Equity card. Should you choose, you may after forty weeks (forty points) take an exam to get your Eligible Performers Card.

3. Open auditions and being selected for a part provide another option. Despite your lack of union affiliation, the director decides you are the correct choice for a part, and casts you.

4. Form your own company, and make your company a union. This takes money, but it is an option.

Casting Agent

A casting agent and/or director auditions actors and makes selections which are then approved or disapproved by the director and/or producer. Regional and other similar organizations have their own staff for this process. Commercial films and television productions hire independent casting agents. Their job involves taking a script and breaking it down into all the parts to be cast. This includes character description and other pertinent information that can be passed along to talent agencies to assist in sending the proper actor to audition. Also, casting agents notify the actor's agent, set up auditions (time and place), rent space, hire readers to do other roles (sometimes done by the stage manager or members of the staff), and interview all union members who request an audition. They are called "EPIs"—Equity Principal Interviews, and are required by Equity. Inasmuch as casting agents are retained for the entire run of the production, they must cast replacements and touring companies—that is, screen candidates before they are seen by the director or production stage manager.

Directing

There is a saying in theatre that if the production is good—"Who's the actor?" If the production is bad—"Who's the director?" The success or failure of a production lies basically with the director. The director is responsible for all aspects of the production and insuring that all of these aspects are evenly blended. This concept is known as synthesis and requires that a director have knowledge of acting, directing, set designing, costuming, lighting, and other areas of production. The director must work with each area's specialist and make sure that these specialists conform to his standard concept of the production.

In the professional theatre, rehearsals last four weeks for a regular play and six weeks for a musical. Before the actual opening, a play will have previews, out of which changes are made "almost daily." Pre-Broadway tryouts were once a standard in Boston, New Haven, Chicago, etc., but today costs are too prohibitive to warrant sending the show out of town for a tune-up. Thus, Broadway tryouts are done a great portion of the time in New York. Once opened, the director's job is technically finished, though he or she may be called to cast throughout productions or even rehearse the company (see chapter on directing).

Stage Managers

When a production opens and the director leaves, the stage manager assumes the director's position. There are different types of stage managers, depending upon their duties, and all belong to "Equity" (AEA).

Production Stage Manager (PSM): This manager's responsibility covers the backstage area including the lights, sets, and sound equipment. In addition, the PSM's duties include coordinating costume fittings, rehearsal schedules, press activi-

Jon Jory, artistic director of the Actors Theatre of Louisville, is the son of noted actor Victory Jory. *Courtesy Actors Theatre of Louisville.*

ties and conducting understudy rehearsals once a week. Sometimes the PSM directs a road company, gives critiques to performers (if they need them), casts replacements, and listens to the actors' personal and professional problems. In other words, the PSM maintains the production after it opens.

Stage Manager (SM): This manager is the one who "calls the show." This means that he or she has the *prompt book* which is a copy of the
• script with all entrances and exits
• cues for lights and sound
• special effects
• scene changes
• all technical plots (scenery, lights, properties, costume, and sound)

From the prompt book, the SM runs or "calls the show." In addition, the SM may have to solve any problems dealing with stage personnel, run auditions, obtain a property list (new "props" are required for a production to replace the rehearsal ones—a union rule), hire crew heads, take down all blocking, work with all designers, oversee rehearsal time, make a rehearsal schedule for the director, rehearse the company once a week after the opening (if needed), go over contracts, and keep track of backstage storage space—what is stored where.

Assistant Stage Managers (ASM): All the jobs the PSM and SM cannot do, from "calling the show" to sweeping the floors, fall to the hands of the ASM. These include:

Designers: All designers belong to USAA (United Scenic Artists of America) and must work with each other as well as the director.

Set Designer: The job of the set (scenery) designer is to create the physical environment for the play and to see that the set is installed within the theatre. In addition, the set designer must create room and appropriate positions for the lights.

Once a designer draws plans and, in some cases makes a three-dimensional model, as many as six scenic shops will inspect the design and then submit a bid for the scenery's construction. The relationship between a set designer and a scenic shop often will determine what shop is chosen, and not necessarily the price submitted. While the set is being built, the scenic designer visits the shop to oversee as well as make any changes. Inasmuch as scenery is the most expensive element in a production (excluding the actors), changes are made in the shop and not the theatre where such changes would cost more. On Broadway, the set designer's first priority is budget; whereas in the Regional Theatres, artistic purposes coexist with budgetary concern and thus money is not the overriding priority.

This production of *Henry VI* by the Royal Shakespeare Theatre in Stratford, England, reflects the importance of the costume designer's task. *Courtesy British Tourist Authority.*

Costume Designer: The costume designer is responsible for every piece of costume whether it is rented, purchased, or designed and put together ("built"). In addition, the designer must have knowledge of fabrics, color, design, and movement. Unlike the set, sound, and light designers, the costumer works directly with the actors. A good costumer consults not only with the director but with the actors as well about the various characters. In this manner, the costumer gains insight about the character as seen though the actor's eyes.

The costumer's job begins with a full scale research using historical books, magazines, newspapers, etc. Sketches are then made and shown to the producer, director, and actors. Adjustments are made and then, as with the set designer, the costumer get bids from the costume shops whose specialty is "building" costumes. These union shops belong to the International Ladies Garment Workers—Theatre Division, and include fabric buyers, dryers, seamstresses, fitters, finishers, trim-

mers, and drapers. Drapers make the pattern called a "muslin" which is a mock-up of the costume. This pattern (muslin) allows the designer to make changes on cheap fabric and not on the expensive costume.

When the "muslin" is completed, actors are brought in for fittings. Unlike in film and television where the costume, hair, wigs, and makeup are divided among several people, in theatre the costumer is responsible for the total look and thus works closely with the hair stylist or wigmaker as well as other specialists. When the costumer is satisfied, he/she will confer with the wardrobe master or mistress and stage manager. Each is given a costume plot (list of each costume accessories, who wears it and when) and how to care for each garment—for example, dry clean or hand wash.

Light Designer (LD): Although the concept of designing lights can be dated to the twentieth century as a separate entity of the production process, light design as a profession was begun in 1947 with *Brigadoon*, and was first recognized as a specialty in the 1976 Tony Awards with *A Chorus Line*.

In order to achieve the proper mood, color, and emotion of a production, the light designer must work closely with the director and set designer. Only when the set designer completes the ground plans can the light designer begin the *light plot* (a blueprint that identifies each light, its position, and the area it is to cover). This is done by tracing paper over the plans, and then through the use of a template (a stenciled pattern of lighting instruments), the light designer draws in the lights. After the plot is completed, it is given to a rental house from which all the lights and props are leased. All equipment for a Broadway production is leased, and the prices are negotiated between the general manager and the rental house. The next step involves hiring a production electrician whose job is to operate the lightboard, to install pipes (battens) in their proper positions and height, and the lights themselves. Inasmuch as lights precede the sets as the first heavy equipment to be put into the theatre, the production electrician works with the house electrician to install the lights as well as the cable for each instrument. The cables are connected to the dimmers which are located in the dimmer banks (DBs). The DBs are connected to the *interconnecting* or *patch panel* which in turn is hooded up to the light board. Modern boards, especially those by Century, have combined the "patch-panel" and the light board into one unit. These units are computerized. Once the lights are "hung" (placed in their proper positions on the pipes), the designer goes to the theatre to check the accuracy of the production electrician's work. He/she has the lights focused—that is, has the lights aimed onto the stage where the action is to take place. Depending upon the production, this takes about twenty hours or longer. A technical rehearsal comes next and then previews. During all of these rehearsals the light designer determines lighting cues—which lights to use at which times and at what intensity. In other words, in the technical rehearsal the light designer lights the show, fixes it in the dress rehearsal, and polishes it during previews.

Sound Designer: Similar to light design, sound design is a relatively new specialty in theatrical productions. Unlike the other designs areas, the sound designer's job is totally subjective for there is nothing a sound designer can draw or write down. A sound designer has to be concerned about the relationship of the voice to the orchestra or any other instrumentation/recordings in a show. He/she is constantly adjusting levels.

Sound equipment is rented for an amount equal to one percent of the equipment's value. *Dream Girls* had sound equipment worth $400,000. In this and other productions, such equipment includes monitors, foot microphones, offstage vocal booth (for a singer to supplement the chorus numbers or to perform off stage), wireless microphones and a console to regulate the total sound.

Working with the director, the sound designer tries to place microphones where actors are blocked. Sometimes restaging is needed to insure proper sound. Throughout the production the sound designer is constantly adjusting the sound; it is an ongoing process and only ceases when the show ends.

Properties, Carpenters, Wardrobe Supervisors and Dressers

The running or operation of a production is placed in the hands of a variety of people behind the scenes. For example, in the commercial theatre, the house (theatre) has its own staff consisting of a house electrician, property person and carpenter. Their contracts extend form Labor Day to Labor Day, but they get paid only when there is a production in the theatre. The contracts are known as "white contracts." When a company tours, production personnel get "pink contracts." The difference is that a pink contract holder belongs to the union IATSE (International Alliance of Theatrical Stage Employees) and is allowed to work without having to join the local union. The additional staff, called "casuals," is hired by the house and paid by the hour, day or week—a week being the same as eight performances.

A "production property person" is responsible for all properties in a show. At times this includes the rehearsal properties, which are supposed to be different from those "props" used in the actual production. Everything except the walls and floor are properties. Thus, the person in charge of "props" is responsible for getting and placing properties, but other members such as the carpenter, electrician, or scenic artists may have to maintain them. In addition to touring with the production, the property person must duplicate all the "props" if there is more than one company.

The house hires its own property person whose title has "house" in front of it, thereby reading "house property person." In addition to working with the production property person, the house property person must maintain the theatre by way of repairs, installations, maintenance of theatre seats, mirrors in dressing rooms, lavatories and most of the theatre's moveable furniture and non-electrical fixtures.

Other staff members include "house electricians" and "house carpenters." House electricians assist production electricians and maintain the house lights as well as being responsible for anything that has to do with water. The house electrician turns the house lights on and off.

The *production carpenter* works with the set designer to install and maintain the seats. The house carpenter and his crew (including the "flyer") install the equipment and raise and lower the scenery. Further jobs of the house carpenter include maintenance of the stage doors, windows and the stage.

As to the costume area in commercial theatre, the two main personnel are *wardrobe supervisor* and *dresser*. The wardrobe supervisor is in charge of all costumes including cleaning and repairing

and supervising the "dressers." The designer's responsibility concludes on opening night at which time the responsibility of the wardrobe supervisor begins.

A *dresser* is responsible for seeing that a performer gets on stage in the right costume at the correct time. By union rules, a "star" is allowed to choose his/her own dresser whether or not the dresser belongs to the Wardrobes Supervisor and Dressers Union. To join this union, the prospective dresser must be sponsored by a member of this union, after which an apprenticeship period of eighteen months must be served. During this time, a dresser may or may not work. It depends upon production needs. The number of dressers depends upon the number of costumes in a production, the difficulty of the changes and how quickly these changes must be made. Only ten to twenty members are selected each year for membership, and thus being a dresser can be a good career if one is willing to put in the time.

Selected Readings

Cohen, Robert. *Acting Professionally.* 4th ed. Mountain View, CA, 1990.

Engel, Lehman. *Getting Started in the Theatre.* New York, 1973.

Greenberg, Jan W. *Theatre Careers.* Holt, NY, 1983.

Henry, Mari Lyn and Rogers, Lynne. *How to Be a Working Actor.* New York, 1986.

Publications:

Art Search, published by the Theatre Communications Group, New York, 355 Lexington Ave., New York, NY 10017

Backstage, 330 W. 42nd St., NY 10036

Show Business, Leo Schull Publications, 134 W. 44th St., NY 10036

Theatre Communications Group, 355 Lexington Ave., NY 10017

Theatre Crafts, 250 W. 57th St., NY, NY 10017

Theatrical Index, Price Berkley, publisher, 888 8th Ave., NY 10019

STUDY QUESTIONS

CHAPTER ONE
Theatre: A Reflective Template

Name _____   Date _____

1. What are the comparative advantages and disadvantages of the four approaches to studying theatre enumerated in this chapter?

2. In what ways can the theatre spectator be regarded as an active rather than a passive participant?

3. How are the three foci that characterize the spectatorship approach to theatre study interrelated?

4. What about the study of theatre spectatorship makes it an appropriate contributor to liberal arts education?

5. How do aspects of the theatre event's "dual nature" weave together to affect the spectator?

(Continued)

6. How do the experiences prior to actual attendance at a performance affect a spectator's responsiveness?

7. What examples can you give illustrating how the aesthetic perceptions of one age or culture differ from those of another age or culture?

8. What implications for the spectator grow directly out of theatre's temporal nature?

9. What are the ways "template thinking" work for and/or against a spectator's perceptivity?

10. What values accrue from the non-valuative description of theatre's illusion, its means, and its stimulation of thought and feeling?

CHAPTER TWO
Origins: Theatre and Drama

Name _____   Date _____

1. Discuss the function of theatre and drama. How have these functions served society?

2. Who was Sir James Frazer? Discuss his ideas.

3. React to the different theories as to the origin of drama.

4. Discuss the relevance of theatre in relationship to other areas of society.

(Continued)

5. As it applies to theatre and drama, what does it mean for a society to be static or dynamic?

6. Looking ahead to Chapter Four, how did the Greeks change theatre from a static to a dynamic form?

7. Discuss the theory of Claude Lévi Strauss as to theatrical originals. Who was Joseph Campbell?

8. What is the relationship between Campbell's ideas about myth and the origins of the theatre?

9. What is ritual? What is myth? Explain their relationship to theatrical origins.

10. Explain why it is imprecise to use the term theatre to include drama.

CHAPTER THREE
Dramatic Structure

Name ———————————————————————————— Date ————————————————

1. Define the term "dramatic structure."

2. Distinguish between "plot" and "story."

3. What are the six basic elements of drama and how are they linked together?

4. Distinguish between theatre and drama.

5. What is the difference between a linear and an episodic plot?

(Continued)

6. What are the specific emotions for each form and how is catharsis achieved in each form?

7. What is the difference between a serious action and a highly serious action?

8. How do these actions affect the outcome in a melodrama and a tragedy?

9. Discuss the difference between probability as Aristotle viewed it and the neoclassical concept of verisimilitude.

10. Discuss style and how it affects the various elements in theatre and drama.

CHAPTER FOUR
The Greek World

Name _____   Date _____

1. Who was Dionysus and what was his relationship to the Greek theatre?

2. Discuss the differences between various Dionysian festivals.

3. Using the City Dionysia as an example, describe how this festival operated. Who was in charge? Describe the various responsibilities.

4. Discuss the different ways that the Greeks used stage scenery.

5. What is the relationship between the Artists of Dionysus and the modern day actor's union?

(Continued)

6. What was "The Three Actor Rule"?

7. Discuss *The Oresteia* and its relevance to modern society.

8. Explain the changes made in the Greek theatre between the fifth and fourth centuries.

9. Is it correct to discuss the Greek theatre and its drama in terms of the Greek world? Or should the discussion focus on Athens solely?

10. What is the great irony between the golden age of Athenian drama and the development of the physical theatre?

CHAPTER FIVE
Rome

Name ———————————————————————————— Date ——————————————————

1. What were the differences between Roman and Greek religion. How did they affect the theatre?

2. Describe the social status of the Roman actor. Was it any different from that of the Greek actor?

3. How did the audiences differ between Rome and Greece?

4. Explain the differences between the Roman physical theatre and that of the Greeks.

5. What were the contributions of the Roman dramatists to modern theatre?

(Continued)

6. Suggest ways in which Seneca's influence appears in Shakespeare's plays.

7. Look up, and then explain, the term "Terentian stage."

8. Compare and contrast the work of Plautus and that of Terence.

9. The place where the audience sat was called the auditorium. What did the Romans suggest by this term?

10. Discuss the minor forms that emerged during this period.

CHAPTER SIX
The Middle Ages

Name _____ Date _____

1. Explain how theatre and drama reemerged.

2. Determine and describe the contributions made by the monasteries to the theatre.

3. Discuss the Feast of Corpus Christi and how it was presented.

4. What forces came into play that caused the change from Latin to the vernacular?

5. How did this change affect theatre and drama?

(Continued)

6. Discuss how industrialism changed the theatre.

7. Define the various secular forms.

8. What is meant by the dual tradiiton in acting? Has it survived today? In what ways?

9. Suggest ways in which ideas from the Middle Ages have influenced modern thinking.

10. How did the east influence the west?

CHAPTER SEVEN
Italian Renaissance

Name _____   Date   _____

1. Discuss humanism and its effect on theatre.

2. Explain the forces that aided the formation of the Renaissance theatre.

3. Identify Serlio, Brunelleschi, Palladio, Aleotti, and Ubaldus. Why are they significant?

4. Discuss Furtenbach's ideas on lighting.

5. Explain the Renaissance notion of perspective and how it was applied to the stage.

(Continued)

6. Identify Torelli and cite his contributions.

7. Explain the "chariot and pole" system of changing scenery.

8. How did literary criticism develop?

9. What was the commedia dell'arte?

10. Suggest ways in which the ideas of the commedia dell'arte influenced modern comedy.

CHAPTER EIGHT
English Theatre and Drama to 1642

Name _____   Date _____

1. Describe how the Golden Age of Elizabethan drama developed.

2. What was the relationship between the University Wits and William Shakespeare?

3. What is the significance of each of the following dates: 1559, 1570, 1572 , 1574?

4. Explain the differences between the public and private theatres.

5. What are two recent discoveries that have altered our theories of Elizabethan theatre and drama?

(Continued)

6. Identify Ben Jonson and Inigo Jones. Cite their contributions.

7. Discuss the rise of the common player and how he achieved status.

8. Were women ever used in acting roles during this period? When were they first accepted as actresses?

9. Was Shakespeare always recognized as a great writer? When did he achieve his recognition?

10. What was the relationship between the theatre and the Elizathethan public? The authorities?

CHAPTER NINE
Birth of Bourgeois Theatre

Name _____   Date _____

1. Describe the physical structure of the Spanish theatre.

2. Choose either Lope de Vega or Pedro Calderón de la Barca and determine his contributions to the Spanish theatre.

3. Discuss Cardinal Richelieu's contribution to French theatre.

4. What is meant by neoclassicism? Consider the concept of verisimilitude and its three basic concepts.

(Continued)

5. What was the controversy surrounding the play, *Le Cid?*

6. How did the Comédie Française come into existence?

7. What were the types of plays written during the Restoration period.

8. Describe the influence that the French fair theatres had on the development of melodrama.

9. Discuss the Licensing Act of 1737. How did it influence the beginning of American theatre?

10. What was burletta?

CHAPTER TEN
The Romantic Ideal

Name _____ Date _____

1. What were the factors contributing to the rise of romanticism?

2. Discuss the philosophy underscoring the romantic movement.

3. What was the Victorian concept of women? How did it affect the theatre?

4. What was the Storm and Stress movement? What writers were involved?

5. What is the relationship between Wilhelm Schlegel and the rise of romanticism in France?

(Continued)

6. Cite three characteristics of the romantic theatre in England.

7. What was the Theatre Regulations Act of 1843?

8. Define the term "native types."

9. Explain how "native types" were reflected on the American stage.

10. What was the Astor Place riot? Who was involved? How did it start?

CHAPTER ELEVEN
Realism and Naturalism in France

Name _____ Date _____

1. Describe the development of historical accuracy and how it affected the theatre in France.

2. Explain the shift away from neoclassicism and how it was demonstrated in theatrical costume.

3. Describe the contribution of Comte and how it altered the perceptions of the dramatists of the period.

4. Discuss the differences between reomanticism, realism, and naturalism.

(Continued)

5. Discuss the changes brought to drama by the works of Dumas *fils,* Augier, Brieux, Becque, Sardou, and Zola.

6. How did these changes affect stage production?

7. Why is Antoine considered a naturalist?

8. What was the comédie rosse?

CHAPTER TWELVE
Realism and Naturalism in Europe and America

Name _____   Date _____

1. What factors contributed to the rise of realism?

2. What is "cultural Darwinism"? How did it affect the theatre?

3. Who was Henrik Ibsen? Discuss his contributions to the theatre.

4. What is meant by Chekovian drama?

5. In order to accommodate the dramatic changes from romanticism to realism, how did theatrical scenery change?

(Continued)

6. Why was the Moscow Art Theatre founded? What influence did it have in the theatre as a whole?

7. Discuss the importance of J. T. Grein and the Independent Theatre in England.

8. Explain the rise of the "star" system in America.

9. What was the Theatrical Syndicate? How was the Syndicate able to get and maintain power?

10. What was the "Little Theatre Movement"? What was the relationship between this movement and the rise of Eugene O'Neill?

CHAPTER THIRTEEN
The Antirealist and the American Renaissance

Name _____ Date _____

1. How did the ideas of Wagner and Nietzsche influence the modern theatre?

2. What were Appia and Craig's contributions to modern set design?

3. What was symbolism? How did it affect the modern theatre?

4. Explain the "art-for-art's-sake" movement.

5. Discuss expressionism and how it manifested itself in the theatre.

(Continued)

6. Discuss Meyerhold and Brecht as revolutionaries in the theatre.

7. What was Brecht's epic theory? How did it differ from Aristotle's concept?

8. Discuss the contributions of African-Americans to the development of musical theatre.

9. Compare and contrast cinema and the theatre.

10. Trace the development of the Royal Court Theatre. What was its relationship to the repeal of censorship that occurred in the theatre?

CHAPTER FOURTEEN
The 1960s and Beyond

Name _____ Date _____

1. What were some of the influences that caused a radical change in theatre practice in the 1960s?

2. Discuss the contributions of Grotowski and Beck to the formation of radical theatre. How are the two similar in their approach? How do they differ?

3. Using two or more groups as examples, discuss the changes that occurred in actor/audience relationships during the 1960s.

4. By what means did agitprop theatre groups engage the attention of audiences who were not traditional theatre goers? What were some of the methods they employed to convey the immediacy of their messages?

(Continued)

5. What is deconstruction? What is its relationship to the feminist theatre movement?

6. Give three categories of feminist dramatic theory and explain the difference between each.

7. Why the term "absurdist theatre"?

8. How does absurdist drama differ from traditional drama?

9. Theatre and drama are a barometer of what is occurring in society. Using the theatre/drama of the 1960s and beyond, support or reject this claim.

10. Compare and contrast the ideas of Grotowski and Stanislavski.

CHAPTER FIFTEEN
Performance Art: An Alternate Form

Name _____   Date _____

1. Trace the development of the form known as "oral interpretation."

2. What was Cunningham's methodology? How is this concept applied to the script?

3. What is the relationship between oral interpretation and readers theatre?

4. According to Adams, what are the four major styles of readers theatre?

5. What is the chief characteristic of each style?

(Continued)

6. Discuss the differences between story theatre and chamber theatre.

7. Compare and contrast chamber theatre and performance art?

8. What is performance art?

9. What is the relationship between performance art, oral interpretation and readers theatre?

10. Adapt a short story into a readers theatre format.

CHAPTER SIXTEEN
Playwriting

Name _____ Date _____

1. What is meant by the playwright's vision?

2. What is meant by the term "scenario"?

3. What is the relationship of "French scenes" to the scenario?

4. Determine ways in which music may be utilized in a play.

5. Compare and contrast the uses of music in a play, movie, or television.

(Continued)

6. Discuss the quotation "A playwright imitates life and the work appears to be life."

7. Is it *always* true that art imitates life? Explain.

8. In order for a play to be produced professionally, certain procedures are necessary. Using the materials in Chapter 21, determine those procedures.

9. Cite the potential markets in which a play might be produced.

10. Choose a modern playwright and research the background on that writer's plays.

CHAPTER SEVENTEEN
The Director and the Actor

Name _____   Date _____

1. "Each production is different from all other productions. Therefore the director's chief responsibility and privilege is to articulate the parameters of a unique production between and among particular artists for a particular audience in a particular theatre at a particular moment in time." Explain.

2. What is the *key to the integrity* of the director's process and product? How does the director work with that key?

3. What three things that can make or break a director happen in the pre-production stage? Explain.

4. Discuss the concept of layering, particularly as applied to work-through rehearsals?

5. Provide a job description for the stage manager. Include his or her relationship with the director.

(Continued)

6. "The liveness of the audience informs the dynamic and rhythm of the production and makes each performance different. It challenges theatre artists and validates theatre art." Explain.

7. What is the aesthetic contract? Who is it between? How does it work?

8. Describe actor homework: (a) before being cast, and (b) after being cast.

9. Define and describe acting as process.

10. Define and explain *subtext, dramatic irony, public solitude,* and *illusion of the first time.*

11. Trust operates on many levels in the theatre. Explain.

12. What is the bottom line of a play? Who are the bottom line magicians in the theatre?

CHAPTER EIGHTEEN
Scenic Actualization and Set Design

Name _____ Date _____

1. Why does the mandala metaphor particularly serve the art of theatre design?

2. How can a visual metaphor assist in developing the symbolic nature of a script?

3. Why are emotions linked specifically to the aesthetic realm of the design process?

4. Define the five primary elements of design.

5. Why is the practical realm often the most critical in terms of the effectiveness of the design process in production?

6. Diagram and/or explain the nature of the "kinetic design process."

(Continued)

7. In what general ways does the director initiate the visual interpretation process.

8. What makes the theatre particularly unique among the visual arts?

9. Demonstrate the triad of the "kinetic design process" with a specific example from *The Architect and the Emperor of Assyria.*

10. It is often said that art imitates life. Can you isolate a personal life experience that reflects the principles of the triad design process?

CHAPTER NINETEEN
The Costume Designer

Name _____ Date _____

1. What is the role of the concept of *individuality* in determining the success of costume design?

2. What are the goals of the costume designer?

3. Explain how costumes communicate both tangible and intangible information to the audience. Give at least three examples of each.

4. What are the three main phases of costume design?

(Continued)

5. What are the six generic components of a total stage costume? Give two examples of each component.

6. Describe each of the four elements of design and explain how a designer uses them in creating costumes.

7. What are the mechanical steps in constructing a stage costume?

CHAPTER TWENTY
Lighting

Name _____   Date _____

1. What are the six functions of stage lighting? How can they be found in everyday life?

2. What are the two basic types of spotlights? What is unique about each and how might a designer use them?

3. What is the purpose of gel?

4. What union oversees the working of designers on Broadway?

5. What are the two types of light plots and what information does each give?

(Continued)

6. What is the purpose of the shop order?

7. What steps does the designer take in putting a show together?

CHAPTER TWENTY-ONE
Managing the Store

Name _____ Date _____

1. What is the function of the Dramatists Guild?

2. Explain how a play is financed.

3. What is the relationship between theatre owners and the unions?

4. Describe the relationship between the unions and the producers.

5. Identify the unions for the costume, light, and scenic designers.

(Continued)

6. Discuss the reasons for a pre-Broadway tryout.

7. The Theatrical Syndicate was discussed earlier in this book. What effect did the Syndicate have on present day management?

8. How does an actor join the unions discussed in this chapter?

9. Suppose you wanted to produce a play. What would it take to produce it?

10. What is a "backer's audition"?

CHAPTER TWENTY-TWO
Careers in Theatre

Name ————————————————————————————   Date ————————————————

1. Why do you suppose a career in theatre is one of dependency?

2. If you were to choose a career in the theatre what would be your choice? Why?

3. Cite the unions for the actors of all media.

4. Describe the functions of the stage manager.

5. What is the relationship between the stage manager and the director?

(Continued)

6. What is the directors' union? Does it govern only directors?

7. Assume you are a director of a non-musical. Discuss your organizational procedures in getting the play ready for production. Discuss procedures for a musical.

8. What is the relationship between a producer and a director? When does the director assume total responsibility?

9. What do you suspect the term "creative team" means?

10. Discuss the nature of the agent in all areas of the theatre. What does it mean that an agent makes a living for two people?

Index